Prentice-Hall International Series in Management

ATHOS AND COFFEY	*Behavior in Organizations: A Multidimensional View*
BALLOU	*Business Logistics Management*
BAUMOL	*Economic Theory and Operations Analysis, 2nd ed.*
BOOT	*Mathematical Reasoning in Economics and Management Science*
BROWN	*Smoothing, Forecasting, and Prediction of Discrete Time Series*
CHAMBERS	*Accounting, Evaluation and Economic Behavior*
CHURCHMAN	*Prediction and Optimal Decision: Philosophical Issues of a Science of Values*
CLARKSON	*The Theory of Consumer Demand: A Critical Appraisal*
COHEN AND CYERT	*Theory of the Firm: Resource Allocation in a Market Economy*
CULLMAN AND KNUDSON	*Management Problems in International Environments*
CYERT AND MARCH	*A Behavioral Theory of the Firm*
FABRYCKY AND TORGERSEN	*Operations Economy: Industrial Applications of Operations Research*
FRANK, MASSY, AND WIND	*Market Segmentation*
GREEN AND TULL	*Research for Marketing Decisions, 2nd ed.*
GREENLAW, HERRON, AND RAWDON	*Business Simulation in Industrial and University Education*
HADLEY AND WHITIN	*Analysis of Inventory Systems*
HOLT, MODIGLIANI, MUTH, AND SIMON	*Planning Production, Inventories, and Work Force*
HYMANS	*Probability Theory with Applications to Econometrics and Decision-Making*
IJIRI	*The Foundations of Accounting Measurement: A Mathematical, Economic, and Behavioral Inquiry*
KAUFMANN	*Methods and Models of Operations Research*
LESOURNE	*Economic Analysis and Industrial Management*
MANTEL	*Cases in Managerial Decisions*
MASSÉ	*Optimal Investment Decisions: Rules for Action and Criteria for Choice*
MCGUIRE	*Theories of Business Behavior*
MILLER AND STARR	*Executive Decisions and Operations Research, 2nd ed.*
MONTGOMERY AND URBAN	*Management Science in Marketing*
MONTGOMERY AND URBAN	*Applications of Management Science in Marketing*
MORRIS	*Management Science: A Bayesian Introduction*
MUTH AND THOMPSON	*Industrial Scheduling*
NELSON (ED.)	*Marginal Cost Pricing in Practice*
NICOSIA	*Consumer Decision Processes: Marketing and Advertising Decisions*
PETERS AND SUMMERS	*Statistical Analysis for Business Decisions*
PFIFFNER AND SHERWOOD	*Administrative Organization*
SIMONNARD	*Linear Programming*
SINGER	*Antitrust Economics: Selected Legal Cases and Economic Models*
VERNON	*Manager in the International Economy*
WAGNER	*Principles of Operations Research with Applications to Managerial Decisions*
ZANGWILL	*Nonlinear Programming: A Unified Approach*
ZENOFF AND ZWICK	*International Financial Management*

Prentice-Hall, Inc.
Prentice-Hall International, Inc., *United Kingdom and Eire*
Prentice-Hall of Canada, Ltd., *Canada*
J. H. DeBussy, Ltd., *Holland and Flemish-Speaking Belgium*
Dunod Press, *France*
Maruzen Company, Ltd., *Far East*
Herrero Hermanos, Sucs, *Spain and Latin America*
R. Oldenbourg, *Verlag*, *Germany*
Ulrico Hoepli Editore, *Italy*

Ronald H. Ballou

Associate Professor of Marketing
Case Western Reserve University

BUSINESS
LOGISTICS
MANAGEMENT

PRENTICE-HALL INC., *Englewood Cliffs, New Jersey*

Library of Congress Cataloging in Publication Data

BALLOU, RONALD H
  Business logistics management.

  Includes bibliographical references.
  1. Physical distribution of goods—Management.
I. Title.
HF5415.7.B34   658.7′8   72–1338
ISBN   0–13–104802–3

© 1973 by Prentice-Hall, Inc., Englewood Cliffs, N.J.

Printed in the United States of America

10   9   8

PRENTICE-HALL INTERNATIONAL, INC., London
PRENTICE-HALL OF AUSTRALIA, PTY. LTD., Sydney
PRENTICE-HALL OF CANADA, LTD., Toronto
PRENTICE-HALL OF INDIA PRIVATE LIMITED, New Delhi
PRENTICE-HALL OF JAPAN, INC., Tokyo

To Carolyn, Kevin, and Brian

Contents

Preface   xiii

**Part
I**

**Introduction and Overview of
Logistics Decision Making**   2

**Chapter
1**
An Overview of Business Logistics   4

      SCOPE OF LOGISTICS. BUSINESS LOGISTICS DEFINED. GENE-
      SIS OF BUSINESS LOGISTICS. THE TOTAL COST CONCEPT.
      APPROACH OF THE TEXT.

**Chapter
2**
Science and Logistics Decision Making   30

      THE CONCEPTUALIZED LOGISTICS PROBLEM. THE MANAGE-
      MENT PROCESS. DIGRESSION ON A GENERAL ANALYTICAL
      DECISION MODEL. LOGISTICIAN'S ATTITUDES TOWARD SCI-
      ENTIFIC ANALYSIS. CONCLUDING COMMENTS.

Chapter
3

The Logistics Information System   56

OVERVIEW OF THE LOGISTICS INFORMATION SYSTEM (LIS).
INPUT DATA AND COMMUNICATIONS. INTERNAL LIS ACTIVI-
TIES. OUTPUT INFORMATION AND COMMUNICATIONS. CON-
CLUDING COMMENTS.

Part
II

The Logistics Environment   **88**

Chapter
4

The Product   90

PRODUCT CHARACTERISTICS. CUSTOMER SERVICE. PRIC-
ING. THE PACKAGE. CONCLUDING COMMENTS.

Chapter
5

The Transportation System—
Facilities and Services   120

IMPORTANCE OF AN INEXPENSIVE TRANSPORTATION SYSTEM.
SCOPE OF THE TRANSPORTATION SYSTEM. SERVICE CHOICES
AND PERFORMANCE CHARACTERISTICS. CONCLUDING COM-
MENTS.

Chapter
6

The Transportation System—
Regulation and Rates   154

TRANSPORT REGULATION. TRANSPORT COST CHARACTER-
ISTICS. RATE PROFILES. LINE-HAUL RATES. SPECIAL SER-
VICE CHARGES. ESTABLISHING AND CHANGING RATES.
DOCUMENTATION. CONCLUDING COMMENT.

Chapter
7

The Storage System   188

NEED FOR THE STORAGE SYSTEM. STORAGE SYSTEM FUNC-
TIONS. STORAGE ALTERNATIVES. MATERIALS-HANDLING
CONSIDERATIONS. STORAGE SYSTEM COSTS AND RATES.
CONCLUDING COMMENTS.

Part III

Logistics Decisions 222

Chapter 8

Facility Location Decisions 224

SINGLE FACILITY LOCATION MODELS. MULTIPLE FACILITY LOCATION MODELS. RETAIL AND PLANT LOCATION. CON-CLUDING COMMENTS.

Chapter 9

Inventory Policy Decisions 278

NATURE OF THE DECISION. RELEVANT COSTS. STOCKING DECISIONS. INVENTORY POLICY DECISIONS. Q-SYSTEM MODELS. P-SYSTEM MODELS. MULTIPLE ITEM, MULTIPLE LOCATION ANALYSIS. CONCLUDING COMMENTS.

Chapter 10

Transport, Production Scheduling, and Order Processing Decisions 334

TRANSPORT DECISIONS. PRODUCTION SCHEDULING. ORDER PROCESSING SYSTEM DECISIONS. CONCLUDING COMMENTS.

Chapter 11

Storage and Materials-Handling Decisions 378

SITE SELECTION. PLANNING FOR DESIGN AND OPERATION. CONCLUDING COMMENTS.

Part IV

Logistics Organization and Control 422

Chapter 12

Organization for Logistics Management 424

ORGANIZATION OF THE LOGISTICS FUNCTION. INTERFUNC-TIONAL MANAGEMENT. INTERORGANIZATIONAL MANAGE-MENT. CONCLUDING COMMENTS.

**Chapter
13**

Logistics Control   446

OVERVIEW OF THE CONTROL PROCESS. CONTROL SYSTEM
DETAILS. CONTROL IN PRACTICE. CONTROL INFORMATION
AND MEASUREMENT. CORRECTIVE ACTION. CONCLUDING
COMMENTS.

**Appendix
A**

The Transportation Method   470

**Appendix
B**

Usemore Soap Company (A):
A Warehouse Location Case Study   478

THE PROBLEM. COMPUTER-ASSISTED ANALYSIS. CONCLUD-
ING COMMENTS.

**Appendix
C**

Usemore Soap Company (B):
An Inventory Policy Case Study   494

INVENTORY CONTROL SYSTEM DESIGN. SYSTEM COSTS AND
ALTERNATIVES. COMPUTER-ASSISTED ANALYSIS.

Preface

Business logistics (physical distribution), a relatively new area of management study and action, draws upon the fields of marketing, production, accounting, and transportation, and the disciplines of applied mathematics, organizational behavior, and economics. Though still a fledgling compared with these more traditional fields, business logistics has come a long way since the early days when it was referred to as "the economy's dark continent."[1] More recently it has been described as being in a state of "semi-maturity."[2] Business logistics stands at the threshold of being recognized as the "third" functional area of business. As such, a great deal of attention in study and research by businessmen and academicians is being directed toward exploiting the opportunities that the management of business logistics activities affords.

This book is primarily about the management of business logistics activities in domestic firms with implications about the management of logistics activities in such areas as the military, service organizations, and non-profit institutions. A systems approach relates the various logistics activities and defines the scope

[1] Peter Drucker, "The Economy's Dark Continent," *Fortune* (April, 1962), pp. 103, 265, 268, and 270.

[2] Donald J. Bowersox, "Physical Distribution in Semi-maturity," *Air Transportation* (January, 1966), pp. 9–11.

of what business logistics management is. That is, the book integrates the activities of transportation, inventory control, materials handling, warehousing, order processing, protective packaging, product scheduling, facility location, and customer service that typically have been fragmented throughout the business firm and managed separately.

The book is organized around the major management activities of planning, organizing, and controlling. The emphasis is on planning, or more specifically, decision making, since it is recognized that decision making is one of the most difficult tasks facing the logistics manager. Further, the amenability of many logistics problems to mathematical treatment and the increasing interest by the modern executive in using mathematical models in the planning process are recognized. Numerous mathematical models and techniques that have been developed and successfully applied to logistics decision problems are presented.

The reader will find that the text breaks down into four major parts. Part I is composed of three chapters. Chapter 1 provides the historical background, definition, scope, perspective of logistics relative to the major functional areas in business, and elements of logistics necessary to establish the place of logistics management in modern business. Chapter 2 deals with the conceptual and analytical framework of logistics management, which is useful in perceiving the similarity of logistics problems and treating them quantitatively no matter where they may occur. Chapter 3 provides an overview of the logistics information system, especially in terms of its relationship to the decision-making process.

In order for the logistician to develop sound logistics plans it is necessary that he understand the conditions and circumstances that surround the selection and implementation of a plan. These conditions and circumstances are broadly referred to as the logistics environment and are the subject of Part II. The environment is divided into three chapters. Chapter 4 concerns the product that flows in the logistics network and looks at the product as the logistician sees it. Chapters 5 and 6 discuss the alternatives, cost and rate structures, and regulatory framework of the transportation system. Similarly, the storage system is discussed in Chapter 7. This discussion of environmental factors is derived from the basic features of the logistics network: the *storage* nodal points, the *transportation* links, and the *product* flow. These are important information inputs to the decision-making process.

Part III deals with the major decision areas of business logistics management. The concern here is with the selection of the best plan of action to achieve logistics goals and a number of quantitative models are introduced as planning aids. Chapter 8 deals with the size, number, and location of retail stores, warehouses, and plants needed in the logistics system. Chapter 9 is devoted to developing inventory policies ranging from single item, single location to multiple item, multiple location problems. Chapters 10 and 11 deal with a wide range of problems, including transportation mode and route selection, order processing, warehousing and materials handling, and production scheduling.

Whereas Parts II and III concern the planning activity in logistics management, Part IV concerns organizing and controlling activities. Plans are of little value unless they are put into action. Implementing plans requires an organization of people. Developing effective organizational relationships both within and beyond the legal boundaries of the firm is the subject of Chapter 12. Chapter 13 concludes with the management activity of control, which helps to assure that the logistics plans will meet the goals for which they were intended.

Since the emphasis of this text is on planning, two case studies (warehouse location and inventory control) using the models actually used by the company are included in the appendices. These cases offer the reader an opportunity to make logistics decisions in a simulated real-world environment.

I would like to acknowledge the many people who directly and indirectly helped to make the writing of this book possible. I wish to thank Professor J. L. Heskett, Harvard University, who, during my formative years of graduate study, encouraged my interest in logistics through the radiation of his own keen interest in the subject. Professors D. Clay Whybark, Purdue University, and Daniel W. DeHayes, Indiana University, read all or portions of the manuscript and offered valuable criticisms. A special thanks goes to the executive staff of the American Warehousemen's Association who read and commented on the storage system chapter. To Professor William E. Cox, Jr., Chairman of the Marketing Department at CWRU, who unselfishly absorbed some of my duties so that the book might progress, and to the students of the physical distribution classes at CWRU who have saved the current reader many agonizing errors, my deep appreciation.

Finally, a special thanks to my wife, Carolyn, for editorial and typing assistance and for moral support and encouragement during the entire project.

RHB
Cleveland, Ohio

BUSINESS LOGISTICS MANAGEMENT

Part
I

Introduction and Overview
of
Logistics Decision Making

Business logistics is the study of how management can best provide a profitable level of distribution service to customers through effective planning, organizing, and controlling of the move-store activities that facilitate product flow. In the first part of this book, the necessary background and framework for this study are developed. Chapter 1 provides an overview of the scope, historical development, economic significance, and key elements of logistics. Chapter 2 discusses the analytical framework that underlies most logistics problems. This framework is the network which is the conceptual representation of the logistics problem and the classical decision theory model, which serves as a basic analytical structure for all decision problems. Chapter 3 integrates the decision process into the logistics information system and discusses it in relation to the logistics environment and to the logistics manager or decision maker.

Chapter

1

An Overview
of
Business Logistics

As far back as man can recall, the goods that he wanted were not produced where he wanted to consume them or they were not available at the time he desired to consume them. Food and other commodities were widely dispersed over the land and were available in abundance only at given times of the year. Early man had the choice of consuming goods at their location when they were available or of moving them to a more preferred location and storing them for later use. Because there were no well-developed transportation and storage systems, the movement of goods was limited to what he could personally move and the storage of perishable commodities was possible for only short periods of time. This limited movement-storage system generally constrained him to live close to the sources of production and to consume a rather narrow range of goods. Even today there are examples of consumption and production taking place only within a very limited geographical region. Striking examples of this can be observed in some countries of Asia and

Africa, where much of the population lives in small, self-sufficient hamlets and most of the goods needed by the residents are produced in the immediate vicinity of the hamlets. Few goods are imported from other areas. Production efficiency and the standard of living are generally low in this type of economy. A major reason is the lack of a well-developed and inexpensive logistics system that would encourage an exchange of goods with other producing areas of the country.

In many countries, logistics systems were gradually improved and consumption and production points began to separate geographically. Areas began to specialize in those commodities which they could produce most efficiently. Excess production could economically be shipped to other producing (or market) areas. Needed goods not produced locally were imported. This exchange process follows the principle of comparative economic advantage which can be easily illustrated. For example, suppose that the people of Ohio and Alabama consume both corn and cotton in the annual amount of two bushels of corn and 10 pounds of cotton per individual. Because of differences in climate, soil conditions, and labor costs, the costs of production in each locality differ (Table 1-1). If the consumers in Ohio and Alabama buy their own locally produced corn and cotton, they pay 2($0.75) + 10($0.20), or $3.50 each to fill their needs. When transportation costs exceed

		TABLE 1-1
	Hypothetical costs for producing corn and cotton in Ohio and Alabama	

	Corn	Cotton
Ohio	$0.75/bu.	$0.20/lb.
Alabama	1.00/bu.	0.15/lb.

the differential in production costs for the products grown in the two areas, there is no advantage in importing, as shown in columns 1 and 2 of Table 1-2. The economy is local in scope. However, even when cheap transportation is available, there is an economic advantage of specializing in the product that can be produced most cheaply and of buying the remaining crop from the other area, where it can be produced most efficiently. Column 4 of Table 1-2 shows that both consumers gain by this practice, as does the entire economy, which in this case consists of the two consumers. Thus, inexpensive transportation or, even more broadly, an efficient and effective logistics system permits the specialization of labor, geographically decouples production from consumption, and encourages competition in distant markets. Clearly, logistics costs have a profound effect on the economic structure of a country.

To the individual firm operating in a high-level economy, logistics activities are critical. Markets are often national in scope, while production may be concentrated at only a few points. Logistics activities provide the "bridge" between the production activities and the markets that are spatially and temporally separated. Effective management of these activities is the major concern of this book.

TABLE 1-2

Comparative economic advantage of producing
or purchasing corn and cotton under expensive
and inexpensive transportation

	Expensive Transportation[a]		Inexpensive Transportation[b]	
	Purchase of In-state Products	Purchase of Out-of-state Products[c]	Purchase of In-state Products	Purchase of Out-of-state Products[c]
Ohio consumer (2 bu corn, 10 lb cotton)	$3.50	$4.00	$3.50	$3.10
Alabama consumer (2 bu corn, 10 lb cotton)	3.50	4.00	3.50	3.20
Cost to economy[d]	$7.00	$8.00	$7.00	$6.30

[a]$0.50/bu on corn and $0.10/lb on cotton.
[b]$0.10/bu on corn and $0.01/lb on cotton.
[c]Alabama cotton purchased by Ohio consumer and Ohio corn purchased by Alabama consumer. Includes the cost of transportation.
[d]The economy consists of a consumer in Ohio and one in Alabama.

Scope of Logistics

Logistics is a term defined by Webster as having to do with moving, supplying, and quartering troops.[1] As stated, logistics would appear to be limited to the military. Recent usage of the term recognizes that the move-store activities so important to the supply arm of the military exist in countless forms throughout the economy. In business, logistics refers to product movement and storage. In communication, logistics activities revolve around message transmission. In metropolitan areas, the movement of people is an important logistics activity. It is probably true that logistics activities are among the most pervasive of all human activities.

Logistics activities, whether they take place in the military, in urban transportation systems, in government supply systems, in business, or in communication processes, are essentially the same. They commonly involve movement and storage for the purpose of having the desired object of flow at the right place at the right time. To study one area has relevance to the others. In this text, the discussion is focused on the logistics problems of the business firm. However, the reader is encouraged to reflect on the broader scope of logistics (military, urban, communication, etc.) to which the discussion, in large part, also applies.

[1] *Webster's New World Dictionary of the American Language*, college edition (New York: The World Publishing Company, 1958), p. 862. For an interesting discussion of the origin of the term logistics, see Graham W. Rider, "Evolution of the Concept of Logistics," *Naval War College Review* (December 1970), pp. 23–33.

Business Logistics Defined

Business logistics is a relatively new field of integrated management study resulting mainly from a reorganization of related activities that previously were scattered among the organizational units within the firm. The newness of the field—the first textbook in the field appeared in 1961[2]—in part explains why no generally accepted definition for logistics has yet emerged. One definition of business logistics has been offered by Heskett, Ivie, and Glaskowsky:

> . . . the management of all activities which facilitate movement and the coordination of supply and demand in the creation of time and place utility in goods.[3]

In addition to not agreeing to a common definition, scholars and practitioners also do not yet agree on an appropriate title for the field. Frequently used and largely synonymous titles for business logistics are marketing logistics, physical distribution, materials management, rhocrematics, and industrial logistics. Using the title of physical distribution, the National Council of Physical Distribution Management has adopted a somewhat more restrictive definition:

> "Physical Distribution" is the term employed in manufacturing and commerce to describe the broad range of activities concerned with efficient movement of finished products from the end of the production line to the consumer, and in some cases includes the movement of raw materials from the source of supply to the beginning of the production line. These activities include freight transportation, warehousing, material handling, protective packaging, inventory control, plant and warehouse site selection, order processing, marketing forecasting and customer service.[4]

Some logisticians prefer a definition with military overtones.

> Logistics is the *Art* and *Science* of *Determining Requirements*; *Acquiring* them; *Distributing* them and finally, *Maintaining* them in an operational ready condition for their entire life.[5]

---

[2] Edward W. Smykay, Donald J. Bowersox, and Frank H. Mossman, *Physical Distribution Management: Logistics Problems of the Firm* (New York: The Macmillan Company, 1961).

[3] J. L. Heskett, Robert M. Ivie, and Nicholas A. Glaskowsky, Jr., *Business Logistics: Management of Physical Supply and Distribution* (New York: The Ronald Press Company, 1964), p. 21.

[4] From a pamphlet distributed by The National Council of Physical Distribution Management, 222 West Adams Street, Chicago, Illinois.

[5] Charles A. Stone, "Logistics: Definition," *The Logistics Review*, Vol. 4, No. 16 (1968), p. 6.

All the above definitions suggest something of the scope and content of the logistics field. However, the definition that will be adopted for our purposes and that seems more in line with the scope of the subsequent discussion in this text and the management theme to be pursued is

> Business logistics management is the planning, organizing, and controlling of all move-store activities that facilitate product flow from the point of raw material acquisition to the point of final consumption, and of the attendant information flows, for the purpose of providing a sufficient level of customer service (and associated revenues) consistent with the costs incurred for overcoming the resistance of time and space in providing the service.[6]

These definitions suggest that business logistics might be viewed as a group of related activities to be managed in much the same way as marketing or production functions. Though not necessary under all circumstances, in many firms logistics has been elevated to a top management position, often of equal ranking with marketing and production. One study found that of 47 companies having a physical distribution (logistics) manager, in 37 (79 percent) of the companies he was either a vice president or reported to a vice president.[7] If no formal organizational structure is created, effective management of the related activities may be realized through cooperation among organizational entities such as by forming coordinating committees.

Logistics is specifically concerned with the flow of goods through the economic system. In the business firm, the logistician is concerned with the inbound movement of goods to supply the production processes of the firm. In this setting, the firm is the customer and anticipates a certain level of distribution service from the suppliers. The firm also is a supplier of finished or semi-finished goods, and the logistician must provide a level of distribution service to the firm's customers. The customer may be another firm or a final consumer. The individual firm represents only one stage in a sequence of economic activities that take place in transforming goods from a raw material state into finished goods. Since these activities are often dispersed geographically, movement and storage take place many times before a finished product is in the hands of the final consumer, as illustrated in Fig. 1-1.

The activities which are referred to as logistics activities are a consequence of the distance and time gap between production's location and the point of consumption and of the inability or the economic undesirability of having production output respond instantaneously to the needs of the market place. Thus, primary logistics activities must be movement and storage. In addition, information flow, especially sales information, is also a key activity, as it sets the logistics system in motion. The logistician sets the level of the move-store activities in a way that gives an optimum balance between the contribution to revenues associated with

---

[6] Adapted with modification from Ronald H. Ballou, "Broadening and Unifying Marketing Logistics," *The Logistics Review*, Vol. 6 (Winter 1970), p. 201.

[7] John F. Spencer, "Physical Distribution Management Finds Its Level," *Handling & Shipping*, Vol. 7 (November 1966), pp. 67–69.

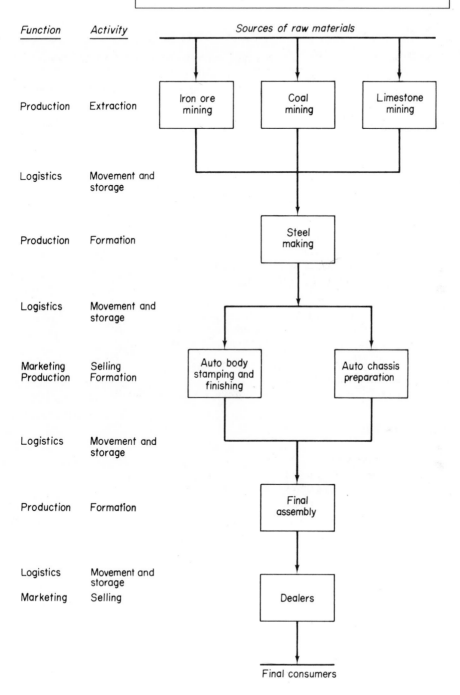

FIGURE 1-1
An abbreviated product flow channel for automobile production, selling, and distribution

Function	Activity	
		Sources of raw materials
Production	Extraction	Iron ore mining / Coal mining / Limestone mining
Logistics	Movement and storage	
Production	Formation	Steel making
Logistics	Movement and storage	
Marketing Production	Selling Formation	Auto body stamping and finishing / Auto chassis preparation
Logistics	Movement and storage	
Production	Formation	Final assembly
Logistics Marketing	Movement and storage Selling	Dealers
		Final consumers

the level of customer service provided and the cost of maintaining the customer service level.

TYPICAL ACTIVITIES

The content of logistics within a firm varies considerably with the type of business and how management perceives the scope of logistics and associated decision problems. A representative list of logistics elements for a firm with substantial logistics costs is as follows.

Key Elements

1. *Transportation*
   a. mode and service selection
   b. carrier routing
   c. vehicle scheduling

2. *Inventories*
   a. finished goods stocking policies
   b. record keeping
   c. supply scheduling (purchasing)
   d. short-term sales forecasting

3. *Customer service*
   Cooperate with marketing in
   a. determining customer needs and wants for service
   b. determining customer response to service

4. *Order processing and information flows*
   a. sales order procedures
   b. information collection, storage, and manipulation
   c. data analysis

Supporting Activities

1. *Warehousing*
   a. space determination
   b. stock layout and dock design
   c. stock placement
   d. warehouse configuration

2. *Materials handling*
   a. equipment selection
   b. equipment replacement policies
   c. order picking procedures
   d. stock storage and retrieval

3. *Protective packaging*
   Design for
   a. handling
   b. storage
   c. protection

4. *Product scheduling*
   Cooperate with production in
   a. specifying aggregate production quantities
   b. sequencing and timing of production
5. *Facility location*
   a. determining location, number, and size of facilities needed
   b. allocating demand to facilities

Maintenance is an activity that conspicuously has been omitted from the list. Though this activity is common in the military logistics organization, it has not generally been a responsibility of the business logistician. It does become important in the evaluation of various system design alternatives such as selection among transportation alternatives (private ownership vs. common carrier). However, the maintenance activity more often is the responsibility of the firm's production function.

LOGISTICS IN MARKETING AND PRODUCTION

It has been the tradition in this country to organize a manufacturing firm around its marketing and production functions. Typically, marketing meant *selling* something and production meant *making* something, though there have been recent attempts to broaden these concepts. Although few businessmen would agree that their organization is so simple, the fact remains that many businesses emphasize these functions while other functions such as traffic, accounting, and engineering are treated as supporting activities. Such an attitude is justified to a degree, because if the firm's products cannot be produced and sold, little else matters. However, such an organization is dangerously simple for many firms to follow, since it fails to recognize the quality of the marketing and production efforts and specifically the activities that must take place between the point and time of production and the point and time of consumption. These are the logistics activities, and they affect the efficiency and effectiveness of both marketing and production.

Both marketing and production people consider logistics activities as part of their responsibilities. For example, the following modern definition of marketing includes physical distribution (logistics):

> Marketing is the process in a society by which the demand structure for economic goods and services is anticipated or enlarged and satisfied through the conception, promotion, exchange, and physical distribution of such goods and services.[8]

Marketing's responsibility for physical distribution often includes field warehousing, customer service, and to some extent inventory management. On the other

---

[8] Theodore N. Beckman and William R. Davidson, *Marketing*, eighth edition (New York: The Ronald Press Company, 1967), p. 4.

hand, production people can also see physical distribution as part of their responsibility, as indicated by the following definition of the production function:

> ... one can conceive of production as a function directly concerned with providing form, time, and place utilities in the product.[9]

Production oversees such logistics activities as traffic, finished goods inventories at the factory, purchasing, product receiving at the plant, and overall production scheduling.

It is clear that there can be potential overlap between marketing and production with regard to the responsibility for logistics activities, and unless the management of the firm takes steps to the contrary, logistics activities as a whole can lack *coordination*. Marketing is likely to be interested in those logistics activities that most directly affect sales, such as field warehousing and local transportation. Production, on the other hand, is likely to be interested in those logistics activities that most directly affect manufacturing activities. Finished goods inventories are of particular interest. Fragmentation of interest in and responsibility for logistics activities as well as lack of coordination among logistics activities as a whole can lead to lower customer service and/or higher total logistics costs than might be necessary. It follows that business logistics represents a regrouping, either by formal organizational structure or conceptually in the minds of management, of move-store activities that frequently are partially under the control of marketing and partially under the control of production.

If logistics is looked upon as a separate area of management study, the relationship of logistics activities to both marketing and production is shown in Fig. 1-2. Marketing would primarily be responsible for market research, promotion, pricing, and product mix. Production's responsibilities would be directed toward creating form value in the product. The important activities for production would include plant layout, detailed production scheduling, quality control, and equipment maintenance. Logistics would concern those activities that give the product time and place values. These latter activities have previously been defined. This separation of the activities into three groupings rather than two is not always necessary or advisable to achieve the coordination of logistics activities that we seek. Marketing and production, when broadly conceived and coordinated, can do an effective and efficient job of managing logistics activities without creating an additional organizational entity. Otherwise, a separate functional area for logistics may be the most effective way of achieving the desired coordination.

Fig. 1-2 also shows activities that are at the interface of marketing and logistics, and production and logistics. The interface is created by the arbitrary division of the firm's activities. This results in certain of these activities not being entirely the responsibility of any one organizational entity. Managing the interface activities by one function alone can lead to suboptimum performance for the firm by subordinating broader company goals to the goals of the individual function.

---

[9] Howard L. Timms and Michael F. Pohlen, *The Production Function in Business*, third edition (Homewood, Illinois: Richard D. Irwin, Inc., 1970), p. 7.

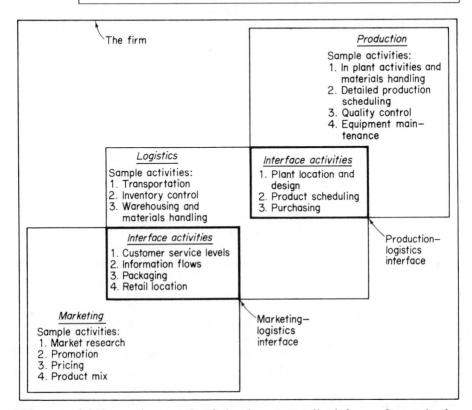

FIGURE 1-2

Regrouping of major activities of the business firm to emphasize logistics activities

This potential danger is a result of the departmentalized form of organization structure so common in companies today. To manage interface activities effectively, some form of cooperation among the functions involved needs to be established. This issue of interfunctional management will be explored in greater depth in the chapter on organization for logistics management. However, it is important to note that establishing a third functional group is not without its cost. The partial cost is an additional functional interface; that is, two now exist where only one between marketing and production previously existed. Some of the most difficult administrative problems arise from the interfunctional conflicts that occur when one is attempting to manage interface activities.

OBJECTIVES OF BUSINESS LOGISTICS

Within the broader objectives of the firm, the business logistician seeks his own functional goals that will move the firm toward its overall objectives. Specifically, he desires to develop a logistics activity mix that will result in the highest possible return on investment over time. There are two dimensions to this goal: (1) the impact of the logistics system design on the revenue contribution and (2) the cost for the system design.

Ideally, the logistician should know how much additional revenue would be generated through incremental improvements in the quality of customer service provided. However, such revenue information is not generally known with great accuracy. Often he must set the customer service level at some value, say 95 percent, that seems acceptable to salesmen and other concerned parties. At this point the analysis turns to a cost analysis rather than profit or return on investment analysis.

Costs involved in the logistics system are broadly of two types: (1) operating costs and (2) capital costs. Operating costs are those that recur periodically or those that vary directly with variations in activity levels. Wages, public warehousing expenses, and administrative and other overhead costs are examples of operating costs. Capital costs are the one-time expenses that do not change with normal variations in activity levels. Examples here are the investment in a private trucking fleet, the construction cost of a privately owned warehouse, and the purchase of materials handling equipment.

If it is assumed that the logistician has knowledge of the impact of his decisions on revenues, his objective can be stated as

$$\text{Max} \sum_i^{N \to \infty} \begin{bmatrix} \text{annual revenue due to customer service level provided} \\ \text{less annual operating cost of the logistics system} \\ \text{annualized investment in the logistics system} \end{bmatrix}_i$$

If the time value of money is great, then maximizing the present value of cash flows or maximizing the internal rate of return of cash flows would be an even more appropriate statement of the objective. Maximizing the cumulative return on investment over time is the single most important objective to assure the *survival* of the firm.

Genesis of Business Logistics

The spirit of the above definitions for logistics is to treat activities related to the physical movement of inventories as an integrated set and to manage them collectively. Though business firms have not denied the importance of distribution, there has been little evidence, until the 1950's, that businesses organized or managed their logistics activities in an integrated way. Educators too have generally given secondary attention to physical distribution and supply activities. Paul D. Converse appraised the state of physical distribution as of 1954:

> ... in the study of marketing and the operation of marketing departments and businesses a great deal more attention is paid to buying and selling than to physical handling. In fact the physical handling of goods seems to be pretty much overlooked by sales executives, advertising men and market researchers.

> ... problems of physical distribution are too often brushed aside as matters of little importance. I have for many years been reading business and economics magazines. Such publications over the years have devoted relatively little space to physical distribution.[10]

In retrospect, Converse was observing from a turning point in the historical development of business logistics. Though the seeds for an integrated treatment of distribution have been traced as far back as 1916 and the work of Arch W. Shaw,[11] the major factors that were instrumental to business logistics emerging as a useful concept were present in the 1950's. The emergence was mainly in the form of a reorganization and rearrangement of the activities related to the task of supplying and distributing goods in order to provide desired customer service levels. The rearrangement of activities and the point of view that resulted were useful because new efficiencies could be gained that previously were overlooked.

REASONS FOR EMERGENCE

Schneider has categorized four major forces that were instrumental to the development of business logistics in industry and the academic world: (1) changes in customer demand patterns, (2) economic pressures on industry, (3) technological change and the application of quantitative techniques to business problems, and (4) the developments in military logistics.[12]

Customer Demand Pattern Shifts. With the prosperity that has occurred in this country since the end of the second world war, prewar consumer demand patterns are no longer relevant. Increasing affluence not only has shifted consumers toward more services, but has also contributed to major geographical changes in population concentrations and to a general proliferation of products and product types offered to consumers.

Population and the market concentrations caused by population movements have at the same time become more concentrated and more dispersed. There has been a market migration of the population seeking the higher-paying jobs of the cities from the rural areas to metropolitan areas that has tended to concentrate markets and reduce the costs of distributing to a dispersed population. However, counterforces, especially the automobile and improved highway networks, have acted to increase the effective size of the metropolitan regions as the population

---

[10] Quoted in Donald J. Bowersox, "Physical Distribution Development, Current Status, and Potential," *Journal of Marketing*, Vol. 33 (January, 1969), p. 63; from Paul D. Converse, "The Other Half of Marketing," *Twenty-Sixth Boston Conference on Distribution* (Boston: Boston Trade Board, 1954), p. 22.

[11] For a summary of this early history, see Bernard J. LaLonde and Leslie M. Dawson, "Pioneers in Distribution," *Transportation and Distribution Management*, Vol. 9 (June 1969), pp. 55–60.

[12] Lewis M. Schneider, "Milestones on the Road of Physical Distribution," reproduced in David McConaughy (ed.), *Readings in Business Logistics* (Homewood, Illinois: Richard D. Irwin, Inc., 1969), pp. 51–63.

has shifted from the cities to surrounding suburban areas. The effect has been to increase the number of retail stocking points and/or to increase the transportation distance and in many cases the time between stores and customers. Marketing through a number of branch stores in shopping centers as compared with a single downtown store can add complexity and usually cost to the associated distribution system.

The combined effect of competition and consumer affluence is probably the major reason for the increasing variety of product items that one can observe throughout the economy. The proliferation of the number of items that must be maintained in inventory increases inventory carrying costs. The increased cost occurs because the sum of the individual inventory levels on a wider range of products and product types exceeds that for a more limited range when the total demand is the same in both cases. Magee observed that replacing one product with three that generate the same level of sales would increase inventories by 60 percent.[13] This upward pressure on inventory costs suggests the need for more careful management.

In summary, Schneider notes:

> . . . physical distribution "dances to the tune" of consumer demand. Because of the shifts in demand patterns, traditional distribution techniques have become increasingly unsatisfactory from a cost and customer service standpoint, and an environment within business has been created in which new techniques and organizational patterns have a greater chance of acceptance.[14]

Economic Pressures. Two economic forces were instrumental in encouraging the movement toward a reorganization for business logistics. First, logistics costs were recognized to be a significant proportion of total costs. Second, reduced profit margins encouraged firms to look for more efficient organizational patterns.

Fragmentation of logistics-related activities among the various organizational entities of the firm has tended to mask the total cost for logistics activities. Accounting systems traditionally have not broken down costs along the lines as we have defined business logistics. However, some data have been gathered that at least indicate the economic magnitude of the logistics problem. At the macroeconomic level, Heskett has estimated that total physical distribution costs in 1960 accounted for 14.9 percent of the United States' gross national product. This was down slightly from 16.4 percent in 1950. Of the total for 1960, 9.2 percent, or approximately two-thirds, went for transportation with the remaining one-third represented primarily by inventory carrying costs.[15] Smykay made a similar estimate for

[13] John F. Magee, "The Logistics of Distribution," *Harvard Business Review*, Vol. 38 (July–August 1960), p. 91.

[14] Schneider, *op. cit.*, p. 54.

[15] J. L. Heskett, "Macroeconomic Cost of Physical Distribution," in *Papers—Third Annual Meeting, American Transportation Research Forum* (Oxford, Indiana: Richard B. Cross Company, 1962), pp. 196–89.

1963 and obtained a lower total cost. Smykay's estimate was a total physical distribution cost of $67.5 billion.[16] As a percentage of the gross national product in current dollars for 1963, physical distribution costs for the entire economy were 11.5 percent.

The potential error in these aggregate estimates is great, and they can be used only as rough guide lines. For example, data on private transportation and inventory carrying costs are not generally reported to governmental agencies and must be estimated. Also, certain classes of logistics activities are not represented, such as local freight transportation by consumers in private automobiles, transmission of utilities (gas, water, and electricity), and government logistics activities. On balance, the above estimates are probably too low rather than too high.

On an individual firm level, logistics costs as a percentage of sales vary widely, depending on the level of logistics activities in a particular industry. In a questionnaire survey of 33 manufacturing concerns, approximately half of which had sales below $5 million, logistics costs were found to be as high as 32 percent of net sales for the food industry and as low as 10 percent for the machinery industry on a two-year (1960–61) average basis.[17] Eight industry categories were cited, as shown in Table 1-3. The expense elements used in this study do not apparently include all the logistics activities that we define as related to the logistics task of the firm. Therefore, these cost estimates tend to be understated. Specifically, costs for information flows, order processing, and purchasing costs are not represented. Also, costs associated with the cost of the money tied up in inventories and the cost of inventory obsolescence and deterioration do not seem to be represented.

A broader study in 1962 involving 270 firms found average physical distribution costs across all industries were 21.8 percent of sales.[18] Table 1-4 shows these costs broken down by functional activity. In this case, the cost breakdown does include the major cost elements of our definition.

While it is clear that business logistics costs are substantial both to the economy as a whole and to many individual firms, the profit squeeze of the postwar period has provided additional impetus to the development of business logistics as a management area. During the postwar period, American business has experienced reduced profit margins compared with prewar years. Major among the reasons for this is the rapid rise of labor costs and the inability to raise prices at a comparable rate. In light of this, business has sought new means of improving the internal efficiency of their operations. Reorganization for business logistics has

---

[16] Edward W. Smykay, "Physical Distribution, Military Logistics, and Marketing Management," reprinted in Norton E. Marks and Robert M. Taylor (eds.), *Marketing Logistics: Perspectives and Viewpoints* (New York: John Wiley and Sons, Inc., 1967), pp. 12–24.

[17] Richard E. Snyder, "Physical Distribution Costs: A Two-Year Analysis," *Distribution Age*, Vol. 62 (January 1963), pp. 45–56.

[18] From a study by A. T. Kearney & Company and reported in Wendell M. Stewart, "Physical Distribution: Key to Improved Volume and Profits," *Journal of Marketing*, Vol. 29 (January 1965), pp. 65–70.

TABLE 1-3
Median percentages of costs to net sales for eight major categories

Expense Element	Food & Food Products Industry			Machinery (Elec. & Nonelec.) Industry			Chemicals, Petroleum, & Rubber Products Industry		
	1960	1961	2-yr. avg.	1960	1961	2-yr. avg.	1960	1961	2-yr. avg.
Common carrier expense—total	10.18	9.63	9.91	8.15	5.29	6.72	10.32	9.31	9.81
Rail shipping expense	6.02	5.63	5.82	1.18	1.04	1.11	5.14	4.76	4.95
Truck shipping expense	2.79	2.80	2.80	5.75	3.60	4.68	3.50	2.94	3.22
Water transportation expense	0.82	0.83	0.83	1.00	0.51	0.75	1.21	1.33	1.27
Air transportation expense	0.55	0.37	0.46	0.22	0.14	0.18	0.47	0.28	0.37
Private trucking expense—total	7.50	5.95	6.73	1.22	0.84	1.03	4.51	3.47	3.99
Truck driver's pay	2.03	1.55	1.79	0.50	0.32	0.41	0.84	0.70	0.77
Equipment leasing charges	3.75	2.97	3.36	0.60	0.40	0.54	2.73	1.98	2.36
Depreciation of equipment	0.89	0.78	0.84	0.01	0.09	0.05	0.01	0.09	0.05
Truck maintenance and supplies (including license fees, insurance, and taxes)	0.83	0.65	0.74	0.02	0.03	0.03	0.62	0.50	0.56
Public warehousing expense (including accessorial charges)[a]	2.37	1.89	2.13	0.29	0.35	0.32	1.55	1.09	1.32
Private warehouse costs—total	5.70	4.02	4.87	0.51	0.53	0.52	3.91	2.88	3.39
At distribution and sales centers	3.52	2.31	2.92	0.11	0.11	0.11	1.59	1.07	1.33
Depreciation	1.04	0.75	0.90	0.11	0.10	0.11	0.60	0.31	0.45
Total overhead, including payroll and maintenance	1.14	0.96	1.05	0.29	0.32	0.30	1.72	1.50	1.61
Materials handling expense—total	2.59	2.34	2.46	0.42	0.36	0.39	1.43	1.41	1.42
Freight handler's pay	0.97	1.17	1.07	0.17	0.16	0.16	0.54	0.51	0.52
Material handling equipment depreciation	0.91	0.57	0.75	0.03	0.03	0.03	0.47	0.49	0.48
Material handling equipment maintenance and supplies	0.71	0.57	0.64	0.22	0.17	0.20	0.42	0.41	0.42
Shipping room costs—total	3.98	3.88	3.93	0.58	0.95	0.76	2.61	2.41	2.51
Payroll	2.05	2.20	2.13	0.35	0.51	0.43	0.53	0.55	0.54
Supplies (including cartons, strapping, etc)	1.37	1.46	1.41	0.16	0.28	0.22	1.45	1.43	1.44
Overhead	0.56	0.22	0.39	0.07	0.16	0.11	0.63	0.43	0.53
Over-short and damaged goods (warehousing and transportation)	0.33	0.27	0.30	0.12	0.02	0.07	0.26	0.19	0.23
Selected administrative expenses related to distribution costs—total	1.77	1.62	1.68	0.11	0.49	0.21	1.36	0.96	1.13
Management: Vice President of traffic	0.34	0.40	0.37	0.05	0.13	0.09	0.99	0.60	0.79
Department heads	0.60	0.38	0.49	0.03	0.09	0.06	0.19	0.20	0.20
Clerical	0.83	0.82	0.82	0.03	0.10	0.06	0.18	0.10	0.14
Others[b]	—	0.02	—	—	0.17	—	—	0.06	—
Total[c]	34.42	29.60	32.01	11.40	8.83	10.02	25.95	21.72	23.80

Expense Element	Paper & Paper Products Industry			Primary & Fabricated Metals Industry			Wood Products (Including Furniture) Industry		
	1960	1961	2-yr. avg.	1960	1961	2-yr. avg.	1960	1961	2-yr. avg.
Common carrier expense—total	4.56	5.60	4.99	5.51	5.14	5.32	9.15	8.81	8.46
Rail shipping expense	2.52	2.80	2.66	1.74	1.64	1.69	4.18	5.07	4.62
Truck shipping expense	2.04	2.60	2.32	2.78	2.52	2.65	3.97	3.71	3.84
Water transportation expense	—	0.20	—	0.80	0.79	0.79	1.00	—	—
Air transportation expense	—	—	—	0.19	0.19	0.19	—	0.03	—
Private trucking expense—total	4.39	2.54	3.45	5.87	3.53	4.70	2.82	2.46	2.64
Truck driver's pay	2.52	1.36	1.94	3.04	1.79	2.42	1.35	1.16	1.25
Equipment leasing charges	1.77	0.96	1.36	0.19	0.24	0.21	0.64	0.25	0.25
Depreciation of equipment	—	0.01	—	0.60	0.35	0.48	0.24	0.25	0.25
Truck maintenance and supplies (including license fees, insurance, and taxes)	0.10	0.21	0.15	2.04	1.15	1.59	0.59	0.39	0.49
Public warehousing expense (including accessorial charges) [a]	2.44	1.40	1.92	—	0.58	—	0.10	0.10	0.10
Private warehouse costs—total	2.85	2.01	2.43	11.30	9.53	10.42	0.70	1.00	0.85
At distribution and sales centers	—	—	—	6.25	4.57	5.41	0.50	0.40	0.45
Depreciation	0.23	0.30	0.27	1.05	0.97	1.01	0.10	0.12	0.11
Total overhead, including payroll and maintenance	2.62	1.71	2.16	4.00	3.99	4.00	0.10	0.48	0.29
Materials handling expense—total	1.41	1.27	1.34	1.61	1.51	1.56	1.08	1.09	1.09
Freight handler's pay	0.84	0.70	0.77	0.71	0.69	0.70	0.75	0.73	0.74
Material handling equipment depreciation	0.38	0.50	0.44	0.80	0.74	0.77	0.15	0.15	0.15
Material handling equipment maintenance and supplies	0.19	0.07	0.13	0.10	0.08	0.09	0.18	0.21	0.20
Shipping room costs—total	3.55	3.01	3.28	3.33	2.49	2.91	1.75	1.43	1.59
Payroll	1.01	0.91	0.96	1.39	1.34	1.36	0.75	0.70	0.72
Supplies (including cartons, strapping, etc)	1.67	1.50	1.58	1.17	0.75	0.96	0.52	0.35	0.44
Overhead	0.87	0.60	0.74	0.77	0.40	0.59	0.48	0.38	0.43
Over-short and damaged goods (warehousing and transportation)	0.21	0.20	0.20	0.02	0.02	0.02	0.22	0.13	0.17
Selected administrative expenses related to distribution costs—total	0.52	0.57	0.53	5.50	3.65	4.30	1.45	0.79	1.09
Management: Vice President of traffic	—	0.03	—	3.50	1.88	2.69	0.15	0.11	0.13
Department heads	0.30	0.29	0.30	—	0.46	—	0.20	0.28	0.24
Clerical	0.22	0.24	0.23	2.00	1.23	1.61	1.10	0.35	0.72
Others [b]	—	0.01	—	—	0.06	—	—	0.05	—
Total [c]	19.93	16.60	18.13	33.14	26.43	29.23	17.27	15.81	15.99

[a] Public warehousing ratios for 1960 included the effect of local distribution.
[b] Not included in the 1960 survey cost accounts.
[c] All totals relating to two-year average figures are additive.
[d] NA (not available).

TABLE 1-3 (cont.)

Expense Element	Textiles Industry			Transportation Equipment Industry		
	1960	1961	2-yr. avg.	1960	1961	2-yr. avg.
Common carrier expense—total	5.42	NAd	NA	NA	5.27	NA
Rail shipping expense	0.65	NA	NA	NA	2.16	NA
Truck shipping expense	3.77	NA	NA	NA	1.44	NA
Water transportation expense	0.50	NA	NA	NA	1.55	NA
Air transportation expense	0.50	NA	NA	NA	0.12	NA
Private trucking expense—total	0.10	NA	NA	NA	1.83	NA
Truck driver's pay	0.10	NA	NA	NA	0.72	NA
Equipment leasing charges	—	NA	NA	NA	0.63	NA
Depreciation of equipment	—	NA	NA	NA	0.22	NA
Truck maintenance and supplies (including license fees, insurance, and taxes)	—	NA	NA	NA	0.26	NA
Public warehousing expense (including accessorial charges) a	1.00	NA	NA	NA	—	NA
Private warehouse costs—total	5.74	NA	NA	NA	0.74	NA
At distribution and sales centers	3.00	NA	NA	NA	0.21	NA
Depreciation	0.65	NA	NA	NA	0.11	NA
Total overhead, including payroll and maintenance	2.09	NA	NA	NA	0.42	NA
Materials handling expense—total	1.00	NA	NA	NA	0.80	NA
Freight handler's pay	0.80	NA	NA	NA	0.58	NA
Material handling equipment depreciation	0.10	NA	NA	NA	0.10	NA
Material handling equipment maintenance and supplies	0.10	NA	NA	NA	0.12	NA
Shipping room costs—total	2.17	NA	NA	NA	1.12	NA
Payroll	0.84	NA	NA	NA	0.63	NA
Supplies (including cartons, strapping, etc)	0.29	NA	NA	NA	0.37	NA
Overhead	1.04	NA	NA	NA	0.12	NA
Over-short and damaged goods (warehousing and transportation)	0.01	NA	NA	NA	0.01	NA
Selected administrative expenses related to distribution costs—total	0.71	NA	NA	NA	0.45	NA
Management: Vice President of traffic	0.13	NA	NA	NA	0.23	NA
Department heads	0.20	NA	NA	NA	0.12	NA
Clerical	0.38	NA	NA	NA	0.09	NA
Othersb	—	NA	NA	NA	0.01	NA
Total c	16.15	NA	NA	NA	10.22	NA

Source: Richard E. Snyder, "Physical Distribution Costs: A Two-Year Analysis," Distribution Age, Vol. 62 (January 1963), pp. 50–51.

		TABLE 1-4
		A. T. Kearney & Company study of the physical distribution costs in 270 companies

Functional Activity		Percentage of Sales[a]
Administration		2.4
Transportation:		
Inbound	2.1	
Outbound	4.3	6.4
Receiving and shipping		1.7
Packaging		2.6
Warehousing:		
In-plant	2.1	
Field	1.6	3.7
Inventory carrying costs:		
Interest	2.2	
Taxes, insurance, obsolescence	1.6	3.8
Order processing		1.2
	Total	21.8%

[a] Average costs across all industries.
Source: Wendell M. Stewart, "Physical Distribution: Key to Improved Volume and Profits," *Journal of Marketing*, Vol. 29 (January 1965), p. 67.

offered some previously unrecognized economics and has been referred to as "the last frontier for cost economies."[19]

Technological Change and Quantitative Models. Technological innovation is not unique to logistics, but the impact of innovation has increased the complexity of logistics problems and, hence, the need for careful management. Complexity refers to the number of alternatives associated with logistics decisions. Though technological change has occurred in materials handling through palletization, containerization, and packaging, and in the data processing system through the addition of electronic data processing capability, the proliferation of transportation services and its effect on service choice is a good illustration of the additional complexity that technological innovation has created. Before 1920, transportation service was primarily limited to the railroad and to water transportation, where it was available. Since that time, there has been a resurgence of water transportation services, and air freight and highway transportation have been developed as new transportation services. Also, the additional modes greatly increase the possibility of combined services, such as highway-rail, rail-water, and highway-rail-water. The best choice of a transportation service is not as obvious as when one or only a few choices exist. Hence, the proliferation of logistics choices through technological innovation encourages reorganization and centralized management of logistics activities to deal more effectively with the increasing complexities.

[19] Donald D. Parker, "Improved Efficiency and Reduced Cost in Marketing," *Journal of Marketing*, Vol. 26 (April 1962), p. 16.

Scientific management techniques and computer technology also have grown along with logistics system components. During the 1950's, there was rapid growth in the application of quantitative methodology to business problems. The digital computer became a useful business tool rather than a laboratory curiosity. These developments were particularly important to the genesis of business logistics. The physical as opposed to behavioral nature of many logistics problems makes them amenable to quantitative analysis. Problems such as facility location and multiple product inventory control are now approached by simulation, mathematical programming, and heuristic methods. This more sophisticated treatment permits and encourages a broader scope towards logistics problems that is essential to effective business logistics management. That is, inventory problems can be analyzed in relation to transportation problems, and combined solutions can be found. A less sophisticated analysis might require that each class of problems be treated as independent with resulting suboptimum decisions.

The Military Experience. The military was and continues to be a source of experience from which the business sector may benefit. Though the problems of each are not identical—that is, the military has the objective to win wars and as a result often established a "customer service" level higher than that usually found among businesses, and the maintenance activity is not generally a logistics responsibility in the private sector—there are a great many similarities. Common military logistics activities include determining requirements, procurement, storage, transportation, and inventory management, all of which are included in the business logistics function.

Military logistics problems are enormous. For example, the military alone maintains inventories valued at about one-third of those held by all United States manufacturers. The experience generated from managing inventory levels of this size is valuable to the business logistician. The research supported through institutions such as the RAND Corporation and many of this country's universities has provided an extensive information base on which business sector logistics has developed.

The Total Cost Concept

Central to the development of business logistics is the so-called total cost concept. The total cost concept is the recognition that the logistics system should be defined broadly enough so that all the relevant costs to a decision problem are considered in the decision process and are balanced at optimum. A narrowly defined problem can lead to solutions that are suboptimum in light of the logistics system as a whole. It seems rather obvious that when more variables are considered in a decision problem, a higher-order optimum solution that is, an optimum solution to a broader problem definition, is possible. If all the activities of the firm could be analyzed simultaneously and their interdependencies accounted for, more comprehensive solutions could be obtained than if selected groups of activities are analyzed within the limits and responsibilities of subdivided organizational entities. However, the scope of decision problems for a functional area tends to be limited by the activities assigned to it. This leads to the important question of interest to us: Which activities should be assigned to the logistics?

If we accept the idea that functional subdivisions of the firm are needed for purposes of effective administration, then the activities that are assigned to a given functional area should be the most relevant selection from among all activities of the firm. Activities are often broadly subdivided on the basis of the major tasks of the firm such as marketing, logistics, and production. Within this broad divisioning, individual activities are assigned on the basis of the strength of their economic interrelationships. The total cost concept suggests that transportation and inventory costs—the major logistics cost activities—should be thought of as related or managed within a single functional area, since their cost patterns tend to be *conflicting*. Other activities in the logistics mix show similar major economic interdependencies and are therefore grouped within the logistics function. It is this reasoning that leads to the list of key logistics elements and activities as noted earlier in the chapter.

AN ILLUSTRATION

The airlines currently are encouraging potential customers in the use of the total cost concept in an attempt to promote freight service. With an unenlightened approach to selecting transportation service, that is, by a comparison of the direct cost of the various services, air freight is generally the most expensive and would not be selected. In fact, the cheapest service is the most likely candidate for selection. A comparison of direct transportation costs neglects the effect of speed and dependability of inventory levels. As a general rule, as the speed and dependability of a service increase, so does the cost of the service. Conversely, the improved quality of the service means lower inventory costs as lead time and demand uncertainties are reduced. Thus, there is a cost conflict or tradeoff situation established, as shown in Fig. 1-3.

Fig. 1-3 might well represent a decision problem of an industrial buyer purchasing goods for resale. The buyer, in this case, selects and pays for the transportation. Suppose that rail, truck, and air are the transportation possibilities with the service quality and cost of service increasing in this same order. The lowest cost service would be rail, but when this low transportation cost is combined with a high inventory cost, the total cost is overly high. If the company buys a premium transportation service, the additional transportation costs can be offset by reduced inventory costs. Inventory costs will drop with the improved transportation service characteristics as less stock needs to be maintained as protection against customer demand and stock replenishment uncertainties. These may be diminishing returns with improved service as the decreasing inventory costs are exceeded by the increasing transportation costs. The best balance between these two conflicting cost patterns is sought. Fig. 1-3 in our example shows this to be

FIGURE 1-3

Generalized cost conflict between transportation and inventory costs as a function of transportation service characteristics

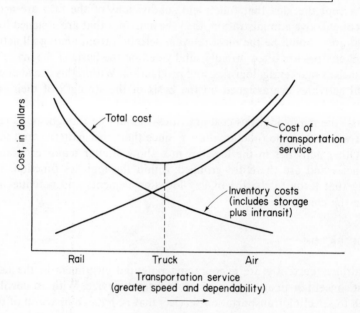

truck service. However, the economics of any particular situation may shift the optimum point. Thus, it is possible that air freight can be the most economical service choice, even though its direct cost is high.

Other Examples. The total cost concept applies to more than the transportation service selection problem. In fact, nearly every logistics problem involves a tradeoff of conflicting costs. This is the decision maker's dilemma. If there were no cost tradeoffs to be concerned with, the solutions to problems would be obvious and there would be little need for management or for this text. Such is not the case, and it should be made perfectly clear that balancing conflicting cost patterns is at the heart of our study of logistics management.

Additional examples of logistics problems and the tradeoff of relevant costs are offered in Fig. 1-4. Fig. 1-4(a) illustrates the problem of setting the customer service level. As customers receive a higher level of service, fewer of them are lost as a result of out-of-stock situations and slow and unreliable deliveries. Expressed another way, the cost due to lost sales decreases with improved customer service. Counterbalancing the lost-sales cost is the cost for maintaining the level of service. Improved service usually means that more must be paid for transportation, order processing, and inventories. The best tradeoff occurs at a point less than 100 percent perfect customer service.

Fig. 1-4(b) shows the basic economic considerations in determining the number of warehouses for a logistics system. Typically, outbound transportation

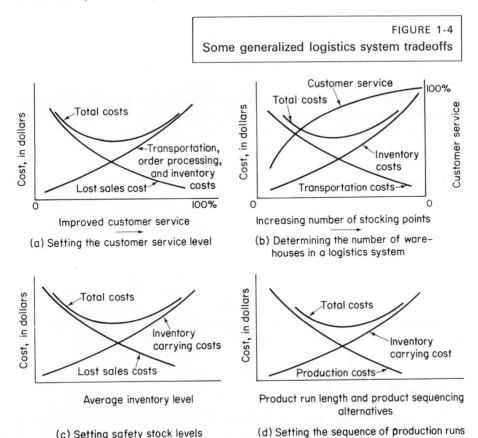

FIGURE 1-4

Some generalized logistics system tradeoffs

(a) Setting the customer service level

(b) Determining the number of warehouses in a logistics system

(c) Setting safety stock levels

(d) Setting the sequence of production runs for multiple products

costs from the warehouse exceed the inbound costs so transportation costs decline with increasing numbers of warehouses. However, as the number of warehouses proliferates, the inventory level for the entire system increases and inventory costs rise. In addition, the customer service level is affected by this decision. The decision problem is one of balancing the combined inventory-transportation costs against the contribution to revenues due to the customer service level provided.

Fig. 1-4(c) illustrates the problem of setting the safety stock level for inventories. Since safety stock increases the average level of inventories and also affects the customer service level through the availability of stock when an order is placed, lost sales cost responds as noted in Fig. 1-4(a). Increasing the average level of inventories will increase the inventory carrying cost. Transportation costs remain relatively unaffected. Again, a balance is sought between these opposing costs.

Finally, Fig. 1-4(d) shows the basic features of a multiproduct scheduling problem. Production costs are affected by the sequence in which the products are produced and the length of production runs. As the production sequence of products is changed, inventory costs will increase, since orders will not necessarily be received at the optimum time they are desired to replenish depleted stocks. The effect is to raise the average inventory level. The best sequence and run length in which to produce the products are found where the combined production and inventory costs are minimized.

The above examples illustrate the total cost concept as applied to the internal problems of the firm and specifically to logistics problems. However, at times decisions made by one firm in the channel of distribution affect the logistics costs of another. For example, the inventory policies of a buyer affect both the inventory costs of the shipper and the operating costs of the carrier. In this case, it is necessary to extend the boundaries of the system beyond either the logistics function or the firm possibly to include several firms. Thus, the total cost equation would be expanded, and the scope of management decision making would extend beyond the legal limits of the firm. The point is, the total cost, or alternately the total system, concept is a concept without clear boundaries. Although one might argue that in some way all activities of the entire economy are economically related to the logistics problem of the firm, to attempt to assess all the various cost tradeoffs that might relate to any decision problem is folly. It is left to the judgment of management to decide which factors to consider relevant and to include them in the system. This defines whether the total cost analysis will include only factors within the logistics function as we have defined it or whether the analysis should be extended to include other factors under the control of the firm or even some beyond the immediate control of the firm.

Approach of the Text

The emphasis in this text will be directed toward the managerial problems associated with moving and storing goods by domestic business firms. Little direct attention will be given to logistics problems as they occur in the military, government supply, private companies primarily engaged in international manufacture or trade, or institutions that are usually not considered to be profit motivated, such as hospitals and universities. However, much that will be discussed is transferable with some modification in problem description to these related areas. The reader is challenged to expand the scope of logistics as he works through this material.

It is assumed that one of the most difficult tasks facing the manager of business logistics activities is decision making, that is, the identification of and selection among alternative courses of action. Fortunately, many logistics problems yield to scientific analysis. It will be the approach in this text to structure logistics problems in as definitive a manner as possible and to apply quantitative methodology along with managerial judgment in seeking optimum solutions to realistic problems. In general, behavioral problems involving motivation and control of personnel will not be emphasized. Though also extremely important to management, behavioral problems cannot effectively be handled within the scope of this text.

Order of Discussion. The layout of the parts of the book reflects an attempt to decompose the logistics decision problem into a basic structure, which is shown in Fig. 1-5. The management functions of planning, organizing, and controlling are recognized and provide a managerial structure to the text. Planning is the most emphasized, since organizing and controlling are in large part variations of planning.

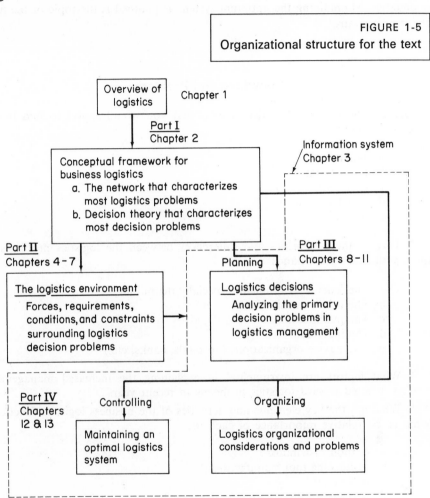

FIGURE 1-5
Organizational structure for the text

Specifically, the discussion is divided into four parts. Part I of the text provides an overview of the logistics system and establishes a framework for logistics problem analysis in terms of the network and classical decision theory. The information system is introduced in this part because it transcends all management functions. Part II presents general descriptive material about the environment in which the logistician makes decisions. This part is a recognition that the logistician needs some basic understanding of the product, the transportation system, and the storage system in order to develop reasonable alternatives and to assess the level of risk associated with his decision problems—in general, to make better decisions. Part

III discusses various analytical approaches to solving common logistics problems. Such problems are transportation mode selection, routing for pickup and delivery, warehouse location, and inventory control. Part IV discusses the organizational concerns of logistics management both within the firm and beyond the firm's legal boundaries. Maintaining the optimum system as planned is the topic of the final chapter on control.

Questions and Problems

Compare the business logistics systems that you would expect to find in the following countries:

    a. Japan
    b. United States
    c. Cambodia
    d. Great Britain
    e. Russia

2. Discuss the similarities and differences between the logistics problems of the manufacturing firm and:

    a. The federal government, especially the military
    b. The urban transit system
    c. The public utilities
    d. The individual
    e. The service organizations (hospitals, banks, etc.)

3. What factors are instrumental in explaining the increased management interest directed toward logistics problems in recent years?

4. What are the key elements and activities of the business logistics function? What is the relative importance of each to:

    a. A food distributor?
    b. A machine tool manufacturer?
    c. A hospital?
    d. A computer hardware manufacturer?
    e. A department store?

5. What is the total cost concept in business logistics management? Why is it so important to business logistics?

6. Establishing logistics as a separate organizational entity within a business firm creates an additional set of interface activities. What are interface activities? Why would the creation of an additional set of interface activities cause concern among most companies?

7. Is survival an appropriate basis for defining the objective for business logistics? What support is there for it? What exceptions are there?

8. Air freight has generally been considered a premium form of transportation and has been used accordingly. As the newly appointed distribution manager for Speedy All-Cargo Airlines, how would you suggest that air transportation service be promoted to manufacturers of such products as electrical machinery, instruments, photographic goods, and leather products? Your hope is to encourage these manufacturers to use air freight on a regular basis, but this is likely to be accomplished only if you can show convincing economic reasons for changing traditional methods of distribution. Specifically, what arguments would you put forth?

9. Differentiate "business logistics management" from

    a. Traffic management
    b. Marketing management
    c. Production management

Selected Bibliography

BOWERSOX, DONALD J., BERNARD J. LaLONDE, and EDWARD W. SMYKAY, *Readings in Physical Distribution Management*. New York: The Macmillan Company, 1969.

BOWERSOX, DONALD J., EDWARD W. SMYKAY, and BERNARD J. LaLONDE, *Physical Distribution Management*, revised edition. New York: The Macmillan Company, 1968.

CONSTANTIN, JAMES A., *Principles of Logistics Management*. New York: Appleton-Century Crofts, 1966.

DANIEL, NORMAN E. and J. RICHARD JONES (eds.), *Business Logistics: Concepts and Viewpoints*. Boston: Allyn and Bacon, 1969.

HESKETT, J. L., ROBERT M. IVIE, and NICHOLAS A. GLASKOWSKY, JR., *Business Logistics: Management of Physical Supply and Distribution*. New York: The Ronald Press Company, 1964.

MAGEE, JOHN F., *Physical-Distribution Systems*. New York: McGraw-Hill Book Company, 1967.

MAGEE, JOHN F., *Industrial Logistics*. New York: McGraw-Hill Book Company, 1968.

MARKS, NORTON E. and ROBERT M. TAYLOR (eds.), *Marketing Logistics: Perspectives and Viewpoints*. New York: John Wiley and Sons, Inc., 1967.

McCONAUGHY, DAVID (ed.), *Readings in Business Logistics*. Homewood, Illinois: Richard D. Irwin, 1969.

MOSSMAN, FRANK H. and NEWTON MORTON, *Logistics of Distribution Systems*. Boston: Allyn and Bacon, 1965.

PLOWMAN, E. GROSVENOR, *Elements of Business Logistics*. Stanford: Stanford University Press, 1964.

SMYKAY, EDWARD W. and BERNARD J. LaLONDE, *Physical Distribution: The New and Profitable Science of Business Logistics*. Chicago: The Dartnell Corporation, 1967.

Chapter 2

Science and Logistics Decision Making

In this text we shall explore many methods that aid in the solution of distribution problems. These methods may appear on the surface to be quite different, yet there is an underlying structure called *decision theory* that links all decision-making methods together. In addition, there is a unifying theme (the *network*) that links all elements of the logistics system together at the conceptual level. Both decision theory and the logistics network are mathematical abstractions of real-world activities, but, as Albert Einstein observed, "How can it be that mathematics, being after all a product of human thought independent of experience, is so admirably adapted to the objects of reality?" This chapter develops conceptualized frameworks for solving real-world logistics problems in a scientific manner.

The Conceptualized Logistics Problem

In the broadest sense, the management of the various logistics activities in the business firm is the singular problem of designing an effective and efficient network configuration. That is, the logistics manager is interested in planning and controlling a distribution network that will permit the products of his firm to be at the right place and at the right time as they are demanded by customers. The objective of the network design is to construct a configuration of warehouses, retail outlets, factories, inventory levels, transportation services, and information processing systems that will achieve an optimum balance between the sales resulting from the level of customer service established by the network design and the costs associated with the creation and operation of the network.

Conceptually, the business logistics problem can be viewed as an abstract network of links and nodes, as shown in Fig. 2-1. The links of the network represent the movement of goods between the various inventory storage points, or nodes, which are usually retail stores, warehouses, or factories. There may be several links between any pair of nodes to represent alternate forms of transportation service, different routes, and different products. Nodes represent points where the flow of inventory is temporarily stopped, for example, at a warehouse, before moving on to the retail store and the final customer.

The above move-store activities for inventory flows are only one part of the total logistics system. In addition there is a network of information flows. Information consists of such data as dollar sales, product costs, inventory levels, transportation data, etc. Links in the information network usually consist of the mail or some electronic means such as telephone or teletype for transmitting information from one geographic point to another. Nodes are the various data collection and processing points, such as a clerk who handles order processing and prepares bills of lading[1] or a computer that updates inventory records.

The information network is conceptually much like the product flow network in that they both can be viewed as a collection of links and nodes. A major difference in the networks is that product mainly flows "down" the channel of distribution (toward the final consumer), whereas information mainly (but not entirely) flows "up" the channel (toward raw material sources), as shown in Fig. 2-1.

The product flow network and the information network combine to form a conceptualized logistics system. These networks are combined because designing each separately can lead to a suboptimum design for the entire system. That is, the networks are not independent. For example, the design of the information network influences the order cycle times for the system. Order cycle times in turn affect the inventory levels that must be maintained at the nodes in the product network. The availability of inventory affects customer service levels, and customer service levels in turn affect order cycle times and the information network design. There are also additional interdependencies that exist between the two networks that require viewing the logistics system as a whole rather than by its parts.

Universality of the Network. The above discussion and the network shown in Fig. 2-1 are directed toward the business logistics system. However, the network can represent many types of logistics systems as well. For example, the military

---

[1] A bill of lading is a contractual agreement between the shipper and carrier setting forth the conditions under which the freight will be moved.

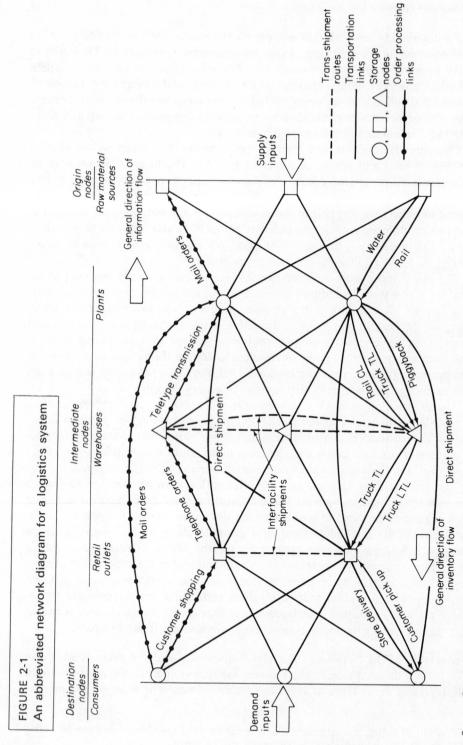

FIGURE 2-1
An abbreviated network diagram for a logistics system

Source: Ronald H. Ballou, "Broadening and Unifying Market Logistics." *The Logistics Review.* Vol. 6 (Winter 1970). p. 8. Reproduced by permission of *The Logistics Review.*

32

logistics system corresponds almost directly to the business logistics system at this conceptual level. Logistics systems at the microeconomic level, such as the flow of goods within a warehouse or the logistics problems between the final consumer and the retail outlet, are also represented by the network. The transportation of people within metropolitan areas (urban logistics) can be described by this same network. The concept of the network pervades all types of logistics activities at all levels of the economy. It is the unifying theme that ties all related logistics areas together, and it is the conceptual framework that underlies the function of business logistics management.[2]

The Management Process

The logistician has the power to change and maintain the network in a desired configuration. He influences the network design and operation through the activity of management. Since this book is about logistics *management*, it makes sense to understand a bit about the management process itself. A normative model of the management process is shown in Fig. 2-2 which relates the primary management activities of analysis for decision making, implementing and controlling to each other as well as to the environment and goals of the firm.

The decision-making (planning) process often is the most difficult part of the overall management activity; that is, deciding what to do with regard to the design and operation of the logistics system when future events are not known for sure. Fortunately, the process can be structured, and the structure in turn provides a common framework for attacking nearly all logistics problems. The elements of planning are shown in the upper two-thirds of Fig. 2-2. Major elements in the planning process include (1) the logistics environment, (2) goals, (3) future events, and (4) analysis. The lower one-third of Fig. 2-2 relates to putting decisions into action and maintaining optimum performance levels. The latter is left for discussion in the last two chapters of the book.

THE LOGISTICS ENVIRONMENT

The first important element in the decision-making process is the logistics environment. The logistics environment is a collective term referring to all factors, constraints, forces, conditions, circumstances, and relationships that surround and impinge on logistics decisions and over which the decision maker has little or no control. It is the logistician's world. More specifically, it includes the transportation rate structure, the available types of transportation and warehousing services, legal restrictions, market structure, technological advances, and more. It is from this environment that logistics problems, alternative courses of action, and constraints relevant to logistics activities are derived. For purposes of this text, the

---

[2] For an expanded discussion of the network as a unifying theme for logistics management, see Ronald H. Ballou, "Broadening and Unifying Marketing Logistics," *The Logistics Review*, Vol. 6 (Winter 1970), pp. 5-23.

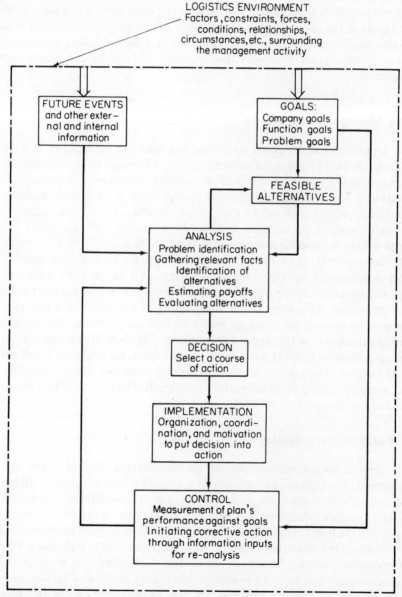

FIGURE 2-2

A normative model of the management activity

LOGISTICS ENVIRONMENT
Factors, constraints, forces,
conditions, relationships,
circumstances, etc., surrounding
the management activity

FUTURE EVENTS
and other exter-
nal and internal
information

GOALS:
Company goals
Function goals
Problem goals

FEASIBLE
ALTERNATIVES

ANALYSIS
Problem identification
Gathering relevant facts
Identification of
alternatives
Estimating payoffs
Evaluating alternatives

DECISION
Select a course
of action

IMPLEMENTATION
Organization, coordi-
nation, and motivation
to put decision into
action

CONTROL
Measurement of plan's
performance against goals
Initiating corrective action
through information inputs
for re-analysis

environment is classified into three major headings. These are (1) the product, (2) the transportation system, and (3) the storage system. The logistician needs a working knowledge of each element if he is to be effective in making decisions that will move the firm toward its ultimate goals. Though no lengthy discussion of the environment is offered at this point, a basic outline is given to show the place of the logistics environment in the making of logistics decisions.

The Product. The product is the center of focus of most logistics activities. Depending on the particular vantage point of the decision maker, the product appears to be different. The person making promotional decisions views the product as a convenience, as a status symbol, or as some other image that can be created in the mind of the consumer. The person responsible for production decisions has an entirely different view. Here the product is seen as a collection of materials that are transformed into desired forms at a minimum cost. However, to the logistician, product definition centers on (1) its phyisical characteristics, such as bulk, weight, and package design, and on special characteristics such as fragility, flamability, and perishability, (2) service requirements from the customer's point of view, such as delivery time and stock availability, and (3) economic characteristics, such as value and price. The point is, the logistician needs an in-depth knowledge of only a portion of the entire business environment to make most decisions. Of course, there are times when logistics decisions interface with the other functions of the business, and in these cases broader knowledge and cooperation with other functional areas will be required.

The Transportation System. The transportation system refers to the entire movement capability available to the company including all the various transportation services—private and public, singular and coordinated. Basically, transportation service is characterized by (1) the average transit time for product movement, (2) the dependability of the service, (3) the quality of movement in terms of loss and damage, (4) service frequency and availability, and (5) the cost of service. Most alternatives that include transportation services embrace these five factors in varying degrees. Underlying these factors is a complex government-regulated rate structure, a system of transport facilities and operation equipment, and a capability to perform at a given level of service.

The Storage System. The final element in the environment for logistics decision making is the storage system. This system includes (1) the maintenance of inventories and (2) the supporting warehouse facilities and materials-handling equipment necessary for inventory holding and processing. In this case, alternative courses of action revolve around different inventory stocking policies, warehouse locational patterns, internal warehouse materials stocking and flow arrangements, and combinations of public and private warehousing.

GOALS

Goals provide the purpose for which decisions are made and are ultimately derived from the needs and wants of society. Goals may be stated differently for different levels in the firm. There are company-wide objectives that the firm as a whole seeks to achieve. Such goals may relate to community goodwill, growth, return on investment, etc. Sometimes different but facilitating goals to the firm's broader goals are established for the firm's logistics function. The single most important objective here should be the maximization of the long-run return on investment. Finally, there are individual problem goals. These often are more limited in scope than either company or function goals, but they too supplement the broader goals of the logistics function and of the firm. Problem objectives may be to minimize costs, maximize short-term profits, maximize customer service, etc. These more narrow objectives are reasonable in many cases because the controllable variables in the problem do not directly influence all the factors that comprise the broader goals. For example, the problem of stock layout in warehouses can appropriately be resolved by using a cost-minimizing objective, since customer service, revenues, community goodwill, and capital investment levels are relatively unaffected by the alternative layout plans that might be selected. Hence, all objectives except those relating to costs are held constant. In those problem areas where a simple quantifiable objective does not adequately meet the goals for the problem solution, it is often effective to retain the limited objective so as to make some initial approximations to the problem solution and then to treat the broader aspects of the objectives as modifying the initial solution.

All goals are derived from the environment and ultimately from the needs and wants of society. Firms exist to serve these needs and wants. In a competitive society, profits are the determiner of a firm's survival. Therefore, the most important decision-making goals should be economic or economically related ones. This is the posture that will be used in approaching logistics problems throughout this text.

FUTURE EVENTS AND OTHER INFORMATION

Logistics decision making involves planning today, when future events are not known for sure, the courses of action that will have a payoff under future conditions. An event (also called a state of nature) for decision-making purposes is any condition or circumstance that affects the future benefits to be derived from various courses of action. Events can be the result of political decisions, weather, and consumer decisions as derived from the environment. More specifically, the particular event or combination of events that take place, say a future level of sales, influence the outcome (the level of profits, for example) of each possible course of action, yet events are not within the control of the decision maker. If some future events are known, then such information merely aids in the preselection of some courses of action over others.

Not all information relates directly to future occurrences. Cost information, risk preference data, historical sales data, market information, and the like represent information obtained both internal and external to the firm. This information is used to help to identify feasible alternative courses of action and to determine the payoff associated with each alternative.

ANALYSIS

Analysis is a broad activity in the decision-making process. It consists of a five-step process: (1) problem identification, (2) gathering the relevent facts about the problem, (3) indicating the feasible alternatives, (4) estimating payoffs for the alternatives, and (5) searching for the best alternative. It is the focal activity where the environment, future events, and goals are brought together with a particular problem to be solved. A problem exists when there is a difference between where the company is or is headed and where it should be or where management desires it to be.

Problem identification is the recognition that certain desired goals are not being achieved. This recognition may come from the measurement activity of the control function (Fig. 2-2) or from the conscious efforts of management in the never-ending process of gathering facts and analyzing the facts against goals. Once the problem has been identified, further fact gathering is required to specify alternatives that are feasible, that is, alternatives that are quickly eliminated because they would be illegal, because they would be beyond the financial means of the company, because the financial return is clearly outside the policy guide lines of the company, etc. Also, additional facts are needed to sharpen predictions of future events and evaluate the payoffs of the feasible alternatives. Estimating payoffs requires establishing some value for each feasible alternative and each possible future event. The data for these payoff values are often easily obtained from the logistics information system, though research studies may have to be conducted to provide the data not already generated or maintained by the total information system of the company. After the decision problem is structured and a choice criterion established, the final step in the decision process is to make a selection. Evaluating alternatives may be done on an intuitive basis by the manager, or the decision problem may be modelled and quantitative techniques may be applied to uncover the best choice. The decision process is now complete.

In summary, decision making has been viewed as a *process*. The process is a normative one which indicates the steps that the logistics manager *should* go through in making decisions rather than the ones he does follow. We cannot be sure what process he actually uses. However, the process described here is rational and can be effective in achieving the economic objective prescribed for logistics.

Digression on a General Analytical Decision Model

The conceptualized network model relates all the elements of logistics management to each other in an integrated system. Selecting among alternative system designs is aided by an additional concept known as *decision theory*. Decision theory provides a general analytical model relating the various key elements of single decision problems in a logical way. Because the decision theory model offers, in a simple way, the concepts that pervade all logistics planning and control models even the most sophisticated ones such as warehouse location, inventory control, or transport routing models, it is worth our time to digress from a direct discussion of logistics matters to develop a decision theory framework. The reader already familiar with the basic ideas of decision theory may wish to skip this section.

Decision theory refers to a mathematical representation of the decision problem that embodies its major elements of future events, alternatives, and payoffs. The simplest of problems can be structured in the form of a two-dimensional matrix, as shown in Fig. 2-3. The alternative courses of action S_i are arrayed along one side with future events or states of nature N_j along the other. There is a probability $P(N_j)$ ranging from 0 to 1 associated with each state of nature, and it represents the likelihood that the state of nature will occur. The payoffs W_{ij} for various alternatives S_i and states of nature N_j are in the body of the matrix. The value of each alternative V_i which is a function of both the states of nature and the payoff values are listed on the right-hand side of the matrix. Computing the value of each alternative and then selecting an alternative among all alternatives depend on the decision criterion established by the decision maker.

FIGURE 2-3
General matrix representation of the decision problem

	States of Nature					
	$P(N_1)$[a]	$P(N_2)$	$P(N_3)$	$\cdots$	$P(N_n)$	*Value of*
	N_1	N_2	N_3	$\cdots$	N_n	*Alternatives*
	S_1	W_{11}[b]	W_{12}	$\cdots$	W_{1n}	V_1[c]
Alternative	S_2	W_{21}	W_{22}	$\cdots$	W_{2n}	V_2
courses of	S_3	W_{31}	W_{32}	$\cdots$	W_{3n}	V_3
action	.	.	.	$\cdots$	.	.
	.	.	.	$\cdots$	.	.
	.	.	.	$\cdots$	.	.
	S_m	W_{m1}	W_{m2}	$\cdots$	W_{mn}	V_m

[a] Probability of the corresponding state of nature where $\sum_{j=1}^{n} P(N_j) = 1$.
[b] Payoff value for a particular alternative and state of nature.
[c] Value of each alternative.

This matrix model of the decision problem is universal in scope, but the final form of the matrix depends on what the decision maker is willing to assume about his knowledge of the future. For example, he may assume complete knowledge of the future, in which case there is only one state of nature. In another case the several states of nature may occur according to a probability distribution. And so it goes. These various cases have been classified into three groups: (1) decision making under *certainty* conditions, (2) decision making under *risk* conditions, and (3) decision making under *uncertainty* conditions. Each case fits into the general theory presented above.

DECISIONS UNDER CERTAINTY CONDITIONS

Rarely does management have perfect information for any decision that it makes. However, management sometimes finds it expedient to assume that future events affecting the decision are known for sure and that all input data to the decision can be specified with certainty. It is not that management is naive about conditions in the real world, quite the contrary. But by assuming certainty, an initial guide line solution may be obtained to decision problems that otherwise may be too complex to analyze in a definitive way. Management then relaxes the restrictive assumptions by performing a *sensitivity analysis* on the key parameters in the problem. Sensitivity analysis will be discussed as a separate topic in a subsequent section of this chapter.

Example.   To illustrate decision making under certainty conditions, consider the problem of supplying three customers from three plants. The product is a large machine tool that can be manufactured at any of three plants with equal production costs. The only difference is that the tool can be shipped at different transportation rates depending on the plant-customer combination. Each customer has purchased one machine tool. The physical distribution manager of the company must decide the cheapest way to ship the tools, that is, which plants should ship to which customers. The shipping costs for this problem are shown in Table 2-1.

TABLE 2-1
Matrix of shipping costs for example distribution problem

		Plant		
		1	*2*	*3*
	A	$100	$150	$225
Customer	B	125	200	160
	C	250	175	110

Though there are formal analytical methods for finding the best routing pattern,[3] it is possible in this case to list all routings and select the one with the lowest cost by visual inspection. There are six possible routings shown in Table 2-2. For example, one possible routing pattern is to supply customer A from plant 1, cus-

TABLE 2-2
All possible plant-warehouse routing patterns with associated shipping costs for the example problem

Possible Routing Pattern No.	Plant			Routing Pattern Cost
	1	*2*	*3*	
(1)	A	B	C	$410
(2)	A	C	B	435
(3)	B	A	C	385 ← Lowest cost
(4)	B	C	A	525
(5)	C	A	B	560
(6)	C	B	A	675

[3] Linear programming is an appropriate technique, and its application to the routing problem will be discussed in the chapter on transport decisions.

tomer B from plant 2, and customer C from plant 3 at a total shipping cost of $100 + 200 + 110 = \$410$. The costs for the remaining five routing patterns can be calculated in a similar way; the results are shown in Table 2-2. The minimum cost pattern is B-1, A-2, C-3 with a total shipping cost of \$385, and we choose this alternative since an appropriate objective in this case is cost minimization.

The above example is an illustration of decision making under certainty conditions, since all the relevant information about the problem is assumed to be known for sure. All shipping costs are known, the requirements of each customer are known, and the supply from each plant is known. There is only one future event or state of nature. That is, the data inputs to the problem will be the same in the future when the actual shipments are made as they are today at the time the decision must be made. Unlike this illustrative problem, which can be solved simply by enumerative procedures, many real-world decision problems under certainty conditions are characterized by one future event with a large number of alternative courses of action, as shown in Fig. 2-4. When many alternatives must be evaluated,

---

FIGURE 2-4

Basic structure of a decision problem under certainty conditions

State of Nature

		N_1[a]
	S_1	W_{11}[b]
	S_2	W_{21}
Alternative	S_3	W_{31}
courses of	.	.
action	.	.
	.	.
	S_m	W_{m1}

[a] The probability of this state of nature is taken to equal 1.
[b] The payoff for each alternative under one state of nature.

---

quantitative techniques become particularly valuable. Techniques such as calculus, mathematical programming, critical path methods, and heuristic programming methods are often applied to logistics problems when they are formulated as decision problems under certainty conditions.

DECISIONS UNDER RISK CONDITIONS

Nearly everyone has played games that utilized playing cards, dice, spinners, or well-balanced wheels. Such game have one important feature in common—they all represent decision situations where the likelihood of the states of nature occurring is given by a probability distribution. The states of nature here are the outcomes of rolling the dice, spinning the wheel, drawing cards, etc., and the design of these devices specifies a probability distribution.

The logistician finds few completely analogous decision problems to those in games. However, it is often possible to assign subjective probabilities to the future events, and from an analytical standpoint the problems are the same. When the future events have assigned probabilities, the decision problem is referred to as decision making under risk conditions. Risk decisions are different from decisions made under certainty conditions in that more than one mutually exclusive future event now becomes possible in the decision problem.

Example. Consider an abbreviated system design problem as a decision problem under risk conditions. The problem involves selecting the type of trucking and the type of warehousing that should be used in a logistics system. At issue are common carrier and privately owned trucking alternatives, and public and private warehousing. There are four distinct alternatives that result from the combination of two types of trucking and two types of warehousing. These are arrayed in matrix form as shown in Fig. 2-5. Which trucking and warehousing combination to use

---

FIGURE 2-5

Matrix representation of a logistics system design problem under risk conditions

---

States of Nature—Annual Sales Level

		Low (N_1) $P(N_1) = 0.20$	Average (N_2) $P(N_2) = 0.60$	High (N_3) $P(N_3) = 0.20$	Expected Contribution to Profit
Alternative	*A*	$5,000,000[b]	$6,000,000	$7,000,000	$6,000,000
system	*B*	3,000,000	6,000,000	10,000,000	6,200,000
design[a]	*C*	−1,000,000	4,000,000	11,000,000	4,400,000
	D	−5,000,000	3,000,000	15,000,000	3,800,000

[a] A = public warehouse, common carrier trucking
  B = public warehouse, privately owned trucking
  C = private warehouse, common carrier trucking
  D = private warehouse, privately owned trucking
[b] Body of matrix represents profit for a given sales level and alternative.
Source: Redrawn from Ronald H. Ballou, "Probabilities and Payoffs: Aids to Distribution Decision Making," *Transportation and Distribution Management,* Vol. 9 (August 1969), p. 28.

---

depends on the level of sales that will occur over the next several years. Obviously, a low sales level suggests that the investment in a fleet of trucks and privately owned warehousing (alternative D) may not be wise, since the high level of fixed investment may not be recovered. Conversely, if a high level of sales were achieved, the better strategy would be cheaper than the alternative that requires the trucking and warehousing services to be purchased outside the firm (alternative A). The remaining alternatives represent more moderate investment levels and would be reasonable choices when sales are at neither of the extremes. The resulting profit for each alternative under the various states of nature is given by

$$\text{Profit} = \text{sales} - \text{logistics costs}$$

These profits are shown in the body of the matrix in Fig. 2-5. Profit in this matrix specifically refers to the contribution made to total firm profit as a result of this decision.

The choice of an alternative would be easy to make if the level of future sales were known for sure. However, under conditions of risk the assumption is that the level of sales is known according to a probability distribution. In this case, a probability distribution of sales comes from a statistical sales forecast. In other risk decision problems the probability of future events may be established by subjective estimates. In either case, the decision problems take on added complexity as compared with certainty decision problems because of the added states of nature that must be considered in selecting an alternative.

Criteria for Selecting an Alternative.   In the above example no alternative was selected, since there was no criterion by which to guide a choice. One popular selection criterion is the expected value. The expected value is equivalent to the arithmetic mean of the payoffs for each alternative. The payoff value for each state of nature is weighted by the probability that the state of nature will occur, and then the weighted payoffs are summed for all states of nature to yield the average or expected value. Mathematically, the expected value is

$$EV_i = \sum_{j=1}^{n} P(N_j)W_{ij} \qquad i = 1, 2, \ldots, m \tag{2.1}$$

where $P(N_j)$ is the probability of state of nature N_j occurring and W_{ij} is the payoff value for alternatives S_i and state of nature N_j. In the above example the expected contribution to total profits for alternative A has the value

$$EV_A = (0.20)(5,000,000) + (0.60)(6,000,000) + (0.20)(7,000,000)$$
$$= \$6,000,000$$

where all values in the calculation come from Fig. 2-5. The expected values for all other alternatives are found in the same way. The alternative having the highest expected value is the one chosen as the initial solution to the decision problem. Had the problem involved cost, the decision criterion would be to select the alternative with the minimum expected value.

It should be noted that the expected value criterion is a long-run decision rule. It is most relevant when there are many such decisions to be made by the firm. Just as with any arithmetic mean, a large sample is required to make it a reasonable measure of central tendency. If this decision is viewed as standing apart from the other decisions of the firm, then a different criterion is likely to be more reasonable. For example, when the decision is made but once as in some types of contract bidding, averaging across several states of nature is not too meaningful. In this case, our concern is with the specific state of nature that is most likely to occur rather than with averaging across several states of nature. Thus, a short-run decision criterion might be to assume that the state of nature with the highest probability will occur, and the alternative with the most favorable payoff if this state of nature is assumed is the one to be selected. In the above example, state N_2 (average sales) has the highest probability, and either alternative A or B would be chosen since their payoffs under this state are equal ($6,000,000).

Alternately, the monetary payoffs in the decision may be replaced by utility values that reflect the decision maker's feeling about risk in the short-run decision problem. The analysis can proceed by optimizing the expected utilities. Determining appropriate utility values is discussed in a subsequent section of this chapter.

DECISIONS UNDER UNCERTAINTY

It is a truism to say that the most difficult decision problems to analyze are those where the least is known about the parameters of the problem. But many logistics problems are of this type. Not only are the probabilities of future events not known, but which events are likely to occur is not definable. Methods for selecting the best alternatives under uncertain conditions are based on the decision maker's view of the world, and the number of such methods is limited only by the number of decision makers that there are. Five of these methods are popular, and they deal only with the case of partial uncertainty. That is, all but the probabilities associated with the future events is unknown. These decision criteria are (1) the maximin rule, (2) the maximax rule, (3) the rule of insufficient reason, (4) the Hurwicz alpha criterion, and (5) Savage's criterion of regret.[4] Since it serves no direct purpose in this text to discuss all these methods, only the maximin rules and the rule of insufficient reason will be presented to indicate the "flavor" of such criteria. Before these methods are presented, consider an illustrative problem of decision making under uncertainty conditions.

Example. Two new hypothetical companies (Able and Baker) will compete in the same markets with essentially the same product line. An important factor in generating sales is the level of physical distribution service[5] provided to the customers. Profits are a function of both the revenue generated because of the level of customer service provided and the cost of producing a given level of service. Able Company wants to set its service level, and three possible levels are to be examined. Baker Company can also adjust its service level, and Able's level of profits depends on Baker's decision. Able assumes that Baker has three service choices, but is uncertain which of these service levels will be selected. The problem is laid out in matrix form in Fig. 2-6. Given this simplified abstraction of a complex real-world decision problem, which service level should Able select?

Maximin Criterion. One philosophy that the decision maker might adopt is that of pessimism. That is, he believes that forces outside of his control will always act against him. In the case of our problem, Able can expect that whichever alternative

---

[4] A more complete discussion of these decision criteria is given in David W. Miller and Martin K. Starr, *Executive Decisions and Operations Research* (Englewood Cliffs, N. J.: Prentice-Hall, Inc., 1960), pp. 85–94.

[5] The concept of physical distribution service will be discussed more thoroughly in the chapter on the product.

FIGURE 2-6
Example decision problem under uncertainty conditions

States of Nature:
Baker's Customer Service Level

		$P(N_1) = ?$ $N_1 = 85\%$	$P(N_2) = ?$ $N_2 = 90\%$	$P(N_3) = ?$ $N_3 = 95\%$
Able's	85%	$6,500,000[a]	5,500,000	4,000,000
customer	90	6,000,000	5,500,000	5,000,000
service level	95	3,000,000	3,700,000	4,500,000

[a] Values in the body of the matrix are Able's profits under various service levels that Baker might establish.

it selects Baker will have chosen a service level that results in minimum profits for Able. It is not important whether Baker actually performs in this manner, what is important is that Able's management thinks that Baker will perform in this way. Given this pessimistic attitude, Able will select the alternative offering the greatest benefit. This leads to the maximin criterion. That is, note the worst or minimum payoff for each alternative and from among these select the one with the highest payoff. Thus, we would have

Alternative	Worst or Minimum Payoff
1—(85%)	$4,000,000
2—(90%)	$5,000,000 ←— Maximin choice
3—(95%)	$3,000,000

Rule of Insufficient Reason. This criterion is based on the principle of insufficient reason, which suggests that if there is no reason for any state of nature to occur more frequently than any other, then the frequency of occurrence will be the same. Each state of nature will be assigned an equal probability of $1/n$, where n is the number of states of nature involved in the decision problem. With this assignment, the decision problem is reduced, computationally at least, from one under uncertainty to one under risk. The selection of an alternative now proceeds as any risk problem. For example, for the problem in Fig. 2-6 the probability of each service level is $\frac{1}{3}$, and the expected value (*EV*) for each alternative is

$$EV_1 = \tfrac{1}{3}(6,500,000) + \tfrac{1}{3}(5,500,000) + \tfrac{1}{3}(4,000,000) = \$5,300,000$$
$$EV_2 = \tfrac{1}{3}(6,000,000) = \tfrac{1}{3}(5,500,000) + \tfrac{1}{3}(5,000,000) = \ 5,500,000$$
$$EV_3 = \tfrac{1}{3}(3,000,000) + \tfrac{1}{3}(3,700,000) + \tfrac{1}{3}(4,500,000) = \ 3,700,000$$

Alternative 2, or a 90 percent service level, would be selected, since it has the highest expected value.

If we had examined the remaining decision criteria, we would have noted that the choice of a particular alternative varies depending on the decision criterion used. Which criterion should we use? The answer is simple, but not very satisfying. The decision maker merely decides on what his particular view of the world is and selects a criterion that best matches his philosophy. Such a procedure offers little more than intuition alone would provide. However, an alternate approach to decision making under uncertainty conditions is to reduce the problem to one of certainty or risk by assuming that conditions surrounding the problem are known, for example, by assigning subjective probabilities to the states of nature. Next, a sensitivity analysis is performed to account for the uncertainties in the input data to the decision problem.

SENSITIVITY ANALYSIS

The use of a sensitivity analysis in conjunction with quantitative decision models is simple in concept and of immense practical value. Sensitivity analysis is the practitioner's way of handling uncertainty and, in a few words, it is nothing more than repeated analysis of the decision problem using different input data. The limits to which the input data are varied represent the range of values that the input data might reasonably assume. What the decision maker seeks from a sensitivity analysis is how likely it is that the selection of an alternative will change with variations in the input data values. Obviously, if the choice of an alternative is not altered with reasonable changes in the input data, the decision maker gains confidence in his choice. Let the future hold what it will, his choice of an alternative remains the same. On the other hand, if the choice of an alternative is highly sensitive to even minor changes in the input data, then this is a strong indication for the decision maker to seek additional information so as to reduce his uncertainty, or it may simply provide a rough guide line as to the extent of the risk associated with selecting an alternative.

Example.   Recall the logistics system design problem shown in Fig. 2-5. In this simple problem, uncertainty can be present in three places: (1) in specifying the states of nature and the associated probabilities, (2) in establishing the payoff value for a given alternative and state of nature, and (3) in selecting an appropriate decision criterion.

The probabilities for the states of nature as shown in Fig. 2-5 represent the most likely probabilities. Suppose that from the opinions that generate the most likely probabilities, estimates are also made of the most pessimistic and most optimistic probability distributions (Table 2-3). With these additional probability distribu-

	TABLE 2-3		
	Subjective probability distributions for example problem		
Annual Sales	*Most Pessimistic Probabilities*	*Most Likely Probabilities*	*Most Optimistic Probabilities*
Low	0.30	0.20	0.10
Average	0.60	0.60	0.50
High	0.10	0.20	0.40
	1.00	1.00	1.00

tions it is possible to calculate the corresponding expected values. These expected values are summarized in Table 2-4, and the highest expected values are noted. In two of the three cases alternative *B* shows the greatest benefit, and *A* is the best alternative in the other. It is not clear at this point whether *A* or *B* should be selected. The analysis may stop here with the decision maker applying subjective judg-

---

TABLE 2-4

Expected values for most pessimistic, most likely, and most optimistic probability distributions for the various alternatives in example problem and their combined weighted averages

Alternatives	$M_1{}^c = 0.30$ Most Pessimistic Probabilities	$M_2 = 0.50$ Most Likely Probabilities	$M_3 = 0.20$ Most Optimistic Probabilities	Combined Weighted Average
A^a	$5,800,000 [b]	$6,000,000	$6,300,000	$6,000,000
B	5,500,000	6,200,000 [b]	7,300,000 [b]	6,240,000
C	3,200,000	4,400,000	6,300,000	4,420,000
D	1,800,000	3,800,000	7,000,000	3,840,000

[a] For a description of these alternatives, see Fig. 2-5.
[b] Bracket encloses highest expected value.
[c] M_j is an assigned factor indicating the relative weight given to each probability distribution.

---

ment to resolve the conflict between the choice of *A* or *B*. However, the decision maker may indicate the relative weight he desires to give to each distribution by applying a weighting factor M_j that has a value between 0 and 1; all weights sum to 1. He may then continue a mathematical evaluation. One possible set of weights is shown in Table 2-4. To find the best alternative, a combined weighted average of the expected values is determined. For example, alternative *A* has a combined weighted average of $0.30(5,800,000) + (0.50)(6,000,000) + (0.20)$ $(6,300,000) = \$6,000,000$. Table 2-4 shows the average expected values for all alternatives, and alternative *B* has the highest average value. Though *B* may appear to be the first choice, the combined weighted average value exceeds that of *A* by only \$240,000. Alternative *A* may be a final choice, since no investment is required and if the \$240,000 is the amount management is willing to pay for flexibility.

The above approach to sensitivity analysis assumes that a range of values for the probabilities is known and that we want to test for sensitivity over this range. We were able to compute expected values and compare the differences between alternatives. However, if a range of probabilities is not known or if the assigning of weights does not seem reasonable, a *parametric analysis* can prove useful. The decision maker's role becomes one of judging boundary values on parameters rather than one of assigning parameter values.

In a parametric analysis, the probabilities are permitted to vary over a range of values. The range of probabilities is established to produce a state of indifference between two courses of action that the decision maker might take. Continuing the above example, we see that indifference between alternatives B and C would occur if the expected values of the two alternatives were equal ($EV_B = EV_C$). To compute the expected values, in general we have

$$EV_i = W_{i1}P(N_1) + W_{i2}P(N_2) + W_{i3}P(N_3) \qquad i = 1, 2, \ldots, 4 \qquad (2.2)$$

We also have the relationship that all states of nature probabilities must sum to 1:

$$P(N_1) + P(N_2) + P(N_3) = 1 \qquad (2.3)$$

For our problem, shown in Fig. 2-5, we can make the following numerical substitutions, utilizing Equations (2.2) and (2.3):

$$EV_B = 3P(N_1) + 6P(N_2) + 10(1 - P(N_1) - P(N_2)) \qquad (2.4)$$

and

$$EV_C = -1P(N_1) + 4P(N_2) + 11(1 - P(N_1) - P(N_2)) \qquad (2.5)$$

Setting $EV_B = EV_C$ and solving for $P(N_1)$ yields

$$P(N_1) = \tfrac{1}{5} - \tfrac{3}{5}P(N_2) \qquad (2.6)$$

Knowing that no $P(N_i)$ can be negative, we can deduce the following ranges of $P(N_i)$ from Equations (2.3) and (2.6):

$$0 \leq P(N_1) \leq 0.20$$
$$0 \leq P(N_2) \leq 0.33$$
$$0.47 \leq P(N_3) \leq 1.0$$

Even if the probability distributions of Table 2-3 are only roughly representative, it is highly unlikely that the probabilities above are reasonable. That is, $P(N_2)$ is very likely to be higher than the upper boundary value of 0.33. Therefore, the decision maker can feel confident that the choice of alternative B is a safe one.

This same analysis is repeated for other combinations of alternatives. If the boundary values on $P(N_i)$ cover a reasonable range, the decision maker cannot easily discriminate between the two alternatives. His direction at this point would be to seek additional information to reduce his uncertainty or to compromise between the alternatives involved.

The sensitivity analyses discussed so far apply equally well to testing uncertainties in payoff values. Selecting an appropriate decision criterion is an even more subjective matter. Instead of maximizing or minimizing expected values, the decision maker may feel that the future event with the highest probability will occur and make his choice accordingly. On the other hand, he may prefer events and alternatives that have large payoffs or conversely those that have only minimum losses, and so it goes with different alternatives being selected by different decision criteria. In general, a choice criterion depends on the decision maker's preferences and perceptions of risk. This leads us to the concept of utility. The concept of utility permits us to retain the expected value choice criterion while incorporating differences in decision maker attitudes and risk perceptions into the decision problem.

UTILITY

In most business decision problems the payoff for an alternative and a future event combination is expressed in monetary terms. Using monetary payoff data is quite adequate when the profit or loss associated with a particular decision does not vary from the usual profit and loss range for such decisions. However, when the consequences of a decision are extreme either in the direction of high return or high loss, ordinary monetary payoffs combined with the expected value criterion fail to represent how the decision maker really acts. In other words, extreme consequences alter how a decision maker views the risk of a particular decision. This distortion in the decision process is corrected by using substitute numbers (called *utiles*) in place of monetary payoff values. Selection of an alternative is then made on the basis of the expected utility value. Since utility is in part an expression of the decision maker's satisfaction, he seeks to maximize his satisfaction and selects alternatives accordingly.

The idea of utility (and disutility) can easily be illustrated. Recall the system design problem in Fig. 2-5. As presented, the profits and losses were within the company's usual range for such decisions, and the choice of a system design is based on the highest expected monetary value. However, suppose that the loss of $5,000,000 for alternative *D* might result in financial disaster for the company. The high disutility for this outcome means that the decision maker will not evaluate this alternative on the basis of its average monetary payoff. The prospect of disaster may not be acceptable, no matter how unlikely it is to occur. The decision maker often rejects such an alternative even if it has a high average payoff. Conversely, if an alternative has an extremely high payoff for one state of nature, the decision maker may be willing to take the "long shot" even though the average payoff is low.

A Utility Curve.   Undoubtedly, decision theory could be improved if a utility curve were known for the decision maker so that monetary values in the decision problem could be replaced with utility values. However, it is very difficult to obtain an accurate utility curve for an individual decision maker. The reason is his inability to express definitively how he feels about risk situations. Not only does it require that the decision maker understand himself, but it also demands that he be able to express this understanding accurately and consistently. This is a tall order, and few managers would be able to oblige. However, von Neumann and Morgenstern[6] developed an ingenious method called the *standard gamble* for generating an individual's utility curve that requires the decision maker only to respond to a

[6] John von Neumann and Oskar Morgenstern, *Theory of Games and Economic Behavior* (Princeton, N. J.: Princeton University Press, 1947).

simple lottery proposition. That is, he is offered an amount of money for sure, or he can risk it in a lottery of the following type:

$$\text{Expected value} = (\$15,000,000)p + (1 - p)(-\$15,000,000) \qquad (2.7)$$

where the payoffs in the game represent extreme payoffs in the decision problem and p is the probability of the payoff. In this case, the decision problem in Fig. 2-5 is used, and since 15,000,000 is the extreme payoff either positive or negative, then this value is used to cover the range of monetary payoffs in the decision problem. For example, suppose that the decision maker is offered \$15,000,000 for sure or he can choose the lottery of the type in Equation (2.7). The decision maker is to tell us the probability (p) that would just make him indifferent between the two alternatives. Obviously, with the cash certain value of \$15,000,000 offered the rational decision maker would likely choose a $p = 1$. He finds no benefit in gambling. Next, a different cash certain value is offered, say \$5,000,000, and the same question is repeated. The decision maker now may choose say $p = 0.70$ such that the expected value is \$6,000,000. We might expect him to pick p so that the expected value is greater than the cash certain value, since there is some price for uncertainty.[7] Repeating this procedure with different cash certain values generates a set of p values. Plotting p against cash certain values as shown in Fig. 2-7 gives the desired

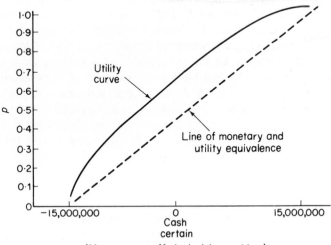

FIGURE 2-7

A utility curve for a mythical decision maker solving the problem presented in Fig. 2-5

(Monetary payoffs in decision problem)

---

[7] Sometimes p values are chosen where the expected value is less than cash certain. The difference is the price for the opportunity to gamble. While this may not seem rational, the number of people frequenting horse races, gambling casinos, and bingo games where the odds favor the house is evidence that decisions are made in this manner.

utility curve. From this curve, the monetary values in the decision matrix are replaced with p values. The selection of an alternative is now based on the expected utility rather than the expected monetary value.

If an accurate utility curve cannot be established, empirical research results suggest that assuming a linear relationship between utilities and monetary values is reasonable. Because most logistics decisions involve only a small proportion of the total assets of the business, catastrophic or extremely beneficial outcomes are usually not present in the decision such that utility values tend to closely follow monetary values. Thus, to optimize expected monetary values is a good approximation to optimizing utility values, and this will be the approach taken throughout the remainder of the book.

It is safe to say that no currently existing quantitative model captures reality in total. As such, a model represents some degree of abstraction from the real world, and management usually does not accept the model solution as the final problem solution. Rather, an often used problem-solving approach is to select or develop a model that is reasonably representative of reality, where model selection is a matter of balancing the benefits of a more sophisticated model against the increased costs of development and use of the model. Once a model solution is obtained, managerial judgment is applied to weigh with the results from the model the factors that are not included in the model but are important to the overall problem solution. In this way management effects a final solution to its problem.

Example.   This approach is easily illustrated by recalling the results of the decision problem shown in Fig. 2-5. The system design alternatives are evaluated according to an expected value criterion. The results from this model show alternative B to have the highest expected value, but alternative A has nearly the same expected value as B. Alternatives C and D might be eliminated from further consideration, since their expected values are not "close" to that of the best alternative. Thus, quantitative analysis helps to reduce the number of alternatives that need to be evaluated further. Of the two alternatives remaining, management may want to consider such additional factors as commitment of company resources required by each alternative, flexibility within each alternative so that changes in future conditions can easily be accommodated, and compatability with the existing system design. The decision process becomes one of tempering the results of a quantitative analysis with qualitative factors in order to achieve a final, practical solution to the logistics decision problem.

INPUT OF UNCERTAIN DATA

One of the often heard criticisms of the scientific approach to solving logistics problems refers to the accuracy of specifying the input data. The criticism is relevant, since all data for decision-making purposes have a degree of uncertainty associated with them, but some more than others. For example, transportation rates, distances, and current sales represent fairly "hard" data, since they are all observable facts. In contrast, out-of-stock costs, stock obsolescence costs, and future sales are examples of "soft" data. That is, a great deal of judgment is required in establishing their values. The answer to data uncertainty is not to throw out the scientific analysis, but to recognize that uncertainty in the data does exist and to deal with it directly.

Once again, sensitivity analysis is the pragmatist's way of handling "soft" data. He tries different input data values ranging between reasonable limits. If he finds that there is little difference in his choice of an alternative, he does nothing about improving the quality of the input data. On the other hand, if there is wide variation in his alternative choices, then this is a clear indication that improved data are needed. How much additional effort should be spent in improving the data base is a matter of balancing the cost for obtaining it with the degree and importance of the reduced uncertainty that is gained.

Logistician's Attitudes toward Scientific Analysis

Because so many logistics problems of the firm are amenable to a scientific analysis, scientific analysis potentially can play a significant role in the management of logistics activities. The question is: What should be the attitude of the logistician toward quantitative approaches to the solution of logistics problems?

In this text, quantitative approaches to problem solution are encouraged. This is not naively to imply that all logistics problems yield to quantitative analysis or that any logistics problem yields completely to a quantitative approach. Rather, quantitative techniques amplify managerial analysis beyond what can often be achieved by intuitive approaches alone. Specifically, scientific analysis helps to uncover alternative courses of action that may not have been obvious or to evaluate more effectively and efficiently alternatives that could not be considered without the aid of quantitative tools. More generally, quantitative analysis works best for the manager if the goals of problem solution can be expressed in economic terms and if the manager believes that scientific analysis can be beneficial.

Mathematical models at best are only approximations to reality. Because of this, there remains a good bit of managerial art in decision making and planning. In this text, a degree of faith in scientific analysis is assumed. Wagner, in his book on the principles of operations research, makes three concluding observations that help to put scientific analysis in perspective.[8] First, decision making should not be abdicated to quantitative models. Effective scientific analysis is often a combination of managerial intuition and quantitative analysis. The two play in concert to improve decision making over what could be achieved by either alone. Above all, scientific analysis does not imply that hunch and intuition should

[8] Harvey M. Wagner, *Principles of Operations Research* (Englewood Cliffs, N.J.: Prentice-Hall, Inc., 1969), p. 7.

be abandoned. Many brilliant decisions still remain the result of chance, hunch, and dreams, rather than formal analysis.

Second, there may be difficulty in demonstrating that a quantitative problem solution is actually an improvement over an intuitive solution to logistics problems. The dynamic environment of business and other related planning decisions prevent holding all else constant so that the effect of a single plan might be observed. Faith in scientific analysis reinforced by past successful applications is the best guarantee that improvement will result.

Third, a scientific analysis must be *well conceived and executed.* Performing a scientific analysis itself will not guarantee good results. As with any analysis, if it is poorly conceived or poorly executed, and if the input data are questionable, the analysis, no matter how good, will also be questionable.

Thus, scientific analysis is a starting point in logistics planning, the results of which must be tempered with good managerial judgment.

Concluding Comments

There is a well-structured framework that underlies a scientific approach to solving many logistics problems. First, logistics activities throughout the economy are composed of move-store activities, where the object of flow is a product, information, or people. These move-store activities can be conceptualized in terms of a network of links and nodes. The network gives a graphic and simple representation of complex logistics activities and their interaction.

Second, there is a formalized structure within which most logistics decision problems may be viewed. This structure is called *decision theory,* which represents a process of activities. To every logistics decision problem, there are four key elements.

    (1) The environment from which goals, data, problem constraints, etc. are derived.

    (2) The specific objectives for the decision problem.

    (3) The future events and information needed to evaluate alternative courses of action.

    (4) The process of analysis which identifies problems, gathers facts, specifies alternatives, estimates payoffs for alternatives, and selects a course of action.

Network analysis and decision theory together comprise the fundamental framework for scientific logistics management. In general, the combined framework is a guide to how logisticians *should* view their decision problems rather than how they actually approach them. Applications of this framework are extensively discussed in Part III on logistics decisions. Special reference is made to the routing and vehicle scheduling problems of Chapter 10 for direct application of network analysis and to the single-order inventory problem of Chapter 9 and the warehouse-sizing problem of Chapter 11 for application of decision theory as presented in this chapter. However, these applications should not be viewed as limiting, since all logistics decision problems and the models to solve them relate to this basic framework, even though the decision models may not appear in a matrix format.

Questions and Problems

1. Sketch a network diagram of the logistics system as represented by:

   a. U. S. Steel Company supplying sheet steel to auto manufacturers.

   b. An oil company supplying heating fuel to the northeast United States.

   c. A food canning company supplying canned beans to a domestic market.

   d. A Japanese electronics firm distributing transistor radios in Europe.

2. Consider the problem of locating a company-owned warehouse that will serve as a regional distribution point for its line of housewares products.

   a. Describe the planning process that the logistician is likely to go through in deciding where to locate the warehouse.

   b. What environmental factors are most important in this decision?

   c. What should the goals be for this problem?

   d. How should the logistician proceed with implementing the chosen plan, and how should he control the performance of the plan once he has implemented it?

3. Typical logistics decisions include transport mode selection, facility location, and order processing system design. Give a general matrix representation of these decision problems. What does this suggest about the fundamental nature of the decision matrix model?

4. What is utility? How is it relevant to the decision-making process?

5. What is sensitivity analysis? What important role does it play in making quantitative techniques useful to the solution of logistics problems?

6. The usefulness of quantitative analysis in the solution of logistics problems depends a great deal on the attitudes that the logistician has about quantitative analysis of the problems. The text notes three important attitudes. What are these? Can you add any?

7. A company is planning its order processing system to transmit order information between field warehouses and headquarters. Three alternatives seem feasible: (1) mail, (2) *W*ide *A*rea *T*elephone *S*ervice (WATS), and (3) teletypewriters using the telegraph network. The best choice depends in large measure on the order throughput to the system. Three levels of order activity seem possible, depending on the near future sales activity. The order activity and the estimated probability of its occurring are given below:

Orders Per Month	Probability
10,000	40%
50,000	35
100,000	25
	100%

The costs for each system depend on the throughput volume and are given below.

Order Volume	System Design		
	Mail	WATS	Teletype
10,000 orders	$3,000	$8,000	$12,000
50,000	23,000	16,000	16,000
100,000	48,000	26,000	21,000

Using the expected value criterion for choice, which design looks the most attractive?

Selected Bibliography

CHERNOFF, H. and L. E. MOSES, *Elementary Decision Theory*. New York: John Wiley & Sons, Inc., 1959.

HOROWITZ, IRA, *An Introduction to Quantitative Business Analysis*. New York: McGraw Hill Book Company, 1965, Chapters 2–3.

JEDAMUS, P. and R. FRAME, *Business Decision Theory*. New York: McGraw-Hill Book Company, 1969.

MILLER, D. W. and M. K. STARR, *Executive Decisions and Operations Research*. Englewood Cliffs, N. J.: Prentice-Hall, Inc., 1960, Chapters 4–5.

NEWMAN, JOSEPH W., *Management Applications of Decision Theory*. New York: Harper & Row, Publishers, 1971.

PRATT, J., H. RAIFFA, and R. SCHLAIFER, *Introduction to Statistical Decision Theory*. New York: McGraw-Hill Book Company, 1965.

SCHLAIFER, R., *Probability and Statistics for Business Decisions*. New York: McGraw-Hill Book Company, 1959.

WAGNER, HARVEY M., *Principles of Operations Research*. Englewood Cliffs, N. J.: Prentice-Hall, Inc., 1969. Especially Chapter 1.

von Neumann, J. and O. Morgenstern, *Theory of Games and Economic Behavior*, 3rd edition. Princeton, N. J.: Princeton University Press, 1953.

Chapter
3

The Logistics
Information System

Between the environment and the logistics manager there exists an information system that aids the logistics manager in his decision process. Berenson defines an information system as

> ...an interacting structure of people, equipment, methods, and controls, which is designed to create an information flow that is capable of providing an acceptable base for management decisions....[1]

Data obtained from the environment are not always in the form needed for decision-making purposes and/or available when and where needed. Thus, the information system facilitates logistics decision making and the provision of logistics services in three ways: (1) by *transforming* data into a more useful form, (2) by *transferring* data to points in the logistics network where they are needed, and (3) by *storing* data until they are needed. This chapter deals with the philosophy, design, and content of the logistics information system.

[1] Conrad Berenson, "Marketing Information Systems," *Journal of Marketing*, Vol. 33 (October 1969), p. 16.

Overview of the Logistics Information System (LIS)

A major purpose of obtaining information is to make decisions. The logistician may develop both informal and formal ways of acquiring the information that he needs. These range from information exchanged over cocktails to well-established procedures for data collection. Since the computer has become an integral part of business operations, there has been a trend toward more formal and highly structured information systems. The capacity of the computer for data storage and manipulation is increasingly making it more central to information system design. However, this is not suggesting that every information system should be computer-oriented, but the computer has unquestionably expanded the manager's information base.

The logistics information system, whether computer-oriented or not, is shown in Fig. 3-1. Three primary activities take place within the system: (1) the communi-

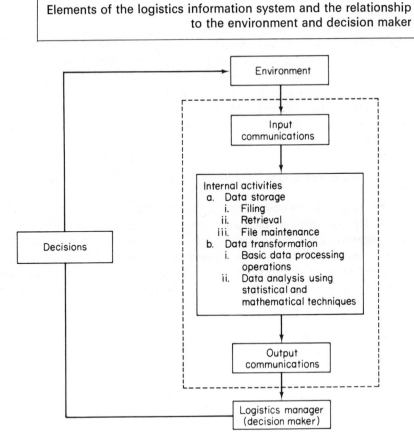

FIGURE 3-1

Elements of the logistics information system and the relationship to the environment and decision maker

---- Limits of the information system

cation of input data, (2) the processing and storage of the input data, and (3) the communication of the data from storage or after it has been processed. The logistics information system described herein might better be referred to as a decision-information system. It is broader in scope than an order processing system that emphasizes data collection, storage, and report functions—basic data processing activities. The LIS also includes various models developed to assist in evaluating logistics system design alternatives as well as standard statistical routines for manipulating data. Order processing, which often is treated as synonymous with the LIS, is only one aspect of the total logistics information system. The decision system within information systems decomposes into two types. The first includes mathematical and statistical models that facilitate analysis of data. This system does not make final decisions and does not initiate any action. It is referred to as a *decision-assisting system*. The second type is referred to as a *control system*. It is similar to the first, except that the decision loop is closed within the system. That is, based on preestablished decision rules, the system will respond to data from the environment and initiate some action. Computerized inventory control systems and computer-controlled materials handling and storage in warehouses are examples.

Control systems compared with decision-assisting systems create a distinct danger for the manager that should be recognized. The manager delegates a certain amount of his decision-making responsibility to a set of rules and procedures. Along with this, he may also lose direct control over the decision activity and ultimately control over the efficiency with which the activity is carried on. Loss of control over computerized inventory control systems offers far too frequent an example of this. Hence, when an information system includes control systems, positive steps need to be taken to prevent managerial loss of control.

TRANSFER, TRANSFORM, AND STORAGE FUNCTIONS

The LIS may take almost any form. It may include a computer, desk calculators, a group of people with a task to perform, filing cabinets, telephones, teletypewriters, magnetic tapes, punch cards, and the mail service. It may range from a manual system to a computer-dominated system. But all information systems perform the same basic functions—they transfer, transform, and store data.

Transferring data involves the movement of data throughout the information network, with the greatest movement being to and from a data processing point. The order transmittal link from customer to order processing location and the network link over which stock orders are sent from a computer to the production facility are common examples of the transfer activity within the LIS.

The transform function is a data conversion activity to create information that the logistics manager can use for decision making. Transformation of data occurs at two levels: (1) basic data processing operations including data sorting, checking, comparing, and manipulating using simple arithmetic operations, and (2) more sophisticated data manipulations using statistical and mathematical techniques.

Transformation activities, unlike transfer activities, usually take place at a single, centralized point in the information network.

The storage function, like the transform function, is often centralized as well. Storage activities involve filing, retrieval, and file maintenance. Data may be maintained in its "raw" state, such as simply storing account data from sales orders, or it may be stored in its transformed state, such as in the form of account summaries. Storage gives information a time dimension that is valuable especially when data are available to the system on a continuous basis but decisions need to be made periodically.

SYSTEM DESIGN SPECIFICATIONS

Designing a logistics information system centers on three factors: (1) the decisions to be made, (2) information system requirements, and (3) control over control systems.

Decisions to be Made. If there were not economic or physical constraints on information systems, the logistician might be tempted to have available to him every decision model and every bit of information possible. Even with constraints, managers seem to suffer from an overabundance of information, most of which is not particularly important to the task they perform. An appropriate way to design the LIS is to analyze the logistics decisions that must be made and structure the LIS to assist in the most important of these. The importance of a decision for LIS design often is judged on how frequently it must be made. As such, inventory control, carrier routing, and order picking in warehouses are frequently occurring decisions that might have top priority in system design, that is, design in terms of information to be stored for easy retrieval, capacity of the system to maintain such information on a regular basis, and equipment necessary for analyzing, transmitting, and disseminating the information. Less frequently occurring decisions such as facility location, warehouse layout, and package design should not exert as great an influence on system design, though some provision may be desirable for analyzing such problems when they do occur and possibly anticipating the information needs. An activity check list of the type shown in Table 3-1 gives an initial indication of the relative frequency of the decisions and those around which the LIS might be designed.

After it has been determined around which decisions the information system is to be designed, the next questions are: Which information should the system retain and in what form? These too are dictated by the decisions to be made. For example, warehouse stock replenishment decisions require demand forecast information, cost data relevant to the stocking decision (that is, inventory carrying cost and procurement costs), information regarding stocking rules, such as when to replenish stock and the order quantity, and the current level of inventory in all warehouses by item. The information should be retained in a form needed in decision analysis or in a form that can easily be converted to a more desirable form.

TABLE 3-1

Hypothetical activity check list for
logistics information system design

Activity	Very Frequently (Daily)	Frequently (Monthly)	Infrequently (Yearly)	Very Infrequently (> Yearly)
Stock replenishment	X			
Transport routing & scheduling	X			
Warehouse order scheduling	X			
Freight bill preparation	X			
Demand forecasting		X		
Freight bill auditing		X		
Warehouse stock layout			X	
Carrier selection review			X	
Materials handling equipment replacement review			X	
Facility location review			X	
Customer demand allocation to warehouse review			X	
Production scheduling rules review			X	
Package design review			X	
Private warehouse sizing review				X
Private transportation equipment review				X

Information System Requirements.   The design of the LIS should also reflect the impact that it has on both customer service and logistics costs. Various system designs differ in the speed with which information is transferred and transformed. Since the speed of transferring order information from the customer to the point where action can be taken on the order affects the overall time between when a customer places an order and when he receives it, customer service will change with system design. Also, the rate of information transformation and the speed of data transmittal determine the extent of the information time lag in the system. In turn, this time lag imparts higher costs for distribution activities through the greater level of uncertainty that is created for decision making.

Speed exacts its price. A system that responds quickly most often is an expensive system, consisting mostly of electronic devices such as computers, teletypewriters, and telephones. Slower-response systems often rely on mail service and manual data processing. Of course, well-designed and well-managed manual systems often can outperform the most sophisticated automated information systems that are poorly conceived and managed.

Control over Control Systems.   When the LIS has within its structure certain subsystems that are automatic decision systems, the LIS should be designed so that the manager does not lose control over them. Though some control systems might be designed to be self-corrective (adaptive), in that they compare system output with actual conditions and automatically take the necessary corrective action, two additional safeguards are needed. The first is the *exception report*. When the control system is not performing according to preset limits, the system should be designed to generate reports about the out-of-control condition. The manager then decides on the corrective action and through manual intervention reestablishes the desired conditions. The second is *managerial understanding* of the system operation. This may seem too obvious to warrant discussion, except that it is so often lacking. As is frequently the case, control systems are established to replace manual systems. With the turnover of personnel and too often poor documentation of such systems, those instrumental in establishing the system are no longer with the company, and the new personnel cannot understand or lack incentive to understand the system. This is costly, as one manufacturer with such a system found out. In this case, an inventory control system was installed along with a new computer. Neither the data processing manager who fed the data to the system nor the traffic manager who oversaw the system output fully understood the system. After several years of operation with field complaints of over-and under-stock situations and accounting reports showing inventory costs exceeding those under previous manual system control, an error was discovered in the original model formulation by an outside consulting group. Thousands of dollars in higher costs and reduced revenues were lost because the system was not fully understood by those responsible for it.

Input Data and Communications

The transfer of input data is a primary activity in the logistics information system. It is a fairly mechanical process that physically relocates the data from their source to a processing point where they are stored or transformed.

DATA SOURCES

Before the transfer process begins, the input data need to be acquired from the environment (recall Fig. 3-1). Data relevant to the logistics decision-making process are obtained both externally and internally to the firm. The important data sources include: (1) the sales order, (2) accounting data, (3) logistics research, (4) published data, and (5) judgment data.

The Sales Order. The sales order is the most important single source of customer data available to the logistician. The typical sales order contains such data as customer location, items demanded, order date, and item weights. More sophisticated order forms also include shipping instructions, customer assignment to warehouse, and credit status. Sales information is the key to initiating product flows, and an information system to handle these data usually is the first form of an LIS that most firms have. In more traditional terms, such a system is the order processing system.

FIGURE 3-2

Simplified sales order information flow in a centralized sales order processing system

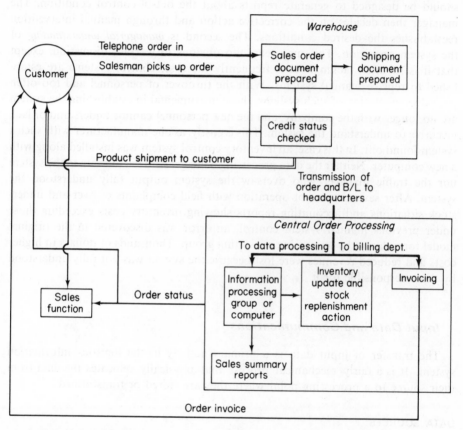

——— Sales information flow (raw data)

In light of the previous discussion, the order processing system is a subset of the total logistics information system. It is essentially a data transfer system with only a relatively minor data manipulation activity. Fig. 3-2 shows a simplified order processing system. Sales data in their raw or unmanipulated form are transmitted to the warehouse and then to headquarters for invoicing and other data processing. Data manipulation may occur only to the extent of preparing sales summary reports, stock replenishment orders, and inventory reports as to level, out-of-stock condition, and unsaleable stock. Though an order processing system might easily be exploded into a complete inventory control system, the main function of an order processing system is to transmit the sales data to a point(s) in the distribution system where customer demands expressed by the order can be acted upon.

Accounting Data. Accounting data are an important source of internal information available to the logistician. Accounting data focus on costs, and, needless to say, cost information is an important input to nearly every logistics decision. An appreciation of the need for a wide variety of cost information can be gained from the flow chart in Fig. 3-3.

The physical distance between the LIS and the accounting system is not great, that is, common equipment may be used for both, and the physical transfer of data does not represent a significant problem. More important, however, is having available the information needed for decision making and having it in a reasonable form.[2]

Logistics Research. Research provides information that neither an operating order processing system nor accounting system is likely to generate. Though there is little formal logistics research carried out by companies, such an effort can be worthwhile by providing new logistics system design alternatives not previously considered feasible (for example, new transportation intermodal combinations), reducing the uncertainties in the decision process, or simply sharpening the information base (for example, determining customer service needs).

Published Information. Much information is available to the logistician that comes from outside the company and should be considered a part of the LIS. Trade journals,[3] government-sponsored research reports,[4] and academic journals[5] are examples of sources for information on trends, technological advances, new decision techniques, costs, and the like.

Judgment Data. Executives within the firm, consultants to the firm, salesmen, operating personnel, and suppliers to the firm all represent sources of information and should be thought of as part of the information system. The suggestion systems within many companies attest to the importance of this information source. An open mind is often the key to unlocking this source.

INFORMATION TRANSFER ALTERNATIVES

Once the information sources have been identified, the next question is how to transfer input data to where they are needed for processing. Considering the wide range of data sources outlined above, there is an equally wide-ranging set of data communications alternatives. These include direct verbal communications, telephone conversations, intercomputer transfers, mail correspondence, video displays, and the like. Though these alternatives for the transfer of all types of

---

[2] For an elaboration of this, see Russell L. Ackoff, "Management Misinformation Systems," *Management Science*, Vol. 14 (December 1967), pp. 147–56.

[3] For example, *Handling and Shipping, Transportation & Distribution Management*, and *Distribution World Wide*.

[4] For example, RAND reports and the many reports available from the Superintendent of Documents, Washington, D. C.

[5] For example, *Journal of Marketing Research, Management Science, The Logistics Review, The Journal of Industrial Engineering*, and *Naval Research Logistics Quarterly*.

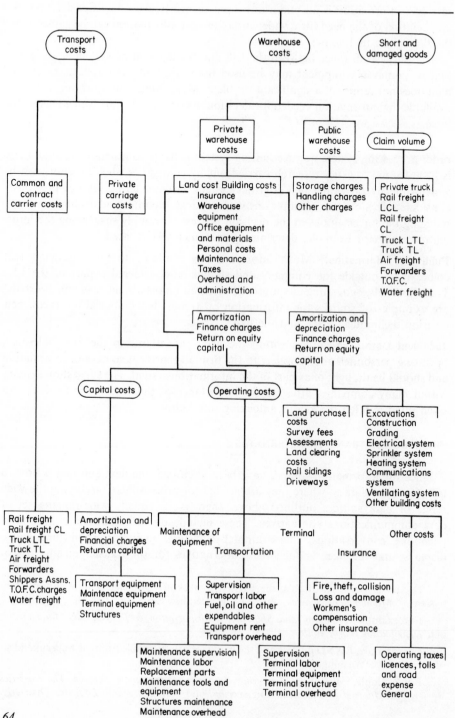

FIGURE 3-3
Areas of cost information needs by the logistics manager

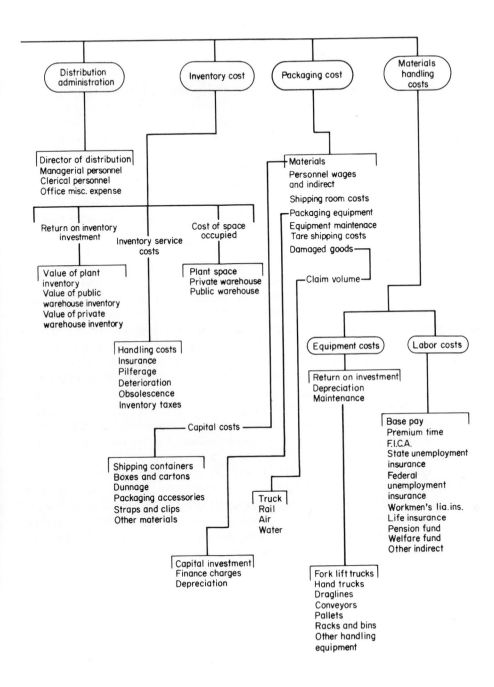

Distribution administration

Inventory cost

Packaging cost

Materials handling costs

Director of distribution
Managerial personnel
Clerical personnel
Office misc. expense

Materials
Personnel wages
and indirect

Shipping room costs

Packaging equipment
Equipment maintenace
Tare shipping costs

Damaged goods

Return on inventory
investment

Inventory service
costs

Cost of space
occupied

Value of plant
inventory
Value of public
warehouse inventory
Value of private
warehouse inventory

Plant space
Private warehouse
Public warehouse

Claim volume

Handling costs
Insurance
Pilferage
Deterioration
Obsolescence
Inventory taxes

Equipment costs

Labor costs

Return on investment
Depreciation
Maintenance

Base pay
Premium time
F.I.C.A.
State unemployment
insurance
Federal
unemployment
insurance
Workmen's lia.ins.
Life insurance
Pension fund
Welfare fund
Other indirect

Capital costs

Shipping containers
Boxes and cartons
Dunnage
Packaging accessories
Straps and clips
Other materials

Truck
Rail
Air
Water

Capital investment
Finance charges
Depreciation

Fork lift trucks
Hand trucks
Draglines
Conveyors
Pallets
Racks and bins
Other handling
equipment

Source: William B. Saunders, "Designing a Distribution System," *Distribution Age* (January 1965), pp. 32–36.

65

data are important, the logistician is probably more often concerned with the transfer of sales data and the specific set of design alternatives that he has available.

As shown in Fig. 3-2, sales order communications involve primarily the movement of data from the customer to a central order processing point. Design of the communications system is a function of both the speed of data transmittal and the number of nodal points through which the data must pass. In other words, the overall speed of data movement is the key to effective data communication design and not the block-to-block speed that may be achieved in any of the communications network links.

All the alternatives that the logistician has available to design such a system are too numerous to mention. However, some of the more popular alternatives can be noted. First, sales order data transmittal is accomplished through salesman order pickup, through the use of postal services, and through the use of some type of electronic device such as a telephone or teletypewriter. The direct cost and speed of the alternatives vary greatly. Mail service is most often the least expensive and also the slowest. Data transmittal by electronic means has the greatest speed of all the alternatives, but the high cost of such devices often limits their use to situations where a high volume of data is generated. Second, the number of nodal points where data transmission is temporarily halted for such activities as sales order form preparation, shipping document preparation, invoicing, out-of-stock checking, and credit checking varies with communications system design. A communications system that transmits order data directly to a central processing point where they are then retransmitted to a field warehouse may be a faster system than the more direct data routing, as shown in Fig. 3-2. This does not eliminate any nodes in the system, but it does permit making sales information available more quickly for inventory level adjustment and demand forecasting. Some nodal point activities, such as credit checking and invoicing, may be relocated in the network so as not to interrupt the data flow from customer to data processing point.

Few generalizations can be made about the best communications system for different situations. The wide variance among firms in the need for data transmission speed, the data volume generated at nodal points, the needed balance with other information system demands within the firm, and constraints on physical location and sequence of billing, credit checking, and out-of-stock checking activities indicates that careful and individual treatment is needed of data communications problems.

Internal LIS Activities

Data storage and transformation are the two primary activities performed at a nodal point within the information network. These activities contribute to the timeliness and usefulness of the data obtained in a "raw" state from the environment. They occur at two levels of sophistication within the information system: (1) the basic data processing level and (2) the decision-assisting analysis level.

However, there is much overlap between the two, and with the addition of certain decision rules, decision-assisting analysis can be made into decision-making analysis, or a control system.

BASIC DATA PROCESSING

The first level of data processing sophistication is to transform "raw" data by means of coding, arithmetic manipulation, sorting, and summarizing. Timeliness is imparted in information through the data storage functions of coding, retrieval, and file maintenance. Basic data processing can be illustrated in the activities of (1) coding, (2) forecasting, and (3) statistical analysis.

Coding. Sales data enter the LIS on a by-customer basis. That is, sales data are obtained from sales orders, which reference all data to a customer name and a street address. It is often more useful to have such data referenced directly on a geographical basis rather than on an account basis. Analysis for transportation decisions, facility location decisions, and inventory stocking decisions depends on a geographical information base.[6] To the logistician an account is a location, a product mix, a shipping weight, a requirement for customer service, and a distance from other accounts. Preferably, he would like to have information related to a geographical customer code.

Geographical coding can be accomplished in a number of ways. The simplest is to place a linear grid overlay on the map of a region and use the horizontal and vertical grid numbers as the code. For example, a grid overlay is placed over the western portion of the United States as shown in Fig. 3-4. Data are then located within the various cells defined by the grid. That is, a customer account located within the crosshatched cell would be aggregated along with other accounts falling within the cell. All are treated as if located at the midpoint of the cell. The location code for this account would be 004019, which is a combination of horizontal and vertical coordinates, and all data would be related to this and similar numbers as shown in Table 3-2. The grid size is a balance between overaggregation of data and the resulting loss of sensitivity, and the needless complexity and cost associated with grid cells so fine that they fail to group like customers and therefore fail to benefit from averaging.[7] Once the grid matrix is established, the distance between grid cells can accurately be determined by using spherical trigonometry:[8]

---

[6] A time-based information system is conceptually more appropriate than a distance-oriented one. Since time depends on so many other variables such as carrier speed, terrain, and vehicle operator variations, it tends to be a "soft" data base and there is some question as to its practicality.

[7] For an elaboration of the criteria for establishing a grid coding system, see Richard J. Lewis, *A Business Logistics Information and Accounting System for Marketing Analysis*, unpublished Ph.D. dissertation held in the library of Michigan State University, East Lansing, Michigan, 1964.

[8] The use of the great circle distance accounts for the curvature of the earth and avoids distance distortions due to the overlay of a two-dimensional grid onto a sphere. For a technical development of the formulation, see William L. Hart, *Plane and Spherical*

FIGURE 3-4

Geographical information coding system based on a simple grid overlay

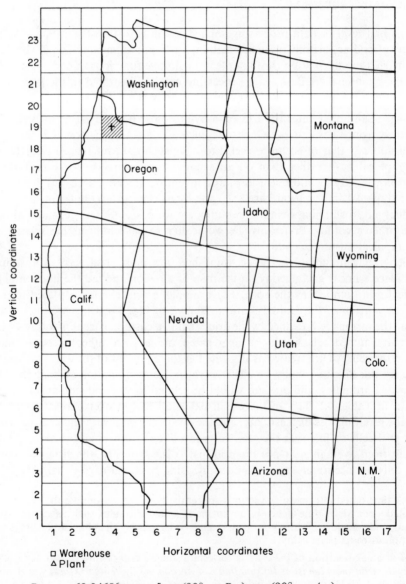

$$D_{A-B} = 69.0468\{\text{arccos } [\cos (90° - B_{\text{lat}}) \cos (90° - A_{\text{lat}})$$
$$+ \sin (90° - B_{\text{lat}}) \sin (90° - A_{\text{lat}}) \cos (A_{\text{long}} - B_{\text{long}})]\} \qquad (3.1)$$

Trigonometry with Applications (Boston: D. C. Heath and Co., 1943), p. 188. This specific formula applies when both points lie within the same spherical quadrant.

TABLE 3-2

An example of hypothetical sales order information summarized around a grid location code

Customer Location-grid Cell Code[a]	No. of Accounts in Cell	Total Annual Sales	Total Annual Shipping Weights	Average Order Size, Units	Average Customer Service Requirement[b]	Location Code of Serving Plant	Location Code of Serving Warehouse
001001	0	$0	0 lb	0	—	—	—
.	.	.	.	.	.	.	.
.	.	.	.	.	.	.	.
003008	123	890,000	600,000	153	1	013010	002009
003009	51	401,000	290,000	136	1	013010	002009
003010	37	295,000	175,000	127	2	013010	002009
.	.	.	.	.	.	.	.
.	.	.	.	.	.	.	.
004019	96	780,000	550,000	156	1	013010	002009
.	.	.	.	.	.	.	.
.	.	.	.	.	.	.	.

[a] Grid numbers are referenced to Fig. 3-4.
[b] Requirements expressed in the number of days for delivery acceptable to the customers.

where

D_{A-B} = great circle distance between grid midpoints A and B in statute miles
A_{lat} = latitude of midpoint A in degrees
A_{long} = longitude of midpoint A in degrees
B_{lat} = latitude of midpoint B in degrees
B_{long} = longitude of midpoint B in degrees

This formula is easily programmed for computer computation and is particularly useful in facility location analysis.

Other coding systems can be developed from such familiar geographical reference systems as the Standard Metropolitan Statistical Areas used by the Bureau of the Census, PICADAD—a point reference system used by the Bureau of the Census, Transportation Division, and Zip Code used by the United States Post Office Department.[9] Like the grid method, important logistics data would be related to the geographic reference numbers. Because the reference numbers refer to either an area or a point, mathematical manipulation of the code numbers is possible to determine distances, travel times, and transportation costs between pairs of areas or points. This ease of data manipulation is of great advantage in facility location analysis and for approximating transportation costs.

Coding generally requires only the simplest of arithmetic operations. As can be noted from Table 3-2, such a listing is produced by sorting the data according to geographical code and by summarizing and averaging data for each information category. This type of coded information is often stored as paper reports, on magnetic tape, on disks, etc., along with other records such as transportation rates, inventory costs, and inventory level records to be retrieved when they are needed for decision making.

Sales Forecasting. Short-term prediction of sales is vital to the maintenance of reasonable inventory levels and is a frequently recurring data processing activity of the information systems. Long-range forecasting is important to the design and maintenance of an optimal logistics system over time. However, short-term forecasting is more often treated as a basic data processing operation, whereas long-term forecasting involves a greater judgment input and is not as amenable to simple arithmetic analysis.

Forecasting is an example of data transformation, but without any accompanying analysis. In general, it is a statement about one of the future events (demand level) that will affect the outcome for a decided course of action. It, therefore, is input information to decision analysis. Short-term sales forecasting is singled out for discussion here because of its particular importance to the logistician, mainly in the planning and controlling of inventory levels in warehouses and for aggregate production scheduling. Long-term forecasting usually is not the singular

[9] For an excellent comparison of the advantages and disadvantages of these reference systems, see Donald J. Bowersox, Edward W. Smykay, and Bernard J. LaLonde, *Physical Distribution Management*, revised edition (New York: The Macmillan Company, 1968), pp. 88–99.

responsibility of the logistician, even though it is essential to such logistics decisions as facility location, private transportation decisions, and facility sizing.

There are many ways in which a demand forecast might be developed. However, they seem to reduce to three basic categories. First are the *subjective* forecasts. Data for the forecasts are solicited from those persons who supposedly have some knowledge of future demand. These persons might be salesmen, executives, suppliers, and experts. Such forecasts are highly judgmental and are not generally subject to rigors of scientific analysis.

Second are *surveys*. Surveys broadly include all types of market samplings, pilot studies, and experiments directed at those who generate or directly influence demand. Although these methods offer an improvement in data quality, they are often expensive, especially if they must be carried out on a periodic basis.

Third are *historical data extrapolations*. That is, forecasts are produced by assuming that future demand will follow the patterns observed in historical data. Since historical data are usually available and relatively inexpensive to obtain, this approach has particular appeal. Also, when the method is used for short-term forecasting purposes as in the case of inventory control, forecasting reliability does not suffer from the projection method used because of the short forecasting interval. In addition, such projection methods are easily programmed for computer computation. The most often used methods are (1) some form of time series analysis, (2) some form of moving average including exponential smoothing, and (3) multiple regression analysis. These are worth exploring in greater detail.

TIME SERIES FORECASTING. Time series forecasting is built on the philosophy that a historical sales pattern can be decomposed into four categories: trend, seasonal variation, cyclical variation, and residual variation. Trend represents the long-term movement in sales caused by such factors as changes in population, changes in marketing performance of the firm, and fundamental changes in market acceptance of the firm's products. Several typical sales trend lines are illustrated in Fig. 3-5. Seasonal variations refer to the regular "hills and valleys" in sales data that usually repeat every 12 months. The forces causing these regular variations in sales include climatic changes, buying patterns pegged to calendar dates, and the availability of goods. Cyclical variations are long-term (greater than 1 year) undulations in the sales pattern. Finally, residual variation is that portion of total sales that is unaccounted for by trend, seasonal, and cyclical variations.

Classical time series combines each type of sales variation in the following way:

$$Y = T \times S \times C \times R \tag{3.2}$$

where

$$Y = \text{sales level, \$}$$
$$T = \text{trend value, \$}$$
$$S = \text{seasonal sales index}$$
$$C = \text{cyclical sales index}$$
$$R = \text{residual sales index}$$

FIGURE 3-5

Examples of several common trend lines found in sales data with a generalized mathematical expression for each trend line

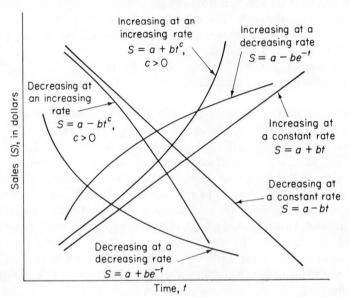

Note: a, b, and c are constants in the equation to be determined from a fit of the equation to the actual sales data. The term e is a constant approximately equal to 2.732.

In practice, the model is often reduced to only trend and seasonal elements. This is done because a well-specified model has a residual index value R of 1.0 and thus does not affect sales S over time, and because it is difficult in many cases to detect cyclical variation and rationally to explain its presence. Treating the cyclical sales index C as equal to 1.0 is not as serious as it first seems, since the model is usually updated as new data become available. The effect of cyclical variation, if business cycles do exist, tends to be compensated for in the updating process.[10]

Trend in sales might simply be determined by fitting a line to historical sales data by "eye." This technique is simple, but trend lines produced by different individuals will differ. A mathematical approach to curve fitting overcomes this disadvantage, and the forecast equation usually can be routinized for easy manual or computer computation. This latter feature is important to the logistician when forecasts must be produced for thousands of product line items. A commonly used mathematical technique is the method of *least squares*, where the line selected is the one that minimizes the sum of the squared differences between the actual sales and sales projected by the trend line. A least squares line can be found for any trend line form, whether linear or nonlinear, that is, for any of the trend lines

[10] The model is sometimes expressed in an additive form of $S = T + S + C + R$ and S, C, and R are stated in absolute sales levels.

shown in Fig. 3-5.[11] Many computer libraries now contain "canned" programs for curve fitting that produce various trend line equations requiring only reading the actual sales data into the computer. The "best" trend line from among all possible trend lines is the one that is closest to all points.[12] Examples of the "eyeball" and least squares methods are shown in Fig. 3-6. Extrapolating the lines to the next month beyond the available data produces the forecast.

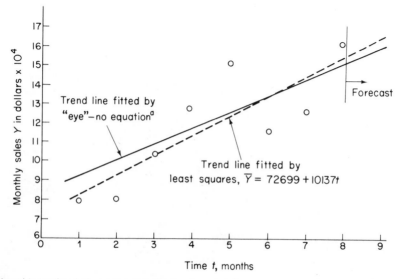

FIGURE 3-6

Straight-line trend lines fitted to sales data by "eye" and by the least squares technique

a Produced by author *before* computing the least squares line.

Seasonal variation in sales is dramatically seen in the sales pattern for room air conditioners (Fig. 3-7). Using only the trend line for sales projection could result in substantial and unnecessary error. However, if the seasonal pattern is a regular one,[13] this knowledge can be used to adjust trend line extrapolations and produce more accurate forecasts. A set of seasonal index values is needed and can be determined by the method of simple averages or the ratio-to-moving average method.[14]

[11] For a discussion of the mathematical procedures for deriving various trend line equations, see most any elementary statistics text or N. R. Draper and H. Smith, *Applied Regression Analysis* (New York: John Wiley & Sons, Inc., 1966), pp. 7–13 and pp. 264–67.

[12] For a more complete discussion of this, see *Ibid.*, pp. 163–67.

[13] Regularity means that the peaks and the valleys of the series occur at approximately the same date each year and are approximately of the same magnitude.

[14] For a discussion of these methods, see Taro Yamane, *Statistics: An Introductory Analysis*, 2nd edition (New York: Harper & Row, Publishers, Inc., 1964), pp. 354–60.

Once both the trend line and seasonal index values are known, the forecast is made by solving the following formula:

$$Y_t = T_t \times S_t \qquad (3.3)$$

To illustrate, suppose that for the time series shown in Fig. 3-7 we have a trend line of $T_t = 1000 + 46t$. We wish to project the sales level for the first week of

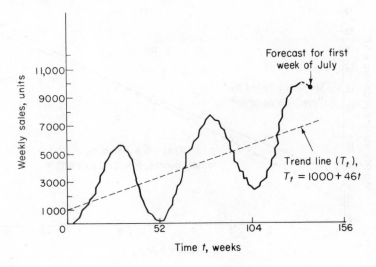

FIGURE 3-7

Generalized sales pattern for room air conditioners, showing a strong seasonal pattern

July of the third year, where $t = 131$ and the seasonal index $S = 1.35$. The forecast would be

$$Y_{t=131} = [1000 + 46(131)] \times 1.35$$
$$= 9485 \text{ units}$$

MOVING AVERAGE FORECASTING. Moving average forecasting, especially exponential smoothing, has had increasing acceptance as a useful method to the logistician for forecasting short-term sales. Sales forecasts are produced by "tracking" sales over time in much the same manner as a radar-controlled gun follows an airplane. That is, most recent sales are compared with the forecast for that period, and corrections are made in the next forecast based on the extent of the error observed and the forecast history. Changes in the forecast for the next period occur because of forecast errors observed in the previous period and, therefore, the forecasting process may lag fundamental changes in sales. On the other hand, an important feature of this type of forecasting is that it is adaptive, or self-correcting. That is, the effects of new sales information are incorporated into the model so that updating is taken care of within the model.

The simplest adaptive type of forecasting model is developed from the basic moving average model:[15]

$$M_t = M_{t-1} + \frac{Y_t - Y_{t-n}}{n} \tag{3.4}$$

where
M_t = moving average for time period t and the expected sales for $t + 1$.
M_{t-1} = moving average for the previous period $(t - 1)$.
Y_t = consecutive observations in the interval to $t + n$.
n = the number of most recent observations.

The value for n is selected as a balance between the amount of data to be retained by the system and the need for quick response. For a series that does not fluctuate a great deal, a large n value offers good stability in the forecast. If the series is subject to frequent trend changes, a more responsive system with a low n value will "track" the actual sales better. If we put economics aside for the moment, the best n is the one that permits the model to "track" the regular or fundamental patterns in the series without "tracking" the random variations.

The application of the model is simple and straightforward. For example, suppose $n = 4$ and the sales in the last five periods were $Y_1 = 8$, $Y_2 = 15$, $Y_3 = 5$, $Y_4 = 20$, and $Y_5 = 25$. The previous average is $M_4 = 12$ and

$$M_5 = 12 + \frac{25 - 8}{4}$$

$$= 16.25$$

If one more period passes and $Y_6 = 10$, the new forecast becomes

$$M_6 = 16.25 + \frac{10 - 15}{4}$$

$$= 15$$

The basic moving average model can be criticized because it weights past observations the same as more recent observations and because it does not provide a convenient means for adjusting the response of the model. The exponential smoothing model is a direct descendant of the moving average model, but it overcomes these objections by permitting a discounting of past observations and adjustment of the extent of discounting. The basic exponential smoothing model is

$$F_t = \alpha(Y_t - F_{t-1}) + F_{t-1} \tag{3.5}$$

[15] For this development, see Robert G. Brown, *Smoothing, Forecasting and Prediction of Discrete Time Series* (Englewood Cliffs, N. J.: Prentice-Hall, Inc., 1962), pp. 98–99.

where

F_t = the forecast.
F_{t-1} = the previous forecast.
Y_t = actual sales in period t.
α = the smoothing constant having a value $0 \leq \alpha \leq 1$.

The term α is similar to $1/n$ in the moving average model. Rearranging terms shows the exponential smoothing model in its more usual form:

$$F_t = \alpha(Y_t) + (1 - \alpha)F_{t-1} \tag{3.6}$$

Since this model and its variations are discussed at some length in Chapter 9, no further discussion or application will be offered at this point.

MULTIPLE REGRESSION MODEL FORECASTING. In the sales forecasting models discussed so far, time is the only variable that has been considered. It is reasonable to expect that additional variables may be useful in forecasting the level of sales. The statistical technique referred to as multiple regression-correlation analysis permits analyzing a number of variables simultaneously and developing a forecasting model with multiple variables.

Consider the supply problem of an apparel manufacturer whose forecasts need to be made approximately four months in advance of the selling season and production. It is least expensive if all cloth can be obtained from suppliers at one time. The perishability of fashion goods left in inventory at the end of the season and the profit opportunities lost when goods cannot be produced and delivered demand accurate forecasting. Because of the four-month forecast interval, the previous methods do not prove entirely satisfactory. However, if a model can include leading indicators or variables that can be projected four months ahead, a useful forecasting model results. For example, a multiple regression model was developed for the summer selling season, which is:

$$\bar{Y} = -3016 + 1211X_1 + 5.75X_2 - 109X_3 \tag{3.7}$$

where

$\bar{Y}$ = estimated average summer season sales in millions of dollars.
X_1 = time in years, 1966 = 1.
X_2 = number of accounts purchasing during the season.
X_3 = monthly change in consumer debt, percent.

This model explained 99 percent ($R^2 = 0.99$) of the total variation in Y and was significant at the five percent level. The model was an accurate predictor of sales. For example, the actual sales for the summer season of 1970 were $16,072,000. The model inputs for 1970 were $X_1 = 5$, $X_2 = 2414$, and $X_3 = 7.44$, and when substituted into Equation (3.7) gave a $\bar{Y}$ of 16,110, or estimated sales of $16,110,000.

Regression models are extremely easy to develop. Nearly every computer installation has a "canned" multiple regression-correlation program as part of the software package that performs the necessary computations for fitting an ordinary least squares model to the data. Unfortunately, such programs do not supply the judgment required to assure a valid model. Several of the problems that should be considered are noted here. First, the relationship expressed in the model should be *logical*. There should be strong reasons for believing that the model's independent variables can explain the variation in the variable in question (dependent variable). An example of a good relationship is the use of a United States Federal Reserve System statistic called change in consumer debt to explain retail sales, and a poor relationship is the use of minister's salaries to explain liquor sales. The former is a well-known leading indicator of retail sales, and it is logical that the consumer's willingness to change his debt commitment would affect retail sales. The latter, however, are not logically related but might appear to be, since both are related to the general level of the economy.

Second, the model should be *correctly specified*. If the model contains too few variables, then strong explanatory variables remain outside the model specification. The effect of their omission shows up in the statistical properties of the model as prediction errors (called residuals).[16] That is, the prediction errors may not have the properties of being random and normally distributed with a mean of zero. Too many variables mean that needless variables will have to be handled and processed, and possibly the accuracy of the model will be reduced, as an additional degree of freedom is lost for each variable.

Third, the model should be based on an *adequate number of observations*. As a rule of thumb, statisticians suggest that five observations are needed for each coefficient that must be estimated in the model. Thus, the model in Equation (3.7) should be based on a minimum of 20 observations.

Fourth, the model variables should not be highly correlated with each other. If they are, there is *multicollinearity* present. The problem created by its presence is that the effect of one model variable cannot be distinguished from another. In addition, there are the economic consequences of servicing variables that do not contribute a great deal to the forecast. Not much can be done about multicollinearity other than to drop one of the correlated independent variables from the model.

Fifth, if the prediction errors in a time series model are correlated with each other over time, *autocorrelation* is said to be present. If autocorrelation is present, there will be an understatement of the variance of the dependent variable, as well as of the variances of the coefficients of the regression model. It is detected by a statistical test known as the Durbin-Watson test.[17] If detected, the problem can

---

[16] The residual r is the difference between the actual values and the values predicted by the model; that is,

$$r_t = Y_t - \bar{Y}_t$$

and

$$\bar{Y}_t = -3016 + 1211X_1 + 5.75X_2 - 109X_3$$

[17] Yamane, *op. cit.*, pp. 809–13.

be reduced or eliminated in several ways, one of which is to develop the model based on first differences of the data.[18]

Three different forecasting model types have been presented. Which should we choose? Obviously, this depends on the application. It also depends on what is known about the underlying forces that create the sales pattern and the capabilities of the information system. The logistician's first need is to forecast for inventory control and production scheduling. This generally involves the forecasting of every item in the product line. With an extensive product line and a substantial history of sales to be maintained by the information system, the record keeping for this activity can be burdensome and time-consuming. This problem is minimized if a moving average model is used, especially the exponential smoothing model. The exponential smoothing model combines all of history for an item in one value—the previous forecast. This feature along with the adaptive nature of the model considerably reduces the data storage requirements and makes it particularly attractive for these applications.

The exponential smoothing model is a type of moving average model and, as it is usually applied, its forecasts tend somewhat to lag actual events. If greater forecasting accuracy is required, a model involving a mathematical expression that can be extrapolated into the future may prove more satisfactory than an adaptive model. The time series and regression models are examples. However, their accuracy is very much dependent on uncovering fundamental relationships in sales and expressing them in a mathematical form. On balance, the exponential smoothing model is probably the best choice, because (1) underlying relationships in sales data are usually not clear, (2) the data handling and storage problem is an important issue in many cases, and (3) the problem of forecast lag is somewhat correctable and the shortness of the forecast interval minimizes the impact of the lag. However, for other planning needs a different set of criteria may dominate.

Statistical Analysis. Information systems can have available in them a number of standard statistical techniques as part of the software package for the computer. These techniques assist in transforming data into a more useful form and examining data for basic relationships. Among these statistical techniques are regression-correlation analysis, nonparametric tests, discriminant analysis, factor analysis, and analysis of variance.[19] They aid in the decision process by providing more relevant information through data analysis and manipulation. Since they do not evaluate or search for the best courses of action, the type of analysis that they provide is included as part of the basic data processing activity.

Regression-correlation analysis is a popular statistical technique useful for manipulating logistics data, and it serves as an illustration of the type of informa-

[18] For a complete discussion of these problems, see Richard C. Clelland, John S. DeCani, Francis Brown, J. Parker Bursk, and Donald S. Murray, *Basic Statistics with Business Applications* (New York: John Wiley & Sons, Inc., 1966), pp. 538–52, and J. Johnston, *Econometric Methods* (New York: McGraw-Hill Book Company, 1963), pp. 177–228.

[19] A complete discussion of these techniques can be found in William S. Peters and George W. Summers, *Statistical Analysis for Business Decisions* (Englewood Cliffs, N. J.: Prentice-Hall, Inc., 1968).

tion to be received from statistical analysis. For example, DeHayes wanted to explain the average transit time and transit time variability in rail carload shipments as part of an information base for evaluating and selecting among different transportation services. Twenty independent variables were initially tested in a regression analysis in an attempt to specify the needed relationships. Six of these variables were found to be significant for explaining average transit time and seven for explaining transit time variability. A significant average transit time relationship was found to be

$$\bar{T} = 2.35 + 1.36X_1 + 1.13X_2 - 0.78X_3 + 0.83X_4 + 0.02X_5 - 0.53X_6 \quad (3.8)$$

where

$\bar{T}$ = mean transit time for rail carload shipments, days.
X_1 = rail rate basis distance, hundreds of miles.
X_2 = average number of carriers.
X_3 = percentage of one product type shipped.
X_4 = east/west direction between origin and destination.
X_5 = population of origin area, in ten thousands.
X_6 = percentage of consignees at destination owned by consignor.

The transit time variability relationship was

$$\bar{V} = 4.41 + 0.15Z_1 + 0.20Z_2 + 0.35Z_3 + 0.52Z_4$$
$$- 0.28Z_5 + 0.26Z_6 - 1.2Z_7$$

where

$\bar{V}$ = transit time variability, days.
Z_1 = rail rate basis distance, hundreds of miles.
Z_2 = average number of carriers.
Z_3 = percentage of one product type shipped.
Z_4 = north/south direction between origin and destination.
Z_5 = rate territories involved between origin and destination.
Z_6 = northeast United States region.
Z_7 = month the average shipment was initiated.

These relationships were found to be statistically significant at the 0.05 significance level.[20] These relationships might next provide input data to a decision analysis, possibly transportation mode selection analysis.

DECISION-ASSISTING ANALYSIS

A number of models and techniques exist that do more than merely manipulate data. These distinguish themselves from the models discussed above in that *they*

[20] Daniel W. DeHayes, Jr., "Industrial Transportation Planning: Estimating Transit Time for Rail Carload Shipments," *Papers—Tenth Annual Meeting, American Transportation Research Forum* (Oxford, Indiana: The Richard B. Cross Company, 1969), pp. 101–13.

evaluate alternative courses of action and may also seek the best possible course of action. They are considered part of the information system because they provide information leading directly to making final decisions. The information generated from decision-assisting models is on a higher level of the decision-making continuum than the information generated from simple data processing activities, since the latter is an input to decision-assisting analyses.

Decision-assisting models are available in the LIS either as standardized models (for example, those in computer libraries) or as models custom-made to the specific logistics problem of the firm. In either case, decision-assisting models can usefully be classified into three groupings: (1) algorithmic models, (2) simulation models, and (3) heuristic models.

Algorithmic Models. Algorithmic models are based on precise mathematical procedures for evaluating alternatives and guarantee that the optimum solution (best alternative) has been found to the problem as proposed. Many of the so-called operations research models are of this type. These include mathematical programming (linear, nonlinear, dynamic, and integer programming), sequencing models, various calculus-dominated models, and equipment replacement models, to note a few. Many algorithmic models have been generalized and are available as canned computer routines.

Although the algorithmic models can guarantee an optimal solution, the price for this is generally a more limited problem definition than required of the other model types. This limitation is a result of the scope of algorithmic models available to handle a large number of variables as well as the computational efficiency of the algorithms. Even so, algorithmic models can still be useful in providing first solutions to complex problems. The basic economic order quantity (EOQ) model for inventory control is an example. This model is a calculus-based model that has been very popular in practical application. Though it is of limited scope, it captures the essence of the inventory problem and continues to be the basic submodel in many broadly based and mathematically sophisticated inventory models. The EOQ model gives the optimum quantity of goods to reorder when inventory drops to a predetermined level. The model is a balance of ordering costs and inventory carrying costs and has the following formulation:

$$Q^* = \sqrt{\frac{2DS}{IC}} \tag{3.10}$$

where
$\quad Q^* =$ the order quantity, units.
$\quad\ \ D =$ annual demand, units.
$\quad\ \ S =$ the order processing cost, \$/order.
$\quad\ \ I =$ annual inventory carrying cost, % of the value of a unit held in
$\qquad\qquad$ inventory.
$\quad\ \ C =$ value of a unit held in inventory.

Further discussion of this model can be found in Chapter 9.

Simulation Models. Simulations are mathematical descriptions of complex real-world systems that usually must be manipulated with the aid of an electronic computer because of the burdensome computational effort required. Simulation is an experimental technique in which after a computer programming model of the system has been developed, the model may be sampled under different input conditions. Sampling reveals how the model and, by implication, the real-world system act under various conditions. The distinct advantage of simulations is that important insights can be gained about complex systems without disturbing the ongoing operation. For the most part, simulation models are tailor-made to the particular problem being analyzed. However, some computer simulation languages do exist that aid in model development. These include SIMSCRIPT,[21] GPSS,[22] SIMULA,[23] and DYNAMO.[24]

Simulation models have been developed to help solve many of the problems facing the logistician. Such models have been reported for facility location decisions,[25] inventory control,[26] and carrier routing decisions.[27] One of the pioneering efforts in simulation modeling is the work of Forrester.[28] His model was a simulation of a production-distribution system involving three levels in the distribution channel: a retailer's inventory, a distributor's inventory, and a factory inventory. Each was interconnected through information flows and flows of goods. Given time delays throughout the system such as order transmission times, order processing times, factory lead time, and shipment delivery times, what would be the response of the system over time to changes in external forces, that is, changes in the level of retail sales? Also, how would the system response change if the delays through the system were changed? By simulating the system, such information could be obtained. Fig. 3-8 illustrates the type of information that the simulation produced when a sudden 10 percent increase in retail sales occurred. As decisions are made to adjust the time lags at various points in the system, the system response and the graph of that response change. Management can continue to play external contingencies against different system time delays to effect the best system in terms of desired response and the cost of that response.

[21] H. Markowitz, B. Hausner, and H. Karr, *Simscript: A Simulation Programming Language* (Englewood Cliffs, N. J.: Prentice-Hall, Inc., 1963).

[22] G. Gordon, "A General Purpose Systems Simulator," *IBM Systems Journal*, Vol. 1 (September 1962), pp. 18–33.

[23] A simulation program for the analysis of discrete event system and a library program for the UNIVAC 1108 computing system.

[24] J. Forrester, *Industrial Dynamics* (Cambridge, Mass.: M.I.T. Press, 1961).

[25] Harvey N. Shycon and Richard B. Maffei, "Simulation—Tool for Better Distribution," *Harvard Business Review*, Vol. 39 (Nov.–Dec. 1960), pp. 65–75.

[26] Samuel Eilon and Joseph Elmaleh, "Adaptive Limits in Inventory Control," *Management Science*, Vol. 16 (April 1970), pp. B-533–B-548.

[27] Richard B. Maffei, "Modern Methods for Local Delivery Route Design," *Journal of Marketing*, Vol. 29 (April 1965), pp. 13–18.

[28] Jay W. Forrester, "Industrial Dynamics: A Major Breakthrough for Decision Makers," *Harvard Business Review* (July–August 1958), pp. 37–66.

FIGURE 3-8

Response of production-distribution system to a sudden
10 percent increase in retail sales

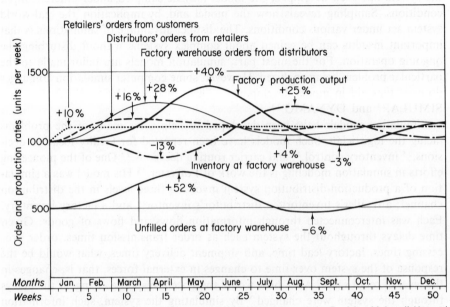

Source: Jay W. Forrester, "Industrial Dynamics: A Major Breakthrough for Decision Makers," *Harvard Business Review* (July-August 1958), p. 43.

Not all simulations need to be as extensive as Forrester's, though all are fundamentally the same. That is, they evaluate the potential impact of various decisions on a real-world system and thereby provide a valuable source of information without disturbing the real-world system.

Heuristic Models.   Heuristic models are something of a blend between the realism in model definition that can be achieved by simulation models and the search for optimum solutions achieved by algorithmic models. They generally achieve a broad problem definition, but do not guarantee optimum problem solutions. The models are built around the concept of the heuristic, which Hinkle and Kuehn define as:

> A heuristic . . . is a short cut process of reasoning . . . that searches for a *satisfactory, rather than an optimal, solution.* The heuristic, which reduces the time spent in the search for the solution of a problem, comprises a rule or a computational procedure which restricts the number of alternative solutions to a problem, based upon the analogous human trial-and-error process of reaching acceptable solutions to problems for which optimizing algorithms are not available.[29]

[29] Charles L. Hinkle and Alfred A. Kuehn, "Heuristic Models: Mapping the Maze for Management," *California Management Review*, Vol. 10 (Fall 1967), p. 61.

A number of interesting logistics problems have now been solved by using the heuristic approach. These include locating warehouses, order consolidation for freight savings, local truck delivery scheduling, and airline scheduling.[30]

Output Information and Communications

The communication of information from the information processing point(s) is an extension of the input data communication network. Many of the same transmission devices and services are used. Only the direction of the information flow differs. Speed remains the important design criterion for output information. The form of the output from the LIS is generally some sort of report, for example, an order status report, a sales forecast, or a distribution cost report. Such reports can be classified as information reports and as action reports.

INFORMATION REPORTS

Summary Reports. Information reports do not directly initiate action. Rather, they provide information upon which the logistics manager may take action. The most common type is the summary. The summary is a report based on simple manipulations of historic and current data. Such reports should be relevant to the decisions facing the logistician and in no more detail than the decisions at hand require. However, there should be associated with the summary reporting system the capability of exploding and isolating more detailed information. Take the distribution cost report, for example. The summary report might include only total logistics costs for the current year and a comparison with previous years. If the costs seem in line with objectives and other cost-absorbing activities of the firm, no further information may be sought. If not, the manager may seek more detailed information by "exploding" the first level report to break down distribution costs into contributing cost activities such as transportation, inventory, order processing, etc. The logistics manager may desire further breakdowns of this information by plant territories, by warehouse territories, or even customer groupings within territories in order to isolate specific activities that are not meeting expectations in terms of cost performance. The explode-isolate type of reporting system has the distinct advantage of not burdening the manager with information that he does not need and in which he can become "lost" just by its sheer volume.

Status Reports. Status reports are special-purpose reports that contribute to a smoothly running logistics operation. Reporting to customers on the status of their orders (for example, when the order was received, date shipped, how shipped, etc.) contributes to customer satisfaction. These reports can be routinized and handled by a clerical staff. Once the reporting system is established, the manager has minimum contact with it.

Exception Reports. The ultimate in information system design would be to establish goals for all logistics activities and then to have the LIS automatically generate

---

[30] *Ibid*, pp. 59–68.

reports regarding the variation of actual conditions from preplanned conditions. Few, if any, information systems have this level of sophistication, but many use the basic idea of an exception report. Reports on the amount of unsaleable stock in warehouses, the amount of lost and damaged stock, and the percentage of orders filled in more than one day are examples of reports that are generated on a periodic basis, but on which no managerial action is taken unless the results appear to be "out of line." No goals are established within the LIS. Rather, the manager has these in mind as he peruses the reports.

Output from Decision-Assisting Models.   The final information report is a result of analyses performed in conjunction with decision models. Conventional output would be in the form of a printed report indicating the most economical alternatives that guide the logistics manager in decision making. Most noteworthy here is the form that this type of output is likely to have in the future. Video-display output will largely replace hard-copy output to gain speed and flexibility. The use of a light pen on a video display unit to alter input parameters to the problem being analyzed offers additional flexibility. For example, a logistician searching for optimum warehouse configuration by means of a simulation approach must define the sales territories to be served by the warehouses. He can use the light pen to partition a map on the video screen into territories and to provide a graphic input to a simulation model. The simulation model makes the necessary evaluations of inventory, order processing, and transportation costs, and the computer gives this information as output. The manager is then ready to evaluate another alternative.

ACTION REPORTS

The second general type of report is the action report. It differs from the information report in that it is a command issued by the LIS to perform some activity. Examples of action reports are stock orders on plants, daily truck sequencing and routing, and the warehouse order picking schedule. Such reports are produced and transmitted on a routine basis, but manual intervention into transmission of the report by the manager is usually possible to effect any changes he thinks necessary and to maintain positive control over actions that are his responsibility.

Action reports are common in automatic control systems within the LIS. Automatic control systems are closed-loop decision systems where decision rules and reference standards have been added to the decision-information system. After input data from the environment have been preprocessed, they are compared to a reference standard (for example, a preestablished "trigger" inventory level for initiation of stock replenishment in the case of warehouse inventory control) to determine if action is needed. When action is needed, the decision-assisting analysis comes into play to determine the best action, for example, the stock replenishment quantity. The action report is a stock order on plants to replenish warehouse stocks. The system is reestablished as a result of the action taken. The basic features of an automatic inventory control system are shown in Fig. 3-9.

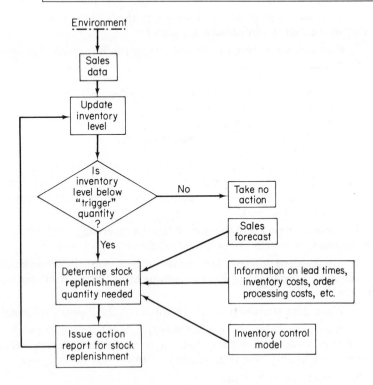

FIGURE 3-9

Basic features of an automatic inventory control system

Concluding Comments

The logistics information system is a subset of the total information system for the firm. It is the focal point within the firm for information that is relevant to logistics decision making. Broadly, the LIS is a data translator, transmitter, and storage system that gives form, time, and place values to information, and may also act as a decision maker when programmed as a control system. It serves as more than a data bank or an order processing system. It also aids in analysis of data through the use of statistical and mathematical models. Information systems may be designed on three levels: (1) a basic data processing level where little analysis takes place, (2) a level where statistical and mathematical models become an integral and useful part of the system for data analysis but no action takes place, and (3) a level where data analysis, decision making, and action are all handled by the system. The LIS interacts with all logistics decisions, and the logistics manager should be extremely careful about abdicating managerial responsibility for decision making to the information system without establishing adequate controls over the system.

Questions and Problems

1. Contrast a logistics information system with an order processing system.

2. To what extent should the logistician relinquish his decision-making responsibility to the logistics information system?

3. Compare the nature or content of logistics information systems you would expect to find in:

    (a) A small common carrier trucking firm.
    (b) A large railroad company.
    (c) A large food producer.
    (d) A medium-sized chemical company.

4. Pick a company with which you are familiar. Which logistics information do you think should be (1) maintained for ready access in computer files, (2) maintained in the company's noncomputerized filing system, and (3) not maintained in any formal way?

5. It has been said that the decisions to be made suggest the design of the logistics information system. To what extent do you agree with this?

6. Contrast the logistics information system with the information systems of marketing and production. What commonality is there? What distinct differences are there?

7. What data sources provide the inputs to the logistics information system?

8. What alternative methods are there for data transmission within the logistics information system? Compare these in terms of their cost, performance, convenience, availability, and compatability with the rest of the system.

9. Explain the following:

    (a) Geographical coding.
    (b) Time series forecasting.
    (c) Exponential smoothing.

How do they relate to the logistics information system?

10. How do statistical analysis models differ from decision-assisting models? What place do these model types have in the logistics information system?

11. Decision-assisting models can be classified as algorithmic, simulation, and heuristic model types. Explain the differences.

12. Contrast information reports with action reports. How are they part of the logistics information system?

Selected Bibliography

BowERSOX, DONALD J., BERNARD J. LaLONDE, AND EDWARD W. SMYKAY (eds.), *Readings in Physical Distribution Management*. New York: The Macmillan Company, 1969, pp. 331–63.

DANIEL, NORMAN E. and J. RICHARD JONES, *Business Logistics: Concepts and Viewpoints.* Boston: Allyn and Bacon, Inc., 1969, Part 8, pp. 301–42.

FORRESTER, JAY W., *Industrial Dynamics.* Cambridge, Mass.: Massachusetts Institute of Technology Press, 1961.

KELLY, JOSEPH F., *Computerized Management Information Systems.* New York: The Macmillan Company, 1970.

MONTGOMERY, DAVID B. and GLEN L. URBAN, *Management Science in Marketing.* Englewood Cliffs, N. J.: Prentice-Hall, Inc., 1969, Chapter 1.

PRINCE, THOMAS R., *Information Systems for Management Planning and Control.* Homewood, Illinois: Richard D. Irwin, Inc., 1966.

RAPPAPORT, A. (ed.), *Information for Decision Making: Quantitative and Behavioral Dimensions.* Englewood Cliffs, N. J.: Prentice-Hall, Inc., 1970.

WILLIAMS, THOMAS H. and CHARLES H. GRIFFIN, *Management Information: A Quantitative Accent.* Homewood, Illinois: Richard D. Irwin, Inc., 1967.

Part II

The Logistics Environment

Logistics decisions are made with due consideration to the constraints, relationships, forces, and conditions that affect decision outcomes but are largely beyond the logistician's influence. Although it would be impractical to discuss all the environmental factors that might in some way impinge on logistics decisions, this part of the book provides background discussion on those environmental considerations most germane to the logistics activity. Chapter 4 gives an overview of the product characteristics, customer service requirements, pricing, and packaging as the logistician sees them. Chapters 5 and 6 are concerned with the transportation system and its physical capabilities, economic characteristics, and legal responsibilities. Finally, Chapter 7 provides an overview of storage system capabilities and economies. The importance of these elements is derived from the basic logistics network, where the product is the object of flow in the network, transportation provides product movement over the links, and the storage system provides for product storage at the network nodal points.

Chapter
4

The Product

A key factor in the business logistics mix is what will broadly be referred to as the *product*. The product is a collection of perceptions by the logistician, by sales people, and by the customer regarding the characteristics of the product, the customer service associated with the product, the product price, and the package. The product is the center of focus to the logistician because the product in its physical form is the object of flow in the logistics system and in its economic form generates the revenues to keep the firm economically healthy. This chapter offers a general description of the product as one of three elements in the environment that are important to logistics decision making.

Product Characteristics

Various characteristics of the product have a direct influence on the logistics system design and on the cost of the design. Such product characteristics are value, weight, bulk, fragility, perishability, flamability, and substitutability. They affect the selection and cost of movement, storage, packaging, handling, and lost sales. For purposes of discussion, these characteristics have been collected into four categories: (1) weight-bulk ratio, (2) value-weight ratio, (3) substitutability, and (4) risk characteristics.

WEIGHT-BULK RATIO

The weight and bulk (volume) of the product are common, interdependent determinants of movement and storage costs. When the ratio of weight to bulk is high, as in such products as books, sheet steel, and lead bars, movement costs tend to be low relative to product sales value as there is complete utilization of the weight-carrying capacity of the transportation equipment. The handling cost component of storage costs also decreases due to full utilization of equipment, and other storage cost components are not greatly affected by high weight-bulk ratios. However, low weight-bulk products such as set-up aluminum patio furniture, bed pillows, and inflated basketballs do not utilize transportation equipment or storage space efficiently. Therefore, logistics costs tend to be higher for these products as a proportion of sales value than for high weight-bulk ratio products of equal value. The combined movement and storage costs, or total cost, tend to decline with increasing weight-bulk ratios, as shown in Fig. 4-1. Since the service provided to customers is not significantly affected by this ratio, the revenue contributed by the logistics system will also be unchanged.

FIGURE 4-1

Effect of product weight-bulk ratios on logistics system costs

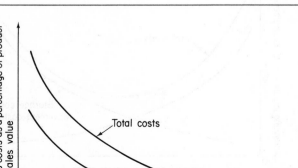

VALUE-WEIGHT RATIO

The value of a product is an important determinant of logistics system design. Generally, the higher the product's value, the better able it is to absorb logistics costs and the more likely it is that a premium logistics system will be used for distribution. However, for one more fully to appreciate the effect of value, it is best compared with product weight in the form of a value-weight ratio ($/lb). Logistics costs are, in large part, pegged to weight, and weight provides a good reference measure for value.

Low value-weight ratio products, such as sand, iron ore, and lumber, compared with high value-weight ratio products, such as electronic equipment, photographic goods, and optical instruments, incur relatively high movement costs. Storage costs tend to be low because the capital tied up in inventories, which is a function of product value, is low, and capital costs represent a significant portion of total storage costs. Also, storage costs are low as a proportion of the product's sales value. As the value-weight ratio increases, movement costs drop and storage costs rise, creating a cost tradeoff, as shown in Fig. 4-2. The level of sales is relatively unaffected by different value-weight ratios.

FIGURE 4-2
Effect of product value-weight ratios on logistics system costs

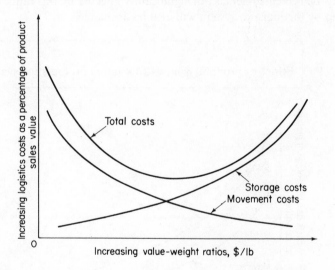

SUBSTITUTABILITY

When one product is not easily distinguished from another either in fact or as the consumer perceives the product, the products are substitutable or, in the economist's vernacular, they are undifferentiated. The degree of product substitutability affects logistics system design choices and costs. Promotional efforts often are directed toward creating in the mind of the consumer a state of product differentiation and ultimately a brand loyalty.

To the logistician, the degree of product substitutability affects the customer's willingness to wait for stock replenishment when a substitute product is readily available. When there is a stockout or the time to acquire the product exceeds that for product substitutes, a lost sale is likely to result. Many food products can be classed as highly substitutable. When there are no substitutes in the form of competing brands, the customer has the choice (1) of waiting until the product is available (backordering), (2) of altering his specifications for the product and choosing another, or (3) of dropping his interest in the product. If it is assumed that he selects the first alternative, the sale is not lost, only delayed. Though selecting either of the remaining two alternatives results in a lost sale for the supplier, the backorder occurs often enough in nearly all types of products to say that lost revenue is less as a percentage of sales for products of low substitutability than for ones of high substitutability.

The logistician has little or no control over product substitutability. He does influence product availability through transportation service and inventory level choices. As product availability changes, so does the extent of lost revenue. Transportation service and inventory level are interdependent, and product availability can be altered by changing either one or both of these variables. In Fig. 4-3,

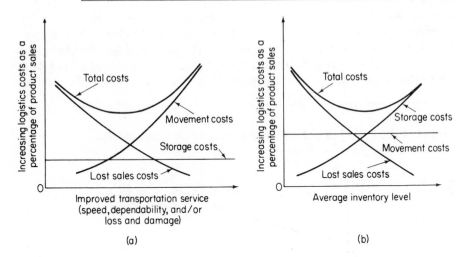

FIGURE 4-3

Effect of transportation service and average inventory level on logistics costs as a percentage of product sales for a product with a given degree of substitutability

Source: Adapted from J. L. Heskett, Robert M. Ivie, and Nicholas A. Glaskowsky, Jr., *Business Logistics* (New York: The Ronald Press Company, 1964), p. 30.

transportation service and inventory level are changed in turn while the other is held constant. Figure 4-3(a) shows that lost revenue declines as faster, more dependable, and safer transportation service is provided. Given a constant average inventory, the time to acquire the product is reduced and the probability of being damaged is less as more premium transportation is used. If a stockout occurs, the time to fill the backorder is less with premium transportation service. Customer service will improve and lost sales costs will decline. Transportation costs generally increase with higher service quality.

Figure 4-3(b) shows the tradeoff between lost sales costs and storage costs when the transportation service is held constant. Increasing average inventory levels result in increased product availability through a reduced probability of being out of stock. Correspondingly, there would be fewer lost sales. Higher inventory levels mean higher storage costs. Again, this is a situation of conflicting cost patterns.

RISK CHARACTERISTICS

Special product characteristics such as fragility, flammability, likelihood of exploding, valuation, and ease of being stolen tend to constrain the logistics system to certain designs, add costs to the system design, or both. For example, perishable products such as fresh fruits or frozen foods must be shipped in refrigerated equipment and stored in refrigerated warehouses. The possibility of deterioration limits the length of time that they may be retained in the logistics system. Valuable products or those easily stolen, such as cigarettes, require special security precautions to be maintained while goods are in transit or are being stored. Hazardous products such as caustic chemicals or explosive petroleum products may require special equipment designed especially for their transport, and storage may require isolated areas with fire equipment or special containers. The point is, products with special characteristics that increase the risk of loss to product, equipment, or personnel above that which might be considered as normal generally increase both storage and movement costs as shown in Fig. 4-4. Packaging costs may, in part, counterbalance the increased storage and movement costs that are due to the higher risk. If risk is compared to product value, say in the form of a

---

FIGURE 4-4

Effect of increasing risk of loss in the product on logistics costs

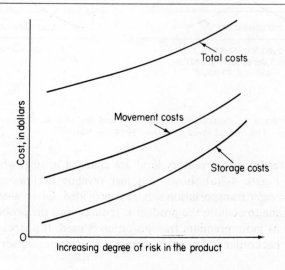

risk-value index, products with higher risk would cause logistics costs to be a higher percentage of the product sales dollar.

A SINGLE ENTITY

The product is a single entity, and the logistician must deal with the combined effect of all product characteristics in designing the logistics system. In any specific case, only a subset of all characteristics will be important; that is, a product may be fragile but not hazardous or bulky and not particularly valuable. It would be impractical to attempt a discussion of all possible product characteristic combinations. However, it is important for the logistician to be conscious of those characteristics that have an impact on logistics system design and to understand the magnitude of the cost tradeoffs among important logistics costs such as movement, storage, and lost sales if he is to approach an optimum system design.

Customer Service

Customer service is one of the most intangible elements in the logistics mix. The fact that far too little is known about its exact nature probably has forced logisticians to deal with it in a superficial way. It is common to find it defined in terms of delivery time or stock availability. That is, customer service may mean the number of days for local delivery from a warehouse. For example, Pillsbury's objective in 1955 was "third morning delivery" anywhere in the United States[1] and the General Electric marketing services decided on a policy of "a 90 percent customer service level—which means 90 percent of the customers would receive shipments the day after the order was received (the other 10 percent on the second day)."[2] On the other hand, customer service often is expressed in terms of inventory availability. For example, the ratio of the average number of units that are out-of-stock to the average demand or a simple frequency measure such as a ratio of the number of weeks when no stockouts occurred to the total number of weeks may be used. The major problems with these measures are (1) they are often treated separately, (2) they do not entirely reflect the customer's feeling and his actions about service, and (3) they do not include the various activities over which the logistician has control and which affect customer service. Treating customer service strictly in terms of delivery time or stock availability potentially suboptimizes the resulting decisions. A broader concept is needed.

NEED FOR CONCERN

Before pursuing the concept question, it is well to ask at this point: What should be the logistician's concern with customer service? In much the same way that

---

[1] "New-fangled Routes Deliver the Goods—Faster and Cheaper," *Business Week* (November 4, 1959), pp. 108–10.

[2] "The Case for 90% Satisfaction," *Business Week* (January 14, 1961), pp. 82–85.

customers respond to price in selecting products, they respond to service, or so it is believed. Generally, the higher the quality of distribution service provided relative to competition, the greater will be the revenue received from any given group of customers. Customer service is the end result of logistics system design and operation. It also is the reason for incurring logistics costs. Since customers are sensitive to even small changes in the service provided,[3] there is reason to believe that supplier patronage (and therefore revenues) may follow. The customer finds an economic advantage in terms of lower inventories from better supplier service,[4] though it is possible that the customer may use personal relationships with suppliers to define his buying patterns and hence nullify service differentials that may be created. To the extent that product revenue is a function of the service provided, the logistician must be concerned with how much service should be provided. He cannot be content to concern himself only with logistics costs and neglect the revenue effects of his decisions when the firm seeks profit as an objective. Neither can he afford to meet the insatiable desire of the customer for service by providing an extremely high customer service level and neglecting logistics costs. He seeks some middle ground where the differences between revenues and costs are maximized.

CUSTOMER SERVICE DEFINED

Customer service is a complex collection of demand-related factors under the control of the firm, but whose importance in determining supplier patronage is ultimately evaluated by the customer receiving the service. If the customer does not know or cannot express his feelings about service or in some way relate through his actions how he patronizes a supplier in relation to service, then only the most crude revenue-service relationships can be established. There is a general lack of research in this area, but researchers have attempted to define the factors that make up customer service.

In a study by Hutchinson and Stolle, customer service factors were classified as those typical to the physical distribution area and additional factors important to the customer. Those of interest to the logistician are

1. *Order processing time:* elapsed time from receipt of customer's order until it is ready for assembly.
2. *Order assembly time:* time required to prepare the order for shipment.
3. *Delivery time:* time in transit to the customer.
4. *Inventory reliability:* stockouts, back orders, percentage of demand filled, omission rate, percentage of orders shipped complete, and so on.
5. *Order-size constraint:* minimum order size and minimum frequency allowed.

[3] Ronald P. Willett and P. Ronald Stephenson, "Determinants of Buyer Response to Physical Distribution Service," *Journal of Marketing Research*, Vol. 6 (August 1969), pp. 279–83.

[4] Ronald H. Ballou and Daniel W. DeHayes, Jr., "Transport Selection by Interfirm Analysis," *Transportation and Distribution Management*, Vol. 7 (June 1967), pp. 33–37.

6. *Consolidation allowed:* ability to consolidate items from several locations into a single shipment.

7. *Consistency:* range of variation in each of the preceding elements.[5]

The customer is concerned with the above factors and with additional factors not directly under the control of the logistician. These same authors note the following elements in the latter category

1. *Frequency of a salesman's visits* to check his customer's needs.

2. *Ordering convenience* (telephone, preprinted forms, and so on).

3. *Order progress information* (order acknowledgement, shipping notices, and so on).

4. *Inventory backup during promotions*, new product introductions, and competitive tests.

5. *Format and organization of the invoice.*[6]

Stephenson and Willett in their study of customer service suggested several factors not specifically included in the above lists. The physical condition of the goods as received by the customer is a factor very directly under control of the logistician. Also noted were claim procedures and billing accuracy and efficiency.[7] However, billing procedures only rarely would be the logistician's responsibility.

A Cooperative Effort.[8]   The above lists suggest that customer service for a customer is not due to the singular efforts of the logistician. Rather, customer service must be a cooperative effort usually between selling and logistics activities, at times also involving the control function of the firm. If salesmen provide good service to the customer in the form of frequent visits, stock checking, and order preparation, this effort might be nullified by poor physical distribution of the goods. Cooperation is needed if the best profit picture is to be produced for the company. As Ivie noted:

> It is not reasonable to assume that the logistics manager can sit at his desk and determine what the optimum system will be for any customer or group of customers without direct contact with them. It goes without saying that this can only be accomplished with the support and cooperation of the marketing function.[9]

[5] William M. Hutchinson and John F. Stolle, "How to Manage Customer Service," *Harvard Business Review* (November–December 1968), p. 88.

[6] *Ibid.*, p. 89.

[7] P. Ronald Stephenson and Ronald P. Willett, "Selling with Physical Distribution Service," *Business Horizons* (December 1968), pp. 75–85.

[8] The discussion in this section is adapted from Ronald H. Ballou, "Cooperation at the Interface of Marketing and Logistics," a paper presented at the American Marketing Association Seminar held at The University of Oklahoma, Norman, Oklahoma, April 22–24, 1970.

[9] Robert M. Ivie, "Information Systems for Logistics Management," reprinted in Norton E. Marks and Robert M. Taylor (eds.), *Marketing Logistics: Perspectives and Viewpoints* (New York: John Wiley and Sons, Inc., 1967), pp. 123–25.

Cooperation among functional areas of the firm is not easy, but the rewards to the firm can be substantial when it can be accomplished. The logistician generally seeks two things from marketing's cooperation: (1) for marketing to provide customer service information and (2) for marketing to make realistic demands for customer service.

Since the customer is the ultimate judge of the customer service level and the salesman has the most frequent and direct contact with the customer, marketing is in a position to provide much valuable information for establishing a level of service or in developing a sales-service relationship. Such information is useful in determining which are the most important factors in the customer service mix. To quote Ivie again:

> . . . the logistician must rely heavily upon marketing's "eyes" and "ears", the salesman, and work with and through him. The logistics manager can review reports from sales representatives to obtain much valuable information about customer service performance and specialized requirements of customers . . .[10]

When salesmen and customers perceive customer service only in light of its most immediate impact, both groups would agree that the customer service level is never high enough. Salesmen do not want any lost sales due to poor service, and customers do not want additional costs to them because of less than the highest possible service level that might be provided. To follow a 100 percent customer service policy can be exceedingly expensive, since logistics costs rise geometrically as high customer service levels are approached (see Fig. 4-5). High logistics costs

---

FIGURE 4-5

Customer service and logistics system costs as a function of logistics system design

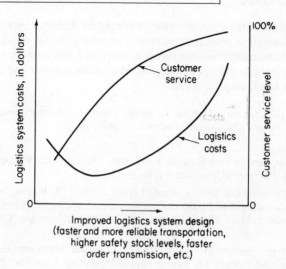

Improved logistics system design
(faster and more reliable transportation,
higher safety stock levels, faster
order transmission, etc.)

[10] *Ibid.*, p. 123.

are reflected in the price of the product. However, if the demand for very high customer service levels is relaxed somewhat, much lower logistics costs could be achieved. The reduced costs might then be reflected in lower prices. In fact, it has been suggested that a price discount schedule be established for different levels of service. The customer would have a chance to choose the best level for his needs, and the logistics manager meets his profit objectives by setting the price discounts in line with the logistics costs to produce the various service levels.

The Order Cycle. It is often practical to deal most directly with those customer service factors under immediate control of the logistician. The primary factors are those that make up order cycle time, that is, order transmittal time, order processing time, order assembly time, stock availability, and delivery time. These factors are primary determinants in such decisions as inventory stocking policies, facility locations, and transportation mode selections. Other factors such as order condition, order-size constraint, and ability to consolidate orders, while of overriding importance in some cases, often act as modifying rather than primary factors in logistics system design. That is, modifying factors are brought into the decision process after order cycle time considerations have first had their influence.

The order cycle is referred to as the length of time between when the customer[11] releases the order and when he receives the order from the supplier and has it available for sale from his own inventory. It is often called the lead time. The order cycle is the combined effect of a number of time-consuming logistics activities which have been noted above and are shown in Fig. 4-6. The order transmittal time may be composed of several time elements depending on the method used for communicating orders. A salesmen-mail communication system would have an order transmittal time composed of the length of time a salesman and the sales office retain the order before mailing it and the length of time the order is in the mail. A customer-prepared order plus telephone transmission would have a total transmittal time essentially of the telephone call. Note that at times it may be important to factor into order cycle time the customer's time for filling out an order form or the time between salesman's visits.

The second major component of order cycle time is the time for order processing and assembly. Order processing involves such activities as a shipping document preparation, inventory record updating, credit clearance coordination, checking the order for errors, communication with customers and interested parties within the company on the status of orders, and dissemination of order information to sales, production, and accounting. Order assembly is the time required to make the shipment ready for delivery after the order has been received and the order information made available to the warehouse or shipping department. It involves picking the order from stock, moving the order to the outbound point in the warehouse, packaging or light manufacturing if necessary, and consolidation with other orders moving in the same direction. Order processing and assembly to a degree take place concurrently, so the total time expended for both activities is not the sum of the times required by each. Rather, both activities overlap, with

[11] The customer used in its broadest sense may also mean the demands of a production line, a warehouse inventory, etc.

FIGURE 4-6

Example of a dual distribution system and the primary
components of order cycle time

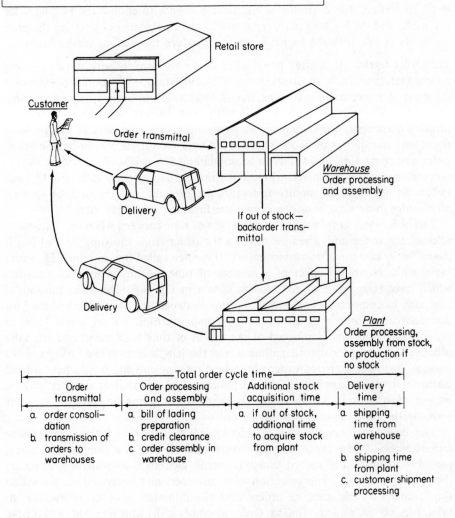

	Total order cycle time		
Order transmittal	Order processing and assembly	Additional stock acquisition time	Delivery time
a. order consolidation b. transmission of orders to warehouses	a. bill of lading preparation b. credit clearance c. order assembly in warehouse	a. if out of stock, additional time to acquire stock from plant	a. shipping time from warehouse or b. shipping time from plant c. customer shipment processing

order processing beginning slightly ahead of assembly due to error checking and
initial handling of the paper work. Shipping document preparation and inventory
updating can be carried out while assembly operations are taking place.

Stock availability has a dramatic effect on total order cycle time, since it often
forces product and information flows out of the established channel. A normal
channel may be to supply customers through a warehouse, as shown in Fig. 4-6.
When stock is not available in warehouse inventories to fill an order, a second or
backup distribution channel may be used. For example, a back order for the out-
of-stock item would be transmitted to the plant to be filled from plant stocks. If

there is no plant stock available, a production order is prepared and stock produced. Delivery is then made directly from the plant to the customer. Many other backup systems are possible depending on customer service requirements. The one shown here is for a highly substitutable product.

Order cycle time increases from back orders because of the additional order processing time, the possible increased order assembly time, especially if the order must be produced, and the added delivery time due to the longer delivery link to the customer. If no backup distribution system has been established, the increased time due to a stockout is the time until the inventory is replenished at the warehouse.

The final primary element in the order cycle over which the logistician has direct control is the delivery time. This is the time required for moving the order from the stocking point to the customer. It also may include the time for loading at the origin point and unloading at the customer's location.

The combined effect of the various factors that make up order cycle time can be represented in a probability distribution, as shown in Fig. 4-7. This is a con-

FIGURE 4-7
Order cycle time distributions as a function
of average order cycle time

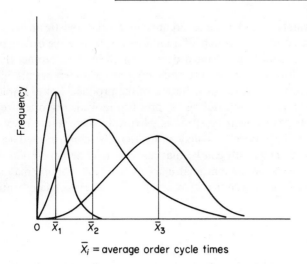

$\overline{X}_i$ = average order cycle times

venient form for decision-making purposes, since the distribution expresses both the average time to receive goods as well as the uncertainty or variation in time to accomplish the various activities in the total order cycle and it can be quantified. The order cycle distribution tends to be skewed for low average order cycle times and more symmetrical as the average increases. These shapes occur because order cycle time cannot go below zero. If a significant number of stockouts occur, the distribution will tend to become bimodal rather than unimodal as the longer order cycle times associated with backorders become important in the distribution of "regular" order cycle times.

Order Processing Priorities.   Order cycle time for an individual customer can vary greatly from the company average, depending on the priority system, or lack of one, that has been established by the firm for processing incoming orders. Distinguishing one customer from another may be necessary when order processing backlogs occur. For example, in processing orders from its industrial customers, a medium-sized paper company noted that when order backlogs occurred and pressure was applied to reduce them, order processing personnel had a tendency to process the smaller and less complicated orders first. This relegated the orders from the larger and more valuable customers to a later time than they normally would be handled, which resulted in an increased order cycle time for these customers.[12] The company unconsciously was reducing its customer service level to its larger customers during order backlog periods because it lacked specific priority rules for processing orders.

Condition of the Order.   Fast and reliable order service can be nullified if the order arrives in a damaged and unusable state. Damage may result from improper handling or from inadequate and poorly designed packaging. While a certain amount of damage will occur in the normal course of doing business, the logistician seeks to balance the negative effects of damage on customer service against the cost of packaging.

Order Constraints.   Under some circumstances, the logistician may find it desirable to limit customers to orders of a minimum size, to have orders placed according to a rigid schedule, or to have orders prepared by the customer that conform to preset specifications. These constraints on the customer permit important economies to be achieved in the distribution of the product. For example, a minimum order size and precise scheduling of product movements often result in lower transportation costs. Such constraints obviously have a negative effect on the customer, but the service loss may more than be compensated for by the cost savings realized. The result can be that markets may be penetrated that otherwise are too costly to serve, or marginal markets with low volume may still be served if the volume from a number of markets can be consolidated into economical movements.

CUSTOMER SERVICE FUNCTION

To effect a good logistics system design, the logistician would like to know the influence that each customer service factor has on producing sales. Better still, he would like a precise, mathematical relationship that expresses revenue as a function of the customer service factors, especially those under his control. However, product differences and differences in the way individual customers respond

[12] Abbott D. Weiss and J. L. Heskett, *East River Pulp and Paper Corp.* (*A*), Intercollegiate Clearing House case Gen. Mgt. 113 (Cambridge, Mass.: Intercollegiate Clearing House, Harvard University, 1966).

to customer service for various products make such a relationship exceedingly difficult to realize.

On a more limited scale, the logistician would find it very useful if the relationship involved only order cycle time. That is, sales would be a function of average order cycle time and order cycle time variability:

Sales due to customer service = *f*(average order cycle time, order
cycle time variability)

This general relationship is commonly known as a *customer service function*. A hypothetical function has been shown in Fig. 4-8. In this case, sales have been related to ratios of the firm's order cycle variables and the order cycle variables of a competitor. Supplier patronage and, therefore, sales follow the buyer's alternatives for service and should be reflected in the customer service function. Though

FIGURE 4-8

A hypothetical customer service function involving
order cycle time factors

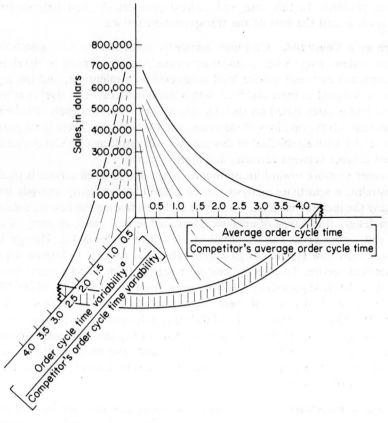

a Variability is expressed in standard deviations.

it might appear that such a function should be discontinuous at the point where our firm's performance falls below that of the competitor's (average order cycle time and variability ratios exceed 1), since all orders would be switched to the competitor, this may not be so. Because the buyer also considers product price, personal relationships with the salespeople and the firm, convenience of doing business, reputation of the supplier firm, and the multitude of other factors that are in the patronage mix, order cycle time is not the sole determinant of sales. Therefore, a company may continue to patronize a supplier even though his customer service does not measure up to that of a competitor's.

To illustrate how the customer service function bears on logistics system design, consider a hypothetical transportation service selection problem of the Gadgets Manufacturing Company. Six transportation services are to be explored for serving the east coast markets from its midwestern stock location point as listed in Table 4-1. Delivery time is the only component of order cycle time that is affected by the transportation service choice. Different order cycle times for the various transportation services, and the sales that are generated from the various customer service levels are also shown in Table 4-1. Deducting all costs against sales revenue and then the cost of the transportation service yields the before-tax profit for this decision problem. In this case, rail carload provides the best balance between sales revenue and the cost of the transportation service.

Service as a Constraint. Customer service is often treated as a constraint on logistics system design when a customer service function cannot be developed. A predetermined customer service level is selected as a minimum, and the logistics system is designed to meet this level with a minimum cost. The level is arbitrarily selected and is often based on such factors as (1) the service levels established by competition, (2) the opinions of salesmen, and (3) tradition. There is no guarantee that a service level established in this manner will result in a system design that is the best balance between revenues and logistics costs.

In order to move toward an optimum system design when service is treated as a constraint, a sensitivity analysis can be helpful. A sensitivity analysis involves changing the factors that make up service and then finding the new minimum-cost system design. If this type of analysis is repeated several times, an array of system costs and service levels can be obtained, as shown in Table 4-2. Though it may not be known how system design affects sales, it is possible to impute the worth of improved service. To improve customer service from an 85 percent level to a 90 percent level, logistics costs will increase from $7,000,000 to $9,000,000 annually. The imputed worth of these five percentage points in customer service is $2,000,000. Thus, a minimum of $2,000,000 in sales plus enough sales revenue to cover nonlogistics costs must be generated to justify the increased expenditures for distribution. It may be easier for salesmen and sales managers to relate to an imputed value for service than to estimate the sales that could be generated from a given level of service.

Service as a Percentage. In the above discussion, customer service was referred to in percentage terms. This is a common practice, albeit a confusing one. Such a

TABLE 4-1
Hypothetical transportation service selection problem of the Gadgets Manufacturing Company

Transportation Service Type[a]	Order Cycle Time[b]		Sales Revenue[d]	All Costs Except Transportation[e]	Transportation Cost	Before-Tax Profit
	Average	Variability[c]				
Less carload, Rail	18	5.5	$100,000	$ 90,000	$ 7,000	$+3,000
Surface freight forwarder	14	2.5	150,000	135,000	12,000	+3,000
Carload, Rail	13	2.3	150,000	135,000	8,000	+7,000
Less truckload	12.5	2.5	200,000	180,000	18,000	+2,000
Truckload	10.5	2.0	300,000	270,000	30,000	0
Air freight	5.5	1.8	400,000	360,000	120,000	−80,000

[a] Carload, less carload, truckload, and less truckload refer to whether or not the particular vehicle is completely filled with gadgets. Quality of delivery service typically varies between load levels as well as between modes.

[b] Competitors average order cycle time is five days, and the order cycle variability is two standard deviations.

[c] Expressed as standard deviations (days).

[d] Developed from the mathematical relationship for the curve shown in Fig. 4-8.

[e] Includes all manufacturing, marketing, and logistics costs except transportation costs.

TABLE 4-2

Logistics system design costs as a function of various customer service levels

Alternative No.	Logistics System Design[a]	Annual Logistics Costs	Customer Service Level[b]
1	Mail order transmittal, water transportation, low inventory levels.	$ 5,000,000	80%
2	Mail order transmittal, rail transportation, low inventory levels.	7,000,000	85%
3	Mail order transmittal, truck transportation, low inventory levels.	9,000,000	90%
4	Mail order transmittal, rail transportation, high inventory levels.	12,000,000	93%
5	Mail order transmittal, truck transportation, high inventory levels.	15,000,000	95%
6	Telephone order transmittal, truck transportation, high inventory levels.	16,000,000	96%

[a] Minimum cost design to produce the stated customer service level.
[b] Percent of customers receiving goods within one day.

percentage figure may mean the percentage of customers within one-day delivery of a warehouse, the probability of an out-of-stock occurring, the percentage of deliveries made "on time," or virtually any other scheme where a percentage value can be developed. Typically, only one of these categories is used, depending on the particular problem at hand. For example, if the problem is one of warehouse location, percent of customers within one-day delivery of a warehouse might be used. If the problem involves setting inventory levels, the probability of a stockout occurring may be appropriate. A broader view of service would be to include the entire order cycle so that order processing time, delivery time, and stock availability are a part of a more comprehensive definition for customer service. One such broader definition would be to interpret customer service as a proportion of the area under the order cycle time distribution curve as shown in Fig. 4-9. For example, a 90 percent customer service level means that on the average 90 percent of the customers have order cycle times of less than or equal to t'. Ten percent will have longer order cycle times.

While this definition does provide greater consistency for a wide variety of logistics decisions and is to be preferred over the fragmented definitions that have been used, shortcomings remain. These shortcomings include: (1) the lack of any

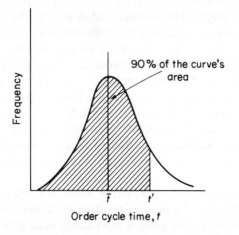

FIGURE 4-9
Customer service as a portion of the area under
the order cycle time frequency distribution

90% of the curve's area

Frequency

Order cycle time, t

relationship between sales and the level of service provided, (2) the omission of those factors that are also a part of service, such as condition of the order and order constraints, and (3) the specific service requirements of individual buyers. Until broad, precise relationships become available, limited definitions of this type are likely to be used in the interim.

Pricing

Setting the price of a product is not usually the responsibility of the logistician. However, since price is in part determined by all costs incurred by the firm and at times are very directly influenced by logistics costs, the logistician can be an important source of information about price-determining costs. His influence is often limited to geographical pricing methods and incentive pricing arrangements based on quantity purchased. Thus, pricing is a factor in the product environment about which the logistician should be knowledgeable and ready to provide advice, at least to the extent that it is within his influence.

GEOGRAPHICAL PRICING METHODS

There are five common pricing methods that are influenced by transportation costs. These are (1) f.o.b., (2) zone, (3) uniform, (4) freight equalization, and (5) basing point pricing arrangements.

F.O.B. Pricing. F.o.b. means "free on board." Under this policy, the product is priced at a particular geographical location. If this location does not correspond with that of the customer's, then the customer must pay for, and usually arrange for, any needed transportation. An infinite number of f.o.b. pricing policies might be devised; however, the two most common are f.o.b. factory or origin and f.o.b. destination or "delivered" price.

The *f.o.b. factory price* is a single price quoted for all customers at the factory location or point of origin. The customer takes title to the goods at this point. Though he usually arranges and pays for transportation, this is not always to his economic advantage. If his orders are small, he may not be able to benefit from transportation price discounts for high-volume shipments. Thus, the customer may make arrangements with the supplier to provide the transportation. The customer still pays the transportation charges, but his costs may be lower if the supplier consolidates the order with other shipments moving in the same direction and reduced per-unit rates are achieved. The f.o.b. factory pricing policy has the primary advantages of treating all customers alike in terms of price, and it also relieves the supplier of the administration of the delivery segment of the distribution channel.

The *f.o.b. destination or delivered pricing policy* is a simple variant of f.o.b. factory pricing. In this case, the product is priced at the customer's door, or in the customer's general vicinity. The price is the factory price plus the transportation charges incurred in the order delivery. The supplier makes the transportation arrangements and merely reflects these charges in the delivered price. This pricing policy is formal recognition that the supplier is in a position to supply the transportation most economically and the customer may lack the expertise or desire to make such arrangements.

Zone Pricing.   When a firm deals with thousands of customers at many different locations that buy hundreds of different product items, the problem of price administration becomes overwhelming. Zone pricing is an attempt to simplify a portion of the pricing problem by treating a large block of customers that are geographically dispersed as if they were all located a given distance from the supply source. A region may be divided into any number of subregions or zones, as shown in Fig. 4-10. Within each zone, transportation costs are averaged and a single price is established.

Zone pricing or transportation cost averaging does not treat all customers equally. If transportation costs are established at a distance midway in the zone, those customers located before the zone midpoint are charged a "phantom" freight cost. That is, these customers pay more than a comparable f.o.b. origin price plus what the transportation cost would be. On the other hand, those customers beyond the zone midpoint pay a lower price than the actual transportation costs would dictate. In this case, the company is said to "absorb" the excess freight charges. Though this is a geographical discriminatory pricing practice (customer's prices do not follow seller's net prices at the factory), the virtues of it may be argued on the basis that simplification of the pricing structure has its compensating economies in other cost areas such as selling, billing, etc. It also is an example of discrimination against a few for the greater good of all.

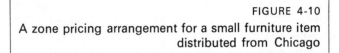

FIGURE 4-10

A zone pricing arrangement for a small furniture item
distributed from Chicago

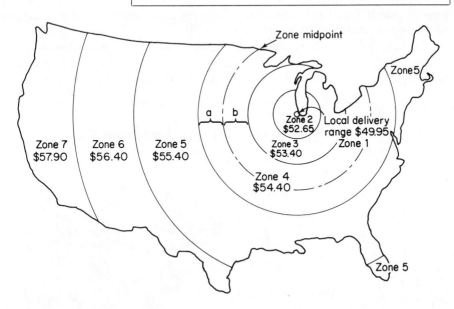

a Company absorbs some freight charges.
b Customers are charged more than actual freight costs.

Uniform Pricing. Uniform pricing is a limiting case of zone pricing where only one zone and one price are used for the entire country. This pricing arrangement has obvious advantages when price is promoted on a national scale. However, it also tends to be more discriminatory than the multiple zone pricing policy. The uniform price is probably most successful where transportation cost represents a small proportion of the product's total value. Products such as jewelry, high-fashion clothing, and electronic equipment lend themselves to a uniform pricing policy.

Freight Equalization. Competing firms are not usually equidistant from all markets such that their transportation costs to place the product in the market will differ. If two firms have the same f.o.b. factory price, the firm with the higher transportation cost to place goods in the same market may absorb enough of the freight charges so that a competitive price may be established in the market place. This practice is referred to as freight equalization and results in different net returns to the seller at the factory.

Basing Point Pricing. The basing point pricing policy is an attempt by a seller to reduce the impact on the market place of his locational disadvantage relative to that of his competitors. He simply does this by basing his pricing calculations on the location of a major competitor as if he were located there. In this way his delivered price will be in line with that of his competitor, since transportation costs radiate from the same point. Such a pricing policy is attractive where (1) the product involved has a high transportation cost relative to its value, (2) there is little preference among buyers as to the supplier of the product (that is, the product is undifferentiated), and (3) there are only a few suppliers and price cutting only leads to retaliation by rivals.

The steel industry offers perhaps the most famous example of basing point pricing. Fig. 4-11 shows a possible situation. Steel is f.o.b. factory priced at Pittsburgh, Pennsylvania, and Gary, Indiana, at $15 per ton. In order to compete

---

FIGURE 4-11

Hypothetical delivered prices for steel from Pittsburgh and Gary

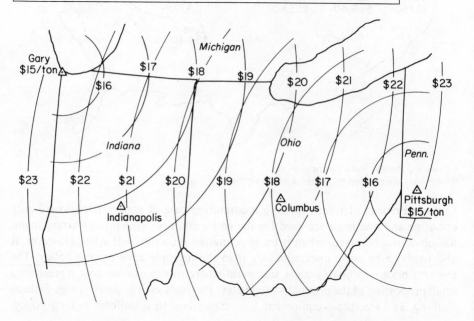

---

directly with the Pittsburgh mills, the Gary mills choose Pittsburgh as a base point. Thus, the delivered price for both mills would be $17.80 per ton in the Columbus, Ohio market. Each mill then competes in the markets on a nonprice basis. However, the effective price at each mill differs, since shipments are made from their actual mill locations. To serve the Columbus market, the Gary mill charges $2.80 per ton for freight but actually incurs $5.20 per ton, as Fig. 4-11 shows. A transportation cost of $2.40 per ton is absorbed. Conversely, Indianapolis is charged $6.10 per ton for freight, while the actual freight expense incurred for delivery by the Gary mill is $3.20 per ton. A phantom freight charge of $2.90 per ton is made to Indianapolis. The Gary mill receives a higher effective price from the customers near to its mill and less from the more distant ones.

Because the prices paid by the buyer do not follow the actual costs of landing the product in the market place, questions have been raised about the legality of basing point pricing systems under the Robinson-Patman Act. However, Beckman and Davidson note that such a delivered pricing practice is probably legal if the following conditions are met:

1. If the seller is willing to sell on an f.o.b. basis when a purchaser so requests.
2. If the seller maintains a uniform delivered price at all points of delivery, as when he charges nationwide uniform delivered prices.
3. If the seller absorbs freight costs, or some portion of them, in order to meet competition, as when his factory price plus actual freight to destination is higher than the amount a customer would have to pay when procuring the same goods from a competitor.
4. If the buyer and/or their customers are noncompetitive.[13]

QUANTITY DISCOUNTS

One often used incentive pricing scheme is the quantity discount. The buyer is encouraged to purchase in larger quantities than he might normally order by a reward system that is graduated to order size. Though the "reward" may take the form of gifts, cash rebates, and credits on future purchases, a common procedure is for the supplier to offer percentage price reductions from a regular price such as follows:

Order Size, Units	Discount from Regular Price
0– 99	0%
100– 499	1
500– 999	2
1000–1999	3
over 2000	4

The exact form of the discount is not as important to the logistician as the magnitude of the incentive for various order sizes. The Federal Trade Commission as authorized under the Robinson-Patman Act requires that quantity discounts follow cost reduction realized from processing orders of different sizes. Economies of scale are often difficult to justify in production operations and selling, but the volume discounts established in the transportation rate structure are well-known. Because of this, logistics costs are frequently used as a guide in setting discount levels and the quantities at which the discounts occur.

To provide information for a quantity discount structure, the logistician examines those logistics costs that are affected by different order quantities from buyers. Chief among these are transportation, order processing, handling, and inventory carrying costs. The nature of each of these costs relative to the quantity purchased

[13] Theodore N. Beckman and William R. Davidson, *Marketing*, eighth edition (New York: The Ronald Press Company, 1967), p. 519.

is shown in Fig. 4-12. Combining these costs into a total cost curve illuminates the break-point quantities. Costs can then be averaged for the range of order sizes between these break-point quantities, as indicated by the C's in Fig. 4-12. The discount percentage is then computed for each order size range as the change in per-unit logistics costs divided by the regular or smallest quantity price. For example, if the regular price P_0 (price for the smallest quantity) is $10 per unit, per-unit

---

FIGURE 4-12

Selected logistics costs as a function of purchase quantity for a given annual demand level

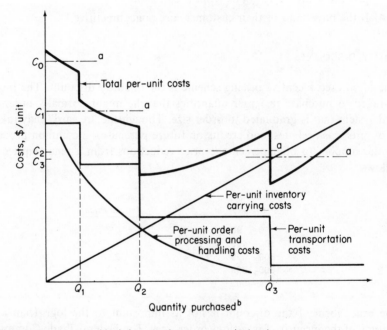

Quantity purchased[b]

[a] The C's denote average total logistics costs between quantity breaks.
[b] The Q's denote break-point quantities.

---

logistics cost (C_0) for the smallest order quantity is $6.50, and per-unit logistics cost C_1 for the purchase quantity range Q_1 to less than Q_2 is $5.00, the maximum discount is

$$\frac{C_0 - C_1}{P_0} = \frac{\$6.50 - \$5.00}{\$10} = 15\%$$

Discounts for the remaining quantity range are computed in a similar manner. These are maximum discounts that can be justified in terms of logistics costs. The actual discount schedule might be adjusted away from the maximum possible discount level so as to share cost economies between the customer and the supplier.

Also, the schedule might be simplified by using more convenient numbers for the discount percentages, and the quantity breaks than are likely to result naturally from the analysis.

The Package

The package is the fourth element in what is broadly thought of as the product. The product package has two important dimensions. The first centers around marketing concerns for product promotion and customer use. The second centers around product protection, which primarily is an engineering and logistics concern. These two dimensions are not independent, which suggests the need for a cooperative effort between marketing, engineering, and logistics in establishing the package design. Freidman summarizes the status of packaging in many firms and notes logistics' responsibility toward it:

> Marketing management continues to look at packaging strictly from a sales point of view. Packaging engineers, frequently reporting to purchasing or manufacturing, look at a package only as a protective device. Only physical distribution management can look at packaging broadly and conceive of changes in design, size, media of transportation, etc., which will contribute to the effectiveness of the distribution system.[14]

The logistician should exert a strong influence over package design because of the impact that the package has on distribution efficiency. For many products, the logistician considers that *the package is the product*. If a refrigerator in a corrugated carton were replaced with rocks and the logistician were not informed of this, he would not handle, store, or transport the product differently. From the logistician's viewpoint, it is the package that has assumed the product characteristics discussed earlier in this chapter. Of course, this is not true for all products, especially those that are not packaged, such as products in bulk, or those that are semipackaged, such as sheet steel on pallets.[15] However, for many goods it is the product in its packaged state that is his concern.

DESIGN CONSIDERATIONS

Package design for logistics objectives should meet four requirements: (1) protect the product, (2) be convenient for handling and storing, (3) be easy to identify, and (4) provide a measure of security.

[14] Walter F. Freidman, "The Role of Packaging in Physical Distribution," *Transportation & Distribution Management* (February 1968), p. 38.

[15] A pallet is a platform usually constructed of wood, with typical dimensions of $40'' \times 48'' \times 5''$ on which goods are stocked, and the platform facilitates moving the goods as a unit.

Product Protection. The most obvious requirement for the package is that it should provide a measure of protection against normal shocks and vibration incurred in handling and transit. Protection may also be needed against water damage, odor contamination, and temperature extremes. A wide variety of packaging materials is available, and engineering studies provide data on such characteristics as strength in tension and compression, moisture resistance, and heat resistance. This information is useful in selecting and evaluating alternative package designs.

To evaluate package designs, it is also necessary to know the likelihood of damage as the product moves from the production line to the consumer. The logistics analyst might determine this exposure by sending test shipments through the distribution system, or he might simulate the exposure by using mechanical equipment. These are probably the most accurate methods for his particular product. However, some data of this type are available external to the firm. Tests performed by the National Safe Transit Committee show relative levels of shock incurred in test shipments handled by various transportation modes (Fig. 4-13). These data provide rough guide lines for package design.

It is interesting to note from Fig. 4-13 that the protective package should be designed to shock levels incurred in handling rather than those occurring enroute. More specifically, it is often claimed that damage in air freight is the lowest among comparable modes. The chart supports this. However, goods must move to and from the aircraft often by truck and by conventional materials-handling equipment, which have high risk levels. Little will be saved in protective packaging costs by using air freight if package design must be pegged to the risk level of ground handling. It may be a misconception that the more damage-free transportation modes offer a relative savings in package costs. Analysis in individual product cases should make this clear.

Handling and Storage Considerations. *Configuration* and *strength* are primary considerations in package design for handling and storage efficiency. The basic dimensions and strength of a package often dictate the type of materials-handling equipment needed, the density of the unit load when a number of packages are grouped together, and the stability of product when stacked for storage. The package cost is in part offset by increased distribution efficiency. The use of higher-strength materials and possibly more expensive configurations that use more packaging materials at times can be justified. Compensating cost savings can often be achieved through more compact unitization of loads so that fewer trips are required to move a given volume of goods and greater utilization of storage space is possible through higher load stacking.

Identification. The package contributes to the ease of product identification and therefore to greater handling efficiencies. When canned soups are offered in "57 varieties," washing machines in five colors, and a style of shoe in 20 sizes, differences in the product may not be easily distinguished from the outward appearance of the shipping package. The result may be an excessive amount of searching for a product throughout the entire distribution process. Specific attention to this

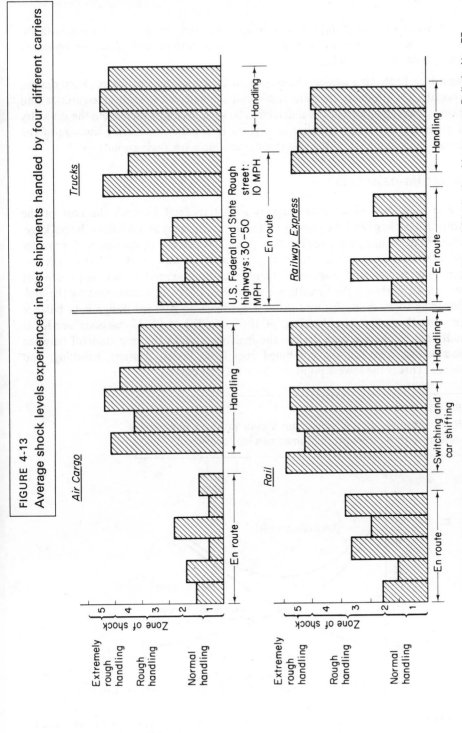

FIGURE 4-13
Average shock levels experienced in test shipments handled by four different carriers

Source: Redrawn from Stuart R. Wallace, "Packaging for Air Transportation," in *Packaging's Role in Physical Distribution.* Management Bulletin No. 77 (New York: American Management Association. 1966), pp. 30–31.

requirement can bring important economic returns, since identification is facilitated in inexpensive ways such as color-coding cartons and stenciling pertinent information on the package.

Security. Protecting against pilferage can be a requirement for package design, especially for products that are small and of high value, such as cigarettes and jewelry. Packaging can act as a deterrent to such losses by increasing the difficulty of pilferage. Banding a number of cartons to a pallet, increasing the size of the carton, or containerizing the goods may be simple packaging solutions.[16]

PACKAGING OBJECTIVES

The logistician views packaging as a cost tradeoff between the cost of the protective package and the gains in distribution efficiency as a result of the package. Attempting to design a package that gives 100 percent protection and provides the maximum in handling and storage efficiency is an "overkill." Although few marketing people and customers would be disappointed in this approach—at least on the surface—the benefits are more than likely far outweighed by the high packaging costs. A much more realistic approach to package design is to balance the costs that affect the decision, as shown in Fig. 4-14. If customer service is unaffected by the package design, the logistician seeks the best tradeoff between the package cost and the combined cost from losses, damage, handling, and storage. This is the lowest point on the total cost curve.

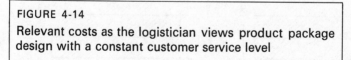

FIGURE 4-14
Relevant costs as the logistician views product package design with a constant customer service level

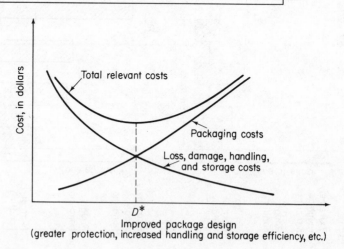

[16] For further discussion, see Robert H. Haskell, "Packaging to Prevent Theft," *Transportation & Distribution Management*, Vol. 10 (July 1970), p. 32.

Concluding Comments

The product is the object of all the logistician's efforts. Although it does have physical features, its important characteristics exist in the minds of those who must deal with it. This chapter attempts to view the product from the logistician's perspective. As such, the product is described in terms of (1) its physical and economic characteristics, (2) its customer service characteristics, (3) its price, and (4) its package. With a perspective of the product, the logistician can more realistically proceed with decisions that may alter the product, especially in the eyes of the customer.

Questions and Problems

1. For logistics purposes, what is a product?
2. Compare the product characteristics of the following items:

   (a) Timex watches
   (b) Rowboats
   (c) Light bulbs
   (d) Coal
   (e) Oriental rugs
   (f) Metal-working lathe

3. What is a customer service function? Of what concern is it to the logistician?

4. How would a company go about determining the customer service function for its product line?

5. Why must customer service be a shared responsibility with marketing?

6. What are the factors that make up order cycle time? Do these factors differ whether orders are filled in a regular distribution channel or are filled through a back up channel when an out-of-stock situation occurs? How?

7. Customer service might be quantified in terms of average order cycle time ($\overline{OCT}$) and order cycle time variability (σ_{oct}), i.e.,

$$\text{Service} = f(\overline{OCT}, \sigma_{oct})$$

Is this a satisfactory expression for customer service?

8. What is the relationship between order cycle time and logistics system design?

9. How should customer service be measured?

10. Why are logistics costs so important in establishing quantity discounts?

11. A rationalized geographical pricing structure would likely follow transportation cost patterns. Any deviations from transportation cost patterns might be considered a form of economic discrimination. To what extent are the following pricing methods discriminatory?

  (a) Basing point pricing
  (b) Uniform pricing
  (c) Zone pricing
  (d) F.o.b. delivered pricing
  (e) Freight equalization pricing

12. Why is packaging considered to be a marketing-logistics interface activity?

13. Package design may require consideration of both promotional and logistics factors. Explain.

Selected Bibliography

Little of the material in this chapter is formally collected in book form. The reader is directed to material cited in the footnotes for further reading.

Chapter
5

The Transportation System—
Facilities and Services

Transportation probably ranks as the most important economic activity in the business logistics mix, consuming typically two-thirds of a firm's dollars spent on all logistics activities.[1] Because of this, the logistician needs a good knowledge of the transportation system, and one that undoubtedly must extend beyond the scope of the two chapters in this book. However, the purpose here is to highlight the aspects of the transportation system that are most necessary for decision making. This chapter focuses on the transportation service alternatives and their performance characteristics.

Importance of an Inexpensive Transportation System

One need only contrast the economies of a "developed" nation with those of a "developing" nation to see the importance that transportation plays in creating a high level of economic activity. It is typical of the "developing" nation to have

[1] J. L. Heskett, "Macroeconomic Cost of Physical Distribution," in *Papers—Third Annual Meeting, American Transportation Research Forum* (Oxford, Inc.: The Richard B. Cross Co., 1962), pp. 169–89.

production and consumption taking place in the same proximity, much of the labor force engaging in agricultural production, and a low proportion of the total population living in urban areas. With the advent of inexpensive and readily available transportation services, the entire structure of the economy changes toward that of "developed" nations. Large cities result from the migration of the population to urban centers, areas limit production to a narrow range of products, and the standard of living usually rises for the average citizen. More specifically, an improved transportation system contributes to (1) greater competition in the market place, (2) greater economies of scale in production, and (3) reduced prices for goods.

Greater Competition. When an improved transportation system is not available, the extent of the market is limited to the areas immediately surrounding the point of production. Unless production costs are extremely low compared with those at a second production point, that is, unless the production cost difference is near to offsetting the transportation costs of serving the second market, little competition is likely to take place. However, with improved transportation, the landed costs for products in distant markets can be competitive with other producers selling in the same markets.

In addition to encouraging direct competition, inexpensive transportation also encourages an indirect form of competition by making available to a market goods that normally could not withstand the cost of transportation. Various fruits and vegetables are examples. When local production of these commodities is out of season, shipments are made into the market from outside areas to meet the demand. This increases the general availability of goods beyond those produced locally and can have a price-stabilizing effect on all goods.

Economies of Scale. The second important effect that cheap transportation has on the business firm is that wider markets permit economies of scale in production. With the greater volume provided by these markets, more intense utilization can be made of production facilities, and specialization of labor usually follows. In addition, cheap transportation also permits decoupling of markets and production sites. This provides a degree of freedom in selecting production sites such that production can be located where there is a geographical advantage.

Reduced Prices. Cheap transportation also contributes to reduced product prices. This occurs not only because of the increased competition in the market place, but also because transportation is a component cost along with production, selling, and other distribution costs that make up the aggregate product cost. As transportation becomes more efficient, as well as offering improved performance, society benefits through a higher standard of living.

Scope of the Transportation System

The domestic transportation system refers to the entire movement capability in the economy. This generally connotes the system for moving freight, though it may include the system for moving intangibles such as electricity, messages, military personnel, etc. The bulk of the freight movement is handled by the five basic modes of transportation (rail, truck, water, pipeline, and air) and the various transportation agencies that facilitate and coordinate freight movement (freight forwarders, railway express, parcel post, air express, and shippers associations). As illustrated in Fig. 5-1, carriers and agencies often interact with each other, and carriers interact among themselves to form more economical arrangements for moving freight. An example is a coordinated service such as piggyback (truck trailers shipped on rail flat cars) that results from truck-rail cooperation.

From a macroeconomic standpoint, the relative importance of the various transportation modes differs considerably at this point in time and, from the

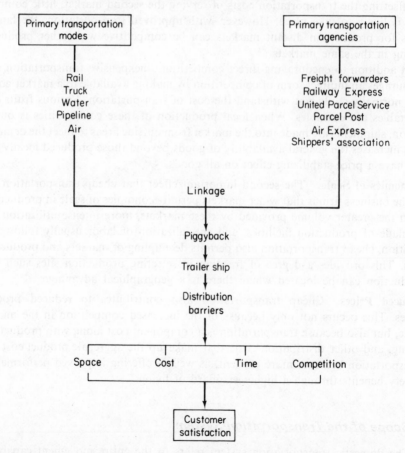

FIGURE 5-1
Transportation system for a business logistics system

Primary transportation modes	Primary transportation agencies
Rail Truck Water Pipeline Air	Freight forwarders Railway Express United Parcel Service Parcel Post Air Express Shippers' association

Linkage

Piggyback

Trailer ship

Distribution barriers

| Space | Cost | Time | Competition |

Customer satisfaction

Source: William Lazer, "The Distribution Mix–A Systems Approach" in Eugene J. Kelley and William Lazer (eds.), *Managerial Marketing: Perspectives and Viewpoints,* 3rd ed. (Homewood, Ill.: Richard D. Irwin, Inc., 1967), p. 529.

direction of current trends, the relative importance of each will change dramatically in the future. As of 1968, railroads hauled the largest percentage of the total ton-miles (one ton moving one mile) shipped, approximately 41 percent, and also the largest absolute number of ton-miles, 757 billion ton-miles (Table 5-1). How-

	TABLE 5-1
	Intercity freight movement in millions of ton-miles by mode for 1968[a]

Transportation Mode	Volume	Percentage of Total Volume
Railroads[b]	757,000	40.7
Trucks[c]	415,000	22.3
Inland waterways[d]	287,000	15.4
Oil pipelines	397,000	21.4
Air[e]	3,100	0.2
	1,859,100	100.0

[a] Estimated.
[b] Railroads all classes including electric.
[c] Ton-miles between cities and between rural and urban areas included, whether private or for hire. Rural-to-rural movements and city deliveries are omitted.
[d] Does not include coastwise and intercoastal ton-miles.
[e] Covers domestic except movements over international waters.
Source: Interstate Commerce Commission, American Trucking Association, and Transportation Association of America.

ever, the percentage of freight moving by rail has been on a gradual decline for the last 40 years (Fig. 5-2), though absolute ton-miles hauled have increased over this period due to the larger market shared by all modes. Trucks and oil pipelines have grown in relative importance over this same period and now account for 22 and 21 percent of the total ton-miles shipped, respectively. Water transportation had grown until 1960, and since then has shown a slight decline to 15 percent of the total ton-miles. Air freight has demonstrated dramatic growth, especially since 1960. The increase between 1967 and 1968 alone was 20 percent. While air freight is likely to be a dramatic growth area for the future, the drama is in large part due to changes in small numbers. Air freight currently accounts for only 0.2 percent of the total ton-miles shipped in the United States.

Products Hauled. The relative importance of each transportation mode and the changes that are occurring in relative importance are partially explained by the composition of the freight hauled and the inherent advantages of the mode. For example, consider pipelines. The pipeline is a highly efficient method for moving products in a liquid or gaseous form over long distances. As such, the use of the pipeline tends to be limited to liquid products (almost entirely oil) moving in high volume and to some products that can effectively be suspended in a slurry and moved as a liquid. For the most part, the latter is experimental. The natural gas pipelines do not compete with other forms of transportation. Thus, the pipeline

FIGURE 5-2

Forty-year trends in usage by mode as a percentage
of the total intercity ton-miles shipped

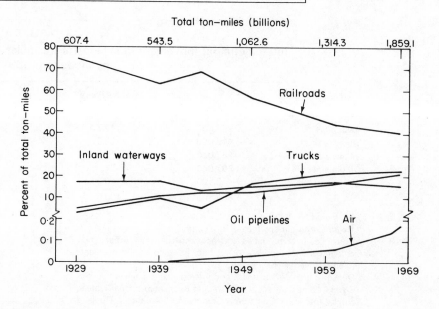

Source : Interstate Commerce Commission, American Trucking Association, and Transportation Association of America.

industry is primarily limited to crude oil and oil products movements. The costs
are low, but the product line is narrow.

In contrast, air freight is not so much limited in scope by technical feasibility
as by the relatively higher rates that must be charged as compared with other
modes. This has tended to limit air freight to products that can effectively tradeoff
the premium costs for improved service. Common products carried are electric
and electronic equipment and parts, wearing apparel, machinery and parts, and
cut flowers. These products generally have high value compared to their weight
or bulk, or speed is important in their distribution.

Water transportation is a major hauler of products in bulk. Coal, ore, coke,
gravel, sand, petroleum, semimanufactured iron and steel, grain, and cement
account for over 90 percent of the traffic on inland waterways. In contrast with
products carried by air, these products are of low value and not perishable, so
storage costs are not excessive and they can withstand the slow seasonal transportation service in exchange for low rates.

By elimination, this leaves rail and truck handling the majority of the manufactured products and over two-thirds of the total ton-miles shipped between cities.
The differences between rail and truck in terms of the products hauled do not
stand in as sharp contrast as do those of the other modes. Rail and truck compete

over essentially the same routes for much of the same freight. Trucking has been an effective competitor since about 1929, and the presence of trucking as an alternative service choice tends to explain the decline of the relative importance of rail and the increasing relative importance of trucking. The products hauled by each, in large part, are divided by the cost-service tradeoff. Rail, with lower rates and a slightly lower level of performance as compared with truck, has concentrated in the lower dollar density and lower value-per-cube products. Chemicals, plastics, and steel products are examples of the freight commonly moved by rail. The opposite is true for trucking. Typical products for trucking are instruments, fabricated metal products, furniture and fixtures, and beverages. Table 5-2 shows some of these differences.

The above discussion has been limited to freight alone. If the relative importance of the transportation modes were judged on the basis of passenger traffic, the results

TABLE 5-2

Sample survey of one million shipping documents of ten thousand manufacturers[a]

	Tons					Ton-Miles				
Group	*Rail*	*Truck*	*Air*	*Water*	*Other*	*Rail*	*Truck*	*Air*	*Water*	*Other*
Food & kindred products	45.8	52.9	—	0.9	0.4	66.1	32.1	—	1.4	0.4
Tobacco products	50.8	47.3	—	—	1.9	67.7	30.4	—	—	1.9
Basic textiles	11.3	87.8	—	—	0.9	22.9	74.4	0.1	0.1	2.5
Apparel & finished textile products	6.6	75.0	0.8	—	17.6	8.6	69.6	1.5	0.1	20.2
Lumber & wood products except furniture	54.3	43.5	—	2.1	0.1	83.7	15.6	—	2.5	0.2
Furniture & fixtures	23.8	75.0	—	—	1.2	43.6	54.4	0.1	0.1	1.8
Pulp, paper, & allied products	52.1	44.7	—	2.1	1.1	72.6	23.6	—	2.4	1.4
Chemicals & allied products	47.0	42.7	—	9.6	0.7	58.4	23.8	0.1	17.0	0.7
Petroleum & coal products	7.5	19.1	—	73.0	0.4	3.8	3.1	—	93.0	0.1
Rubber & miscellaneous plastic products	21.3	76.4	0.2	0.3	1.8	32.2	64.0	0.2	0.8	2.8
Leather & leather products	9.7	82.2	0.3	0.3	7.5	18.8	66.9	0.5	0.3	13.5
Stone, clay & glass products	30.4	63.0	—	6.4	0.2	46.5	44.6	—	8.5	0.4
Primary metal products	51.1	35.9	—	10.5	3.0	65.5	26.1	—	7.8	0.5
Fabricated metal products	31.7	64.9	0.1	1.4	1.0	43.6	50.5	0.3	5.4	3.3
Machinery, except electrical	36.5	60.3	0.3	0.5	2.4	46.7	48.5	0.7	0.5	3.6
Electrical machinery & equipment	28.5	66.2	0.8	0.5	4.0	40.4	51.4	1.4	0.9	5.9
Transportation equipment	50.3	58.6	0.1	0.3	0.7	69.2	29.5	0.2	0.3	0.8
Instruments, photographic goods, optical goods, watches & clocks	14.2	77.5	0.9	0.3	7.1	27.9	61.8	1.6	0.4	8.3

[a] Data based on sample interviews and subject to normal sampling errors. Tabled values are in percentages.
Source: U. S. Department of Commerce, Bureau of the Census, *Census of Transportation, 1963*, pp. 4–45.

would be in sharp contrast with that of freight. Excluding travel by private auto, airlines move the bulk of the intercity passenger traffic (7.1 percent of total intercity traffic during 1966). Railways have increasingly taken a lesser role in passenger traffic (Table 5-3) and in 1966 moved only 1.8 percent of the intercity passenger traffic as compared with 6.4 percent in 1950 and 2.8 percent in 1960. Little passenger traffic moves by water, but buses move nearly one-fourth of the nonauto intercity traffic. Private autos account for approximately 90 percent of the total intercity passenger miles.

TABLE 5-3
Intercity passenger-miles by transportation mode, 1950–1966

Mode	1950	1960	1966
Motor			
Private auto	86.2%	90.1%	88.2%
Commercial motor vehicles	5.2	2.5	2.5
Railroads[a]	6.4	2.8	1.8
Airways[b]	2.0	4.3	7.1
Inland waterways[c]	0.2	0.3	0.4
	100.0%	100.0%	100.0%

[a] Includes electric railways.
[b] Includes domestic commercial revenue service and private pleasure and business flying.
[c] Includes Great Lakes.
Source: U. S. Bureau of the Census, *Statistical Abstract of the United States: 1968*, 89th edition (Washington, D. C., 1968), p. 541.

PHYSICAL PLANT AND EQUIPMENT

The transportation system is physically composed of the networks over which freight is moved and of the equipment used to transport freight. The system includes vehicles, terminals, pipes, highways, waterways, ships, canals, airways, and railroad trackage. The total net public and private investment in the five modes has been estimated at $210 billion of which two-thirds is for motor transport.[2]

Rail. There are approximately 209,000 miles of railroad lines in the United States. This is the aggregate roadway of all line-haul railroads. If multiple main tracks, yard tracks, and sidings are included, the total of railroad track mileage is about 340,000 miles.[3] Railroad line mileage has been gradually shrinking from its maximum length of 250,000 miles in about 1920. Fig. 5-3 shows the existing railroad network. Note the concentration of trackage in the heavily industrialized and populated sections of the country. This concentration would be further accentuated if multiple tracks were indicated in the figure.

[2] Dudley F. Pegrum, *Transportation: Economics and Public Policy*, revised edition (Homewood, Illinois: Richard D. Irwin, Inc., 1968), Chapter 2.

[3] *Yearbook of Railroad Facts*, 1969 edition (Washington: American Association of Railroads, 1969), p. 60.

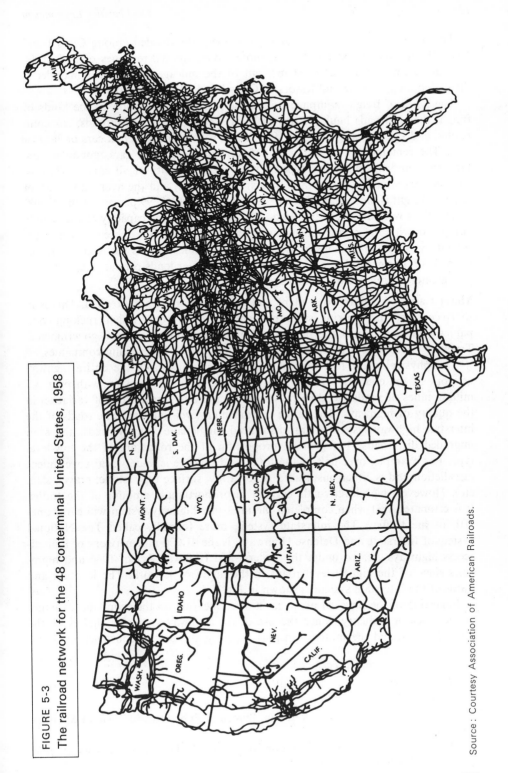

FIGURE 5-3
The railroad network for the 48 conterminal United States, 1958

Source: Courtesy Association of American Railroads.

The ownership of the above mileage is unequally divided among Class I and Class II railroads. Class I railroads, those having annual revenues of $5,000,000 or more, own approximately 86 percent of the mileage, while the remainder is divided among Class II and lessors of Class I and Class II railroads.

The types of freight equipment available is a direct reflection of the kinds of freight that railroads haul. Of the 1,802,787 cars[4] owned by railroads, car companies, and shippers at the end of 1968, about 63 percent were box cars or hopper cars. The remainder were flat cars, refrigerator cars, stock cars, gondola cars, tank cars, and miscellaneous types. The average capacity of all cars is 65 tons, with new cars having an average capacity of 81 tons, and the average weight of carload freight is more than 52 tons.[5] At the close of 1968, 99 percent of the 27,400 locomotives were diesel-electric units. The greater handling capacity of these units compared with the steam locomotive partially explains the increase in average freight train load (1768 tons in 1968) and the number of cars per average freight train (70).[6] The general trend has been toward greater loads per car, longer trains, and greater average daily car mileage.

Motor Carrier. The railroad plant and equipment is privately owned. This is in sharp contrast with trucking, since the highway network over which trucking companies operate is owned and maintained by federal, state, and local governments. Trucking equipment is most generally privately owned by trucking companies.

The physical plant for the trucking industry consists of the entire highway network in the country. The highway network is quite extensive, with over 3.7 million miles of roads.[7] Unlike railway lines, there is a great deal of variation in the quality of highways. The range is from high-level, multiple-lane roads of the interstate highway system to gravel-surfaced, single-lane country roads, and even ungraded dirt roads. The greatest proportion of the roads are of the low-level type. For example, over half of the total road mileage is under local government jurisdiction and is either unsurfaced or of a low surface type (stone, gravel, slag, etc). However, high-level roads carry a disproportionate amount of the traffic. It is estimated that when completed the interstate highway system will carry one-fifth of the traffic.[8] The interstate system, more formally called The National System of Interstate and Defense Highways, is the 41,000-mile network of limited-access highways created under the Federal-Aid Highway Act of 1956 and represents some of the highest-level roads in the highway network. The location and status of the interstate system is shown in Fig. 5-4.

Financing of the physical plant has a direct bearing on the economic structure of the trucking industry. Since the use of the highway system is shared by the general public and the motor transport industry, the cost of construction, main-

[4] *Yearbook of Railroad Facts, op. cit.*, p. 65.

[5] *Ibid.*, pp. 66, 50.

[6] *Ibid.*, p. 48.

[7] U. S. Department of Transportation, Bureau of Public Roads, *Highway Statistics*, 1967, p. 166.

[8] U. S. Department of Transportation, Bureau of Public Roads, *Highway Statistics of the United States, 1963*, p. 144.

tenance, and operation of the system is usually initially financed by a governmental agency and then charged back to the users. The three common cost recovery methods are (1) general taxation (for example, property taxes to support local roads and streets), (2) user taxes such as motor fuel taxes, vehicle registration fees, and weight-mile taxes, and (3) tolls levied on certain roads such as the Chicago Skyway and the Ohio Turnpike. As a result of the financing method, individual trucking firms have no capital investment in the roadway over which they operate. Capital investment by trucking companies is mainly in terminals and facilities and in transport equipment.

The equipment used in the motor transport industry is basically of two types: (1) operating equipment and (2) over-the-road equipment. The first refers to pickup-and-delivery equipment used for short hauls between terminals and customers. Operations usually involve small loads over short distances (up to a maximum of 20 to 30 miles). As such, operating equipment tends to be small and often versatile to accommodate a wide range of shipment sizes and handling situations. Motor-trucks and short tractor-trailer combinations are most common.

Over-the-road equipment is the standardized but sometimes specialized equipment for intercity hauls. Tractor-trailer combinations are most often used, and the units are of greater length and hauling capacity than equipment used in local pickup and delivery operations. Maximum equipment dimensions are usually specified by law for reasons of highway safety. In the midwest, trailers of 40-foot lengths and 8-foot widths are common. The effective height of the load runs between 8 and 9 feet. Experimentation is now proceeding to develop larger and more powerful equipment for use on high-level highways such as those in the interstate system. The use of two trailers connected to form a train—called "double bottoms"—is permitted in several states and nearly doubles the maximum payload to 85,000–90,000 pounds. Even longer trains are being tested, but their use may well depend on whether more efficient power plants can be used (turbine power, for example), whether the equipment can be made interchangeable for use off the turnpike system, and whether terminals can be located at highway interchange points.

Water. The physical plant for inland water carriage is made up of all the natural waterway systems in the country. There are about 25,000 miles of inland water-ways, excluding the Great Lakes, on which inland water traffic flows. Approximately 14,000 miles of this have the channel of 9 feet or greater needed by modern barge equipment. In addition to the waterways, the water physical plant includes the ports, terminals, and navigational aids as well. The greatest portion of the initial cost for the plant is borne mostly by the federal government and to a lesser extent by state and local governments.

Locklin[9] has classified the inland waterway system into five categories: (1) the Great Lakes system, (2) the Mississippi River system, (3) coastal rivers, (4) intra-coastal waterways, and (5) the New York State Barge Canal. These waterways are shown in Fig. 5-5.

---

[9] D. Philip Locklin, *Economics of Transportation*, 6th edition (Homewood, Illinois: Richard D. Irwin, Inc., 1966), pp. 715–17.

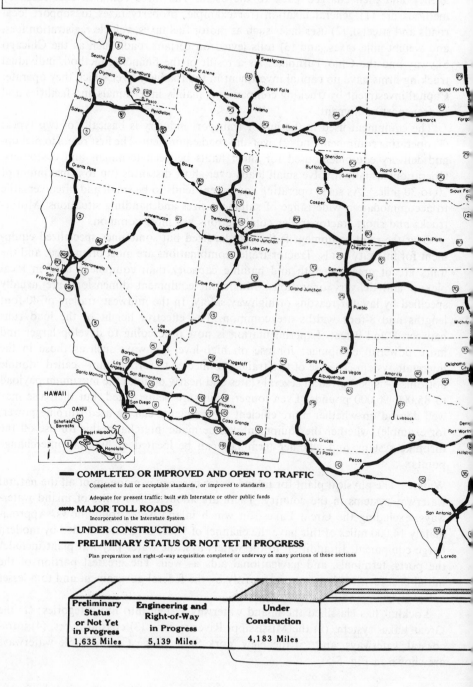

FIGURE 5-4
The National System of Interstate and Defense Highways with status as of June 30, 1968

COMPLETED OR IMPROVED AND OPEN TO TRAFFIC
Completed to full or acceptable standards, or improved to standards
Adequate for present traffic; built with Interstate or other public funds

MAJOR TOLL ROADS
Incorporated in the Interstate System

UNDER CONSTRUCTION

PRELIMINARY STATUS OR NOT YET IN PROGRESS
Plan preparation and right-of-way acquisition completed or underway on many portions of these sections

Preliminary Status or Not Yet in Progress	Engineering and Right-of-Way in Progress	Under Construction	
1,635 Miles	5,139 Miles	4,183 Miles	

U.S. DEPARTMENT OF TRANSPORTATION
FEDERAL HIGHWAY ADMINISTRATION
BUREAU OF PUBLIC ROADS

Scale of map does not permit showing of status
in urban areas and for very short sections

INTERSTATE

TOTAL

42,500

MILES

Open to Traffic

31,543 Miles

35,726 Miles

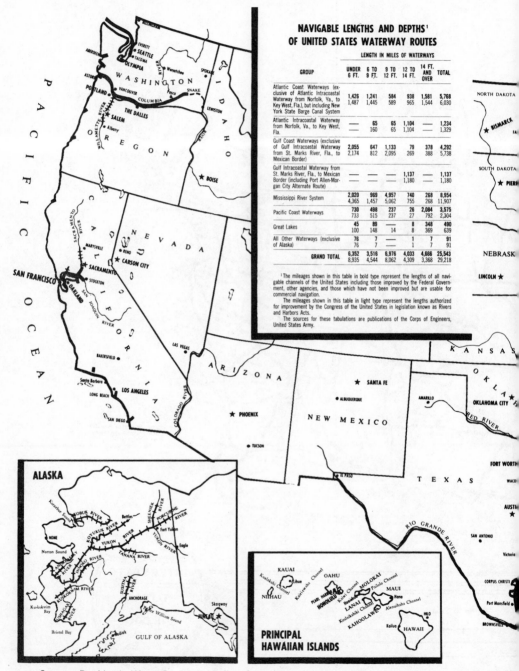

FIGURE 5-5
The principal inland waterway system of the United States

**NAVIGABLE LENGTHS AND DEPTHS[1]
OF UNITED STATES WATERWAY ROUTES**

GROUP	UNDER 6 FT.	6 TO 9 FT.	9 TO 12 FT.	12 TO 14 FT.	14 FT. AND OVER	TOTAL
Atlantic Coast Waterways (exclusive of Atlantic Intracoastal Waterway from Norfolk, Va., to Key West, Fla.), but including New York State Barge Canal System	1,426	1,241	584	938	1,581	5,768
	1,487	1,445	589	965	1,544	6,030
Atlantic Intracoastal Waterway from Norfolk, Va., to Key West, Fla.	—	65	65	1,104	—	1,234
	—	160	65	1,104	—	1,329
Gulf Coast Waterways (exclusive of Gulf Intracoastal Waterway from St. Marks River, Fla., to Mexican Border)	2,055	647	1,133	79	378	4,292
	2,174	812	2,095	269	388	5,738
Gulf Intracoastal Waterway from St. Marks River, Fla., to Mexican Border (including Port Allen-Morgan City Alternate Route)	—	—	—	1,137	—	1,137
	—	—	—	1,180	—	1,180
Mississippi River System	2,020	969	4,957	740	268	8,954
	4,365	1,457	5,062	755	268	11,907
Pacific Coast Waterways	730	498	237	26	2,084	3,575
	733	515	237	27	792	2,304
Great Lakes	45	89	—	8	348	490
	100	148	14	8	369	639
All Other Waterways (exclusive of Alaska)	76	7	—	1	7	91
	76	7	—	1	7	91
GRAND TOTAL	**6,352**	**3,516**	**6,976**	**4,033**	**4,666**	**25,543**
	8,935	4,544	8,062	4,309	3,368	29,218

[1] The mileages shown in this table in bold type represent the lengths of all navigable channels of the United States including those improved by the Federal Government, other agencies, and those which have not been improved but are usable for commercial navigation.

The mileages shown in this table in light type represent the lengths authorized for improvement by the Congress of the United States in legislation known as Rivers and Harbors Acts.

The sources for these tabulations are publications of the Corps of Engineers, United States Army.

Source: President's Water Resources Policy Committee, *A Water Policy for the American People* (Washington, D. C., U. S. Government Printing Office, 1950), Vol. 1, pp. 206–7.

COMMERCIALLY NAVIGABLE
WATERWAYS
OF THE
UNITED STATES

CONTROLLING DEPTHS
9 FEET OR MORE
UNDER 9 FEET
AUTHORIZED EXTENSIONS

The Great Lakes system is 95,000 square miles of natural waterways that were instrumental in the development of the industrial area of the midwest. This system is important in its own right, since 80 percent of the iron ore produced in this country moves from the upper lake docks to Chicago, Detroit, Gary, and Cleveland. About 40 percent of the total inland waterway traffic moves on the Great Lakes. In addition, it connects with the Mississippi River system by a canal into the Illinois River and can accept ocean-going vessels from domestic ports on the coasts and foreign ports via the St. Lawrence Seaway.

The Mississippi River system refers to the Mississippi River and to the various rivers that connect with it such as the Ohio River, the Missouri River, and the Illinois River, to name a few. About 35 percent of the waterway traffic moves on this system.

There are numerous coastal rivers that flow into the Atlantic and Pacific Oceans, as shown in Fig. 5-5. Connecting with these are the various bays, inlets, canals, and protected channels that make up an intracoastal waterway system along the coastline. Nearly all the remaining 25 percent of the traffic moves over these waterways.

Finally, the New York State Barge Canal, formerly the Erie Canal, is the most successful of the man-made waterways. Though the total traffic on this canal does not come close in volume to that of the natural waterways, it is interesting because it is the only major canal that survived from the time of the canal-building era from approximately 1800 to 1840. The strategic location of the canal as a waterway link between the Great Lakes and the Atlantic Ocean via the Hudson River continues to be a major reason for its success.

The variety of equipment used on the waterway system is mainly of two types resulting from the kind of freight carried and the characteristics of the waterway. The types generally are not interchangeable. On the Great Lakes, large vessels are used that are specially designed for handling of bulk cargo such as grain, coal, ore, etc. In contrast, barges are used on the Mississippi River. The shallow draft of these carriers is particularly advantageous, since much of the system has a 9–12-foot depth and cannot accommodate the type of vessel used on the Great Lakes. A number of barges are tied together and pushed by a towboat. Thirty or even forty barges can be lashed together as a single unit or "tow." A single barge can carry 1400 tons, so a 40-barge "tow" is equivalent to the capacity of about sixteen 100-car freight trains. They also can be loaded and unloaded by mechanical methods.

Air.   Airways and airports are the main ingredients in the physical plant for air transportation. Air space in which aircraft operate is a natural resource, and no investment is required. However, many navigational aids such as radio signal stations, beacon lights, radar approach facilities, control towers, etc. have been established at government expense to guide aircraft between airports. Designated pathways in the sky have been defined, and most flights move along these. The navigational aids are concentrated along the approximate 160,000 miles of airways, as shown in Fig. 5-6. No specific taxes are levied on the users of these facilities to recover their cost, though certain taxes on air passenger fares and jet fuel indirectly are considered payment for the airways. Not all costs of the airways would likely be charged back to the users, since the military makes extensive use of them as well.

Airports, like the airways, are publically owned and require little or no capital investment in these facilities on the part of the users. Airports, for the most part, are owned by municipalities, and users are charged for their use through landing fees, purchase of aviation fuel, rentals, etc.

Air equipment is mainly the aircraft with supporting ground equipment for moving people and freight from the terminal to the aircraft. The high cost of a commercial aircraft (the Boeing 747 costs about $20 million) and the relatively small amount of freight hauled compared with passenger traffic has not encouraged a wide variety of aircraft. To date, most aircraft used to carry cargo were designed primarily for passenger service. However, some airplanes are a compromise between the use as passenger carriers and freight haulers, and at times military use as troop and cargo carriers is considered in or may predominate the design, as in the C5A. Some commercial aircraft have a multiple-use design and may be used for passenger service in the daytime and then be easily converted to use as cargo carrier at night; for example, the Boeing 727QC is a quick change convertible jet. From a practical standpoint, aircraft do vary in capacity and in performance characteristics. However, aircraft for commercial use are not designed to handle products with special requirements, as would be a refrigerated railroad boxcar or dry bulk handling tank truck.

Pipeline.   Unlike the other four modes, for pipeline there is only a physical plant consisting of pipes, pumping stations, and storage tanks. No equipment separate from the pipeline network exists.[10] The pipeline plant designed mainly for handling crude oil in 1967 included 165,478 miles of trunk and gathering oil pipelines.[11] About one-half of this mileage was trunk pipelines, and the geographical distribution is shown in Fig. 5-7. Most trunk lines use pipes between 8 and 12 inches in diameter.[12] Gathering lines average about 4 inches in diameter.[13] Since larger-diameter pipe is more efficient than small-diameter pipe, replacement pipes are in the 18–26-inch diameter range.[14] Product pipelines add approximately 50,000 miles to the total pipeline network.

Pipelines have similar economic characteristics to that of the railroads, in that the physical plant of each is privately owned. Most of the pipeline mileage is owned by or affiliated with major oil companies producing enough volume to make

[10] The exception, of course, are the containers being proposed to move high-density products in pipelines. These are experimental at present.

[11] U. S. Bureau of the Census, *Statistical Abstract of the United States: 1969*, 90th edition (Washington, D. C., 1969), p. 564.

[12] *Moody's Transportation Manual* (New York: Moody's Investor's Service, Inc., 1969), p. a68.

[13] W. G. Messner, *Crude-Oil and Refined-Products Pipeline Mileage in the United States*, January 1, 1959, Bureau of Mines, U. S. Department of the Interior, Information Circular 7942 (1959).

[14] *Moody's Transportation Manual, op. cit.*

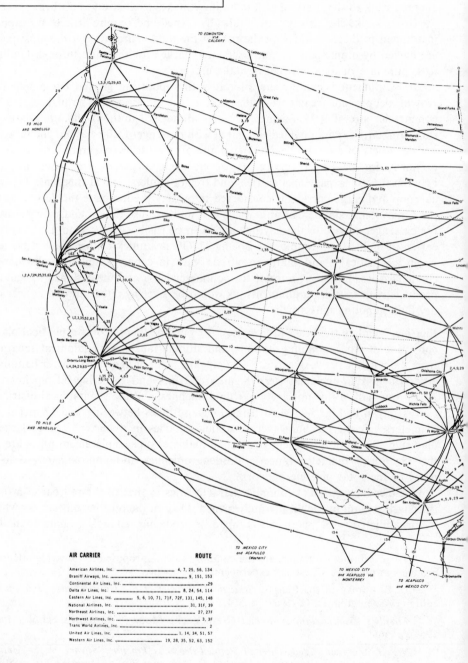

FIGURE 5-6
United States trunk airline routes, 1960

AIR CARRIER	ROUTE
American Airlines, Inc.	4, 7, 25, 56, 134
Braniff Airways, Inc.	9, 151, 153
Continental Air Lines, Inc.	29
Delta Air Lines, Inc.	8, 24, 54, 114
Eastern Air Lines, Inc.	5, 6, 10, 71, 71F, 72F, 131, 145, 148
National Airlines, Inc.	31, 31F, 39
Northeast Airlines, Inc.	27, 27F
Northwest Airlines, Inc.	3, 3F
Trans World Airlines, Inc.	2
United Air Lines, Inc.	1, 14, 34, 51, 57
Western Air Lines, Inc.	19, 28, 35, 52, 63, 152

Source: Civil Aeronautics Board.

NOTES

* Seasonal point

✱ Point authorized by temporary exemption

Route descriptions are based on certificate
as issued and do not purport to represent
flights permissible by non-stop operations.

All points to which the holder's authority has
been suspended under Section 401 (g) of the
Act, have been deleted from the Carrier's
route description.

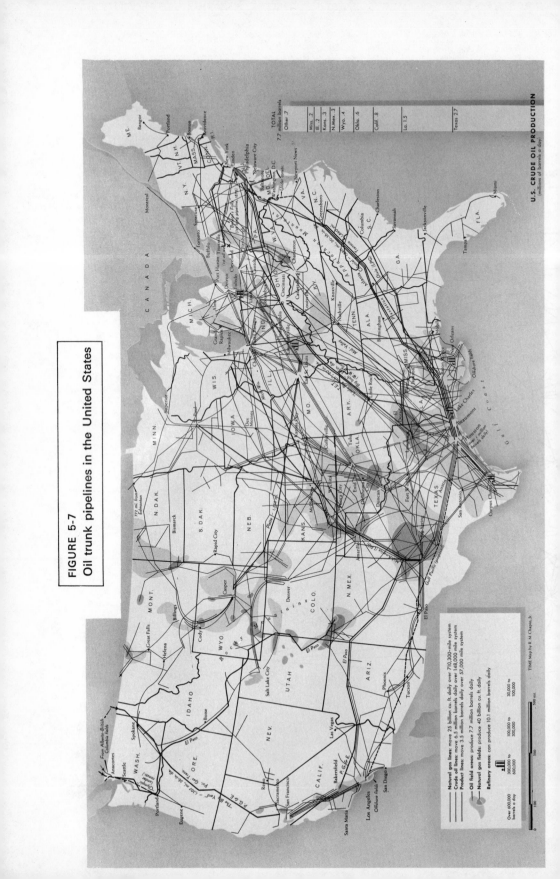

FIGURE 5-7
Oil trunk pipelines in the United States

U.S. CRUDE OIL PRODUCTION
(millions of barrels a day)

TOTAL
7.7 million barrels
Other .7

Miss. .2
Ill. .2
Kans. .3
N.Mex. .3
Wyo. .4
Okla. .6

Calif. .8

La. 1.5

Texas 2.7

TIME Map by R. M. Chapin, Jr.

Natural gas lines: move 25 billion cu. ft. daily over 710,300-mile system
Crude oil lines: move 6.5 million barrels daily over 148,000 mile system
Product lines: move 3.3 million barrels daily over 57,000 mile system
Oil field areas: produce 7.7 million barrels daily
Natural gas fields: produce 40 billion cu. ft. daily
Refinery areas: can produce 10.1 million barrels daily

Over 600,000 barrels a day
300,000 to 600,000
100,000 to 300,000
30,000 to 100,000

pipeline transportation economically feasible. These pipelines are classified as common carriers and report their operations to the Interstate Commerce Commission.

Service Choices and Performance Characteristics

The user of transportation has a wide range of services at his disposal, all revolving around the five basic modes. The variety is almost limitless as (1) the five modes may be used in combination, (2) agencies, associations, and brokers may be used for their indirect services, or (3) a single transportation mode may be used exclusively. From among this plethora of service choices, the user must select a service that provides the best balance between the quality of service provided and the cost of the service. The task of service choice is not as forbidding as it first sounds, since the circumstances surrounding a particular shipping situation often reduce the choice to only a few reasonable service possibilities. To aid in solving the problem of transportation service choice, transportation service may be viewed in terms of characteristics that are basic to all services. These criteria are (1) cost of service, (2) average delivery time, (3) transit-time variability, and (4) loss and damage. It is presumed that the service is available and can be supplied with a frequency that makes it attractive as a possible service choice.

Cost of Service. Cost of service to a shipper is simply the line haul cost for transporting goods plus any accessorial or terminals charges for additional service provided. In the case of for-hire service, the rate charged for the movement of goods between two points plus any additional charges such as for pickup at origin, delivery at destination, insurance, or the cost of preparing the goods for shipment would make up the total cost of service. When the service is owned by the shipper, the cost of service is an allocation of the relevant costs to the shipment in question. Relevant costs would include such items as fuel, labor, maintenance, depreciation of equipment, and administrative costs.

Cost of service varies greatly from one type of service to another. Table 5-4 gives a cost comparison between the various modes on a ton-mile basis. It shows that air is the most expensive, and water the least expensive. Trucking is several

	TABLE 5-4
	Average ton-mile costs by transportation mode

Mode	Cost c/ton-mile
Rail	1.3
Truck	6.0
Water	0.3
Pipe	0.4
Air	19.8

Source: *Moody's Transportation Manual, 1969.*

times more expensive than rail, and rail is three to four times more expensive than water or pipeline movement. These figures are averages that result from the ratio of all revenue generated to the total ton-miles shipped for the particular mode and can only serve as general indicators of cost differences. Cost comparisons for the purpose of transportation service selection must be made on the basis of actual charges that reflect the specific commodity being shipped, the distance and direction of the movement, and any special handling required.

Delivery Time and Variability.   Two related performance characteristics that must be considered when one is selecting a transportation service are speed and variability. Delivery time refers to the average time that it takes for a shipment to move between origin and destination points. For the purpose of comparing transportation services, speed is best measured "door to door," that is, from the time that the shipment leaves the shipper's dock until it arrives at the consignee's dock. Variability refers to the normal variation that can be expected in shipments by the various modes. All shipments having the same origin and destination points are not necessarily in transit for the same length of time due to the effects of weather, traffic congestion, number of stopoffs, and differences in time to consolidate shipments. Transit time variability is a measure of the uncertainty in carrier performance.

Statistics on carrier performance are only beginning to be collected by businesses as computer facilities now make this kind of activity practical and as the impact of carrier performance on inventory costs and customer service is becoming better appreciated. A rough comparison of several methods of transportation has been offered by Peterson and Cutler and is shown in Table 5-5. Data for Table 5-5 were obtained from a sample of 21,000 shipments in 1960 as recorded by the Military

TABLE 5-5

A comparison of transit time estimates by several transportation services based on Department of Defense experience

Transportation Service[a]	Average Transit Time Estimate (days)	Standard Error of Estimate (days)	Correlation Coefficient
Carload	$T = 6.327 + 0.00270d$[b]	1.25	+0.87
Less carload	$T = 10.917 + 0.00311d$	4.48	+0.49
Truckload	$T = 3.197 + 0.00309d$	1.55	+0.84
Less truckload	$T = 5.152 + 0.00335d$	1.03	+0.94
Air freight	$T = 3.404 + 0.00083d$	0.80	+0.64
Surface freight forwarder	$T = 7.025 + 0.00273d$	1.53	+0.80

[a] Carload, less carload, truckload, less truckload refer to whether or not the particular vehicle is completely filled with a company's goods.
[b] d = straight-line distance between origin and destination points.
Source: Keene Peterson and Herschel Cutler, "Transportation and MILSTRIP: Transport Service and Routing Decisions," in *Contributed Papers, American Transportation Research Forum, 1961,* (Multilithed), p. IX-11.

Traffic Management Agency.[15] Simple linear regression analysis was used to estimate average transit time as a function of the straight-line distance between origin and destination points. Transit time variability, or the standard error of the estimate in common statistical terminology, is the dispersion of the transit time data about the average transit time line. Consider truckload shipments moving 700 miles. The average time T is estimated as:

$$T = 3.179 + 0.00309(700)$$
$$= 3.179 + 2.163$$
$$= 5.342 \text{ days}$$

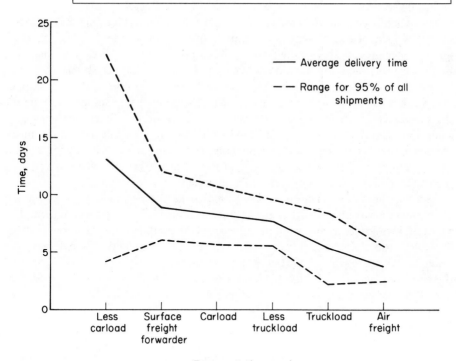

FIGURE 5-8

Comparison of average delivery time and transit-time variability for a 700-mile delivery distance for several transportation modes ranked according to average delivery time

Source: Table 5–5.

[15] For a more detailed discussion of this study, see Keene Peterson and Herschel Cutler, "Transportation and MILSTRIP: Transport Service and Routing Decision," in *Contributed Papers, American Transportation Research Forum, 1961* (Multilithed), pp. IX-1 to IX-17.

If the normal distribution curve is followed, ± 2 standard deviations from the average transit time would include approximately 95 percent of all shipments. For truckload, one standard error of the estimate equals 1.55 days. Thus, it is estimated that 95 percent of all truckload shipments between origin and destination points that are 700 miles apart will have a transit time of

$$2.2 \leq T(\text{days}) \leq 8.4$$

Repeating these computations for the remaining transportation services gives a service performance comparison as shown in Fig. 5-8. It is also worthwhile to note from the Peterson and Cutler study that absolute variability in transit times is somewhat proportional to the average delivery time when distance is used in the prediction of delivery times.

Loss and Damage.   Carriers differ in their ability to move freight loss- and damage-free. Because of this, loss and damage become a factor in selecting a carrier.

Regulated carriers are liable under law to move freight with reasonable dispatch and to do so using reasonable care so as to avoid damage. They are often released from the liability if loss and damage are a result of an act of God, the act or default of the shipper, or other causes not within control of the carrier. Though carriers, upon proper presentation of the facts by the shipper, incur the direct loss sustained by the shipper, there are certain imputed costs that the shipper should recognize before making a carrier selection. The potentially most serious loss that the shipper may sustain has to do with customer service. The goods being shipped may be for the purpose of replenishing a customer's inventory or for direct customer consumption. Delayed shipments or goods arriving in unusable condition mean inconvenience for the customer, or possibly higher inventory costs arising from a greater number of stockouts or back orders that may result when anticipated replenishment stocks are not received as planned.

Second, the claims procedure takes time to gather pertinent facts about the claim, takes effort on the part of the shipper to prepare the proper claim form, ties up capital while claims are being processed, and sometimes involves a considerable expense if the claim can only be resolved through court action. Obviously, the fewer the claims against a carrier, the more favorable will the service appear to the user. A reaction to a high likelihood of damage is to provide improved protective packaging. This expense must be borne by the user as well.

SINGLE SERVICE CHOICES

Each of the five basic transportation modes sells its services directly to users. This is in contrast to the use of a "transportation middleman" like a freight forwarder who sells transportation services but does not own any movement capability. Single mode service is also in contrast to those services involving two or more individual transportation modes.

Rail.   The railroad is basically a long haul and slow mover of raw materials and of low-valued manufactured products. The average length of haul was 518 miles in

1968[16] with an average train speed of 20.4 miles per hour.[17] Average daily car mileage was 53.9 miles per day in line-haul service.[18] This relatively slow speed and short distance traveled in a day reflects the fact that about 89 percent of freight car time is spent in loading and unloading operations, moving from place to place within terminals, being classified and assembled into trains, or standing idle during seasonal slump in car demand.

Rail service exists in two legal forms, common carrier or private. A common carrier sells its transportation services to all shippers and is subjected to economic and safety regulations by the government. In contrast, private carriers are owned by the shipper and serve only the owner. Because of the limited scope of the private carrier's operations, no economic regulation is needed. Nearly all rail movement is of the common carrier type.

Common carrier line-haul rail service is basically either carload (CL) or less than carload (LCL). A carload quantity refers to a predetermined shipment size such that if shipments equal or exceed this size, a particular rate applies. The carload quantity rate is less than the LCL rate to reflect the reduced handling required for volume shipments. Most rail freight today moves under the carload classification. This is part of a general trend toward volume movement. Larger freight cars are being used with an average new freight car capacity of 81 tons compared with a 57-ton average for cars retired,[19] and single-commodity trains, called unit trains, of 100 cars or more per train are being used with rate reductions of 25 to 40 percent.

Railroads offer a diversity of special services to the shipper. These range from the movement of bulk commodities such as coal and grain to refrigerated products and new automobiles, which require special equipment. Other services include expedited service to guarantee arrival within a certain number of hours, various stop-off privileges which permit partial loading and unloading between origin and destination points, pickup and delivery, and diversion and reconsignment, which allows circuitous routing and changes in ultimate destination of a shipment while en route.

Truck. In contrast with rail, trucking is a short-range transportation service of semifinished and finished products, the average length haul in 1968 being 255 miles for common carrier trucks and 132 miles for privately owned trucks.[20] Also, trucking moves freight with smaller average shipment sizes. More than half of the shipments by truck are less than 10,000 pounds, i.e., less than truckload volume (LTL). The inherent advantage of trucking is its door-to-door service such that no loading or unloading is required between origin and destination, as is often true of rail and air modes, its frequency and availability of service, and its door-to-door speed and convenience.

[16] *Motor Truck Facts*, 1969, (Detroit: Automobile Manufacturers Association), p. 50.

[17] *Yearbook of Railroad Facts, op. cit.*

[18] *Ibid.*, p. 55.

[19] *Ibid.*, p. 66.

[20] *Motor Truck Facts, op. cit.*, p. 50.

Truck and rail services show some distinct differences, even though they compete for many of the same product shipments. First, in addition to the common and private legal class, trucking offers services as contract and exempt carriers as well. Contract carriers do not hold themselves out to service all shippers, but rather they work with a limited number of shippers on a long-term contract basis. Shippers enter into a contractual arrangement to obtain a service that better meets their particular needs without incurring the capital expense and administrative problems associated with private ownership of a trucking fleet. Contract carriers are regulated, but less closely than common carriers. Exempt motor carriers are free from economic regulation. Examples of such exempt carriers are those vehicles operated and controlled by farmers and farm cooperatives used to transport agricultural commodities, vehicles used to transport freight associated with the transport by air, occasional transfer of property by motor vehicles, and vehicles transporting freight primarily within municipalities.

Second, trucks can be judged less capable of handling all types of freight than rail mainly due to highway safety restrictions that limit the dimensions of shipments and their weight. Most shipments must be shorter than the common 40-foot van and be less than 8 feet wide and 8 feet tall to assure road clearance. Specially designed equipment can accept loads in different dimensions than these.

Third, trucking offers reasonably fast and dependable delivery for LTL shipments. The trucker needs to fill only one van before moving the shipment, whereas a railroad must be concerned with a train load. On balance, trucking has a service advantage in the small shipment market.

Air. Air transportation is being considered by increasing numbers of shippers for regular service, even though air freight rates exceed those of trucking by more than three times and those of rail by 15 times. The appeal of air transportation is its unmatched origin-destination speed. Commercial jets have cruising speeds between 545 and 585 miles per hour, though airport-to-airport average speed is somewhat slower than cruising speed because of taxi and holding time at each airport and the time needed to ascend to and descend from cruising altitude. But this speed is not directly comparable with other modes, since it does not include pickup and delivery times as well as ground handling time. When all these time elements are combined, door-to-door air delivery time results. Since surface freight handling and movement are the slowest portion of total door-to-door delivery time, overall delivery time is reduced so that a well-managed truck and rail operation often can match the schedule of air. Of course, this is not true in all cases.

Air service dependability and availability can be rated as good under normal operating conditions. Delivery time variability is low in absolute magnitude, even though air traffic is quite sensitive to mechanical breakdown, weather conditions, and traffic congestion. Variability when compared with average delivery time can rank air as one of the least dependable modes.

The capability of air has been greatly constrained by the physical dimensions of the cargo space in the aircraft and its lifting capacity. However, this will increasingly become less of a constraint as larger aircraft are put into service. For example, airplanes like the Boeing 747 and Lockheed 500 (commercial version of the military's C5A) will have a cargo capacity of 125–150 tons. At the same time, door-to-door ton-mile costs are anticipated to drop to eight to ten cents. This could make air a serious competitor of surface transportation.

Air transportation has a distinct advantage in terms of loss and damage. According to a study by Lewis, Culliton, and Steele in the early 1950's, the ratio of claim costs to freight revenue were only about 60 percent of those for truck or rail.[21] In general, less protective packaging will be required for air freight, provided that ground handling does not offer a higher exposure to damage than the en route phase of the movement and airport theft is not excessive.

Air transportation service exists in common, contract, and private legal forms. Direct air service is offered in six general carrier types, which are (1) regular domestic trunk-line carriers, (2) all cargo carriers, (3) local service airlines, (4) supplemental carriers, (5) air taxis, and (6) international carriers. Eleven airlines are currently certified by the Civil Aeronautics Board (CAB) for operation over the most heavily traveled routes. These airlines offer cargo-carrying services in addition to their regularly scheduled passenger operations. All cargo carriers are certified common carriers of freight only. Service is concentrated at night and rates average 30 percent less than those for domestic trunk-line carriers. Local service airlines provide a "connecting" service with domestic trunk-line carriers for less populated centers. They provide both cargo and passenger services. Supplemental carriers operate much as do trunk-line carriers except they have not acquired permanent certification from the CAB. Air taxis are small aircraft offering a shuttle service for passengers and cargo between downtown areas and airports, namely helicopters and small fixed-wing aircraft. They are unregulated and often have only irregular service. International carriers transport freight and passengers beyond the borders of the United States and its territories. The largest is Pan American World Airways.

Water. Water transportation service is limited in scope for several reasons. Domestic water service is confined to the inland waterway system, which requires shippers to be located on the waterways or to use another transportation mode in combination with water. Also, water service on the average is slower than rail. The average speed on the Mississippi water system is between 5 and 9 miles per hour, depending on direction.[22] The average length of haul is 543 miles.[23] Availability and dependability are greatly influenced by the weather. Movement on the waterways in the northern part of the country during the winter is impossible, and service is interrupted by floods and droughts, as is frequently the case on the Mississippi River system. There is tremendous capacity available in water carriers

---

[21] Howard T. Lewis, James W. Culliton, and Jack D. Steele, *The Role of Air Freight in Physical Distribution* (Boston: Division of Research, Graduate School of Business Administration, Harvard University, 1956), p. 82.

[22] The American Waterways Operators, Inc., *Big Load Afloat*, 1965, p. 15.

[23] Corps of Engineers, *Waterborne Commerce of the United States*, (Vicksburg, Miss.: The Division Engineer, U. S. Army Engineer Division Lower Mississippi Valley, 1967), p. 121.

with barge tows up to 40,000 tons, and there are individual barges with standardized dimensions of 26 × 175 ft and 35 × 195 ft. Capability and handling are being increased as barge-carrying ships are being developed, and such improvements as radar, refined depth finders, and better steering controls mean around-the-clock service.

Water services are provided in all four legal forms, but most commodities move free of economic regulation. In addition to unregulated private carriage, liquid cargoes in bulk moving in tank vessels and commodities in bulk such as coal, sand, and grain, which make up over 75 percent of the total annual ton-miles by water, are exempt.[24] Outside of the handling of bulk commodities, water carriers, especially those in foreign service, do move some higher-valued commodities. This freight moves in containers[25] on containerized ships to reduce handling time and better to effect intermodal transfer.

Loss and damage costs due to transporting by water are considered to be low relative to other modes, because damage is not much of a concern to low-valued, bulk products, and losses due to delays are not serious as large inventories are often maintained by buyers. Claims where high-valued goods are transported, as in ocean service, are much higher (approximately four percent of ocean ship revenues). Substantial packaging is needed to protect goods, mainly against rough handling during the loading-unloading operation.

Pipeline.   To date, pipeline transportation offers a very limited range of services and capability. The most economically feasible products to move by pipeline are crude oil and refined petroleum products. However, there is some experimentation with moving solid products suspended in a liquid called a "slurry" or containing the solid products in cylinders that in turn move in a liquid. If these innovations prove to be economical, pipeline service could be greatly expanded.

Product movement by pipeline is very slow, only about two to three miles per hour. This slowness should be tempered by the fact that products move 24 hours a day and seven days a week. This makes the effective speed much greater when compared with other modes. Pipeline capacity is high, considering that a 3-mph flow in a 12-inch diameter pipe can move 89,000 gallons per hour.

Relative to transit time, pipeline service is the most dependable of all modes, since there are few interruptions to cause delivery-time variability. Weather is not a significant factor, and pumping equipment is highly reliable. Also, the availability of pipeline capacity is limited only by the use that other shippers may be making of the facilities at the time capacity is desired.

Loss and damage for pipelines is low because (1) liquids and gases are not subject to damage to the same degree as manufactured products and (2) losses are minimal due to the limited number of dangers that can befall a pipeline operation. There is liability for such loss and damage when it does occur, since pipelines have

----

[24] *Ibid.*

[25] Containers are standardized "boxes," usually 8 × 8 × 20 ft or 8 × 8 × 40 ft in which freight is handled as a unit and which are easily transferred as a unit to other transportation modes.

the status of common carriers, even though many are private carriers in form.

To summarize the quality of the services offered by the transportation industry, Table 5-6 shows a ranking of the various modes using the four cost and performance characteristics set forth at the beginning of this section. These rankings are the author's estimates for average performance over a variety of circumstances. It should be recognized that under specific circumstances of product type, carrier management, user-carrier relationships, shipping distance, and weather conditions these rankings may change.

TABLE 5-6

Relative rankings of cost and operating performance characteristics by transportation mode[a]

		Performance Characteristics			
			Delivery-Time Variability		
Transportation mode	*Cost[b]* *1 = Highest*	*Average Delivery Time[c]* *1 = Fastest*	*Absolute* *1 = Least*	*Percent[d]* *1 = Least*	*Loss and Damage* *1 = Least*
Rail	3	3	4	3	5
Truck	2	2	3	2	4
Water	5	5	5	4	2
Pipe	4	4	2	1	1
Air	1	1	1	5	3

[a] Service is assumed to be available.
[b] Cost per ton-mile.
[c] Door-to-door speed.
[d] Ratio of absolute variation in delivery time to average delivery time.
Source: Author's estimates.

COORDINATED SERVICES

In recent years, there has been renewed interest in the idea of coordinating the services of more than one transportation mode. The major feature of coordination is the free exchange of equipment between modes. For example, a truck trailer is carried aboard an airplane, or a rail car is hauled by a water carrier. Such equipment interchange creates transportation services that are not available to a shipper using a single transportation mode. Coordinated services usually are a compromise of the services offered by the cooperating carriers individually. That is, cost and performance characteristics rank between those of the participating carriers.

There are ten possible coordinated service combinations. These are (1) rail-truck, (2) rail-water, (3) rail-air, (4) rail-pipeline, (5) truck-air, (6) truck-water, (7) truck-pipe, (8) water-pipe, (9) water-air, and (10) air-pipe. Not all of these combinations are currently feasible. Some that are feasible have gained little acceptance. Only rail-truck, called "piggyback," has seen widespread use. Truck-water combinations, referred to as "fishyback," are gaining acceptance. To a much lesser extent, truck-air and rail-water combinations are feasible but have seen little use.

TOFC. Trailer-on-flat car (TOFC) or "piggyback" refers to transporting truck trailers on railroad flat cars usually over longer distances than trucks normally haul. TOFC is a blending of the convenience and flexibility of trucking with the long-haul economy of rail. The cost is less than for trucking alone and has permitted trucking to extend its range. Rail has been able to share in some traffic that normally would move by truck alone. The shipper benefits from the convenience of door-to-door service over long distances at reasonable rates. These features have made piggyback the most popular coordinated service. The number of rail cars loaded with highway trailers has shown a steady and dramatic increase from 168,150 in 1955 to 1,337,149 in 1968.[26]

TOFC service is offered under five different plans, depending on who owns the highway and rail equipment and the rate structure established. These plans are

Plan I.   Railroad transports the trailers of highway common carriers. Billing is through the highway carrier, and the railroad charges a portion of the highway carrier's rate or a flat fee for moving the trailer.

Plan II. Railroads use their own trailers and transport these on their own flat cars to provide a door-to-door service. Shippers deal only with railroads and receive rates comparable to those of highway common carriers.

Plan III. Shippers or freight forwarders can place their own trailers on railroad flat cars for a flat rate, and the trailers may be empty or loaded. The rate is for ramp-to-ramp; that is, pickup and delivery are the responsibility of the shipper.

Plan IV. Shippers furnish not only the trailers or containers, but also the railroad equipment on which the trailers or containers move. The railroad charges a flat rate for moving the cars empty or loaded. The rate is to the railroad for use of the rails and for pulling power.

Plan V.   A TOFC service based on joint rail-truck rates (rates quoted by two or more carriers). Each carrier may solicit freight for the other, which has the effect of extending the territory of each into that served by the other.

Containerized Freight. Under a TOFC arrangement, the entire trailer is transported on a railroad flat car. However, it is also possible to visualize the trailer in two parts, that is, (1) as a container or box in which the freight is packaged and (2) as the trailer's chassis. In a truck-rail combination service, it is possible to haul only the container, thus saving the dead weight of the understructure and wheels. Such a service is called COFC, or container-on-flat-car.

The standardized container is a piece of equipment that is transferable to all

---

[26] *Yearbook of Railroad Facts, op. cit.*, p. 33.

surface transportation modes with the exception of pipeline. Because containerized freight avoids costly rehandling of small shipment units at the point of intermodal transfer and offers a door-to-door service capability when combined with truck, water carriers now have container ships, so combinations of water-truck service can be provided. This type of service is in its infancy, but it is expanding. The container can also be used in combination services with air. The most promising to date is the air-truck combination. The container is important to air transportation, since the high movement costs prohibit transporting the chassis of a highway trailer. The use of large containers has been limited by the dimensions of the existing aircraft and the small shipment sizes that air transportation predominantly handles, but as air freight rates are reduced with the larger aircraft being put into service, coordinated air-truck service will expand.

The services of coordinated transportation services will hinge on the container size that is adopted as standard. A container that is too large for trucking or is incompatable with trucking equipment will exclude trucking from participating. The same argument holds for the other modes. The container sizes that are emerging are the 8 $\times$ 8 $\times$ 20 ft and the 8 $\times$ 8 $\times$ 40 ft. Both are compatable with the standard 40-foot highway trailer and with the other modes with the exception of air. The square cross section in a round fuselage creates a space utilization problem for air.

AGENCIES AND SMALL SHIPMENT SERVICES

Several agencies exist that offer transportation services to shippers but do not own any line-haul equipment. They primarily handle numerous small shipments and consolidate them into vehicle load quantities. Rates competitive with those for LTL and LCL are charged, and the agency, through its consolidation of shipments from many small shipments it handles, can obtain vehicle load rates. The freight rate differential helps to offset operating expenses. In addition to consolidation, agencies provide pickup and delivery services to shippers. Transportation agencies include freight forwarders, parcel post, REA Express, and shipper associations.

Freight forwarders are considered to be common carriers of freight and have the rights and obligations as such. They do own some equipment, but this is mainly for pickup and delivery operations. They purchase long-distance services from motor, rail, and water carriers. A major advantage of freight forwarder service is that it takes the responsibility of selecting the best combination of pickup, long-distance, and delivery services by selling its services directly to the shipper. Though freight forwarders can quote rates on shipments up to 30,000 pounds, the average shipment weight handled is only about 300 pounds.

Parcel post is a small shipment delivery service offered by the United States Post Office. Shipments of any weight up to 70 pounds and 100 inches in size[27]

---

[27] Size refers to the sum of the length (longest dimension), plus girth (twice the width, plus twice the depth). These limits are further reduced for first class post offices.

are accepted, and delivery is made to all points in the United States. Rates are based on the distance that delivery is made from the point of origin. Surface parcel post uses the surface line-haul carriers except pipeline. Air parcel post is available at a higher cost and with a higher service level. United Parcel Service is a similar service to parcel post with competitive rates. Pickup service is available, but delivery is made in only 28 states.

REA Express provides small package services that can compete with parcel post and the trucking industry. Owned largely by the railroads and regulated as a common carrier, this agency originally offered rail services that were competitive with trucking by offering pickup and delivery, rapid terminal handling, and fast line-haul movement. Services have been expanded, and railroads are no longer used exclusively as the line-haul mover. Air carriers cooperate with REA Express to create an air express service that is fast and reliable though fairly high-priced on all but the smallest shipments.

Shippers' associations are cooperative organizations operating on a nonprofit basis. They are designed to perform services similar to freight forwarders. They act as one shipper to gain volume rates. Each shipper pays a portion of the total freight bill based on the amount to be shipped.

In addition to agencies that are created to provide small shipment services, line-haul carriers also move small shipments. There usually is a flat charge when the shipment weight is less than a certain minimum weight, usually 100 pounds for trucking. Service is usually less favorable than for large shipments. A qualitative comparison for various small shipment services is summarized in Table 5-7.

COMPANY-CONTROLLED TRANSPORTATION

An alternative that is available is to provide transportation service through company ownership of equipment or contracting for transportation services. Ideally, the user hopes to gain better operating performance, greater availability and capacity of transportation service, and a lower cost. At the same time, a certain amount of financial flexibility is sacrificed, since the company must invest in a transportation capability or must commit itself to a long-term contractual arrangement. If the shipping volume is high, it may be more economical to own the transportation service than to rent it. However, some companies are forced to own or contract for transportation even at higher costs because the special requirements for service cannot be adequately met through purchase of common carrier services. Such requirements might include (1) fast delivery with very high dependability, (2) special equipment not generally available, (3) special handling of the freight, and (4) a service that is available when needed. Common carriers serve many customers and cannot always meet the specific transportation requirements of individual users.

Concluding Comments

The transportation system of the United States is composed of equipment in which people, goods, and services are moved and the physical network over which movement occurs. There are five basic modes of transportation that transport

TABLE 5-7

A comparison of small shipment transportation services

Carrier	Relative Service	Relative Cost	Pickup	Delivery	Minimum[a] Charge	Features
Parcel post	Fair	Low cost	No	Yes	None	Varying restrictions on size and weight. Must be prepaid.
United Parcel Pkg. Service	Good	Cheapest under 40 pounds	Yes	Yes	Weekly charge	Maximum 50 lb = 108 inches. Liability $100 per pkg.
REA Express	Good	Economical from 41–60 pounds & on special rates	Yes	Yes	$4.85	No tracing of shipments. Liability 50c/lb or $50.
Greyhound Pkg. Exp. Service	Good	Economical under 50 pounds	Extra	Extra	None	Pickup & delivery only in key cities at extra charge.
Motortruck	Good	Moderate on 65 pounds or more	Yes	Yes	$5.00 & higher	Variance in charges and service by carriers. Some surcharges to small communities.
Freight forwarder	Good	Moderate on 65 pounds or more	Yes	Yes	$5.50 & higher	May have surcharges to smaller communities.
LCL-rail	Slow	Economical	Varies	Varies	Often 6000 lb	Not generally available for smaller retail traffic.
Air parcel post	Fast	Expensive	No	Yes	None	Generally cheaper than air express under 10 lb.
REA—Air Express	Very fast	Expensive	Yes	Yes	$5.50 & higher	Generally less than air freight under 35 lb.
Air freight forwarder	Fast	High—good on 35–100-lb range	Usual	Usual	$6.50 & higher	Does not service all towns.
Air freight	Fast	High—usually best on over 100 lb	Extra	Extra	$6.00 & higher	Does not service all towns.
Water	Slow	Cheap	No	No	$15.00	Limited in area served.
Garment carriers	Good	Expensive—rates per piece	Yes	Yes	$1.65	Saves packaging costs and receiving expenses.

[a] Minimum charges shown are approximations only and may vary by carrier, by region, or by length of haul.
Source: Courtesy American Retail Federation.

intercity freight and people. These are the railroads, highway carriers, inland waterways, oil pipelines, and air carriers. These carriers moved nearly 1.9 trillion ton-miles of intercity freight in 1968. This does not include the enormous volume of goods that is transported within metropolitan areas and the movement of goods taking place by private auto, by foot, etc., that is unaccounted for in transportation statistics.

In the United States, the user of transportation services has a number of choices. He can choose any of the services offered by the five basic carriers, select a coordinated service between several carriers, work through a transportation agent or user of transportation services, or own or lease equipment to provide his own service. To the user, transportation service is reducible to several quantifiable cost and performance characteristics, which are (1) direct cost of service, (2) average delivery time, (3) delivery time variability, and (4) loss and damage. Data on these characteristics for various services provide information to the logistician's decision-making process.

Questions and Problems

1. Why is inexpensive transportation a key to a high-level economy?

2. Broadly, what does the logistics manager need to know about transportation?

3. What additional modes of transportation can you think of besides the commonly recognized ones and their combinations? Do you think that significant product flow takes place with these? Under what circumstances should the logistician be concerned with them?

4. Why has there been a decline since the 1920's in the relative importance of rail as a freight carrier?

5. What is transportation service? Contrast the following in terms of speed, reliability, availability, loss and damage, and cost of service.

   (a) Truck and rail
   (b) Rail and inland water
   (c) Piggyback and truck
   (d) Piggyback and rail
   (e) Company-owned trucking with common carrier trucking
   (f) Air and truck

6. There are ten possible coordinated transportation service combinations of five modes taken two at a time. Speculate why only two of these have gained any significant popularity.

7. What does piggyback offer as a transportation service that is not offered by truck or rail alone?

8. Construct a performance characteristics table like that of Table 5-6 for the five basic modes of transportation for distances of 80, 100, 500, 1000, and 3000 miles and for the following products: (1) electronic equipment, (2) fuel oil, and (3) canned food products.

9. Why has containerization become such a popular idea today? What prevents it from being used more extensively?

10. When would company-owned transportation be attractive as an alternative to for-hire transportation?

Selected Bibliography

DAGGETT, S., *Principles of Inland Transportation*. New York: Harper & Bros., 1955.

FAIR, M. L. and E. W. WILLIAMS, JR., *Economics of Transportation*, revised edition. New York: Harper & Bros., 1959.

FLOOD, K., *Traffic Management*. Dubuque, Iowa: Wm C. Brown & Co., 1963.

FREDERICK, J. H., *Commercial Air Transportation*, 5th edition. Homewood, Ill.: Richard D. Irwin, Inc., 1961.

GERMANE, G. E., N. A. GLASKOWSKY, and J. L. HESKETT, *Highway Transportation Management*. New York: McGraw-Hill Book Company, Inc., 1963.

LANSING, J. B., *Transportation and Economic Policy*. New York: The Free Press, 1966.

LOCKIN, P. D., *Economics of Transportation*, 6th edition. Homewood, Ill.: Richard D. Irwin, Inc., 1966.

MOSSMAN, F. H. and N. MORTON, *Principles of Transportation*. New York: The Ronald Press Company, 1957.

NORTON, H. S., *Modern Transporation Economics*. Columbus, Ohio: Charles E. Merrill Books, Inc., 1963.

SAMPSON, R. J. and M. T. FARRIS, *Domestic Transportation: Practice, Theory and Policy*. Boston: Houghton Mifflin Company, 1966.

TAFF, C. A., *Commercial Motor Transportation*, 3rd edition. Homewood, Ill.: Richard D. Irwin, Inc., 1961.

_____, *Management of Traffic and Physical Distribution*, 3rd edition. Homewood, Ill.: Richard D. Irwin, Inc., 1964.

Chapter 6

The Transportation System— Regulation and Rates

This chapter is a continuation of the previous one. The emphasis remains on describing the transportation system as part of the environment in which the logistician makes decisions to achieve both distribution and company objectives. The logistician requires relevant information about his environment. Of concern here is transportation cost and rate information. To understand rates, it is necessary to understand governmental regulation that sets the tone of the rate structure of the for-hire carriers. After a discussion of regulation and rates, brief mention is made of the documents used by the transportation industry.

Transport Regulation

During the second half of the nineteenth century, there was a boom in railroad building that opened the interior of the country to unparalleled prosperity. Many investors pinned hopes on making fortunes on railroad ventures, and shippers envisioned tremendous market growth. Failure of a number of the railroads resulted from ill-conceived projects, financial manipulation, and overexpansion. Lost were the fortunes of many investors as well as public funds used to support the railroads. Shippers were faced with prejudicial treatment by the railroads and discrimination in the rate structure. By 1870, abuses of these types and unfulfilled expectations as to what the railroads could achieve were major reasons behind governmental regulation that was to follow. Railroads had a near monopoly of inland transportation, and this was pointed to as an underlying cause for many of the abuses.

REGULATION BEFORE 1920

Up to 1920, the railroad was the primary transporter of intercity freight. Therefore, early transport regulation was railroad-oriented. Water transportation was not included initially. Regulation at the federal level began with the Act to Regulate Commerce of 1887. Though some modifications have been made in subsequent legislation, the general result has been to strengthen the act rather than to change its substance. The Act of 1887 was addressed to a number of common abuses and established the Interstate Commerce Commission. The Act had the following major features that still hold today:[1]

> *Reasonable rates.* All rates were to be just and reasonable. This was a statutory enactment of a long-standing common law.
>
> *Personal discrimination.* This prohibited one person from being charged differently for a like service under substantially the same conditions and circumstances.
>
> *Undue preference or prejudice.* This was a blanket prohibition of undue or unreasonable preference or advantage of any form to any person, place, or kind of traffic. It was a limitation of what might be considered just and reasonable.
>
> *Long haul, short haul clause.* This prohibited any carrier from charging or receiving any greater compensation for the transportation of passengers or of like kind of property under substantially similar circumstances and conditions for a shorter than for a longer distance over the same line, in the same direction where the shorter is included within the longer distance.
>
> *Pooling.* Common carriers were not to enter into any contract, agreement, or combination for the pooling of freight, or for the division of net proceeds.
>
> *Publication of rates.* All common carriers were required to publish their schedules of rates and fares, and these were to be made available for public inspection and filed with the Interstate Commerce Commission. There was to be strict adherence to these schedules.
>
> *The Interstate Commerce Commission.* The act established the Interstate Commerce Commission (ICC) to administer the law. The ICC was given

[1] This summary follows that provided by Dudley F. Pegrum, *Transportation: Economics and Public Policy*, revised edition (Homewood, Ill.: Richard D. Irwin, Inc., 1968), pp. 296–98.

the power to inquire into the management of common carriers, require testimony of witnesses, order the preparation of annual reports, prescribe a uniform system of accounts, and undertake investigations. In addition, the Commission could order common carriers to cease violation of the law and could prescribe penalties for such violations.

Regulation up to 1920 was basically negative in tone and did little to protect the earnings of the carriers under governmental control. Legislation between 1887 and 1920 was directed toward strengthening the ICC by putting it on a sound legal basis.

REGULATION AFTER 1920

There was a distinct change in the transportation climate after 1920. Whereas before 1920 the railroads had monopolies in the territories in which they operated, after 1920 there was a resurgence of water transportation, trucking became a serious competitor, air transportation was introduced, and pipelines underwent rapid growth—all of which eliminated this advantage. The financial difficulties experienced by the railroads were only aggravated by this new competition. Regulation took a more positive tone with the famous rule of rate-making. English common law provided that regulated industries had a right to reasonable earnings, and the rule of rate-making gave the Commission guide lines on what a fair return on fair investment was.[2] Though originally set at 6 percent maximum, this legal limit was later dropped.

Regulation was extended to all modes of transportation. All modes except air were placed under the regulatory control of the ICC. Economic regulation of air is under the Civil Aeronautics Board (CAB). Unfortunately, carriers were brought under a law that was essentially directed toward railroad problems and economics. Both truck and water exhibit more competitive characteristics, such as a large number of small companies and low fixed investment, than does rail. Possibly these modes should not be regulated. There is some recognition of this as most recent transportation acts are stressing greater reliance on competition as the regulatory force and preservation of the inherent advantages of each mode.

To each transportation mode, regulation today means the following:

> *Degree of regulation.* There are five legal forms of transportation: (1) common carriers, (2) contract carriers, (3) private carriers, (4) exempt carriers, and

---

[2] The commission uses the formula

$$\text{return} = \frac{\text{earnings}}{\text{investment}}$$

to judge rate levels for railroads, where rate levels affect earnings. A ratio of operating expenses to revenues is used to judge the reasonableness of rates for those carriers with low fixed investments, as in trucking. The ROI ratio proves too sensitive to slight changes in rates for low investment carriers.

(5) brokers. Common carriers hold themselves out to serve all shippers and are under full regulation of the ICC or CAB. Contract carriers sell their services to a limited number of shippers and are regulated less closely than are common carriers. Private carriers refer to transportation facilities owned by the same company owning the product. The services of private carriers are not sold outside the company, and no economic regulation is needed. Some carriers may be exempt from economic regulation by virtue of the products they haul. Farm products, products in bulk, and freight moving in pickup and delivery operations are some examples of exempted freight. Brokers such as freight forwarders are treated as common carriers serving the public even though they own no long distance (line haul) equipment.

Rate regulation. If a carrier is classified as a regulated carrier, he is subject to the rate control of the ICC or CAB. The regulatory agency does not establish most of the rates. Rather, the rates are initiated by the carrier, and the agency oversees the justice and reasonableness of the rates when there is cause for investigation, such as under complaint of another carrier or under complaint of a shipper. The agency does have the power if necessary to set maximum or minimum rate limits as well as the absolute rate. Regulated carriers are required to publish their rates.

Discrimination. Service discrimination and rate discrimination are prohibited.

Ownership. Regulated carriers are generally prohibited from owning competing transport facilities. For example, a railroad owning a truck line operating parallel to the railroad and competing for essentially the same business is not allowed. Mergers, consolidations, and acquisitions must have ICC or CAB approval.

Entry and expansion. Competition in the industry is controlled by requiring regulated carriers to acquire the regulatory agency's approval for entry or expansion. New carriers or carriers expanding their territory must show a need for the service and must show a capability of supplying the service before a permission will be granted and the carrier can begin operations. Permission in the form of certificates may be suspended, changed, or revoked for proven violations of the law.

In contrast, nonregulated carriers are free to set rates, need not publish their rates, and in general act as any free enterprise. However, they can be subject to a degree of safety regulation.

Transport Cost Characteristics

Understanding the prices that a logistician must pay for transportation services is keyed to the cost characteristics of each type of service. Just and reasonable transportation rates tend to follow the costs of producing the service. Since each service has different cost characteristics, under any given set of circumstances there will be potential rate advantages of one mode that cannot be effectively matched by other services. Transportation costs can be explained in terms of variable and fixed cost elements.

VARIABLE AND FIXED COSTS

Producing a transportation service incurs a number of costs, such as labor, fuel, maintenance, terminal, roadway, administration, and others. This cost mix

---

FIGURE 6-1

Generalized railroad costs (and revenues) as functions of volume and distance

---

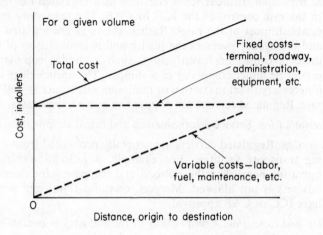

(a) Generalized railroad costs as a function of distance

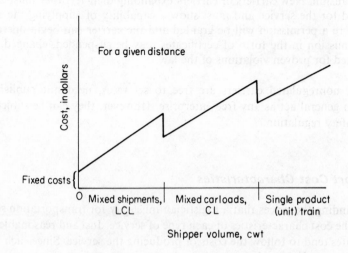

(b) Generalized railroad costs as a function of volume

can arbitrarily be divided into those costs that vary with services or volume (variable costs) and those that do not (fixed costs). Of course, all costs are variable costs if a long enough time period and a great enough volume are considered. However, for purposes of transport pricing it is useful to take costs that are constant over the "normal" operating volume of the carrier as fixed. All other costs are treated as variable. Specifically, fixed costs are roadway acquisition and maintenance, costs of terminal facilities, transport equipment costs, and carrier administration. Variable costs usually include line-haul costs, such as fuel and labor, equipment maintenance, handling, and pickup and delivery. This is not a precise allocation between fixed and variable costs, since there are significant cost differences between transportation modes, and there are different allocations depending on the dimension being examined. The reason is that all costs are partly fixed and partly variable, and allocation of cost elements into one class or the other is a matter of individual perspective.

There are two important dimensions on which line-haul transportation rates are based: (1) distance and (2) shipper volume. In each case, what is considered a fixed and a variable cost is slightly different. To illustrate, consider the cost characteristics of a railroad. Total costs for service vary with the distance over which the freight must be transported, as shown in Fig. 6-1. This is to be expected, since the amount of fuel used depends on distance, and the amount of labor for the haul is a function of distance (time). These are the variable costs. Fixed costs are substantial for rail, since railroads own their roadways, terminals and switching yards, and equipment. These latter costs are treated as invariant with distance traveled. The sum of the fixed and variable cost elements gives the total cost.

In contrast, Fig. 6-1 shows a railroad's cost function based on the shipper's volume. In this case, line-haul labor is not variable, but handling costs are treated as variable. Significant reductions in the handling of shipments of at least CL quantities or train-load quantities cause discontinuities in the total cost curve. These discontinuities occur between LCL and CL shipment sizes and train-load and less-than-train-load shipment sizes. Volume rate reductions are usally pegged to these drops in costs.

COMMON OR JOINT COSTS

It has been mentioned previously that reasonable transport rates are those that follow the costs of producing the service. Beyond the problem of deciding whether a cost is fixed or variable, determining what the actual costs are for a particular shipment requires some arbitrary cost allocations even though the total costs of operating may not be known. The reason is that many transportation costs are indivisible. Many shipments in different sizes and weight move *jointly* in the same haul. How much of the cost should be assigned to each shipment? Should the costs be assigned on the basis of shipment weight to total load, on the proportion of total cubic footage used, or on some other basis? There is no simple formula for cost allocation, and production costs on a per shipment basis remains a matter of judgment.

The back haul that all carriers experience with the exception of pipeline represents a case in point. Carriers rarely can balance perfectly the traffic between the forward movement and the return, or back haul, movement. The back haul is the light traffic direction. Shipments in the back haul may be allocated their fair share of total costs of producing the back haul. This makes the cost per shipment high compared with the forward haul. The back haul may be treated as a by-product of the forward haul, since it results from producing the forward haul. All or most of the costs are then allocated to forward haul shipments. Back haul costs would be considered zero or assigned only the direct costs to move a shipment in the back haul direction. There are several dangers in this latter approach. First, rates on the forward haul may have to be set at a level that would restrict volume in this direction. Second, back haul rates could be set low to help cover some fixed expenses. The effect may be that the back haul gains significantly in volume and possibly surpasses the forward haul volume. A carrier then may find himself not meeting his fixed expenses and faced with rate adjustments that could greatly alter the traffic balance. The by-product has now become the main product. In addition, a significant difference in cost allocation and in rates that follow these costs may lead to questions of discrimination between forward haul and back haul shippers. The key to unlawful discrimination is whether the service in both directions is judged to be under essentially the same conditions and circumstances.

COST CHARACTERISTICS BY MODE[3]

The type of services that a carrier is likely to emphasize is indicated by the nature of the general cost function under which he operates and by the relationship of this function to those of other carriers.

Rail. As a transporter of freight and passengers, the railroad is characterized as a high fixed-cost, relatively low variable-cost carrier. Loading, unloading, billing and collecting, and yard switching of multiple-product, multiple-shipment trains contribute to high terminal costs for rail. Increased per-shipment volume and its effect on reducing terminal costs result in some substantial economies of scale, that is, lower per-unit costs for increased per-shipment volume. Roadway maintenance and depreciation, terminal facilities' depreciation, and administrative expenses also add to the level of fixed cost. Railroad line-haul or variable costs typically include wages, fuel, oil, and maintenance. Variable costs by definition vary proportionately with distance and volume; however, a degree of indivisibility does exist in some variable costs (labor, for example), so variable costs per unit will decrease slightly. Traditionally, variable costs have been taken as one-half to one-third of total costs, though there is a great deal of controversy on the exact proportion.

The net effect of high fixed costs and relatively low variable costs is to create significant economies of scale in railroad costs. Distributing the fixed costs over

[3] This section relies heavily on John R. Meyer, Merton J. Peck, John Stenason, and Charles Zwick, *The Economics of Competition in the Transportation Industries* (Cambridge: Harvard University Press, 1959), Chapters 3–5.

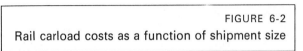

FIGURE 6-2
Rail carload costs as a function of shipment size

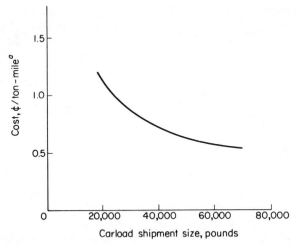

Carload shipment size, pounds

[a] Costs are in 1955 dollars.
Source: John R. Meyer, Merton J. Peck, John Stenason, and Charles Zwick, *The Economics of Competition in the Transportation Industries* (Cambridge, Mass.: Harvard University Press, 1959), p. 152.

greater volume reduces the per-unit costs on the order of magnitude shown in Fig. 6-2. Similarly, rail ton-mile costs drop when fixed costs are allocated over increasing lengths of haul.

Highway. Motor carriers show contrasting cost characteristics with rail. Fixed costs are the lowest of any carrier, because (1) motor carriers do not own the roadway over which they operate, (2) truck-trailer represents a small economic unit, and (3) terminal operations do not require expensive equipment. On the other hand, variable costs tend to be high, since highway construction and maintenance costs are charged to the users in the form of fuel taxes, tolls, and weight-mile taxes.

Trucking costs are mainly divided into terminal expenses and line-haul expenses. Terminal expenses, which include pickup and delivery, platform handling, and billing and collecting, are 15 to 25 percent of total trucking expenses. These expenses on a dollar per ton basis are highly sensitive to shipment sizes less than 2000–3000 pounds. Terminal expenses for shipments larger than 3000 pounds continue to drop as pickup and delivery and handling costs are spread over larger shipment sizes. However, the reduction is far less dramatic than for small shipment sizes, as shown in Fig. 6-3.

Line-haul trucking costs are 50 to 60 percent of total costs. It is not clear that per-unit line-haul costs necessarily decrease with distance or volume. However, total unit trucking costs do decrease with shipment size and distance as terminal costs and other fixed expenses are spread over more ton miles, but not as dramatically as rail costs.

FIGURE 6-3

Trucking terminal costs as a function of shipment size

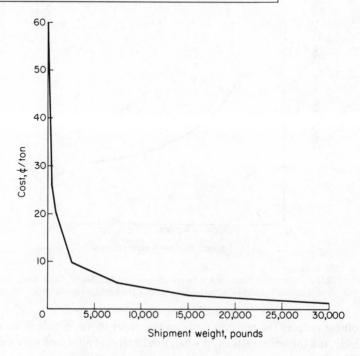

Source: Data from John R. Meyer, Merton J. Peck, John Stenason, and Charles Zwick, *The Economics of Competition in the Transportation Industries* (Cambridge, Mass.: Harvard University Press, 1959), p. 90.

Water. The major capital investment that a water carrier makes is in transport equipment and to some extent terminal facilities. Waterways and harbors are publicly owned and operated. Little of this cost, especially for inland waterway operations, is charged back to water carriers. The predominant fixed costs in a water carrier's operations are associated with terminal operations. Terminal costs include the harbor fees as the carrier enters a seaport, and the costs for loading and unloading cargo. Loading-unloading times are particularly slow for water carriers, and high stevedoring costs make terminal costs almost prohibitive for all but bulk commodities where mechanized material-handling equipment can be used effectively.

These typically high terminal costs are somewhat offset by very low line-haul costs. Without user charges for the waterways, variable costs include only those costs associated with operating the transport equipment. Operating costs (excluding labor) are particularly low because of the minimal drag to movement at slow speeds. With high terminal costs and low line-haul costs, ton-mile costs drop significantly with distance and shipment size. Thus, water is one of the least-cost carriers of bulk commodities over long distances and in substantial volume.

Air. Air transportation has many of the same cost characteristics as water and highway carriers. Air terminals and the air space are generally not owned by the airline companies. Airlines purchase airport services as needed in the form of fuel, storage, space rental, landing fees, etc. If we include ground handling and pick-up and delivery in the case of air freight operations, these costs are the terminal costs for air transportation. In addition, airlines own their own equipment, which when depreciated over its economic life becomes an annual fixed expense.

In the short run, airline variable expenses are influenced more by distance than by shipment size. Since an aircraft has its greatest inefficiency in the takeoff and landing phases of operation, variable costs are reduced by the length of haul. Volume has indirectly influenced variable costs as greater demand for air transportation services has brought about larger aircraft that have lower operating costs per available ton-mile.

Combined fixed and variable expenses generally make air transportation a premium service, especially for short distances. However, distribution of terminal expenses and other fixed charges over increased volume offers some reduction in per-unit costs. Substantial per-unit cost reductions come from operating aircraft over long distances.

Pipeline. Pipeline parallels the railroad in its cost characteristics. Pipeline companies or the oil companies that own the pipelines own the pipe and terminal and

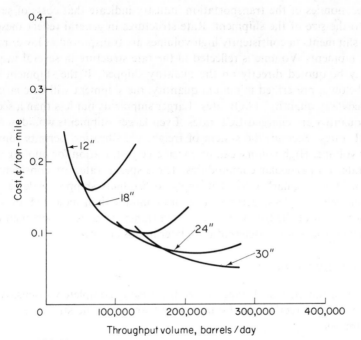

FIGURE 6-4

Pipeline costs as functions of line diameter and throughput volume

Source: *Ibid.,* pp. 129–31.

pumping facilities. They may own or lease the right-of-way for the pipe. These fixed costs plus others give pipeline the highest ratio of fixed cost to total cost of any mode. To be competitive, pipelines must work on high volume so as to "spread" these high fixed costs.

Variable costs mainly include power to move the product (usually crude oil or refined petroleum products) and costs associated with the operation of pumping stations. Power requirements vary markedly depending on the line throughput and the diameter of the pipe. Larger pipes have disproportionately less circumference to cross-sectional area as compared with smaller pipes. Frictional losses, and therefore pumping power, increases with the pipe circumference, while volume increases with the cross-sectional area. As a result, costs per ton-mile decrease substantially with larger pipes, provided that there is sufficient throughput to justify the larger pipe. There are also diminishing returns to scale if too large a volume is forced through pipe of a given size. These general cost characteristics are shown in Fig. 6-4.

Rate Profiles

Transportation rates are the prices that for-hire carriers charge for their services. Various criteria are used in developing rates under various pricing situations. The most common rate structures are related to volume, distance, and demand.

VOLUME-RELATED RATES

The economies of the transportation industry indicate that costs of service are related to the size of the shipment. Rate structures in general reflect these economies, as shipments in consistently high volumes are transported at lower rates than smaller shipments. Volume is reflected in the rate structure in several ways. First, rates may be quoted directly on the quantity shipped. If the shipment is small, that is, below a prescribed minimum quantity, the shipment will be charged a flat rate called "any-quantity" (AQ) rates. Larger shipments but less than a second minimum quantity are charged LCL rates. Even larger shipments would move under lower CL rates. Second, the system of freight classification permits some allowance for volume. High volume can be considered justification for quoting a shipper special rates on particular commodities. These special rates are considered deviations from the "regular" rates that apply to products shipped in lesser volume.

Volume-related rate structures are more complex than indicated above. However, since much of the following section on transport rates is concerned with volume, further discussion is deferred until later in this chapter.

DISTANCE-RELATED RATES

Rates as a function of distance range from being completely insensitive to distance to varying directly with distance. However, most rate structures lie between these extremes.

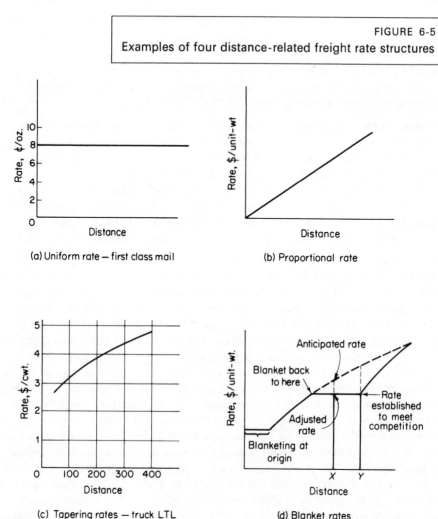

FIGURE 6-5

Examples of four distance-related freight rate structures

(a) Uniform rate — first class mail

(b) Proportional rate

(c) Tapering rates — truck LTL

(d) Blanket rates

Uniform Rates. Simplicity can be a key factor in establishing a rate structure. The simplest of all is the uniform rate structure where there is one transport rate for all origin-destination distances [Fig. 6-5(a)]. An example is the first class postage rates in the United States. The uniform rate structure for mail is justified, since a large portion of the total cost for delivering mail is in handling. Handling costs are not distance-related. On the other hand, to use a uniform rate structure for truck transportation, where line-haul costs are at least 50 percent of total cost, would raise serious questions of rate discrimination.[4]

Proportional Rates. For those carriers with significant line-haul cost components (truck and, to a lesser extent, air), a compromise between rate structure simplicity

---

[4] Discrimination is assumed to occur whenever rates do not follow the costs of producing the service in question.

and service costs is the proportional rate structure [shown in Fig. 6-5(b)]. By knowing only two rates, one could determine all other rates for a commodity by a straight-line extrapolation. Though there are some obvious advantages to this simple structure, it does adversely discriminate against the long-haul shipper in favor of the short-haul shipper. Terminal charges are not recovered on the short haul. This rate structure is not generally used.

Tapering Rates.   A common rate structure is built upon the tapering principle. Because in this country terminal charges are included in line-haul charges, a rate structure that follows costs will show rates increasing with distance but at a decreasing rate, as shown in Fig. 6-5(c). A major reason for this is that, with increased distance of the shipment, terminal costs and other fixed charges are distributed over more miles. The degree of taper will depend on the level of fixed costs that a carrier has and the extent of economies of scale in line-haul operations. Thus, we logically would expect greater taper for rail, water, and pipe than for truck and air.

Blanket Rates.   Meeting rates of competitors and a desire to simplify rate publications and administration lead carriers to establish blanket rate structures. Blanket rates are merely single rates that cover a wide area at the origin, destination, or both. The resulting rate structure is illustrated in Fig. 6-5(d) with the plateaus as the area of rate grouping or blanketing. Blanket rates are most common for products that are hauled over long distances and whose producers or markets are grouped in certain areas, such as for grain, coal, lumber, and produce from California that is sold in eastern markets. Even parcel post rates that are quoted for wide zones radiating from the origin are a form of blanket transportation rates. Blanketing is a form of rate discrimination, but the benefits of simplification of the rates for both the carriers and shippers outweigh the disadvantages. Also, it generally offers the users of transportation services a broader selection of carriers.

Competition at times forces rates along a route to be lower than would normally be predicted from the general rate structure and the cost profile, for example, point Y in Fig. 6-5(d). To offer the lower rate at Y can create a situation where points ahead of Y such as X suffer from discrimination. This is clearly a form of long-haul–short-haul discrimination, which is a violation of the Act to Regulate Commerce of 1887. Carriers may eliminate this type of discrimination by making the rate for X and for all other points ahead of Y that would have a rate greater than that of Y equal to Y's rate. This process is called "blanketing back."

VALUE-OF-SERVICE RATES

Demand may also dictate a level of rates that bears little resemblance to the costs of producing the transportation service. Recognized here is the fact that users of transportation view transportation as only so valuable to them. Thus, there is an upper limit which the rates cannot exceed if the user is to move his goods with the carrier in question. Two dimensions suggest the value of transportation service to a customer: (1) his own economic circumstances and (2) the alternative transportation services available to him.

Consider Fig. 6-6 as an illustration. Producers *A* and *B* manufacture and promote a product that sells for $1.00/lb in market *M*. *A*'s expenses other than transportation costs are 85¢/lb and *B*'s are 75¢/lb. *B* can make a 5¢/lb profit on the product selling for $1.00/lb. Since *B* establishes the price, the maximum that *A* can rationally pay for transportation is 15¢/lb, and at that he would make no profit. This is the maximum that transportation service is worth to him. If rates are set above this level, the product will not move.

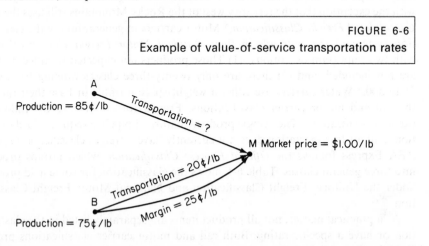

FIGURE 6-6

Example of value-of-service transportation rates

The second dimension is seen in the two service alternatives that *B* has. If it is assumed that both transportation service alternatives have equal performance characteristics, the value of the service to *B* is the cheapest rate. The higher-priced service would have to meet the 20¢/lb rate to be competitive and move some of the product. Thus, demand, or competition, establishes the rate level. Competitive rates based on value of service tend to distort cost-oriented rate structures and increase the complexities of rate quotation, administration, and publication.

Line-haul Rates

Transport prices can be classified as (1) rates for line-haul services and (2) special service charges. Line-haul rates refer to the charges incurred between origin and destination terminals, or door-to-door in the case of motor carrier service. Special service charges are prices for additional services such as terminal services, stop-off services, and detention of carrier equipment. Line-haul rates may be usefully classified (1) by product, (2) by shipment size, (3) by routing, and (4) miscellaneous.

BY TYPE OF PRODUCT

If an individual rate were quoted for each product item between all possible origin-destination points for all transport services, an impossibly large number of rates to be published and administered would result. To substantially reduce the number of rates needed, a rail classification system has been devised in which most product items are assigned to one of 31 classes ranging from Class 13 to Class 400. Rates are quoted for Class 100, and rates on products with different class ratings are found as a percentage of the Class 100 rate.

At one time a number of classifications existed that differed depending on the territory of the country to which it applied. Since the mid-1950's, the railroads have adopted a single classification code in the *Uniform Freight Classification*, with the exception that the territory west of the Rocky Mountains still uses the older *Consolidated Freight Classification*.[5] Motor carriers in general follow the classification system of the railroads in their *National Motor Freight Classification* but with two important exceptions: (1) Those products not expected to move by truck are not included, and (2) there are only twenty-three classes ranging from Class 35 to 500.[6] Water carriers use either a weight-space formula or base their rates on the rail and motor carrier classifications. Freight forwarders use the rail-motor carrier classifications. The "single product" nature of pipeline requires no classification, and air transportation does not currently have a freight classification system. REA Express follows the *Official Express Classification*, which groups products into three general classes. Table 6-1 shows the classification for some acid products under the Uniform Freight Classification and National Motor Freight Classification.

As a practical matter, not all product items are separately listed in the classification or have a specific rating. Both rail and motor carrier classifications provide for this by collecting all products not separately described in the classification under one heading and denoting these products by the letters NOIBN[7], which mean "Not Otherwise Indexed By Name." All NOIBN products have a single rating. Several examples of the NOIBN classification appear in Table 6-1.

Under certain circumstances, product ratings deviate from those listed in the classification and are referred to as "exceptions to the classification." These exceptions take precedence over the published ratings and are generally lower than the class rate. They are established to reflect special conditions, especially competition and operating conditions that cannot be realized under a classification that must provide an average rating for products shipped under average circumstances.

A number of factors are taken into account in establishing a rating. These include:

(1) Shipping weight per cubic foot.
(2) Shipping value per pound as shipped.

---

[5] The Consolidated Freight Classification uses slightly different classification letters and numbers than does the Uniform Freight Classification. An excellent discussion of the differences can be found in Charles A. Taff, *Management of Traffic and Physical Distribution*, 3rd edition (Homewood, Ill.: Richard D. Irwin, Inc., 1964), pp. 121–27.

[6] New England motor carriers use the Coordinated Motor Freight Classification, which classifies freight into eight classes based on shipping weight per cubic foot.

[7] NOIBN is specifically used in the Uniform Freight Classification. The letters NOI are used in the National Motor Freight Classification to mean the same thing.

(3) Fragibility, perishability, and susceptibility to theft.
(4) Hazards of carriage.
(5) Ease of handling.
(6) Ratings on similar products.
(7) Value of service.
(8) Shipping dimensions.
(9) Competitive factors.

TABLE 6-1

Class ratings of acid products under the Uniform Freight Classification and the National Motor Freight Classification

Product	Uniform Freight Classification		National Motor Freight Classification	
	LCL	CL	LTL	TL
Acids:				
Abietic, in barrels	55	$22\frac{1}{2}$	55	35
Acetic, glacial or liquid				
In carboys	100	45	100	45
In glass, in barrels, or boxes	$77\frac{1}{2}$	40	$77\frac{1}{2}$	40
In bulk, in barrels, in packages and in tank trucks	70	30	70	35
Acids, NOIBN,[a] dry				
In glass or in cans or cartons in barrels or boxes	$92\frac{1}{2}$	55	$92\frac{1}{2}$	55
In bulk, in barrels, boxes, steel pails or 5-ply paper bags	85	50	85	50
Acids, NOIBN,[a] liquid				
In carboys	100	60	100	60
In glass, in barrels, and boxes	$92\frac{1}{2}$	55	$92\frac{1}{2}$	55
In bulk, in barrels, also CL, in tank cars	85	50	85	50
Adipic, in bulk in barrels, boxes, steel pails or 5-ply multiple-wall paper bags, also CL, in bulk, in covered hopper cars	65	30	NC[b]	NC[b]
Arsenic, fused, in barrels or boxes, or in bars wrapped in paraffined paper in wooden boxes only	70	$37\frac{1}{2}$	70	$37\frac{1}{2}$
Arsenic, other than fused				
In carboys	100	45	100	45
In barrels, also CL, in tank cars	70	$37\frac{1}{2}$	70	$37\frac{1}{2}$
Azelaic, from animal or vegetable fats, in bags, barrels, or boxes	65	30	65	30
Boric (boracic)				
In glass, in barrels, or boxes	85	45	85	45
In cans, or cartons, in barrels or boxes, or in bulk in bags, barrels, boxes, or steel pails; also CL, in double-wall paper bags or in bulk	70	35	70	$37\frac{1}{2}$
Carbolic (phenol)				
In carboys	100	55	100	55
In glass or in metal cans, in barrels, or boxes	$77\frac{1}{2}$	40	$77\frac{1}{2}$	40
In bulk, in barrels, or in metal drums, in barrels, or boxes; also CL, in tank cars	70	$37\frac{1}{2}$	70	$37\frac{1}{2}$

[a] NOI is used in the National Motor Freight Classification.
[b] Not classified.

Class Rates.   Companion to the freight classifications is a tariff or transportation price list. Once a product has a class rating and the Class 100 tariff is known, then line-haul charges can be determined. To illustrate, suppose a rail carload of boric acid in glass containers is to move between New York and Cleveland. The class 100 tariff is $2.50 cwt. The class rating from Table 6-1 is 45, or 45 percent of the Class 100 tariff. Therefore, the class rate is $2.50 \times 0.45 = \$1.13$/cwt.

The class tariff is a function of the distance between origin-destination points. Determining shipping distances has been simplified somewhat by "rate bases" tables which are laid out much like road mileage charts in highway maps. It would be impractical to list all combinations of origin-destination points. As a result, the principal tonnage point in an area of about 40 miles square is the point listed in the rate bases table, and other points in the square are assumed to be the principal tonnage point for distance computation purposes.

A second table in the freight tariff, or table of rates, gives the tariffs as a function of mileage blocks. The origin-destination distance found in the rate bases table is then used to find the rate per cwt for these points. The rate table usually computes the rate for the most-used class ratings so that further calculation is not required.

Though the class rate system provides the general pricing structure for transportation service, only a small fraction of the railroads total revenue (about 7 percent) or total tonnage moves under this sytem. Nearly 79 percent of the revenue is generated, and about 80 percent of the total tonnage for the railroads is hauled under a special rate structure referred to as the commodity rate structure. The remaining revenue (13 percent) comes from exception rates.

Commodity Rates.   Commodity rates are special rates quoted on particular product items. They represent deviations from the regular freight classification system for the purpose of meeting specific circumstances such as unusually high volume, competition, etc. These rates may or may not be built on a systematic basis.

Freight-All-Kinds.   When carriers quote single rates for a shipment regardless of the classification of the commodities that make up the shipment, the rate is referred to as a "Freight-all-kinds" (FAK) or "All-commodity rate" (ACR). Freight forwarders are frequent users of this rate, since they primarily deal with mixed shipments. The rates follow the costs of providing the transportation service rather than on the "value of service."

BY VOLUME SHIPPED

Rates and actual transportation charges vary depending on the quantity tendered, that is, shipment size. Rates are quoted on a dollars-per-100-lb basis and can be different depending on where the shipment size falls in relation to prescribed minimum quantities that are established in the rate tariff. Any number of minimum quantities may appear in the tariff. There may be multiple minimum quantities, for example, 5,000-lb, 10,000-lb, 20,000-lb, and 30,000-lb minimum. There may be only a single rate for all quantities, which is referred to as "any quantity" (AQ) rates. Railroads, truckers, and transportation brokers customarily have a lower quantity limit on which to base charges, or they have a flat minimum charge such that actual charges cannot drop below this minimum. It is common to find rates quoted by class rating and with a minimum charge. Since class *ratings* are for less-than-vehicle loads and vehicle loads with a single minimum vehicle load *quantity*, then there also is a less-than-vehicle load *rate* and a vehicle-load *rate* in addition to the minimum charge. Examples A–G of Table 6-2 show how these rates are used in determining actual freight charges under different shipping circumstances.

		TABLE 6-2		
		Examples of truck transportation charge computations for different shipment combinations of class ratings, distances, and shipment weights		

Example	Shipment Specifications	Rate, $/cwt	Calculation of Charges	Actual Freight Charges
A	Class 200 (LTL), distance = 400 miles, quantity = 85 lb, minimum charge = $6.95	8.42	0.85 × 8.42 = $7.15	$7.15
B	Class 200 (LTL), distance = 400 miles, quantity = 50 lb, minimum charge = $6.95	8.42	0.50 × 8.42 = $4.21 pay minimum charge	$6.95
C	Class 100 (LTL), distance = 150 miles, quantity = 150 lb, minimum charge = $6.37	3.43	1.5 × 3.43 = $5.15 pay minimum charge	$6.37
D	Class 100 (LTL), distance = 150 miles, quantity = 300 lb, minimum charge = $6.37	3.43	3 × 3.43 = $10.29	$10.29
E	Class 100 (LTL), distance = 300 miles, quantity = 10,000 lb, minimum quantity = 30,000 lb at Class 60 (TL)	LTL = 4.22 TL = 2.76	100 × 4.22 = $422.00	$422.00
F	Class 100 (LTL), distance = 300 miles, quantity = 27,000 lb, minimum quantity = 30,000 lb at Class 60 (TL)	LTL = 4.22 TL = 2.76	270 × 4.22 = $1139.40[a] 300 × 2.76 = $ 828.00[b] pay lowest charge	$828.00
G	Class 60 (TL), distance = 300 miles, quantity = 35,000 lb, minimum quantity = 30,000 lb	2.76	350 × 2.76 = $966.00	$966.00
H	Class 60 (TL), distance = 300 miles, quantity = 35,000, minimum quantity = 30,000 lb. In excess rate offered	TL = 2.76 EX = 2.30[c]	300 × 2.76 = $828.00 50 × 2.30 = $115.00 Total = $943.00	$943.00

[a] Shipment moves at LTL rate.
[b] Shipped as if 30,000 lb and at the TL rate.
[c] Rate applies to all weight in excess of the minimum quantity. The minimum quantity moves at the TL rate.

Though truck rates are used in the examples, the methods of computation are generally applicable to the other transportation modes as well.

Other Incentive Rates.   There are additional incentive rates beyond the vehicle load minimums. One such rate is the *in excess rate* shown in Table 6-2, example H. In excess rates are rates that are lower than the vehicle load rates and apply to only those quantities that exceed the vehicle load minimums. This rate encourages shippers to increase shipment size and allows carriers better to utilize the capacity of their equipment.

Carriers further encourage shippers to ship quantities greater than vehicle load minimums through *multiple-vehicle rates* and even *trainload rates*. Carriers can effect economies of scale on larger loads and pass these economies along to shippers as incentive rates. They are also a competitive weapon against other carriers. The railroads have been very effective in meeting pipeline competition for the movement of coal by the use of single-commodity trains (unit trains) and trainload rates.

In some instances railroads have established *annual volume rates*. Reduced rates are offered if a minimum *annual* tonnage is moved. Coal is a commodity frequently moved under this rate.

BY ROUTING

All rates are either *local* rates or *joint* rates. Local rates apply to shipments made entirely over the routes of a single carrier. Joint rates apply to shipments when more than one carrier is involved in the line-haul movement of the shipment regardless of shipping distance. When a single rate is published in a tariff for specific origin and destination points, it is referred to as a through rate. If the rate only involves a single carrier, it is a "local through rate," and if it involves more than one carrier, it is a "joint through rate."

Proportional Rates.   A proportional rate is a "manufactured" rate that combines an existing rate with a portion of another established rate. Proportional rates frequently involve more than one carrier and are often established for competitive reasons. Fig. 6-7 illustrates a situation where there are competing routes involving carrier *A* and a combination of carriers *A* and *B*. Commodities can move between points *X* and *Z* at a rate of \$1.00/cwt. Carrier *A* also establishes the rate from

---

FIGURE 6-7
Example of a proportional rate

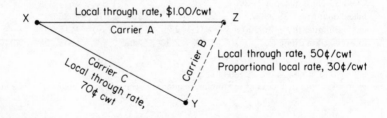

X to *Y*. Because carrier *B*'s local through rate from *Y* to *Z* is 50¢/cwt which, when combined with the rate from *X* to *Y*, exceeds the local through rate from *X* to *Z*, traffic is not likely to move over the *XYZ* route. To protect its traffic, carrier *B* establishes a proportional rate of 30¢/cwt on shipments destined for *Z* but that have *prior movement from X to Y*. Since the combined rate is now $1.00/cwt, carrier *B* protects its traffic on the *XYZ* route and also maintains its through local rate on the *YZ* route.

Combination Rates. When two or more rates are added together to form a single rate, it is referred to as a combination rate. The combination rate may be made up of class, local, joint, proportional, or other rates. It is used only when no published rate exists.

Differential Rates. Rates may be established by adding or subtracting an increment or "differential" from a rate that is considered to be a standard. Such rates are quoted most often for routes that are circuitous or of inferior service compared with faster and more direct routes. Hence, differential rates are usually lower than the standard rates from which they are derived.

Similar to the differential rate is the *arbitrary* rate. The arbitrary rate is a combination of a fixed amount and a standard rate. The fixed amount may be added to establish a rate for a minor destination point that lies beyond a major destination point for which a rate is already established.

Aggregate of Intermediates. Under Section 4 of the Act to Regulate Commerce of 1887, when there is a difference in the published rate between two points and the sum of the published rates for those points intermediate to the first two points, the lower of the two applies. For example, if the rate between *X* and *Z* is $2.00/cwt and the rate between *X* and *Y* is 90¢/cwt and between *Y* and *Z* is 85¢/cwt, the rate of 90¢ + 85¢ = $1.75/cwt would be charged.

MISCELLANEOUS RATES

A number of rates do not fit into the above classifications. These remaining rates are simply collected under "miscellaneous."

Cube Rates. The class rating structure is an average of many different product characteristics. When articles are very light and bulky, class ratings do not fully compensate the carrier for the costs incurred for transporting these items, so cube rates are used. Cube rates are based on space occupied rather than weight.

Import-Export Rates. To encourage foreign trade, special rates—called import or export rates—are established on inland shipments originating from or destined to foreign points. Shipments move over domestic transportation routes at lower rates than comparable shipments with origins and destinations entirely inland. These rates take precedence over class or commodity rates applicable to shipments via the same route.

Deferred Rates. At times the shipper is willing to accept the possibility of increased delay in delivery compared with regular service in exchange for lower rates. The shipper is promised that delivery will be made no later than a given date. Carriers use such freight to fill out available space. Deferred service is used most often in air and water transportation.

Released Value Rates.   Under the Act to Regulate Commerce of 1887, common carriers are responsible for the value of the goods while in their keeping. If goods are lost or damaged, the shipper can claim up to the full value of the goods. Normally, rates are based on this unlimited liability. In contrast, common carriers are permitted to establish rates based on limited liability, called "released value" rates. Under released value rates, the carrier's liability is limited to some fixed figure. For example, movers of household goods commonly limit claim for loss and damage to 60¢/lb. Released value rates are particularly useful where the actual value of the goods is difficult to estimate.

Special Service Charges

In addition to line-haul charges, carriers frequently provide special services for which extra charges are made. Though some of these charges may be included in the line-haul rates, they may be added to the freight bill over and above line-haul charges. There are many such special services, and they can be classified as (1) special line-haul services and (2) terminal services. Only the more frequently used services are discussed.

SPECIAL LINE-HAUL SERVICES

Diversion and Reconsignment.   Diversion of a shipment refers to changing the destination of a shipment while en route. Reconsignment refers to changing the consignee of a shipment, usually after it has reached the original destination. In practice, however, no distinction is made between the terms.

Shippers have frequently used the diversion and reconsignment privilege in two ways. First, when the commodities are perishable, such as in the case of fruits and vegetables, the shipper may start a carload or truckload toward the general market area and when the exact destination has crystallized, the shipment will be diverted to that market. The shipper potentially can gain much from this privilege in terms of flexibility in meeting dynamic market conditions (both demand and price) at a nominal charge of between $5 and $20 per carload.

Second, the carrier can be used as a warehouse. Through circuitous routing, the shipper may substantially increase the time in transit from that normally required. When a demand for the goods develops, the shipment can then be routed directly to the market. Because this practice, if abused, can greatly increase carrier costs, rail carriers especially have questioned its desirability.

Transit Privileges.   Rail carriers, and to a lesser extent motor carriers, have established a special service that permits shipments to be stopped while in transit for processing or storage before moving on to the final destination. A shipment is treated as if it moves directly from an origin to a destination, and the freight charge is composed of the through rate from origin to destination plus a small additional charge for the stop. Without such a stop-off (in transit) privilege, shippers would pay the sum of the through rate from the origin to the stop-off point plus the through rate from the stop-off point to the final destination, which is generally higher than the transit privilege costs. This privilege clearly reduces locational disadvantages of processors and allows the carrier better to meet competition by commiting the shipper to using the carrier for both segments of the haul. Grain is a product that is frequently processed (milled) and transported under this privilege.

A related service is the stop-off privilege to complete loading or partially to unload. To complete loading, a shipper may request that the carrier stop at an intermediate point between the origin and destination points, though the intermediate point need not necessarily be on a direct line between the origin and destination points. The advantage of this privilege to the shipper is that he can obtain a rate on the shipment as if it originated entirely from the origin point plus a nominal stop-off charge. This is usually less than the sum of individual rates. To illustrate, consider the example in Fig. 6-8. A shipment of 18,000 lb is originated at point *I* with an

| FIGURE 6-8 |
| Example of stop-off privilege to complete loading |

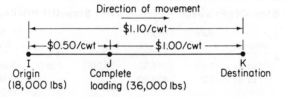

additional 36,000 lb to be combined at point *J* with the 18,000 lb, and both shipments are to move on to point *K*. Rather than the shipper's paying the individual rates between each point, where tariffs permit the shipper may elect to pay the rate from *I* to *K* on the entire shipment plus a stop-off charge. If the rate from stop-off point to the final destination is higher than the rate over the entire route, then the *J* to *K* rate would govern. Table 6-3 shows a comparison of the freight charges with and without a stop-off privilege.

The stop-off privilege applied to partial unloading is similar to that of complete loading. At times it is cheaper for the shipper to consolidate several shipments moving to different destinations in order to take advantage of substantial volume rate breaks while only incurring modest stop-off charges. Stop-offs for partial unloading are of two types: (1) all unloading is made from the equipment in which the shipment was originally loaded [Fig. 6-9(a)] and (2) transfer at a transloading point is made to different equipment before moving on to the final destinations [Fig. 6-9(b)]. Carriers do not charge for transloading; rather, the charges are made as if the partial unloading occurred entirely from the original equipment.

Rates for the stop-off privilege are based on the consolidated shipment weight moving to the final destination point. A fixed charge is added for each stop made. To illustrate the differences in freight charges with and without a stop-off privilege,

TABLE 6-3

Freight charges for example problem
with and without a stop-off privilege

	Loading	Route	Rate	Charges without Stop-Off Privilege	Rate	Charges with Stop-Off Privilege
	18,000 lb at *I*	*I* to *J*	$0.50/cwt	$90.00	—	—
additional	36,000 lb at *J*	*I* and *J* to *K*	1.00/cwt[a]	540.00	$1.10/cwt[b]	$594.00
			stop-off charge	—	stop-off charge	25.00
				$630.00		$619.00

[a] Based on the combined weight of 54,000 lb.
[b] Rate applies from point *I* on complete load.

TABLE 6-4

A comparison of total freight charges for partial unloading
of two points with and without a stop-off privilege

Without Stop-Off Privilege				With Stop-Off Privilege			
Load (lb)	Points	Rate $/cwt	Freight Charges	Load (lb)	Points	Rate $/cwt	Freight Charges
8,000	*I* to *J*	3.05	$244.00	30,000	*I* to *L*	3.00	$900.00
12,000	*I* to *K*	3.35	402.00			2 stop-offs at $15.00/ stop	30.00
10,000	*I* to *L*	3.60	360.00				
Total 30,000		Total charges	$1,006.00			Total charges	$930.00

consider the example shown in Fig. 6-9(a), where $J = 8000$ lb, $K = 12,000$ lb, and $L = 10,000$ lb with a 30,000-lb minimum quantity. Table 6-4 shows the cost comparisons. When the stop-off privilege is used, carriers require that the charges, $930.00 in this example, be collected at only one time. Commonly up to three stops to unload are permitted, but some piggyback tariffs allow up to five stops for unloading.

Protection. Many articles because of their particular physical characteristics require some type of protection in transit in addition to that normally provided. Perishable commodities may need refrigeration, icing, ventilation, or heating. Fragile commodities may require extra packing or dunnage.[8] In these cases, carriers may furnish special equipment such as damage-free cars, refrigerated cars and heaters as well as the necessary labor and materials needed to provide the protective service. Whereas some of the extra service needed for some commodities is reflected

---

[8] Dunnage refers to the cross bracings in a railroad car to prevent the load from shifting during transit and causing damage to the load.

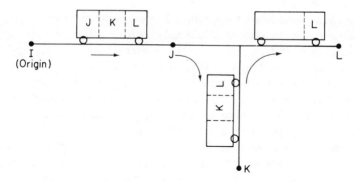

FIGURE 6-9

Examples of stop-off privilege to partially unload

(a) Unloading from a single car

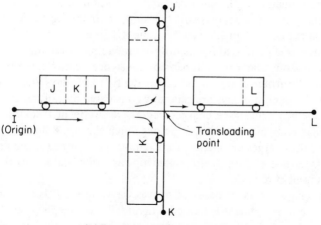

(b) Transfer to different cars before unloading at destinations

in the class rating for the commodities, carriers often add charges to the freight bill to reflect their increased costs for the protective services.

TERMINAL SERVICES

Additional charges may be made to the freight bill for services that take place around the terminal points in a carrier's routing network. Major among these terminal services are pickup and delivery, switching, and demurrage and detention.

Pickup and Delivery. Many carriers provide pickup and delivery service as a part of their regular service and include the charges as part of the line-haul rates. However, this practice is not universal. Some carriers do not provide a pickup and delivery service (e.g., in some water carrier service), and when it is, it may be offered at an extra charge (e.g., in air freight service). When the pickup and delivery service is "free," tariffs usually limit the service to the immediate area of the carrier's terminal, that is, within the corporation limits of the city or within a mile of the terminal, where there is no town.

Switching.   The "line haul" for a railroad involves the movement between terminals or stations. The movement of railroad cars from private sidings and junctions to rail terminals or stations, or vice versa, is referred to as "switching." Switching is similar to pickup and delivery, except that only railroad cars are involved. Line-haul railroads do not always have lines connecting directly to shippers and consignees and have worked out reciprocal switching agreements with other railroads serving these points. Many railroads absorb the switching charges and the shipper pays nothing above the line-haul rate, provided that the line-haul shipment produces a certain level of revenue. If the transportation charge is not sufficient to permit the carrier to absorb the switching charge, or if no reciprocal arrangements can be made to serve the siding or junction, the shipper or consignee pays the switching charge on a flat-charge-per-car basis.

Demurrage and Detention.   "Demurrage" and "detention" are equivalent terms referring to penalty charges imposed on the shipper or consignee for retaining a carrier's equipment beyond an allowed free time. In the case of rail cars, 48 hours is the standard free time permitted for loading or unloading. If retention of the equipment is due to reasons under the shipper's or consignee's control, the railroad may impose a daily demurrage charge of $4.00 for the first four days and $8.00 per day thereafter. Sundays and holidays are generally considered part of free time, but may be charged for once demurrage charges begin. Detention of trucking equipment follows a similar plan, except that free time is much shorter, 8 hours on truckload quantities, and the charges are higher; for example, the charge for the first 24-hour period after free time is $10. A graduated upward rate scale is used for longer periods of equipment retention.

Demurrage charges may be assessed in two ways. The first is the *straight plan*, where each piece of equipment is treated individually for the purpose of determining demurrage charges. Each piece of equipment is charged on the basis of the length of time it is detained. In contrast, the *average plan* represents an agreement between the carrier and the shipper to "average" the shipper's detention performance over a monthly period and to charge accordingly. Under this plan, releasing a rail car within the first 24-hour period carries an allowance of one "credit." For each day a car is retained after the free time period, one "debit" is assessed. If the sum of debits and credits at the end of the month results in debits, the demurrage charge is $4 per debit day for the first four days and $8 per debit day thereafter. A net credit balance results in no demurrage charge.

Establishing and Changing Rates

Establishing and changing rates for regulated carriers follow a formal procedure that may require a minimum of two to three months up to several years before new rates become effective. This is in sharp contrast with nonregulated carriers, who

FIGURE 6-10
Flow diagram of rate-making procedure

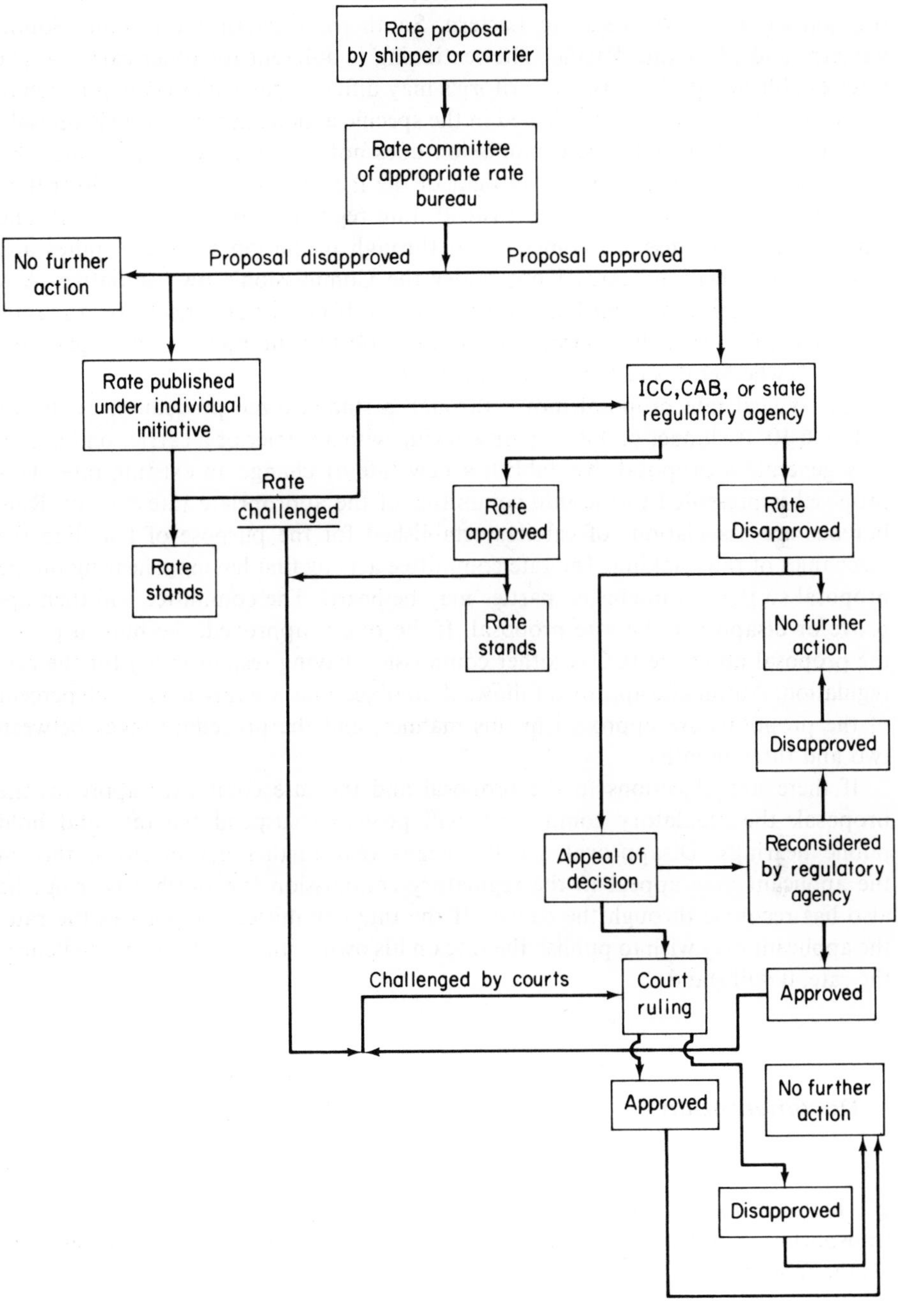

are free to change rates at will, as in the case of exempt carriers or in contrast with private carriers where rates per se do not exist, only various types of costs.

For the purpose of rate-making and reporting, the Interstate Commerce Commission divides the country into sections referred to as rate territories. For example, the railroad rate territories are Eastern, Southern, Western Trunk Line, Southwestern, and Mountain Pacific. The sectioning is different for other carriers. The rates established in the various territories may differ as particular economic conditions and rate problems are reflected in the specific actions taken on rate proposals.

The Interstate Commerce Commission does not establish every rate, since this would be an overwhelming task in light of the fact that there are over 40 trillion rates on file with the ICC alone. Instead, rate regulation by the ICC, CAB, and various state commissions comes about through mediation of rate disputes and through investigations carried out under the Commission's own initiative. Any regulated carrier may publish any rate it desires. If no dispute arises over the rate, it stands. Of course, the appropriate commission has the right to investigate any rate as to whether it is just and reasonable.

The typical rate proposal moves through a standardized procedure, as shown in Fig. 6-10. A shipper on his own or working with a carrier or a carrier on his own may generate a proposal to establish a new rate or change an existing rate. This proposal is presented to the rate committee of the appropriate rate bureau. Rate bureaus are associations of carriers established for the purpose of handling the mechanics of rate-making. The rate committee acts by first having a hearing on the proposal so that all interested parties may be heard. The committee will then approve or disapprove the rate proposal. If the rate is approved, the bureau passes the proposal on to the ICC or other commission having responsibility for the rate regulation. Automatic approval follows if no objections are raised. Over 90 percent of the proposals are approved in this manner, and the procedure takes between two and three months.

If there are objections to the proposal and the rate committee approves the proposal, the regulatory commission will probably suspend the rate and hold public hearings. Disapproval usually means that further action stops, though the applicant may appeal to the regulatory commission for another hearing; he also has recourse through the courts. If the rate committee disapproves the rate, the applicant may wish to publish the rate on his own initiative. If no one challenges the rate, it will stand.

Documentation

There are three basic types of documents that are most commonly used in transportation of freight. These are (1) the bill of lading, (2) the freight bill, and (3) the freight claim.

THE BILL OF LADING

The bill of lading is the key document on which freight moves. It is a legal contract between the shipper and the carrier for the movement of the designated freight with reasonable dispatch to a specified destination and to do it free of damage. According to Taff, the bill of lading has the following three purposes:

(1) It serves as a receipt for goods subject to the classifications and tariffs that were in effect on the date that the bill of lading was issued. It certifies that the property described on the bill of lading was in apparent good order except as noted on the bill of lading. The bill of lading should be signed by both the shipper and an agent for the carrier, but a carrier cannot avoid its liability because it does not issue a receipt or bill of lading.

(2) It serves as a contract of carriage . . . (and) . . . identifies the contracting parties and prescribes the terms and conditions of the agreement. . . .

(3) It serves as documentary evidence of title. It is necessary, however, to qualify this statement. Although this is true of a negotiable bill of lading, in the case of the straight bill of lading, the person who has possession of this type of bill of lading *may* have title to the goods. That, however, depends upon the facts in the individual case. Such matters as the terms of sale have influence in establishing title to the goods covered by the straight bill of lading.[9]

The *straight bill of lading*, shown in Fig. 6-11, as contrasted with the *order bill of lading*, is a nonnegotiable legal document. Under the straight bill of lading, the goods are consigned only to the specific person noted in the document. This bill cannot be traded or sold. Under the order bill of lading, the goods are consigned to the order of a person. This instrument may be traded or sold by endorsing the order to another person other than the one specified in the original bill. A main advantage of being able to change title allows the shipper to obtain payment for the goods before they reach their destination by endorsing the order bill of lading over to his bank and receiving payment. His bank in turn passes the document on to the consignee's bank, the consignee, and finally the carrier. The procedure works in much the same manner as bank drafts filter through the banking system.

FREIGHT BILL

The bill of lading ordinarily does not contain information about the freight charges, though some altered forms do include these charges. More frequently, the charges appear on a separate document commonly referred to as a freight bill. The freight bill (an invoice of carrier charges) contains, in addition to freight charges, much of the same information as a bill of lading, such as shipment origin

[9] Taff, *op. cit.*, p. 95.

FIGURE 6-11
Example of a straight bill of lading

(Uniform Domestic Straight Bill of Lading, National Motor Freight Classification No. 5, Effective Dec. 31, 1940.)

UNIFORM STRAIGHT BILL OF LADING
ORIGINAL—NOT NEGOTIABLE—DOMESTIC

CONSOLIDATED FREIGHTWAYS

Shipper's No. _____

Agent's No. _____

RECEIVED, subject to the classifications and tariffs in effect on the date of the issue of this Bill of Lading,

_____, Date _____, 19___

From _____

At _____ , _____ , _____ , _____
          Street   City   State   Zip Code

the property described below, in apparent good order, except as noted (contents and condition of contents of packages unknown), marked, consigned, and destined as shown below, which said company (the word company being understood throughout this contract as meaning any person or corporation in possession of the property under the contract) agrees to carry to its usual place of delivery at said destination, if on its own railroad, water line, highway route or routes, or within the territory of its highway operations, otherwise to deliver to another carrier on the route to said destination. It is mutually agreed as to each carrier of all or any of said property over all or any portion of said route to destination, and as to each party at any time interested in all or any of said property that every service to be performed hereunder shall be subject to all the conditions not prohibited by law, whether printed or written, herein contained, including the conditions on back hereof, which are hereby agreed to by the shipper and accepted for himself and his assigns.

Consigned to _____

Street _____ County of _____

Destination _____ State of _____

Routing _____ ZIP CODE _____

Collect on Delivery $ _____ and remit to:

_____ , _____ , _____ , _____
          Street   City   State   ZIP CODE

C.O.D. charge to be paid by } Shipper ☐   Consignee ☐

Subject to Section 7 of conditions, if this shipment is to be delivered to the consignee without recourse on the consignor, the consignor shall sign the following statement:
The carrier shall not make delivery of this

No. Packages	Kind of Pkg.	DESCRIPTION OF ARTICLES, SPECIAL MARKS, AND EXCEPTIONS	*Wgt. (Sub. to Correct.)	Class or Rate	Check Column

shipment without payment of freight and all other lawful charges.

_____
(Signature of Consignor)

If charges are to be prepaid write or stamp here "To be Prepaid."

Received $_____
to apply in prepayment of the charges on the property described hereon.

_____
Agent or Cashier

Per _____
(The signature here acknowledges only the amount prepaid.)

Charges Advanced:

$_____

| | | CF Rev | CL Rev | |

*If the shipment moves between two ports by a carrier by water, the law requires that the bill of lading shall state whether it is "carrier's or shipper's weight."

NOTE — Where the rate is dependent on value, shippers are required to state specifically in writing the agreed or declared value of the property.

The agreed or declared value of the property is hereby specifically stated by the shipper to be not exceeding_____per_____.

Shipper:

Per_____

Permanent postoffice address of Shipper:_____Street_____City_____State_____ZIP CODE

SIGNATURES BY INITIALS ONLY NOT ACCEPTED, OR PRINTED SIGNATURE UNLESS SUBSIGNED WITH FULL NAME OF SHIPPER'S REPRESENTATIVE.
(This Bill of Lading is to be signed by the shipper and agent of the carrier issuing same.)

Form 32   C F PRINTING & SUPPLY

FIGURE 6-12
Example of a freight bill

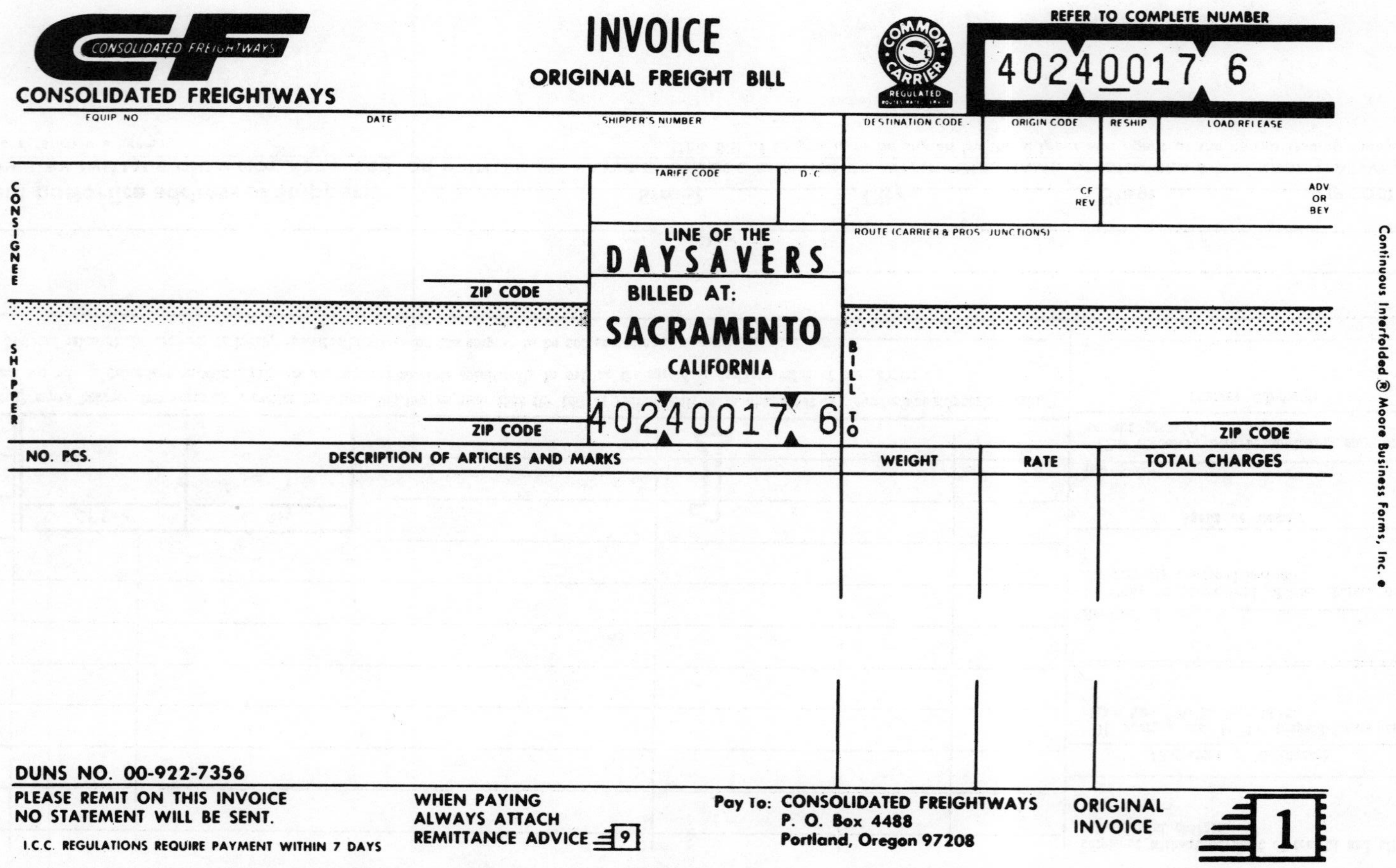
CONSOLIDATED FREIGHTWAYS

INVOICE
ORIGINAL FREIGHT BILL

COMMON CARRIER REGULATED

REFER TO COMPLETE NUMBER
40240017 6

EQUIP NO	DATE	SHIPPER'S NUMBER	DESTINATION CODE	ORIGIN CODE	RESHIP	LOAD RELEASE

TARIFF CODE | D-C | CF REV | ADV OR BEY

CONSIGNEE — ZIP CODE

LINE OF THE DAYSAVERS
BILLED AT:
SACRAMENTO
CALIFORNIA
40240017 6

ROUTE (CARRIER & PROS JUNCTIONS)

SHIPPER — ZIP CODE

BILL TO — ZIP CODE

NO. PCS.	DESCRIPTION OF ARTICLES AND MARKS	WEIGHT	RATE	TOTAL CHARGES

81 (3/71)

MADE IN U.S.A.

DUNS NO. 00-922-7356
PLEASE REMIT ON THIS INVOICE
NO STATEMENT WILL BE SENT.
I.C.C. REGULATIONS REQUIRE PAYMENT WITHIN 7 DAYS

WHEN PAYING
ALWAYS ATTACH
REMITTANCE ADVICE 9

Pay To: CONSOLIDATED FREIGHTWAYS
P. O. Box 4488
Portland, Oregon 97208

ORIGINAL
INVOICE
1

Continuous Interfolded ® Moore Business Forms, Inc.

and destination, quantity shipped, product, and the persons involved. See Fig. 6-12 for an example.

The freight charges may be prepaid by the shipper or billed collect from the consignee. Payments for rail service are to be made before delivery, except that credit is extended to financially responsible shippers. Credit terms vary depending on the carrier involved. For example, users of rail services may be allowed up to 96 hours on carload shipments and up to 120 hours for LCL shipments to make payment. Motor carriers must present shippers with freight bills within seven days, and shippers have seven days to pay after receiving the bill. Transportation agencies can extend credit up to seven days. Domestic water carriers generally allow credit to 48 hours and sometimes up to 96 hours.

FREIGHT CLAIMS

Generally, two types of claims are made against carriers. The first arises from the carrier's legal responsibilities as a common carrier, and the second occurs because of overcharges.

Loss, Damage, and Delay Claims. A common carrier has the responsibility to move freight with "reasonable dispatch" and without loss or damage. The bill of lading specifically defines the limits of carrier responsibility. For example, the carrier is not liable for loss, damage, or delay as a result of an act of God, negligence of the shipper, act of a public enemy, or legal action taken against the shipper of the goods. Otherwise, the carrier is liable for the full value of the goods that are lost or damaged unless the extent of the carrier's liability is specifically limited by the bill of lading. Losses due to "unreasonable" delay or failure to meet guaranteed schedules are recoverable to the extent of the reduction in value as a direct result of the delay.

Overcharges. A claim against a carrier for overcharges results from some form of misbilling. A number of reasons for misbilling have been cited: (1) application of incorrect classification, (2) failure to use the correct rates, (3) use of incorrect distance factors or basing points, (4) simple arithmetic errors, (5) carrier misrouting of joint line shipments, (6) duplicate collection of freight charges, (7) errors in determining item weights, and (8) differences in interpretations of rules and tariffs.[10] Normal bill auditing may detect these errors before payment is made, and another corrected freight bill may be issued. Otherwise, up to three years is allowed for overcharge claims on interstate shipments.

The reparation claim is a type of overcharge. Since common carriers are required by law to charge reasonable rates, the published rate paid by the shipper may later be declared by the regulatory agency or the court to be unreasonable. The shipper may make a claim against the carrier within two years for the difference between the published rate and the rate determined to be reasonable.

---

[10] Paul E. Jamison, "Overcharges: How to Prevent Them, How to Collect Them," *Transportation & Distribution Management*, Vol. 7 (January 1967), pp. 23–26.

Concluding Comment

The intent of this as well as the previous chapter has been to provide an overview of the transportation environment. A reasonable understanding of the legal and economic forces that shape the transportation system and some knowledge of the specific services provided, performance characteristics, and costs associated with various transportation modes is essential to generating transportation service alternatives and evaluating them.

Questions and Problems

1. Trace transportation regulation from the late 1800's to the present. Of what interest is transportation regulation to the manager of logistics activities?

2. What problems are encountered in setting back-haul rates?

3. Contrast the cost characteristics of the five transportation modes. Especially discuss the reasons for the differences between fixed and variable cost proportions of each.

4. Distinguish between uniform rates, proportional rates, tapering rates, and blanket rates.

5. How do value-of-service rates differ from distance-related rates? From volume-related rates?

6. What is the relationship between freight classification and class rates? What is meant by exception to classification, and how is it useful?

7. If a product is Class 55 and the Class 100 rate is $2.00/cwt, what is the transportation rate for this product?

8. Compute the transportation charges for the situations below.

Shipment Specification	Rate, $/cwt
Class 100, distance 500 miles, quantity = 40,000 lb, minimum quantity = 20,000 lb	9.20
Class 55 (LTL), distance 100 miles, quantity 50 lb, minimum charge = $5.00	2.25
Class 200 (TL), distance 1000 miles, quantity 45,000 lb, minimum quantity = 30,000 lb, in excess rate offered	TL = 3.45 EX = 3.00
Class 60 (LTL), distance 200 miles, quantity = 25,000 lb, minimum quantity = 30,000 lb at Class 35 (TL)	LTL = 6.50 TL = 4.75

9. What are the reasons for the difference between vehicle-load and less-than-vehicle load rates, e.g., TL vs. LTL, CL vs. LCL, etc.?

10. Contrast local rates with joint rates.

11. How does the diversion and reconsignment privilege permit carrier equipment to act as a warehouse?

12. A 35,000-pound truckload quantity is to be delivered to three destination points shown schematically below.

	Unload 10,000 lb	Unload 20,000 lb	Unload 5,000 lb
0	A	B	C

The following transportation rates are known.

Load	Origin-Destination	Rate, $/cwt
10,000	O-A	1.50
20,000	O-B	1.75
5,000	O-C	3.00
35,000	O-C	2.00

Should advantage be taken of a stop-off privilege if it costs $20.00 per stop?

13. Distinguish between the following documents:

   (a) Straight bill of lading.
   (b) Order bill of lading.
   (c) Freight bill.

Selected Bibliography

FLOOD, KENNETH, *Traffic Management*. Dubuque, Iowa: Wm. C. Brown & Company, 1963.

FREDERICK, J. H., *Commercial Air Transportation*, 5th edition. Homewood, Illinois: Richard D. Irwin, Inc., 1961.

LEWIS, HOWARD T., JAMES W. CULLITON, and JACK D. STEELE, *The Role of Air Freight in Physical Distribution*. Boston: Division of Research, Graduate School of Business Administration, Harvard University, 1956.

LOCKLIN, PHILIP D., *Economics of Transportation*, 6th edition. Homewood, Illinois: Richard D. Irwin, Inc., 1966.

MEYER, JOHN R., MERTON J. PECK, JOHN STENASON, and CHARLES ZWICK, *The Economics of Competition in the Transportation Industries*. Cambridge, Mass.: Harvard University Press, 1959.

PEGRUM, DUDLEY F., *Transportation: Economics and Public Policy*, revised edition. Homewood, Illinois: Richard D. Irwin, Inc., 1968.

SAMPSON, ROY J. and MARTIN T. FARRIS, *Domestic Transportation: Practice, Theory and Policy*. Boston: Houghton Mifflin Company, 1966.

TAFF, CHARLES A., *Commercial Motor Transportation*, revised edition. Homewood, Illinois: Richard D. Irwin, Inc., 1955.

_____, *Management of Traffic and Physical Distribution*, 3rd edition. Homewood, Illinois: Richard D. Irwin, Inc., 1964.

WILSON, G. LLOYD, *Traffic Management*. Englewood, Cliffs, N. J.: Prentice-Hall, Inc., 1956.

Chapter
7

The
Storage System

In contrast with transportation, storage takes place primarily at the nodal points in the distribution network. As one analyst put it, storage is "little more than transportation at zero miles an hour."[1] This chapter focuses on the service alternatives, characteristics, and costs of the warehousing and materials-handling activities. Together, these activities comprise the major portion of what will be referred to as the storage system. On the average, the activities of the storage system, excluding inventory-carrying costs, absorb one-fifth of the logistics' dollar and are worthy of careful consideration.

Need for the Storage System

Storage is an *economic convenience* rather than a necessity in the logistics system. Goods can be placed at demand points without the aid of storage facilities (and

[1] Paul E. Jamison, "The Role of the Public Warehouse in Physical Distribution," *Transportation & Distribution Management*, Vol. 6 (August 1966), p. 19.

inventories). However, the effect may be erratic production schedules, poor customer service, and inefficient use of transportation services, all of which contribute to either lost revenue or increased costs. Seasonal or uncertain consumption patterns, variations in production levels, and fluctuations and uncertainties in the price of goods, along with the high cost of instantaneously responding to uncertain economic conditions, are the primary reasons for a storage system. The need for the storage system can further be discussed along three lines: (1) customer service considerations, (2) production considerations, and (3) as a hedge against future expectations.

CUSTOMER SERVICE CONSIDERATIONS

Storage is said to give goods time value. When goods are available at one location and desired at another, goods are separated from customers by time, and customer service suffers. Sales may be lost if transportation is not provided of a quality to prevent lost sales. This transportation service may be expensive, and if some storage had been provided, the goods could have been available at the time they were desired. If the increased revenues associated with improved customer service do not offset the costs of maintaining an inventory, they may be offset by the lower cost of transportation required to provide a given level of customer service.

PRODUCTION CONSIDERATIONS

Demand patterns for products often display marked seasonal variations as well as a degree of uncertainty. Without inventories, either goods will not be available for sale at certain times when the demand rate exceeds the production rate or production must be scheduled to "track" demand. Both conditions can be economically undesirable for the firm if demand shows much volatility. The capacity for goods storage permits a smoothing of production output and avoiding production extremes that result in overtime costs and costs associated with labor force cutbacks. That is, storage decouples production from the fluctuations and uncertainties in demand.

HEDGE AGAINST FUTURE EXPECTATIONS

Price and supply fluctuations can bring about the need for storage capacity. At times firms will purchase more stock than is needed for meeting production requirements or customer demands because the stock can be purchased at a "good" price or there may be an anticipated shortage of stock in some future period. Thus, inventories may be used as a hedge against future conditions, and storage capacity must be provided to accommodate these stocks. The storage cost is justified on the difference between current and future prices for goods and the economic consequences associated with being unable to acquire supplies.

Storage System Functions

The storage system can be separated into two important functions—inventory holding (storage) and materials handling. These functions can be "seen" by tracing product flow through a typical food products warehouse, as shown in Fig. 7-1. Materials handling refers to those activities of loading and unloading, moving the product to and from various locations within the warehouse, and order picking.

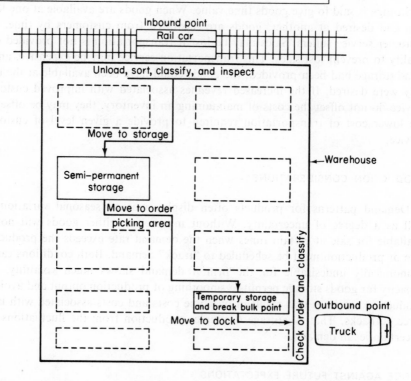

FIGURE 7-1
Move-store activities of a typical food products warehouse

Storage is simply the accumulation of inventory for a period of time. Different locations in the warehouse and different lengths of time are chosen depending on the purpose for storage. Within the warehouse, these move-store activities are repetitive and are analogous to the move-store activities occurring between various levels of the distribution channel (recall Figs. 1-1 and 2-1). Thus, the storage system in many ways is a microlevel distribution system. Specific identification of the major storage system activities promotes understanding of the system as a whole and helps provide a basis for generating design alternatives.

STORAGE FUNCTIONS

Storage facilities are designed around four primary functions: (1) holding, (2) consolidation, (3) break bulk, and (4) mixing. Warehouse design and layout often reflect the particular emphasis on satisfying one or more of these needs.

Holding. The most obvious use for storage facilities is to provide protection and orderly storage for inventories that accumulate there. The length of time that the goods are likely to be maintained in the facility and the requirements under which the storage is to take place dictate the exact nature of the facility's design and layout. Facilities range from long-term, specialized storage (aging liquors, for example) to general-purpose merchandise storage offered by the many public warehouses. Products stored include finished goods ready for the market, semi-manufactured goods awaiting assembly or further processing, and raw materials.

Consolidation. Transportation rate structures, especially rate breaks, influence the use made of storage facilities. If goods originate from a number of sources, it may be economical to establish a collection point or warehouse for the purpose of consolidating the small shipments into larger ones (Fig. 7-2). This assumes that the buyer does not purchase enough to warrant volume shipments from each source. The freight differential may more than offset the field warehousing charges. For example, suppose the buyer in Fig. 7-2 normally receives shipments from the four manufacturers in quantities of 10,000 lb, 8000 lb, 15,000 lb, and 7000 lb, respectively. If all shipments are made LTL to the customer, the total distribution cost would be $966 per shipment, as shown in Table 7-1(a). By consolidating shipments at a distribution warehouse, the total distribution cost is reduced to $778

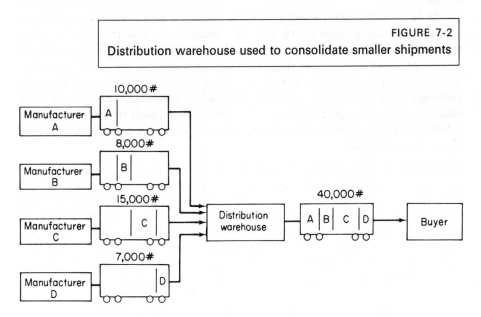

FIGURE 7-2

Distribution warehouse used to consolidate smaller shipments

TABLE 7-1

Example of the potential cost savings associated
with consolidating shipments at a distribution warehouse

(a) Without consolidation

Manufacturer	Shipping Weight	LTL Rate to Customer	Cost
A	10,000 lb	$2.00/cwt	$200
B	8,000	1.80	144
C	15,000	3.40	510
D	7,000	1.60	112
Total	40,000		$966

(b) With consolidation

Manufacturer	Shipping Weight	LTL Rate to Distribution Center	Total LTL	Distribution Warehouse Charge	TL Rate from Distribution Warehouse to Customer	Total TL	Cost
A	10,000 lb	$0.75/cwt	$75	$10	$1.00/cwt	$100	$185
B	8,000	0.60	48	8	1.00	80	136
C	15,000	1.20	180	15	1.00	150	345
D	7,000	0.50	35	7	1.00	70	112
Total	40,000						$778

per shipment, as shown in Table 7-1(b). In this case, a savings of $188 per shipment results.

The term "distribution warehouse"[2] has been used here primarily to present a contrast with the storage warehouse. The difference is a matter of how much emphasis is placed on storage activities and the length of time goods are stored. A storage warehouse implies that much of the warehouse space is devoted to semipermanent or long-term storage, as shown in Fig. 7-3(a). In contrast, in the distribution warehouse most space is allocated to temporary storage and more attention is given to speed and ease of product flow through the warehouse [Fig. 7-3(b)]. Obviously, many warehouses operate in both capacities, and the difference is a matter of degree.

Break Bulk. Using storage facilities to break bulk is the opposite of using them to consolidate shipments. A generalized break bulk situation is illustrated in Fig. 7-4. Low transportation rate, volume shipments are moved to the warehouse and then are reshipped in smaller quantities as required by customers. Breaking bulk is a common use of distribution warehouses, especially when inbound transportation rates to the warehouse exceed the outbound rates, customers order in small quantities, and the distance between manufacturer and customers is great. The transportation rate differentials tend to favor a distribution warehouse location

---

[2] A synonomous term currently in use is "distribution center."

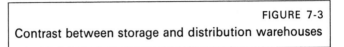

FIGURE 7-3
Contrast between storage and distribution warehouses

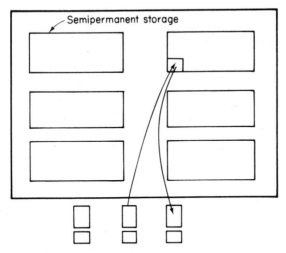

(a) Warehouse with emphasis on long-term storage

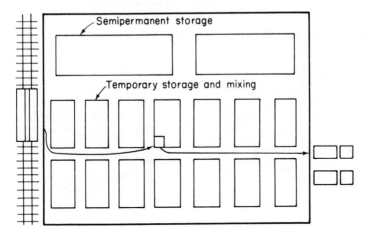

(b) Warehouse with emphasis on short-term storage,
mixing, and materials flow

near customers for break bulk operations; the opposite is true for freight consolidation.

Mixing. The use of storage facilities for product mixing is shown in Fig. 7-5. Firms that purchase from a number of manufacturers to fill a portion of their product line at each of a number of plants may find that establishing a warehouse as a product-mixing point offers transportation economies. Without a mixing point, customer orders might be filled directly from producing points at high

FIGURE 7-4
Distribution warehouse used to break bulk

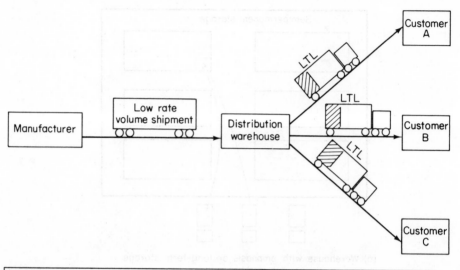

FIGURE 7-5
Generalized example of using a distribution warehouse for product mixing

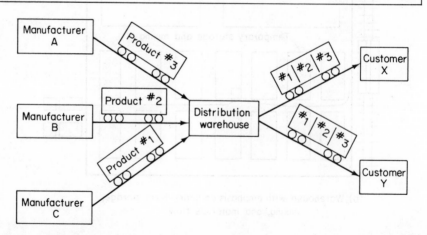

transportation rates on small volume shipments. A mixing point permits volume shipments of portions of the product line to be collected at a single point and then assembled into orders and reshipped to customers.

MATERIALS-HANDLING FUNCTIONS

Materials-handling functions within a storage system reduce to three primary activities: (1) loading and unloading, (2) movement to and from storage, and (3) order filling.

Loading and Unloading.   The first and last activities in the materials-handling chain of events are loading and unloading (recall Fig. 7-1). When the goods arrive at a warehouse they must be offloaded from the transportation equipment. In many cases, unloading and movement to storage are handled as one operation. In others, they are separate processes, sometimes requiring special equipment. For example, ships are unloaded at dock side by cranes, and hopper cars are turned upside down by mechanical unloaders to empty coal or ore. Even when unloading equipment is not different from the equipment used to move goods to storage, unloading may be treated as a separate activity since goods may be offloaded and then sorted, inspected, and classified before moving on to a storage location.

Loading is not dissimilar from unloading. However, several additional activities may take place at the loading point. A final check as to order content and order sequencing may be carried out before loading onto the transportation equipment. Also, loading may include an additional effort to prevent damage by bracing and packing the load.

Movement to and from Storage.   Between the unloading and loading points in a storage facility, goods may be moved several times. Movement first is from the unloading point to a storage area. Next, movement may be to the shipping dock or to an order-picking area for stock replenishment. Using an order-picking area results in an additional movement link and nodal point in the storage system network, as shown in Fig. 7-1.

The actual movement activity can be accomplished by any number of the many types of materials-handling equipment available. These range from manual push trucks to fully automated conveyor systems.

Order Filling.   The final materials-handling activity is that of order filling. This is the selection of stock from the storage areas according to customer requests. Order selection may take place directly from semipermanent storage areas or from areas (called order-picking areas) especially laid out to enhance the orderly flow of materials and, therefore, to promote efficient order selection. Order filling is often the most critical of the materials-handling functions, because the handling of small-volume orders makes this labor intensive and because the speed at which orders are selected directly affects customer service.

Storage Alternatives

Storage may take place under a number of financial and legal arrangements. Each presents a different alternative to the logistician in evaluating his logistics system design mix. Four distinct alternatives seem important, though combinations of the four in both number and degree can create an almost infinite variety of storage alternatives. The basic alternatives are (1) private ownership, (2) public warehousing, (3) contracted space, and (4) storage in transit.

PRIVATE OWNERSHIP

Private ownership of storage facilities refers to warehouses and materials-handling equipment under the financial and administrative control of the firm. These facilities may include production-oriented warehouses or field warehouses from which customer orders are primarily filled. The facility may be a general-purpose structure or a highly specialized building if the company's product line requires it.

Private ownership is an attractive alternative under a number of specific conditions:

1. If the product line requires special handling and storage, such as with certain chemicals and drugs, it may be necessary carefully to train and control the operating personnel and acquire specialized equipment and facilities for handling and storage to assure the quality of warehousing needed.

2. It offers less expensive warehousing when there is a high and stable volume of demand flowing through the facility such that full utilization of the facility is possible.

3. Private warehousing offers a high degree of control over warehousing operations that helps assure efficient warehousing and a high level of customer service.

4. All the benefits of real estate ownership accrue to private warehousing.

5. The warehouse may later be converted to a manufacturing facility, especially a warehouse located next to production facilities.

6. The private warehouse often serves as the base for the company's private truck fleet, sales office, traffic department, and purchasing organization.

In summary, private warehousing has the potential for offering better control, lower costs, and greater flexibility as compared with rented warehouse space, especially under substantial and constant demand conditions or where special warehousing skills are needed.

PUBLIC WAREHOUSING

Thousands of firms in this country are in the business of providing warehousing services to other business firms on a short-term fee basis. They perform many of the same services that are carried out under a private warehousing arrangement; that is, receiving, storage, shipping, and other activities. The public warehouse is similar to the common carrier in transportation service and holds essentially the same relationship to the private warehouse as the common carrier holds to private truck fleet ownership.

Types of Warehouses. An almost infinite variety of warehouse types exists for company-owned warehouses because of customized designs that follow specialized needs. In contrast, a public warehouse holds itself out to serve a wide range of customer needs. Thus, public warehouses do not show the same variety as private warehouses and can be classified into a limited number of groups. Jenkins has used five groups.[3]

[3] Creed H. Jenkins, *Modern Warehouse Management* (New York: McGraw-Hill Book Company, 1968), p. 29.

1. *Commodity warehouses.* These are warehouses that limit their services to certain commodity groupings. The warehouses may specialize in storing and handling such commodities as lumber, cotton, tobacco, and grain as well as other products that are easily spoiled.

2. *Bulk storage warehouses.* Some warehouses offer storage and handling of products in bulk, such as liquid chemicals, oil, highway salts, and syrups. They also mix products and break bulk as part of their service.

3. *Cold storage warehouses.* These are controlled, low-temperature warehouses. Perishables, such as fruits, vegetables, and frozen foods, as well as some chemicals and drugs require this type of storage for preservation.

4. *Household goods warehouses.* Storage and handling of household items and furniture are the specialty of these warehouses. Though furniture manufacturers may use these warehouses, the major users are the household goods moving companies.

5. *General merchandise warehouses.* These warehouses handle a broad range of merchandise and are the most common type. The merchandise usually does not require the special facilities or the special handling noted in the warehouses above.

Obviously, there is no clear dividing line between these warehouse types. Some warehouses may offer several of these services, such as a general merchandise warehouse that has a small refrigerated section.

Inherent Advantages. Public warehousing offers many advantages, a number of which are opposites of those noted for private warehouses. The more important of these are noted below:

1. *No fixed investment.* The use of public warehousing requires no investment for the firm renting space. All warehousing costs are variable, that is, in direct proportion to the amount of warehousing service used. No investment is valuable when a firm has better uses for its capital or cannot afford to make the necessary investment in such facilities.

2. *Lower costs.* Public warehousing generally offers lower costs than private or leased warehousing when inventory volume is low and/or inventory patterns are seasonal. The private warehouse experiences inefficiencies due to under- and overutilization of space. The public warehouse attempts to counterbalance seasonal inventory patterns of a number of manufacturers and benefit from relatively constant and full utilization of capacity, as shown in Fig. 7-6.

3. *Location flexibility.* Because arrangements made with a public warehouse are usually on a month-to-month basis, it is easy to change warehouse locations as markets shift. This lack of a long-term commitment offers important flexibility to maintaining an optimal logistics system.

4. *In-transit privilege.* Storage in a public warehouse can carry with it the side benefit that the warehouse may be the point at which an in-transit privilege is granted. Recall that the in-transit privilege refers to the granting of a single transportation rate from origin to destination even though goods are temporarily stored in the public warehouse. The single rate is

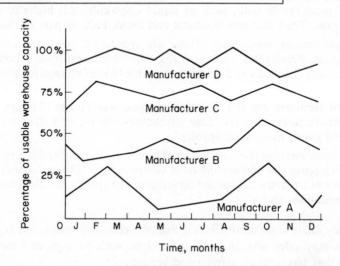

FIGURE 7-6

Balancing seasonal peaks and valleys in inventory levels among several manufacturers to maintain full utilization of usable capacity in public warehouses

Source: Redrawn from Kenneth B. Ackerman, Robert E. House, and Lee P. Thomas, "Distribution Centers: How to Use Them Effectively," *Transportation & Distribution Management* (September 1968), p. 34.

lower than the combination of the two rates from origin to warehouse and from warehouse to destination.

There may also be a tax benefit to goods stored in public warehouses. Some states do not assess personal property taxes on goods stored in public warehouses or do not tax those goods in transit.[4]

Services. Public warehouses provide a wide range of services that supplement and substitute for the logistics activities provided by many companies. A number of the more common services have already been alluded to, such as receiving, storing, shipping, consolidating, breaking bulk, mixing, and in-transit storage. The American Warehousemen's Association offers a detailed list of the types of services that might be expected from a public warehouse.

> Handling, storage, and distribution services, per package or hundred-weight
> In-transit storage
> U. S. Customs bonded storage
> U. S. Internal Revenue bonded storage
> Controlled temperature and humidity space

[4] For an excellent summary of personal property taxes for all states, see "Digest of State Tax Laws Affecting Goods in Storage," *Transportation & Distribution Management*, Vol. 7 (August 1967), pp. 31–38.

Space rental on a square foot basis
Office and display space; special clerical and telephone service
Traffic information
Handling and distribution of pool cars and consolidated shipments
Physical inventories
Modern data facilities
Freight consolidation plan
Packaging and assembly service
Fumigation
Marking, tagging, stenciling, wrapping
Parcel post and express shipments
Dunnage and bracing
Loading and unloading of cars and trucks
Repairing, coopering, sampling, weighing, and inspection
C.O.D. collections
Compiling special stock statements
Maintenance of and delivery to accredited customer lists
Local and long distance trucking
Appliance delivery and installation
Warehouse receipts forms—negotiable and nonnegotiable
O. S. & D. reports prepared
Proration of freight charges
Prepaying of freight bills
Credit information
Loans on stored commodities
Field warehousing services
Waterborne freight terminal services
Storage of machinery, steel, and other items requiring special handling
   equipment
Yard storage
Dry bulk commodity handling, storage, and bagging
Liquid bulk handling, storage, drumming, and bottling
Handling and storage of containerized materials.[5]

Selected services are discussed in greater detail below.

Public warehouses assist in bonding arrangements made with the government for certain goods, such as tobacco and liquor, on which taxes or duties are levied. The arrangement is between the owner of the merchandise and the government, whereby the goods cannot be removed from the warehouse (unless to another bonded warehouse) until the required taxes or duties are paid. The owner of the goods benefits by not having to pay the taxes or duties until the time the goods are sold. The public warehousemen act as an agent to assure the government that the goods are in the warehouse. The concept of bonding also extends to goods stored in private warehouses as well.

Field warehousing, in effect, is the conversion of private warehouse space to

[5] American Warehousemen's Association, 1971 Membership Directory, 222 West Adams Street, Chicago, Illinois.

public warehouse space for the purpose of securing credit. The public warehouse company usually leases from the owner of the goods a portion of the private warehouse in which the goods are stored and issues a warehouse receipt. The owner then can use the receipt to obtain credit, using the goods as collateral for a loan. Since the goods are in the legal custody of the public warehouse, the public warehouse company acts as a third party to guarantee that the collateral for the loan exists. Establishing the warehouse on the owner's property saves the expense of moving the goods to a public warehouse and storage expenses. The arrangement is usually temporary, lasting the duration of the loan.

Stock spotting is a collective term for a number of activities related to order filling and is an extension of the break bulk function. Public warehouses have responded to manufacturers' increasing need to provide a high level of customer service to wholesalers and retailers who engage in hand-to-mouth buying. Manufacturers "spot" an assortment of their goods in public warehouses close to their markets. The public warehouses then assume the responsibility for storage handling, order assembly, record keeping, delivery, bill of lading preparation, and repacking and marking. The public warehouse serves as a branch warehouse by performing all the functions normally handled by a manufacturer's own warehouse. The order cycle time is considerably shortened compared with more distant centralized private warehousing that may be used by the manufacturer. The cost for stock spotting services may be very reasonable in light of the fact that many such branch warehouses can be set up throughout the country.

The public warehouse may also assist in *inventory control*. With many stocks spotted around the country in public warehouses, keeping accurate records on the inventory can be a problem even if the company has its own record-keeping system. Public warehouses help in this regard by such activities as keeping perpetual inventory balances, noting unsaleable stock, noting stock damaged in transit, keeping records on when stock arrives at the warehouse, and listing disbursements. In many instances, public warehouses are now using computer facilities for record keeping.

Documentation and Legal Considerations. Public warehouses hold themselves out to be custodians of public property. In light of this responsibility, some public warehouses are regulated by the Public Utilities Commissions of their states. Regulation is not as extensive as it once was and now involves warehouses only in the states of California, Minnesota, and Washington. The Uniform Commercial Code, which covers public warehouses in all states except Louisiana, defines the responsibilities of the public warehouseman and establishes uniformity in issuing warehouse receipts. In Louisiana, the Uniform Warehouse Receipts Act provides similar responsibilities.

The legal responsibility of the public warehouseman is to exercise reasonable care in the handling and storage of the goods in his custody. If the damages or losses could not have been avoided by the exercise of reasonable care, the warehouseman is not held liable unless specific contractual arrangements have been made to the contrary. As with any blanket statement of liability to cover a wide range of situations, liability is not precisely defined. The owner of the merchandise may wish to extend his protection against liability and casualty losses through insurance protection or by writing into his contract with the public warehouse a provision for added liability for which the warehouseman makes an additional charge.

The contract between the owner of the merchandise and the public warehouseman, in addition to spelling out the extent of the warehouseman's liability, indicates the condition of goods to be deposited in the warehouse, the basis on which storage, handling, and special services charges will be made, and the conditions under which delivery will be made from the warehouse. A standard contract is commonly used by a public warehouseman. The terms and conditions for merchandise warehousemen as agreed to by the American Warehousemen's Association are shown in Fig. 7-7.

FIGURE 7-7

Standard contract terms and conditions for merchandise warehousemen

---

(Approved and Promulgated by the American Warehousemen's Association, October 1968)

ACCEPTANCE—Sec. 1

(a)   This contract and rate quotation including accessorial charges endorsed on or attached hereto must be accepted within 30 days from the proposal date by signature of depositor on the reverse side of the contract. In the absence of written acceptance, the act of tendering goods described herein for storage or other services by warehouseman within 30 days from the proposal date shall consitute such acceptance by depositor.

(b)   In the event that goods tendered for storage or other services do not conform to the description contained herein, or conforming goods are tendered after 30 days from the proposal date without prior written acceptance by depositor as provided in paragraph (a) of this section, warehouseman may refuse to accept such goods. If warehouseman accepts such goods, depositor agrees to rates and charges as may be assigned and invoiced by warehouseman and to all terms of this contract.

(c)   This contract may be cancelled by either party upon 30 days written notice and is cancelled if no storage or other services are performed under this contract for a period of 180 days.

SHIPPING—Sec. 2

Depositor agrees not to ship goods to warehouseman as the named consignee. If, in violation of this agreement, goods are shipped to warehouseman as named consignee, depositor agrees to notify carrier in writing prior to such shipment, with copy of such notice to the warehouseman, that warehouseman, named as consignee is a warehouseman and has no beneficial title or interest in such property and depositor further agrees to indemnify and hold harmless warehouseman from any and all claims for unpaid transportation charges, including undercharges, demurrage, detention or charges of any nature, in connection with goods so shipped. Depositor further agrees that, if it fails to notify carrier as required by the next preceding sentence, warehouseman shall have the right to refuse such goods and shall not be liable or responsible for any loss, injury or damage of any nature to, or related to such goods. Depositor agrees that all promises contained in this section will be binding on depositor's heirs, successors and assigns.

FIGURE 7-7 cont.

TENDER FOR STORAGE—Sec. 3

All goods for storage shall be delivered at the warehouse properly marked and packaged for handling. The depositor shall furnish at or prior to such delivery, a manifest showing marks, brands, or sizes to be kept and accounted for separately, and the class of storage and other services desired.

STORAGE PERIOD AND CHARGES—Sec. 4

(a)   All charges for storage are per package or other agreed unit per month.

(b)   Storage charges become applicable upon the date that warehouseman accepts care, custody and control of the goods, regardless of unloading date or date of issue of warehouse receipt.

(c)   Except as provided in paragraph (d) of this section, a full month's storage charge will apply on all goods received between the first and the 15th, inclusive, of a calendar month; one-half month's storage charge will apply on all goods received between the 16th and last day, inclusive, of a calendar month, and a full month's storage charge will apply to all goods in storage on the first day of the next and succeeding calendar months. All storage charges are due and payable on the first day of storage for the initial month and thereafter on the first day of the calendar month.

(d)   When mutually agreed by the warehouseman and the depositor, a storage month shall extend from a date in one calendar month to, but not including, the same date of the next and all succeeding months. All storage charges are due and payable on the first day of the storage month.

TRANSFER, TERMINATION OF STORAGE, REMOVAL OF GOODS—Sec. 5

(a)   Instructions to transfer goods on the books of the warehouseman are not effective until delivered to and accepted by warehouseman, and all charges up to the time transfer is made are chargeable to the depositor of record. If a transfer involves rehandling the goods, such will be subject to a charge. When goods in storage are transferred from one party to another through issuance of a new warehouse receipt, a new storage date is established on the date of transfer.

(b)   The warehouseman reserves the right to move, at his expense, 14 days after notice is sent by certified or registered mail to the depositor of record or to the last known holder of the negotiable warehouse receipt, any goods in storage from the warehouse in which they may be stored to any other of his warehouses; but if such depositor or holder takes delivery of his goods in lieu of transfer, no storage charge shall be made for the current storage month. The warehouseman may, without notice, move goods within the warehouse in which they are stored.

(c)   The warehouseman may, upon written notice to the depositor of record and any other person known by the warehouseman to claim an interest in the goods, require the removal of any goods by the end of the next succeeding storage month. Such notice shall be given to the last known place of business or abode of the person to be notified. If goods are not removed before the end of the next succeeding storage month, the warehouseman may sell them in accordance with applicable law.

(d)   If warehouseman in good faith believes that the goods are about to deteriorate or decline in value to less than the amount of warehouseman's lien before the end of the next succeeding storage month, the warehouseman may specify in the notification any reasonable shorter time for removal of the goods and in case the goods are not removed, may sell them at public sale held one week after a single advertisement or posting as provided by law.

(e)   If as a result of a quality or condition of the goods of which the warehouseman had no notice at the time of deposit the goods are a hazard to other property or to the warehouse or to persons, the warehouseman may sell the goods at public or private sale without advertisement on reasonable notification to all persons known to claim an interest in the goods. If the warehouseman after a reasonable effort is unable to sell the goods he may dispose of them in any lawful manner and shall incur no liability by reason of such disposition. Pending such disposition, sale or return of the goods, the ware-

FIGURE 7-7 cont.

houseman may remove the goods from the warehouse and shall incur no liability by reason of such removal.

HANDLING—Sec. 6

(a)   The handling charge covers the ordinary labor involved in receiving goods at warehouse door, placing goods in storage, and returning goods to warehouse door. Handling charges are due and payable on receipt of goods.

(b)   Unless otherwise agreed, labor for unloading and loading goods will be subject to a charge. Additional expenses incurred by the warehouseman in receiving and handling damaged goods, and additional expense in unloading from or loading into cars or other vehicles not at warehouse door will be charged to the depositor.

(c)   Labor and materials used in loading rail cars or other vehicles are chargeable to the depositor.

(d)   When goods are ordered out in quantities less than in which received, the warehouseman may make an additional charge for each order or each item of an order.

(e)   The warehouseman shall not be liable for demurrage, delays in unloading inbound cars, or delays in obtaining and loading cars for outbound shipment unless warehouseman has failed to exercise reasonable care.

DELIVERY REQUIREMENTS—Sec. 7

(a)   No goods shall be delivered or transferred except upon receipt by the warehouseman of complete instructions properly signed by the depositor. However, when no negotiable receipt is outstanding, goods may be delivered upon instructions by telephone in accordance with a prior written authorization, but the warehouseman shall not be responsible for loss or error occasioned thereby.

(b)   When a negotiable receipt has been issued no goods covered by that receipt shall be delivered, or transferred on the books of the warehouseman, unless the receipt, properly indorsed, is surrendered for cancellation, or for indorsement of partial delivery thereon. If a negotiable receipt is lost or destroyed, delivery of goods may be made only upon order of a court of competent jurisdiction and the posting of security approved by the court as provided by law.

(c)   When goods are ordered out a reasonable time shall be given the warehouseman to carry out instructions, and if he is unable because of acts of God, war, public enemies, seizure under legal process, strikes, lockouts, riots and civil commotions, or any reason beyond the warehouseman's control, or because of loss or destruction of goods for which warehouseman is not liable, or because of any other excuse provided by law, the warehouseman shall not be liable for failure to carry out such instructions and goods remaining in storage will continue to be subject to regular storage charges.

EXTRA SERVICES (SPECIAL SERVICES)—Sec. 8

(a)   Warehouse labor required for services other than ordinary handling and storage will be charged to the depositor.

(b)   Special services requested by depositor including but not limited to compiling of special stock statements; reporting marked weights, serial numbers or other data from packages; physical check of goods; and handling transit billing will be subject to a charge.

(c)   Dunnage, bracing, packing materials or other special supplies, may be provided for the depositor at a charge in addition to the warehouseman's cost.

(d)   By prior arrangement, goods may be received or delivered during other than usual business hours, subject to a charge.

(e)   Communication expense, including postage, teletype, telegram, or telephone, will be charged to the depositor if such concern more than normal inventory reporting or if, at the request of the depositor, communications are made by other than regular United States Mail.

FIGURE 7-7 cont.

BONDED STORAGE—Sec. 9

(a) A charge in addition to regular rates will be made for merchandise in bond.

(b) Where a warehouse receipt covers goods in U. S. Customs bond, such receipt shall be void upon the termination of the storage period fixed by law.

MINIMUM CHARGES—Sec. 10

(a) A minimum handling charge per lot and a minimum storage charge per lot per month will be made. When a warehouse receipt covers more than one lot or when a lot is in assortment, a minimum charge per mark, brand, or variety will be made.

(b) A minimum monthly charge to one account for storage and or handling will be made. This charge will apply also to each account when one customer has several accounts, each requiring separate records and billing.

LIABILITY AND LIMITATION OF DAMAGES—Sec. 11

(A) THE WAREHOUSEMAN SHALL NOT BE LIABLE FOR ANY LOSS OR INJURY TO GOODS STORED HOWEVER CAUSED UNLESS SUCH LOSS OR INJURY RESULTED FROM THE FAILURE BY THE WAREHOUSEMAN TO EXERCISE SUCH CARE IN REGARD TO THEM AS A REASONABLY CAREFUL MAN WOULD EXERCISE UNDER LIKE CIR-CUMSTANCES AND WAREHOUSEMAN IS NOT LIABLE FOR DAMAGES WHICH COULD NOT HAVE BEEN AVOIDED BY THE EXERCISE OF SUCH CARE.

(B) GOODS ARE NOT INSURED BY WAREHOUSEMAN AGAINST LOSS OR INJURY HOWEVER CAUSED.

(C) THE DEPOSITOR DECLARES THAT DAMAGES ARE LIMITED TO _____, PROVIDED, HOWEVER, THAT SUCH LIABILITY MAY AT THE TIME OF ACCEPTANCE OF THIS CONTRACT AS PROVIDED IN SECTION 1 BE INCREASED ON PART OR ALL OF THE GOODS HEREUNDER IN WHICH EVENT A MONTHLY CHARGE OF _____ WILL BE MADE IN ADDITION TO THE REGULAR MONTHLY STORAGE CHARGE.

NOTICE OF CLAIM AND FILING OF SUIT—Sec. 12

(a) Claims by the depositor and all other persons must be presented in writing to the ware-houseman within a reasonable time, and in no event longer than either 60 days after delivery of the goods by the warehouseman or 60 days after depositor of record or the last known holder of a nego-tiable warehouse receipt is notified by the warehouseman that loss or injury to part or all of the goods has occurred whichever time is shorter.

(b) No action may be maintained by the depositor or others against the warehouseman for loss or injury to the goods stored unless timely written claim has been given as provided in paragraph (a) of this section and unless such action is commenced either within nine months after date of delivery by warehouseman or within nine months after depositor of record or the last known holder of a nego-tiable warehouse receipt is notified that loss or injury to part or all of the goods has occurred which-ever time is shorter.

(c) When goods have not been delivered, notice may be given of known loss or injury to the goods by mailing of a registered or certified letter to the depositor of record or to the last known holder of a negotiable warehouse receipt. Time limitations for presentation of claim in writing and maintaining of action after notice begin on the date of mailing of such notice by warehouseman.

Source : Courtesy American Warehousemen's Association.

The public warehouseman uses a number of documents to communicate with the warehouse user. These include the warehouse receipt, the bill of lading, the over, short, and damage report, and the inventory report. The most important of these is the warehouse receipt, since it specifically notes the commodities in question, their stored location, the owner of the commodities, to whom they are to be delivered (that is, to bearer, to a designated person, or to the order of the owner), and the terms and conditions of the contract. The contract terms and conditions appear on the back of the warehouse receipt. The required content of the receipt is specified under both the Uniform Commericial Code and the Uniform Warehouse Receipts Act.

Warehouse receipts may be negotiable or nonnegotiable. The difference lies in the ease of passing the goods from one person to another. A nonnegotiable receipt is issued to a designated person or company. The goods cannot be passed to another person without written instructions to the warehouse to release the goods. An example of this type of receipt is shown in Fig. 7-8. In contrast, the negotiable receipt is issued to the order of a person or company, or it is not specifically issued to any particular person. The receipt may simply pass from one person to another by endorsement of the receipt, and the warehouse will release the goods to whomever holds the receipt. The negotiable feature of the receipt facilitates using the goods as collateral for loans.

The over, short, and damage (O.S. & D.) report is issued upon receipt of the goods and only if goods do not arrive in good condition or as stated on the bill of lading. The O.S. & D. report serves as a basis for filing a claim with the carrier.

The inventory report shows the inventory position in the warehouse at the end of the month in terms of item, quantity, and weight. It may also doubly serve as an invoice for monthly storage charges.

The bill of lading is a shipping document rather than a warehouse document, and it was previously discussed in Chapter 6. However, the warehouse often prepares the bill of lading and in the case of in-transit storage the bill of lading releases goods from storage. Therefore, it affects the warehouseman's liability to the extent of the goods listed on the bill. The bill of lading also provides general documentation on what was shipped from the warehouse.

In summary, the documentation system in a warehouse serves four basic purposes. These are (1) to record receipts, (2) to note exceptions, (3) to list releases, and (4) to provide a regular inventory status report.[6]

CONTRACTED SPACE

Contracting for, or leasing, warehouse space provides an intermediate alternative between private ownership and public warehousing. Leased space may be obtained in a number of ways, including contracting with a public warehouse for

[6] For a more complete discussion of this documentation system, see Kenneth B. Ackerman, Robert E. House, and Lee P. Thomas, "Distribution Centers: How to Use Them Effectively," *Transportation & Distribution Management* (November 1968), pp. 35–38.

FIGURE 7-8
Example of a nonnegotiable warehouse receipt

AMERICAN WAREHOUSE COMPANY STREET ADDRESS • CITY & AMERICA 00000 TELEPHONE: (312) – 123-4567	ORIGINAL NON-NEGOTIABLE WAREHOUSE RECEIPT	DOCUMENT NUMBER 6077

AMERICAN WAREHOUSE COMPANY claims a lien for all lawful charges for storage and preservation of the goods; also for all lawful claims for money advanced, interest, insurance, transportation, labor, weighing, coopering and other charges and expenses in relation to such goods, and for the balance on any other accounts that may be due. The property covered by this receipt has NOT been insured by this Company for the benefit of the depositor against fire or any other casualty.

DATE: 12/22/71

RECEIVED FROM
Major Chemical Corp.
Anywhere, Michigan

CUSTOMER NUMBER: 207-936

CUSTOMER ORDER NO.: 372

THIS IS TO CERTIFY THAT WE HAVE RECEIVED the goods listed hereon in apparent good order, except as noted herein (contents, condition and quality unknown), SUBJECT TO ALL TERMS AND CONDITIONS INCLUDING LIMITATION OF LIABILITY HEREIN AND ON THE REVERSE HEREOF. Such property to be delivered to THE DEPOSITOR upon the payment of all storage, handling and other charges. Advances have been made and liability incurred on these goods as follows:

FOR ACCOUNT OF
Consumer Products, Inc.
Somewhere, Ohio

WAREHOUSE NO.: 2

DELIVERING CARRIER	CARRIER NUMBER	PREPAID/COLLECT	SHIPPERS NUMBER
CRR	736920	Prepaid	67032

QUANTITY	SAID TO BE OR CONTAIN (CUSTOMER ITEM NO., WAREHOUSE ITEM NO., LOT NUMBER, DESCRIPTION, ETC.)	WEIGHT	RATD EE	STORAGE RATE / HANDLING RATE	DAMAGE & EXCEPTIONS
500 cs	Hand soap in bars -- 48/case	20,000#		.07/cs .10/cs	
TOTALS		20,000#			

NO DELIVERY WILL BE MADE ON THIS RECEIPT EXCEPT ON WRITTEN ORDER.

AMERICAN WAREHOUSE COMPANY
BY *R.W. Carson*
AUTHORIZED SIGNATURE

Source: Courtesy American Warehousemen's Association.

a longer term than the usual month period, leasing space from another manufacturer who may have excess capacity in his own private warehouse, selling and leasing back one's own private warehouse, or contracting with a company in the business to offer this kind of space. Leasing combines the advantages (and disadvantages) of owning and renting. Primarily, it offers control over warehouse operations without requiring the large initial investment of private warehousing.

STORAGE IN TRANSIT

Storage in transit is not to be confused with the storage-in-transit privileges offered by transportation companies. What is referred to here is the inventory that remains in transportation equipment during the time from when it is shipped to when it is received. The transportation equipment in effect becomes a warehouse for a period of time. Storage in transit is a valid warehousing alternative, because the logistician can control the length of time that the goods are in transit. Control is achieved through circuitous routing of a shipment where diversion and reconsignment are offered as a transportation privilege. Second, the length of time in transit may be altered by the choice of carriers. For example, rail shipments generally require longer shipping times than air freight. Through careful planning it is possible to reduce or eliminate the need for any conventional warehousing, especially for products shipped over long distances and where customer service levels are not extremely high. Also, inventory carrying costs associated with in-transit storage would be lower than for conventional storage methods, as the expense of the warehouse is eliminated.[7]

Materials-handling Considerations

Materials-handling considerations are an integral part of the storage space decision. If the choice is public warehousing, compatability of the company's materials-handling system with that of the public warehouse is a prime consideration. If a company-controlled warehouse is selected, the efficiency of the entire materials-handling operation is of concern. Materials handling is largely a cost-absorbing activity, though it has some impact on order cycle time and therefore, customer service. Thus, the objectives for materials handling are cost-centered, that is, to reduce handling cost and to increase space utilization. Improved materials-handling efficiency develops along four lines: (1) load unitization, (2) space layout, (3) storage equipment choice, and (4) movement equipment choice.

LOAD UNITIZATION

A fundamental principle in materials handling is: "Material handling economy is generally directly proportional to the size of load handled."[8] That is, as the size of the load increases, the fewer the number of trips required to store a given quantity of goods, the greater the economy. The number of trips relates directly to the labor time necessary to move the goods as well as the time that the materials-

---

[7] For an interesting discussion of the accounting problems associated with inventories in transit, see Lewis M. Schneider, "Inventory In Transit—Fact or Phantom?" *Transportation & Distribution Management* (January 1969), pp. 29–32.

[8] Stanley M. Weir, *Order Selection* (New York: American Management Association, 1968), pp. 4–5.

handling equipment is in service. Efficiency often can be improved by consolidating a number of small packages into a single load and then handling the consolidated load. This is referred to as a load unitization and is most commonly accomplished through palletization and containerization.

Palletization. A pallet (or skid) is a portable platform, usually made of wood or corrugated cardboard, on which goods are stacked for transportation and storage. Figure 7-9 shows several types. Goods are often placed on a pallet at the time of manufacture and remain palletized until order filling requires breaking the bulk. Palletization aids movement by permitting the use of standardized mechanical materials-handling equipment to handle a wide variety of goods. Further, it aids in load unitization with a resulting increase in weight and volume of materials handled per man-hour. It also increases space utilization by providing more stable stacking and hence higher stacks in storage.

Pallets may be made in any desired size. The most popular is 40 × 48 in., with 32 × 40 in., 36 × 48 in., and 48 × 48 in. also in common use. Pallet size and configuration depend on the size, shape, weight, and crushability of the goods, and capacity of the movement equipment. In addition, choosing pallet size should take into account compatability within one's own materials-handling system and compatability with materials-handling systems outside the firm that must also handle the goods, such as public warehouses used by the firm as well as the firm's customers. Once these needs are accounted for, the largest suitable pallet size should be selected so as to minimize the number of pallets required and to minimize handling. Loading the pallet should take into consideration the distribution of weight and the stability of load.

The pallet is an added cost item to the materials-handling system. It must be justified on the basis of the savings achieved by its use.

Containerization. The ideal in load unitization and materials-handling system compatability is the container. Containers are large boxes in which the goods are stored and transported. Containers can be waterproofed and locked for security so that ordinary warehousing is not necessary. Storage can take place in an open yard. Standardized materials-handling equipment can be used to move the containers, and the containers are interchangeable among different transportation modes. Standardization of container sizes will be the key to widespread use of containers. Because of the many interest groups throughout the storage-transportation systems of this country and of the world, container size standards are still under controversy. Containers are expensive, and probably some cost-sharing plan and container exchange program will need to emerge before containerization becomes the common materials-handling method.

SPACE LAYOUT

Location of stock in the warehouse directly affects the total materials-handling expense of all goods moving through the warehouse. What we seek is a balance between the materials-handling costs and the utilization of warehouse space.

FIGURE 7-9
Examples of several pallet types

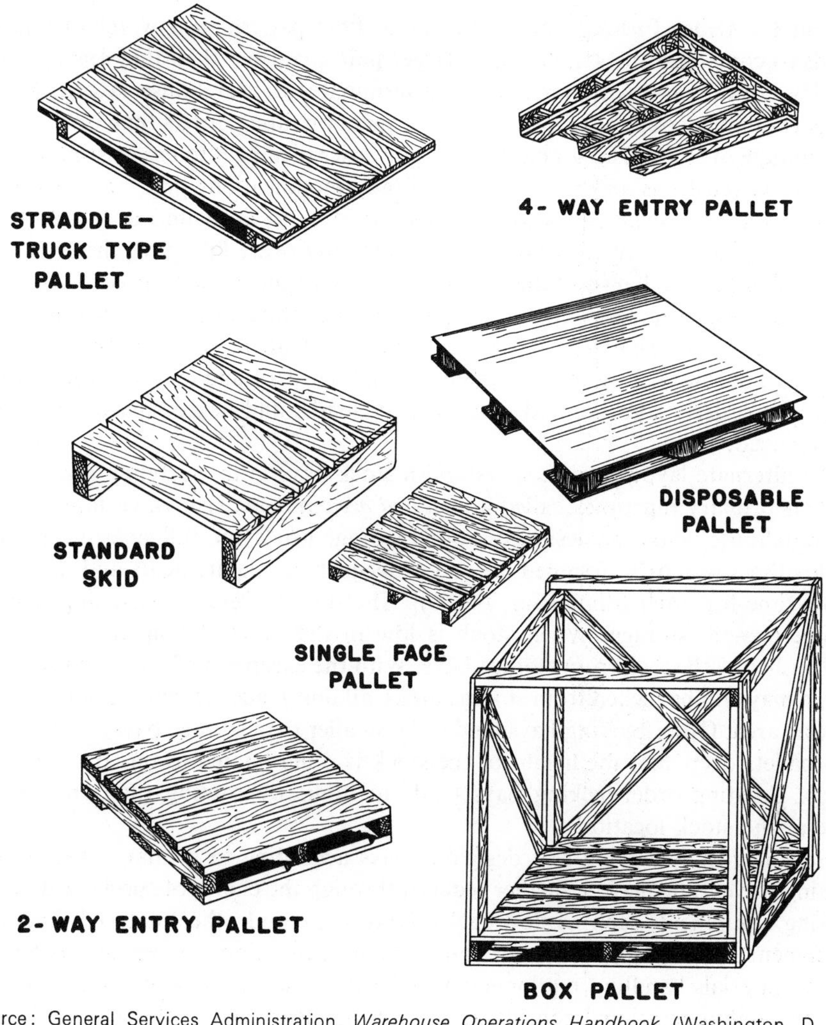

STRADDLE-
TRUCK TYPE
PALLET

4-WAY ENTRY PALLET

STANDARD
SKID

DISPOSABLE
PALLET

SINGLE FACE
PALLET

2-WAY ENTRY PALLET

BOX PALLET

Source: General Services Administration, *Warehouse Operations Handbook* (Washington, D. C.:
U. S. Government Printing Office, 1953), p. 30.

Specifically, there are storage space and order-picking considerations in the internal
design of a warehouse.

Layout for Storage.   In warehouses where the turnover is low, the primary concern
is to lay out the warehouse for storage. Storage bays may be both wide and deep,
and stacking may be as high as ceiling height or load stability permits. Aisles may
be narrow. This layout assumes that the extra time required to move stock in and
out of storage areas is more than compensated for by the full utilization of the

space. As stock turnover increases, such a layout becomes progressively less satisfactory, and modifications must be made to keep handling costs reasonable. Thus, aisles will tend to become wider and the height of the stack may be decreased. These reduce the time spent placing and removing the stock.

Layout for Order Picking. Since the usual flow pattern in a warehouse is for goods to come into the warehouse in larger unit quantities than they leave, order-picking considerations become prime determinates of warehouse layout. A disproportionate amount of labor time can be spent on filling orders than on receiving and storage of stock. The simplest layout for order picking it to use existing storage areas (referred to as an *area system*) with any modifications that may be needed such as stacking height, location of goods relative to outbound docks, and bay size [Fig. 7-10(a)]. If turnover of goods is high and order filling requires breaking bulk, using storage bays to fulfill both storage and order-picking needs may result in higher than necessary costs for materials handling and poor utilization of warehouse space. That is, the traveling time is great, as long distances are encountered in routing through the warehouse to fill orders, and unit loads are broken such that orderly stacking and placement of loads, and hence, space utilization, are reduced.

An alternate layout plan is to establish stock bays in the warehouse according to their primary function—called a *modified area system*. That is, certain areas of the warehouse would be designed around storage needs and full space utilization, while others would be designed around order-picking requirements and minimum travel time for order filling [Fig. 7-10(b)]. The storage (reserve) bays are used for semipermanent storage. When stock is low in the order-picking bays, they are replenished with stock from storage bays. With the exception of large, bulky items, which may still be picked from storage areas, all unit loads are broken in the order-picking area. Order-picking bays tend to be smaller than storage bays, usually only two pallets deep, and the height of the stock is often limited to one or two pallet loads. Creating order-picking bays tends to minimize routing time and service time at the stock location.

Beyond just specifying and designing bays according to primary need, order-picking travel time may be further reduced through the choice of specialized order-picking equipment, such as flow racks, conveyors, and other materials-handling equipment, and by operational design, such as sequencing, zoning, and batching. Since materials-handling equipment will be discussed in a later section of this chapter, only operational considerations will be mentioned at this point.

Sequencing is the arrangement of items on orders to be filled in the sequence in which they appear on the order-picking route through the warehouse. Order-picking time is saved by avoiding backtracking. This technique may be applied to both area and modified area systems. It does carry the penalty that the sequencing must occur on the sales order through cooperation with customer or salesman, or product item data must be sequenced after the order is received.

Zoning refers to the assigning of individual order pickers to serve only a limited number of the stock items instead of routing them through the entire stock. An

---

FIGURE 7-10

A generalized representation of order picking from storage areas as compared with order picking from separately designated bays

---

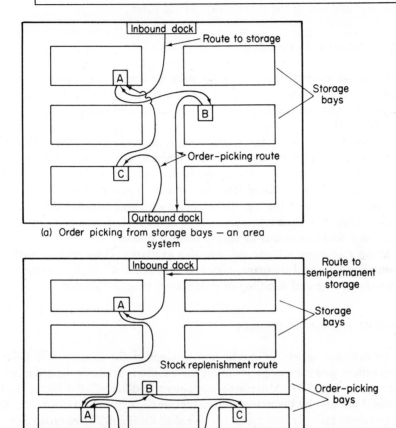

(a) Order picking from storage bays — an area system

(b) Order picking from order — picking bays with stock replenishment from storage bays — a modified area system

order picker may pick only the stock in a single aisle, and he usually fills only a portion of the total customer order. Although zoning permits labor specialization and minimum travel time in order picking, it also has some shortcomings. First, it requires that stock be located between zones according to ordering frequency, item weight, etc., so that the work load of the order picker is balanced. Second, original sales orders must be subdivided and a picking list for each zone developed. Third, the various portions of the orders must be reassembled into a complete order before leaving the warehouse. If the order filling proceeds from one zone to another to avoid the problem of reassembly, then order picking pace becomes dependent on the pace of order picking in other zones.

Batching is the selection of more than one order on a single pass through the stock. This practice would obviously reduce travel time, but it also adds to the complication of reassembling orders and partial orders for shipment. It also may increase order-filling time for any one order, since its completion is dependent on the number and size of the other orders in the batch.

STORAGE EQUIPMENT CHOICES

Storage and materials handling often must be considered in concert. In a way, storage is simply a temporary halt in the flow of materials through a warehouse. Storage aids promote the full utilization of space and improve the efficiency of materials handling.

Probably the most important storage aid is the *rack*. Racks are shelves usually of angle iron on which goods are stored. When a wide variety of items in small quantities must be stored, stacking loads one on top of another is inefficient. Racks promote floor-to-ceiling stacking, and the items on the bottom shelf are as accessible as those on the top, though items with high turnover should be placed near the bottom to reduce total service time at the rack. Racks also aid in rotating stock as in a first-in-first-out inventory control system.

A number of other storage aids are also available. These include shelf boxes, horizontal and vertical dunnage, bins and U-frames. All such equipment assists the orderly storage and handling of products of irregular shapes.

MOVEMENT EQUIPMENT CHOICES

A tremendous variety of mechanical equipment for loading and unloading, picking orders, and moving goods in the warehouse is available. Selected examples are shown in Fig. 7-11. Movement equipment is differentiated by its degree of specialized use and by the extent that manpower is required to operate it. Rather than discussing each piece of equipment, we shall distinguish three broad categories: (1) manual equipment, (2) power-assisted equipment, and (3) fully mechanized equipment. A mixture of these categories is generally found within a materials-handling system rather than a single category used exclusively.

Manual Equipment. Hand-operated materials-handling equipment, such as two-wheel hand trucks and four-wheel platform trucks, provides some mechanical advantage in movement of goods and requires only a modest investment. Much of this equipment can be used for a great many goods and under a wide variety of circumstances. Some of this equipment, however, is designed around specialized uses, for example, carpet handling, furniture handling, and pipe handling.

In general, the flexibility and low cost makes manual equipment valuable when the product mix in a warehouse is dynamic and the volume flowing through the warehouse is not high, and when investment in more mechanized equipment is not desirable. However, the use of the equipment is somewhat limited to the lifting and pushing capacity of the operator.

FIGURE 7-11
Selected examples of materials-handling equipment

Courtesy of Eaton, Inc., and Rex Chainbelt, Inc.

Power-Assisted Equipment.   Materials handling can be speeded up and the output per man-hour can be increased with the use of power-assisted materials-handling equipment. Such equipment includes cranes, industrial trucks, elevators, hoists, and many others. However, the workhorse of the industry is the forklift truck and its variations.

The forklift truck is usually only one part of a materials-handling system. It is combined with palletized loading and sometimes pallet racks. The power-assisted equipment permits high stacking of loads (over 12 feet) and the movement of loads of substantial size. The most common forklift truck has a capacity of about 3000 lb. The use of the forklift truck, pallet, and rack in a modified area warehouse layout is shown in Fig. 7-12.

FIGURE 7-12

Pallet-rack-forklift truck materials-handling system in a modified area warehouse layout

---

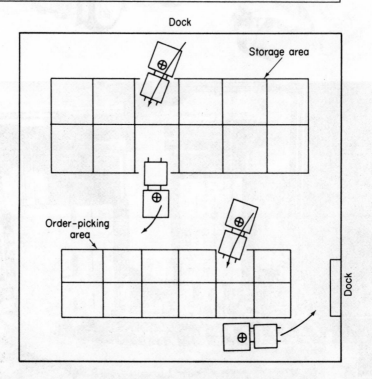

The pallet-forklift truck materials-handling system has high flexibility. The pallet permits a variety of goods to be moved with standard handling equipment. The system as a whole is not likely to become obsolete or require expensive modification as storage requirements change. Since, in addition, only a modest investment is required, the system is a popular one.

Fully Mechanized Equipment. Opposite to manual materials-handling equipment is fully automated materials-handling equipment. With computerized controls and sophisticated conveyors, some materials-handling systems have been developed that come close to full automation. For example, the huge S & H Green Stamp Distribution Center in Hillsdale, Illinois, serves more than 150 redemption centers, stocks 2000 items from 700 suppliers, and processes over 16,000 cartons on a single $7\frac{1}{2}$-hour shift. A computerized conveyor system is used to move goods from order-picking areas, police the flow of orders through the conveyor system, and control the accumulation of orders at the dock.[9] The handling system at the Rohr Corporation, which handles 90,000 aircraft parts, represents a step closer to a fully automated warehouse. With the exception of the shipping and receiving area, and the audit area for paper work and loading checking, incoming loads are moved via conveyor to storage racks, stored in racks by automated cranes, and retrieved by the reverse process. A schematic diagram of this system is shown in Fig. 7-13.

"Gee whiz" stories like these excite the imagination, but fully mechanized materials-handling systems are not good alternatives for most warehouse operations. Unless a constant and substantial volume flows through a warehouse, it is difficult to justify the large investment required for such systems. In addition, they impart inflexibilities into warehouse operations in terms of future product mix and volume, mechanical failures that can shut down the entire system, and warehouse location. However, given favorable circumstances for its development, the fully mechanized warehouse offers the potential for lower operating costs and faster order picking than any other type of materials-handling system.

FIGURE 7-13
Schematic diagram of an automated warehouse

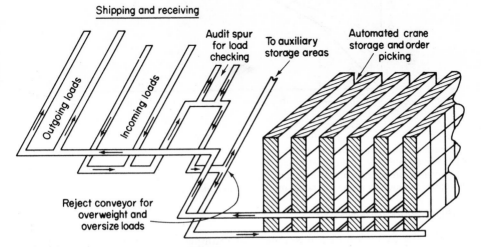

Shipping and receiving

Audit spur
for load
checking

To auxiliary
storage areas

Automated crane
storage and order
picking

Outgoing loads

Incoming loads

Reject conveyor for
overweight and
oversize loads

[9] "Computer/Controls Police Distribution Center Material Flow," *Transportation & Distribution Management*, Vol. 9 (January 1969), pp. 21–28.

Storage System Costs and Rates

A company must pay for storage system costs either through rates charged by an outside firm offering such services or through internal costs generated from operating a company-owned storage system. The expense is also determined by the particular materials-handling system chosen in a company-controlled warehouse. To provide an overview of the various storage system costs, four different systems will be noted: (1) public warehousing, (2) leased warehouse, manual handling, (3) private warehouse, pallet-forklift truck handling, and (4) private warehouse, automated handling. Each represents a different level of fixed and variable costs, as shown in Fig. 7-14, but is not to be considered an exhaustive list of all possible combinations of space alternatives and handling methods.

FIGURE 7-14

Generalized total cost curves for four alternative storage systems

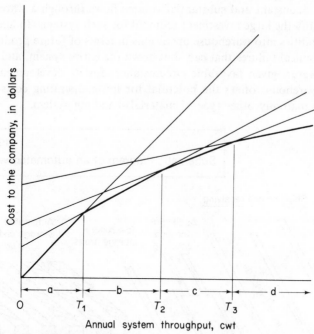

Annual system throughput, cwt

a Economical range for public warehousing.
b Economical range for leased warehousing, manual handling.
c Economical range for private warehousing, pallet-forklift truck handling.
d Economical range for private warehousing, automated handling.

PUBLIC WAREHOUSING

With the exception of a few states (for example, California, Washington, and Minnesota) where public warehouse rates are disclosed to the public, establishing warehouse rates is a matter of negotiation between the warehouseman and the customer. The rate decided upon will be based on such factors as the volume of goods to be handled and stored, the length of time a certain volume of warehouse space will be needed, the number of separate items in the product mix, any special requirements or restrictions for storage, the average outbound order size, and the amount of clerical work required, including inventory record keeping and the preparation of the bill of lading. These cost factors are generally grouped into three basic categories: (1) storage, (2) handling, and (3) clerical costs. Each exhibits different characteristics, and often separate rates are quoted in the three levels. Specifically, storage rates are often quoted on a per-hundredweight-per-month basis. The monthly rate reflects the time dimension of storage. In contrast, handling rates are usually quoted on a per-hundredweight basis. The number of times that the goods must be handled is the important dimension in handling costs. Clerical costs are charged to the customer on a direct basis. For example, bill of lading preparation costs are charged on a per-bill basis.

Several other methods of quoting rates may also be used by public warehousemen. These are

1. On a per-case basis for storage with an in/out per-case charge for handling.
2. By the amount of actual space occupied by the merchandise, usually computed by the square foot or cubic foot.
3. By a lease agreement for space and a contract for the handling function by the warehouse personnel.[10]

In all cases except method 3 above, the customer is billed monthly unless other arrangements have been made.

Public warehousing to the customer is an all-variable-cost storage system alternative. If a company generates a substantial and steady volume of business, public warehousing may become more expensive than private warehousing. Flexibility and improved customer service may be reasons for selecting public warehousing even if costs are higher than those for another alternative.

LEASED WAREHOUSING, MANUAL HANDLING

A second possible storage system is to combine leased warehousing space with manual materials handling. Though leasing is a long-term commitment compared with public warehousing, the charges for the space are incurred at regular intervals, so leased space can be treated as variable cost for a given warehouse throughput. Handling equipment requires a modest investment, if the equipment is company-owned, that must be amortized over a period of time. Labor cost tends to be substantial for this system, which imparts a strong variable cost component into the total storage system cost curve (Fig. 7-14).

---

[10] Jamison, *op. cit.*, p. 23.

PRIVATE WAREHOUSING, PALLET-FORKLIFT TRUCK HANDLING

This is a commonly chosen alternative to public warehousing. All costs within this system are internal company costs, provided that handling equipment is not leased or rented. Owning both warehouse and equipment introduces a substantial fixed-cost level in the total cost curve, as shown in Fig. 7-14. The greater degree of mechanization in handling and the low direct costs for operating a private warehouse mean low variable costs. However, substantial volume is needed before this alternative becomes an economically viable alternative compared with the previous alternatives noted above.

The pattern of throughput for a private (or leased) warehouse is important in assessing the costs for the storage system. Seasonal variations in warehouse usage cause under- and overutilization of a warehouse. During periods of low utilization, there is idle capacity and indivisibilities of some labor units that create high variable costs. Conversely, straining the capacity limits of the warehouse again causes high variable costs as materials-handling inefficiency and damage to the stored goods increase. The typical per-unit cost curve for a private warehouse is shown in Fig. 7-15. Therefore, the exact level of cost associated with storage under the private warehousing, pallet-forklift truck storage system depends on the extent of warehouse utilization and the diseconomies caused by fluctuating throughput in the warehouse.

FIGURE 7-15
Typical per-unit cost curves for a privately owned storage system

---

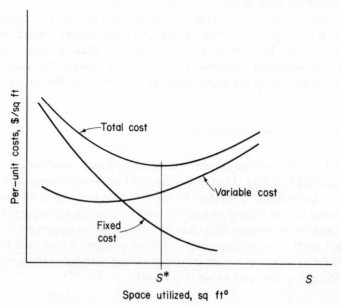

Space utilized, sq ft[a]

[a] The minimum total cost point S^* occurs at about 70–85 percent of the total space available for storage.

TABLE 7-2
Allocation of a set of warehouse expense items into basic storage system cost categories

Acct. Code	Account Name	Total	Storage	Handling	Clerical	G & A[b]
1	Rent	$16,281	$13,980	$ 1,345	$ 506	$ 450
2	Taxes—payroll[a]	2,390[a]	63[a]	1,187[a]	810[a]	330[a]
3	Taxes—highway	10		7	3	
4	Taxes—real estate	2,259	1,852	313	94	
5	Taxes—franchise	1,775	275			500[a]
6	Maintenance—bldg.	225	25		200	
7	Maintenance—elevator	50	50			
8	Maintenance—tools and equipment	185	70	115		
9	Maintenance—furniture	60			50	10
10	Maintenance—air conditioning	1,500	1,400	50	50	
11	Utilities	950	380	190	380	
12	Insurance—liability[a]	222[a]	4[a]	75[a]	101[a]	42[a]
13	Insurance—compensation[a]	691[a]	35[a]	652[a]	3[a]	1[a]
14	Insurance—other	80	25	26	29	
15	Insurance—group[a]	847[a]	24[a]	434[a]	262[a]	127[a]
16	Labor[a]	34,170[a]	1,200[a]	23,550[a]	9,420[a]	
17	Salaries	6,500				6,500
18	Dues and subs.	150				150
19	Motor equipment	500				500
20	Demurrage	110	110			
21	Donations	25				25
22	Legal and accounting	100				100
23	Loss and damage	700	10	690		
24	Miscellaneous	573	33	4		536
25	Packing materials	295		295		
26	Postage	175		25		150
27	Bad accounts	210				210
28	Stationery—supplies	350			350	
29	Telephone—telegraph	1,125				1,125
30	Subcontracts	500	500			
31	Equipment rental	175		175		
32	Travel	800				800
33	Equipment interchange		200	(200)		
34	Gasoline and oil	400		300	100	
35	Amortization—organization expense	500				500
36	Tires and tubes	30		30		
37	Depreciation expense	4,857	507	4,209	141	
38	Garage	500		500		
39	Subtotals	79,270	20,743	33,972	12,499	12,056
40	Prorata G & A		3,721	6,093	2,242	(12,056)
41	Total expense	$79,270	$24,464	$40,065	$14,741	

a Denotes labor and labor-related expenses.
b General and administration expenses.
Source: Howard Way and Edward W. Smykay, "Warehouse Cost Analysis and Control," *Transportation & Distribution Management,* Vol. 4 (July 1964), p. 32.

PRIVATE WAREHOUSE, AUTOMATED HANDLING

In terms of costs, the private warehouse, automated handling storage system is a limiting case of the above alternatives. It represents a high level of fixed investment in the warehouse and the automated handling equipment, such as computer-controlled conveyors, cranes, etc., and a low level of variable costs, as the system requires little in the way of manpower, light, heat, etc. As Fig. 7-14 shows, at very high warehouse throughput levels private warehousing with automated handling has the potential for being the lowest-cost storage system.

Beyond simply comparing one storage system against another, it is useful for further analysis and control to break down total costs into the three basis cost components in a storage system—storage, handling, and clerical costs. For the public warehouse these costs provide the basis for establishing rates. In the private warehouse they are valuable in controlling the various expenses and providing a ready comparison with the public warehousing alternative. Allocation of the various costs incurred in warehouse operation requires a good deal of judgment. One such allocation is illustrated in Table 7-2. Once total storage, handling, and clerical costs are obtained, they can be expressed on a per-hundredweight basis, a square-foot basis, or any other basis that may be useful.

Concluding Comments

This chapter provides a brief overview of the storage system in the logistics network. The discussion is directed toward the types of systems available, the functions they serve, their inherent advantages, storage and handling alternatives, and the costs associated with the various alternatives. This is the storage system environment. Logistics decision making draws upon this information in generating reasonable courses of action.

Questions and Problems

1. Why is the storage system considered by the logistician to be an economic convenience rather than a necessity?

2. Why is the storage system a *micro* logistics system problem? Compare the storage system with the logistics system network in Fig. 2-1.

3. Compare and contrast private ownership of storage space with rented storage space with reference to:

   (a) The services that can be obtained with each.
   (b) The cost for storage.
   (c) The degree of administrative control.
   (d) The flexibility for meeting future uncertainties.

Under what general circumstances is private warehousing the better choice?

4. How is storage in transit an alternative to conventional warehousing?

5. What benefits does containerization offer over more conventional forms of load unitization? Why is it not more widely used?

6. Indicate whether an area or a modified area layout system would likely be used and why in the following warehousing situations:

    (a) A food distribution center.
    (b) A furniture warehouse.
    (c) Storage of major appliances.
    (d) Storage of a steel company's products.
    (e) Storage of redemption items for S & H Green Stamps.

7. Explain or define the following:

    (a) Stock spotting.
    (b) Negotiable warehouse receipt.
    (c) O. S. & D. report.
    (d) Containerization.
    (e) Palletization.
    (f) Bonding.
    (g) Field warehousing.
    (h) Order picking.
    (i) Storage in transit.
    (j) Breaking bulk.
    (k) Zoning.

8. How does storage contribute to the time utility in goods? Explain.

9. What in general should a logistician know about the storage system?

Selected Bibliography

ACKERMAN, KENNETH B., ROBERT E. HOUSE, and LEE P. THOMAS, "Distribution Centers: How to Use Them Effectively," *Transportation and Distribution Management.* A seven-part series from September 1968 to March 1969.

AMMER, D. S., *Materials Management.* Homewood, Illinois: Richard D. Irwin, Inc., 1962.

BRIGGS, ANDREW J., *Warehouse Operations Planning and Management.* New York: John Wiley & Sons, 1960.

FREDERICK, JOHN H., *Using Public Warehouses.* Philadelphia: Chilton Co., 1957.

HAYNES, D. OLIPHANT, *Materials Handling Equipment.* Philadelphia: Chilton Co., 1957.

HAYNES, D. OLIPHANT, *Materials Handling Applications.* Philadelphia: Chilton Co., 1958.

JENKINS, CREED, *Modern Warehouse Management.* New York: McGraw-Hill Book Co., 1968.

TAFF, CHARLES A., *Management of Traffic and Physical Distribution*, 3rd edition. Homewood, Illinois: Richard D. Irwin, Inc., 1964, especially Chapters 21 and 22.

WEIR, STANLEY M., *Order Selection.* New York: American Management Association, 1968.

Part
III

Logistics Decisions

We now direct our attention to the major decision areas facing the logistician. To this point, the discussion has related to information inputs to the decision-making process. Our interest turns to the problems of identifying feasible alternative courses of action, estimating their payoffs, and selecting among the alternatives for the best course of action. A quantitative approach is taken where possible.

Logistics decisions are grouped into four broad categories. The first is facility location. Location of retail stores, warehouses, and plants acts as constraints on the daily operation of the logistics system. Good location decisions are imperative for efficient operation of the system. In Chapter 8, the methods for determining the size, number, and location of facilities are discussed.

The second is the inventory policy decision. Major policy questions involve how much to order and when to place the order. Chapter 9 deals with these questions for the single item at a single location and multiple items at multiple locations.

The third category groups several important logistics decisions into one chapter, Chapter 10. First, there are the transport decisions, which include transportation service selection decisions, carrier routing, and vehicle scheduling. Second, there is the logistics-production interface problem of production scheduling. Third, order-processing decisions are considered.

The final category is the warehousing decisions. These refer to the design and operation of the warehouse, which includes sizing storage space, stock layout, equipment selection and replacement policies, and dock design. These are the topics of Chapter 11.

Chapter
8

Facility Location
Decisions

In the broadest sense, the logistician is interested in locating inventories at strategic points in the distribution network. Whenever inventories are not in transit, a network nodal point is created (Fig. 8-1). In practice, a nodal point often represents a retail store, a public or private field warehouse, or a factory warehouse. For some products, especially bulk products, there may not be a fixed physical structure for sheltering the inventories. That is, these inventories may be stored in an open yard or even under ground. In any case, where the inventories should temporarily be stopped in the distribution network and facilities provided for storage is an important decision for the logistician, since both customer service and logistics costs are affected.

Where to locate the nodal points in the network is a highly complex decision problem. Until recently such problems were solved intuitively, since neither mathematical models nor computer technology was advanced enough to handle the many variables and the accompanying data necessary to analyze a network containing even as few as 10 facility locations. A number of analytical techniques now exist that are useful in providing management with initial solutions to the problem.

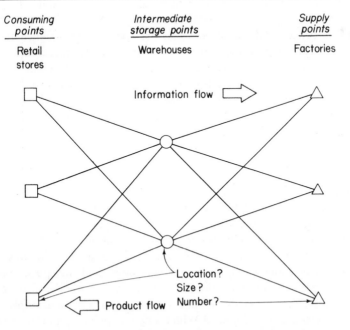

FIGURE 8-1

An industrial logistics network with emphasis on nodal point decisions

Analytical methods have been developed that aid in the three basic location problems of concern to the business logistician, that is, the location of retail sites, warehouses, and plants. Of the three, warehouse location has received the greatest attention by logistics analysts, since logistics costs—transportation and inventory costs—are often of relatively greater importance in the location decision than they are for many retail store and plant location decisions. Because of this, the main discussion on location will be focused on the warehouse location problem. In the final sections, retail site and plant location problems will be discussed in contrast with warehouse location.

Single Facility Location Models

Rarely does a firm have only one warehouse in its distribution network. However, in many cases it is possible clearly to separate all or a part of the territories being served by the warehouses and then to analyze the problem as one or a series of single warehouse location problems. An example of this concerns a firm having several regional warehouses located throughout the country. The western and southwestern regions of the country have market concentrations mainly on the west coast with a limited market potential eastward to the Mississippi River. Since western markets can be conveniently delineated from those east of the Mississippi

River, little error would be expected in assigning western markets to western regional warehouses and eastern markets to eastern regional warehouses.

When the warehouse location problem can reasonably be reduced to a number of single location problems, some conceptual and computational difficulties are overcome. For example, the problem of deciding the volume to flow through the warehouse is concurrently resolved when the markets are assigned to the warehouse. Also, depending on the nature of customer service requirements, many of the inventory policy decisions can be handled independently of the location decision. Most single warehouse location analyses are concerned with minimizing the sum of those transportation costs for products moving into and out of the warehouse, but in some cases the effect of location (delivery time) on customer service and revenue is reflected in the analysis.

AN EARLY APPROACH

A classic approach to the single warehouse location problem is an early analysis by Weber,[1] Palander,[2] and Hoover[3] that will be referred to as Weber's graphic method. The method utilizes the two-dimensional graph and has the important feature of being able to handle nonlinear transportation costs. The problem is to find the minimum transportation-cost location for a single warehouse when the demand assigned to the warehouse is predetermined and transportation costs are an important determinant of location. Weber's graphic method is a straightforward location analysis and can easily be understood by means of an example.

Suppose a warehouse is supplied Widgets by one plant P_1 and the warehouse in turn serves retail stores in two markets M_1 and M_2. The annual volume in M_1 is 20,000 cwt, and in M_2 it is 50,000 cwt. There is no weight loss or gain in the distribution system, so the plant supplies $M_1 + M_2$, or 70,000 cwt. Transportation rates are nonlinear with distance from the plant or to the markets. The transportation cost is the transportation rate times the volume of product moving. Transporttion costs can be represented by concentric circles (called isocost lines) radiating from each market or plant locations. These isocost lines have been constructed in Fig. 8-2 and represent the transportation cost for moving the given volume the distance of the radiating line from (to) the associated supply or market point. Note that the distance between the lines is not constant so as to reflect the nonlinear transportation rates and also that the lines radiate from each market or plant location.

Now, we seek the point where the sum of the inbound and outbound transportation costs is a minimum. This is the suggested location for the warehouse. To find

---

[1] Alfred Weber, *Über den Standort der Industrien* (Mohr, Tübingen, 1909), translated by Carl J. Friedrich as *Alfred Weber's Theory of the Location of Industries* (Chicago: University of Chicago Press, 1929).

[2] T. Palander, *Hritrage Zur Standortstheorie* (Uppsala, 1935).

[3] Edgar M. Hoover, *Location Theory and the Shoe and Leather Industries* (Cambridge, Massachusetts: Harvard University Press, 1957), pp. 42–52.

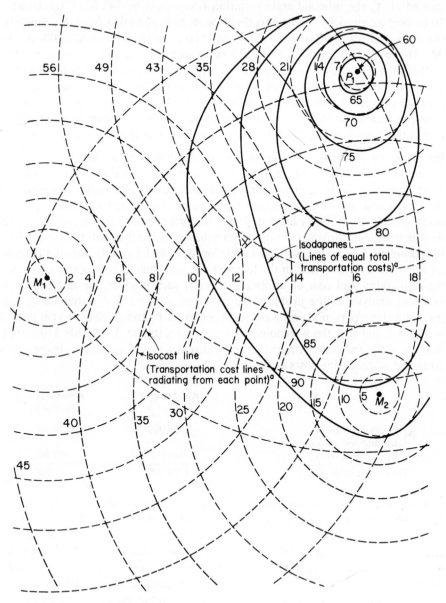

FIGURE 8-2

A graphic technique for locating the minimum total transportation cost point, given a single plant P_1 and two markets M_1 and M_2

Isodapanes
(Lines of equal total transportation costs)[a]

Isocost line
(Transportation cost lines radiating from each point)[a]

[a] Transportation costs in thousands of dollars.
Source: Redrawn from Ronald H. Ballou, "Locating Warehouses in a Logistics System," *The Logistics Review*, Vol. 4, No. 19 (September-October 1968), p. 27.

this location, Weber suggested the construction of the lines of equal total transportation costs which he called isodapanes. Constructing the isodapanes first requires finding the total transportation costs for a number of points scattered over the location map. Consider point X on the map (Fig. 8-2). If the warehouse were located at X, the inbound transportation cost would be \$42,000 (70,000 cwt $\times$ \$0.60/cwt) as given by the intersecting isocost lines radiating from P_1. Similarly, the outbound transportation costs are \$12,000 to serve M_1 and \$32,000 to serve M_2. The total transportation cost for X is the sum of these three costs, or \$86,000.

Repeating the above computations for other arbitrarily selected points and then connecting those points with the same total transportation cost by new lines will generate a series of cost contours or isodapanes. The isodapanes converge on the least-cost warehouse location. In the case of our example, the best warehouse location is the same point as P_1 with a minimum total transportation cost of \$60,000.

Improving the Analysis. The graphic method offers serveral distinct advantages to providing an initial solution to the single warehouse location problem. Perhaps most important is the graphic picture that is created. Not only is an optimum location found, but from the graphic picture of the isodapanes nearly optimum solutions can also be easily located. This is important because managers must often deviate from the mathematical optimum solution as the final solution to the location problem. The reason is that a simple location model usually does not consider all of the factors important in the location decision such as land costs, wages, and the availability and cost of utilities. However, such costs can be included in an extended analysis of the problem. To illustrate, suppose that warehousing costs (excluding transportation costs) are \$2.25 per cwt at P_1 and \$2.00 per cwt at point X in Fig. 8-2 and that the warehouse is currently located at X. It costs \$100,000 to relocate the warehouse. A more complete analysis would combine transportation costs and warehousing costs as follows:

	Warehouse at Location X	Warehouse at Location P_1
Transportation costs	\$ 86,000	\$ 60,000
Labor, utilities, and other direct warehousing costs	140,000	157,500
Total direct costs	\$226,000	\$217,500

If the warehouse were located at P_1, there is an annual savings of \$226,000 — \$217,500 = \$8,500 against a relocation investment of \$100,000. There is a simple return on investment before tax of 8.5 percent, which is probably too low to encourage management to relocate the warehouse. Thus, because the isodapanes give a contour of transportation costs over the location map, Weber's graphic approach facilitates a more complete analysis beyond the model solution.

A previously noted advantage of Weber's graphic method is that nonlinear transportation costs can be handled. This can be important when the mode of transportation has a high fixed cost. A high fixed cost generally creates a taper in transportation rates with distance.

A notable disadvantage of Weber's approach limits it from gaining widespread use as a technique for locating multiple facilities. The method is computationally burdensome when many market and supply points are encountered.

GRID MODEL

The grid model[4] overcomes some of the computational difficulties noted above and is perhaps the easiest of all single facility location models to use. The method gives a good first approximation to a least-cost solution and will give the optimum single facility location when there is perfect symmetry in the arrangement of market and supply points; that is, the points form the pattern of a perfect square, equilateral triangle, regular polygon, etc., and the mathematical product of demand times the transportation rate is equal for all points. Vergin and Rogers estimate that on the average the grid method will give results that are 6.2 percent higher than the optimal location costs.[5] A 6 percent error may be worth accepting for the benefits of a simple and easy-to-use location methodology.

Example. Consider the problem of two plants supplying the warehouse of Limited Distributors, Inc., which in turn supplies three demand centers. The spatial arrangement of the plants and market points is shown in Fig. 8-3 and we seek the location for the single warehouse that will minimize transportation costs. A grid overlay on a highway map is used as a convenience in establishing the relative location of each point. Each location may be expressed as a geometric coordinate point, which is useful for analytical purposes. Although a grid overlay and coordinate system is very appealing, it must be cautioned that when the distribution network is extensive, say, for example, that it covers the continental United States, some distortions and resulting errors in distance computations may occur. This is due to laying a plane over a sphere. The extent of the distortion depends on the particular map projection on which the grid coordinates are constructed.[6]

Different volumes of the same product (A & B) are sold on a per-hundred-weight basis. The truck mode is used for both inbound and outbound movement from the warehouse, though movement into the warehouse is in truckload (TL) quantities, whereas the outbound movement is in less than truckload (LTL) quantities. On outbound movement the products move together and carry the same class rate. Demand, transportation rates, and location coordinates are summarized in Table 8-1.

---

[4] See Donald J. Bowersox, "An Analytical Approach to Warehouse Location," *Handling & Shipping*, Vol. 2 (February 1962), pp. 17–20; and Edward W. Smykay and Ward A. Fredericks, "An Index Based Method for Evaluating Warehouse Locations," *Transportation Journal* (Fall 1963), pp. 30–34.

[5] Roger C. Vergin and Jack D. Rogers, "An Algorithm and Computational Procedure for Locating Economic Facilities," *Management Science*, Vol. 13 (February 1967), pp. B-240–B-254.

[6] For a discussion of various map projection techniques and associated problems, see Erwin Raisz, *General Cartography* (New York: McGraw-Hill Book Company, Inc., 1948).

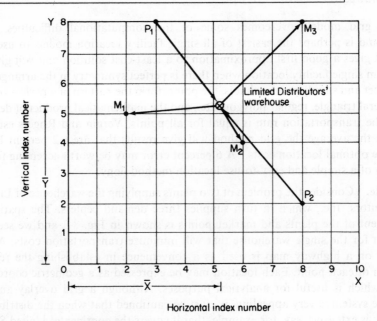

FIGURE 8-3

Location map of plants P_1 and P_2 and markets M_1, M_2, and M_3 for Limited Distributors, Inc., with the grid model location noted by X

Horizontal index number

Scale: 1 = 10 miles

TABLE 8-1

Volume, transportation costs, and grid index numbers for market and supply points (Limited Distributors)

(i)	Point (i)	Product(s)	Total Volume Moving V_i (cwt)	Transportation Cost, ($/cwt/mi)[a]	Grid Index Number X_i	Y_i
1	P_1	A	2000	$0.05	3	8
2	P_2	B	3000	0.05	8	2
3	M_1	A & B	2500	0.075	2	5
4	M_2	A & B	1000	0.075	6	4
5	M_3	A & B	1500	0.075	8	8

[a] Determined by dividing a representative quoted rate ($/cwt) by the distance (miles) over which the rate applies.

The center of gravity for the network is found by solving the following independent expressions for the coordinates of the warehouse $(\bar{X}, \bar{Y})$ to be located.

$$\bar{X} = \frac{\Sigma_i V_i R_i X_i}{\Sigma_i V_i R_i} \qquad (8.1)$$

and

$$\bar{Y} = \frac{\Sigma_i V_i R_i Y_i}{\Sigma_i V_i R_i} \tag{8.2}$$

where

V_i = volume (in cwt) flowing from (to) point i.
R_i = transportation rate (in \$/cwt/mi) to ship V_i from (to) point i.
X_i, Y_i = coordinate points or index numbers for point i.
$\bar{X}, \bar{Y}$ = coordinate point or index number for the warehouse.

Solving for the warehouse location in the horizontal direction $\bar{X}$, we have

$$\bar{X} = \frac{\begin{aligned}&2000(0.05)(3) + 3000(0.05)(8) + 2500(0.075)(2) + 1000(0.075)(6)\\&+ 1500(0.075)(8)\end{aligned}}{2000(0.05) + 3000(0.05) + 2500(0.075) + 1000(0.075) + 1500(0.075)}$$
$$= 5.16$$

And solving for the warehouse location in the vertical direction $\bar{Y}$, we have

$$\bar{Y} = \frac{\begin{aligned}&2000(0.05)(8) + 3000(0.05)(2) + 2500(0.075)(5) + 1000(0.075)(4)\\&+ 1500(0.075)(8)\end{aligned}}{2000(0.05) + 3000(0.05) + 2500(0.075) + 1000(0.075) + 1500(0.075)}$$
$$= 5.18$$

The warehouse location suggested by the grid model has the coordinates $\bar{X} = 5.16$ and $\bar{Y} = 5.18$; this location is shown in Fig. 8-3. The total transportation costs are summarized in Table 8-2 and are determined by

					TABLE 8-2
			Calculation of transportation costs for grid model solution		

Col. (1) i	Col. (2) Point (i)	Col. (3) Volume V_i (cwt)	Col. (4) Transportation Cost R_i (\$/cwt/mi)	Col. (5) Distance d_i (miles)[a]	Col. (6) Cost (\$) Col. (3) × Col. (4) × Col. (5)
1	P_1	2000	0.05	35.6[b]	\$3560
2	P_2	3000	0.05	42.8	6420
3	M_1	2500	0.075	31.6	5920
4	M_2	1000	0.075	14.5	1080
5	M_3	1500	0.075	40.2	4520
				Total transportation cost	\$21,500

[a] $d_i = K[(X_i - \bar{X})^2 + (Y_i - \bar{Y})^2]^{1/2}$
[b] These distances have been rounded to the nearest 1/10 mile.

$$TC = \Sigma_i V_i R_i K[(X_i - \bar{X})^2 + (Y_i - \bar{Y})^2]^{1/2} \tag{8.3}$$

where K is a scale factor to convert index numbers to miles.

The above problem does not fit the conditions under which the grid model would give the optimum or least-cost warehouse location. The reason for this is that the grid model treats horizontal and vertical distances as independent of each other when in fact the hypotenuse of the distance triangle is the relevant distance on which to base the location analysis. This shortcoming can be overcome by formulating a more exact model, but the price paid for the more accurate model is increased computational complexity. In most cases the grid model will not produce excessive error. However, for those cases where greater precision is desired and the use of the computer can inexpensively handle the increased computational difficulties, an exact model is offered.

AN EXACT LOCATION MODEL

An exact location model begins with the total transportation cost expression shown in Equation (8.3). To find the $\bar{X}$, $\bar{Y}$ values, we can use the techniques of differential calculus, which will give the following results.[7]

$$\bar{X}^{k+1} = \frac{\Sigma_i V_i R_i X_i / D_i^k}{\Sigma_i V_i R_i / D_i^k} \tag{8.4}$$

$$\bar{Y}^{k+1} = \frac{\Sigma_i V_i R_i Y_i / D_i^k}{\Sigma_i V_i R_i / D_i^k} \tag{8.5}$$

where $D_i = [(X_i - \bar{X})^2 + (Y_i - \bar{Y})^2]^{1/2}$ and k is the iteration number. Since $\bar{X}$ and $\bar{Y}$ cannot be solved for directly because they are not independent of each other, then $\bar{X}$ and $\bar{Y}$ must be solved for by some iterative procedure, such as Newton's approximation method,[8] steepest descent method,[9] and various random

[7] The warehouse location coordinate expressions are found by taking the first partial derivatives of the total transportation cost expression with respect to $\bar{X}$ and $\bar{Y}$ and setting them equal to zero. Thus,

$$\frac{\partial TC}{\partial \bar{X}} = \Sigma_i \{ V_i R_i K(X_i - \bar{X}) / [(X_i - \bar{X})^2 + (Y_i - \bar{Y})^2]^{1/2} \} = 0$$

and

$$\frac{\partial TC}{\partial \bar{Y}} = \Sigma_i \{ V_i R_i K(Y_i - \bar{Y}) / [(X_i - \bar{X})^2 + (Y_i - \bar{Y})^2]^{1/2} \} = 0$$

Rearranging the terms in each equation yields

$$\bar{X} = \frac{\Sigma_i V_i R_i X_i / [(X_i - \bar{X})^2 + (Y_i - \bar{Y})^2]^{1/2}}{\Sigma_i V_i R_i / [(X_i - \bar{X})^2 + (Y_i - \bar{Y})^2]^{1/2}}$$

and

$$\bar{Y} = \frac{\Sigma_i V_i R_i Y_i / [(X_i - \bar{X})^2 + (Y_i - \bar{Y})^2]^{1/2}}{\Sigma_i V_i R_i / [(X_i - \bar{X})^2 + (Y_i - \bar{Y})^2]^{1/2}}$$

[8] See Thomas L. Saaty, *Mathematical Methods of Operations Research* (New York: McGraw-Hill Book Co., 1959), pp. 101–3, 106.

[9] See G. E. P. Box and K. B. Wilson, "On the Experimental Attainment of Optimum Conditions," *Journal of Royal Statistical Society, Series B*, Vol. 13, No. 1 (1951), pp. 1–45.

methods.[10] One easily understood method that is discussed here is the method of successive approximations, though it is not always the most efficient in the sense of leading quickly to the optimum solution. All of these methods search for the optimum warehouse location by converging on the solution in progressive computational steps.

Before the iterative search process toward solution can begin, initial values for $\bar{X}$, $\bar{Y}$ need to be established. An often used starting solution is the grid model or center-of-gravity solution.[11] Variations of the grid model solution have been suggested as even more efficient starting points.[12]

Continuing the previous example, we set the grid model warehouse coordinates $\bar{X}^0$ and $\bar{Y}^0$ into Equation (8.4). Thus, we have

$$\bar{X}^1 = \frac{\Sigma_i V_i R_i X_i / [(X_i - \bar{X}^0)^2 + (Y_i - \bar{Y}^0)^2]^{1/2}}{\Sigma_i V_i R_i / [(X_i - \bar{X}^0)^2 + (Y_i - \bar{Y}^0)^2]^{1/2}} \tag{8.6}$$

$$= \frac{\dfrac{2000(0.05)(3)}{\sqrt{(-2.16)^2 + (2.82)^2}} + \dfrac{3000(0.05)(8)}{\sqrt{(2.84)^2 + (-3.18)^2}} + \dfrac{2500(0.075)(2)}{\sqrt{(-3.16)^2 + (-0.18)^2}}}{\dfrac{2000(0.05)}{\sqrt{(-2.16)^2 + (2.82)^2}} + \dfrac{3000(0.05)}{\sqrt{(2.84)^2 + (-3.18)^2}} + \dfrac{2500(0.075)}{\sqrt{(-3.16)^2 + (-0.18)^2}}}$$

$$\qquad + \dfrac{1000(0.75)(6)}{\sqrt{(0.84)^2 + (-1.18)^2}} + \dfrac{1500(0.075)(8)}{\sqrt{(2.84)^2 + (2.82)^2}} \qquad + \dfrac{1000(0.075)}{\sqrt{(0.84)^2 + (-1.18)^2}} + \dfrac{500(0.075)}{\sqrt{(2.84)^2 + (2.82)^2}}$$

$$= 5.04$$

At this point X^0 is replaced with the newly computed value of $\bar{X}^1$ in the computation of $\bar{Y}^1$. That is,

$$\bar{Y}^1 = \frac{\Sigma_i V_i R_i Y_i / [(X_i - \bar{X}^1)^2 + (Y_i - \bar{Y}^0)^2]^{1/2}}{\Sigma_i V_i R_i / [(X_i - \bar{X}^1) + (Y_i - \bar{Y}^0)^2]^{1/2}} \tag{8.7}$$

$$= \frac{\dfrac{2000(0.05)(8)}{\sqrt{(-2.16)^2 + (2.82)^2}} + \dfrac{3000(0.05)(2)}{\sqrt{(2.84)^2 + (-3.18)^2}} + \dfrac{2500(0.075)(5)}{\sqrt{(-3.16)^2 + (-0.18)^2}}}{\dfrac{2000(0.05)}{\sqrt{(2.16)^2 + (2.82)^2}} + \dfrac{3000(0.05)}{\sqrt{(2.84)^2 + (-3.18)^2}} + \dfrac{2500(0.075)}{\sqrt{(-3.16)^2 + (-0.18)^2}}}$$

$$\qquad + \dfrac{1000(0.075)(4)}{\sqrt{(0.84)^2 + (-1.18)^2}} + \dfrac{1500(0.075)(8)}{\sqrt{(2.84)^2 + (2.82)^2}} \qquad + \dfrac{1000(0.075)}{\sqrt{(0.84)^2 + (-1.18)^2}} + \dfrac{1500(0.075)}{\sqrt{(2.84)^2 + (2.82)^2}}$$

$$= 5.06$$

[10] See Samuel H. Brooks, "A Discussion of Random Methods for Seeking Maxima," *Operations Research*, Vol. 6 (March–April 1958), pp. 244–51.

[11] Among those suggesting the center-of-gravity start are Leon Cooper, "Solutions of Generalized Locational Equilibrium Models," *Journal of Regional Science*, Vol. 7, No. 1 (1967), pp. 1–18; and Vergin and Rogers, *op. cit.*

[12] L. A. Goldstone, "A Further Note on Warehouse Location," *Management Science*, Vol. 15 (December 1968), pp. B-132–B-133.

This completes the first iteration with a new set of warehouse coordinate values. These new coordinates become the inputs to the next computational cycle (iteration). The iterative process is continued until the coordinate values repeat, at which point the optimum solution is found, or until the changes in successive $\bar{X}$ and $\bar{Y}$ values are so small that further computational effort is not warranted. Several additional iterations have been carried out, and the results are summarized in Table 8-3. As can be noted, for this example the grid model gives a total cost

TABLE 8-3
Summary of warehouse locations and associated total transportation costs

Iteration (k)	Warehouse Coordinates, $\bar{X}^k$, $\bar{Y}^k$	Total Cost ($)[a]
0	5.16, 5.18	$21,500
1	5.04, 5.06	21,431
2	4.99, 5.03	21,427
3	4.97, 5.03	21,426
4	4.95, 5.04	21,425
.	.	.
.	.	.
.	.	.
30	4.91, 5.06	21,425

[a] Computed from Equation (8.3).

($21,500) very close to the optimum warehouse location cost ($21,425).

SERVICE ELASTICITY OF DEMAND

The above warehouse location models have assumed that the location problem is one of minimizing costs; that is, the revenue generated by the distribution system is unaffected by warehouse location. But to the extent that warehouse location affects delivery time to the customer and the customer is sensitive to different delivery times, the effects of customer service need to be included in the location decision.

The notion of the interdependence between warehouse location and the revenue generated by the physical distribution system is appealing, though relatively little has been done to establish the exact nature of service elasticity of demand.[13] Intuitively, the more removed a warehouse is from the point of demand, the longer will be the order cycle time. The longer order cycle time will be due to the intransit component of the cycle. Since longer and more uncertain delivery times mean increased inventory carrying costs, customers are likely to allocate their purchases

[13] For a definitive study on some of the variables that are significant to developing a customer service function, see Ronald P. Willett and P. Ronald Stephenson, "Determinants of Buyer Response to Physical Distribution Service," *Journal of Marketing Research*, Vol. 6 (August, 1969), pp. 279–83.

among those competing warehouses offering the best service. Consequently, selecting warehouse locations that are distant from markets may result in the least transportation costs, but these sites may be a poor choice when revenue losses to competitors are considered in the decision.

Both the grid model and the exact model formulation have been expanded to account for the effects of delivery time. In the grid model speed is brought in as a weighting factor to differentiate various market points. The model is a simple extension of Equations (8.1) and (8.2) and can be expressed as

$$\bar{X} = \frac{\Sigma_i V_i R_i X_i / M_i}{\Sigma_i V_i R_i / M_i} \tag{8.8}$$

and

$$\bar{Y} = \frac{\Sigma_i V_i R_i Y_i / M_i}{\Sigma_i V_i R_i / M_i} \tag{8.9}$$

where

$M_i =$ the average over-the-road speed from computed warehouse location to market i and equal to d_i / t_i.

$d_i = [(X_i - \bar{X})^2 + (Y_i - \bar{Y})^2]^{1/2}$.

$t_i =$ the time from the warehouse location to market i.[14]

Since M_i depends on the distance d_i from the warehouse location that is to be determined, an iterative solution procedure is needed, such as the method of successive approximations as previously discussed, in conjunction with solving Equations (8.4) and (8.5).

A direct approach to handling customer service in a location model is to establish a revenue function and then subtract locational costs. One revenue function that has been suggested which is a blend of empirical results and the classical definition of price elasticity of demand is

$$V = V_0 b^{-at/t_0} \tag{8.10}$$

where

$V =$ the volume ordered with delivery time t.

$V_0 =$ the volume ordered with instantaneous delivery time $t = 0$.

$b =$ a constant (≥ 1) for a specific market area and market mix.

$t_0 =$ the competitor's delivery time.

$t =$ the delivery time for the firm in question.

$a =$ a proportionality factor for a specific market area.[15]

[14] This model was developed to locate a warehouse serving a number of supermarkets and is discussed in greater detail by Donald J. Bowersox, "An Analytical Approach to Warehouse Location," *Handling & Shipping*, (February 1962), pp. 17–20.

[15] This is a slightly modified version of the revenue function used in Frank H. Mossman and Newton Morton, *Logistics of Distribution Systems* (Boston: Allyn and Bacon, Inc., 1965), pp. 245–56.

This function is plotted in Fig. 8-4 and shows that sales on a warehouse decay as it is located farther from a market relative to a competing warehouse. This revenue function is highly abstract, since it does not account for such factors as delivery time variability, delivery time tradeoff with inventory availability, and the personal relationship between buyer and seller. However, the function seems to be reasonably valid in suggesting how sales are affected by at least one aspect of service. In a broader examination of customer service, Willett and Stephenson found that:

> ... buyers perceived diminishing marginal utility from constant incremental reductions in service times on orders.[16]

Hence, this simple function should be useful, at least, in location model conceptualization.

FIGURE 8-4

Total volume demanded in a market as a function of delivery time to the market relative to a competitor's delivery time

---

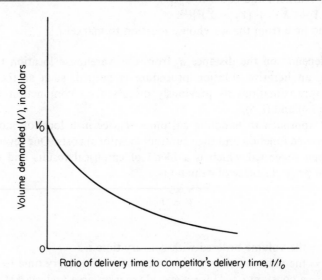

Ratio of delivery time to competitor's delivery time, t/t_o

In practice it often is not possible to develop a sophisticated mathematical representation of the customer service function because of the intangible nature of many of the customer service variables. Because of this, customer service is sometimes treated as a *constraint* which the warehouse location must meet. That is, a restriction may be placed on the warehouse location decision requiring that the warehouse be no farther than 300 miles from the markets so that one-day delivery service can be provided. Another way of handling customer service is to treat it

---

[16] Ronald P. Willett and P. Ronald Stephenson, "Customer Service: A Physical Distribution Variable," unpublished (December 1967).

as an opportunity or penalty cost. An added factor can be included in the location model which will tend to penalize location decisions in proportion to the distance or time that they are removed from the consuming points. Avoiding the difficult problem of estimating the exact nature of the customer service function has the obvious benefit of keeping the location decision problem computationally more manageable.

Ideally, warehouse location should be expressed as a profit-maximizing rather than a cost-minimizing problem. For example, using the revenue function in Equation (8.10) and the transportation cost model of Equation (8.3), we have

$$
\underset{\text{to profit}}{\text{Contribution}} = \overbrace{\sum_{i=1}^{i=3} P_i V_{0i} b_i^{-a_i t_i / t_{0i}}}^{\substack{\text{Total revenue from} \\ i \text{ markets}}} - \overbrace{\sum_{i=1}^{i=3} R_i K d_i V_{0i} b_i^{-a_i t_i / t_{0i}}}^{\substack{\text{Transportation costs} \\ \text{from warehouse to } i \text{ markets}}}
$$

$$
- \overbrace{\sum_{k=1}^{k=2} V_k' R_k' K d_k'}^{\substack{\text{Transportation cost from} \\ k \text{ plants to the warehouse}}} \tag{8.11}
$$

where

P_i = price in market i.

V_k' = volume transported from plant k to warehouse $\bar{X}, \bar{Y}$ and

$$
V_k' = \sum_i V_{0i} b_i^{-a_i t_i / t_{0i}}.
$$

R_k' = transportation rate (\$/cwt/mi) to ship V_k' from plant k to warehouse $\bar{X}, \bar{Y}$.

d_k' = distance from plant k to warehouse $\bar{X}, \bar{Y}$.

All other terms have previously been defined. Again, an iterative search procedure is needed to find the warehouse location $\bar{X}, \bar{Y}$ that will yield the highest average contribution to profit.

APPRAISAL OF SINGLE FACILITY MODELS

Of the several models that have been discussed, some offer greater realism while others are easier to handle computationally. It is clear that no single model is likely to have all of the features desired so that the solution to the model would automatically lead to a final management decision and management could merely delegate location decisions to an analyst. Therefore, these models only provide guide-line solutions, and the effective use of them requires a good understanding of their strengths as well as their shortcomings.

The benefit of these particular location models is quite clear. They aid the search for the best solution to the location problem, and they capture enough of the reality of the actual problem so that the solution is meaningful to management. The shortcomings may not be so obvious, and they need to be spelled out. Though almost any model will exhibit some shortcomings in the real problem situation, this does not mean that the model is not useful. What is important is the sensitivity that the location decision has to misrepresentations of reality. If a simplifying assumption such as linearity in transportation rates has little or no effect on where the warehouse is located and on the associated distribution costs, a simpler model will prove to be more effective from a use standpoint than a more realistic and often more complex one.

The simplifying assumptions of greatest concern are as follows. First, demand is assumed to be concentrated at a single point, when in fact demand is generated from a number of retail stores or individual customers dispersed over a wide area. The market center of gravity is often used as the demand focal point, but this is subject to error when demand is not uniformly distributed over the region. Second, these single facility location models are based on variable costs only and make no distinction between capital cost differences required for establishing a warehouse at various locations and other costs such as labor, inventory carrying costs, and utilities associated with operating a warehouse at different locations. Third, total transportation costs increase proportionately with distance. This may be a reasonable assumption if motor carrier service is used, since rates tend to be reasonably linear, at least over short distances. On the other hand, if rail service is used, the greater taper in the rate structure may require a careful examination of the linearity assumption. Fourth, straight-line routes are assumed between the warehouse and other network points. This is rarely true, but a proportionality factor can be included in the model to convert straight-line distances to highway miles, rail miles, or whatever. For example, calculated straight-line miles should be increased by 21 percent to get highway direct-route miles and by 24 percent to get rail short-line miles. Fifth, there is some concern that location models such as these are not dynamic; that is, they do not find a solution that reflects future changes in revenues and costs. A common dynamic approach is to update the location decision when economic conditions warrant. Another approach based on the dynamic programming technique is discussed in the next section on multiple facility location models. Sixth, all products are grouped into one homogeneous category, which results in a good location for all products taken together, but a potential suboptimum location for any one product in the mix.

Multiple Facility Location Models

The typical and more complex location problem occurs when two or more warehouses must be located simultaneously. This problem is typical, because most companies have a number of warehouses in their distribution system. It is complex because these warehouses cannot reasonably be treated as economically independent, and the number of possible warehouse spatial configurations becomes enormous. As an example of a large-scale distribution problem, one company of industrial cleaning compounds with annual sales of approximately $50 million sold its products in approximately 2000 counties of the United States, used 105 warehouses, and manufactured its products in four plants. There are over 800,000 possible plant-warehouse-customer alternatives if only the existing locations are used. Finding an optimum warehouse configuration is further complicated by the several hundred product items and several modes of transportation that the company uses. Problems of this magnitude strongly indicate the need for some analytical means to aid management in finding the best warehouse location configurations.

The multiple warehouse location problem breaks down into several basic questions. These are

(1) How many warehouses should there be in a distribution system?
(2) How should the demand be allocated to the warehouses?
(3) Where should the warehouses be located?
(4) What size should the warehouse be in terms of demand throughput?
(5) How should the demand be allocated to the plants in a distribution system?

A number of location models have been developed that aid in answering all or most of these questions. By necessity, all must be programmed on a large-scale computer for effective use as a management tool. These location models can be classified as (1) algorithmic, (2) simulation, or (3) heuristic types.

ALGORITHMIC MODELS

An algorithmic location model is characterized by its mathematical structure to which a solution of known accuracy can be found. Generally, such models have been limited in the number of variables that can be handled effectively. The value of such models is in knowing that the optimum location can be determined or that it can be converged upon within the scope of the model's definition.

A Calculus Model. An algorithmic model for locating multiple facilities can be developed as an extension of the exact formulation for a single location model in Equation (8.3).[17] As a cost-minimizing model, the model is

$$TC = \sum_{j=1}^{m} \sum_{i=1}^{n} V_{ij} R_{ij} K[(\bar{X}_j - X_i)^2 + (\bar{Y}_j - Y_i)^2]^{1/2} \tag{8.12}$$

where there are $j = 1, 2, \ldots, m$ warehouses to be located and there are $i = 1, 2, \ldots, n$ supply and market points. V_{ij} is the volume flowing from plant to warehouse and from warehouse to customer, R_{ij} is the transportation rate on a per-unit distance basis, X_i, Y_i are the coordinates of the supply and market points, $\bar{X}_j$,

---

[17] This model has also been extended to include the effect of cost nonlinearities in Leon Cooper, "An Extension of the Generalized Weber Problem," *Journal of Regional Science*, Vol. 8, No. 2 (1968), pp. 181–97.

$\bar{Y}_j$ are location coordinates for the warehouses, and K is a constant to convert coordinate-based distances to miles. Using calculus techniques[18] yields

$$\bar{X}_j^{k+1} = \frac{\sum_{i=1}^{n} V_{ij} R_{ij} X_i / D_{ij}^k}{\sum_{i=1}^{n} V_{ij} R_{ij} / D_{ij}^k} \qquad j = 1, 2, \ldots, m \qquad (8.13)$$

and

$$\bar{Y}_j^{k+1} = \frac{\sum_{i=1}^{n} V_{ij} R_{ij} Y_i / D_{ij}^k}{\sum_{i=1}^{n} V_{ij} R_{ij} / D_{ij}^k}$$

where

$$D_{ij} = [(\bar{X}_j - X_i)^2 + (\bar{Y}_j - Y_i)^2]^{1/2}$$

and k is the iteration number.

These equations can be solved by the method of successive approximations that previously was discussed. The solution will give the best locations for a given number of warehouses and a given allocation of demand and supply to the potential warehouses. Since this method does not automatically increase or decrease the number of warehouses in the system, then alternate numbers of warehouses and supply-demand allocations will need to be suggested and the solution procedure repeated.

EXAMPLE. Suppose that four west-coast demand centers are to be supplied by warehouses on the west coast. The factory supplying the warehouses is located in the eastern United States, so the effect of warehouse inbound transportation costs are the same throughout the area and can be neglected. The coordinate locations and the annual volume demanded by each location are shown in Fig. 8-5. The transportation rate for all points is $1/unit/100 miles.

The solution procedure begins with several judgmental decisions. The first is the number of warehouses to be analyzed. In this limited example we might have as few as one, but no more than four (one in each market). For illustrative purposes, two warehouses will be used. Second, once the number of warehouses has been established, the next decision is to assign markets to them. Since the final warehouse sites are not yet known, only a guess can be made as to their locations. Assuming that the warehouses might be finally located in the neighborhood of coordinates (5, 5) and (7, 10), we might then assign markets to the nearest warehouse. Hence, markets M_1 and M_2 would be assigned to the first warehouse location (5, 5) and markets M_3 and M_4 would be assigned to the second warehouse location (7, 10). This market assignment may have to be adjusted and the solution procedure repeated once the warehouse locations have been determined.

Given the number of warehouses and the market assignments to these warehouses, the coordinate points for each warehouse are determined by solving for the location as separate and independent problems. Hence, the problem

---

[18] Take the partial derivatives with respect to $\bar{X}_j$ and $\bar{Y}_j$, set equal to zero, and rearrange terms.

FIGURE 8-5

Four retail stores located on a grid map with two warehouses to serve them

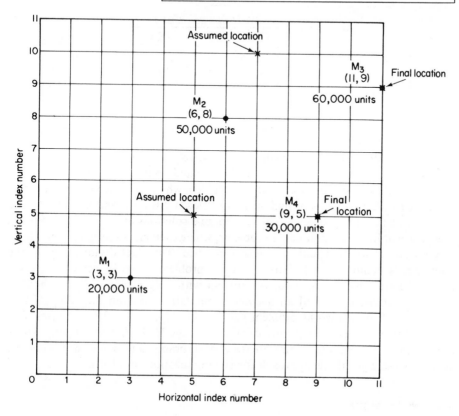

Scale: 1 = 100 miles

reduces to solving two single warehouse location problems. Table 8-4 summarizes the solution procedure beginning with an initial solution ($k = 0$) provided by a grid model solution and using the method of successive approximations to search for the optimum solution.

However, this analysis alone does not lead to very useful results until inventory costs are balanced with transportation costs. Since the model includes only transportation cost factors, minimum transportation costs occur with the maximum number of warehouses possible, which is four in this case. Inventory costs may be introduced outside the model and added to transportation costs. The minimum of the sum indicates the best warehouse location pattern. Table 8-5 summarizes such computations and shows that two warehouses located at coordinates (11, 9) and (9, 5) would be the best initial choice for warehouse locations, given that inventory carrying costs are $500,000\sqrt{N}$, where N is the number of warehouses.

TABLE 8-4

Computational example of the two-warehouse location problem shown in Figure 8-5

| Iteration (k) | Warehouse Coordinates | | Total Cost |
	$\bar{X}_1^k, \bar{Y}_1^k$	$\bar{X}_2^k, \bar{Y}_2^k$	
0	8.72, 8.54	6.60, 4.20	$429,917
1	8.95, 8.59	7.15, 4.38	421,799
2	9.16, 8.63	7.62, 4.54	414,589
.	.	.	.
.	.	.	.
.	.	.	.
∞	11.00, 9.00	9.00, 5.00	$381,458

Branch-and-Bound Models. Another and relatively new algorithmic approach to the facilities location problem is that of branch and bound. The location problem is formulated as an integer-programming problem which may include fixed charges associated with a facility's being "open" or "closed." Branch and bound refers to the way in which the problem is solved. Optimal solutions are achieved by solving a sequence of linear programming problems, where each moves progressively closer to the optimal solution until it is finally reached. The chief disadvantage of the approach is computational. Large location problems become prohibitively expensive to treat by this method. A problem with only 4 plants, 50 warehouses, and 200 customers required an average computation time on the IBM 7094 of 10 minutes.[19] A real-world problem can involve 15 plants, 40 warehouses, and 4000 customers, as is subsequently discussed for the H. J. Heinz Company. However, as more efficient algorithms are developed, branch and bound will become a very valuable algorithmic approach for solving location problems.[20]

SIMULATION MODELS

For the purposes of warehouse location, a simulation model refers to a mathematical representation of the distribution system in terms of simple algebraic and logic statements that are manipulated with the aid of a computer. There are important reasons for the popularity of simulations as managerial decision-making aids. The simulation model usually replicates reality to a much better degree and requires fewer approximations than does a comparable algorithmic model. A primary purpose of a warehouse location simulation is to evaluate various locational patterns in the hope of finding the most economical configurations. Simulation models are unlike algorithmic location models, in that the analyst or manager

---

[19] M. A. Efroymson and T. L. Ray, "A Branch-Bound Algorithm for Plant Location," *Operations Research* (May-June 1966), pp. 361–68.

[20] Some encouragement in this regard has been offered by B. M. Khumawala and D. C. Whybark, "A Comparison of some Recent Warehouse Location Techniques," *The Logistics Review*, Vol. 7, No. 31 (Spring 1971), pp. 3–19.

TABLE 8-5

Analysis of transportation cost and inventory cost tradeoffs for various warehouse combinations in example problem

Number of Warehouses N	Best Assignment of Markets to N Warehouses[a]	Minimum Outbound Transportation Cost Locations	Total Outbound Transportation Costs[b]	Inventory Carrying Costs[d]	Total Costs
1	M_1, M_2, M_3, M_4	8.09, 7.44	$519,505	$500,000	$1,019,505
2	$M_1, M_2; M_3, M_4$	6, 8; 11, 9	141,161	707,000	848,161 ←
3	$M_3; M_4; M_1, M_2$	11, 9; 9, 5; 6, 8	6,997	865,000	871,997
4	$M_1; M_2; M_3; M_4$	3, 3; 6, 8; 11, 9; 9, 5	0[c]	1,000,000	1,000,000

a The minimum cost combination of markets to the given number of warehouses.
b Inbound transportation costs are not included, since the location decision is not sensitive to them.
c No delivery costs are assumed to be incurred when the warehouse is located in a market. This neglects any local delivery costs.
d Computed as $500,000 $\sqrt{N}$.

must supply the locational patterns to be evaluated; the model itself does not seek the best solution. Whether optimal or nearly optimal locational patterns are uncovered depends on the set of warehouse configurations selected for evaluation. There is no guarantee that the optimum configuration is contained in this set.

One of the best-known simulations of a physical distribution system was developed for the H. J. Heinz Company[21] and later applied to the distribution problems of The Nestlé Company. The simulation provided answers to the basic warehouse location questions (number, location, allocation of demand to warehouses, etc.) and could handle up to 4000 customers, 40 warehouses, and 10 to 15 factories. Contrasted with the above algorithmic models, the simulation model has a much broader scope. The major distribution cost elements included in the Heinz Company simulation are

1. The customers
   The characteristics of the customers that affect distribution costs are
   a. Customer location
   b. Annual volume of demand
   c. The types of products purchased. Different products fall into various commodity classifications and will, therefore, call for different freight rates. When there are regional variations in product mix, as was the case in both studies reported here, an average rate for all products will not do.
   d. The distribution of the size of orders. Different size shipments call for different freight rates.

2. Warehouses
   The characteristics of the warehouses that affect costs are
   a. Fixed investment in company-owned warehouses. Some companies prefer public warehousing, implying a relatively small fixed investment.
   b. Fixed annual operation and administrative costs.
   c. Variable costs of storing, handling, stock rotation, and data processing.

3. Factories
   The location of the factories and the products available at each factory are the elements that most affect distribution costs. Certain warehousing and handling charges at the factory may be properly attributable to distribution costs, but insofar as these costs are largely independent of the warehouse configuration, they may be excluded from the analysis.

4. Transportation costs
   The freight costs of moving product from factory to warehouse are termed "transportation" costs. These depend on the location of the factory and warehouse involved, the size of the shipment, and the commodity classification of the product.

[21] Harvey N. Shycon and Richard B. Maffei, "Simulation–Tool for Better Distribution," *Harvard Business Review*, Vol. 39, No. 6 (November–December 1960), pp. 65–75. A simulation of more recent development is reported in Edward W. Smykay, "Anatomy of a Ready-Made PD Simulation Program," *Handling & Shipping*, Vol. 9 (February 1968), pp. 62–64; (April 1968), pp. 76–77; and (July 1968), pp. 55–57.

5. Delivery costs
   The costs of moving the product from warehouse to customer, termed "delivery" costs, depend upon the size of shipment, the location of the warehouse and customer, and the commodity classification of the product.[22]

The general computer processing procedure was first to introduce the computer source program representing the simulation model into the computer. Next, customer data and warehouse locations were read in. The computer manipulates the data according to the programmed instructions and gives results of the calculations and comparisons in the form of output.

More specifically, data processing was handled in two parts. First, a preprocessing program separated customer orders that could be filled via a warehouse from those orders that were sufficiently large to be economically filled directly from a plant. Next, the test or main program computes distances from customers to warehouses and plants to warehouses from a longitude-latitude coordinate system.[23] Customers were assigned to warehouses by examining the five closest warehouses and then selecting the warehouse offering the least cost in terms of delivery costs from warehouse to customer, handling and storage at the warehouse, and transportation costs from plant to warehouse. The computer then performed the necessary computations to evaluate a particular warehouse configuration, given the assigned product flows through the warehouse system and geographical data read into the test program. A linear programming approach was used to resolve any capacity limitations at the factories. The test run was repeated for as many warehouse location configurations as were desired to be evaluated. Fig. 8-6 gives a flow diagram of the model's operation.

A shortcoming of warehouse location simulation as a decision-making aid lies in the method of selecting the number of warehouses and their locations. That is, warehouse configurations are supplied externally to the model by management instead of the model's providing a search routine to find the best or near-optimum configuration within the scope of the model. Thus, simulations are somewhat cumbersome to use, since repeated computer runs must be made in order to establish good location patterns, which is not necessarily the most efficient use of computer time. The effectiveness of simulations depends heavily on management's ability to suggest near-optimum warehouse location configurations for evaluation.

Simulation models and algorithmic models possess different characteristics. Simulation models offer good flexibility in modeling the problem but are not very effective for searching out optimum or near-optimum location patterns for large-scale location problems. On the other hand, algorithmic models are generally

[22] Martin L. Gerson and Richard B. Maffei, "Technical Characteristics of Distribution Simulators," *Management Science*, Vol. 10 (October 1963), pp. 62–69.

[23] This coordinate system limits errors between actual and computed distances to about two percent. For the grid reference systems such as Picadad and the REA Express system, see Donald J. Bowersox, Edward W. Smykay and Bernard J. LaLonde, *Physical Distribution Management* (New York: The Macmillan Company, 1968), pp. 92–99.

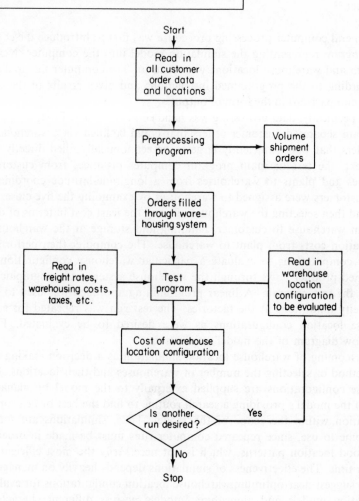

FIGURE 8-6

Flow chart for a warehouse location simulation developed for the H. J. Heinz Company

Start

Read in all customer order data and locations

Preprocessing program → Volume shipment orders

Orders filled through ware-housing system

Read in freight rates, warehousing costs, taxes, etc. → Test program ← Read in warehouse location configuration to be evaluated

Cost of warehouse location configuration

Is another run desired?   Yes

No

Stop

Source: Harvey Shycon and Richard B. Maffei, "Simulation—Tool for Better Distribution," *Harvard Business Review*, Vol. 38 (November-December 1960), p. 73.

efficient in locating optimum or near-optimum warehouse locations, but the scope of the problem that can be handled is limited by the mathematical procedures available to solve the problem. It is clear that a more powerful analytical tool would be available if the best of these model types could be merged. The heuristic model attempts to do just this.

HEURISTIC MODELS

A heuristic has been referred to as "any principle or device that contributes to the reduction in the average search to a solution"[24] and sometimes as a rule of thumb that guides problem solving. More broadly, heuristic decision making represents a way of approaching a decision that contrasts sharply with the more "conventional" approach to problem solving. The conventional approach refers to the process of first solving an abstract model of a problem and then using managerial judgment to modify the model solution in order to effect a final, practical solution to the problem. This procedure recognizes that the model does not adequately reflect all the important variables, but does give an initial solution that is useful in narrowing the search for a final solution. Heuristic decision making turns the conventional approach around by calling on management or the analyst to provide some rules of thumb or heuristics that will substantially reduce the number of alternatives that need to be examined *before* analysis begins and that will guide the search for solution toward an optimum termination. Solving a heuristic model involves searching only those alternatives that finally would be considered as practical. The heuristic approach cannot guarantee that the optimum solution will be found, any more than a simulation approach can. However, with the use of heuristics to guide the search among alternatives, near-optimum solutions often result. Sometimes optimum solutions can be achieved, depending on the quality of the heuristics used.

Kuehn-Hamburger Model.[25]   Kuehn and Hamburger have developed a computer program that will determine the number and location of warehouses in a large-scale distribution network. The construction of the model closely resembles a simulation model like that for the Heinz Company, but it also contains at least three important heuristics that are used to reduce the combinatorial difficulty of the problem and to guide the model toward an optimal solution. The heuristics used can be paraphrased as follows:

(1) Locations with the greatest promise are those at or near concentrations of demand.
(2) Near-optimum warehousing systems can be developed if at each stage the warehouse offering the greatest cost savings is added.
(3) Only a small subset of all possible warehouse locations needs to be evaluated to determine which warehouse should be added.[26]

[24] A. Newell, J. C. Shaw, and H. A. Simon, "The Processes of Creative Thinking," The RAND Corporation Paper, P-1320, (August 1958), p. 22.

[25] Alfred A. Kuehn and Michael J. Hamburger, "A Heuristic Program for Locating Warehouses," *Management Science* (July 1963), pp. 643–66. For an extension of this model, see E. F. Feldman, A. Lehrer, and T. L. Ray, "Warehouse Location Under Continuous Economies of Scale," *Management Science*, Vol. 12 (May 1966), pp. 670–84.

[26] Kuehn and Hamburger, *op. cit.*, p. 645.

The first heuristic recognizes that many sites have a very low probability of being acceptable. Such sites might be restricted for commercial use, undeveloped in terms of adequate resources to operate the warehouse, or politically unattractive. Specifically, the heuristic points the analysis directly toward population centers as potential warehouse locations. This greatly reduces the number of warehouse sites that needs to be examined. The remaining two heuristics guide the solution procedure so that all warehouse site combinations do not have to be examined. That is, warehouses are added to the warehouse configuration one at a time, and the warehouse added at each stage is the one contributing the greatest cost reduction. Of those warehouses not yet in the configuration, only a few need to be evaluated in detail for one to decide which warehouse to add. A flow diagram of the computational procedure used is shown in Fig. 8-7.

The Kuehn-Hamburger warehouse location model is one of the most comprehensive available today. Because of this, it is of value to note what has been included in the model and its formulation. The important features contained in the model are

(1) Multiple products.
(2) Fixed and variable warehousing costs.
(3) Warehouse capacity.
(4) Factory capacity.
(5) Effect of delivery time on customer service.
(6) Actual transportation rates.

The complete mathematical statement of the problem is as follows:

$X_{h,i,j,k}$ = the quantity of good h ($h = 1, \ldots, p$) shipped from factory i ($i = 1, \ldots, q$) via warehouse j ($j = 1, \ldots, r$) to customer k ($k - 1, \ldots, s$).

$A_{h,i,j}$ = the per-unit transportation cost of shipping good h from factory i to warehouse j.

$B_{h,j,k}$ = the per-unit transportation cost of shipping good h from warehouse j to customer k.

$C_{h,j}(\sum_{i,k} X_{h,i,j,k})$ = total cost of warehouse operation associated with processing good h at warehouse j. Without loss of generality we may express this function as the sum of $S_{h,j}$ and F_j defined below.

$D_{h,k}(T_{h,k})$ = explicit or imputed cost due to a delay of T time units in delivery of good h to customer k. When the customer imposes a maximum delivery time (constraint), D becomes infinite whenever the indicated time limit is reached.

F_j = fixed cost per time period of operating warehouse j. Note that this is a planned fixed cost to be incurred and not a sunk cost.

$S_{h,j}(\sum_{i,k} X_{h,i,j,k})$ = semivariable cost of operating warehouse j per unit of good h processed, including variable handling and administrative costs, storage costs, taxes, interest on investment,

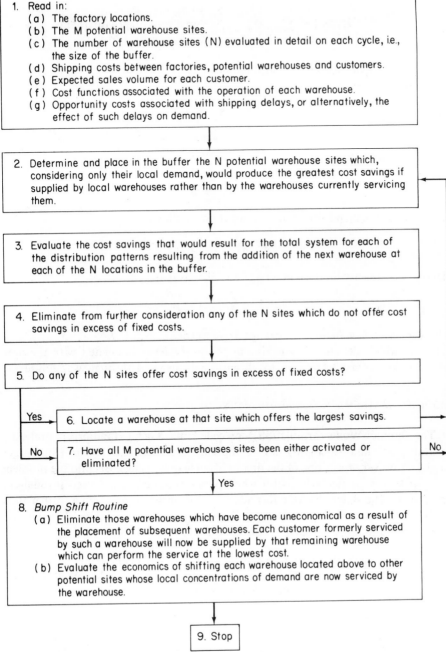

FIGURE 8-7

Flow diagram of the solution procedure in the Kuehn-Hamburger
heuristic program for locating warehouses

1. Read in:
   (a) The factory locations.
   (b) The M potential warehouse sites.
   (c) The number of warehouse sites (N) evaluated in detail on each cycle, i.e.,
       the size of the buffer.
   (d) Shipping costs between factories, potential warehouses and customers.
   (e) Expected sales volume for each customer.
   (f) Cost functions associated with the operation of each warehouse.
   (g) Opportunity costs associated with shipping delays, or alternatively, the
       effect of such delays on demand.

2. Determine and place in the buffer the N potential warehouse sites which,
   considering only their local demand, would produce the greatest cost savings if
   supplied by local warehouses rather than by the warehouses currently servicing
   them.

3. Evaluate the cost savings that would result for the total system for each of
   the distribution patterns resulting from the addition of the next warehouse at
   each of the N locations in the buffer.

4. Eliminate from further consideration any of the N sites which do not offer cost
   savings in excess of fixed costs.

5. Do any of the N sites offer cost savings in excess of fixed costs?

Yes → 6. Locate a warehouse at that site which offers the largest savings.

No → 7. Have all M potential warehouses sites been either activated or
         eliminated?   No

↓ Yes

8. *Bump Shift Routine*
   (a) Eliminate those warehouses which have become uneconomical as a result of
       the placement of subsequent warehouses. Each customer formerly serviced
       by such a warehouse will now be supplied by that remaining warehouse
       which can perform the service at the lowest cost.
   (b) Evaluate the economics of shifting each warehouse located above to other
       potential sites whose local concentrations of demand are now serviced by
       the warehouse.

9. Stop

Source: Redrawn from Alfred A. Kuehn and Michael J. Hamburger, "A Heuristic Program for Locating
Warehouses," *Management Science*, Vol. 9 (July 1963), pp. 643–66.

pilferage, and so on (the homogeneous portion of the very general function $C_{h,j}$).

$Q_{h,k}$ = quantity of good h demanded by customer k.

W_j = capacity of warehouse j.

$Y_{h,i}$ = capacity of factory i to produce good h.

Z_j = 1 if $\sum_{h,i,k} X_{h,i,j,k} > 0$ and zero otherwise (that is, $\sum Z_j$ = the number of warehouses used).

The problem then becomes one of minimizing total distribution costs, an objective function of the form

$$f(X) = \sum_{h,i,j,k}(A_{h,i,j} + B_{h,j,k})X_{h,i,j,k} + \sum_j F_j Z_j$$
$$+ \sum_{h,j}S_{h,j}(\sum_{i,k} X_{h,i,j,k}) + \sum_{h,k} D_{h,k}(T_{h,k}),$$

subject to constraints of the following form:

$$\sum_{i,j} X_{h,i,j,k} = Q_{h,k}$$

(customer k's demand for product h must be supplied),

$$\sum_{j,k} X_{h,i,j,k} \leqq Y_{h,i}$$

(factory i's capacity limit on good h cannot be exceeded),

$$I_j(\sum_{h,i,k} X_{h,i,j,k}) \leqq W_j$$

(the capacity of warehouse j cannot be exceeded), where $I_j(\sum_{h,i,j} X_{h,i,j,k})$ is a function which denotes the maximum inventory level associated with the flow of all goods from all factories to all customers serviced through warehouse j.[27]

MODIFIED MATHEMATICAL PROGRAMMING

The Baumol-Wolfe formulation[28] preceded the Kuehn-Hamburger model by several years and is slightly less comprehensive than the Kuehn-Hamburger model. However, it was one of the first to bring warehousing costs into the problem analysis and is particularly useful when public warehouses are used throughout the system. The Baumol-Wolfe formulation uses linear programming (rather than decision rules) for finding the best warehouse location configuration. The use of a linear programming approach is appealing for several reasons:

(1) The method is based on the rigor of mathematical proofs.
(2) Linear programming routines are readily available, so the job of programming for computer analysis is reduced.

[27] *Ibid*, pp. 657–58.

[28] This section adapted from William J. Baumol and Philip Wolfe, "A Warehouse-Location Problem," *Operations Research*, Vol. 6 (March-April 1958), pp. 252–63.

(3) Efficient linear programming routines permit the model also to be economical in its use of computer time for fairly large problems.
(4) The logic of the method is easily understood.
(5) The model can be developed by an analytical group within the firm.

For these reasons it is of value to examine the Baumol-Wolfe model as an alternative to the Kuehn-Hamburger type of approach.

The Baumol-Wolfe model is a blend of algorithmic and heuristic procedures and might logically be classified as either type. It is classified here as heuristic because the effectiveness of the model greatly depends on the set of potential warehouse sites that are presented to the model for evaluation. The model does not and cannot evaluate every possible warehouse site in most realistic problems.

This model manipulates two types of costs—linear transportation costs and nonlinear warehousing costs. Transportation costs from plant to warehouse and from warehouse to customer increase linearly with volume. This assumption is reasonable if the rate breaks between LTL and TL, LCL and CL, etc. are not too great and the taper in the rate structure is not too pronounced. Warehousing costs exhibit nonlinearities from at least two sources. First, the fixed costs of operating a warehouse when spread over increasing volume show some economies of scale that are reflected in costs or warehousing rate structures. Second, larger inventories do not require proportionately larger safety stocks. So, as volume is decreased in the warehouses by increasing the number of warehouses in the distribution system, the costs for supporting the inventories will increase but at a decreasing rate. Fig. 8-8 shows this effect when demand is constant and all warehouses have equal throughput.

FIGURE 8-8

Effect on total warehousing costs of increasing the number of warehouses in the logistics system for a given level of demand

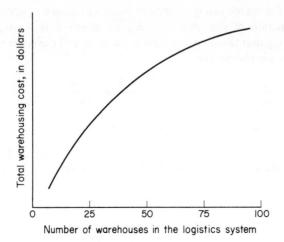

Number of warehouses in the logistics system

Example. Understanding the Baumol-Wolfe model can best be accomplished through the solution of a small-scale problem. Consider the problem of determining the number, location, and size of warehouses and of the demand to be assigned to both plants and warehouses for eight demand points r, two factories f, and five potential warehouse sites w shown in Fig. 8-9. Each factory can produce up to 40

FIGURE 8-9

Spatial arrangement of factories f, potential warehouses w, and retailers r in the example problem

---

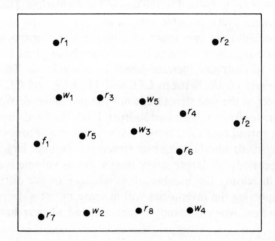

and 50 units, respectively. There is no effective capacity limits on warehouses, since public warehousing is used. The units demanded by the retailers r are

$r =$	1	2	3	4	5	6	7	8
demand $=$	10	10	10	15	5	15	10	15

The total cost for warehousing z units at each warehouse is approximated by a square-root function of the form $C = K\sqrt{z_w}$, where K is a constant and z_w is the annual throughput (loading) on warehouse w. Specifically, the warehouse cost relationships by warehouse are

$w =$	1	2	3	4	5
cost $=$	$75\sqrt{z_1}$	$80\sqrt{z_2}$	$75\sqrt{z_3}$	$80\sqrt{z_4}$	$70\sqrt{z_5}$

The marginal warehousing cost at each warehouse is[29]

[29] The marginal warehousing cost functions are found by taking the first derivative of total warehousing cost C with respect to the warehouse volume z. For example,

$$C = 75\sqrt{z_1}$$

The derivative of C is

$$\frac{dC}{dz_1} = \frac{1}{2} \cdot 75 \frac{1}{\sqrt{z_1}} = \frac{75\sqrt{z_1}}{2z_1}$$

$w =$	1	2	3	4	5
marginal cost $=$	$\dfrac{75\sqrt{z_1}}{2z_1}$	$\dfrac{80\sqrt{z_2}}{2z_2}$	$\dfrac{75\sqrt{z_3}}{2z_3}$	$\dfrac{80\sqrt{z_4}}{2z_4}$	$\dfrac{70\sqrt{z_5}}{2z_5}$

The transportation cost in dollars per unit between factories f and warehouses w is in the following matrix which we will call A.

$f =$	$w =$	1	2	3	4	5
	1	7	7	8	12	11
	2	14	12	9	6	8

Similarly, the transportation costs in dollars per unit between warehouses w and retailers r are

$w =$	$r =$	1	2	3	4	5	6	7	8
	1	5	11	3	8	5	10	11	11
	2	14	16	8	9	4	7	4	4
	3	10	11	3	5	2	5	9	5
	4	15	13	9	6	7	2	10	2
	5	9	7	3	2	6	5	12	8

This matrix we will call B.

The solution procedure is an iterative one, where we first solve the location problem based on transportation costs alone; that is, we initially assume warehousing costs are zero. Next, we add marginal warehousing costs determined for the warehouse volumes from the previous iteration to the transportation costs. The computations are again carried out. Additional iterations are performed until the warehouse loadings do not change from one iteration to the next. Now, consider the procedure in more detail.

Form a three-dimensional matrix of transportation costs to specify the total transportation cost of moving units from any factory to any warehouse to any customer. This matrix is found by adding together the costs from the factory-warehouse and warehouse-customer transportation cost matrices. For example, the transportation cost for one unit moving from factory 1 through warehouse 1 to retailer 1 is 7 (northwest corner element in matrix A) plus 5 (northwest corner element in matrix B) for a total of 12. Other elements in the three-dimensional matrix are developed in a similar fashion, different route combinations being used. The completed matrix, displayed in two parts to show the hidden elements, is given in Fig. 8-10.

INITIAL CYCLE

The initial computational cycle begins with the cost matrix in Fig. 8-10. The first step is to find the minimum cost routes from any factory to any retailer via a particular warehouse. These routes and their associated costs are found by examining each row in Fig. 8-10 and by picking the cell with the minimum cost. For the first plant $f = 1$ and the first retailer $r = 1$ the best warehouse to ship through is

$w = 1$, since it has the lowest cost (12) of any of the five warehouses. Repeating this procedure will result in a two-dimensional cost matrix[30] and a matrix of warehouse numbers associated with these costs. That is,

		Minimum Transportation Costs from *f* to *r*										**Warehouse Numbers Associated with Minimum Costs**							
	$r =$	1	2	3	4	5	6	7	8		$r =$	1	2	3	4	5	6	7	8
$f =$	1	12	18	10	13	10	13	11	11	$f =$	1	1	5	1	5	3	3	2	2
	2	17	15	11	10	11	8	16	8		2	5	5	5	5	3	4	4	4

Next, the two-dimensional cost matrix is treated as a standard linear programming problem (transportation class), and optimum solution is through the use of the transportation algorithm. The transportation linear programming problem solution procedure is discussed in Appendix A, and only the final results are presented here. Thus, the initial cycle solution would be

$r =$		1	2	3	4	5	6	7	8	Factory Supply
$f =$	1	12 / 10	18	10 / 10	13	10 / 5	13	11 / 10	11 / 5	40
	2	17	15 / 10	11	10 / 15	11	8 / 15	16	8 / 10	50
Retail Demand		10	10	10	15	5	15	10	15	

[30] The three-dimensional transportation cost matrix can be reduced in this simple manner to a two-dimensional matrix, because there are no capacity restrictions on the warehouses. If there are capacity constraints on the warehouses, the problem can be restated in a two-dimensional form and solved as an ordinary transportation problem. For example, suppose the capacity constraints on these five warehouses are 20, 15, 10, 20, and 25, respectively. The transportation problem will have the following form:

		Warehouses					Customers								Plant & Warehouse Constraints
		1	2	3	4	5	1	2	3	4	5	6	7	8	
Plants	1	7	7	8	12	11	∞	∞	∞	∞	∞	∞	∞	∞	40
	2	14	12	9	6	8	∞	∞	∞	∞	∞	∞	∞	∞	50
	1	0	∞	∞	∞	∞	5	11	3	8	5	10	11	11	20
	2	∞	0	∞	∞	∞	14	16	8	9	4	7	4	4	15
Warehouses	3	∞	∞	0	∞	∞	10	11	3	5	2	5	9	5	10
	4	∞	∞	∞	0	∞	15	13	9	6	7	2	10	2	20
	5	∞	∞	∞	∞	0	9	7	3	2	6	5	12	8	25
Warehouse & Customer Constraints		20	15	10	20	25	10	10	10	15	5	15	10	15	

where the main body of the matrix contains the appropriate transportation costs between plants and warehouses and between warehouses and customers.

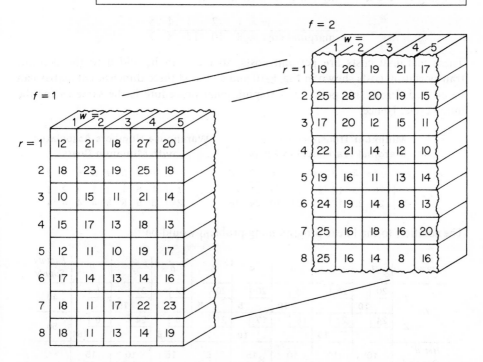

FIGURE 8-10

Matrix of transportation costs for all factory-warehouse-retailer combinations for initial computational cycle

where the solution is given in bold type. Referring back to the matrix containing the warehouse numbers, we see that the following loadings are accumulated for each warehouse. The warehousing cost is determined from the warehouse cost relationship for each warehouse and the transportation costs from the transportation cost matrix in Fig. 8-10.

		Warehouse Loadings z_w	Warehousing Cost $C = K\sqrt{z_w}$
$w =$	1	20	$336
	2	15	310
	3	5	168
	4	25	400
	5	25	350
		Warehousing cost	$1564
		Transportation cost	935
		Total cost	$2499

FIRST ITERATION

Given the above warehouse loadings, the marginal warehousing cost can be determined from the marginal warehousing cost relationships previously developed. Since warehouse loadings were initially taken as zero, marginal warehousing cost will also be zero. With the new loadings, a new estimate can be made of marginal warehousing costs. For example, the loading on warehouse 1 is 20 units, so the marginal warehousing cost is $(75/2)(\sqrt{20}/20) = 8.4$, rounded to 8. Repeating for all warehouses gives the following marginal cost matrix.

$w =$	1	2	3	4	5
marginal cost $=$	8	10	17	8	7

These marginal costs are per-unit costs, so they can be added to the per-unit transportation costs shown in Fig. 8-10 and a revised three-dimensional matrix can be created. From this point the computational procedure is the same as for the initial cycle. Hence,

Minimum Transportation & Marginal Warehousing Costs

$r =$	1	2	3	4	5	6	7	8
$f = $ 1	20	25	18	20	20	22	21	21
2	24	22	18	17	21	16	24	16

Warehouse Numbers Associated with Minimum Costs

$r =$	1	2	3	4	5	6	7	8
$f = $ 1	1	5	1	5	1	4	2	2
2	5	5	5	5	4	4	4	4

The solution to the linear programming problem would be

$r =$	1	2	3	4	5	6	7	8	Factory Supply
$f = $ 1	20 10	25	18 10	20 5	20 5	22	21 10	21	40
2	24	22 10	18	17 10	21	16 15	24	16 15	50
Retail Demand	10	10	10	15	5	15	10	15	

and the revised warehouse loadings and costs are

Warehouse Number, w	Warehouse Loadings z_w	Warehousing Costs $C = K\sqrt{z_w}$
1	25	$375
2	10	253
3	0	0
4	30	439
5	25	350
	Warehousing cost	$1417
	Transportation cost	945
	Total cost	$2362

SECOND ITERATION

New marginal warehouse costs based on warehouse loadings of the first iteration are

$w =$	1	2	3	4	5
marginal cost $=$	8	13	∞	7	7

Adding these marginal costs to the transportation costs of Fig. 8-10 develops a revised three-dimensional cost matrix. Repeating the computations based on this revised cost matrix yields

Revised Minimum Transportation & Marginal Warehousing Costs

$r =$	1	2	3	4	5	6	7	8
$f = 1$	20	25	18	20	20	21	24	21
2	24	22	18	17	20	15	23	15

Revised Warehouse Numbers Associated with Minimum Costs

$r =$	1	2	3	4	5	6	7	8
$f = 1$	1	5	1	5	1	4	2	4
2	5	5	5	5	4	4	4	4

The solution to the linear programming problem would be

$r =$	1	2	3	4	5	6	7	8	Factory Supply
$f = 1$	20	25	18	20	20	21	24	21	40
	10		10		5	5		10	
$f = 2$	24	22	18	17	20	15	23	15	50
		10		10		15		15	
Retail Demand	10	10	10	15	5	15	10	15	

The warehouse loadings are

	Warehouse Loadings z_w
$w = 1$	25
2	10
3	0
4	30
5	25

FIGURE 8-11

A possible total cost function for the warehouse location problem

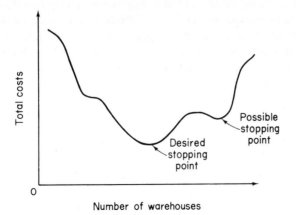

Since the warehouse loadings are identical for two successive iterations, a solution is found. That is, the marginal warehousing costs will not change, so no further cost reductions can be found by this method. The final total cost is $2326, but it should be noted that this is not necessarily the lowest possible cost that might be achieved. Because the total cost function in a complex problem of this type may have hills and valleys (Fig. 8-11), we cannot be sure that the procedure will not stop at a local optimum point. The dropping of warehouses in a sequential manner simplifies the solution of a complex problem, but it also makes the solution procedure "nearsighted" in its search for the lowest-cost warehouse configuration. This can cause the procedure to err in favor of too many warehouses rather than too few. However, the procedure does lead to substantial improvements in the design of many distribution systems.

APPRAISAL OF MULTIPLE WAREHOUSE LOCATION MODELS

Current warehouse location models like those discussed above attempt to find the least-cost warehouse configurations by trading transportation costs for warehousing or inventory costs. The large number of possible warehouse configurations to be evaluated even in small distribution networks makes the location decision a particularly difficult one, and the nature of the cost functions involved results in a complex mathematical problem that cannot be handled with complete satisfaction by current analytical techniques. However, the techniques that are discussed above show that analysis has come a long way in terms of problem definition and problem solution technique from those proposed by Weber and others. Atkins and Shriver have compared each of these multiple facility location methods, including a manual approach to their concept of the ideal analysis requirements desired by management (Table 8-6). Their appraisal provides some useful guide lines on when each type of analysis may be most appropriate.

All warehouse location methods discussed in this chapter suffer from the fact that they do not consider the impact of inventory stocking policies on the facility location decision. Inventory stocking decisions affect the average inventory level and hence the carrying costs, and the plant-to-warehouse transportation costs, which are inputs to the location decision. Conversely, the location decision affects order lead time and warehouse throughput, which are determinants of inventory policy. Thus, the future direction in facility location model development likely will be to create models that effectively trade off warehouse location configuration and inventory policy interdependencies.[31]

[31] Heskett has suggested that such comprehensive models should be temporally oriented to follow traditional inventory analysis rather than the spatial dimensions of location models. See J. L. Heskett, "Spatial and Temporal Aspects of Physical Distribution" in Peter D. Bennett (ed.), *Marketing and Economic Development*, Proceedings, American Marketing Association (Chicago: American Marketing Association, 1965), pp. 679–87.

DYNAMIC LOCATION ANALYSIS[32]

The location models discussed so far represent the type of sophisticated research that is being conducted to assist logisticians in solving warehouse location problems. Though many improvements have been made in the models to make them more representative and computationally efficient, they still remain essentially static in nature. That is, they do not provide optimal location patterns over time.

Demand and cost patterns shift over time, so implementing a location model solution today may prove to be a suboptimal warehousing configuration under tomorrow's economic conditions. Typically, the impact of changing conditions is handled in one of several pragmatic ways. First, the future conditions can be forecast over a reasonable planning horizon. One of the static location models can then be applied to the average of these data. A sensitivity analysis on the model can be applied for a reasonable range of the forecast data. A single warehouse location or a single configuration of warehouses would be selected for the entire planning horizon. The method is simple, but under dynamic conditions this average solution will produce some error. Second, it is possible continually to update a short-range model solution as conditions change sufficiently to warrant a reevaluation. This procedure is particularly appropriate (1) if forecasts cannot be made with accuracy beyond one or two years, (2) if the cost of relocating warehouses is minimal as in changing among public warehouses, and (3) if the decision to relocate requires less time to implement than the time span of an accurate forecast. However, it often requires substantial lead time to effect such location changes as land purchase, construction, lease negotiation, financing, and the time lags associated with closing down one warehousing operation and starting another. Also, it is an arbitrary decision as to how much conditions must change before the location configuration is updated.

Ideally, a model that could effectively handle data about future conditions while maintaining the scope achieved in a number of the static models is sought. None currently exists, and, because of computational difficulties, efficient models that provide optimal solutions to the problems are not likely forthcoming in the near future. However, it is possible to develop a heuristic procedure based on existing static location models that were presented earlier in this chapter. The procedure utilizes the technique of dynamic programming and gives a schedule of *when* the warehousing configuration should be changed and *to what* configuration the change should be made. It can use either single facility model results or multiple facility model results, depending on the problem under analysis.

Example. To illustrate the dynamic location procedure, consider a hypothetical but representative problem, as shown in Fig. 8-12. A plant at Granville ships to a number of markets through a single warehouse. Over time, demand is increasing and the center of gravity of demand is shifting westward. Outbound per-unit trans-

---

[32] This section is based on Ronald H. Ballou, "Dynamic Warehouse Location Analysis," *Journal of Marketing Research*, Vol. 5 (August 1968), pp. 271–76.

TABLE 8-6

Comparison of the more popular methods used in multiple warehouse location studies

Ideal Analysis Requirements Desired by Management	Conventional Manual Approach	Mathematical Simulation	Linear Programming	Heuristic Programming
1. No restriction on the number of plant and warehouse sites and the number of customers.	1. The restriction is usually simply a matter of time and manpower. In most instances gross simplifications of the problem statement are necessary.	1. There is, in effect, no theoretical limit to the size of problem that can be handled by simulation. More than a hundred potential warehouse sites, as well as thousands of customer demand centers, might be considered. This fact in itself, however, results in a tendency for analysts to incorporate too much detail in simulation models, to the extent that a study may simply bog down, or it may be no longer possible to "validate" the answers produced by the model.	1. In addition to the practical limitation in terms of the time to amass the data required, computer running time and the costs thereof can also be a limiting factor. Most often, the number of customer demand centers will be limiting, and as a general rule it will perhaps not exceed 500.	1. As with simulation, there is no theoretical limit to problem size. However, the nature of heuristic programming presupposes the use of more discretion in screening out unnecessary details than does simulation.
2. Would like it to represent explicitly any significant production or storage capacity limitations.	2. In most business systems of reasonable size it is difficult to represent adequately more than one or two capacity restrictions.	2. Capacity restrictions can be considered on an empirical or rule-of-thumb basis rather than on an optimal basis.	2. The capability to deal with capacity limitations in an optimal sense is one of the most important capabilities of linear programming.	2. Capacity restrictions can be considered on an empirical or rule-of-thumb basis, rather than on an optimal basis.
3. Would like it to be broad in scope, to include such things as the impact on inventory requirements and customer service.	3. Conventional analyses tend to be carried out along functional or single-product lines rather than interfunctional and multiproduct lines. The conclusions that result are often inconsistent and may be far from optimal for the company as a whole.	3. There is no theoretical limit to the possible scope of a simulation model. As in No. 1 above, this can be either an advantage or disadvantage, depending on the skills and experience of the analysts.	3. Another important capability of linear programming is the facility it provides for dealing with complex interactions between functions and between products in broad-scope applications.	3. Theoretically, there is no limit to the scope of a heuristic program. But there are practical limitations, primarily in terms of development effort and computer running time.

Ideal Analysis Requirements Desired by Management	Conventional Manual Approach	Mathematical Simulation	Linear Programming	Heuristic Programming
4. May wish it to reflect day-to-day scheduling problems, particularly in those situations where customers are supplied along continually changing distribution routes.	4. This is computationally impractical to consider doing by hand in most situations.	4. Simulation is probably most useful where scheduling factors are a major concern. There are, in fact, many situations where scheduling is such a predominant factor that simulation is the only reasonable alternative to conventional methods.	4. In general, linear programming cannot be used effectively to analyze complicated scheduling problems.	4. From a practical standpoint, heuristic programming is apt not to be used in situations where scheduling is important.
5. Would like it to provide the optimum solution, taking into account all of the above factors, plus the timing of investments, as well as plant and warehouse costs which may reflect increasing economies of scale.	5. Even in the rare situation where a conventional approach may produce the best possible answer to complex facility location problem, there is no assurance that the best answer has been found. Furthermore, the simplifying assumptions used are often difficult for management to accept, with the result that action may be deferred for prolonged periods.	5. The inability to proceed systematically to an optimum solution is perhaps the main drawback of simulation. Many months, or even years, may go into the development of a simulation model. Once it is developed, it must provide answers that are at least better than those obtainable by conventional analysis. While this goal is usually achieved, one never knows how much additional improvement is possible.	5. LP does produce optimum solutions for the problems as stated. However, the present state of the art does not allow the problem statement to incorporate conveniently either fixed costs or the effects of increasing economies of scale.	5. Optimum answers cannot be guaranteed, but computer-based procedures search automatically and systematically through possible decision alternatives in order to find improved solutions. As a consequence, where this approach is applicable, it should produce better solutions than can be obtained through simulation.
6. Would like to achieve all of the above objectives to the maximum possible extent in the shortest possible time and at the lowest possible cost.	6. While failing to meet any of the above requirements to the degree desired by management, conventional analyses can certainly be carried out in the shortest possible time at the lowest possible cost. Hence even minor improvements may justify the analysis many times over.	6. Simulation models for facility location planning can be an expensive and time-consuming undertaking. Typically, total costs may range from $50,000 to $100,000 or more.	6. LP is simple in its basic concepts, yet it is nonetheless one of the most sophisticated tools of management science in terms of the need for experienced, trained personnel. It is likely, therefore, to be expensive if it is to be used properly.	6. Some "canned" procedures have been developed which can be used at relatively low cost, perhaps less than $10,000 to $20,000 to carry out a study.

Source: Adapted from Robert J. Atkins and Richard H. Shriver, "New Approach to Facilities Location," Harvard Business Review, Vol. 46 (May–June 1968), pp. 72–73.

FIGURE 8-12

Plant-market location map with maximum profit warehouse location points (+) for each of five years

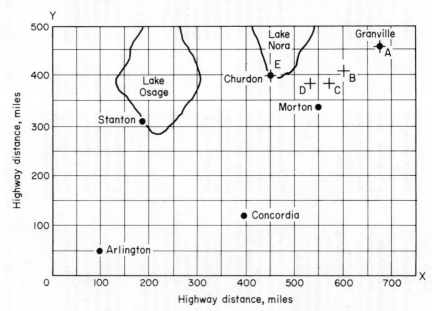

Source: Ronald H. Ballou, "Dynamic Warehouse Location Analysis," *Journal of Marketing Research*, Vol. V (August 1968), p. 273.

portation costs are higher than inbound costs, so the optimal warehouse location each year is also shifting westward. The problem is limited to a planning horizon of five years for exposition, though much longer time periods can be handled with-

TABLE 8-7

Projected discounted profits for each location in each year of the planning period with maximum profits along the main diagonal

Warehouse Location Alternatives	Year from Present				
	1st	2nd	3rd	4th	5th
A	$194,600[a]	$356,100	$623,200	$671,100	$1,336,000
B	176,500	372,000[a]	743,400	750,000	1,398,200
C	172,300	344,700	836,400[a]	862,200	1,457,600
D	166,700	337,600	756,100	973,300[a]	1,486,600
E	159,400	303,400	715,500	829,800	1,526,000[a]

[a] These alternatives are the maximum profit locations for each year of the planning period and are shown in Fig. 8-12.

Source: Ronald H. Ballou, "Dynamic Warehouse Location Analysis," *Journal of Marketing Research*, Vol. 5 (August, 1968), p. 274.

out greatly increasing computation time. Table 8-7 shows the results from applying a static location model to find the optimum warehouse location to each of the annual demand and costs as projected for each year in the planning horizon. The optimum warehouse locations throughout the five years, based on single-period data alone, are given in Fig. 8-12 and lettered *A* through *E*. These five points are the maximum profit points in each year. At this point, we state the important heuristic used in the solution procedure: *A reasonable set of location-relocation alternatives is composed of the optimum locations for each of the future periods.* Thus, the maximum profit points for the five years are listed as the alternatives in Table 8-7, and the maximum profit value is inserted into the cell intersecting that location and the year of the data. That is, the maximum profit values appear along the main diagonal of the table. The rest of the table is filled out by generating the profit level associated with each remaining location and each year's data. In this case, the static model is used to provide profit information under given locations and data inputs. The values in the table are then discounted to the present at the appropriate cost of capital to make all future profits comparable at time zero, when the location-relocation decision must be made. We also know that it costs $100,000 to change from any location configuration to another and that the cost of capital is 20 percent.

Problem Solution. Finding the best location-relocation plan requires searching Table 8-7, after accounting for the appropriate moving charges, for the maximum profit path. This is not an easy task, since even for this small problem there are $5^5 = 3125$ possible location-relocation plans. However, the technique of dynamic programming can be applied here, and it will reduce the number of required computations to find the optimum plan to $5 \times 5 = 25$. Dynamic programming permits us to recast this multiperiod problem into a series of single-decision events. According to Bellman's principle of optimality:

> In a sequence of decisions, whatever the initial decision, the remaining decisions must constitute an optimum policy for the state resulting from the initial decision.[33]

That is, an optimal path through the table considering the cost of moving from one alternative to another can be found by making a first decision, then making a second decision based on the first, then making a third decision based on the second, etc. until the complete five years have been evaluated.

Applying this technique to our problem, we begin with the last (fifth) year of the planning horizon and work backwards to the first. We ask ourselves: Given a particular alternative, should we stay in that location or should we relocate and where? To start, consider location *A*. Is it more profitable to stay at location *A* and gain $1,336,000 (see Table 8-7, location *A* and year 5), or is it better to relocate at another alternative and gain that location profit while incurring the moving

---

[33] Richard E. Bellman and Stuart E. Dreyfus, *Applied Dynamic Programming* (Printon, N. J.: Princeton University Press, 1962).

expense? The following table can be constructed to examine the profit in year 5 at location A, that is, $P_5(A)$:[34]

$$P_5(A) = \max \begin{bmatrix} A \\ B \\ C \\ D \\ E \end{bmatrix} \begin{matrix} \text{Alternative } (x) & \text{Location profit} & \text{Moving cost} & \text{Net profit} \\ \$1,336,000 & - & 0 & = & \$1,336,000 \\ 1,398,200 & - & \$48,225 & = & 1,349,975 \\ 1,457,600 & - & 48,225 & = & 1,409,375 \\ 1,486,000 & - & 48,225 & = & 1,438,375 \\ 1,526,000 & - & 48,225 & = & 1,477,775 \end{matrix}$$

The location profit for each alternative is found in Table 8-7, and the moving cost is $100,000 discounted at 20 percent for four years. The net profit for each alternative is computed as the difference between location profit and moving cost. Scanning the net profit figures for all alternatives, we see that location E has the highest profit at $1,477,775. This means that *if* we were at location A at the beginning of year 5, we should move to location E. This outcome is entered into Table 8-8 in the northeast corner [cell $P_5(D)$], and the policy is M_E (move to E). Next, a similar set of computations is carried out for location B in year 5 to determine $P_5(B)$ and its associated policy. Again the results are entered into Table 8-8. Similarly, $P_5(C)$, $P_5(D)$, and $P_5(E)$ are also analyzed.

The computations proceed to year 4, year 3, etc. For years other than year 5 the computations are slightly more complicated, since the cumulative effect of the

---

[34] The mathematical statement of this procedure is given as follows: The cumulative profit $P_j(x)$ for a portion of the planning period starting in year j and location x and following an optimal policy is given by

$$P_j(x) = \max \begin{bmatrix} S_x : P_{jx} + aP_{j+1}(x) \\ M_i : P_{ji} - F_j + aP_{j+1}(i) \\ \text{for all } i \text{ except } i = x \end{bmatrix}$$

where

x = the location being evaluated.

j = the year from present date.

i = an alternative location other than x.

$P_j(x)$ = location x in year j being evaluated.

P_{jx} or P_{ji} = discounted profits due to location from Table 8-7 for location x (or i) in year j.

$P_{j+1}(x)$ or $P_{j+1}(i)$ = profit element from Table 8-8 for location x (or i) in year $j + 1$.

F_j = discounted cost of moving at beginning of year j.

S_x = policy designation for "staying" in location x.

M_i = policy designation for "moving" to location i.

a = factor between 0 and 1 to reflect uncertainty about the future (taken as 1 for computational convenience in our example).

TABLE 8-8

Location-relocation plans for a five-year planning period with optimum cumulative discounted profits due to location for year j to year 5

Year from Present Date j

Warehouse Location Alternatives x	1st $P_1(x)$	Policy[a]	2nd $P_2(x)$	Policy[a]	3rd $P_3(x)$	Policy[a]	4th $P_4(x)$	Policy[a]	5th $P_5(x)$	Policy[a]
A	$3,719,686	S_A	$3,525,086	S_A	$3,168,986	M_C	$2,402,030	M_D	$1,477,775	M_E
B	3,717,486	S_B	3,540,986	S_B	3,168,986	M_C	2,402,030	M_D	1,477,775	M_E
C [b] →	3,755,430 →	S_C	3,583,130 →	S_C	3,238,430	S_C →	2,402,030	M_D	1,477,775	M_E
D	3,720,300	S_D	3,553,600	S_D	3,216,000	S_D	2,459,900 →	S_D →	1,486,600	S_D
E	3,659,197	S_E	3,499,797	M_C	3,168,986	M_C	2,418,800	S_E	1,526,000	S_E

[a] Policy symbol refers to "staying" S in the designated location or "moving" M to a new location as indicated.

[b] Arrows indicate maximum profit location plan when warehouse is initially located at C.

Source: Ronald H. Ballou, "Dynamic Warehouse Location Analysis," Journal of Marketing Research, Vol. 5 (August, 1968), p. 275.

subsequent years' decisions needs to be included in our computations. To illustrate, consider $P_3(D)$ in Table 8-8. The computations are as follows:

Alternative (x)	Profit due to location	Moving cost	Net cumulative profit for subsequent years $P_4(x)$	Net cumulative profit for year 5 $P_3(D)$

$$P_3(D) = \max \begin{bmatrix} A \\ B \\ C \\ D \\ E \end{bmatrix} \begin{array}{lllll} \$623{,}200 & - & \$69{,}444 & + & \$2{,}402{,}030 & = & \$2{,}955{,}786 \\ 743{,}400 & - & 69{,}444 & + & 2{,}402{,}030 & = & 3{,}075{,}986 \\ 836{,}400 & - & 69{,}444 & + & 2{,}402{,}030 & = & 3{,}168{,}986 \\ 756{,}100 & - & 0 & + & 2{,}459{,}900 & = & 3{,}216{,}000 \\ 715{,}500 & - & 69{,}444 & + & 2{,}418{,}800 & = & 3{,}064{,}856 \end{array}$$

The only difference from year 5 computations is that the cumulative profit for all subsequent years is now included. These profits are combined into a single value $P_{j+1}(X)$. In our computations for $P_3(D)$, these values are $P_4(X)$ and are represented as column 4 in Table 8-8. In the same manner as before, we choose the maximum profit alternative, which is location D. Since our assumption was that we were at location D, our policy is to stay at D, that is, S_D. The profit of \$3,216,000 and the policy of S_D are entered into the $P_3(D)$ cell of Table 8-8. Similar computations are carried out until Table 8-8 is complete.

Interpretation of Results. The best location-relocation plan is found in the profits of Table 8-8, column 1 and the policies for each year. Given that the warehouse can initially be located anywhere as in the case of a new warehouse, we prefer a plan that will yield optimum total profits throughout the entire planning horizon. Such a plan is found by searching the $P_1(X)$ column of Table 8-8 for the maximum profit level. This is to locate initially at C. The policy is to stay at C during the first year, as indicated by S_C. Moving horizontally in the table to year 2, we find that the policy is S_C. No relocation is required. Continuing to move horizontally in the table, we see that no move is required until the beginning of the fourth year, when the policy is M_D. This indicates that relocation should be to location D. We now move horizontally in row D, and no further moves are indicated. The arrows in Table 8-8 trace the plan, which for the five years should be C, C, C, D, D with a total profit of \$3,755,430.

A different plan should be followed if an existing warehouse is already located at or near one of the five alternatives noted. For example, if an existing warehouse is located at D, the best plan under this condition would be D, D, D, D, D, as found by tracing the policies through Table 8-8 beginning in row D. No relocations are suggested, since the gain in profits achieved by a move is more than outweighed by the cost of moving. The profit for this plan is $P_1(D) = \$3,720,300$, slightly lower than that for the previously noted plan, where $P_1(C) = \$3,755,430$. Note that there is no benefit to moving at time zero, since a moving cost of \$100,000 would be incurred against a savings of $P_1(C) - P_1(D) = \$35,130$.

Conditions and Extensions. The example above is hypothetical, and to apply the technique in the real world requires an understanding of the conditions on which the technique is developed. Several of these are discussed.

SELECTION OF ALTERNATIVES. It has been taken as a heuristic rule that the optimal location of a single warehouse or the configuration of multiple warehouses during each period serves as a possible alternative in the problem. The alternatives to be evaluated need not be limited to these. An existing location or configuration of warehouses may serve as an additional alternative. Other alternatives that management may find particularly attractive may also be added to the list for evaluation.

PLANNING HORIZON AND FORECAST ACCURACY. Choosing the appropriate planning horizon depends on the magnitude of future sales, the discount rate, and the accuracy of the forecasts. Each reflects on the importance or the validity of any future period. Increasing profits will tend to increase the importance of future periods, while high discount rates diminish the impact of future profits rapidly. Though a clear cutoff point on the number of years to include in the planning horizon is not available, a comparison of the magnitude of discounted profits of later years with those of subsequent years can provide indications of future years that can be eliminated from consideration.

Forecast accuracy affects the confidence we can have in the profits of future years. Our confidence usually decreases as the profits must be projected farther into the future. The confidence we feel in the profit projections can be imparted into the calculations in a pragmatic way by weighting the profit-for-all-subsequent-years factor $P_{j+1}(X)$ in each computation of $P_j(X)$ with a number between zero and one. It is expected that the factor will approach zero for the later years of the planning horizon.

CAPITAL COSTS. When the location problem involves privately owned warehouses, the time period over which the investment costs should be amortized cannot be known in advance of the analysis. It is initially assumed that the annualized investment cost is constant for each year regardless of the location-relocation plan. Actually, the cost is $I_c = (I_o - S_N)/N$, where

I_c = annual cost due to the initial investment in the warehouse.
I_o = initial investment cost of warehouse.
S_N = resale value of the warehouse in year N.
N = number of years warehouse is used.

Thus, annualized investment cost could change, if there were nonlinearities in salvage costs over time. A sensitivity analysis can be performed to determine if the desired plan would be different under different assumptions about the annualized investment costs. Also, a recursive scheme can be used whereby the dynamic analysis is repeated under different assumptions about N and the value of I_c that results. When the assumed N and the actual N resulting in the optimal plan are equal, the computation is complete. The optimal or nearly optimal plan without the constant investment should be found.

Retail and Plant Location

The extent to which the logistician should become involved in the location of retail outlets and the location of manufacturing facilities depends a great deal on whether logistics costs bear significantly on the location decision. Factors that are typically of concern to the logistician after the basic transportation-inventory cost considerations are proximity to competition, population makeup, customer traffic patterns, and local zoning laws in the case of retail site selection; and manufacturing labor costs and availability, tax environment, and availability of schools, churches, and housing and community attitudes toward industrial development in the case of plant location. When such factors become of prime importance to the location decision, logisticial analysis has far less impact on the final decision than it would for most warehouse location decisions. In those retail or plant location situations where logistics costs are important, the analytical techniques developed for locating warehouses will also apply here.

Retail Site Selection. A great deal has been written about selecting good retail locations, but little has been done to develop comprehensive models that will aid in the location decision. To date, the focus of retail site analysis has not directly been on selecting retail locations, but rather on determining the potential revenue (drawing power) that the site might generate or the overall desirability of a particular site.[35] Methods of the latter have centered around one technique. As one recent survey study on market potential stated:

> Market potential, community of interest, and retail gravitation are terms used to identify trade flow theories which try to explain why individuals are attracted to a particular community or market center from surrounding areas. Attempts to measure this influencing force have been numerous; yet, most of the methods devised revert directly or with slight modification to one of the oldest, although still most popular techniques today—Reilly's Law of Retail Gravitation.[36]

Reilly's law is stated as:[37]

$$\frac{B_a}{B_b} = \frac{P_a}{P_b}\left(\frac{D_b}{D_a}\right)^2 \tag{8.14}$$

where

B_a = the retail trade that city A draws from intermediate town T.
B_b = the retail trade that city B draws from intermediate town T.

[35] Jac L. Goldstucker, "A Systems Framework for Retail Location" in *Science, Technology, and Marketing* (Chicago: American Marketing Association, 1966), pp. 412–29.

[36] James E. Suelflow, *Market Potential—Its Theory and Application* (Madison, Wisconsin: University of Wisconsin, Bureau of Business Research and Service, 1967), p. 1.

[37] William J. Reilly, *The Law of Retail Gravitation* (New York: The Knickerbocker Press, 1931).

P_a = population of city A.
P_b = population of city B.
D_a = distance of city A from intermediate town T.
D_b = distance of city B from intermediate town T.

This basic formulation has undergone some modification over the years. Population has been replaced with store size or selling space, and distance has been replaced with customer travelling time to the store.[38] If B_a is set equal to B_b and the relationship solved for D_b, the resulting expression would give the dividing distance between two competing trading areas.

Reilly's law and its modifications are not the only approaches to the retail location problem. Other methods, including correlation-regression analysis, economic and location theory, empirical analysis, image maps, and consumer-behavior analysis, provide alternative approaches to defining retail trade areas.[39] However, such approaches have traditionally been little concerned with costs that are considered to be logistics costs. The important question then becomes to what extent the logistician should become involved in retail location decisions.

The answer to the above question may, in a great many cases, be "not at all" or "very little." However, it should be realized that the retail location problem involves many of the same cost tradeoffs as the warehouse location problem. Of course, the difference is in the importance placed on specific variables in the location mix. To illustrate the similiarities, consider the problem of the large chain retailer having a number of stores to cover his trading area. The most profitable configuration is sought by deciding on the number of stores needed, their sizes, their locations, and what their stocking policies should be. These are the same questions raised regarding a warehouse configuration, so much of the warehouse location analysis already may be reasonably transferable to those retail location problems where logistics costs are not overwhelmed by demand considerations. Figure 8-13 shows the conflicting inventory and transportation costs typical to the problem of determining the optimum number of facilities in a network. However, variables such as proximity to complementary stores, merchandise mix in the store, and available parking space are a few of the variables that must be considered in retail location and that are not of great importance in a warehouse-location analysis.

Any wholesale transfer of warehouse location analysis to the retail location problem must be cautioned against. As one analyst points out, an acceptable retail location decision model "requires a theory which is exceedingly precise in its predictive powers."[40] That is, the retail location model often must be able to dis-

[38] See David L. Huff, "A Computer Program for Location Analysis" in Raymond M. Haas (ed.), *Science, Technology, and Marketing* (Chicago: American Marketing Association, 1966), pp. 371–79. For an even more sophisticated version of this, see William I. Baumol and Edward A. Ide, "Variety in Retailing," *Management Science*, Vol. 3 (October 1956), pp. 93–101.

[39] For an excellent summary of these methods, see Donald L. Thompson, "Future Directions in Retail Area Research," *Economic Geography*, Vol. 42 (January 1966), pp. 1–18.

[40] Goldstucker, *op. cit.*, p. 413.

FIGURE 8-13

Generalized logistics cost functions as related to
the number of retail stores in a network

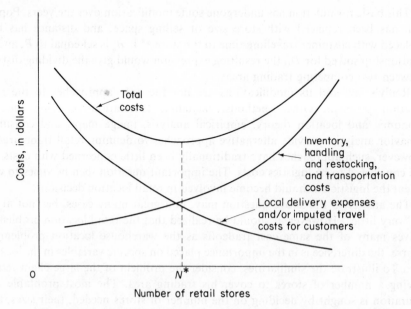

Given: Fixed store size, constant merchandise mix, and fixed revenue potential

criminate between street corners. In contrast, warehouse location models may
require no greater discrimination than between cities.

Plant Location.   The location of a manufacturing facility often involves both logistical and manufacturing considerations. The logistician is concerned with the
inbound transportation cost associated with raw materials and the outbound transportation cost on finished product plus the costs associated with a factory inventory
of finished product. A significant portion of the total logistics bill may be closely
associated with the location of the plant site, but, more importantly, nearly all
manufacturing costs will be incurred here. Because such factors as availability and
cost of labor, availability of real estate, and degree of unionization outweigh logistical concerns at this point, manufacturing considerations become of prime importance, and the logistician often does not have the primary responsibility for the
final plant location decision.[41] He may, quite appropriately, act in an advisory
capacity, much the same as he would in retail location decisions. If plant location
is heavily influenced by inbound and/or outbound transportation costs, as may be

[41] One study of the reasons for plant location or expansion in the states of Kentucky,
Tennessee, and Mississippi found that transportation costs rank ninth behind such
reasons as labor availability and cost, convenience to markets, availability of real estate
and raw materials, adequate power, local cooperativeness, and less unionization. See
Thomas P. Bergin and William F. Eagan, "How Effective Are Industrial Development
Programs?" *Michigan Business Review*, Vol. 12 (January 1960), pp. 23–28.

the case for chemical or beverage production, the logistician may have a strong influence on plant location. Conceptually, the logistician sees the plant location problem as similar to warehouse and retail location in terms of the basic cost trade-offs involved. Again, the degree to which he becomes active in the plant location decision depends primarily on the extent to which the location choice is sensitive to logistics costs as compared with other cost considerations in the problem.

Concluding Comments

Locating inventories in the logistics network is one of the more complex problems that the logistician must face. Inferential treatment of the problem may fail to uncover the most promising network configurations, and the aid of analytical techniques to help search for lower-cost (higher-profit) solutions is appealing. A number of analytical location methods have been presented that help determine the number, size, and spatial configuration of inventory storage facilities. Only the basic elements of these models have been presented, and it would be rare if they could be transferred without some modification to an actual problem situation. Therefore, this chapter should be viewed as an examination of some of the more popular analytical techniques used in searching for optimum distribution system designs, and when these techniques are modified to reflect the realities of the actual problem situation, they can provide some useful guide lines for effective logistics system design.

Questions and Problems

1. Two plants are to serve seven customers through four potential warehouses. The following per-unit transportation costs are given between plants and warehouses, and between warehouses and customers.

		Warehouse			
		1	2	3	4
Plant	1	10	7	5	9
	2	8	11	8	6

and

		Warehouse			
		1	2	3	4
	1	6	8	9	7
	2	5	7	7	9
	3	4	8	6	10
Customer	4	5	6	5	9
	5	6	7	8	8
	6	7	5	7	5
	7	8	9	6	9

The plants can produce 40 and 40 units, respectively, and the markets demand 10, 5, 20, 15, 10, 15, and 5 units, respectively.

Per-unit (marginal) warehousing costs and total warehousing costs are nonlinear, a function of volume V flowing through the warehouse, and are given by the formulas below.

		Per-Unit Cost Formula, $/Unit	Total Cost, $
	1	$40\sqrt{V_1}/V_1$	$80\sqrt{V_1}$
	2	$30\sqrt{V_2}/V_2$	$60\sqrt{V_2}$
Warehouse	3	$50\sqrt{V_3}/V_3$	$100\sqrt{V_3}$
	4	$25\sqrt{V_4}/V_4$	$50\sqrt{V_4}$

Using the Baumol-Wolfe iterative method for locating multiple warehouses, find:

(a) Which warehouses should be used.
(b) The volume flowing through each warehouse.
(c) The total cost for the final configuration.

FIGURE 8-14
Location of plants and markets with grid overlay

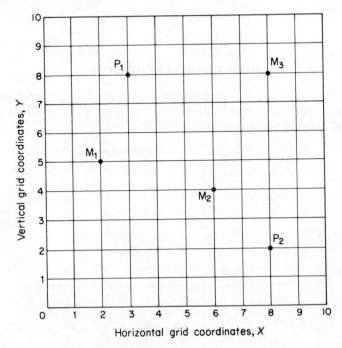

Vertical grid coordinates, Y

Horizontal grid coordinates, X

Scale: 1 = 10 miles

2. The grid overlay shown in Fig. 8-14 notes the spatial location of three markets and two plants. Volume either flowing to or from each point and the associated transportation cost are given below.

Point No.	Point i	Volume V_i (cwt)	Transportation Cost R_i ($/cwt/mi)
1	P_1	5000	0.04
2	P_2	7000	0.04
3	M_1	3500	0.095
4	M_2	3000	0.095
5	M_3	5500	0.095

(a) Use the center-of gravity (grid) method to find the location of a single warehouse.
(b) Evaluate the quality of the solution obtained in terms of optimality, usefulness, factors included or not included in the model, how management might use the solution, etc.
(c) If two warehouses are to serve these markets, how would you proceed to select the best sites?

3. The Fad Products Company has developed a new product that is expected to have a three-year life. The geographical center of demand is expected to shift rather substantially over the three-year period, thus causing the least-cost warehouse location to be different in each year. Because of the short product life, the company uses public warehouse space.

The physical-distribution manager for the company has made demand forecasts and has determined the most feasible warehouse location alternative in each year. The costs due to location in each year in each location are presented in the following table.

Location Alternative	Year from present date		
	1	2	3
A	5072	7063	8900
B	7921	2076	3760
C	6220	4450	1076

The cost of relocating is $4000 per move. For simplicity assume a zero discount rate. Using the technique of dynamic programming, answer the following.

(a) If the company is free to select any initial location, find the optimum location—that is, specify what the plan is and the total cost for the plan.
(b) If the company has a warehouse initially at location A, what would your answer be to part (a)?

4. The Roca-Cola Bottling Company obtains powders, liquid concentrates,

and bottling supplies from a supply point S_1. The company services two markets, M_1 and M_2. Each market demands annually approximately 150,000 cwt and 250,000 cwt, respectively. Annual purchases are 50,000 cwt. Water, which is available everywhere, makes up the weight difference between supply and total demand. The location of each point and the isocost transportation rate ($/cwt) lines are shown on the accompanying map (Fig. 8-15).

FIGURE 8-15
Transportation isocost lines for Roca-Cola Bottling Company problem

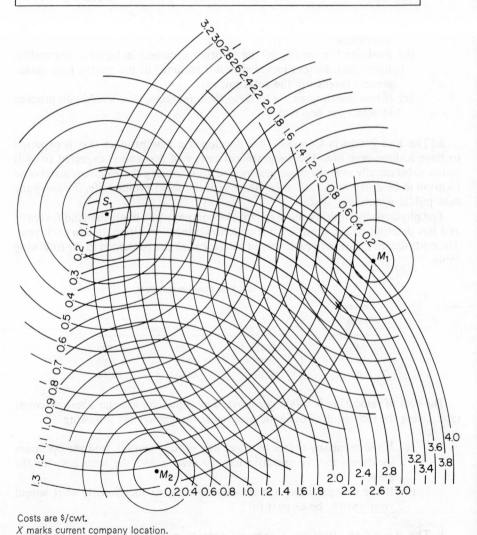

Costs are $/cwt.
X marks current company location.

(a) Suggest the company location that will minimize total transportation costs.

(b) Labor costs, land costs, building costs, etc. vary, depending on the site selected. Suppose these additional costs are $11.00 per cwt of product produced at the optimum location point as compared with $10.00 per cwt at the existing location X. If it costs $1,000,000 to relocate the plant in addition to the above costs, would you suggest a move to the optimum location at this time? If a move is made, no further moves would be anticipated for at least 10 years.

5. Facility location models (as well as other design models) can be classified as either algorithmic, simulation, or heuristic types. Expalin the differences between these and cite examples of each type. Be sure to indicate why your example does illustrate the type.

6. Bottoms-Up, Inc., is a small company that manufactures and sells a beer under the Old Wheez label. The company was examining the possibility of penetrating the North Shore City metropolitan market area. A plant location that would serve the area was sought. A grid overlay was placed over a map of the area, as shown in Fig. 8-16. North Shore City is E, and the surrounding suburbs were designated as A to I except E. A market research study indicated the following potential volumes for Old Wheez.

FIGURE 8-16

Grid overlay of North Shore City metropolitan area

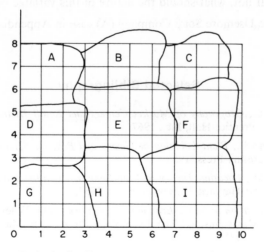

Scale: 1 = 2 miles

Area	Annual Volume, cwt
A	10,000
B	5,000
C	70,000
D	30,000
E	40,000
F	12,000
G	90,000
H	7,000
I	10,000

Demand came primarily from dealers that were scattered uniformly over the area. Transportation costs were estimated at $0.10/cwt/mile.

(a) If the center-of-gravity approach is used, where should the plant be located?

(b) What would you determine the annual transportation bill to be?

(c) The center-of-gravity solution is generally regarded as an approximate solution. How would you proceed to find a more exact solution?

7. Contrast the retail store and plant location problems with the warehouse location problem. To what extent are warehouse location decision models appropriate and applicable to these other location problems?

8. To date many facility location models have not included customer service as a specific variable to be balanced against location costs. Others have used delivery distance or time between warehouse and customer as a customer service variable. Is delivery distance or time an adequate variable to describe customer service? If it is, how must it be treated in the models to achieve this adequate representation? If not, what should the nature of this variable be?

9. Prepare the Usemore Soap Company (A) case in Appendix B.

Selected Bibliography

BERRY, BRIAN J. L., *Geography of Market Centers and Retail Distribution*. Englewood Cliffs, N. J.: Prentice-Hall, Inc., 1967.

GREENHUT, MELVIN L., *Plant Location in Theory and Practice*. Chapel Hill: University of North Carolina Press, 1956.

HOOVER, EDGAR M., *Location Theory and the Shoe and Leather Industries*. Cambridge, Massachusetts: Harvard University Press, 1957.

ISARD, WALTER, *Location in Space-Economy*. New York: John Wiley & Sons, Inc., and Cambridge, Massachusetts: The Technology Press of the Massachusetts Institute of Technology, 1956.

MARKS, NORTON E. and ROBERT M. TAYLOR., *Physical Distribution and Marketing Logistics: An Annotated Bibliography*. Chicago: American Marketing Association, 1966, especially Section II.

Mossman, Frank and Newton Morton, *Logistics of Distribution Systems.* Boston: Allyn & Bacon, Inc., 1965.

Nelson, R. L., *The Selection of Retail Locations.* The Dodge Corporation, 1958.

Weber, Alfred, *Über den Standort der Industrien.* Mohr, Tübingen, 1909. Translated by Carl J. Friedrich as *Alfred Weber's Theory of the Location of Industries.* Chicago: University of Chicago Press, 1929.

Chapter
9

Inventory
Policy Decisions

One reason inventories exist in the logistics system is because it would be either too expensive or impossible to provide the kind of transportation service needed to have goods at the place and at the time they are desired by consumers. In certain cases, as in the distribution of spare parts, where demand is infrequent but customer service demands are high, or in the distribution of high-fashion clothing, where obsolescence rates are high, transportation costs are substituted for inventory costs by using premium transportation and keeping inventories low. Conversely, in the distribution of bulk materials it is often more economical to maintain large inventories so that less expensive transportation can be used. The logistician seeks an economical balance between transportation and inventory costs where inventories represent an important alternative to the creating of time and place utility in the product.

Traditionally, the inventory-transportation cost tradeoff and the inventories maintained to smooth production processes have favored substantial inventory accumulations in this country. It was estimated in 1966 that the total dollar investment in inventories for both government (includes military) and private enterprise was on the order of $285 billion.[1] The cost of carrying these inventories in the business sector is conservatively estimated to be about 22 percent of the annual average inventory value, or about $5\frac{1}{2}$ percent of GNP[2] and has been noted to vary among firms from 18 to 30 percent of annual average inventory value.[3] For the individual firm, inventory costs average about one-third of total physical distribution costs, or about 7.5 percent of sales.[4] These are nationwide estimates and may not be typical for any one firm, but they do indicate the economic magnitude of the problem faced by the logistician and the need for careful management of these inventories. It is not uncommon to find that the most dramatic cost savings among logistics activities come from improved inventory policies.

Inventory policy decisions revolve around two basic questions. First, *how often* should the order for stock replenishment be placed? Second, *what quantity* should be ordered? Although the decision questions are easily stated, the answers are far from obvious. Inventory analysts have spent considerable effort, most since World War II, developing models that aid in making inventory decisions. From the substantial body of literature that has evolved, a selected sampling will be made of those models most useful to the practicing logistician.

Nature of the Decision

Like so many logistical problems, the inventory problem is one of balancing conflicting costs. Typically, procurement and out-of-stock costs are balanced against inventory carrying costs (Fig. 9-1). These costs are controlled by varying the quantities ordered and the timing of the placement of the order. For example, if the inventory policy is to order in large quantities but infrequently, we may be paying more to maintain a high average inventory level than is saved by having low total procurement cost and a low exposure to out-of-stock situations. Conversely, if the policy is to order less but more often, the cost of carrying inventory will be low because the average inventory level is low. However, such savings in carrying costs may be more than offset by increased procurement and out-of-stock costs. Fig. 9-2 shows these policy extremes. What the logistician desires is to establish the order quantity level and the timing of the placement of the order that will minimize total inventory costs.

This is an extremely simple statement of an inventory decision problem, and it

[1] U. S. Bureau of the Census, *Business Statistics: 1967*, 16th edition (Washington, D. C., 1967), p. 23; and U. S. Bureau of the Census, *Statistical Abstract of the United States: 1968*, 89th edition (Washington, D. C., 1968).

[2] J. L. Heskett, "Macroeconomic Cost of Physical Distribution," in *Papers—Third Annual Meeting, American Transportation Research Forum* (Oxford, Ind.: The Richard B. Cross Co., 1962), pp. 169–89.

[3] Ronald S. Foster, *What Does It Cost to Carry Inventory?* (Washington, D. C.: The National Association of Wholesalers).

[4] Wendall M. Stewart, "Physical Distribution: Key to Improved Volume and Profits," *Journal of Marketing*, Vol. 29 (January 1965), pp. 65–69.

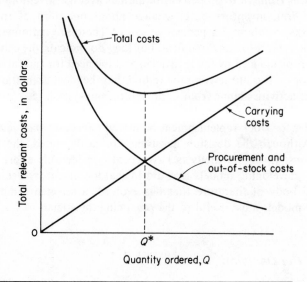

FIGURE 9-1

Basic inventory cost tradeoffs for a common inventory situation

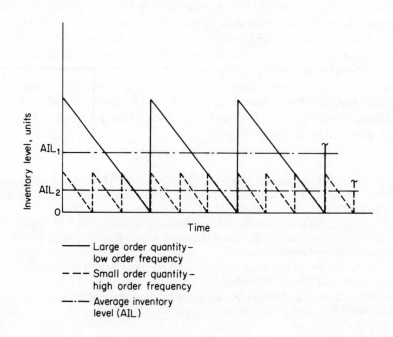

FIGURE 9-2

Effect of extreme inventory policies on inventory level under constant demand and constant lead time conditions does not indicate anything about the environment in which the decision must be made. For example, nothing is said about the effect of production costs on inventory levels or the decision problem of controlling inventories for multiple echelons in the logistics channel. Nothing is indicated about the nature of demand and order cycle times (certain or uncertain), whether demand changes over time, or if there are multiple products to be controlled. Each condition represents a different problem to be analyzed. However, much about each problem is the same and relates back to these basic cost tradeoffs. It would be impossible to examine every inventory decision problem that might arise, but several different situations will be discussed to indicate possible approaches toward developing inventory policies. The analyst must remain flexible and imaginative in the application of inventory theory to real problem situations. Theoretical inventory models rarely transfer directly to real problems. However, basic concepts usually transfer quite well.

Our starting point in developing inventory decision policies is to assume that the facility location decisions have been made so that the market for the products in question have been divided among the facilities in the logistics system.[5] Inventory policies may be required for each nodal point in the logistics network (e.g., a retail, warehouse, or plant location), or a policy may need to be developed for all points collectively. Our primary emphasis will be on developing single-facility decision models, but we shall briefly discuss the multiple point (multi-echelon) problem. Before beginning, we need a basic understanding of the relevant costs on which inventory decision policies are developed.

Relevant Costs

There are three classes of costs that we need to consider, since they are affected to some degree by inventory policy decisions. These are (1) procurement costs, (2) carrying costs, and (3) out-of-stock costs.

PROCUREMENT COSTS

The first class of costs is associated with acquiring replenishment stock for inventories. When a stock order is placed, a number of different costs can be incurred in processing and handling the order. More specifically, procurement costs include (1) the cost of processing an order through the accounting and purchasing departments, (2) the cost of transmitting the order to the supplier, usually by mail or by some electronic means, (3) the cost of transporting the order when transportation charges are not included in the purchased goods, and (4) the cost of any materials handling or processing of the order at the receiving dock. When the firm is self-supplied, as in the case of a factory replenishing its own

---

[5] Location decisions and inventory policy decisions are actually economically interdependent and can only be treated as independent with some risk of creating a suboptimum logistics system.

finished goods inventories, procurement costs are altered to reflect production setup costs. Transportation and receiving costs may not be relevent to the inventory decision problem, depending on the particular circumstances.

Some of the above procurement costs are fixed per order and do not vary with the order size. Others, such as transportation and materials-handling costs, vary to a degree with order size. Each case requires slightly different analytical treatment.

CARRYING COSTS

Carrying costs result from storing or holding goods for a period of time and are roughly proportional to the quantity of goods on hand. A number of cost items are included under this general heading. First, there is the storage or the out-of-pocket cost for space. This may be the warehouse rental charge if the space is rented, or it may be the direct operating expenses if the space is owned. Space cost may be nonexistent if the goods are in transit. Second, there is the capital cost. Inventories tie up capital that may be used in other ways to earn a return. Putting a dollar figure on capital costs depends on the company's philosophy about their investment opportunities and may range from the interest paid on short-term capital (e.g., the prime interest rate) to the target rate of return expected on all investment opportunities of the firm. Proctor and Gamble recently had a return on investment of 16.5 percent,[6] and a large auto manufacturer allegedly uses a target return of 20 percent. The final figure will likely depend on what management agrees to. Third, there are insurance and taxation costs. Insurance is maintained as protection against inventory losses such as fire and theft, and premiums paid will reflect the level of inventories maintained. Inventory taxes are levied on the inventory levels found on the day of assessment. Although this level may only crudely reflect the average inventory level experienced throughout the year, taxes are usually a relatively minor portion of carrying costs, so relating taxes to average inventory levels results in only small errors. Fourth, there are the costs of deterioration or obsolescence. In the course of maintaining inventories a certain portion of the stock will become dead stock. It may become contaminated, damaged, spoiled, or otherwise unfit for sale as a new product. The product may lose value, or additional costs may be incurred to make the product fit for sale. In contrast to deterioration, some of the products may become obsolete in the sense of being superseded by newer products. The cost of obsolescence is the difference between the original value and the salvage value of the product.

OUT-OF-STOCK COSTS

Out-of-stock costs are incurred when a customer places an order and the order cannot be filled from the inventory to which it is normally assigned. There are two kinds of out-of-stock costs that can be distinguished: (1) lost sales costs and (2) backorder costs. Each presupposes certain actions on the part of the customer,

---

[6] "Is the Soap Leader Getting Soft?" *Business Week* (July 19, 1969), p. 52.

and because of their intangible nature, they are very difficult to measure accurately.

A *lost sales cost* occurs when the customer, faced with an out-of-stock situation, chooses to withdraw his order for the product. The cost is the profit that would have been made on this particular sale and may also include an additional cost for the negative effect that the stockout may have on future sales. Highly substitutable products such as bread or cigarettes are most likely to incur the lost sales cost.

The *backorder* case assumes that the customer will wait for his order to be filled so that the sale is not lost, only delayed. However, backorders can create additional clerical and sales costs for order processing and additional transportation and handling costs when such orders are not filled through the normal distribution channel. These costs are fairly tangible, so measurement is not too difficult. There also may be the intangible cost of lost future sales, and this cost is very difficult to measure. Products that can be differentiated in the mind of the consumer (e.g., automobiles and appliances) are more likely to be backordered than substituted for.

Stocking Decisions

A first step in developing inventory policies is to take a broad look at the distribution system, which may contain hundreds of inventory nodal points and many times that number of product items. When one is designing the system configuration, it is often not possible to give each product item special attention. Rather, all product items or broad classes of items are treated collectively. As such, any stocking point might be carrying a full product line. With the wide differences in demand levels and demand variation, maintaining all product items at all stocking points may not be the most economical stocking procedure. Generally, a more economical procedure is to stock high-volume items at retail points, moderately moving items only at warehouses, and low-volume items only at centralized stocking points. This three-level stocking procedure is an extension of the ABC method of inventory control so frequently encountered in production.

What is behind the ABC method? Two things, basically. First, in almost any company's product line a few items account for most of the sales. A rule of thumb is that 20 percent of the items account for 80 percent of the sales, hence, the "20–80" rule. Though it would be rare for any company's sales to fit the "20–80" rule exactly, a disproportionality between sales volume and product items does generally exist.[7] Table 9-1 shows a ranking of a company's 14 product items by sales volume and the percentage of total sales compared with the percentage of the product item list. Fig. 9-3 plots these data and we can see, in this case, that 20 percent of the items account for approximately 68 percent of the total sales volume, 50 percent of the items account for about 89 percent of sales, etc. This wide differ-

---

[7] The item-demand distribution often follows the log normal probability distribution as shown by John F. Magee, *Physical Distribution Systems* (New York: McGraw-Hill Book Company, 1967), pp. 36–40.

TABLE 9-1

ABC classification of 14 products of a chemical company

Rank[a]	Product Item Number	Monthly Sales (000's)	Cumulative Percentage of Total Sales	Cumulative Percentage of Items	Classification of Items by ABC Method
1	D-204	$5,056	36.2%	7.1%	
2	D-212	3,424	60.7	14.3	A
3	D-185-0	1,052	68.2	21.4	
4	D-191	893	74.9	28.6	
5	D-192	843	80.5	35.7	B
6	D-193	727	86.0	42.8	
7	D-179-0	451	89.2	50.0	
8	D-195	412	92.2	57.1	
9	D-196	214	93.5	64.2	
10	D-186-0	205	95.0	71.5	C
11	D-198-0	188	96.5	78.6	
12	D-199	172	97.8	85.7	
13	D-200	170	99.0	92.9	
14	D-205	159	100.0	100.0	
		$13,966			

[a] Ranked according to sales volume.

ence between high- and low-volume items suggests that they might be handled differently in the inventory system.

Second, the amount of safety stock (that extra amount of stock carried as a protection against demand and lead time uncertainties as well as contingencies) in the distribution system is less when low-volume items are stocked at centralized locations. By stocking low-volume items at many points in the distribution system, the total demand for these items is divided among the stocking points. At each of these points a safety stock is provided which, when summed for the entire system, exceeds the safety stock required at one or a few stocking points. Again, since safety stock is in part a protection against demand variability and there is greater variability in demand when it is subdivided, total system safety stock will increase with the number of stocking points. For example, suppose that two warehouses have a demand for a particular item that is normally distributed with a mean of 100 units and a standard deviation (σ) of 10 units. If the policy were to carry two standard deviations of safety stock, each warehouse would have a 20-unit safety stock and a system safety stock of 40 units (2×20). If the stock were consolidated at one location, the demand distribution would have a mean of 200 and a standard deviation of $\sqrt{(10)^2 + (10)^2} = 14.1$ units.[8] Using the same inventory policy, we see that the system safety stock would be 28.2 or (2×14.1) units, which is less than the 40 units for two warehouses.

[8] This is a result of convoluting the two independent demand distributions, which is discussed in G. Hadley and T. M. Whitin, *Analysis of Inventory Systems* (Englewood Cliffs, N. J.: Prentice-Hall, Inc., 1963), pp. 118–26.

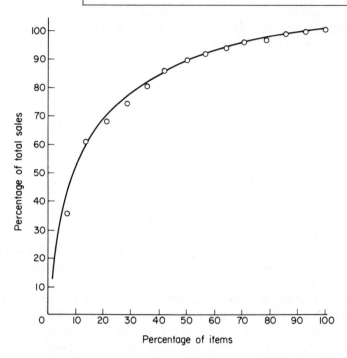

FIGURE 9-3

Cumulative distribution of percentage of sales versus percentage of items

Source: Table 9-1.

Magee[9] has established an empirical formula describing the effect on demand variability when demand territories are being combined. It is

$$\sigma = gD^\alpha \qquad (9.1)$$

where

σ = standard deviation of the distribution of annual demand, units.

D = average annual demand level, units.

g = a constant to be determined, dimensionless.

α = constant to be determined, dimensionless.

Since α usually has a value between 0.6 and 0.9, demand variability and associated inventory levels (and carrying costs) increase, but at a decreasing rate as demand increases due to the consolidation of demand territories.[10] This empirical relation-

---

[9] Magee, *op. cit.*, p. 141.

[10] Recall that it is this idea that is behind the inventory cost functions used in the Baumol-Wolfe method of locating warehouses, as discussed in the previous chapter and behind Fig. 8-8.

ship suggests that from an inventory cost standpoint few stocking points are less costly than many when demand is uncertain.

This suggests that only centralized warehouses should be used for all products to minimize inventory costs, but the effect on transportation costs has not yet been considered. Stocking high-volume items at centralized warehouses may result in high delivery charges and poor customer service. For low-volume items that have been consolidated into a few warehouses, the delivery costs may be high, but the lower warehouse inbound transportation costs due to large inbound shipments and lower inventory carrying costs often balance high delivery costs in favor of consolidation. Also, customer service can actually improve when low-volume items are consolidated by decreasing the probability of a stockout, especially when the inventories at the decentralized points have not been well managed.

The ABC method provides rough guide lines for deciding which of the items should be classified as high-, moderate-, and low-volume for locating the stock in various echelons of the logistics system. An arbitrary breakdown for the items shown in Table 9-1 might be 15–35–50; i.e., the top 15 percent of the items should be stocked primarily at the retail point, the next 35 percent of the items should be stocked at the distribution or regional warehouses, and the remaining 50 percent should be stocked only at the factory warehouse. It should be mentioned again that the percentage breakdown is arbitrary, as is the threefold classification (e.g., AB or ABCD may be appropriate in some cases). What is important is to recognize the relevant cost tradeoffs and balance these when the stocking policy is developed.

The stocking policy decision further refines the demand patterns for the various product items beyond initial location decision allocations. It also focuses the inventory control decision on particular levels of the logistics system so that differences in customer service requirements, inventory costs, and transportation costs at each level can be taken into account.

Inventory Policy Decisions

In deciding when and in what quantities orders should be placed, the logistician may face an overwhelming set of difficult circumstances, such as uncertain demand, uncertain lead time, multiple products, quantity discounts, changing demand levels, and multiple stocking points. A number of models and techniques have been devised to aid in the selection of the best inventory policies under the various circumstances. The more important of these circumstances along with analytical techniques to deal with them will be discussed.

SINGLE-ORDER CASE

The first inventory problem that we shall consider arises when product demand generally occurs over a short time period, and the placement of an order is made just *once*. Since only one order is placed, when to order is not at issue. The question of how much to order is the important issue. Examples of such single-order problems are wholesale buying of Christmas trees, stocking spare parts for aircraft that are produced in limited quantities, and purchasing newspapers for a newstand.

Example. A small millinery store will place an order for high-fashion ladies' hats that are likely to sell only in the immediate season. The hats can be purchased for $15 and will be sold for $25. Any leftover hats will be placed on sale for $10 (assume that all leftovers can be disposed of at this price). The retailer anticipates the demand for these hats to be

Number of Hats	Probability of Sale
0	0.10
1	0.15
2	0.20
3	0.30
4	0.20
5	0.05
>5	0.00
	1.00

This is a simple and straightforward decision problem under risk conditions and can be represented in the form of a decision matrix, as shown in Table 9-2. We are seeking the order quantity that will yield the highest average profit. The highest average profit objective is a long-run strategy and assumes that this or similar decisions will continue to be made by the firm in the future.

TABLE 9-2

Decision matrix for the one-order inventory problem

States of Nature
(Demand)

	D \\ Q	0 P_1=0.10	1 P_2=0.15	2 P_3=0.20	3 P_4=0.30	4 P_5=0.20	5 P_6=0.05	Expected Average Profit
Order quantity (ALTERNATIVES)	0	0	0	0	0	0	0	0
	1	−5	10	10	10	10	10	8.50
	2	−10	5	20	20	20	20	14.75
	3	−15	0	15	30	30	30	18.00 ⟸ Best alternative
	4	−20	−5	10	25	40	40	16.75
	5	−25	−10	5	20	35	50	12.50

$D \geq Q$

$D < Q$

Since the basic construction and use of the decision matrix was discussed in the second chapter of this book, we can now concentrate on solving the problem. The first step is to establish the states of nature and the alternatives. For this problem, the states of nature are the various demand levels D that can occur. The alternatives are the different quantities of hats that can be ordered Q. Next, the payoff or expected profit value for each demand level and each order quantity has to be computed. For example, consider the profit that would be made if the total demand were for four hats and only three hats were stocked. Since demand exceeds supply, only three can be sold. The net profit is $10 per hat, so the total profit would be $30. If Q exceeds D, then there will be some leftover stock to be disposed of. Suppose two hats were demanded and four were stocked. The two hats could be sold at a profit of $20 and the remaining two hats sold at a loss of $10 for a net gain of $10. Repeating this type of analysis for every cell in the decision matrix is required, but the analysis can be simplified by developing formulas for computing the payoff values based on the various demand D and order quantity Q values. Two different formulas are needed to account for those situations when overstock does and does not occur. The formulas are

	Demand Exceeds Stock $D \geq Q$	Demand Less Than Stock $D < Q$
Sale of hats	$+25Q$	$+25D$
Cost of hats	$-15Q$	$-15Q$
Clearance of hats	—	$+10(Q - D)$
Total	$10Q$	$15D - 5Q$

Once the decision matrix is filled out (Table 9-2), the average profit for each order quantity is computed. Recall that this is done by multiplying each payoff value by the probability that the payoff will be realized and then summing across the appropriate row of the matrix. For example, the expected average profit for an order quantity of four hats is

$$(-20)(0.10) + (-5)(0.15) + (10)(0.20) + (25)(0.30) + (40)(0.20)$$
$$+ (40)(0.05) = \$16.75$$

After repeating this calculation for every alternative, the alternative having the highest expected average profit is selected. In this case, the order would be placed for three hats, and the expected return would be $18.00 However, $Q = 2$ and $Q = 4$ are also alternatives with near-optimum expected profit values, and they might be considered as possible final solutions, especially when there are some doubts about the accuracy of the probability distribution of demand.

Now that the method has been presented, the careful reader may find it difficult to see how this method balances the conflicting costs noted at the beginning of this chapter. The reason for the difficulty lies in the subtlety of the cost tradeoffs. In this one-order problem, order processing costs that are constant per order can be neglected, since the decision does not in any way depend on them. The method balances the costs of overstock against those of understock. When $Q > D$, there is an implied overstock cost equal to the difference between what the item could have sold for and what it did sell for as leftover stock. When $Q < D$, there was not enough stock on hand, and an opportunity cost incurred equal to the profit foregone. Seeking the optimum balance of opportunity costs leads to the same results as are obtained by balancing the more easily expressed carrying costs and stockout costs of Fig. 9-1.

REORDER CASE

The more common inventory problem is a natural extension of the one-order problem; that is, the demand for a product item projects well into the future, and many orders will be placed over time as stocks are depleted. The question of when an order should be placed now becomes relevant along with the order quantity question. A basic model for solving the multiple-order problem dates as far back as 1915, when Ford Harris of the Westinghouse Electric Company first formulated it.[11] Though based on a number of assumptions, it still remains a fundamental model for solving this problem. It is often referred to as the *Economic Order Quantity* (EOQ) model.

The EOQ formulation represents one of the two basic approaches to the multiple-order problem that are in use. One is called the *Q*-system and the other the *P*-system. The *Q*-system has a variable review period and a fixed order quantity. More specifically, when the stock level falls to a predetermined level, an order is placed in the amount of the economic order quantity (EOQ). A disadvantage of this system is that it requires close monitoring of the on-hand inventory. This suggests that high-valued items might be a good choice for this system, since they probably would be monitored closely anyway and they can more readily withstand the high monitoring costs than can low-valued items. However, an offsetting cost is that the *Q*-system generally carries a slightly lower safety stock than the *P*-system.

The *P*-system is a fixed review period, variable order quantity system. That is, the inventory level will be reviewed only at preset times. Whatever the stock level is found to be, an order is placed equal to the difference between some predetermined maximum level and the amount on hand. The *P*-system has several advantages over the *Q*-system. The monitoring of stock level often is less frequent and can be scheduled to fit with other of the firm's activities. Also, when more than one product is being monitored, it is often possible to coordinate the review of all products at the same time. The order is placed at the same time, and if a number of products are being shipped from the same supply point, it may be possible to effect lower transportation rates because of the quantity moving together. Again, the major disadvantage is the slightly higher average inventory level than is required under the *Q*-system.

[11] Ford Harris, *Operations and Cost*, Factory Management Series (Chicago: A. W. Shaw Co., 1915), pp. 48–52.

Q-system Models

In many business situations a simple inventory decision model can prove more useful to management than a complex one. The simple model often provides broad guide lines for inventory control with only modest data requirements and understanding of higher mathematics. The basic EOQ model is of this type.

THE BASIC MODEL

The EOQ model is based on the situation where demand, lead time, and all relevant costs are known and constant over time. Further, no stockouts are permitted, which is reasonable since demand and lead time are known, and the entire order is received at one time.[12] Fig. 9-4 shows control of the inventory system under certainty conditions. That is, when the inventory level drops to the reorder point, which is determined by the amount of stock needed to cover the

---

FIGURE 9-4
Control of an inventory under certainty conditions

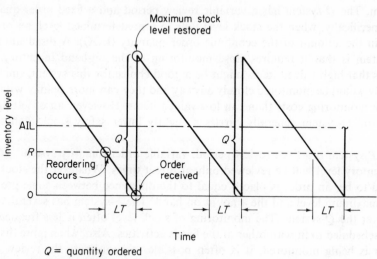

Q = quantity ordered
LT = lead time
AIL = average inventory level
R = reorder point quantity

---

[12] A variant of this model has been developed for those situations where the order quantity is received over a period of time rather than at a single instant. For a discussion of the problem formulation, see John H. Magee and David M. Boodman, *Production Planning and Inventory Control*, 2nd edition (New York: McGraw-Hill Book Company, 1967), pp. 66–72.

demand during the lead time period,[13] an order is placed. The order is assumed to be received when the last item leaves the inventory and the inventory level is restored to a level equal to the amount ordered. The pattern is repeated over time.

Recall that the inventory policy decision is to determine the optimum order quantity (Q^*) and when the order should be placed. We approach this decision problem by first establishing the total relevant cost equation. There are two types of costs in this equation—procurement costs and carrying cost—which oppose each other as the size of the order is altered. Figure 9-1 shows the nature of these costs, excluding the out-of-stock costs, since they are not a part of this simple model. The total cost equation for an annual period is

$$TC(Q) = \frac{D}{Q}S + IC\frac{Q}{2} \tag{9.2}$$

where

$TC(Q)$ = annual total relevant inventory cost depending on the value of variable Q, \$.

Q = size of each order to replenish inventory, units.

D = annual demand, units.

S = procurement cost, \$/order.

C = value of a unit carried in inventory, \$/unit.

I = carrying costs as a percentage of C, %.

The term $(D/Q)S$ refers to the procurement costs, and $IC(Q/2)$ refers to the carrying costs. Next, we seek the order quantity that will minimize total costs, that is, Q^*. This search is easily made by the use of differential calculus, which yields[14]

$$Q^* = \sqrt{\frac{2DS}{IC}} \tag{9.3}$$

Thus, Q^* is the order size that should be placed when reordering occurs.

---

[13] Lead time is defined as the time between when the order is placed and when it is received.

[14] The optimum Q is found by taking the first derivative of $TC(Q)$, setting the derivative equal to zero, and solving for Q. Thus,

$$TC(Q) = \frac{D}{Q}S + IC\frac{Q}{2}$$

Taking the derivative and setting it equal to zero, we obtain

$$\frac{dTC(Q)}{dQ} = \frac{-DS}{Q^2} + \frac{IC}{2} = 0$$

Solving for Q gives

$$Q^* = \sqrt{\frac{2DS}{IC}}$$

When should reordering take place? In the Q-system of inventory control, enough stock must be anticipated to cover sales that will occur during the time that the order is being processed and transported. Therefore, if the lead time is 10 days, then a 10-day stock level should remain when reordering occurs. The optimum number of times per year N that orders will be placed is given by

$$N^* = \frac{D}{Q^*} \tag{9.4}$$

Example. Suppose that an inventory control problem has the following specifications for a particular item.

$D = 50$ units per week or $50 \times 52 = 2600$ units per year.
$I = 10\%$.
$S = \$10$.
$C = \$5$.
$LT =$ lead time of three weeks.

The optimum order quantity according to Equation (9.3) would be

$$Q^* = \sqrt{\frac{2(2600)(10)}{(0.10)(5)}}$$
$$= 322 \text{ units}$$

An order for 322 units should be placed when the current inventory level falls to a three-week supply, or $3 \times 50 = 150$ units. Orders should be placed $2600/322 = 8.07$ times per year, according to Equation (9.4). This is an order about every $6\frac{1}{2}$ weeks. Following Equation (9.2), we find that the total cost for the example problem is

$$TC(Q^*) = \frac{(2600)(10)}{322} + \frac{(0.10)(5)(322)}{2}$$
$$= 80.70 + 80.50$$
$$= \$161.20$$

Sensitivity. The basic EOQ model is sometimes viewed with suspicion because of the rather restrictive assumptions that are made. Rarely would we find a situation where demand is constant and known with certainty and costs are known precisely. However, simplifying assumptions are of great concern only when the policy decisions are affected by the assumptions made. At least to the input data assumptions, the EOQ model solution is relatively insensitive. To illustrate this, consider in the previous example what would happen if the exact yearly demand level were not known for sure. Suppose that we vary demand ± 20 percent to observe the effect on the order quantity and total cost. Table 9-3 summarizes the comparison, and from it we can see that there is a less than proportional change in Q^* and $TC(Q)$ with changes in demand. For example, if demand actually turns out to be 20 percent higher than we used in the example problem, we can expect the optimum order quantity to increase by 9.4 percent, and the minimum total inventory costs

TABLE 9-3

Sensitivity of economic order quantity and inventory costs to uncertainty in demand for an example inventory problem

(1) Demand D	(2) Percentage Change in D from Expected Demand	(3) Order Quantity Q*	(4) Percentage Change in Q* from Expected Demand	(5) Total Cost TC(Q)	(6) Percentage Change in TC(Q) from Expected Demand	(7) Total Cost if Q=322 Used instead of Q*	(8) Percentage Change in Total Cost If Q=322 Used Instead of Q*c
2080	−20%	288	−10.6%a	$144.30	−10.5%b	$145.10	+0.55
2340	−10	306	− 5.0	153.00	− 5.1	153.20	+0.13
2600	0	322	0	161.20	0	161.20	0
2860	+10	337	+ 4.7	169.20	+ 5.0	169.30	+0.06
3120	+20	353	+ 9.4	176.80	+ 9.7	177.30	+0.28

a Computed from Column (3) values as [(288 − 322) × 100]/322.
b Computed from Column (5) values as [(144.30 − 161.20) × 100]/161.20.
c Computed by the formula Column (8) = [(Column (7) − Column (5)) × 100]/Column (5)

293

would increase by 9.7 percent. If we follow the $Q^* = 322$ policy based on the expected annual demand of 2600 units and demand actually is 20 percent higher, inventory costs would be only 0.28 percent higher than if the optimum Q were used. From this comparison, and similar comparisons also could be made for the other input data, it is clear that policy decision on the amount to order is not sensitive to rather wide fluctuations in demand levels. This insensitivity suggests that the model can reasonably be applied even when the input data are not known with great certainty and undoubtedly accounts in part for the popularity of this basic inventory control model.

QUANTITY DISCOUNTS

There are often economies of scale in production and transportation that are, in part, passed along to customers in the form of price discounts. The amount of the discount depends on the quantity ordered and thus affects inventory policy decisions. This situation can be analyzed as a variant to the basic EOQ model.

There are two popular ways in which price discounts occur. First is the sequential or "in excess" discount, where one price is in effect for an order size from zero to some limit amount and a lower price applies to the amount exceeding this limit. Any number of quantity-price echelons can be created in the pricing schedule. Second is the retroactive discount, where the reduced price applies to all units ordered, even those in previous price-quantity classes. Since there seems to be greater incidence of the retroactive discount, an example will highlight this form.

Example. The Acme Manufacturing Company purchases compressors as components in a particular room air conditioner model which it manufactures. The company purchases these compressors from Navajo Compressors on an f.o.b. origin price basis, and Acme arranges for transportation. Navajo does not have a price-discount schedule, and simply charges $30 per compressor regardless of the amount purchased. Acme can select LTL, TL, or CL shipping methods, each with a different cost. The shipping cost schedule is given in Table 9-4. The service characteristics of each transportation method are assumed to be equal for this example. Acme expects to manufacture 10,000 air conditioners of this model per

---

TABLE 9-4

Transportation costs on compressors by alternative shipping methods and the effective compressor price to Acme Manufacturing Company

Number of Compressors Purchased	Method of Transportation	Transportation Rate, $/Unit[a]	Effective Price to Acme, $/Unit[b]
0–799	Truck, LTL	$4	$34
800–1599	Truck, TL	3	33
1600+	Rail, CL	2	32

[a] These rates are somewhat inflated to show contrast in the example.
[b] The sum of the f.o.b. origin price plus transportation costs.

year. Order-processing and assembly-line-setup costs are $1000 per run, and carrying costs are 25 percent of the average value of a unit in stock.

The best order quantity, as well as the best method of transportation, can be found by examining the total cost curves for each transportation price category *i*. Modifying Equation (9.2), we would have

$$TC(Q)_i = \frac{D}{Q}S + IC_i\frac{Q}{2} \tag{9.5}$$

Varying Q while holding all parameters constant will generate a total cost curve. Changing C_i for the various price categories *i* and repeating the computational

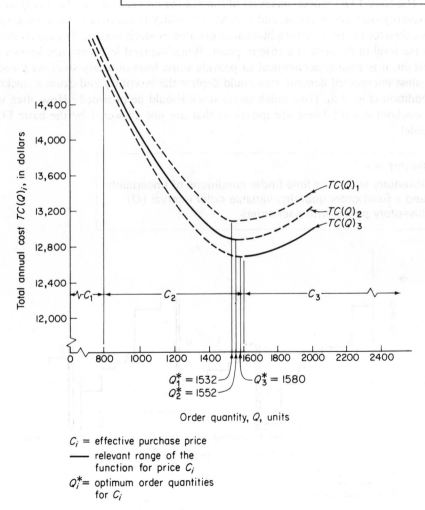

FIGURE 9-5

Total inventory cost curves for Acme Manufacturing under different effective purchase prices C_i

Order quantity, Q, units

$Q_1^* = 1532$
$Q_2^* = 1552$
$Q_3^* = 1580$

C_i = effective purchase price
—— relevant range of the function for price C_i
Q_i^* = optimum order quantities for C_i

process will generate a family of curves such as those plotted in Fig. 9-5 for the example. From this graph we can easily see that the optimum order quantity is 1600 units shipped by rail. Though $Q_3^* = 1580$ would appear to give a slightly lower cost, the purchase cost of $C_3 = \$33$, which generates Q_3^*, does not apply for 1580 units. Therefore, we must seek *feasibility* along with optimality in selecting the best order quantity under conditions of purchase discounts.

Though it is laborious to plot total cost curves, especially when a large number of discount categories are present, the procedure can be shortened. Generally, it is necessary to examine only the limiting values of discount categories as possible Q values and the Q^* values obtained from the EOQ formula. This eliminates the need for plotting the curves and reduces the procedure to only a few calculations.

UNCERTAIN DEMAND

The basic EOQ model makes no allowance for uncertainties in the inputs to the inventory decision problem, and if inventory policy is sensitive to these uncertainties, then for proper control a more sophisticated model is needed. The uncertainties in the level of demand is a case in point. When demand levels are not known for certain, it is usually economical to provide some level of safety stock as a hedge against unexpected demand that could deplete the inventory and cause a stockout condition (Fig. 9-6). How much safety stock should be provided? How often will a stockout occur? These are questions that are not answered by the basic EOQ model.

FIGURE 9-6

Inventory level over time under conditions of uncertainty and a fixed order quantity, variable order interval (*Q*) inventory policy with backorders

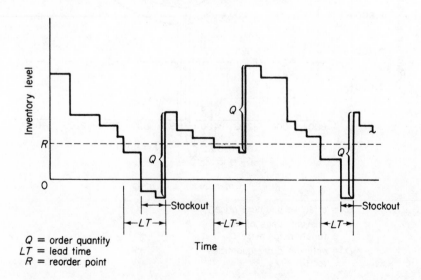

Q = order quantity
LT = lead time
R = reorder point

In developing a more sophisticated analysis we need to recognize two types of inventory levels: (1) the inventory level needed to meet the expected demand and (2) the inventory level needed for variations in demand from the expected level. Again, our objective is to find the fixed quantity that should be ordered and the minimum amount of stock that triggers the placement of an order. However, the analysis will be based on the assumption that there is no interaction between the order quantity and the reorder point quantity. This approximate analysis will yield results that are reasonably close to the optimum inventory policy and at the same time the higher order mathematics needed to produce the optimum solution can be avoided[15].

The approximate Q-system analysis can best be illustrated by means of an example. Suppose that the weekly demand for an inventory item is normally distributed with a mean of 50 units and a standard deviation of 10 units. Inventory carrying cost I is 10 percent, procurement cost S is \$10 per order, and the item value C is \$5. The procurement lead time is three weeks. The first step is to calculate the inventory policy necessary to meet the average annual demand. We appeal to the basic EOQ model [Equation (9.3)]:

$$Q^* = \sqrt{\frac{2(2600)(10)}{(0.10)(5)}}$$
$$= 322 \text{ units}$$

and on the average there will be $\frac{2600}{322} = 8.07$ orders per year.

The second step is to determine the safety stock and reorder point quantities. There is no safety stock required for the time between stock replenishment and the reorder order point, since any fluctuations that occur in demand during this period are adjusted for by varying the order interval. However, for the time interval between order placement and order receipt—the lead time—demand fluctuations can result in a stockout situation, and some level of safety stock may be desirable. In order to determine the amount of safety stock required, it is necessary to have the distribution of demand during lead time. We have the demand distribution for one week, but the lead time is three weeks long. Through a process of convoluting the one-week probability distribution, a three-week distribution of demand can be developed without observing the demand over three-week periods.[16] Convoluting recognizes that if the demand in each week is random, normally distributed, and independent, the three-week distribution must also be normally distributed with a mean of $\bar{X}n$ and a standard deviation of $s\sqrt{n}$, where $\bar{X}$ and s are the mean and standard deviation of the original or one-week demand distribution, respectively, and n is the number of convolutions of the original

[15] For development of optimal Q-system, see Martin K. Starr, and David W. Miller, *Inventory Control: Theory and Practice* (Englewood Cliffs, N. J.: Prentice-Hall, Inc., 1962), pp. 122–25.

[16] For a complete discussion of convolutions for the normal distribution as well as other popular distributions, see Hadley and Whitin, *op. cit.*

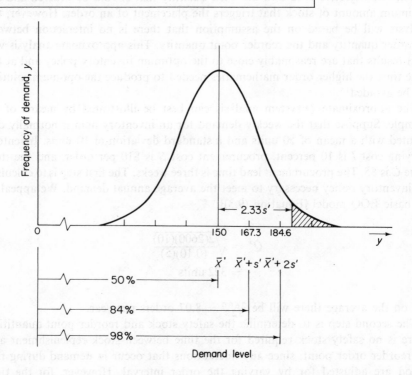

FIGURE 9-7
Area under normal distribution of demand *y* during lead
time for the example problem

distribution, which is three in this case. Hence, the properties of the three-week
demand distribution (Fig. 9-7) would be

$$\text{Mean } (\bar{X}') = 3(50) = 150 \text{ units}$$
$$\text{Standard deviation } (S') = 10\sqrt{3} = 17.32 \text{ units.}$$

To this point in the development of the analysis, no mention has been made
of the cost of being out of stock. The reason is that the analysis might go in different directions at this point. That is, we could estimate the cost of being out of
stock and then set the safety stock level to just balance stockout costs with the
cost of carrying the safety stock. The probability of having a stockout during an
order interval is a result of this economic balance. The second approach is to
specify an acceptable stockout level and then to set the safety stock level. Though
the stockout cost is not specified in this latter case, management by its action is
implying a stockout cost. Consider the latter case first.

Assigned Customer Service Level. Suppose management has established the
policy that on the average there should be only one chance in one hundred of a
stockout occurring during the lead time period, that is, only one stockout in

every 100 lead times. We are looking for the demand level y such that there is 1 percent of the area under the probability curve for the normal distribution to the right of this point, as shown in Fig. 9-7. From Table 9-A at the end of this chapter, this point is 2.33 standard deviations from the mean $\bar{X}'$. Thus, the safety stock quantity r is $2.33S' = (2.33)(17.32)$, or about 40 units. The reorder point R is $\bar{X}' + r = 150 + 40 = 190$ units.

To summarize the inventory policy, an order should be placed when stock is depleted to 190 units. The order quantity is 322 units, and orders will be placed about eight times per year. Management can expect that, on the average, a stockout will occur in only one out of 100 order intervals.

Known Stockout Costs. Knowledge of the stockout costs leads us to a slightly different problem formulation than when customer service levels are assigned. The customer service level will be determined by an economic balance of the inventory costs rather than by management policy.

There are two types of out-of-stock costs that we want to consider. First, there is the cost that is constant for each out-of-stock unit and is expressed on a per-unit basis. This representation is most appropriate when items are ordered one at a time and each order (item) requires separate processing and handling. The second type is the fixed cost for each stockout period. Stockout costs may be treated as constant per stockout period when a large number of items appear on a few orders, when a minimum staff level must be maintained to process backorders, or when stockouts, regardless of level, have a constant negative affect on goodwill. In practice, stockout costs do not clearly fall into either of these two extremes; rather, some combination of both is more likely. However, the relative insensitivity of inventory policy decisions to precise specification of stockout costs means that the more appropriate of these stockout types can be used with a low risk of making a poor policy decision. The per-unit stockout cost case is illustrated below.

Finding the best inventory policy with known per-unit stockout costs k begins with building a total relevant inventory cost expression. The components are

$$\frac{D}{Q}S = \text{annual procurement cost, \$.}$$

$$IC\frac{Q}{2} = \text{annual carrying cost to meet average demand, \$.}$$

$$ICr = \text{annual carrying cost for } r \text{ units of safety stock, \$.}$$

$$\frac{D}{Q}kS'N(z) = \text{annual stockout cost, \$.}$$

where $N(z)$ is called the *unit normal loss integral* with values tabulated in Table 9-B. The inventory cost model is constructed by summing the individual cost components into a single expression involving the decision variables of order quantity Q and safety stock r. That is,

$$TC(Q, r) = \frac{D}{Q}S + IC\frac{Q}{2} + ICr + \frac{D}{Q}kS'N(z) \tag{9.6}$$

where $S'N(z)$ is the expected number of units out of stock in an order interval with r units of safety stock in the inventory system.[17] The application of the concepts of differential calculus will yield expressions whereby Q and r can be found.[18] Hence,

$$Q^* = \sqrt{\frac{2D[S + kS'N(z)]}{IC}} \tag{9.7}$$

and

$$P_{r^*} = \frac{Q^*IC}{Dk} \tag{9.8}$$

where P_{r^*} is the probability of having a stockout when the safety stock level is r^*. The asterisk * refers to an optimum value.

Though we would like to solve these two expressions simultaneously to find the best Q and r values, this cannot be done with respect to Q directly. Therefore, we resort to an iterative solution procedure. An approximate value for Q can be found by solving the basic EOQ model [Equation (9.3)]. In the previous example, Q was found to be 322 units, and we use this as an initial value for Q. With an initial Q value and the stockout cost k estimated to be \$2/unit, we can solve Equation (9.8). Thus,

$$P_{r^*} = \frac{(322)(0.10)(5)}{(2600)(2)}$$

$$= 0.031$$

[17]
$$S'N(z) = \int_{\bar{X}'+r}^{\infty} (y - \bar{X}' - r)f(y)\,dy$$

[18] The partial derivative with respect to Q of the total cost expression would be

$$\frac{\partial TC(Q,r)}{\partial Q} = -\frac{DS}{Q^2} + \frac{IC}{2} + 0 - \frac{Dk}{Q^2}\int_{\bar{X}'+r}^{\infty} (y - \bar{X}' - r)f(y)\,dy = 0$$

and solving for Q gives

$$Q = \sqrt{\frac{2D\left[S + k\int_{\bar{X}'+r}^{\infty} (y - \bar{X}' - r)f(y)\,dy\right]}{IC}}$$

Then the partial derivative of the total cost expression with respect to r gives

$$\frac{\partial TC(Q,r)}{\partial r} = 0 + 0 + IC + \frac{Dk}{Q}\int_{\bar{X}'+r}^{\infty} (-1)f(y)\,dy = 0$$

and solving for $\int_{\bar{X}'+r^*}^{\infty} f(y)\,dy$ gives

$$\int_{\bar{X}'+r^*}^{\infty} f(y)\,dy = \frac{Q^*IC}{Dk} = P_{r^*}$$

This derivation requires taking the derivative of an integral, which is discussed in Maurice Sasieni, Arthur Yaspan, and Lawrence Friedman, *Operations Research—Methods and Problems* (New York: John Wiley & Sons, Inc., 1959), pp. 304–6.

Technically, the term P_{r^*} is the probability of demand y equaling or exceeding the average demand during lead time plus the safety stock $(\bar{X}' + r)$, as shown in Fig. 9-8. We are seeking the amount of safety stock r, and we can find how many standard deviations that r lies from the mean $\bar{X}'$ by using the normal distribution table (Table 9-A). For $P_{r^*} = 0.031$, r lies 1.87 standard deviations z away from the mean of the demand during lead time distribution. Since there are 17.32 units S' per standard deviation, $r = z \times S'$, or 32.4 units. Recall that S' is the number of units in a standard deviation of the demand during lead time distribution.

FIGURE 9-8

Safety stock level r shown on the demand during lead time distribution

---

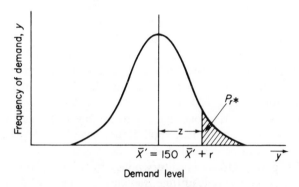

Now with a first estimate of the safety stock level, the order quantity determined from Equation (9.7) can now be found. Since we know that r lies 1.87 standard deviations z from the mean of the demand during lead time distribution, the value of the normal loss integral is $N(1.87) = 0.01195$, from Table 9-B. Substituting into Equation (9.7), we have

$$Q^* = \sqrt{\frac{2(2600)[10 + 2(17.32 \times 0.01195)]}{(0.10)(5)}}$$
$$= 329 \text{ units}$$

This completes the approximate solution. The best estimate of the optimum order quantity is 329 units and of the reorder point quantity (R) is $150 + 32.4$, or 182 units. If greater accuracy is desired, use the updated Q value to find the new r value from Equation (9.8). With the new r value, a new Q value can be found from Equation (9.7). And so the iterative procedure goes until two successive Q and r values repeat. At this point the true optimum policy will be found.

The total cost [Equation (9.6)] for the approximate solution is

$$TC(Q^*, r^*) = \frac{(2600)(10)}{329} + \frac{(0.10)(5)(329)}{2} + (0.10)(5)(32.4)$$
$$+ \frac{(2600)(2)(17.32)(0.01195)}{329}$$
$$= \$180.80$$

Note that the substitution of the unit normal loss integral has been made into the above equation. Also note that the total inventory costs have increased from $161.20 for the certainty case to $180.80. The difference is the price we pay for uncertainty.

UNCERTAIN DEMAND, UNCERTAIN LEAD TIME

The decision analysis developed to this point has assumed a constant lead time for stock replenishment. However, it is rare to find a situation in practice where lead time is known exactly. The factors that make up lead time—order processing and transmittal time, production time and in-transit time—are each subject to random variation such that lead time is better described by a probability distribution than by a single value.

We need to be concerned about uncertainty in lead time for the same reason that we were concerned about demand uncertainty. That is, an out-of-stock situation can occur because of our inability to plan for exactly the demand level that will take place. Since in this case both lead time and demand uncertainties are accounted for simultaneously, a joint probability distribution is created that gives the probabilities for various lead time length and a demand level combinations. To handle this case in a rigorous mathematical way is extremely difficult, and consequently only models of limited applicability have been developed. However, if some information can be generated about the demand distribution during lead time, it would be possible to set inventory policy by the approximate method used in the previous section, where lead time was known. One procedure of generating the lead time distribution is by using Monte Carlo methods and computer simulation to form the joint probability distribution.[19] The concepts behind the development of such a simulation are not complicated, but the programming effort may become quite extensive if each of the distributions is simulated in great detail.

To determine the properties of the demand during lead time distribution, Brown[20] has shown that for the case where average demand is constant and the demand and lead time distributions are independent, the variance of demand during lead time is given by[21]

$$S'^2 = \bar{t} \cdot S_D^2 + \bar{X}^2 \cdot S_{LT}^2 \tag{9.9}$$

where

S'^2 = variance of demand during lead time distribution.

[19] A discussion of how to program the computer for this case is given in Claude McMillan and Richard F. Gonzalez, *Systems Analysis: A Computer Approach to Decision Models* (Homewood, Illinois: Richard D. Irwin, Inc., 1965), pp. 81–114.

[20] Robert G. Brown, *Smoothing, Forecasting and Prediction of Discrete Time Series* (Englewood Cliffs, N. J.: Prentice-Hall, Inc., 1962). pp. 366–67.

[21] If demand and lead time distributions are not independent, the variance of demand during lead time is given by

$$S'^2 = \bar{t}^2 \cdot S_D^2 + \bar{X}^2 \cdot S_{LT}^2 + S_D \cdot S_{LT}$$

$\bar{X}$ = average demand for the original or one-period demand distribution.
S_D^2 = variance of the original demand distribution.
$\bar{t}$ = average lead time length expressed in the number of demand periods.
S_{LT}^2 = variance of lead time distribution.

The average demand during lead time is $\bar{t}\bar{X}$. For example, if a lead time distribution has a mean $\bar{t}$ of two weeks with a variance (S_{LT}^2) of 1.5 weeks, and the weekly demand distribution has a mean $\bar{X}$ of 100 units and a variance S_D^2 of 70 units, the distribution of demand during lead time would have a mean $(\bar{X})'$ of 2(100) = 200 units. The variance of the demand during lead time distribution would be

$$S'^2 = 2.0(70) + (100)^2(1.5)$$
$$= 15{,}140 \text{ units}$$

or a standard deviation of 124 units.

Compared with the demand distribution, the lead time distribution gives the logistician a greater degree of control. He can select among several transportation services with different operating characteristics, install various order processing systems ranging from manual to computerized, or build supply inventories, all of which effect the lead time distribution. Purely from an inventory standpoint, the logistician would like consistent lead times as well as short average lead times. Both permit safety stock levels and stockout costs to be at a minimum. However, these lower inventory costs are traded for the higher costs needed to realize improved lead time performance. Clearly, lead time is a control variable that can be used in balancing opposing costs at a lower total cost level.

P-system Models

Recall that the P-system of inventory control, in contrast with the Q-system as illustrated in Fig. 9-6, refers to a fixed order interval, variable order quantity policy. That is, the stock level of an item is reviewed at preset times, and if the quantity on hand is below a desired maximum, then the difference is placed on order (Fig. 9-9). This system is particularly appropriate when the stock level review can be coordinated for a number of items so that inventory maintenance is kept to a minimum. In addition, transportation cost savings may be possible as a result of ordering a number of items together so that advantage can be taken of the weight breaks in the transportation rate structure.

Two P-system models will be discussed. The first involves uncertain demand and constant costs. The second involves known demand and costs that fluctuate over time.

UNCERTAIN DEMAND MODEL

This P-system model is very similar to the Q-system model under uncertain demand conditions. However, one important difference in the P-system is that all demand fluctuations (both order period and lead time) must be protected against,

FIGURE 9-9

Inventory level over time under uncertain demand conditions and a variable order quantity, fixed order interval (*P*-system) inventory policy with back orders

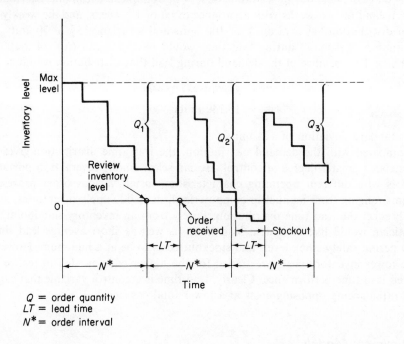

Q = order quantity
LT = lead time
N^* = order interval

whereas only demand fluctuations during the lead time period are important in calculating safety stock in the Q-system. This makes the P-system model even more complex to formulate precisely than the Q-system model, but an approximate solution will provide reasonable answers while considerably reducing the complexity of the decision problem.

To solve the P-system model, we need to know the time between stock level reviews and the maximum stock to be carried. We begin with the simplification that a reasonable solution can be found by providing enough safety stock to protect against demand fluctuations for one order interval plus the lead time period. A second simplification is that the decision about the order interval length can be made independently of the safety stock decision. Let us continue with the same example used in the development of the Q-system model, which had the following specifications:

S = procurement cost, \$10/order.
I = carrying cost, 10%.
C = unit value, \$5/unit.
D = weekly demand normally distributed, mean = 50 units, standard deviation = 10 units.

k = stockout cost, \$2/unit backordered.

LT = lead time, 3 weeks.

A good approximation to the optimum order interval is obtained from the basic EOQ model [Equations (9.3) and (9.4)]. The order quantity is

$$Q^* = \sqrt{\frac{2(50)(52)(10)}{(0.10)(5)}}$$

$$= 322 \text{ units}$$

and the order interval is

$$N^* = \frac{D}{Q^*}$$

$$= \frac{2600}{322}$$

$$= 8.07 \text{ orders/year}$$

The stock level would be reviewed every $52/8.07 = 6.45$ weeks.

Next we need to develop the relevant distribution of demand for the order interval of 6.45 weeks plus the lead time of three weeks. Thus, the weekly demand distribution is convoluted for 9.45 weeks. The average demand for the convoluted demand distribution would be $\bar{X}' = 9.45(50)$ or 473 units, and the standard deviation would be $S' = 10\sqrt{9.45}$ or 30.8 units. Now, we can find the amount of safety stock r required by balancing the carrying costs for the safety stock with the stockout costs. The cost expression is only a function of r and can be stated as follows:

Total relevant cost = cost of carrying safety stock + out-of-stock costs or

$$TC(r) = ICr + \frac{D}{Q}kS'N(z) \tag{9.10}$$

Taking the derivative with respect to r and setting it equal to zero yields the same result as Equation (9.8), or

$$P_{r^*} = \frac{Q^*IC}{Dk} \tag{9.11}$$

Solving for P_{r^*}, which is the right tail area under the normal distribution curve from the point $\bar{X}' + r$, gives

$$P_{r^*} = \frac{(322)(0.10)(5)}{(2600)(2)}$$

$$= 0.031$$

From Table 9-A, we find that for the right tail area to be 0.031, r must lie 1.87 standard deviations away from the mean of the distribution. Since $S' = 30.8$, $r = 30.8(1.87)$ or 57.6 units. This completes the computations, but what have we found?

When an order is placed every $6\frac{1}{2}$ (6.45) weeks, we need enough stock to cover the lead time period or 150 units plus the safety stock of $r = 57.6$ units plus the stock needed to cover the normal demand for the time between order arrivals of 322 units. This gives a total of approximately 530 units that should be on hand at the time of review. Thus, the number of units to be ordered is the difference between 530 and the quantity on hand. Recalling Fig. 9-9, we would have $N^* = 6.45$ weeks, Max level $= 530$ units, and $Q = $ Max level $-$ inventory on hand at time of review. The total cost for the P-system is $193.30, according to Equation (9.6), compared with $180.80 for the Q-system.

A DYNAMIC P-SYSTEM MODEL

The inventory policy for products that have demand values that will terminate in the near future (aircraft spare parts), that have inventory values that fluctuate significantly over time (scrap copper), or that have demand rates that fluctuate significantly over time (raw materials) cannot appropriately be established by using the above static analysis. Yet nearly every real inventory problem falls into this category, since conditions are constantly changing and elements of the problem interact. Often assumptions such as constant demand and constant costs are reasonable to make and do not substantially affect the inventory policy decision. However, when such assumptions are not acceptable, some other method is needed. Dynamic inventory problems of this type have been solved by the use of calculus,[22] linear programming,[23] and dynamic programming. The concept of dynamic programming will be discussed as a useful approach to making inventory policy decisions under dynamic data conditions.

Example. The distribution manager of the mythical Regal Piping Company makes a brand of pipe for use in highly corrosive environments. Pipe style 203T is sold to contractors for special installations. Regal has firm contracts to produce different quantities of 203T over the next three months. This production will require 8, 16, and 20 tons of Zudnium, an important raw material in the production of 203T. Zudnium is in short supply and is purchased in the open market. The company anticipates that the price per ton will be given by $(1)p^2$, where p is the amount purchased. It will cost $4 per ton to carry the raw material in inventory from one month to the next. The distribution manager desires to establish a purchasing plan that provides the needed raw material. The lead time is sufficiently short that the purchase decision does not have to be made until the beginning of each month. There are currently two tons of Zudnium on hand, but none is desired to be in stock at the end of the three months.

We can easily find the best ordering policy by analyzing the decision to be made each month beginning with the last month and following the rules of dynamic

---

[22] See Daniel Teichroew, *An Introduction to Management Science: Deterministic Models* (New York: John Wiley & Sons, Inc., 1964), pp. 563–65.

[23] See A. S. Cahn, Jr., "The Warehouse Problem," (Abstract) *Bulletin of the American Mathematical Society*, Vol. 54 (1948), p. 1973.

programming. Let p_i be the amount of Zudnium purchased in month i and z_i be the amount carried over from the previous month into month i.

THIRD MONTH. The amount to be purchased in the third month is the difference between the amount of p_3 needed to meet production demand and the amount of stock z_3 carried over from the second month. That is,

$$p_3^* = 20 - z_3 \tag{9.12}$$

The cost incurred in the third month is the sum of the purchase costs and the inventory carrying costs. Hence,

$$C_3 = 4z_3 + p_3^2 \tag{9.13}$$

Since we know the optimum purchase quantity, at least in terms of z_3, the optimum third month cost is

$$C_3^* = 4z_3 + (20 - z_3)^2 \tag{9.14}$$

resulting from substituting Equation (9.12) into Equation (9.13).

SECOND MONTH. We now proceed with similar computations for the second month. First, we express the amount of stock z_3 carried over to month 3 as equal to the stock carried over to month 2 plus the amount purchased less the amount used in the second month's production. That is,

$$z_3 = z_2 + p_2 - 16 \tag{9.15}$$

The monthly cost is

$$C_2 = 4z_2 + p_2^2 \tag{9.16}$$

The best second-month purchase decision can be found from combining the second month's costs C_2 [Equation (9.16)] and the optimum cost for the third month C_3^* [Equation (9.14)]. Hence,

$$\begin{aligned} C_{2,3} &= C_2 + C_3^* \\ &= 4z_2 + p_2^2 + 4z_3 + (20 - z_3)^2 \end{aligned} \tag{9.17}$$

We want the value for p_2 that will make $C_{2,3}$ a minimum. Though we might try various values of p_2 and observe $C_{2,3}$, using differential calculus leads us to p_2^*. That is,

$$p_2^* = 17 - \frac{z_2}{2} \tag{9.18}$$

Substituting this result back into Equation (9.17) gives the following optimum cost expression for *both* the second and third month.

$$\begin{aligned} C_{2,3}^* &= 4z_2 + \left(17 - \frac{z_2}{2}\right)^2 + 4\left(z_2 + 17 - \frac{z_2}{2} - 16\right) + \left(36 - z_2 - 17 + \frac{z_2}{2}\right)^2 \\ &= 6z_2 + \left(17 - \frac{z_2}{2}\right)^2 + 4 + \left(19 - \frac{z_2}{2}\right)^2 \end{aligned} \tag{9.19}$$

The solution pattern is now well established. We repeat it for the first month. The monthly cost is

$$C_1 = 4z_1 + p_2^2 \tag{9.20}$$

and the inventory carryover is

$$z_2 = z_1 + p_1 - 8 \tag{9.21}$$

The combined cost for all three months is given by the sum of Equations (9.19) and (9.21):

$$C_{1,2,3} = C_1 + C_{2,3}^*$$
$$= 4z_1 + p_1^2 + 6z_2 + \left(17 - \frac{z_2}{2}\right)^2 + 4 + \left(19 - \frac{z_2}{2}\right)^2 \tag{9.22}$$

Substituting Equation (9.21) into Equation (9.22) yields

$$C_{1,2,3} = 4z_1 + p_1^2 + 6(z_1 + p_1 - 8) + \left(17 - \frac{z_1 + p_1 - 8}{2}\right)^2$$
$$+ 4 + \left(19 - \frac{z_1 + p_1 - 8}{2}\right)^2 \tag{9.23}$$

Using the concepts of differential calculus gives us p_1^*. The result is

$$p_1^* = \frac{38 - z_1}{3} \tag{9.24}$$

Since we know the current inventory level, our optimum inventory policy can be found by working backward through the computations. The value for $p_1^* = 12$ since $z_1 = 2$ [Equation (9.24)]. This information is substituted into Equation (9.21) to yield $z_2 = 6$. Now Equation (9.18) can be solved to give $p_2^* = 14$. Continuing in the same manner, we obtain $z_3 = 4$ and $p_3^* = 16$. The minimum cost according to Equation (9.22) would be $C_{1,2,3}^* = \$644$. It is interesting to note that to follow the policy of directly ordering for production without any inventory carryover would result in a total cost of \$692, $7\frac{1}{2}$ percent higher than the optimum policy.

At this point it may seem that all inventory problems should be approached by means of a dynamic analysis. To a degree this is true, since the future is another important dimension to the problems that cannot be neglected. However, there are shortcomings to this dynamic analysis that should be realized. First, it is assumed that we have knowledge of the demand and cost levels for significant periods in the future. If the future is highly uncertain, applying and reapplying the static *P*- or *Q*-system models in each future period may provide better policies, since the decision information does not have to be projected far into the future. Second, the problem involved must be fairly simple to be handled by current analysis techniques. That is, there must be few interdependencies between periods, and there cannot be many time periods involved. Analytical techniques to handle the dynamic inventory problem will undoubtedly improve and reduce these shortcomings. In the meantime the logistician should be conscious of the time dimension when establishing inventory policies. If a dynamic analysis like that illustrated above cannot be used, plans should be made to review inventory policies periodically so that they remain relevant to current conditions.

Multiple Item, Multiple Location Analysis

The inventory problem faced by the logistician in the real world is truly the large-scale problem. It often involves hundreds of product items located at numerous warehouses. The demand for the items varies among warehouse territories, and not all items are maintained at each warehouse. Product is supplied to the warehouses from a number of plants, and several different transportation services are used in the course of moving the product from plant to warehouse to customer. In many cases the complex problem suggested here can be solved by using the various techniques previously discussed in this chapter. One approach is to subdivide the large-scale problem into a number of independent single-item, single-location problems and then apply one of the *Q*- and *P*-system models. This approach is no more complex than finding the best inventory policy for one item or a homogeneous group of items.[24] Since these models have already been discussed in some detail, we explore an integrated approach to the large-scale problem. The integrated approach uses many of the previously discussed concepts and requires management to specify customer service levels. It does not necessarily produce optimum inventory policies, but at the same time few simplifying assumptions are necessary. The method to be discussed is an automatic inventory control system with a digital computer being used to update inventory records, print reports, and take action in the form of stock orders according to preset decision rules. The method is general and could be used with only slight modification in many different situations. It was actually used by a manufacturer of industrial cleaning compounds, who will be referred to as the Usemore Soap Company.

The Usemore Soap Company sold over 200 products with more than 750 line items for cleaning applications of all types. Restaurants, schools, hospitals, car washes, and industrial firms were examples of customers for soap, and Usemore had more than 71,000 individual customers. Sales in 1968 were $50 million, or about 180 million pounds of soap. Sixty percent of these sales were processed through 105 public warehouses located throughout the United States. The problem was to establish the operating policies that would provide the desired level of customer service while incurring a minimum inventory cost.

A schematic diagram of Usemore's inventory control system is shown in Fig. 9-10. The normal information flow is to have orders placed through salesmen or by telephone to the warehouse. The sales information is forwarded to headquarters, where the computer updates the inventory records. When stock is depleted at a

[24] Some models have been developed to analyze the multiple product, multiple facility problem as a single problem, but the models remain at the theoretical level. For a survey of such models, see Donald L. Iglehart, "Recent Results in Inventory Theory," *Journal of Industrial Engineering*, Vol. 17 (January 1967), pp. 48–51.

FIGURE 9-10

Inventory control and information system for the Usemore Soap Company

---

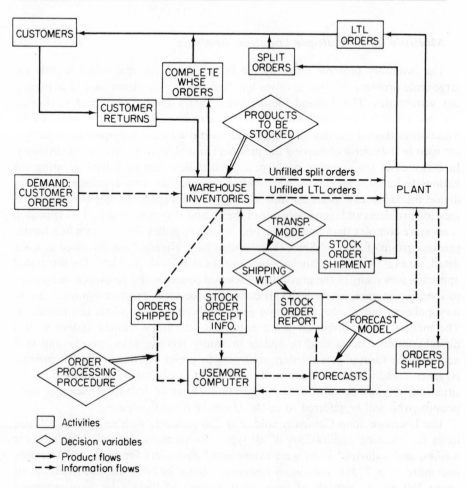

Activities

Decision variables

Product flows

Information flows

Courtesy of Logistics Systems, Inc.

warehouse, a stock order is issued on the plant by the computer. When replenishment stocks arrive at the warehouse, the computer is informed and the inventory record is adjusted. To maintain adequate stock in each warehouse at all times, the computer is called upon to forecast item sales each month and, if necessary, to alter the amount of stock flowing to the warehouse. The system is keyed to the sales forecast, so we begin discussion of the inventory control system design at this point.

Central to any large-scale automatic inventory control system is the short-range forecast of item sales. Random events, seasonal influences, and general economic activity all affect the level of sales. Forecasting the level of sales is essential to good inventory planning because the time lags in replenishing stock do not always permit having enough stock on hand to meet all possible demand levels. By anticipating the demand that will occur, excessive over- and understock costs may be avoided. We do not seek a forecasting method that will predict the exact level of future demand. Contingencies like weather, strikes, and riots impart such random fluctuations in sales that to follow this random pattern in sales could cause wild fluctuations in inventory levels if we based our inventory planning on a model with the sensitivity to follow these random variations in sales. Conversely, a forecasting method so insensitive that fundamental changes in the level of sales go undetected is equally as unsatisfactory. Inventory planning based on such a highly overdamped (insensitive) forecast model might result in long periods of large overstock and understock, especially if a significant rising or falling trend is occurring in sales. Obviously, the most economical inventory system will be achieved when it is based on a forecast method that will generate values between these extremes.

There are four popular mathematical models that might be used to project sales. These are (1) a moving average model, (2) a time series model, (3) a multiple regression model, and (4) an exponential smoothing model. The latter is a widely accepted predictive method for inventory control applications, partly because of the minimum amount of data that needs to be stored in the computer. For example, the exponential smoothing model requires that only the previous forecast and the current actual sales level be retained, whereas a 12-month moving average would require retention of 12 sales values for the last 12 months. This is a sizable reduction when thousands of items are involved. Because of this, the discussion will center on the exponential smoothing model. Discussion of the other methods can be found in almost any textbook on elementary statistics[25] and in the chapter of this text on information systems.

The Basic Model. Like most forecasting techniques, the exponential smoothing model uses historical data as a basis for predicting the future. It is a kind of moving average, except that past observations are not given equal weight. Rather, the weight given to past observations decreases geometrically with the age of the data; that is, more recent observations are weighted more heavily than less recent observations. Such a geometric weighting system can be reduced to a rather simple expression involving only the forecast from the most recent period and the actual demand for the current period. Thus, the predicted demand level for the next period is given by

$$\text{New forecast} = \alpha(\text{actual demand}) + (1 - \alpha)(\text{previous forecast}) \qquad (9.25)$$

where α is a weighting factor having values between 0 and 1, and is commonly referred to as the exponential smoothing constant. Note that the effect of all previous data is included in the previous forecast figure, so that only one number needs to be retained by a computer to represent the demand history.

[25] For example, see Samuel B. Richmond, *Statistical Analysis*, 2nd edition (New York, The Ronald Press Company, 1964), pp. 347–50, 424–71.

Suppose that a demand level of 1000 units was forecast for the current month. Actual demand for the current month is 950 units. The value for the smoothing constant is $\alpha = 0.3$. The expected value for demand next month according to the above formula would be

$$\text{New forecast} = 0.3(950) + 0.7(1000)$$
$$= 985 \text{ units}$$

This forecast becomes the previous forecast when the procedure is repeated one month from now. And so it goes.

Choosing the proper value for the exponential smoothing constant is in large part a matter of judgment. The higher the value of α, the greater is the weight placed on current sales levels and the quicker the response to changes in the sales level. The lower the α value, the greater is the weight given to past sales levels in predicting future sales levels and the longer is the lag time in responding to changes in the level of sales. Guide-line values for α range from 0.1 to 0.3, though higher values may be used for short times when anticipated changes will occur, such as a recession, an aggressive but temporary promotional campaign, discontinuing some products in the line, or starting the forecasting procedure when few historical sales results are available. A good rule to follow when searching for an α value is to choose a value that will allow the forecast model to track the major changes occurring in demand and average the random fluctuations.

Improving the Model. The basic forecast model described above gives good performance when a high degree of accuracy is not required or when the sales pattern is similar to Fig. 9-11(a). However, when there is trend in the data or a significant seasonal pattern (the seasonal pattern is discernible from the random fluctuations in the data), knowledge of the nature of these factors can be used to improve the tracking of the forecast model. Remember, we want the forecast model to follow fundamental changes in sales but generally not random fluctuations.

One possible trend line in sales data is illustrated in Fig. 9-11(b). Here a straight line is shown, though the long-term growth or decline in sales might take any shape. If the basic model is used in this situation, a predicted value will lag the change in actual values. However, the basic model can be modified to reduce the lag. The addition (or subtraction) to sales for amount due to trend is estimated by the difference between the new forecast and the previous forecast. Exponentially smoothing the trend values yields

$$\text{New trend} = \alpha(\text{new forecast} - \text{previous forecast})$$
$$+ (1 - \alpha)(\text{previous trend}) \tag{9.26}$$

Combining this with the basic model gives

$$\text{Corrected forecast} = \text{new forecast} + \left(\frac{1-\alpha}{\alpha}\right)(\text{new trend}) \tag{9.27}$$

FIGURE 9-11
Examples of common sales patterns

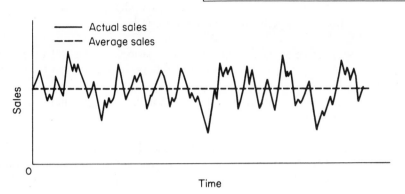

(a) Random sales pattern with no trend or seasonal element

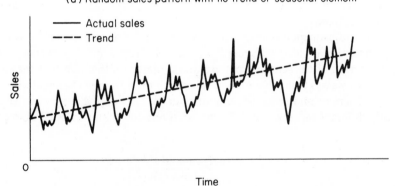

(b) Random sales pattern with an increasing trend in sales,
but no seasonal element

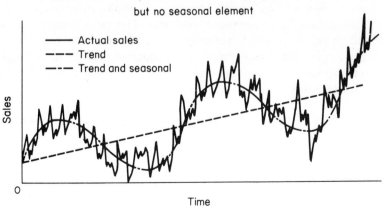

(c) Random sales pattern with both trend and seasonal elements

313

where $(1 - \alpha)/\alpha$ times the magnitude of the trend is the extent of the error in the steady state.[26]

Correction for seasonality is the second major modification that might be made to the basic forecast model. However, before the model with seasonal corrections is developed, Brown suggests that two conditions be met.

1. There must be a known reason for the periodic peaks and valleys in the demand pattern, and these peaks and valleys should occur at the same time every year.
2. The seasonal variation in demand should be larger than the random variations, or "noise."[27]

If seasonal demand is not stable and significant as these conditions suggest, then it becomes extremely difficult to develop a model that will predict the direction and magnitude of the next period's sales. Seasonal demand is not discernible from random variations. If these conditions hold, knowledge of major changes occurring in the demand pattern can be used in the forecast model to anticipate similar future changes in demand.

Seasonal adjustments usually involve some form of an index or ratio where the actual demand is divided by some base value such as a moving average for one complete period of the seasonal pattern and centered on the month of the year for which the forecast is being made. In keeping with the notion of exponential smoothing and a desire to minimize the amount of data stored in the computer, we create a slightly different ratio with a different interpretation than suggested above. That is,

$$\text{Ratio} = \frac{\text{actual demand this month}}{\text{base value}} \qquad (9.28)$$

where the base value may be the demand in the corresponding period one year ago or the average demand over several periods in situations where the seasonal peaks tend to shift slightly from one year to the next. This ratio requires that demand data for 12 periods be retained, whereas data for 19 periods are required when the moving average is used. The demand ratio [Equation (9.28)] can be manipulated in the usual exponential smoothing manner to yield a forecast value. For example, the basic relationship is

$$\text{New forecast ratio} = \alpha(\text{current demand ratio}) + (1 - \alpha)\text{previous}$$
$$\text{forecast ratio} \qquad (9.29)$$

[26] For a development of this function see Robert G. Brown, *Smoothing, Forecasting and Prediction of Discrete Time Series* (Englewood Cliffs, N. J.: Prentice-Hall, Inc., 1962), p. 114.

[27] Robert G. Brown, "Less Risk in Inventory Estimates" reprinted in Norton E. Marks and Robert M. Taylor, *Marketing Logistics: Perspectives and Viewpoints* (New York: John Wiley & Sons, Inc., 1967), p. 166.

Correcting for trend, we have

$$\text{New trend} = \alpha(\text{new forecast ratio} - \text{previous forecast ratio})$$
$$+ (1 - \alpha)\text{previous trend} \tag{9.30}$$

The trend-corrected forecast ratio becomes

$$\text{Corrected forecast ratio} = \text{new forecast ratio} + \left(\frac{1 - \alpha}{\alpha}\right)\text{new trend} \tag{9.31}$$

Converting the corrected forecast ratio to a demand level, we multiply it by the base value. Hence,

$$\text{Forecast next period} = \text{corrected forecast ratio} \times \text{demand one}$$
$$\text{year ago next period} \tag{9.32}$$

A caution should be made at this point about the use of the seasonally corrected model. This model is highly sensitive to even a moderate degree of random variation in the demand pattern, so the forecasts tend greatly to "overshoot" the actual demand levels. However, good performance can be expected when random variations in demand are minimal. Otherwise, the basic model with or without trend correction and using a high α value may produce better forecasts than the seasonally corrected model.

Forecast Error. Because an exponential smoothing model is based on historical data, prediction of future demand will generally be in error to some degree. If we know the extent of the errors in the forecasts on the average, a level of safety stock can be provided to protect against such errors.

The error in the forecast is defined as the difference between the actual demand level and the forecasted demand level. If these errors are plotted for a large number of forecasts, a frequency distribution will be generated like that shown in Fig. 9-12. The distribution of forecast errors usually approximates the normal distribution. The dispersion of the error about the mean error, which should be zero if our forecast model averages the random variation in demand as we would like and forecast errors are normally distributed, can be expressed in some common form such as the standard deviation, variance, or mean absolute deviation. The latter will be favored in our discussion to closely follow the work of Brown,[28] but there is no difficulty in converting to another form. That is, the mean absolute deviation (MAD) multiplied by 1.25 equals the standard deviation for the normal distribution, and, of course, the standard deviation squared gives the variance. The absolute deviation is defined as

$$\text{Absolute deviation} = |\text{actual demand} - \text{forecasted demand}| \tag{9.33}$$

where $||$ denotes the absolute value (the magnitude of the number only) of the expression contained within. The mean absolute deviation is the average of a

---

[28] *Ibid.*, pp. 159–70.

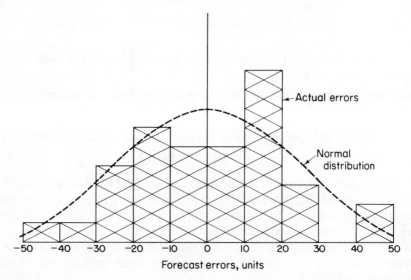

FIGURE 9-12

Example of a frequency distribution of forecast errors

number of individual forecast errors, where the average may be created by equally weighting or exponentially weighting forecast errors. For purposes of planning safety stock levels, we are interested in a projection of the expected forecast error dispersion in the coming period. MAD is a measure of the dispersion and is forecasted by means of an exponential smoothing model in precisely the same manner as demand. That is,

$$\text{New MAD forecast} = \alpha \,|\, \text{current actual demand} - \text{forecasted demand} \,|$$
$$+ \, (1 - \alpha)(\text{previous MAD forecast})$$

Example. Item 601T in the Usemore Soap line is a powdered floor cleaning compound sold mainly to schools for janitorial purposes. Sales are made in 550-pound drum units. The sales pattern for this product is strongly influenced by the school year, and the level of sales has been increasing. The sales pattern for the three-year period ending in 1969 as shown in Fig. 9-13 was replicated by simulating the trend, seasonal, and random factors in the demand pattern. This was done so that we might have the benefit of knowing the mean values of the random variations, which are also plotted in Fig. 9-13. Our objective in this example is to select a good forecast model, that is, one that best tracks the mean of the random variations in demand.

Three forecasting models were tested, different exponential smoothing constants being used. The three models were (1) the basic model, (2) the basic model with trend correction, and (3) the basic model with trend and seasonal corrections. The α values tested ranged from 0.1 to 1.0.

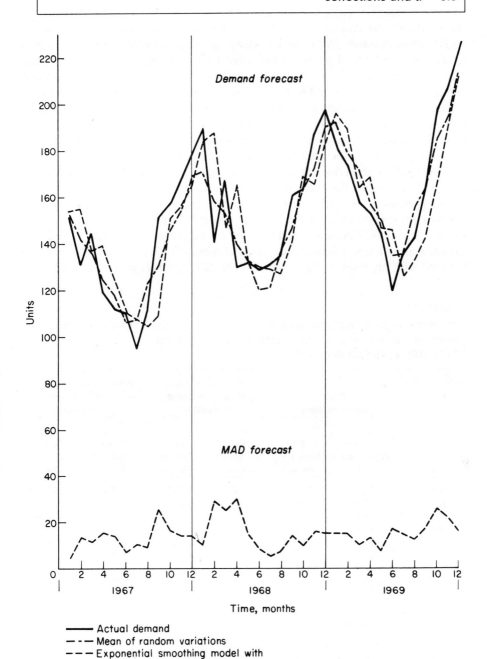

FIGURE 9-13

Demand and MAD forecasts for Usemore Soap Company's item number 601T, using an exponential smoothing model with trend and seasonal corrections and α = 0.5

Demand forecast

MAD forecast

Time, months

Units

————— Actual demand
—·—·— Mean of random variations
————— Exponential smoothing model with
   trend and seasonal corrections

317

Next, we need some guide lines for choosing the model and α value. A good rule of thumb to follow in this regard is to look for the model that tracks the major changes in demand and averages the random variations. If we could always effectively separate major changes and random demand, as shown in Fig. 9-13, we would merely choose the model that best tracks the mean of the random variations in demand. Since this knowledge is seldom available, two quantitative guide lines can be used instead. First, since on the average we desire a minimum error in the forecast, the model having the lowest standard deviation or MAD of forecast errors over a period of time is most desirable. Concurrently, we want the sum of the errors to cancel over a period of time so that no bias remains in the distribution of forecast errors. This is necessary if we are to interpret the normal error distribution in the usual way. Table 9-5 shows these two factors for the three models being tested. The standard deviation and sum-of-the-forecast errors values are averaged for 36 periods after the models have been allowed to stabilize for 24 periods to minimize the effect of initial conditions. From this test, the seasonal model appears to be the best model, though this is not unexpected, since the demand pattern shows a strong seasonal element. The seasonal model has both the lowest standard deviation and the sum of the errors nearest zero. The best α for the seasonal model is not so easily determined. The lowest standard deviation is found with an α value of 0.5, whereas the sum of errors nearest zero has an α

TABLE 9-5

An error performance comparison of three exponential smoothing forecast models for predicting sales of Usemore Soap Company's product item 601T

α	Basic Smoothing Model		Basic Smoothing Model with Trend Correction		Basic Smoothing Model with Trend & Seasonal Corrections	
	Standard Deviation of Forecast Errors	Sum of Forecast Errors	Standard Deviation of Forecast Errors	Sum of Forecast Errors	Standard Deviation of Forecast Errors	Sum of Forecast Errors
0.1	29.7	511	27.0	125	27.8	−416
0.2	27.2	430	26.4	94	20.7	−30
0.25	26.5	237	25.5	92	19.8	13[b]
0.3	25.8	205	24.4	90	19.2	35
0.4	24.3	163	22.5	87	18.7	53
0.5	22.8	136	20.7	85	18.6[a]	61
0.6	21.5	116	19.6	81	18.7	64
0.7	20.4	101	19.2	77	18.8	67
0.8	19.7	89	19.2	74	19.0	68
0.9	19.4	79	19.4	71	19.2	70
1.0	19.3	70	19.3	70	19.3	70

[a] Lowest standard deviation of forecast errors.
[b] Lowest sum of forecast errors.

value of 0.25. This suggests a range of values that might be appropriate. Using the standard deviation as the more appropriate measure of the two for setting the alpha value, $\alpha = 0.5$ is favored. This model is shown against demand for the 36 test periods in Table 9-6 and Fig. 9-13. It should also be noted from Tables 9-5 and 9-6 that the basic model and the trend-corrected model give good results when an α of approximately 0.9 is used.

Initial Conditions. The question of initial conditions needs to be raised before we return the discussion to issues more directly concerned with inventory control. When a new product is introduced or when historical sales data are not available for existing products, beginning a forecast without the benefit of past records can cause rather poor forecasts in the initial periods until a history is generated. There are several things that might be done during these initial periods. First, some artificial values might be used as past trend and forecast values. If these values are representative of the future, then the forecast will give good performance from the outset. Second, a high value of alpha may be used so that historical data are given little or no weight in future predictions. The value could then be lowered when the historical records are established. Third, several periods may be set aside where demand data are collected but no forecasts are made. During these periods, inventory stock levels are determined by the sales or distribution departments.

SETTING STOCK LEVELS

Usemore Soap had established a multi-item, multi-installation inventory control system that was neither the fixed order interval system or a fixed order quantity system, but closer to the former. Usemore Soap wanted to take advantage of transportation rate breaks and quantity stock order processing at both warehouses and plants, so replenishment of warehouse stocks did not occur until a predetermined shipping weight was reached. Shipping weight was the difference between the maximum stock level maintained and the actual stock level for all items in the warehouse. The required shipping weight might vary between 20,000 pounds and 80,000 pounds, depending on (1) the type of transportation used, (2) the rate break schedule, and (3) the frequency with which stock orders were accumulated. Because the particular date on which a stock order was released by the computer was a function of sales for all items stocked at the warehouse, the order cycle time could vary for any one item. Thus, the inventory control system actually was a variable order interval, variable order quantity system for individual items, as shown in Fig. 9-14.

This inventory system is guided by four variables: (1) the shipping weight (and transportation mode), (2) the level of customer service, (3) the items to be stored in a warehouse, and (4) the maximum inventory level in the warehouse. Given that the first three decisions have been made by management, now can we make the decision regarding the fourth? We begin by estimating the lead time. An average figure for lead time can be determined by summing the times associated with the

TABLE 9-6

A comparison with demand of the three exponential smoothing forecast models for predicting item 601T sales with all models using their best exponential smoothing constant (α) value[a]

Year	Month	Actual Demand	Mean of Random Variations	Basic Model ($\alpha = 0.9$) Demand Forecast	MAD Forecast	Error (e)	Basic Model with Trend Correction ($\alpha = 0.9$) Demand Forecast	MAD Forecast	Error (e)	Basic Model with Trend & Seasonal Correction ($\alpha = 0.5$) Demand Forecast	MAD Forecast	Error (e)
1967	1	151	152	152	3	-1	153	3	-2	154	4	-3
	2	131	141	151	18	-20	151	18	-20	155	13	-23
	3	145	136	134	12	12	132	14	13	137	11	8
	4	119	124	144	23	-25	145	24	-26	139	15	-20
	5	112	118	122	11	-9	120	9	-7	125	14	-12
	6	110	106	114	3	-3	112	2	-2	110	7	1
	7	95	107	111	15	-16	111	14	-16	107	10	-12
	8	112	122	97	15	15	95	16	17	104	9	8
	9	151	130	111	38	41	112	37	40	109	26	42
	10	157	145	147	13	11	151	10	7	151	16	7
	11	167	154	157	11	11	158	9	9	156	14	12
	12	178	169	167	12	12	168	11	11	165	14	13
1968	1	190	171	177	14	14	178	12	13	184	10	7
	2	141	158	189	45	-48	191	46	-50	188	29	-47
	3	168	153	146	25	23	142	29	27	147	25	21
	4	130	140	166	35	-36	168	36	-37	166	30	-35
	5	132	133	134	5	-2	131	5	1	132	15	0
	6	129	120	133	3	-3	132	3	-3	130	8	3
	7	131	121	130	2	2	129	2	2	129	5	3
	8	135	138	132	4	4	132	4	4	127	7	9
	9	161	147	135	24	26	136	24	26	141	14	21
	10	164	164	159	8	6	161	6	4	169	9	-4
	11	188	173	164	22	24	165	21	23	166	16	22
	12	198	191	186	14	13	188	11	10	183	15	15

Year	Month	Actual Demand	Mean of Random Variations	Basic Model (α = 0.9)			Basic Model with Trend Correction (α = 0.9)			Basic Model with Trend & Seasonal Correction (α = 0.5)		
				Demand Forecast	MAD Forecast	Error (e)	Demand Forecast	MAD Forecast	Error (e)	Demand Forecast	MAD Forecast	Error (e)
1969	1	181	193	197	15	−15	198	16	−17	197	15	−15
	2	174	179	183	9	−9	182	8	−7	189	15	−14
	3	158	172	175	16	−17	175	15	−16	164	10	−6
	4	153	157	160	8	−7	159	6	−5	169	13	−16
	5	144	150	154	9	−10	154	9	−9	147	7	−2
	6	120	135	146	24	−26	145	23	−25	146	17	−26
	7	136	136	123	15	14	120	17	17	126	14	11
	8	143	155	135	9	8	136	8	7	133	12	10
	9	164	165	143	20	21	144	19	20	142	17	23
	10	199	185	162	35	37	164	33	35	165	26	34
	11	208	195	195	16	13	199	12	10	191	22	18
	12	224	215	207	17	17	209	15	15	213	16	11

a The results from all models for the first 24 months are disregarded so that the effect of start up conditions on model performance is diminished.

FIGURE 9-14

Variable order interval, variable order quantity inventory control system
for one stock item used by the Usemore Soap Company

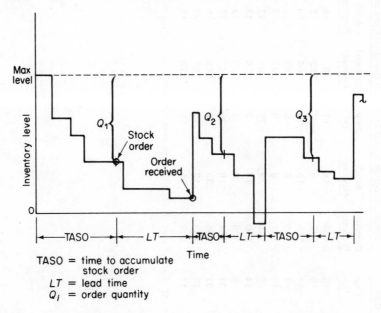

TASO = time to accumulate stock order
LT = lead time
Q_i = order quantity

various independent parts of lead time. For example, Usemore Soap had the
following lead time breakdown:

		Lead Time, Days	
Lead Time Factors	*Max.*	*Average*	*Min.*
(1) Lag in updating computer inventory records due to bills of lading preparation, invoicing, etc.	7	5	3
(2) Processing of stock order by Traffic Department	4	3	2
(3) Production of stock order	12	10	8
(4) Transit time	9	7	5
Totals	32	25	18

Lead time represents only one of two sources of variability that must be taken
into account when one is setting an inventory policy. Demand variability must also
be taken into account. As was previously pointed out, handling both lead time
and demand variability is a complex mathematical problem. What is sought is the
distribution of demand during lead time plus one order cycle. This distribution can
be determined accurately enough for most problems by an approximate method.

Since we are dealing with a fixed order interval inventory control system for all items together, we need to provide safety stock protection for one order cycle plus lead time. First, an estimate of the average order cycle time is needed. Though the order cycle is variable in length for individual items, a satisfactory inventory control system can be achieved by averaging the individual item order cycle lengths over a reasonable period of time. An estimate of order cycle length in months is

$$\text{Order cycle length for warehouse } j = \frac{\text{stock order shipping weight}}{\substack{\text{forecasted monthly demand} \\ \text{for all items in warehouse } j}} \qquad (9.35)$$

To illustrate, suppose that Usemore Soap stocks only four items in a particular warehouse. The monthly demand forecast for the four items shows expected sales of 2000, 15,000, 5000, 18,000 pounds, respectively. The required shipping weight is 20,000 pounds. Hence, the warehouse order cycle length (or time to accumulate a stock order) is

$$\frac{20,000}{2000 + 15,000 + 5000 + 18,000} = 0.5 \text{ month}$$

or approximately 10 days, given a month of 20 working days.

Given that one of the items in the warehouse has an expected monthly demand of 2000 pounds and a variation represented by MAD = 400 pounds, the distribution of demand during lead time plus one order cycle can now be estimated. If it is assumed that the forecast error is normally distributed and the range is represented by ± 2 standard deviations from the mean forecast, the maximum and minimum monthly demands are $2000 \pm 2(1.25)$MAD, where 1.25 MAD converts mean absolute deviation to a standard deviation. Thus, the maximum and minimum monthly forecast range is 3000 to 1000 units. Now, the approximate range of the distribution of demand during lead time plus one order cycle is

$$
\begin{aligned}
\text{Maximum demand} &= \frac{\text{maximum monthly demand}}{\text{working days per month}} \\
&\quad \times (\text{maximum lead time} + \text{order cycle time}) \\
&= \tfrac{3000}{20}(32 + 10) = 6300 \text{ pounds} \qquad (9.36)
\end{aligned}
$$

and

$$
\begin{aligned}
\text{Minimum demand} &= \frac{\text{minimum monthly demand}}{\text{working days per month}} \\
&\quad \times (\text{minimum lead time} + \text{order cycle time}) \\
&= \tfrac{1000}{20} \times (18 + 10) = 1400 \text{ pounds} \qquad (9.37)
\end{aligned}
$$

If the lead time and forecast error distributions are normally distributed, there will be only a small error in approximating the demand during an order cycle plus lead time by a normal distribution. Thus, over 99 percent of the distribution is within ± 3 standard deviations of the mean, that is, a range of 6.[29] An easily obtained estimate of the standard deviation from which to determine safety stock is

$$S' = \frac{(6300 - 1400)}{6}$$

$$= 816 \text{ pounds}$$

The above method for determining the standard deviation of the demand-lead time distribution on which safety stocks are based is noticeably crude. The method tends to overstate the standard deviation (and the safety stock), but the benefits of a simple computational method can outweigh higher costs due to slightly higher safety stock than necessary for adequate customer service. However, if greater accuracy is desired, there are several possibilities for improvement: (1) increase the range value from 6 to 8 or 10, (2) use computer simulation to generate a more accurate picture of the demand-lead time distribution, and (3) apply Equation 9.9 instead.

Safety Stock. Setting the safety stock level depends on the definition of customer service that is adopted. Suppose that customer service is based on the probability of having a stockout. If the service level is set at 98 percent or approximately two standard deviations away from the mean such that the probability of having a stockout is less than $2\frac{1}{2}$ percent (Fig. 9-15), the amount of safety stock r needed is $2S'$ or $2(816) = 1632$ pounds.

If the service level is set on the basis of the *number of units* out of stock per month rather than on the *probability* of a stockout occurring during an order cycle plus lead time period, the safety factor can be quite different. For example, if management desires a 98 percent service level, then for one order cycle plus lead time period, 2 percent out of the expected demand of $\frac{2000}{20} \times (25 + 10) = 3500$ units on the average may be backordered. To set the safety stock level, $(0.02 \times 3500) = 70$ out-of-stock units (pounds) needs to be translated into a standard deviation on the distribution of forecast errors curve. This is simply done by recalling Equation (9.6) and that $S'N(z)$ gives the expected number of units out of stock. Hence,

$$S'N(z) = 70 \text{ pounds}$$

and

$$N(z) = \frac{70}{816}$$

$$= 0.086$$

---

[29] The astute reader will note that simply adding the max and min of individual lead time factor's distributions inaccurately states the max and min for the combined distribution. If the distributions can be assumed to be normal, a more accurate approach would be to determine the max and min for the combined distribution from the square root of the sum of the squared differences between max and min. In this case, the Max(Min) = Avg $\pm \sqrt{(\text{Max-Min})^2} = 25 \pm \sqrt{(7-3)^2 + (4-2)^2 + (12-8)^2 + (9-5)^2}$ Thus, Max = 32.2 and Min = 17.8.

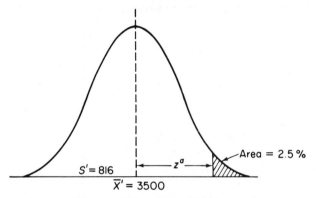

FIGURE 9-15

The approximate distribution of demand during one order cycle
plus lead time based on the expected demand and
an estimate of the standard deviation

Demand during one order cycle plus lead time

$$a_z = \frac{(\bar{X}' + r) - \bar{X}'}{S'}$$

The standard deviation z for a unit normal loss integral of 0.086 is found in Table 9-B. Thus, $z = 0.98$. The safety stock level based on this definition of customer service would be $0.98S'$, or 800 pounds of this particular soap item. The result is a more moderate safety stock level than under the previous customer service definition based on probability, even though the customer service levels on the surface were roughly the same (98 percent). This indicates the need to carefully define customer service.

Max Level. The amount of stock needed to meet the average demand during the order cycle plus lead time is

Regular stock $=$ (monthly forecast)

$$\times \left(\frac{\text{average order cycle length} + \text{average lead time}}{\text{number of working days per month}} \right) \quad (9.38)$$

Continuing the above example, we would need $(2000)(\frac{35}{20}) = 3500$ pounds. The max level (see Fig. 9-14) is the regular stock $\bar{X}'$ plus safety stock r or $3500 + 1632 = 5132$ pounds, if the first definition of customer service is used. Thus, the computer keeps track of the deficit between this max level and the current stock level for this item. When similar deficits for all items carried in the warehouse accumulate to the shipping weight, replenishment orders are placed on the plant to the extent of the deficit for each item. Stock in other warehouses is handled computationally in precisely the same manner as has been described above.

Concluding Comments

Inventories represent the second largest logistics cost item for the average firm. It is obvious that good management is essential. Extensive work has been carried out to improve the management of inventories, and this chapter summarizes the basic inventory control theory that has proved useful in practice. A number of models are presented because of the varied circumstances under which inventories are managed, and they can be classified as (1) *Q*-system or *P*-system types, (2) one-order or repeat-order types, (3) static or dynamic in nature, and (4) whether the input data to the models are known for sure or known only in a probabilistic way. These models deal with a single item and a single stocking point, which is a segmentation of the large-scale inventory problems usually faced by business firms. However, to show how these models of limited scope are useful in guiding inventory policies, the chapter concludes with a discussion of an inventory control procedure developed for a multiple time, multiple installation inventory system actually in use.

Before we leave the subject of inventory control, one further observation should be made. Much of the effort expended in the management of inventories is associated with forecasting, bookkeeping, order placement, etc., for possibly thousands of product items. The routine nature of much of inventory management as well as its similarity among many firms has encouraged the development of standardized computer packages for dealing with inventory control system design and operation. Most major computer manufacturers list such programs in their libraries. To note several, there are IBM's IMPACT program, NCR's REACT program, and Honeywell's PROFIT program.[30]

Questions and Problems

1. The following estimates are made about a certain inventory item:

> Demand: normally distributed with a mean of 100 units per week and
> a standard deviation of 20 units
> Inventory carrying cost: 20%
> Order costs: $20/order
> Item value: $20
> Lead time: 1.5 weeks

Determine the order quantity and reorder point in a *Q*-type inventory system for

[30] For an excellent summary discussion of these three programs, see Donald J. Bowersox, Edward W. Smykay, and Bernard J. LaLonde, *Physical Distribution Management*, revised edition (New York: The Macmillan Company, 1968), pp. 224–27.

(a) An assigned service level where there would be only a 10 percent chance of a stockout during any order period.

(b) A known stockout cost of $4/unit.

2. Repeat question 1, but assume that lead time is also variable. It is estimated that lead time is approximately normally distributed with a mean of 1.5 weeks and a standard deviation of $\frac{1}{3}$ week.

3. From the data from question 1(b), determine the maximum inventory level and the review interval for a *P*-type inventory control system.

4. Compute the total relevant cost of the inventory policies of question 1(b) and question 3. Why is the total cost of the *P*-system policies slightly higher than for those of the *Q*-system?

5. Prepare the Usemore Soap Company (B) case in Appendix C.

6. Sally's Flower Shop must plan its supply of flowers for a coming holiday season. A review of her own sales records plus her subjective judgment about the sales potential for long-stemmed white roses results in the following probability distribution.

Demand, Doz.	Probability
1	0.05
2	0.10
3	0.15
4	0.20
5	0.20
6	0.15
7	0.10
8	0.05
	1.00

Sally can buy roses for $3 per dozen. She sells them for $6 per dozen. Costs of wrapping and delivery are $0.50 per dozen. When the holiday has passed, all leftover roses are sold to institutions at $0.50 per dozen. How many roses should Sally order? How sensitive is your recommendation to Sally's estimate of the demand distribution?

7. You wish to establish a fixed order interval, variable order quantity inventory control system for a low-cost item. You gather the following information.

Procurement cost = $10/order.

Unit price = $10/unit.

Inventory carrying cost = 25 percent per year.

Stockout cost = $5/unit.

Daily demand: minimum = 20, average = 40, maximum = 60 units, and normally distributed.

Working days per week = 5.

Working weeks per year = 48.

Lead time: minimum = 5, average = 10, maximum = 15 working days, and normally distributed.

What should the inventory policy decision rules be?

8. Discuss the relevance of the following in:

(a) Order processing costs
    (i) accounting costs
    (ii) requisition costs
    (iii) receiving costs
    (iv) purchase costs
    (v) invoicing costs
    (vi) transportation
    (vii) make-ready costs

(b) Carrying costs
    (i) inventory taxes
    (ii) insurance
    (iii) property taxes
    (iv) cost of money
    (v) materials handling
    (vi) space costs
    (vii) stock refurbishing costs

(c) Out-of-stock costs
    (i) expediting costs
    (ii) order processing costs
    (iii) goodwill
    (iv) lost future profits
    (v) lost sales

Of those costs you consider to be relevant, how would you estimate them?

9. The weekly demand for an item is normally distributed with a mean equal to 100 and a standard deviation equal to 8. The ordering cost is $10, and the carrying cost is 12 percent per year. The price per item is $12. There is a predictable two-week lag between order placement and delivery. Assume that there is a per-unit understock cost of $15.

(a) Using the approximate method of analysis, find the optimal P-system inventory control policy for the item.
(b) Using the approximate method of analysis, find the optimal Q-system inventory control policy for this item.
(c) Compare the total relevant costs of both policies in parts (a) and (b). Explain any differences noted.
(d) Repeat part (b), but in this case assume that there is to be no more than a 10 percent chance of a stockout during a lead time period. What is the implied worth of an out-of-stock unit under this policy?

10. Under what circumstances would you envision that a dynamic inventory policy analysis would be most important? Describe some of these problem situations.

TABLE 9-A Areas under the Normal Distribution Curve

$z = \dfrac{X' - \bar{X}'}{S}$, where X' = random variable
$\bar{X}'$ = mean of random variable
S = standard deviation

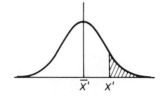

z	.00	.01	.02	.03	.04	.05	.06	.07	.08	.09
.0	.5000	.4960	.4920	.4880	.4840	.4801	.4761	.4721	.4681	.4641
.1	.4602	.4562	.4522	.4483	.4443	.4404	.4364	.4325	.4286	.4247
.2	.4207	.4168	.4129	.4090	.4052	.4013	.3974	.3936	.3897	.3859
.3	.3821	.3783	.3745	.3707	.3669	.3632	.3594	.3557	.3520	.3483
.4	.3446	.3409	.3372	.3336	.3300	.3264	.3228	.3192	.3156	.3121
.5	.3085	.3050	.3015	.2981	.2946	.2912	.2877	.2843	.2810	.2776
.6	.2743	.2709	.2676	.2643	.2611	.2578	.2546	.2514	.2483	.2451
.7	.2420	.2389	.2358	.2327	.2296	.2266	.2236	.2206	.2177	.2148
.8	.2119	.2090	.2061	.2033	.2005	.1977	.1949	.1922	.1894	.1867
.9	.1841	.1814	.1788	.1762	.1736	.1711	.1685	.1660	.1635	.1611
1.0	.1587	.1562	.1539	.1515	.1492	.1469	.1446	.1423	.1401	.1379
1.1	.1357	.1335	.1314	.1292	.1271	.1251	.1230	.1210	.1190	.1170
1.2	.1151	.1131	.1112	.1093	.1075	.1056	.1038	.1020	.1003	.0985
1.3	.0968	.0951	.0934	.0918	.0901	.0885	.0869	.0853	.0838	.0823
1.4	.0808	.0793	.0778	.0764	.0749	.0735	.0721	.0708	.0694	.0681
1.5	.0668	.0655	.0643	.0630	.0618	.0606	.0594	.0582	.0571	.0559
1.6	.0548	.0537	.0526	.0516	.0505	.0495	.0485	.0475	.0465	.0455
1.7	.0446	.0436	.0427	.0418	.0409	.0401	.0392	.0384	.0375	.0367
1.8	.0359	.0351	.0344	.0336	.0329	.0322	.0314	.0307	.0301	.0294
1.9	.0287	.0281	.0274	.0268	.0262	.0256	.0250	.0244	.0239	.0233
2.0	.0228	.0222	.0217	.0212	.0207	.0202	.0197	.0192	.0188	.0183
2.1	.0179	.0174	.0170	.0166	.0162	.0158	.0154	.0150	.0146	.0143
2.2	.0139	.0136	.0132	.0129	.0125	.0122	.0119	.0116	.0113	.0110
2.3	.0107	.0104	.0102	.0099	.0096	.0094	.0091	.0089	.0087	.0084
2.4	.0082	.0080	.0078	.0075	.0073	.0071	.0069	.0068	.0066	.0064
2.5	.0062	.0060	.0059	.0057	.0055	.0054	.0052	.0051	.0049	.0048
2.6	.0047	.0045	.0044	.0043	.0041	.0040	.0039	.0038	.0037	.0036
2.7	.0035	.0034	.0033	.0032	.0031	.0030	.0029	.0028	.0027	.0026
2.8	.0026	.0025	.0024	.0023	.0023	.0022	.0021	.0021	.0020	.0019
2.9	.0019	.0018	.0018	.0017	.0016	.0016	.0015	.0015	.0014	.0014
3.0	.0013	.0013	.0013	.0012	.0012	.0011	.0011	.0011	.0010	.0010
3.1	.0010	.0009	.0009	.0009	.0008	.0008	.0008	.0008	.0007	.0007
3.2	.0007	.0007	.0006	.0006	.0006	.0006	.0006	.0005	.0005	.0005
3.3	.0005	.0005	.0005	.0004	.0004	.0004	.0004	.0004	.0004	.0003
3.4	.0003	.0003	.0003	.0003	.0003	.0003	.0003	.0003	.0003	.0002
3.5	.0002	.0002	.0002	.0002	.0002	.0002	.0002	.0002	.0002	.0002
3.6	.0002	.0002	.0001	.0001	.0001	.0001	.0001	.0001	.0001	.0001
3.7	.0001	.0001	.0001	.0001	.0001	.0001	.0001	.0001	.0001	.0001
3.8	.0001	.0001	.0001	.0001	.0001	.0001	.0001	.0001	.0001	.0001
3.9	.0000	.0000	.0000	.0000	.0000	.0000	.0000	.0000	.0000	.0000
z	.00	.01	.02	.03	.04	.05	.06	.07	.08	.09

TABLE 9-B
Table of Unit Normal Loss Integrals $N(z)$ [a]

Examples: $N(z) = N(0.85) = 0.11$

$N(-z) = z + N(z)$

$N(-0.79) = 0.79 + 0.1223 = 0.9123$

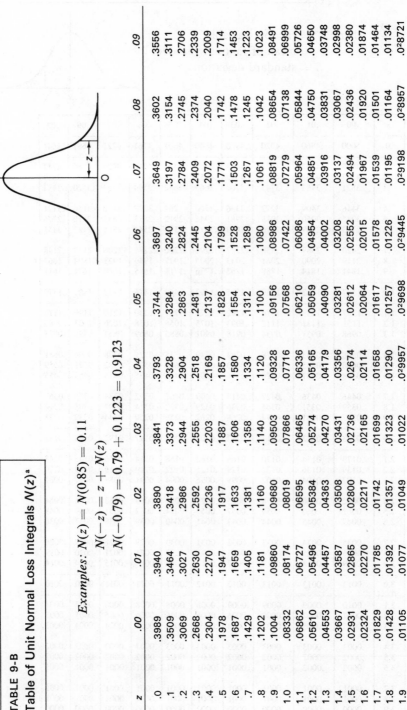

z	.00	.01	.02	.03	.04	.05	.06	.07	.08	.09
.0	.3989	.3940	.3890	.3841	.3793	.3744	.3697	.3649	.3602	.3556
.1	.3509	.3464	.3418	.3373	.3328	.3284	.3240	.3197	.3154	.3111
.2	.3069	.3027	.2986	.2944	.2904	.2863	.2824	.2784	.2745	.2706
.3	.2668	.2630	.2592	.2555	.2518	.2481	.2445	.2409	.2374	.2339
.4	.2304	.2270	.2236	.2203	.2169	.2137	.2104	.2072	.2040	.2009
.5	.1978	.1947	.1917	.1887	.1857	.1828	.1799	.1771	.1742	.1714
.6	.1687	.1659	.1633	.1606	.1580	.1554	.1528	.1503	.1478	.1453
.7	.1429	.1405	.1381	.1358	.1334	.1312	.1289	.1267	.1245	.1223
.8	.1202	.1181	.1160	.1140	.1120	.1100	.1080	.1061	.1042	.1023
.9	.1004	.09860	.09680	.09503	.09328	.09156	.08986	.08819	.08654	.08491
1.0	.08332	.08174	.08019	.07866	.07716	.07568	.07422	.07279	.07138	.06999
1.1	.06862	.06727	.06595	.06465	.06336	.06210	.06086	.05964	.05844	.05726
1.2	.05610	.05496	.05384	.05274	.05165	.05059	.04954	.04851	.04750	.04650
1.3	.04553	.04457	.04363	.04270	.04179	.04090	.04002	.03916	.03831	.03748
1.4	.03667	.03587	.03508	.03431	.03356	.03281	.03208	.03137	.03067	.02998
1.5	.02931	.02865	.02800	.02736	.02674	.02612	.02552	.02494	.02436	.02380
1.6	.02324	.02270	.02217	.02165	.02114	.02064	.02015	.01967	.01920	.01874
1.7	.01829	.01785	.01742	.01699	.01658	.01617	.01578	.01539	.01501	.01464
1.8	.01428	.01392	.01357	.01323	.01290	.01257	.01226	.01195	.01164	.01134
1.9	.01105	.01077	.01049	.01022	$.0^2 9957$	$.0^2 9698$	$.0^2 9445$	$.0^2 9198$	$.0^2 8957$	$.0^2 8721$

z	.00	.01	.02	.03	.04	.05	.06	.07	.08	.09
2.0	$.0^2 8491$	$.0^2 8266$	$.0^2 8046$	$.0^2 7832$	$.0^2 7623$	$.0^2 7418$	$.0^2 7219$	$.0^2 7024$	$.0^2 6835$	$.0^2 6649$
2.1	$.0^2 6468$	$.0^2 6292$	$.0^2 6120$	$.0^2 5952$	$.0^2 5788$	$.0^2 5628$	$.0^2 5472$	$.0^2 5320$	$.0^2 5172$	$.0^2 5028$
2.2	$.0^2 4887$	$.0^2 4750$	$.0^2 4616$	$.0^2 4486$	$.0^2 4358$	$.0^2 4235$	$.0^2 4114$	$.0^2 3996$	$.0^2 3882$	$.0^2 3770$
2.3	$.0^2 3662$	$.0^2 3556$	$.0^2 3453$	$.0^2 3352$	$.0^2 3255$	$.0^2 3159$	$.0^2 3067$	$.0^2 2977$	$.0^2 2889$	$.0^2 2804$
2.4	$.0^2 2720$	$.0^2 2640$	$.0^2 2561$	$.0^2 2484$	$.0^2 2410$	$.0^2 2337$	$.0^2 2267$	$.0^2 2199$	$.0^2 2132$	$.0^2 2067$
2.5	$.0^2 2004$	$.0^2 1943$	$.0^2 1883$	$.0^2 1826$	$.0^2 1769$	$.0^2 1715$	$.0^2 1662$	$.0^2 1610$	$.0^2 1560$	$.0^2 1511$
2.6	$.0^2 1464$	$.0^2 1418$	$.0^2 1373$	$.0^2 1330$	$.0^2 1288$	$.0^2 1247$	$.0^2 1207$	$.0^2 1169$	$.0^2 1132$	$.0^2 1095$
2.7	$.0^2 1060$	$.0^2 1026$	$.0^3 9928$	$.0^3 9607$	$.0^3 9295$	$.0^3 8992$	$.0^3 8699$	$.0^3 8414$	$.0^3 8138$	$.0^3 7870$
2.8	$.0^3 7611$	$.0^3 7359$	$.0^3 7115$	$.0^3 6879$	$.0^3 6650$	$.0^3 6428$	$.0^3 6213$	$.0^3 6004$	$.0^3 5802$	$.0^3 5606$
2.9	$.0^3 5417$	$.0^3 5233$	$.0^3 5055$	$.0^3 4883$	$.0^3 4716$	$.0^3 4555$	$.0^3 4398$	$.0^3 4247$	$.0^3 4101$	$.0^3 3959$
3.0	$.0^3 3822$	$.0^3 3689$	$.0^3 3560$	$.0^3 3436$	$.0^3 3316$	$.0^3 3199$	$.0^3 3087$	$.0^3 2978$	$.0^3 2873$	$.0^3 2771$
3.1	$.0^3 2673$	$.0^3 2577$	$.0^3 2485$	$.0^3 2396$	$.0^3 2311$	$.0^3 2227$	$.0^3 2147$	$.0^3 2070$	$.0^3 1995$	$.0^3 1922$
3.2	$.0^3 1852$	$.0^3 1785$	$.0^3 1720$	$.0^3 1657$	$.0^3 1596$	$.0^3 1537$	$.0^3 1480$	$.0^3 1426$	$.0^3 1373$	$.0^3 1322$
3.3	$.0^3 1273$	$.0^3 1225$	$.0^3 1179$	$.0^3 1135$	$.0^3 1093$	$.0^3 1051$	$.0^3 1012$	$.0^4 9734$	$.0^4 9365$	$.0^4 9009$
3.4	$.0^4 8666$	$.0^4 8335$	$.0^4 8016$	$.0^4 7709$	$.0^4 7413$	$.0^4 7127$	$.0^4 6852$	$.0^4 6587$	$.0^4 6331$	$.0^4 6085$
3.5	$.0^4 5848$	$.0^4 5620$	$.0^4 5400$	$.0^4 5188$	$.0^4 4984$	$.0^4 4788$	$.0^4 4599$	$.0^4 4417$	$.0^4 4242$	$.0^4 4073$
3.6	$.0^4 3911$	$.0^4 3755$	$.0^4 3605$	$.0^4 3460$	$.0^4 3321$	$.0^4 3188$	$.0^4 3059$	$.0^4 2935$	$.0^4 2816$	$.0^4 2702$
3.7	$.0^4 2592$	$.0^4 2486$	$.0^4 2385$	$.0^4 2287$	$.0^4 2193$	$.0^4 2103$	$.0^4 2016$	$.0^4 1933$	$.0^4 1853$	$.0^4 1776$
3.8	$.0^4 1702$	$.0^4 1632$	$.0^4 1563$	$.0^4 1498$	$.0^4 1435$	$.0^4 1375$	$.0^4 1317$	$.0^4 1262$	$.0^4 1208$	$.0^4 1157$
3.9	$.0^4 1108$	$.0^4 1061$	$.0^4 1016$	$.0^5 9723$	$.0^5 9307$	$.0^5 8908$	$.0^5 8525$	$.0^5 8158$	$.0^5 7806$	$.0^5 7469$
4.0	$.0^5 7145$	$.0^5 6835$	$.0^5 6538$	$.0^5 6253$	$.0^5 5980$	$.0^5 5718$	$.0^5 5468$	$.0^5 5227$	$.0^5 4997$	$.0^5 4777$
4.1	$.0^5 4566$	$.0^5 4364$	$.0^5 4170$	$.0^5 3985$	$.0^5 3807$	$.0^5 3637$	$.0^5 3475$	$.0^5 3319$	$.0^5 3170$	$.0^5 3027$
4.2	$.0^5 2891$	$.0^5 2760$	$.0^5 2635$	$.0^5 2516$	$.0^5 2402$	$.0^5 2292$	$.0^5 2188$	$.0^5 2088$	$.0^5 1992$	$.0^5 1901$
4.3	$.0^5 1814$	$.0^5 1730$	$.0^5 1650$	$.0^5 1574$	$.0^5 1501$	$.0^5 1431$	$.0^5 1365$	$.0^5 1301$	$.0^5 1241$	$.0^5 1183$
4.4	$.0^5 1127$	$.0^5 1074$	$.0^5 1024$	$.0^6 9756$	$.0^6 9296$	$.0^6 8857$	$.0^6 8437$	$.0^6 8037$	$.0^6 7655$	$.0^6 7290$
4.5	$.0^6 6942$	$.0^6 6610$	$.0^6 6294$	$.0^6 5992$	$.0^6 5704$	$.0^6 5429$	$.0^6 5167$	$.0^6 4917$	$.0^6 4679$	$.0^6 4452$

TABLE 9-B cont.

z	.00	.01	.02	.03	.04	.05	.06	.07	.08	.09
4.6	$.0^6 4236$	$.0^6 4029$	$.0^6 3833$	$.0^6 3645$	$.0^6 3467$	$.0^6 3297$	$.0^6 3135$	$.0^6 2981$	$.0^6 2834$	$.0^6 2694$
4.7	$.0^6 2560$	$.0^6 2433$	$.0^6 2313$	$.0^6 2197$	$.0^6 2088$	$.0^6 1984$	$.0^6 1884$	$.0^6 1790$	$.0^6 1700$	$.0^6 1615$
4.8	$.0^6 1533$	$.0^6 1456$	$.0^6 1382$	$.0^6 1312$	$.0^6 1246$	$.0^6 1182$	$.0^6 1122$	$.0^6 1065$	$.0^6 1011$	$.0^7 9588$
4.9	$.0^7 9096$	$.0^7 8629$	$.0^7 8185$	$.0^7 7763$	$.0^7 7362$	$.0^7 6982$	$.0^7 6620$	$.0^7 6276$	$.0^7 5950$	$.0^7 5640$

[a] These tables of "Unit Normal Loss Integral" appear in *Probability and Statistics for Business Decisions* by Robert Schlaifer, published by McGraw-Hill Book Company, Inc., 1959. They are reproduced here by specific permission of the copyright holder, The President and Fellows of Harvard College.

Selected Bibliography

BROWN, ROBERT G., *Statistical Forecasting for Inventory Control*. New York: McGraw-Hill Book Company, Inc., 1959. A lightly written text on the use of the exponentially smoothed moving average as a short-term forecast method for controlling inventories.

————, *Smoothing, Forecasting and Prediction of Discrete Time Series*. Englewood Cliffs, N. J.: Prentice-Hall, Inc., 1963. A comprehensive and mathematically rigorous treatment of mathematical forecasting methods with heavy emphasis on exponential smoothing concepts.

BUCHAN, JOSEPH and ERNEST KOENIGSBERG, *Scientific Inventory Management*. Englewood Cliffs, N. J.: Prentice-Hall, Inc., 1963.

FETTER, ROBERT and WINSTON C. DALLECK, *Decision Models for Inventory Management*. Homewood, Illinois: Richard D. Irwin, Inc., 1961.

HADLEY, GEORGE and THOMAS W. WHITIN, *Analysis of Inventory Systems*. Englewood Cliffs, N. J.: Prentice-Hall Inc., 1963. A rigorous mathematical presentation of basic inventory control theory.

MCMILLAN, CLAUDE and RICHARD F. GONZALEZ, *Systems Analysis: A Computer Approach to Decision Models*. Homewood, Illinois: Richard D. Irwin, Inc., 1965. Especially see Chapter 6 for a discussion of how to use the computer to simulate an inventory system under uncertainty conditions.

SCARF, HERBERT E., DORTHY M. GILFORD, and MAYNARD W. SHELLY (eds.), *Multistage Inventory Models and Techniques*. Stanford, Calif.: Stanford University Press, 1963.

STARR, MARTIN K. and DAVID W. MILLER, *Inventory Control: Theory and Practice*. Englewood Cliffs, N. J.: Prentice-Hall, Inc., 1962. This is an introductory text.

Chapter
10

Transport, Production Scheduling, and Order Processing Decisions

In addition to location and inventory decisions discussed in the previous two chapters, the logistician frequently becomes involved in a variety of resource allocation and scheduling decisions. Important among these are transport decisions, including transportation service selection, carrier routing, and vehicle scheduling, production scheduling decisions, which require coordination between inventory policy decisions and production sequencing decisions, and order processing decisions, which refer to the selection and operation of the order processing system. These will be individually discussed in this chapter.

Transport Decisions

Transport decisions are important to the logistician because of their frequently recurring nature. Constantly changing requirements force continual reconsideration of transport decisions. Questionable decision-making practices can lead to large diseconomies as small diseconomies are compounded over a period of time. Fortunately, many such decisions are amenable to quantitative treatment, which aids in the search for optimal decisions and helps to routinize decision making. Service selection, carrier routing, and vehicle scheduling are the most common of these decisions.

TRANSPORT SERVICE SELECTION

A variety of transportation services exist, not only as represented by different modes, but within modes as well. Selecting a service to move a good or a mixture of goods is a difficult task complicated by the number of both tangible and intangible factors that need to be considered. Wilson noted a number of factors that influence service choice, and these are paraphrased below:

1. Rates and total charges via the various available types of services.
2. The time involved in the service or combination. Faster or slower service may be important under certain circumstances.
3. The convenience of a given method of shipment. Packaging requirements, location of carrier's facilities relative to the firm's shipping and receiving points, availability of in-transit services, availability of special equipment for efficient handling of goods, availability of direct services, and availability of pickup and delivery services are all convenience considerations.
4. Experience regarding a carrier's safe delivery performance and reliability in handling goods requiring special treatment such as refrigeration and security.
5. Business policy may influence the choice. For example, a policy may be established that traffic is to be divided equitably among various carriers[1].

Currently, there are two general approaches to selecting a transport service that include a number of these factors. The first is a direct cost approach, and the second is an inventory-theoretic approach.

Direct Cost Approach. Traffic managers have been solving the transportation service selection problem for years. The approach has been to treat the problem intuitively by balancing transportation cost against the benefits of speed, convenience, availability, carrier relations, special services, etc. in light of a cost-minimizing objective. Intuition, as when applied to any problem, has the advantages of potentially being broad in scope, of capturing both tangible and intangible factors in the analysis, and of being adaptive to a wide variety of specific circumstances. In practice, however, the tendency too often has been to view transport selection in a narrow sense by considering transportation cost as the primary factor in the decision. Because the effect of transport service on revenues and on

---

[1] G. Lloyd Wilson, *Traffic Management* (Englewood Cliffs, N. J.: Prentice-Hall, Inc., 1956), pp. 187–88.

costs outside of the traffic department has been little understood, analysis becomes limited to those factors immediately under the control of the decision maker. The result has been that many carriers are selected more on the basis of direct cost of the service than on a tradeoff of cost and service.[2] Undoubtedly, the direct cost approach is inadvertently encouraged if the scope of traffic department responsibilities is narrowly defined and if the pressures for cost performance are great.

Inventory-Theoretic Approach. An alternative approach is to view the transport service selection problem in terms of cost-service tradeoffs. Nearly every transport service can be effectively described in terms of quantifiable characteristics: (1) cost of service, (2) average door-to-door delivery time, (3) transit-time variability, and (4) loss and damage.[3] The performance characteristics associated with a transport service reflect on the costs incurred by the consignee (receiver of the goods) and the supplier. In turn, transport service choice can affect the consignee's patronage of the supplier. Thus, an appropriate approach to the selection problem is to balance the direct costs of service against those costs indirectly affected by service choice.

SEPARATE DECISION ENTITIES. A critical point to realize in this analysis is that service selection should be a cooperative effort between the supplier and the consignee when they are separate legal or decision entities. Suppose that the

---

FIGURE 10-1

Consignee's inventory pattern under variable and nonvariable lead time caused by uncertainties in transport service quality

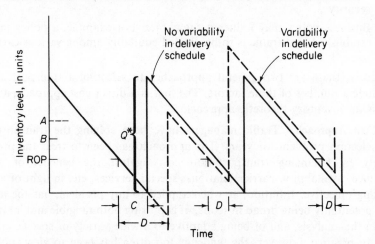

Source: Redrawn from Ronald H. Ballou and Daniel W. DeHayes, Jr., "Transport Selection by Interfirm Analysis," *Transportation and Distribution Management*, Vol. 7 (June 1967), p. 36.

[2] For a more complete discussion of the transport selection problem in a traditional setting, see Wilson, *Traffic Management*, pp. 185–213.

[3] See Chapter 5 for an elaboration of these performance characteristics.

supplier is responsible for making the transportation choice. To provide improved transportation service and therefore lower the consignee's average inventory level (Fig. 10-1), the supplier will pay more in transportation costs (Fig. 10-2). Without any motivation in the form of competitive standards for service or compensating incentives from the consignee, the choice that the supplier makes is likely to be the least costly, poorest quality service. This is a disadvantage for the consignee. However, the consignee may exercise some control over the selection through the sales orders that he places with the supplier. If the consignee responds to improved service with additional orders, the supplier experiences higher sales and possibly higher profits. Thus, the supplier has a motivation to provide improved service. A cooperative effort can result in higher profits for both parties, and the economic equilibrium established between the two determines the transport service to be used.

To illustrate this concept, consider an example involving the ABC Electronics Company and Community Distributors, a large dealer in electronic supplies.[4]

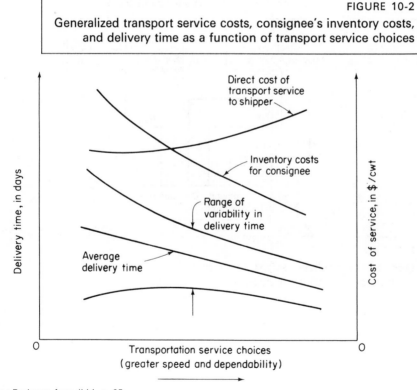

FIGURE 10-2

Generalized transport service costs, consignee's inventory costs, and delivery time as a function of transport service choices

Source: Redrawn from *ibid.,* p. 35.

[4] Based on an example in Ronald H. Ballou and Daniel W. DeHayes, Jr., "Transport Selection by Interfirm Analysis," *Transportation and Distribution Management* (June 1967), pp. 33–37.

Community purchases a line of electronic tubes from ABC and also from Brown Manufacturing Company, a competing supplier. Prices are on a delivered basis, and the suppliers make the carrier selection decision. The problem centers around the mode that supplier *A* (ABC) should choose to supply Community. Three choices are feasible—air, truck, and rail. Each offers a different level of service in terms of speed and dependability, and the cost of the service differs as well. Supplier *B* is currently using rail. The situation is illustrated in Fig. 10-3. Loss and damage considerations between modes are negligible, since packaging costs do not vary significantly between these transportation services.

The performance characteristics of each mode are shown in Table 10-1. The differences noted in delivery time variability are more important in this example than average delivery time. The reason is that Community has a relatively stable demand pattern such that different average delivery times require only a shift in

---

FIGURE 10-3

Example mode selection problem involving two suppliers, a consignee, and three possible transport service choices

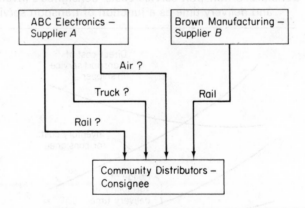

TABLE 10-1

Door-to-door delivery schedule characteristics and costs of service for the transportation services available to shipper *A*

Transportation Service	Average Delivery Time, Days	Delivery Time Variability, Days[b]	Delivery Cost per Case, $/Case
Air	2	1	2
Truck	4	2	0.7
Rail	7	4	0.5
Rail[a]	7	3	—

[a] Transportation service that *B* currently is using.
[b] Represents the range of transit-time variability about the mean delivery time for 95 percent of all shipments.
Source: Ronald H. Ballou and Daniel W. DeHayes, Jr., "Transport Selection by Interfirm Analysis," *Transportation and Distribution Management*, Vol. 7 (June 1967), p. 37.

the consignee's reorder point quantity (if it is assumed that a basic fixed order quantity, variable order interval inventory control system is used) with no resulting changes in the average inventory level. Delivery time variability is the important decision variable, since it creates uncertainty in Community's inventory lead time. Lead time uncertainty directly relates to the level of safety stock that Community must maintain and to the cost for carrying its inventory. Community purchases from its suppliers 2555 cases of tubes per year for $100 per case. It divides its orders among the two suppliers on the basis of the customer service offered, which in this case is delivery time variability or specifically the absolute value of the difference between the absolute values of the delivery time variabilities of the two suppliers ($|V_B| - |V_A|$). When no difference is present ($|V_B| - |V_A|$) = 0, because each supplier provides transportation service of equal dependability, and Community orders an equal amount per year from each supplier, that is, 1278 cases from each. For each day that delivery time variability is reduced relative to that offered by supplier B, Community's policy is to increase the quantity purchased from supplier A by 5 percent of the total tubes purchased as a motivation for better service from its suppliers. Table 10-2 provides a schedule of profits that

			TABLE 10-2
	A schedule of profits, orders, and transportation charges to A as a function of the difference in transit-time variability between A and B		

Difference in Variability ($|V_B| - |V_A|$)[a]	Cases per Year Ordered from A	Profit to A Before Transportation Charges, $/Year[b]	Total Transportation Charges		
			Air	Truck	Rail
1	1150	23,000	$2300	$ 805	$575
0	1278	25,560	2556	895	639
1	1405	28,100	2810	984[c]	703
2	1533	30,660	3066	1073	767
3	1660	33,200	3320	1162	830
4	1790	35,800	3580	1253	895

[a] Represents a possible range of differences in transit-time variability.
[b] Twenty percent of gross revenue.
[c] For example, 1405 cases × $0.7/case = $984.
Source: Ronald H. Ballou and Daniel W. DeHayes, Jr., "Transport Selection by Interfirm Analysis," *Transportation and Distribution Management*, Vol. 7 (June 1967), p. 37.

supplier A can generate by creating various levels of service differences through mode selection and the associated transportation costs incurred for a particular shipment volume.

Choice of a mode now becomes a simple matter of examining the profit levels that result for each modal choice and selecting the one with the highest profit. Profit values are determined by

$$\text{Net profit to ABC} = \left(\begin{array}{c}\text{profit to ABC before} \\ \text{transportation charges}\end{array}\right) - \left(\begin{array}{c}\text{transportation} \\ \text{charges}\end{array}\right) \quad (10.1)$$

Using the figures from Table 10-2, we can generate the following decision matrix:

Alternatives	State of Nature-Certainty Probability = 1.0
Air	$P_A = \$30,660 - 3066 = \$27,594$ ⟵
Truck	$P_T = 28,100 - 984 = 27,116$
Rail	$P_R = 23,000 - 575 = 22,425$

That is, for air, $(|V_B| - |V_A|) = 3 - 1 = 2$ from Table 10-1. From Table 10-2 for $(|V_B| - |V_A|) = +2$, the profit to A before transportation charges equals $30,600. Correspondingly, in Table 10-2, the transportation charges are $3066. Net profit for air is $27,594. Profits for the other alternatives are calculated in a similar manner. Air offers the highest profit to ABC and would be the choice. Community also gains from this choice through improved service and lower inventory costs.

There is a question of how much motivation should be provided. If Community does not alter its ordering pattern, ABC has no motivation to select a higher-quality transport service. The highest net profit to ABC occurs with the choice of rail, as shown below:

Alternatives	State of Nature-Certainty Probability = 1.0
Air	$P_A = \$25,560 - 2556 = \$23,004$
Truck	$P_T = \$25,560 - 895 = 24,665$
Rail	$P_R = \$25,560 - 639 = 24,921$ ⟵

On the other hand, Community might switch all orders to ABC if it perceives any favorable difference in service and thereby provide the maximum incentive to ABC. It also would result in the lowest possible inventory cost for itself. However, the obvious benefits of maintaining two sources of supply will tend to keep Community's order switching policy between these two extremes. In any case, the policy should at least be favorable enough to encourage ABC toward choosing higher-quality transport service.

It should be recognized that the mode choice described above is a *static* solution to the problem. That is, any retaliation by Brown precipitated by a loss of his sales has not been considered. It is possible that counter moves may be made by Brown in an attempt to recover the lost sales. ABC may make further counter moves. Though it is possible that the decision over time may be a series of choices and counter choices, the final choices will tend to stabilize around the inherent advantages of the two competing suppliers.[5] Due to locational advantages that one competitor may have relative to the other and due to some transport service

---

[5] This dynamic decision process is characterized by the two-person, nonzero sum game. For further elaboration of game theory, see C. West Churchman, Russell L. Ackoff, and E. Leonard Arnoff, *Introduction to Operations Research* (New York: John Wiley & Sons, Inc., 1957), pp. 519–58.

alternatives being available to one supplier and not to the other, some positive service advantage is likely to exist that favors one of the suppliers. A supplier should seek this advantage and stabilize his service choice at this point, and the consignee should promote this choice. Further choices and counter choices only add to the costs of all parties involved.

This simple example has attempted to illuminate the transport service selection problem under the most difficult circumstances, that is, where the supplier-decision maker and the consignee-service receiver are separate legal or decision entities and where competition is present. The theory for making optimum transport service choices is easily outlined as has been done. However, successful implementation of the theory requires that all parties in the decision system be rational and understand the circumstances under which each must make his decisions. Otherwise, transport service selection will tend to follow the traditional or direct cost minimization approach to the problem, which can be to the economic disadvantage of both the supplier and consignee.

SINGLE DECISION ENTITY. A somewhat simpler yet common transportation service selection problem is the case where the shipper and the receiver are under the control of a single firm. Such a case would be a firm's plant supplying its own regional warehouse, where the plant is the shipper and the warehouse is the recipient of the goods. The transport service choice is the conceptually simple matter of balancing the relevant costs. Competition among alternative suppliers is not at issue, since the warehouse is a captive buyer of the supplying plant.

Baumol and Vinod[6] have suggested the general form of a relationship to deal with transportation service selection under these circumstances. They take the relevant costs to be (1) direct shipping cost, (2) in-transit inventory carrying costs,[7] (3) ordering cost, and (4) consignee's inventory cost, including base stock plus safety stock. Again, transport service is treated in terms of its quantifiable characteristics of cost, average delivery time, and delivery time variability. The cost tradeoffs as a function of these characteristics are shown in Fig. 10-4, and the total relevant cost expression is

Cost = direct shipping cost + in-transit inventory carrying cost
+ ordering cost + consignee's inventory carrying cost

Notation useful in developing a more explicit form of this expression is

C = total relevant annual cost, \$.
D = total annual demand in inventory and total amount transported per year, units.
r = shipping cost, \$/unit.
t = average delivery time for a single shipment, years.

---

[6] W. J. Baumol and H. D. Vinod, "An Inventory Theoretic Model of Freight Transport Demand," *Management Science*, Vol. 16 (March 1970), pp. 413–21.

[7] In-transit inventory costs were not singled out in the analysis for separate legal entities. These costs can be treated in the same manner as transportation costs or simply included within transportation costs.

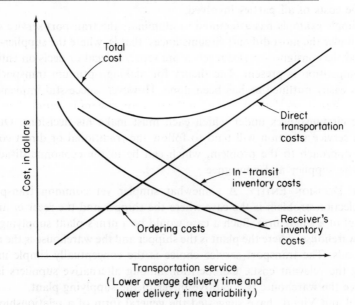

FIGURE 10-4

Generalized cost tradeoffs for transportation service selection in a single-entity inventory-transportation system

s = average time between shipments, years.
u = carrying cost of in-transit inventory, \$/unit/year.
w = carrying cost of consignee's inventory, \$/unit/year.
a = order processing cost, \$/order.
i = average inventory level.
Q = consignee's base stock order quantity, units.

The direct shipping cost is given by the (unit shipping cost) × (the amount shipped), or rD. The in-transit inventory carrying cost is the (cost per unit of time) × (transit time) × (amount shipped), or utD. The ordering cost is the (cost per order) × (number of shipments), or aD/Q or a/s. The receiver's inventory carrying cost is the (cost per unit per year) × (average inventory level), or wi or $wsT/2$. Finally, the safety stock costs may be approximated as $wk[(s + t + k'\sigma)D]^{1/2}$, where $[(s + t + k'\sigma)D]^{1/2}$ is an approximation for a standard deviation of inventory requirements if it is assumed that the stochastic demand and lead time elements satisfy a Poisson probability distribution, k is the number of standard deviations to provide out-of-stock protection at a certain level, σ is delivery time variability expressed as a standard deviation, and k' is the number of σ from the mean in the lead time distribution. Now the total cost expression can be restated as

$$C = rD + utD + \frac{a}{s} + \frac{wsD}{2} + wk[(s + t + k'\sigma)D]^{1/2} \qquad (10.2)$$

If the receiver follows a fixed order quantity, variable order interval inventory control system (Q-system), then $s = Q/D$. Thus

$$C = rD + utD + \frac{aD}{Q} + \frac{wQ}{2} + wk(Q + tD + k'\sigma D)^{1/2} \qquad (10.3)$$

In this expression, r, σ, and t characterize each mode and are treated as unknowns. The consignee's order quantity Q is also an unknown but can be determined from his inventory policy regarding base stock. Finding the set of r, σ, and t (a specific transport service) that will minimize C is mathematically complex. However, when it is realized that in most cases only a limited number of transport services are feasible, a trial-and-error solution procedure is satisfactory. Thus, the solution procedure might be

(1) Approximate Q, using a formulation without safety stock considerations such as Equation (9.3) of chapter 9. Insert Q into Equation (10.3).
(2) Test combinations of r, σ, and t as represented by various transport services for the minimum C.

For example, suppose that the same carriers are available as in the example for ABC Electronics having the following characteristics:

Air: $r_A = \$2,$ $\quad t_A = \frac{2}{365}$ years, $\quad \sigma_A = \frac{0.5}{365}$ years

Truck: $r_T = 0.7,$ $\quad t_T = \frac{4}{365}$ years, $\quad \sigma_T = \frac{1.0}{365}$ years

Rail: $r_R = 0.5,$ $\quad t_R = \frac{7}{365}$ years, $\quad \sigma_R = \frac{2.0}{365}$ years

In addition, we have the following known values:

$D = 10,000$ units.
$a = \$10/\text{order}.$
$w = \$5/\text{unit}/\text{year}.$
$k = 2.3.$
$k' = 1.96$, if it is assumed that the lowest 5 percent of the shipments are neglected and the delivery time distribution approaches a normal distribution.
$u = \$3/\text{unit}/\text{year}.$

First, the inventory order quantity would be

$$Q^* = \sqrt{\frac{2Da}{w}} = \sqrt{\frac{2(10,000)(10)}{5}} = 200 \text{ units}$$

Then, from Equation (10.3):

$$\text{Air:}\quad C_A = 2(10,000) + \frac{3(2)}{365}(10,000) + \frac{10(10,000)}{200} + \frac{5(200)}{2}$$

$$+ 1(2.3)\left[200 + \frac{2}{365}(10,000) + 1.96\left(\frac{0.5}{365}\right)(10,000)\right]^{1/2}$$

$$= \$21,203$$

$$\text{Truck:}\quad C_T = 0.7(10,000) + 3(\tfrac{4}{365})(10,000) + 500 + 500$$

$$+ 2.3[200 + (\tfrac{4}{365})(10,000) + 1.96(\tfrac{1}{365})(10,000)]^{1/2}$$

$$= \$8372$$

$$\text{Rail:}\quad C_R = 0.5(10,000) + 3(\tfrac{7}{365})(10,000) + 500 + 500$$

$$+ 2.3[200 + \tfrac{7}{365}(10,000) + 1.96(\tfrac{2}{365})(10,000)]^{1/2}$$

$$= \$6626$$

Rail offers the lowest total cost and would be the best choice in this case.

Appraisal. It would be naive to believe that the inventory-theoretic approach captures the transportation service problem in its entirety. Rather, it sets forth some of the basic tradeoffs to be considered in the service selection problem. That is, while transportation is a cost that must be incurred in moving the product to a point in the distribution channel where it is desired, the effect of the quality of the service on customer costs and in turn its effect on their patronage should be considered in the decision. A broader problem scope that combines both service and costs is suggested.

Exploiting the cost-service tradeoffs can depend on a number of additional factors, not all of which are directly under the control of the manager making the service selection. For example, effective cooperation is encouraged if a reasonable knowledge of the other party's costs is present. If the supplier and the consignee are separate legal entities, it is doubtful that perfect cost information is possible unless some form of information exchange is worked out. In any case, a sensitivity to the other party's reactions to either service choice or patronage should indicate the direction of cooperation.

Second, where there is a competing supplier, the consignee and the supplier should act rationally to affect optimum cost-service tradeoffs. Rationality among the parties cannot be guaranteed, however.

Third, price effects have not been considered. If the supplier were to provide a higher-quality transportation service, he might raise the product price to at least in part compensate for his added cost. The consignee should consider both price and service when determining patronage.

Fourth, transportation rate changes, changes in product mix, and inventory cost changes as well as possible transport service retaliation by a competing supplier add a dynamic element to the problem that is not directly considered.

CARRIER ROUTING

One way in which the logistician seeks to improve distribution efficiency is through the maximum utilization of transportation equipment and manpower. The length of time that goods are in transit reflects on the number of shipments that can be made with a vehicle within a given period of time and on the total transportation cost for all shipments. To reduce transportation costs, and also to improve customer service, routings are sought that will minimize time or distance. Two types of routing problems are common. First is the routing through a transportation network where the origin and destination points are different, as in selecting the best highway trip plan for a truck moving between New York and Los Angeles. Second is routing through a network where the origin and destination points are the same, as in sequencing the stops for a delivery truck making local product deliveries.

Separate and Single Origin-Destination Points.   Consider the problem of routing a truck from Amarillo, Texas to Fort Worth, Texas. The primary highway network with approximate driving times for each link is shown in Fig. 10-5. The objective

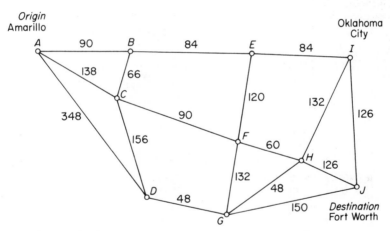

FIGURE 10-5

Schematic representation of the highway network between Amarillo and Fort Worth, Texas, with approximate driving times

Note: All link times are in minutes.

is to minimize the traveling time through the network. The return route is a separate problem.

A number of techniques exist for solving this problem, including the use of dynamic programming, linear programming, and others.[8] To solve the problem as proposed above, Dantzig's shortest-route tree method is simple and reasonably

---

[8] For a discussion and appraisal of these methods, see Stuart E. Dreyfus, "An Appraisal of Some Shortest-Path Algorithms," *Operations Research*, Vol. 17 (1969), pp. 395–412; Maurice Pollack and Walter Wiebenson, "Solutions of the Shortest-Route Problem—A Review," *Operations Research*, Vol. 1 (March-April 1960), pp. 224–30; and Stanley Zoints, "Methods for Selection of an Optimum Route," in *Papers—American Transportation Research Forum* (Oxford, Indiana: American Transportation Research Forum, 1962), pp. 25–36.

efficient in terms of computation time. A more general approach known as the "matrix method" gives the optimal route between *any* two nodal pairs in the network rather than just the designated origin-destination points.[9] However, because of the large amount of information that must be retained during computation, the latter method is not particularly efficient for large-scale problems. Therefore, the shortest-route tree method, though slightly more limited in scope, will be described here.[10]

FIGURE 10-6

Computation procedure for solving the routing problem in Figure 10-5

Ⓐ	Ⓑ	Ⓒ	Ⓓ	Ⓔ	Ⓕ	Ⓖ	Ⓗ	Ⓘ	Ⓙ
AB–90	BC–66	CB–66	DG–48	EB–84	FH–60	GH–48	HF–60	IE–84	
AC–138	BE–84	CF–90	DC–156	EI–84	FC–90	GF–132	HJ–126	IJ–126	
AD–348		CD–156		EF–120	FE–120	GJ–150	HI–132	IH–132	
					FG–132	GD–48	HG–48		

(a) Initial setup

90

Ⓐ	Ⓑ	Ⓒ	Ⓓ	Ⓔ	Ⓕ	Ⓖ	Ⓗ	Ⓘ	Ⓙ
(AB–90)	BC–66	CB–66	DG–48	EB–84	FH–60	GH–48	HF–60	IE–84	
AC–138	BE–84	CF–90	DC–156	EI–84	FC–90	GF–132	HJ–126	IJ–126	
AD–348		CD–156		EF–120	FE–120	GJ–150	HI–132	IH–132	
					FG–132	GD–48	HG–48		

(b) First step

90   138

Ⓐ	Ⓑ	Ⓒ	Ⓓ	Ⓔ	Ⓕ	Ⓖ	Ⓗ	Ⓘ	Ⓙ
(AB–90)	BC–66	CB–66	DG–48	EB–84	FH–60	GH–48	HF–60	IE–84	
(AC–138)	BE–84	CF–90	DC–156	EI–84	FC–90	GF–132	HJ–126	IJ–126	
AD–348		CD–156		EF–120	FE–120	GJ–150	HI–132	IJ–132	
					FG–132	GD–48	HG–48		

(c) Second step

90   138   174

Ⓐ	Ⓑ	Ⓒ	Ⓓ	Ⓔ	Ⓕ	Ⓖ	Ⓗ	Ⓘ	Ⓙ
(AB–90)	BC–66	CB–66	DG–48	EB–84	FH–60	GH–48	HF–60	IE–84	
(AC–138)	(BE–84)	CF–90	DC–156	EI–84	FC–90	GF–132	HJ–126	IJ–126	
AD–348		CD–156		EF–120	FE–120	GJ–150	HI–132	IH–132	
					FG–132	GD–48	HG–48		

(d) Third step

---

[9] The matrix method is described in Zoints, *ibid.*, pp. 29–31.

[10] Description of this method follows that appearing in Frederick S. Hillier and Gerald J. Lieberman, *Introduction to Operations Research* (San Francisco: Holden-Day, Inc., 1967), pp. 218–22.

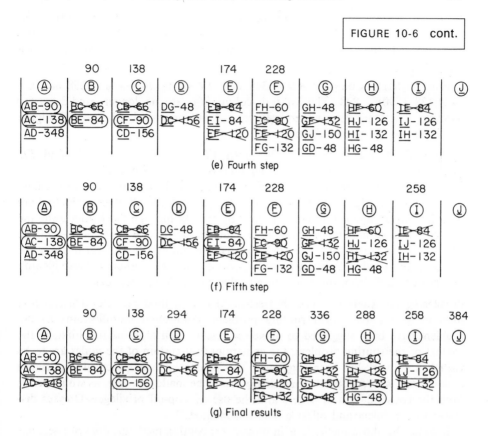

(e) Fourth step

(f) Fifth step

(g) Final results

With regard to the problem in Fig. 10-5, the shortest-route tree method begins with a list of all nodes and the associated links and link values for the links leading from each node. For computational efficiency the link values should be listed in ascending order for each node, as shown in Fig. 10-6(a). Do not include links into the origin or out of the destination.

FIRST STEP: Identify the node nearest the origin in time by examining the link values at the origin, or Ⓐ column. Choose the minimum-valued link and circle the entry. This is link *AB*. Write this link value above node *B*, that is, column Ⓑ, to identify the column as preparation for the next step. Cross out all links which lead *into* *B* in all columns in which they appear so that they cannot be selected later. This completes the first step, and the revised list is shown in Fig. 10-6(b).

SECOND STEP: To select the next node, compare a new link from *A* with a combination of *AB* and the *lowest-valued link* the identified column Ⓑ. That is, *AC* = 138 and *AB* + *BC* = 90 + 66 = 156, so choose *AC*. Circle *AC* in column Ⓐ, write 138 above column Ⓒ, and cross out all links leading into *C*. The updated list is shown in Fig. 10-6(c).

THIRD STEP: Compare the new link $AD = 348$ with BE via A $(90 + 84) = 174$ and CF via A $(138 + 90) = 228$ and choose BE. Note that BE and CF are the lowest-valued links in the identified columns. Circle it and update the listing. See Fig. 10-6(d).

FOURTH STEP: Compare $AD = 348$ with EI via $B(174 + 84) = 258$ and CF via $A(138 + 90) = 228$. The links in column Ⓑ are no longer candidates for selection, since they have either been crossed out or circled. Choose CF. Figure 10-6(e) shows the updated listing.

FIFTH STEP: Compare $AD = 348$ with EI via $B(174 + 84) = 258$ and FH via $C(228 + 60) = 288$. Choose EI. Update listing as shown in Fig. 10-6(f).

The solution procedure is now well established and we skip ahead to the final results shown in Fig. 10-6(g). Since point J is reached and all other paths to J are excluded, an optimum solution is found. By tracing through the listing using the circled links, we find the shortest time route to be $A \rightarrow B \rightarrow E \rightarrow I \rightarrow J$. The minimum total travel time to Fort Worth is 384 minutes. If we wish to carry the computations until all links are circled or crossed out, the method will also identify the shortest path from the origin to all other points in the network.

Broadening the Analysis. The shortest-route tree method provides a useful first solution to the real-world routing problem. Additional modifications to the problem have been suggested to make the results even more useful. First, in the context of the routing problem, the constraint that certain of the nodes are to be visited in network has been suggested. This constraint is of practical importance to situations where stop-offs for delivery are to be made en route, as would result from the consolidation of orders and the use of stop-off privileges. Dreyfus discusses this problem and offers a solution method.[11]

Second, the above method, as in most other routing methods, does not account for travel-time variability. All use average travel time. Although the method does give the least average travel-time route, this route may be a high time-variance route. Some alternative routing may have a higher average travel time but lower variance. When both average travel time and travel-time variability are important, Zoints has suggested that "... the route-minimizing method be applied to the average plus a multiple of the standard deviation .... The multiple of the standard deviation used determines the weight given to the minimizing of the variance."[12]

Third, single origin-destination routing is often part of a larger problem involving multiple origin-destination points. A common problem occurs when the supply from several origin points is to be distributed among a number of demand points, such as factories supplying warehouses (Fig. 10-7). Each potential factory-warehouse link represents a route to be optimized by the above method. The multiple origin-destination problem involves the additional question of the volume that is to be shipped along each route. Optimizing the volume shipped along each

[11] Dreyfus, *op. cit.*, pp. 408–9. Routing for order consolidation has also been approached by heuristic programming, as reported in Charles L. Hinkle and Alfred A. Kuehn, "Heuristic Models: Mapping the Maze for Management," *California Management Review*, Vol. 10 (Fall 1967), pp. 59–64.

[12] Zoints, *op. cit.*, p. 35.

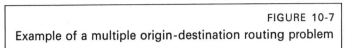

FIGURE 10-7

Example of a multiple origin-destination routing problem

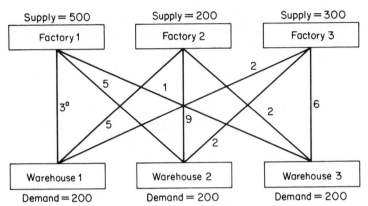

a The cost in $/unit for an optimal routing between Factory 1 and Warehouse 1.

route is easily solved as a special class of linear programming problem called the transportation problem. Solution to the problem posed in Fig. 10-7 and a discussion of a solution method are given in Appendix A.

Coincident Origin-Destination Points. The logistician commonly encounters routing problems in which the origin point is the same as the destination point. Familiar examples are the routing of delivery trucks from a warehouse to retail points and return (for example, serving retail food stores from a central warehouse), the tour design of local delivery trucks from retail stores to customers (for example, United Parcel pickup and delivery, and home delivery by department stores), and the routing of school buses. This decision problem is an extension of the separate origin-destination points problem, but the requirement that the tour is not complete until the vehicle returns to its starting point adds a complicating dimension to the problem. The objective in these problems is to find the best routing *sequence* that will minimize travel time or distance. Operations researchers have labeled this general class of problems as "traveling salesman problems."

A number of methods exist for evaluating various routing alternatives and selecting optimum or nearly optimum tours. Some of the methods used are branch and bound,[13] graphics,[14] heuristics,[15] and dynamic programming,[16] to note a few.

[13] John D. C. Little, Katta G. Murty, Dura W. Sweeney, and Caroline Karel, "An Algorithm for the Traveling Salesman Problem," *Operations Research*, Vol. 11 (November–December 1963), pp. 972–89.

[14] L. L. Barachet, "Graphic Solution of the Traveling-Salesman Problem," *Operations Research*, Vol. 5 (December 1957), pp. 841–45.

[15] Robert L. Karg and Gerald L. Thompson, "A Heuristic Approach to Solving Travelling Salesman Problems," *Management Science*, Vol. 10 (January 1964), pp. 225–48.

[16] M. Held and R. M. Karp, "A Dynamic Programming Approach to Sequencing Problems," *Journal of the Society for Industrial and Applied Mathematics*, Vol. 10 (March 1962), pp. 196–210.

Which to choose is a matter of balancing the efficiency with which the method seeks a solution and the "quality" of the solution obtained. That is, branch and bound procedures guarantee that an optimal solution will be obtained, but they often require a considerable amount of computational time, especially for large-scale problems. In contrast, heuristic procedures often provide "good" or nearly optimum solutions, and they are conservative in their requirements for computational time. As Tellman and Cochran note: ". . . the methods based on heuristic programming are the only algorithmic approaches that are computationally feasible for large problems."[17] This encourages us to explore a heuristic approach to this type of routing problem.

To illustrate a heuristic solution procedure, consider a simple problem that can be worked through by hand computation.[18] A delivery truck is to start at a warehouse *W*, make stops at four customer locations *A*, *B*, *C*, and *D*, and return to the warehouse. The problem is shown in Fig. 10-8 along with the travel times between all points. The decision problem is to find the sequence of stops so that the total travel time will be minimized. Karg and Thompson[19] offer a heuristic procedure that may be paraphrased as follows:

1. Choose any two points and list them $(i_1 i_2)$ in any arbitrary order.
2. Assume that a nondisconnected arrangement $(i_1 i_2 \ldots, i_k)$ of k points, where $2 \leq k < n$, has been constructed, where n is the total number of points in the network. Choose at random one of the remaining points; call it point *h*. For *j* running from 1 to *k*, compute the quantities

$$d_j = a_{i_j,h} + a_{h,i_{j+1}} - a_{i_j,i_{j+1}} \qquad (10.4)$$

FIGURE 10-8

Example delivery problem with travel times in minutes

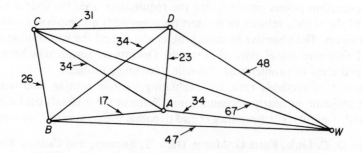

---

[17] Frank A. Tillman and Harold Cochran, "A Heuristic Approach for Solving the Delivery Problem," *The Journal of Industrial Engineering*, Vol. 14 (July 1968), pp. 354–58.

[18] Data for this example problem are obtained from Richard B. Maffei, "Modern Methods for Local Delivery Route Design," *Journal of Marketing*, Vol. 29 (April 1965), pp. 13–18.

[19] Karg and Thompson, *loc. cit.*

where we define i_{k+1} to be i_1 when $j = k$. The a's represent distance, time, cost, etc. between pair points.

3. Let j^* be any value of j such that d_{j^*} is a minimum of the quantities computed in step 2.

4. Relabel i_j as i_{j+1} for $j = j^*, \ldots, k$ and label h as i_{j^*}; that is, insert h into the list of i_k points and reorder the list to accommodate the entry.

5. A new arrangement $(i_1, i_2, \ldots, i_{k+1})$ of $k + 1$ points has now been made. If $k + 1 = n$, stop; otherwise replace k by $k + 1$ and cycle through the procedure once again by returning to step 2.

The thrust of this procedure is to begin with two points and then insert a third into the tour such that time, distance, cost, or some other appropriate measure is minimized. After three points have been established, a fourth is added so as to minimize the resulting four-point tour. And so it goes.

Applying this method to our five-point tour problem of Fig. 10-8, we begin by selecting two points at random, say A and C. That is, $i_1 = A$ and $i_2 = C$. Since there are two points initially, $k = 2$. The new point to enter the tour is *randomly* selected to be B. Now, compute d_j according to Equation (10.4) and Fig. 10-8.

For $j = 1$:

$$d_1 = a_{i_1,B} + a_{B,i_2} - a_{i_1,i_2}$$
$$= a_{A,B} + a_{B,C} - a_{A,C}$$
$$= 17 + 26 - 34$$
$$= 9$$

For $j = 2 = k$:

$$d_2 = a_{i_2,B} + a_{B,i_1} - a_{i_2,i_1}$$
$$= a_{C,B} + a_{B,A} - a_{C,A}$$
$$= 26 + 17 - 34$$
$$= 9$$

Since d_1 is one minimum,[20] $j^* = 1$. Our new tour is $i_1 = A$, $i_2 = B$, $i_3 = C$. Since $k + 1 = 3 < n = 5$, repeat the cycle.

The new point randomly selected to enter the tour is W. With the addition of point B, $k = 3$.

For $j = 1$:

$$d_1 = a_{i_1,W} + a_{W,i_2} - a_{i_1,i_2}$$
$$= a_{A,W} + a_{W,B} - a_{A,B}$$
$$= 34 + 47 - 17$$
$$= 64$$

[20] Arbitrarily select among tied minimum d_j.

For $j = 2$:

$$d_2 = a_{i_2,W} + a_{W,i_3} - a_{i_2,i_3}$$
$$= a_{B,W} + a_{W,C} - a_{B,C}$$
$$= 47 + 67 - 26$$
$$= 88$$

For $j = 3 = k$:

$$d_3 = a_{i_3,W} + a_{W,i_1} - a_{i_3,i_1}$$
$$= a_{C,W} + a_{W,A} - a_{C,A}$$
$$= 67 + 34 - 34$$
$$= 67$$

Minimum $d_j = d_1$, so $j = 1$. The new tour is $i_1 = A$, $i_2 = W$, $i_3 = B$, $i_4 = C$. Since $k + 1 = 4 < n = 5$, one more cycle is needed.

The remaining point is D. The value of k is 4.

For $j = 1$:

$$d_1 = a_{A,D} + a_{D,W} - a_{A,W}$$
$$= 23 + 48 - 34$$
$$= 37$$

For $j = 2$:

$$d_2 = a_{W,D} + a_{D,B} - a_{W,B}$$
$$= 48 + 34 - 47$$
$$= 35$$

For $j = 3$:

$$d_3 = a_{B,D} + a_{D,C} - a_{B,C}$$
$$= 34 + 31 - 26$$
$$= 39$$

For $j = 4 = k$:

$$d_4 = a_{C,D} + a_{D,A} - a_{C,A}$$
$$= 31 + 23 - 34$$
$$= 20$$

Finally, the minimum $d_j = d_4$ such that $j^* = 4$. We then introduce D as i_5 and increase all i's greater than $j^* + 1 = 5$ by 1. The tour is $i_1 = A$, $i_2 = W$, $i_3 = B$, $i_4 = C$, $i_5 = D$. The final tour is $W \rightarrow B \rightarrow C \rightarrow D \rightarrow A \rightarrow W$. Unfortunately, this is not the optimal tour. The optimal tour is $W \rightarrow A \rightarrow B \rightarrow C \rightarrow D \rightarrow W$.

This unlucky outcome should not be alarming and could have been anticipated, since the solution depends on the choice of the initial two points and on the order in which additional points are selected to enter the tour. Since only a small amount of computation time is required to generate solutions and also since there is a high probability in a small problem of finding the optimum (probability $\cong 0.6$ for $n = 5$), a suggestion is simply to repeat the procedure a finite number of times and take the best of these solutions. If this does not yield the optimum, it nonetheless should improve on the first solution.

But what about large-scale problems? As the number of points on a tour increases, the probability that a single solution to the problem will produce the optimum decreases. To improve the accuracy of the procedure, large problems can be divided into a number of subproblems and each can be solved individually. Experience with the procedure has indicated that it works best on the convex part of the tour (tour surface curves outward) and when the problem is small. Thus, the large problem is "cut" into several smaller problems that are convex or nearly convex. For a "cut" to produce an eight-point subproblem, see Fig. 10-9. Karg and Thompson note that "the only requirement on the solutions to the series of subproblems so defined is that the common link (the dashed line from i_1 to i_8 in Fig. 10-9) must be traversed once in the solutions to both (complementary) subproblems."[21] Each subproblem is then solved by the above heuristic procedure.

FIGURE 10-9

Example of a convex cut of a large traveling salesman type problem

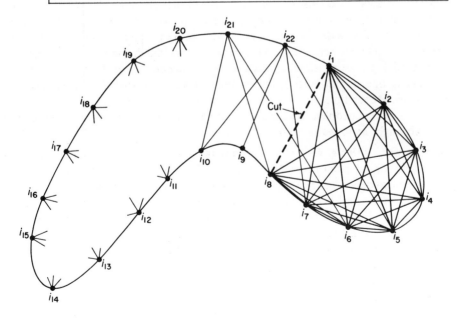

[21] Karg and Thompson, *op. cit.*, p. 230.

Broadening the Analysis. Several additional considerations may be brought into the delivery problem more accurately to reflect actual circumstances. First, the optimal tour may be too long or too short effectively to fit within the standard work day. Therefore, it may be necessary to add or delete points on the tour in order to establish a territory of reasonable size.

Second, the total time associated with a tour is affected by the time required for serving each point. Loading, unloading, and document preparation all add to the total tour time. Though the optimal tour is not affected by these considerations, the number of points that can be included on a tour may be. In some models, especially heuristic and simulation ones, a limitation on total tour time can be introduced.

Third, if time is to be minimized in the delivery problem, the time value of each network link may vary depending on time of day, direction of travel, and terrain. Though the solution method does permit different link values, say from *A* to *B* compared with *B* to *A*, only a static set of link values is handled directly.

Incorporating these real-world considerations into the analysis is a matter of judgment. Often the model and these additional factors are worked in concert to achieve a more practical solution.

VEHICLE SCHEDULING

In the above delivery problems, it was assumed that there was more than enough vehicle capacity to complete the tour. When the tour has many stop-off points and reasonably large quantities are demanded at each point, more than one vehicle is needed to complete the tour, or, alternately, a single vehicle must be routed several times to meet the demand requirements of the tour. Vehicle capacity is an important consideration in real-world routing problems, and it will be considered in two forms here. First, vehicle capacity will be introduced as a constraint on minimizing routing time or distance for the delivery problem. Second, the problem is one of minimizing the number of vehicles needed to meet demand requirements over time when route distance or travel time is less of a consideration. This second problem is relevant when per-mile costs are low and fleet capital costs are high, as in water transportation.

Routing with Vehicle Capacity Constraints. The logistician commonly faces the scheduling problem in which a number of customers are to receive deliveries from a central depot, or freight pickup is to be made at many points and the vehicle returned to a central depot. He wishes to route the delivery or pickup vehicles to minimize travel time, distance, cost, etc. So far, this is just the "traveling salesman problem" noted in the previous section. However, to serve these points, he may have a fleet of vehicles with various capacities. Thus, in addition to selecting the most efficient route, he would also like to know which vehicles should be used on the route (tour).

The number of alternative routes and combinations of vehicles for even a small-size problem is staggering and requires some mathematical aid to find the best solutions. Several mathematical formulations of the problem and solution methods exist,[22] but probably the best all-around solution method in terms of accuracy and computation time is the "savings" method by Clarke and Wright.[23] In testing several methods, Christofides and Eilon found that the "savings" method required substantially less computational time than comparable methods and on the average produced tours that were only 3.2 percent longer than the optimal tours in 10 problems tested.[24] The method is simple and is suitable for hand computation or computer programming.

EXAMPLE. Consider the problem of routing gasoline delivery trucks from a supply depot to 12 auto service station customers. Each customer demands an amount q_i ($i = 1, 2, \ldots, 12$) and is located at P_i and a distance $d_{y,z}$ from the depot at P_0 and other customer points. A fleet of trucks is available to make deliveries, and each has a capacity C_i ($i = 1, 2, \ldots, n$). The capacity of each truck is much less than the total customer demand. The objective is to minimize the total distance traveled by the trucks.

The computational procedure may be paraphrased as follows:

1. Initially, assume that enough vehicles are available and allocate one to a customer. If a single customer demand exceeds the capacity of the vehicle, split the load and consider only the remainder of the load. Set up a vehicle allocation table like that in Table 10-3. In the problem at

				TABLE 10-3
				Available truck capacity and initial allocation of capacity to customers in example problem

Trucks	Up to 4000 gal	Over 4000 gal	Over 5000 gal	Over 6000 gal
Available	∞	7	4	0
Allocated	12	0	0	0

hand there are three trucks that have a 5000-gallon capacity and four trucks of 6000 gallons capacity. We assume an unlimited supply of 4000-gallon trucks. One truck of the smallest capacity is initially allocated to each customer and provides an initial feasible solution to the problem.

2. For hand computation, set up a matrix as shown in Fig. 10-10. The load to be delivered to each customer P_i is listed in column q. The right-hand value in each cell is the distance $d_{y,z}$ between P_y and P_z, where y and z are specific customers. The left-hand value represents the savings $S_{y,z}$ in distance associated with P_y and P_z when P_y enters the tour. $S_{y,z}$ is determined by

$$S_{y,z} = d_{0,y} + d_{0,z} - d_{y,z} \qquad (10.5)$$

[22] Some of these methods are surveyed in N. Christofides and S. Eilon, "An Algorithm for the Vehicle-dispatching Problem," *Operational Research Quarterly*, Vol. 20 (1969), pp. 309–18.

[23] G. Clarke and J. W. Wright, "Scheduling of Vehicles from a Central Depot to a Number of Delivery Points," *Operations Research*, Vol. 11 (1963), pp. 568–81.

[24] Christofides and Eilon, *loc. cit.*

FIGURE 10-10

Matrix setup for a vehicle scheduling problem where q is customer demand, P_i is customer or depot identification, cell right-hand value is distance between designated points, cell left-hand value except column P_0 is savings $S_{y,z}$, and the middle value in column P_0 is a link designator $t_{y,z}$.

$z \longrightarrow$

$y \downarrow$

Load, q	P_0	P_1	P_2	P_3	P_4	P_5	P_6	P_7	P_8	P_9	P_{10}	P_{11}	P_{12}
1200	2 / 9	P_1											
1700	2 / 14	18 5	P_2										
1500	2 / 21	18 12	28 7	P_3									
1400	2 / 23	10 22	20 17	34 10	P_4								
1700	2 / 22	10 21	20 16	22 21	26 19	P_5							
1400	2 / 25	10 24	16 23	16 30	20 28	38 9	P_6						
1200	2 / 32	10 31	20 26	26 27	30 25	44 10	50 7	P_7					
1900	2 / 36	10 35	20 30	20 37	24 35	42 16	50 11	58 10	P_8				
1800	2 / 38	10 37	16 36	16 43	20 41	38 22	50 13	54 16	68 6	P_9			
1600	2 / 42	10 41	20 36	32 31	36 29	44 20	50 17	64 10	72 6	68 12	P_{10}		
1700	2 / 50	10 49	20 44	34 37	42 31	44 28	50 25	64 18	72 14	76 12	84 8	P_{11}	
1100	2 / 52	10 51	20 46	34 39	46 29	44 30	50 27	64 20	72 16	70 20	84 10	92 10	P_{12}

Customers q [a]

[a] Customers are identified and ranked for convenience according to the savings $S_{y,z}$.

Source: Problem given in G. Clarke and J. W. Wright, "Scheduling of Vehicles from a Central Depot to a Number of Delivery Points," *Operations Research*, Vol. 11 (1963), pp. 568–581.

The value in the middle of the cell $t_{y,z}$ indicates whether the customer combination P_y and P_z are in the tour. The designator has the following values:

$t_{y,z} = 1$ if two customers are linked on a truck route.
$t_{y,z} = 0$ if the customers are not linked on a truck route.
$t_{y,z} = 2$ if the customer is served exclusively by a single truck.

In the initial problem setup all $t_{y,0} = 2$, meaning that one truck is used to serve one customer. For ease of computation, the matrix is ordered from left to right on the basis of increasing savings $S_{y,z}$.

3. Search the matrix for the largest savings subject to the following conditions for any cell (y, z):

   a. $t_{y,0}$ and $t_{z,0}$ are > 0.

   b. P_y and P_z are not already allocated on the same truck run.

   c. Amending Table 10-3 by removing the trucks allocated to loads q_y and q_z and adding a truck to cover the load $q_y + q_z$ does not cause the trucks allocated to exceed the trucks available in any column of Table 10-3.

4. Select a cell where there are two tours that can be combined into a single tour. A value of $t_{y,z} = 1$ is placed in the cell and all $t_{y,z}$ values are adjusted so that the sum of $t_{y,z}$ across a row plus $t_{y,z}$ down the column where $y = z$ is always equal to 2. Where $t_{j,0} = 0$, set $q_j = 0$ and make q_j equal the total load on the tour for all other j. Stop when no other links are possible.

To illustrate this procedure, consider our problem at an intermediate point in the solution. Fig. 10-11 and Table 10-4 show this point. Fig. 10-11 has been streamlined to show only savings and not distances. We search for the cell showing

TABLE 10-4

Intermediate allocation of trucks in example problem

Trucks	Up to 4000 gal	Over 4000 gal	Over 5000 gal	Over 6000 gal
Available	∞	7	4	0
Allocated	4	2	2	0

FIGURE 10-11

Intermediate step in the solution of example problem

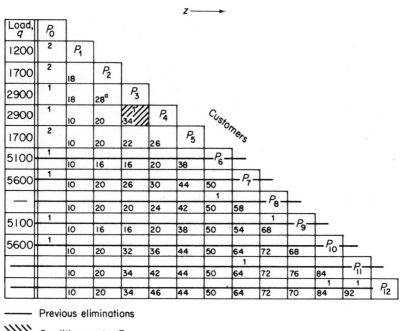

———— Previous eliminations

⊠ Condition a, step 3

▨ Condition b, step 3

✕ Condition c, step 3

[a] Cell 2, 3 is next choice to combine tours.

the next highest savings among those that have not been eliminated under the three conditions of step 3. This is cell 2, 3. Now we assign $t_{2,3} = 1$ and adjust row $y = 3$ and column $z = 3$ so that the t's sum to 2. This forces $t_{3,0} = 0$ as well as $t_{2,0} = 1$ and $t_{4,0} = 1$. The tour $P_0P_2P_0$ is now combined with the tour $P_0P_3P_4P_0$ to form the tour $P_0P_2P_3P_4P_0$ with a total load of $1700 + 2900 = 4600$ gallons. The need for two 4000-gallon trucks is eliminated, and these are replaced with a 5000-gallon truck. The allocation now is updated as shown in Fig. 10-12 and Table 10-5.

FIGURE 10-12
Revised solution matrix for example problem

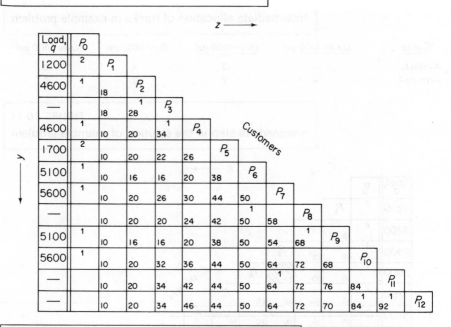

TABLE 10-5
Revised truck allocation table for example problem

Trucks	Up to 4000 gal	Over 4000 gal	Over 5000 gal	Over 6000 gal
Available	∞	7	4	0
Allocated	2	3	2	0

TABLE 10-6
Truck requirements for gasoline truck scheduling problem

Trucks	Up to 4000 gal	Over 4000 gal	Over 5000 gal	Over 6000 gal
Available	∞	7	4	0
Allocated	1	3	3	0

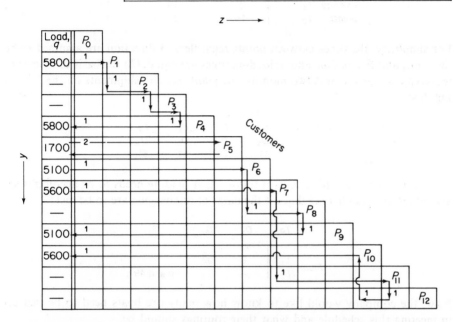

FIGURE 10-13

Final routing for the gasoline truck scheduling problem

Finally, choosing cell 2, 1 produces a solution, which is given in Fig. 10-13 and Table 10-6. Four tours are required, which are $P_0 \rightarrow P_1 \rightarrow P_2 \rightarrow P_3 \rightarrow P_4 \rightarrow P_0$, $P_0 \rightarrow P_5 \rightarrow P_0$, $P_0 \rightarrow P_6 \rightarrow P_8 \rightarrow P_9 \rightarrow P_0$, and $P_0 \rightarrow P_7 \rightarrow P_{11} \rightarrow P_{12} \rightarrow P_{10} \rightarrow P_0$ and trucks with capacity of 6000 gallons, 4000 gallons, 6000 gallons, and 6000 gallons, respectively. The total distance covered in the four tours is 290 units.

Minimizing Carrier Requirements. Carrier capacity may be an overriding consideration to distance or travel time when capacity is very expensive. Thus, the logistician may seek to minimize the number of carriers required to meet a routing schedule over time. Capacity is treated here as the capacity of all vehicles over time rather than the capacity of individual vehicles at any given time. A small problem is presented as an illustration of how much larger problems of this type might be approached.

Consider a supply problem of a steel producer with three plants D_1, D_2, and D_3 on the Great Lakes. The company obtains iron ore from two points L_1 and L_2 in the upper Great Lakes area. The ore is moved between the loading and discharge points by ore boats. The sailing time in days between ports plus time required for loading and unloading are consolidated in the following table.[25]

---

[25] Data for this example were obtained from S. Vajda, *Readings in Mathematical Programming* (New York: John Wiley & Sons, Inc., 1962), pp. 34–35.

		Discharge Points	
	D_1	D_2	D_3
Loading L_1	21	19	13
points L_2	16	15	12

For simplicity, the times between points regardless of direction are assumed to be the same, and the loading and unloading times are equal. On the basis of inventory requirements for the next two months, the plants require shipments on the following days:

From	L_2	L_1	L_1	L_2
at	D_3	D_1	D_2	D_3
Day	12	29	51	61

Due to loading and sailing time, it follows that loading needs to be accomplished according to the following dates if the dates of discharging are to be met:

To	D_1	D_2	D_3
From L_1	8	32	—
L_2	—	—	0 and 49

Now, the company would like to know how many ore boats need to be tied up in meeting this schedule and what their routings should be.

Dantzig and Fulkerson[26] have formulated this as a linear programming problem. The problem can then be solved as a transportation problem, as shown in Appendix A. The problem is set up by noting first the combination loading point and time of loading as an initial state i, and the discharge point and time of unloading as a terminal state j. In our problem, there are four initial states [$(L_2, 0)$, $(L_1, 8)$, $(L_1, 32)$, and $(L_2, 49)$] and four terminal states [$(D_3, 12)$, $(D_1, 29)$, $(D_2, 51)$, and $(D_3, 61)$].

The general problem is stated as[27]

$$\sum_j X_{ij} \leq a_i \qquad i = 1, 2, \ldots, n \tag{10.6}$$

and

$$\sum_i X_{ij} \leq b_j \qquad j = 1, 2, \ldots, m \tag{10.7}$$

where

X_{ij} = number of ore boats in terminal state j redirected to state i.
a_i = number of initial states i.
b_j = number of terminal states j.

[26] G. B. Dantzig and D. R. Fulkerson, "Minimizing the Number of Tankers to Meet a Fixed Schedule," *Naval Research Logistics Quarterly*, Vol. 1 (1954), pp. 217–22.

[27] Notation closely follows Vajda, *loc. cit.*

To put it in the form of a transportation problem, slack variables X_a and X_b are added to Equations (10.6) and (10.7). They become

$$\sum_j X_{ij} + X_a = a_i \qquad i = 1, 2, \ldots, n \qquad (10.8)$$

and

$$\sum_i X_{ij} + X_b = b_j \qquad j = 1, 2, \ldots, m \qquad (10.9)$$

The objective function is to maximize the number of ore boats redirected, or

$$z_{max} = \sum_i \sum_j X_{ij} \qquad (10.10)$$

The problem now has a standard transportation problem format and can be expressed in matrix form, as shown in Fig. 10-14. The rows are the terminal states, and the columns are the initial states. The rim values a_i and b_j are the number of times each state occurs. In our case, all a_i and b_j equal 1. Next, we must recognize that only certain cells or X_{ij} represent possible solution values. For example, $X_{4,2}$ is not feasible, since a boat cannot be directed from unloading at day 61 to meet a loading date at day 8. All cells are explored in this manner, and those that are infeasible are given a very high cell cost to lock them out of solution, say 100 units. Feasible cells are assigned low costs, say 1 unit. Slack cell costs should be moderately high to discourage assignments to them, say 10 units. An initial feasible solution to our problem can be achieved by making all initial assignments to the slack cells. Of course, this solution represents the maximum number of boats that might be needed.

FIGURE 10-14

Transportation problem setup of the ore boat scheduling problem

---

Initial States i

Discharge Date \\ Load Date	L_2 0	L_1 8	L_1 32	L_2 49	Slack	b_j
D_3 12	100	100	1	1	10 [1]	1
D_1 29	100	100	100	1	10 [1]	1
D_2 51	100	100	100	100	10 [1]	1
D_3 61	100	100	100	100	10 [1]	1
Slack	10 [1]	10 [1]	10 [1]	10 [1]	10 [0]	4
a_i	1	1	1	1	4	

Terminal states j

FIGURE 10-15

Solution matrix for the ore boat scheduling problem

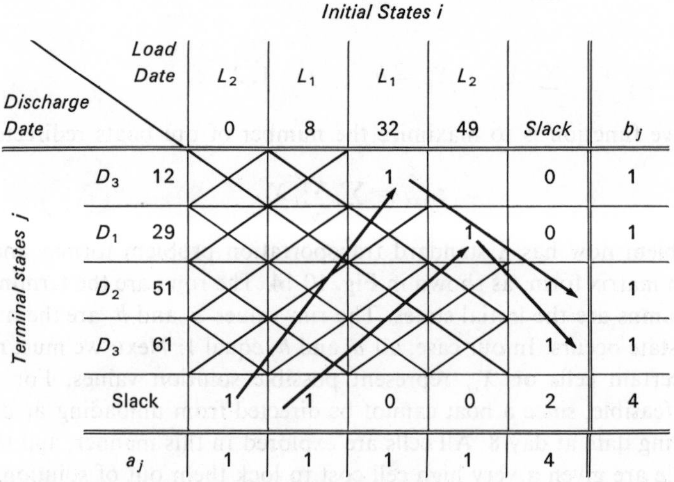

Initial States i

inadmissible X_{ij} or loading-discharge point combinations.

Following the transportation solution method yields the solution matrix of Fig. 10-15. To read the solution, we start with initial state 1 and then find the $X_{ij} = 1$ associated with terminal state 1. This is cell $i = 3$, $j = 1$. Next, we look for an $X_{ij} = 1$ for $j = 3$. This is now a slack cell, and we stop. The first routing as shown in Fig. 10-15 is a connected path of L_2, $0 \rightarrow D_3$, $12 \rightarrow L_1$, $32 \rightarrow D_2$, 51. Starting with the second initial state, we trace a similar path of L_1, $8 \rightarrow D_1$, $29 \rightarrow L_2$, 49 $\rightarrow D_3$, 61. A minimum of two ore boats is required.

Several additional assumptions of the method should be noted, as they may bear on the usefulness of the results. First, it was assumed that all boats were identical and interchangeable. Second, the boats were permitted to end up anywhere. If a specific final destination point is desired, it may be introduced as an artificial state. This, of course, may increase the number of boats required. Third, it was assumed that the entire load was picked up and delivered by one boat. This is not necessary, since the loads can be divided into any number of separate states each with identical dates. Fourth, the objective was to minimize the number of carriers required. It is possible to restate the problem so that total sailing time is minimized for a given number of boats. Fifth, the level and timing of inventory requirements are known. As has been noted here, it is not particularly difficult to modify or even eliminate many of the assumptions by the judicious use of the model.

Production Scheduling

Particularly difficult management problems are those that occur at the interface between two areas of managerial responsibility. Such an interface exists between logistics and production. The interface problem is production scheduling, that is, *what* to make, *how much* to make, and *when* to make it.

Production and logistics share an interest in finished-goods inventories. Production uses them to help smooth production operations under uncertain or seasonal demand conditions. Likewise, logistics uses inventories to balance against the cost and performance of transportation; that is, if transportation could provide instantaneous service, time and space barriers would disappear. Different managerial problems arise in the area of production scheduling, depending on the functional area having responsibility for inventory policy. Of concern here is the case where the logistics function of the firm has the responsibility for finished-goods inventories and goods are produced to order. The logistician can influence the production schedule through inventory policy, and the production schedule adopted in turn affects the average inventory level. The case where production has the primary responsibility for inventories is well documented and is beyond the scope of this text.[28] Also, production to customer demand forecasts is of little interest, since the logistician merely accepts the consequence of such production schedules without direct influence over them.

When the logistician sets inventory policy, he may force certain diseconomies onto the production operations, since the effect of inventory policy is to specify a product demand level and an input sequence for production. That is, inventory policies are in large part production schedules. From a total company standpoint, it is best to balance inventory costs against those production costs directly affected by inventory policy. These production costs act as cross charges against logistics so as to encourage a wider base on which to establish inventory policies. It is because of the impact of logistically determined inventory policy on production costs and because of the need in the logistics system to maintain given customer service levels through inventory reorder policies that the logistician becomes involved in production scheduling. He does not usually become involved in more detailed matters of production operations, such as employment levels, in-process materials flow, equipment layout, and the like. Only indirectly does he influence these.

EXAMPLE. To firm up these ideas, consider a scheduling example. The situation is shown in Fig. 10-16. Orders for three chemical products are placed on the warehouse, and production is scheduled when plant orders for stock replenishment at the warehouse are issued. If demand and lead time certainty and a fixed order quantity are assumed, and if variable order interval warehouse inventory control system is used, the optimum order quantity Q^* and the order interval N^* can be determined from the costs given in Table 10-7. Thus, if only logistics costs are of concern, inventory policy would suggest that product 1 should be ordered in quantities of $Q_1^* = 447$ approximately $N_1^* = 22$ times a year, product 2, $Q_2^* = 39$

---

[28] For a discussion of this point of view, see Robert E. McGarrah, *Production and Logistics Management: Text and Cases* (New York: John Wiley and Sons, Inc., 1963), pp. 105–34; and Elwood S. Buffa, *Production-Inventory Systems* (Homewood, Illinois: Richard D. Irwin, Inc., 1968), pp. 49–200.

FIGURE 10-16

Production scheduling problem for three products produced to inventories

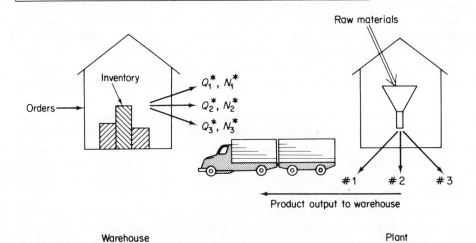

Note: Q's and N's are order quantities and order frequencies.

TABLE 10-7

Demand, inventory costs, and inventory reorder policy for three products in example

Product	Annual Demand D_i	Procurement Costs S_i[a]	Inventory Carrying Cost C_i	Order Quantity Q_i^*[b]	Order Frequency N_i^*[c]
#1	10,000 units	$10/order	$1/unit/yr	447 units	22 times/yr
2	1,000	15	20	39	26
3	100,000	5	0.25	2000	50

[a] Costs represent an average figure independent of production sequence.
[b] See Equation (9.3).
[c] See Equation (9.4).

and $N_2^* = 26$, and product 3, $Q_3^* = 2000$ and $N_3^* = 50$. No particular production scheduling problem occurs. Thus, the production sequence desired by the logistician is shown in Fig. 10-17. That is, the sequence would be $\#3231 \mid 3231 \mid 3231 \mid 323 \ldots$ over the near future. Production is assumed to be instantaneous.

The three chemical products are produced in a single kettle. Because there is a degree of incompatability between the products, after each product run the kettle must be washed and prepared for the next run. The amount of preparation time and expense depends on the sequence that the products are produced. For example, product 3 is an acid-based product and can readily contaminate either products 1 or 2. Thus, the cost of sequencing from 3 to 1 or 3 to 2 is high. Other sequence

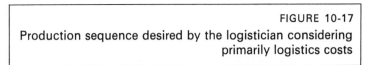

FIGURE 10-17

Production sequence desired by the logistician considering primarily logistics costs

FIGURE 10-18

Production sequence cost matrix for example problem

		To Product		
		1	*2*	*3*
	1	$0	$20	$10
From Product	*2*	0	0	10
	3	100	100	0

combinations are less expensive. A sequence cost matrix for these three products is given in Fig. 10-18.

Production scheduling is now a problem of balancing sequencing costs against inventory costs. In our example problem, there are three unique production sequences. With their corresponding sequence costs developed from Fig. 10-18, these are

Sequence	Sequence Cost
3231 3231 ···	$220
3321 3321 ···	110
1233 1233 ···	130

That is, sequence 3231 has a sequence cost of $1 \rightarrow 3$, $10 plus $3 \rightarrow 2$, $100 plus $2 \rightarrow 3$, $10, and $3 \rightarrow 1$, $100, or $220.

The question now becomes: If a more favorable sequence is chosen, say 3321, over the sequence based on logistics cost considerations alone, say 3231, can it be justified in terms of the higher inventory costs that will occur? The sequence cost savings would be $(220 - 110) \times \frac{52}{2} = \$2860/\text{year}$. That is, the sequence repeats approximately every two weeks (see Fig. 10-17), so the savings will occur $\frac{52}{2} = 26$ times a year.

To change to sequence 3321 from 3231 would force suboptimum inventory levels in the warehouse. The sequence 3231 will have the lowest possible inventory costs, since it was developed strictly from inventory cost considerations. On the other hand, if sequence 3321 is adopted, the order frequency noted by N_i^* in Table 10-7 cannot be maintained. Suboptimality occurs when production and shipments to the warehouse must be made at undesirable times. For example, since two batches of product 3 are produced in sequence, suppose they are produced as a double batch and shipped at the same time. The effect is to increase the average inventory level of product 3 from $Q_3/2$ to $(2Q_3)/2$. The increased carrying cost per year would be $0.25(Q_3/2) = 0.25(\frac{2000}{2}) = \$250$. Balanced with the sequencing cost saving of \$2860, a net savings of $\$2860 - 250 = \$2610$ is realized. If the production of product 3 can be spaced out while the optimum order frequency for the remaining products is still maintained, the increase in inventory will be less.

Broadening the Analysis. The above example has been presented under rather strict assumptions about the real world. In reality, inventory policies must be generated in light of demand and lead time uncertainties, seasonal variations in demand, and varying customer service requirements. If the inventory reorder policies are adaptive to changing conditions in order to maintain optimal or nearly optimal inventory levels, these dynamic policies will be reflected in production costs. More than just production sequence costs will now be involved. Labor costs, administrative costs, power costs, etc. may all come into play. Again, a schedule of cross charges to logistics based on cost differentials relative to optimal production policies can be established, but now additional production costs are included in the cross charges. The same basic tradeoff analysis shown in the example above still applies.

The type of broad, interfunctional analysis suggested for production scheduling carries with it the possibility that the logistics function may absorb higher inventory costs than it might if a more narrow view of the problem were taken. Such added costs are charges against the firm as a whole. Top management should not view these costs as entirely under the control of the logistician, but rather as costs resulting from a combined logistics-production effort. The logistician should not be penalized for his cooperation.

Order Processing System Decisions

The order processing system is a subsystem of the total logistics information system. However, because order information is vital to the effective planning and operation of the logistics system, order processing is generally the most important of the information system activities. Several decisions concern its overall design, which include (1) order transmission, (2) order sequencing, (3) central system design, and (4) order scheduling.

SYSTEM DESIGN

Order Transmission Selection. As noted in Chapter 3, the order processing system deals with raw sales order data and transmits it from the point of generation to the point where customer demands can be acted upon. Thus, the order processing system is basically a data transmission system, and system design revolves around the different means of transmitting the order data.

Common among order transmission alternatives are telephone, mail, salesman pickup and dropoff, and teletype, as shown in Fig. 10-19. Selecting one or a combination of transmission alternatives is a problem of balancing cost against performance. Speed, reliability, and accuracy are the desirable performance characteristics. In general, the greater the performance, the higher the customer service level. That is, order transmission time is a component of order cycle time or inventory lead time, and order cycle time affects customer service and/or inventory costs through the inventory levels that must be maintained. Higher-performance devices in terms of speed and accuracy, such as teletypewriters and dataphones, are generally more expensive than mail or salesman transmission.

Though it is easy to state the problem as one of balancing costs and performance, establishing the assignable costs and revenues to the problem is particularly difficult. The reason is that such transmission devices, especially more sophisticated ones, often are not used solely for communicating order information, but may also

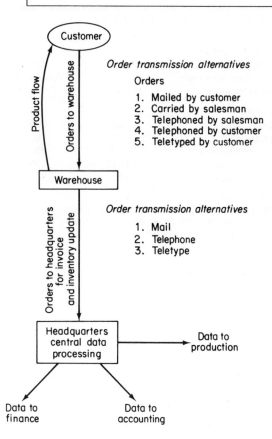

FIGURE 10-19

A simple order processing system with some alternative means of order transmission

Order transmission alternatives

Orders

1. Mailed by customer
2. Carried by salesman
3. Telephoned by salesman
4. Telephoned by customer
5. Teletyped by customer

Order transmission alternatives

1. Mail
2. Telephone
3. Teletype

Customer

Product flow

Orders to warehouse

Warehouse

Orders to headquarters for invoice and inventory update

Headquarters central data processing

Data to production

Data to finance

Data to accounting

be used as a link to the centrally located computer for data analysis or may be part of the total information system of the firm and may be used for a multitude of data transmission purposes, such as credit reports, sales analysis reports, and messages. Allocating the common costs to the various uses is a matter of judgment, though accountants have established guide lines.

Even more difficult than establishing relevant costs is determining the impact on revenues of various transmission devices and order processing system designs. Direct revenue effects are generally not known. However, they sometimes can successfully be imputed from the inventory costs required to meet a given customer service level under various order processing system designs. Order transmission affects inventory costs through its effect on inventory lead time and through its effect on order information availability for inventory updating resulting from the level of uncertainty that information lags create in the inventory system.

The sales order processing transmission selection problem from Fig. 10-19 is depicted in Table 10-8. Choosing the best alternative for transmitting order information from customer to warehouse and on to central data processing is a matter

---

TABLE 10-8

Hypothetical annual costs relevant to a series of sales order transmission alternatives shown in Fig. 10-19

Mode of Sales Order Information Transmission from Customer to Warehouse and from Warehouse to Central Data Processing	(1) Revenue Effects[b]	(2) Assignable Costs, $[c]	(3) Net Costs[d]
Salesman carry-mail[a]	$ 0	$1000	$1000
Salesman telephone-mail	−500	2000	1500
Customer telephone-mail	−600	1500	900
Customer telephone-telephone	−900	3000	2100
Salesman telephone-teletype	−1000	5000	4000
Customer teletype-teletype	−1200	7000	5800

[a] Used as a reference alternative.
[b] Imputed from inventory costs and referenced to the first alternative. Expressed as opportunity costs where negative costs are revenues.
[c] Based on a given annual volume of sales orders processed.
[d] Sum of columns (1) and (2).

---

of balancing revenue effects of the alternative against the assignable costs for order information transmission. In this hypothetical example, the customer telephoning his order to the warehouse and then mailing orders to central data processing shows the greatest promise.

Order Sequencing. The above example has given a rather limited view of alternatives available for changing data transmission speed. To the logistician, transmission speed is affected by the sequence in which the data becomes available at various collection points, in addition to electronic methods of speeding transmission. With reference to Fig. 10-19, it may be possible to increase transmission speed by sending customer orders directly to the central data processing point and then on to the warehouse for order filling. Inventory records can be updated more quickly with a reduction in the level of uncertainty and lower safety stocks. If an electronic form of data transmission is used, the time lapse at the warehouse is small, and customer service will not change perceptively. Such alternatives should also be factored into the selection problem.

Along this same line, the sequence in which the various functions of the business have access to the data can increase logistics costs. In one company, sales orders were sent from the warehouse, where orders were filled, to headquarters, where inventory records were updated and replenishment orders were released to plants. Upon receipt of the orders at headquarters, a bill of lading was matched with the sales order and an invoice was prepared. The order was then sent to data processing for the inventory records to be updated. Resequencing the order information first through data processing reduced the information lag by several days and improved the control over inventories. Very often, logistics costs are more sensitive to information time lags than those of accounting, manufacturing, or marketing. Therefore, logistics needs generally should be met first when one is deciding on the sequence of order information availability.

Central System Design.   A certain amount of data manipulation is part of the order-processing system. Included are such activities as bill of lading preparation, inventory updating, stock order preparation, sales record keeping, and inventory reports. Systems for handling these activities range from manual systems to fully automated ones. System design criteria include the volume of orders handled in terms of its magnitude and fluctuation over time, as well as the requirements for flexibility in system size, speed of data processing, and the acceptable level of error in information handling. Systems that primarily process order information by hand have the potential of handling a small volume of orders efficiently and usually can be expanded or contracted at low cost to meet a fluctuating volume of orders through the system. Such systems are generally slow speed and have a higher error level than corresponding automated systems, except in those cases of spectacular automated system failure. In contrast, systems aided by the use of electronic data processing equipment require higher initial costs to establish, have less flexibility to meet changing conditions at low cost, and have high penalty costs associated with record loss. However, the electronically assisted system can process a high volume of orders quickly, at low cost, and relatively error-free. System design selection is the balancing at optimum the fixed and variable costs of a system and the revenue and cost effects associated with the system's performance.

Order Scheduling.   A final consideration in the design of the order-processing system is the data collection procedure for introducing order information into the system. Collecting and processing orders as they are generated may cause periods of high loading on the operating logistics system as well as slack periods. Order processing can be smoothed with resulting lower costs for processing, filling, and shipping orders if the times that order information is introduced into the system can be staggered. Staggering of orders usually can be accomplished by the times that a salesman is scheduled to call on customers or the times that customers are required to submit orders. This type of scheduling offers significant logistics cost reduction with little change in the level of customer service provided.

Concluding Comments

This chapter has looked at several decision areas that confront the logistician. Transport decisions are frequently occurring problems that include transport service selection, carrier routing, and vehicle scheduling. Fortunately, these problems submit to mathematical analysis and can be routinized to a large extent. Production scheduling is an interfunctional decision requiring the cooperation of production and logistics to effect economies for the firm. Mathematical analysis can provide decision guide lines for both. Finally, order processing decisions represent a subset of logistics information system decisions. Important decisions here are order transmission design, central data processing design, and order scheduling. No specific mathematical models have yet been developed to handle these latter problems.

Questions and Problems

1. Selecting a mode of transportation is a decision problem of concern to both the consignor and the consignee when the consignor actually makes the selection decision. Why is this so? Can the consignee influence the choice? If so, how and under what circumstances?

2. If you were to develop a transport mode selection model, list the factors you think are important to the mode selection decision. Which factors do you think could formally be included in the model? Would you judge such a model as useful or impractical?

3. When would the direct cost approach to transportation service selection be satisfactory? When would the concepts of the inventory-theoretic approach be more appropriate?

TABLE 10-9

Door-to-door delivery characteristics and costs of service for transportation services available to Wagner

Transportation Service	Average Delivery Time, Days	Delivery-Time Variability (V), Days
Rail	16	5
Piggyback	10	4
Truck	4	1
Piggyback[a]	9	3

[a] Transportation service used by Bradley.

TABLE 10-10

A schedule of orders, profits, inventory costs, and transportation charges to Wagner as a function of the difference in transit-time variability between Wagner and Bradley

Difference in Variability, $(V_W - V_B)$	Profit to Wagner before Inventory & Transportation Costs, $/yr[a]	Quantity Ordered from Wagner, Units	Wagner's Inventory Cost, $/yr	Total Transportation Charges, $/yr		
				Rail	Piggyback	Truck
−3	70,000	35,000	30,000	5,000	10,000	25,000
−2	80,000	40,000	29,000	7,500	13,000	30,000
−1	90,000	45,000	27,000	10,000	17,000	36,000
0	100,000	50,000	24,000	12,500	22,000	44,000
+1	110,000	55,000	20,000	15,000	28,000	52,000
+2	120,000	60,000	15,000	17,500	35,000	60,000
+3	130,000	65,000	9,000	20,000	44,000	66,000
+4	140,000	70,000	7,000	22,500	54,000	73,000

[a] Price is assumed to be constant.

4. The Wagner Company competes with Bradley Electric Company in supplying electric motors to Electronic Distributors, Inc. Wagner sells on a delivered price basis, and has the responsibility for providing transportation.

The traffic manager has three transportation service choices for delivery—rail, piggyback, and truck. To help select among these, he has compiled information on profits, costs, and operating characteristics of the three alternatives plus information on the current delivery service provided by Bradley. This information is shown in Tables 10-9 and 10-10.

   (a) Which of the three alternatives should Wagner choose if Electronic's demand for motors is reasonably certain?
   (b) Would your decision be different if you anticipate that Bradley will retaliate to your choice? How?
   (c) Would price play a role in the final decision?
   (d) If Electronic Distributors follows a fixed buying pattern from Wagner and Bradley in order to maintain two sources of supply, how will Wagner's decision be affected?
   (e) What role does cooperation between Wagner and Electronic play in selecting a transportation service?

5. The Transcontinental Trucking Company wishes to route a shipment from Buffalo, New York to Duluth, Minnesota over major highways. Since time and distance are closely related, the company dispatcher would like to find the shortest route. A schematic network of the major highway links and mileages between the two cities is shown in Fig. 10-20. Find the shortest route through the network by using Dantzig's shortest-route tree method.

FIGURE 10-20
Feasible routes for Transcontinental Trucking Company problem

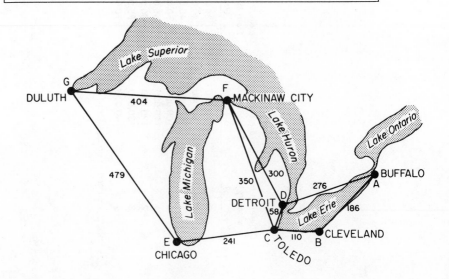

6.[29] In December 1965, the U. S. Army Material Command was preparing final arrangements to move its M113 Full Tracked Armored Personnel Carrier from various subcontractor manufacturing facilities to intermediate storage facilities at Letterkenny, Pennsylvania for those units destined for Europe or to several army bases within the United States. The production schedule for December plus the units on hand at the plant and the requirements for December are shown below.

Production Schedule for December

Cleveland, Ohio	150 units plus 250 on hand
South Charleston, W. Va.	150
San Jose, Calif.	150

Requirements for December

U. S. Army, Europe via Letterkenny, Pa.	300 units
Fort Hood, Texas	100
Fort Riley, Kansas	100
Fort Carson, Colorado	100
Fort Benning, Georgia	100

FIGURE 10-21

Transportation network with associated costs for U.S. Army Material Command problem

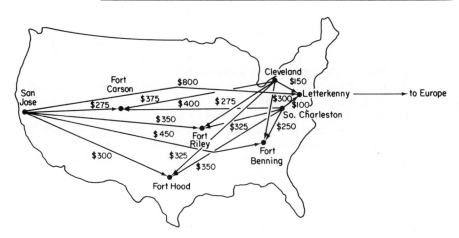

Fig. 10-21 shows the locations of the supply and demand points as well as the per-unit transportation costs from supply to demand points.

Find the least-cost routing schedule for December to meet the requirements, but do not exceed the available supplies.

[29] This problem is adapted from a case study by Colonel James Piercy.

7.[30] A bakery delivers daily to five large retail stores in a defined territory. The route man for the bakery loads goods at the bakery, is to make deliveries to the retail stores, and return to the bakery. A schematic diagram of the territory is shown in Fig. 10-22. The associated network travel times in minutes are

		To				
		B	1	2	3	4	5
	B	0	24	50	38	55	20
	1	24	0	32	23	45	18
From	2	50	32	0	15	21	60
	3	38	23	15	0	14	25
	4	55	45	21	14	0	42
	5	20	18	60	25	42	0

FIGURE 10-22
Territory map for bakery routing problem

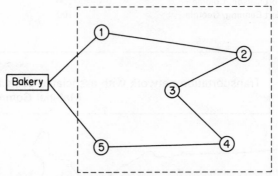

(a) What is the best routing sequence for the delivery truck?
(b) If loading or unloading times are significant, how would they be included in the analysis?
(c) Retail store number 3 is located in a densely populated urban area such that the travel times to and from this point may increase by as much as 50 percent depending on the time of day. Travel times for the other points remain relatively unchanged. Would the solution in part (a) be sensitive to such variations?

8. B & K Stores is a chain of supermarkets that are serviced daily by a single distribution center. A fleet of trucks is used to make these deliveries. The distribution center has available a large number of 10,000-pound trucks, four 20,000-pound trucks, and three 30,000-pound trucks. The daily demand from each store is as follows.

---

[30] This problem is adapted from Richard B. Maffei, "Modern Methods for Local Delivery Route Design," *Journal of Marketing*, Vol. 29 (April 1965), pp. 13–18.

Store	Daily Demand, lb
1	6,000
2	3,000
3	4,000
4	7,000
5	5,000
6	2,000
7	3,000
8	8,000
9	10,000

A matrix of travel times in minutes between the distribution center and other store points is as follows.

	D. C.	1	2	3	4	5	6	7	8	9
D. C.	0	10	20	5	5	20	25	25	30	5
1	10	0	5	10	5	10	15	15	20	10
2	20	5	0	20	15	5	10	10	15	15
3	5	10	20	0	5	20	25	25	30	10
4	5	5	15	5	0	15	25	25	25	5
5	20	10	5	20	15	0	10	5	15	15
6	25	15	10	25	25	10	0	5	5	20
7	25	15	10	25	25	5	5	0	5	20
8	30	20	15	30	25	15	5	5	0	25
9	5	10	15	10	5	15	20	20	25	0

One round trip can be made.

(a) Find the best routing schedules for the fleet of trucks to minimize total travel time.
(b) How many trucks will be needed and at what capacity?

9. Queens Lines operates a fleet of tankers to transport crude oil throughout various parts of the world. One scheduling problem concerns the movement of oil from two Middle East ports to four European ports in England, France, and Germany. The sailing time in days between ports is

Middle East Ports	European Discharge Points			
	A	B	C	D
1	20	18	12	9
2	17	14	10	8

Within the next three months, deliveries are to be made according to the following schedule.

From loading port	1	2	1	2	1	2
At discharge port	D	C	A	B	C	A
Day	10	15	36	39	52	86

Assume that ships are available to start anywhere and can end up at any point.

How many ships are needed to meet the schedule, and how should they be deployed?

10.   An assembly division of a large company orders four items from one of the producing divisions within the company to meet its own production needs. Pertinent demand and inventory cost data are summarized below.

Product	Annual Demand	Procurement Costs	Inventory Carrying Costs
1	20,000 units	$16/order	$2/unit/yr
2	2,000	25	15
3	50,000	7	20
4	200,000	4	0.5

Demand is relatively constant throughout the year.

Plant production set up and sequencing costs are estimated as shown in the following matrix.

		To Product			
		1	2	3	4
	1	0	50	150	175
From	2	60	0	0	50
Product	3	100	0	0	125
	4	200	75	60	0

(a) What should be the product sequence that the logistician should select if he is cross charged for the proportion of production cost due to sequencing?

(b) If production sequencing costs are not cross charged to logistics, which sequence is the logistician likely to choose? What is the worth of production-logistics cooperation?

11. What arguments can you put forth as to why logistics should receive sales order information before production, marketing, or accounting when such information cannot be made available simultaneously to all parties?

12. A wine manufacturer uses direct selling to generate orders. Each salesman calls upon a number of accounts within a defined territory. All orders are filled through a central distribution point. Discuss the impact of the following order scheduling schemes on logistics costs.

(a) Telephone orders to distribution center after 10 are accumulated.
(b) Mail orders to distribution center as obtained.
(c) Mail all orders to distribution center once a week.
(d) Have customer prepare and mail orders to distribution center.

Selected Bibliography

FORD, L. R., JR. and D. R. FULKERSON, *Flows in Networks*. Princeton, N. J.: Princeton University Press, 1962.

WAGNER, HARVEY M., *Principles of Operations Research*. Englewood Cliffs, N. J.: Prentice-Hall, Inc., 1969, especially Chapter 7.

WILSON, G. LLOYD, *Traffic Management*. Englewood Cliffs, N. J.: Prentice-Hall, Inc., 1956, especially Chapter 13.

Chapter
11

Storage
and
Materials-Handling Decisions

The logistician often becomes involved with activities that supplement the primary move-store activities of the firm. Such activities affect the overall efficiency of logistics system operation, but often do not have as dramatic an impact on customer service or system costs as do transportation and inventory carrying costs. These activities are considered to be supporting in nature. Warehousing activities, that is, storage and materials handling at the point of inventory accumulation in the logistics network, are of this type.

This is not to imply that warehousing activities are unimportant and can be assumed away. As previously noted, storage and materials-handling activities account for roughly one-fifth of the logistics dollar (recall Table 1-4). This estimate excludes the cost of carrying inventories. Neglecting effectively to manage these activities can result in inefficiencies that outweigh gains in good management of such key activities as transportation, inventory control, and information flow.

Many storage and materials-handling activities are repetitive, so careful management can produce substantial economies over a period of time.

In this chapter we want to consider the problems of planning for the design and operation of the nodal points in the logistics network. Nodal points usually are characterized by warehouses but also may refer to inventory accumulations in whatever form they may take place, whether held outdoors, underground, or within partially protecting shelters. The major emphasis will be on warehouse design and its operation with implications to other methods of storage, since warehousing is the most complex and widely used storage form. Specifically, this chapter deals with planning for facility design, which includes (1) facility sizing, (2) facility configuration, (3) dock design, (4) materials-handling system selection, and (5) stock layout. This discussion is a continuation of that initiated in Chapter 7 on the storage system.

Site Selection

Before a discussion of the detailed decisions about warehouse design and operation can logically proceed, the question of where the warehouse is to be located must be resolved. In Chapter 8, a number of mathematical models were presented that give a first approximation to final location in terms of a region, metropolitan area, or city. Within the defined area, the specific site must be selected. Site selection is more of an art than a well-defined process. It involves weighing a number of tangible and intangible factors. Chief among these factors are:

1. The cost or rent of the land on which the warehouse is to be constructed.
2. The real estate and local government taxes associated with the site.
3. Labor climate, productivity, and costs for the area.
4. The availability, adequacy, and cost of the various utilities, such as water, electricity, gas, and sewage disposal.
5. Community attitudes toward the project.
6. Zoning restrictions associated with the proposed warehouse.
7. The availability of transportation services in the form of rail spurs and highways.
8. Potential for later expansion.

Of course, when the warehouse already exists, as in the case of a public warehouse or a facility to be leased, selection is usually restricted to the available facilities. Site selection is more concerned with rates and services to be provided when selection is among the public warehouses. Selecting a facility to be leased involves many of the factors noted above, but the physical characteristics of the buildings to be leased act as constraints on warehouse operations. Planning the private warehouse offers the maximum design flexibility of all the warehousing alternatives, and the planning for design and operation of the next section is directed toward, but not limited to, the private warehouse.

Planning for Design and Operation

Planning for facility design concerns the long-range decision making required to establish the facilities necessary for the efficient temporary storage of products and the flow of products through the facility. Such decisions often require a substantial capital investment that commits the company to a design for years. Careful design planning can mean years of efficient warehouse operation.

SIZING THE FACILITY

The first and probably the most important decision in designing a storage facility concerns its size. Once warehouse size is determined, it acts as a constraint on warehouse operations that may last 20 years or longer. Whereas the internal layout of the facility may be changed with relative ease, changing the overall size of the warehouse is much more involved. Though the facility may be expanded at a later date or extra space may be leased to other users, the resulting quality of the space may not be ideal. In general, the result of poor planning of warehouse size is either to cause higher than necessary materials-handling costs in the warehouse in the case of underbuilding or to force unnecessary space costs on the logistics system in the case of constructing more space than needed.

Specifically, what is size? Size simply refers to the overall cubic content of the warehouse building—its length, width, and height. Determining the needed volume of the building is a task complicated by the many factors that impinge on the size decision. Such factors as the type of materials-handling system to be used, aisle requirements, stock layout arrangements, dock requirements, local building codes, office area, and product throughput both at the present and in the future influence the final choice of a warehouse size. A starting point is the minimum space required for accommodating the inventory stored in the warehouse over time. The remaining factors influence size by adding to the basic, inventory-determined size.

Let us look at inventory-determined size under two assumptions. The first is to consider that there will not be significant changes in the need for space in 10 years or longer. No trend in space needs is expected. However, in the short term there will be seasonal changes in the need for space as sales through the warehouse and replenishment of warehouse stock vary throughout the year. The second is to consider the sizing problem when average inventory levels are anticipated to change over a period of years. This is the dynamic sizing problem that seeks the best size for the warehouse in each year of the planning horizon. Before a detailed sizing analysis is carried out, a company typically has made its location decision. In the location analysis, it is necessary to assign sales territories to warehouses (recall Chapter 8). Assigning sales territories determines the product throughput and the inventory accumulation for each warehouse in the logistics system. Rough warehouse size approximations can be made from these inventory needs, and further analysis begins with this preliminary information.

The No-Trend Sizing Problem.   An approach to solving the sizing problem when there is no trend in average inventory levels over time can best be illustrated by means of an example. Consider the problem of the Bradley Electric Company. Bradley is a one-product-line company specializing in room air conditioners. A company-owned warehouse is to be constructed to serve the major sales region of the country. The sizing problem is complicated by the uncertainty in the sales level and the wide seasonal swings in sales throughout the year. Bradley's need for warehouse space is estimated by month for a typical year, as shown in Table 11-1.

	TABLE 11-1
	Most likely, pessimistic, and optimistic monthly sales estimates and resulting warehouse space requirements for Bradley Electric Company

(a) Most Likely Sales Projection, Probability of Occurrence = 0.50.

	(1) Beginning Inventory on Hand, Units	(2) Sales During Month Through Warehouse, Units[a]	(3) Production During Month to Warehouse, Units	(4) End-of- Month Inventory, Units[b]	(5) Total Space Required, sq ft[c]
January	119,750	6,650	27,190	140,290	70,145
February	140,290	32,800	25,140	132,630	66,315
March	132,630	104,850	49,700	77,480	38,740
April	77,480	214,100	180,050	43,430	21,715
May	43,430	282,000	282,150	43,580	21,790
June	43,580	239,500	240,460	44,540	22,270
July	44,540	130,300	143,760	58,000	29,000
August	58,000	46,090	75,790	87,700	43,650
September	87,700	9,990	42,460	120,170	60,035
October	120,170	1,530	25,960	144,600	72,300
November	144,600	30,220	21,920	136,300	68,150
December	136,300	55,670	39,120	119,750	59,875
		1,153,700	1,153,700		

(b) Pessimistic Sales Projection, Probability of Occurrence = 0.25.

	(1) Beginning Inventory on Hand, Units	(2) Sales During Month Through Warehouse, Units[a]	(3) Production During Month to Warehouse, Units	(4) End-of- Month Inventory, Units[b]	(5) Total Space Required, sq ft[c]
January	119,750	5,000	20,400	135,150	67,575
February	135,150	24,600	18,800	129,350	64,675
March	129,350	78,500	37,300	88,150	44,075
April	88,150	161,000	135,000	62,150	31,075
May	62,150	212,000	212,000	62,150	31,075
June	62,150	179,000	180,010	63,250	31,625
July	63,250	97,700	107,700	73,250	36,625
August	73,250	34,600	56,900	95,550	47,775
September	95,550	7,500	31,900	119,950	59,975
October	119,950	1,150	19,550	138,350	69,175
November	138,350	22,700	16,400	132,050	61,025
December	132,050	41,700	29,400	119,750	59,875
		865,450	865,450		

(c) Optimistic Sales Projection, Probability of Occurrence = 0.25.

	(1) Beginning Inventory on Hand, Units	(2) Sales During Month Through Warehouse, Units[a]	(3) Production During Month to Warehouse, Units	(4) End-of-Month Inventory, Units[b]	(5) Total Space Required, sq ft[c]
January	119,750	9,300	36,100	146,550	73,275
February	146,555	45,900	36,100	136,750	68,375
March	136,750	146,800	68,500	58,450	29,225
April	58,450	300,000	252,000	10,450	5,225
May	10,450	394,000	393,000	9,450	4,725
June	9,450	335,000	346,000	20,450	10,225
July	20,450	184,000	200,000	36,450	18,225
August	36,450	64,500	104,000	75,950	37,975
September	75,950	14,000	59,400	121,350	60,675
October	121,350	2,140	35,440	154,650	77,325
November	154,650	42,300	30,600	142,950	76,475
December	142,950	77,900	54,700	119,750	59,875
		1,615,840	1,615,840		

[a] Excludes those sales shipped direct to customers.
[b] Computed as the sum of columns (1) and (3) less (2).
[c] Based on an average packaged unit size of 8.0 cubic feet and an average safe stacking height of 16 feet; that is, $\frac{16}{8} = 2$ units per square foot of floor area.

Approximate space needs for each month are given by the end-of-the-month inventory level in the warehouse. This level is computed by the difference equation:

$$\text{End-of-the-month inventory} = \text{inventory at beginning of the month}$$
$$\text{less sales from warehouse during month}$$
$$\text{plus production shipped to warehouse}$$
$$\text{during month} \qquad (11.1)$$

Space requirements in square feet of floor space for each month is determined by converting units in inventory to required square feet of floor space, as shown in column 5 of Table 11-1.

The exact level of sales, and therefore the exact space requirements, cannot be known for sure. Yet a single warehouse size is to be selected. To account for uncertainty in needed space, optimistic and pessimistic sales projections are also made, as shown in Table 11-1(b) and (c). All projections are assigned a probability according to management's subjective judgment as to the likelihood of occurrence of each. In this case, probabilities of 0.25, 0.50, and 0.25 are assigned to the pessimistic, most likely, and optimistic sales projections, respectively.

Determining the best warehouse means to meet the above space requirements is a matter of balancing the economic effects of different alternative methods for acquiring space. These alternative methods include private ownership of space, leasing of space (direct leasing or leasing through a sale-lease-back arrangement), renting space in a public warehouse, or various combinations of these. If a private warehouse is to be constructed to entirely meet the space needs, the sizing decision is a fairly easy one though it does not necessarily result in the least expensive size. That is, if just private warehousing is to be used, the warehouse is sized to meet the peak space requirements. This size will be an efficient choice if there is a relatively nonfluctuating and certain need for space. When space needs fluctuate and cannot be known with great certainty, diseconomies in private warehousing designed to meet peak loads can result from underutilization of the available warehouse space during nonpeak loading periods. Conversely, a warehouse sized to nonpeak loads can result in high costs due to stock crowding in the warehouse during peak loading periods. The most economical plan may be the one that sizes the warehouse according to the best combination of private warehousing and rented or leased space. The peak requirements for space are met through temporary use of outside services.

What is the best warehouse size? Finding the best warehouse size is a complicated mathematical problem. However, the problem solution is simplified if we deal with it as a decision problem under risk conditions using the methods shown in Chapter 2. Table 11-2 shows the problem layout for the Bradley Electric Company. Across the top of the decision matrix are possible future events, which in this case are the projections of space needs by month. Three different projections are used for each month to reflect the pessimistic, most likely, and optimistic sales estimates. The space requirements have already been calculated and are shown in Table 11-1. The subjective probabilities for each event in the decision matrix is the weight given to each month $(\frac{1}{12})$ times the subjective probability of the event occurring. For example, in January the event of 67,575 square feet of needed space is a pessimistic estimate for January and has a probability of 0.25. Therefore, the probability p_1 equals (0.25) $(\frac{1}{12})$ or $\frac{1}{48}$. The other event probabilities (p_j) are calculated in a similar manner. Across all months, $\sum_{j=1}^{j=36} p_j = 1$.

The alternatives to be evaluated are different warehouse sizes expressed in terms of space available for storage. This is the space within the storage bays and thus excludes space required for aisles, structural members, and the like. The gross square footage to be constructed is a sum of the space required plus the additional space needed for aisles, docks, roof supports, etc.

The most complicated aspect of the problem concerns the cost associated with each event and alternative. Bradley can use public warehousing at a cost of $3.0/sq ft in combination with whatever privately owned warehousing is built. Thus, for a given size, the first question is: What portion of the space can most economically be used? Better still, what is the private warehouse utilization that offers the best balance between variable private warehousing costs and public warehousing costs? The variable cost curve for a private warehouse is somewhat U-shaped, so variable costs decline gradually to a point where about 70–85 percent of the available storage space is being utilized. Further use of the existing space causes variable costs to increase sharply as crowding of stock results in a greater incidence of damaged goods, increased difficulty in rotating stock, increased materials-handling time required to service a given volume of stock, and the like. For Bradley, the minimum variable cost point is 75 percent of capacity. Unless public warehousing

TABLE 11-2
A decision matrix for sizing a private warehouse for Bradley Electric Company

Available Space for Storage S_i, sq ft[a]	Month Weighting P_j Total Req'd Space L_j	January $P = \frac{4}{8}$ 67,575[e]	$P = \frac{2}{4}$ 70,145[f]	$P = \frac{4}{8}$ 73,275[g]	February $P = \frac{1}{48}$ 64,675	$P = \frac{2}{4}$ 66,315	$P = \frac{4}{8}$ 68,375
O, all public storage	Total cost[b] C_{ij}	$203,025	$210,435	$219,825	$194,025	$198,945	$205,125
	In private[c] Q_{ij}	0	0	0	0	0	0
	In public[d] $(L_j - Q_{ij})$	67,675	70,145	73,275	64,675	66,315	68,375
20,000	Total cost	199,275	206,686	216,076	190,275	195,195	201,375
	In private	15,000	15,000	15,000	15,000	15,000	15,000
	In public	52,675	55,145	58,275	49,675	51,315	53,375
25,000	Total cost	198,038	205,748	215,138	189,333	194,258	200,438
	In private	18,750	18,750	18,750	18,750	18,750	18,750
	In public	48,825	51,395	54,525	45,925	47,565	49,625
30,000	Total cost	197,100	204,810	214,200	188,400	193,320	199,500
	In private	22,500	22,500	22,500	22,500	22,500	22,500
	In public	45,075	47,645	50,775	42,175	43,815	45,875
35,000	Total cost	196,151	203,861	213,251	187,451	192,371	198,551
	In private	26,250	26,250	26,250	26,250	26,250	26,250
	In public	41,325	43,895	47,025	38,425	40,065	42,125
40,000	Total cost	195,225	202,935	212,325	186,525	191,445	197,625
	In private	30,000	30,000	30,000	30,000	30,000	30,000
	In public	37,575	40,145	43,275	34,675	36,315	38,375
60,000	Total cost	191,445	199,185	208,575	182,775	187,695	193,875
	In private	45,000	45,000	45,000	45,000	45,000	45,000
	In public	22,565	25,145	28,275	19,675	21,315	23,375

Available Space of Storage S_i, sq ft[a]	Month Weighting P_j Total Req'd Space L_j	March $P = \frac{1}{48}$ 44,075	$P = \frac{1}{24}$ 38,740	$P = \frac{1}{48}$ 29,225	April $P = \frac{1}{48}$ 31,075	$P = \frac{1}{24}$ 21,715	$P = \frac{1}{48}$ 5,225
0, all public storage	Total cost[b] C_{ij}	132,225	116,220	87,675	93,225	65,145	15,675
	In private[c] Q_{ij}	0	0	0	0	0	0
	In public[d] $(L_j - Q_{ij})$	44,075	38,740	29,225	31,075	21,715	5,225
20,000	Total cost	128,475	112,470	83,925	89,475	61,395	33,919
	In private	15,000	15,000	15,000	15,000	15,000	5,225
	In public	29,075	23,740	14,225	16,075	6,715	0
25,000	Total cost	127,538	111,533	82,988	88,538	60,458	41,419
	In private	18,750	18,750	18,750	18,750	18,750	5,225
	In public	25,325	19,990	10,475	12,325	2,965	0
30,000	Total cost	126,600	110,595	82,050	87,600	61,286	48,919
	In private	22,500	22,500	22,500	22,500	21,715	5,225
	In public	21,575	16,240	6,725	8,575	0	0
35,000	Total cost	125,651	109,646	81,101	86,651	68,786	56,419
	In private	26,500	26,250	26,250	26,250	21,715	5,225
	In public	17,825	12,490	2,975	4,825	0	0
40,000	Total cost	124,725	108,720	81,918	85,725	76,286	63,918
	In private	30,000	30,000	29,225	30,000	21,715	5,225
	In public	14,075	8,740	0	1,075	0	0
60,000	Total cost	123,056	119,055	111,918	113,306	106,286	93,918
	In private	44,075	38,740	29,225	31,075	21,715	5,225
	In public	0	0	0	0	0	0

TABLE 11-2 cont.

Available Space of Storage S_i, sq ft[a]	Month Weighting P_j Total Req'd Space L_j	May $P = 4\frac{1}{8}$ 31,075	May $P = 2\frac{1}{4}$ 21,790	May $P = 4\frac{1}{8}$ 4,725	June $P = 4\frac{1}{8}$ 31,625	June $P = 2\frac{1}{4}$ 22,270	June $P = 4\frac{1}{8}$ 10,225
0, all public storage	Total cost[b] C_{ij}	93,225	65,370	14,175	94,875	66,810	30,675
	In private[c] Q_{ij}	0	0	0	0	0	0
	In public[d] $(L_j - Q_{ij})$	31,075	21,790	4,725	31,625	22,270	10,225
20,000	Total cost	89,475	61,620	33,544	91,125	63,060	37,669
	In private	15,000	15,000	4,725	15,000	15,000	10,225
	In public	16,075	6,790	0	16,625	7,270	0
25,000	Total cost	88,538	60,683	41,044	90,188	62,123	45,169
	In private	18,750	18,750	4,725	18,750	18,750	10,225
	In public	12,325	3,040	0	12,875	3,520	0
30,000	Total cost	87,600	61,343	48,543	89,250	61,702	52,669
	In private	22,500	21,790	4,725	22,500	22,270	10,225
	In public	8,575	0	0	9,125	0	0
35,000	Total cost	86,651	68,842	56,044	88,301	69,202	60,169
	In private	26,250	21,790	4,725	26,250	22,270	10,225
	In public	4,825	0	0	5,375	0	0
40,000	Total cost	85,725	76,342	63,543	87,375	76,702	67,668
	In private	30,000	21,790	4,725	30,000	22,270	10,225
	In public	1,075	0	0	1,625	0	0
60,000	Total cost	113,306	106,342	93,543	113,718	106,702	97,668
	In private	31,075	21,790	4,725	31,625	22,270	10,225
	In public	0	0	0	0	0	0

386

Available Space for Storage S_l, sq ft	Month Weighting P_j / Total Req'd Space L_j	July			August		
		$P = \frac{1}{48}$, 36,625	$P = \frac{1}{24}$, 29,000	$P = \frac{1}{48}$, 18,225	$P = \frac{1}{48}$, 47,775	$P = \frac{1}{24}$, 43,650	$P = \frac{1}{48}$, 37,975
0	Total cost	$109,875	$ 87,000	$ 54,675	143,325	130,950	113,925
	In private	0	0	0	0	0	0
	In public	36,625	29,000	18,225	47,775	43,650	37,975
20,000	Total cost	106,125	83,250	50,925	139,575	127,200	110,175
	In private	15,000	15,000	15,000	15,000	15,000	15,000
	In public	21,625	14,000	3,225	32,775	28,650	22,975
25,000	Total cost	105,188	82,313	51,169	138,638	126,263	109,238
	In private	18,750	18,750	18,225	18,750	18,750	18,750
	In public	17,875	10,250	0	29,025	24,900	19,225
30,000	Total cost	104,250	81,375	58,669	137,700	125,325	108,300
	In private	22,500	22,500	18,225	22,500	22,500	22,500
	In public	14,125	6,500	0	25,275	21,150	15,475
35,000	Total cost	103,301	80,426	66,169	136,751	124,376	107,351
	In private	26,250	26,250	18,225	26,260	26,250	26,250
	In public	10,375	2,750	0	21,525	17,400	11,725
40,000	Total cost	102,375	81,750	73,668	135,825	123,450	106,425
	In private	30,000	29,000	18,225	30,000	30,000	30,000
	In public	6,625	0	0	17,775	13,650	7,975
60,000	Total cost	117,468	111,750	103,668	132,075	122,737	118,481
	In private	36,625	29,000	18,225	45,000	43,650	37,975
	In public	0	0	0	2,775	0	0

TABLE 11-2 cont.

Available Space for Storage S_i, sq ft[a]	Month Weighting P_j Total Req'd Space L_j	September			October		
		$P = \frac{1}{48}$ 59,975	$P = \frac{1}{24}$ 60,035	$P = \frac{1}{48}$ 60,675	$P = \frac{1}{48}$ 69,175	$P = \frac{1}{24}$ 72,300	$P = \frac{1}{48}$ 77,325
0	Total cost	179,925	180,105	182,025	207,525	216,900	231,975
	In private	0	0	0	0	0	0
	In public	59,975	60,035	60,675	69,175	72,300	77,325
20,000	Total cost	176,175	176,366	178,275	203,775	213,150	228,225
	In private	15,000	15,000	15,000	15,000	15,000	15,000
	In public	44,975	45,035	45,675	54,175	57,300	62,325
25,000	Total cost	175,238	175,418	177,338	202,838	212,213	227,288
	In private	18,750	18,750	18,750	18,750	18,750	18,750
	In public	41,225	41,285	41,925	50,425	53,550	58,575
30,000	Total cost	174,300	174,480	176,400	201,900	211,275	226,350
	In private	22,500	22,500	22,500	22,500	22,500	22,500
	In public	37,475	37,535	38,175	46,675	49,800	54,825
35,000	Total cost	173,351	173,531	175,451	200,951	210,326	225,401
	In private	26,250	26,250	26,500	26,250	26,250	26,250
	In public	33,725	33,785	34,425	42,925	46,050	51,075
40,000	Total cost	172,425	172,425	174,525	200,025	209,400	224,475
	In private	30,000	30,000	30,000	30,000	30,000	30,000
	In public	29,975	29,975	30,675	29,175	42,300	47,325
60,000	Total cost	168,675	168,855	170,775	196,275	205,650	220,725
	In private	45,000	45,000	45,000	45,000	45,000	45,000
	In public	14,975	15,035	15,675	24,175	27,300	32,325

Available Space for Storage S_i, sq ft [a]	Month Weighting P_j / Total Req'd Space L_j	November $P=\frac{1}{48}$ 61,025	November $P=\frac{1}{24}$ 68,150	November $P=\frac{1}{48}$ 71,325	December $P=\frac{1}{48}$ 59,875	December $P=\frac{1}{24}$ 59,785	December $P=\frac{1}{48}$ 59,875	Weighted Average Annual Cost [h]
0	Total cost	183,075	204,450	213,975	179,625	179,355	179,625	$141,805
	In private	0	0	0	0	0	0	
	In public	61,025	68,150	71,325	59,875	59,785	59,875	
20,000	Total cost	179,325	200,700	210,225	175,875	175,605	175,875	139,220
	In private	15,000	15,000	15,000	15,000	15,000	15,000	
	In public	46,025	53,150	56,325	44,875	44,785	44,875	
25,000	Total cost	178,388	199,763	209,288	174,938	174,668	174,938	138,828
	In private	18,750	18,750	18,750	18,750	18,750	18,750	
	In public	42,275	49,400	52,575	41,125	41,035	41,142	
30,000	Total cost	177,450	198,825	208,350	174,000	173,730	174,000	138,754
	In private	22,500	22,500	22,500	22,500	22,500	22,500	
	In public	38,525	45,650	48,825	37,375	37,285	37,375	
35,000	Total cost	176,501	197,876	207,401	173,051	172,781	173,051	139,566
	In private	26,250	26,250	26,250	26,250	26,250	26,250	
	In public	34,775	41,900	45,075	53,625	33,535	33,625	
40,000	Total cost	175,575	196,950	206,475	172,125	171,855	172,125	140,525
	In private	30,000	30,000	30,000	30,000	30,000	30,000	
	In public	31,025	38,150	41,325	29,875	29,785	29,875	
60,000	Total cost	171,825	193,200	202,725	168,375	168,105	168,375	149,326
	In private	45,000	45,000	45,000	45,000	45,000	45,000	
	In public	16,025	23,150	26,325	14,875	14,785	14,875	

[a] Refers to the private space required for storage only. Excluded is the space required for aisles, structural members, docks, etc. [b] The combined cost C_{ij} for meeting space requirements L_j in both private and public warehouses. [c] The space Q_{ij} is the amount of space used in the private warehouse of size S_i in meeting the total space requirement L_j. [d] The amount of the total space requirement L_j allocated for storage in a public warehouse equal to $(L_j - Q_{ij})$. [e] Most pessimistic space need for month from Table 11-1. [f] Most likely space need for month from Table 11-1. [g] Most optimistic space need for month from Table 11-1. [h] The weighted average annual cost for each warehouse size is $\sum_j P_j C_{ij}$ for $i = 1, 2, \ldots, n$.

costs are very much higher than private warehouse variable costs, the best utilization will be near the point of minimum variable costs.[1] All space required over 75 percent of the total available space for any given-size warehouse is to be stored in a public warehouse. Now, the total cost for a particular space requirement L_j and a space allocation policy Q_{ij} on an annual basis is the sum of the fixed costs for a given warehouse size plus the private warehouse variable costs plus the public warehousing storage costs. For Bradley, we have

$$C_{ij} = (\$1.5/\text{sq ft})(S_i) + (\$0.75/\text{sq ft})Q_{ij} + (\$3.0/\text{sq ft})(L_j - Q_{ij}) \quad (11.2)$$

where

C_{ij} = combined annual cost of warehouse size S_i, space allocation policy Q_{ij}, and space requirement L_j, \$.

S_i = warehouse size in terms of available space for storage, sq ft. The associated cost of \$1.5/sq ft is inflated to include the cost for aisles, docks, etc. and also includes an increment for return on investment.

L_j = total space required for a given month, sq ft.

Q_{ij} = space required in the private warehouse of size S_i, sq ft. If $0.75S_i \geq Q_{ij}$, then $Q_{ij} = L_j$. If $0.75S_i \leq Q_{ij}$, then $Q_{ij} = 0.75\,S_i$.

$L_j - Q_{ij}$ = space required in the public warehouse, sq ft. The associated cost is expressed in square feet for purposes of this sizing analysis, though it is customary to separate storage and handling charges and express them in \$/cwt.

All costs in the function are expressed on an annual basis.

[1] The actual minimum cost point can be determined as follows. The total variable cost for combined private and public storage is

$$VC_{ij} = f(Q)_i + K(L_j - Q_{ij})$$

where

VC_{ij} = total variable cost, \$.

$f(Q)_i$ = the private variable cost function.

K = the public warehousing in \$/sq ft.

L_j = total space requirement, sq ft.

Q = amount of space used in private warehouse, sq ft, where $Q \leq L_j$.

Now, differentiating with respect to Q gives

$$\frac{dVC_{ij}}{dQ} = \frac{df(Q)_i}{dQ} + (-K) = 0$$

$$\frac{df(Q)_i}{dQ} = K$$

Given the variable cost function, we would then solve for Q.

To compute the annual charges for each event and warehouse size shown in Table 11-2, we must first decide on the allocation of space between private and public warehouses and then compute the costs according to Equation (11.2). As an illustration, consider the event of $L_1 = 67,575$ sq ft and a warehouse size of $S_4 = 30,000$ sq ft of private available storage space. The maximum space that can economically be used in a warehouse of this size is $0.75(30,000) = 22,500$ sq ft. Therefore, $Q_{4,1} = 22,500$ sq ft and $67,575 - 22,500 = 45,075$ sq ft is allocated to a public warehouse. The total annual cost if this strategy is followed throughout the year is:

$$C_{4,1} = 1.5(30,000) + 0.75(22,500) + 3.0(45,075)$$
$$= \$197,100$$

Similar calculations are completed for all the events shown in Table 11-2 and for all size alternatives under consideration.

The best private warehouse size is found by weighting all possible annual costs C_{ij} for a given warehouse size S_i by the weighting factor P_j and then finding the minimum weighted annual cost EC_i among all possible warehouse sizes. More succinctly, we seek

$$EC_i = \min_{1 \le i \le m} \sum_{j=1}^{n} P_j C_{ij} \qquad (11.3)$$

for m warehouse sizes and n space requirement levels. For example, consider the alternative of all public storage; that is, $S_i = 0$. From Table 11-2, we can make the following calculations:

$$EC_1 = \tfrac{1}{48}(203,025) + \tfrac{1}{24}(210,435) + \tfrac{1}{48}(219,825)$$
$$+ \tfrac{1}{48}(194,025) + \cdots + \tfrac{1}{48}(179,625)$$
$$= \$141,805$$

Applying Equation (11.3) to all reasonable warehouse sizes, we seek the minimum weighted average annual cost. For Bradley, this is 30,000 sq ft of available storage space, as shown in Table 11-2. The lowest annual cost is $138,754. Selecting 30,000 sq ft of private warehouse space (recall that the actual building size may well exceed this by a factor of 2 or more) gives lower expected costs than to meet all space needs through public warehousing and meets the company's required return on investment.

In addition to suggesting a warehouse size, the above analysis also gives us the anticipated loading pattern on the warehouse throughout the year. The pattern is given in Table 11-2 for each warehouse size in rows labelled *In private Q_{ij}* and *In public $(L_j - Q_{ij})$*. Figure 11-1 shows the loading pattern for a 30,000-sq ft warehouse and the most likely space requirement projections [recall Table 11-1(a)]. That is, the first 22,500 sq ft of space requirements are met by the private warehouse. The remaining needs are met through public warehouse space. For Bradley, the private warehouse should be sized to just meet the minimum space needs. A relatively small warehouse is suggested because of the favorable public warehousing

---

FIGURE 11-1

Loading 30,000 sq ft of available private warehouse storage
space for Bradley Electric Company

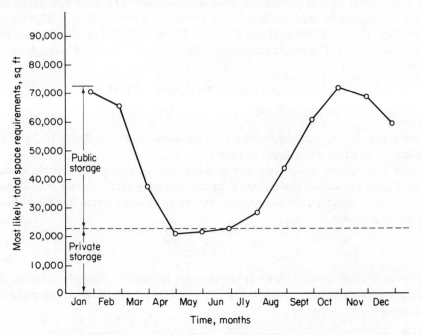

cost as compared with the cost for private storage. The timing of the public warehouse space needs is also defined by the sizing analysis, as shown in Fig. 11-1.
Such timing information is valuable when one is negotiating with the public
warehouseman.

Sizing with Trend.   Warehouse sizing is a strategic or long-run planning problem.
When the trend in space requirements is not constant over time, as was assumed
in the no-trend sizing analysis, we should be prepared to factor fundamental
changes in space requirements into our analysis. The problem now becomes a
dynamic one, so we must consider the additional questions of *when should the
warehouse size be changed and by how much.* This problem is similar to the more
familiar equipment replacement or investment problems that have interested
management scientists for some time. Most of the models have used some form
of the present value concept to account for the time value of money but have
differed greatly in their approaches to finding the best sizing plan through time.[2]

    [2] Compare the models of Arnold Reisman and Elwood S. Buffa, "A General Model
for Investment Policy," *Management Science*, Vol. 8 (1962), pp. 304–10; James M. White,
"A Dynamic Model for the Analysis of Expansion," *The Journal of Industrial Engineering*,
Vol. 17 (May 1966), pp. 275–81; and Robert M. Lawless and Paul R. Haas, Jr., "How to
Determine the Right-Size Plant," *Harvard Business Review* (November–December 1962),
pp. 97–112.

Finding the best dynamic sizing plan presents some difficult combinatorial problems. However, the computational difficulties can be greatly reduced by approaching the problem in a heuristic fashion. In doing this, we shall call on the form of dynamic analysis used for warehouse location introduced in Chapter 8.

Determining the best dynamic plan for private warehouse space over time is a matter of balancing several types of costs that will be incurred over the period of the planning horizon. Recall that the planning horizon is that future period of time over which economic data have a significant impact on a choice of an alternative and are specifically included in the decision analysis. The important costs are (1) the capital costs of acquiring space, (2) the fixed and variable costs for storing goods in the private warehouse as well as the rental costs for public warehousing space used, (3) the costs associated with changing from one warehouse size to another, which includes such costs as design costs, engineering costs, start-up costs, capital costs, and divestiture costs, and (4) the salvage or resale value of the warehouse space. These costs are incurred at different times and are discounted at the rate of the cost of capital to time zero when the sizing plan is established. Specifically, these costs are combined into a relationship of the form

$$PVC = I_{i0} + \sum_{j=1}^{N_1} \frac{EC_{ij}}{(1+r)^j} + \frac{\Delta I_{(i-i'),N_1}}{(1+r)^{N_1}} + \sum_{j=N_1+1}^{N_2} \frac{EC_{i',j}}{(1+r)^j}$$

$$+ \frac{\Delta I_{(i-i''),N_2}}{(1+r)^{N_2}} + \cdots - \frac{S_T}{(1+r)^T} \qquad (11.4)$$

where

$PVC =$ the present value of all investment, period, and resale costs, \$.

$\Delta I_{(i-i'),N_1} =$ the cost of changing from warehouse size S_i to $S_{i'}$ at the end of year $j = N_1$, \$.

$I_{i0} =$ the initial outlay for warehouse size S_i at time $j = 0$.

$EC_{ij} =$ the cost due to warehousing for warehouse size S_i at the end of year j, \$.

$S_T =$ resale value for warehouse size chosen for last year of planning period $j = T$, \$.

$r =$ cost of capital.

$N_1 - N_2 =$ the number of years in which warehouse size $S_{i'}$ is used.

$T =$ the total number of years in the planning horizon.

We seek the sizing plan that will give a minimum *PVC*. Although this formulation may seem a little forbidding, the solution procedure for selecting the minimum is straightforward.

First, the length of the planning horizon is defined. It is usually safe to omit that portion of the future that has little impact on the current sizing decision. Any particular length is affected by the uncertainties associated with forecasting for long periods in the future and by the discount rate used. Discounting reduces the importance of costs in later years relative to early years, and the higher the discount rate, the greater is this effect. Though the length of the planning horizon should be determined for each individual case, a 10-year planning horizon is often reasonable, with 20 to 30 years as an outside limit.

Second, a set of sizing alternatives is defined for each year of the planning horizon. Solving the problem is facilitated if the number of sizing alternatives is limited to those that seem most reasonable. Though subjective judgment may be used to select these alternatives, a set that will give an optimal or nearly optimal solution is the set defined by the solution of one-period (one-year) problems. That is, a reasonable set of warehouse size alternatives is determined for each year of the planning horizon by applying the analysis described in the previous section of the no-trend sizing problem to the forecasted space requirements within each year. These alternatives are the alternatives to be evaluated in the dynamic problem analysis, as shown in Table 11-3. The minimum annual costs associated with these alternatives form the main diagonal of the table.

Third, the costs associated with a warehouse size S_i used in the years for which S_i is not the best choice are computed next. These costs are found by computing the expected annual costs as done in Table 11-2 for the particular warehouse size S_i and the particular space requirements of year j. These costs complete the body of Table 11-3.

TABLE 11-3
A problem set up for the dynamic warehouse sizing problem

Warehouse Size Alternatives[a]	Years in Planning Horizon, j				
	1	2	3	$\cdots$	n
S_1	EC^*_{11}	EC_{12}	EC_{13}	$\cdots$	EC_{1n}
S_2	EC_{21}[b]	EC^*_{22}	EC_{23}	$\cdots$	EC_{2n}
S_3	EC_{31}	EC_{32}	EC^*_{33}	$\cdots$	EC_{3n}
i $\vdots$	$\vdots$	$\vdots$	$\vdots$	$\vdots$	$\vdots$
S_n	EC_{n1}	EC_{n2}	EC_{n3}	$\cdots$	EC^*_{nn}

[a] The warehouse size S_i as determined from the forecasted space requirements for year j only and having the minimum annual expected cost EC^*_{ij} for $i = j$. S_i and EC^*_{ij} are found by applying the analysis described in the previous section on the no-trend sizing problem. The EC^*_{ij} for $i = j$ are placed along the main diagonal of the table.
[b] The annual expected cost that is associated with size S_2 and the space requirement conditions of year 1. In a similar manner, all other nondiagonal elements represent the annual expected cost of S_i and the space requirements in year j.

Fourth, the costs in Table 11-3 are discounted at the cost of capital that is appropriate for the company. In addition, the costs ΔI associated with changing the warehouse size from S_i to $S_{i'}$ in any year is discounted at the cost of capital.

Finally, a dynamic programming approach can be used to find the best dynamic plan for warehouse size over time. The same methodology is used as described in Chapter 8 for dynamic warehouse location. We systematically search among the discounted costs to find the minimum present value of the expected costs due to warehousing and the costs of changing warehouse size. The result is a plan for

(1) the warehouse needed initially and (2) the warehouse size needed in each year of the planning horizon.

Appraisal of the Sizing Method. The method of sizing a warehouse as presented here represents somewhat of a departure from existing methods. Though few methods exist that specifically deal with warehouse sizing, the general problem of "investment" decisions or "buy-lease" decisions has been studied more extensively.[3] In contrast with existing methods, the method above offers the following major benefits:

1. The method specifically draws attention to the problem of seeking the best privately owned warehouse size in terms of a combination of own-rent alternatives rather than providing capacity in the form of either all owned space or all rented space.
2. The variability of space requirements due to seasonal fluctuations in supply and demand and the uncertainties associated with forecasting are dealt with.
3. The timing and magnitude of public warehouse space needs are defined and can be planned for.
4. The timing and magnitude of private capacity needs are defined at present to permit lead time for planning and/or construction of capacity changes.

No single planning model for warehouse sizing is a panacea. For good planning, it is useful to understand the limitations of the method as well as its benefits. The more important of these limitations are

1. Inventory levels are used as the primary determinant of space needs. The space requirements for aisles, docks, staging areas, and order-picking areas are approximated and incorporated into the cost for a given warehouse size.[4] They are not treated as variables. Therefore, our sizing method provides only an approximation to the final size to be built.
2. As with any dynamic model, long-range forecasts are required. Any errors in the plan due to inaccurate forecasts must be weighed against the alternative approach of changing the warehouse size as changes in space requirements are observed.
3. The method is heuristic and does not guarantee that the optimum warehouse size will be found, rather that a good solution will be determined. The selection of the sizing alternatives to be examined is based on judgment. As such, some size combinations may not be explored by the

[3] For examples, see White, *op. cit.*; Edward H. Bowman and Robert B. Fetter, *Analysis for Production and Operation Management*, 3rd edition (Homewood, Illinois: Richard D. Irwin, Inc., 1967), pp. 381–412; and Paul A. Weeks, John C. Chambers, and Satinder K. Mullick, "Lease-Buy Planning Decisions," *Management Science*, Vol. 15 (February 1969), pp. B-295–B-307.

[4] An interesting model that incorporates a number of these features is given in C. E. Hancock and H. F. Kraemer, "The Economic Sizing of Warehouses—A Comparison of Evaluation Models," a paper presented before the TIMS-ORSA Joint National Meeting, Minneapolis, Minnesota, October 7–9, 1964.

analysis. However, the improvement to be gained from additional size alternatives in the analysis should be minor.

FACILITY CONFIGURATION

Warehouses come in various shapes as well as various sizes. Any given warehouse size may be accommodated in different length, width, and height combinations. Since it is now assumed that the basic warehouse size has been established, the question is: What is the best configuration for the warehouse?

Ceiling Height.   In the previous sizing analysis, we assumed a given usable ceiling height. Determining what this height should be depends on construction costs, materials-handling costs, and load stacking characteristics. If we were to double the ceiling height of a warehouse, thereby doubling the cubic content, the construction costs would not necessarily double. The roof and floor remain the same in both cases. Balancing construction costs, however, are the added materials-handling costs due to the greater service time required for stacking and picking loads at a greater average height. Finally the characteristics of the goods to be stored can influence the desired ceiling height. Stability of the goods stacked individually in columns or in pallet-load units may put an upper limit on the height. Of course, storage racks are often used to increase the utilization of ceiling height and overcome product limits. Height limitations may then shift from the product characteristics to the characteristics of storage and materials-handling equipment. Local building codes may also influence the final ceiling height.

Choosing a ceiling height is a matter of trading off construction and equipment costs with materials-handling costs in light of product, equipment, and legal constraints. In addition, there should be a minimum of wasted space between the goods and the effective warehouse ceiling. Exactly how much wasted space is desirable must be judged in relation to the uncertain needs of the future.

Length vs. Width.   The length and width, or configuration, of the warehouse building should be decided in relation to the materials-handling costs of moving products through the warehouse and to warehouse construction costs. Francis explored the question of configuration design in a theoretical way.[5] He examined configuration with the inbound-outbound dock located at X and then at Y, as shown in Fig. 11-2. The warehouse uses rectangular aisles, stores n different item types, and has a total floor area of S. The optimum width W^* and length L^* are found by balancing materials-handling costs against warehouse perimeter costs. Perimeter costs are defined as the annual construction and maintenance costs per foot of warehouse perimeter. For the dock located at X, Francis concluded that the optimum width W^* is

$$W^* = \left[\frac{C + 8k}{2C + 8k}\right]^{1/2} S^{1/2} \tag{11.5}$$

[5] Richard L. Francis, "On Some Problems of Rectangular Warehouse Design and Layout," *The Journal of Industrial Engineering*, Vol. 18 (October 1967), pp. 595–604.

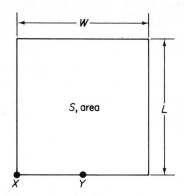

FIGURE 11-2

Outline of a warehouse with width *W* and length *L* and with possible inbound-outbound dock locations at *X* and *Y*

and the optimum length *L** is

$$L^* = \frac{S}{W^*} \tag{11.6}$$

where

$C = \sum_j u_j t_j$, where t_j is the total cost per foot to move the item type *j* in and out of storage and u_j is the expected number of items of item type *j* going in and out of storage per year, $/ft.

k = the annual perimeter cost per foot, $/ft.

S = required floor area of the warehouse, sq ft.

For the dock centered in the warehouse at location *Y*, the optimum width is

$$W^* = S^{1/2} \tag{11.7}$$

and the optimum length is

$$L^* = S^{1/2} \tag{11.8}$$

That is, the warehouse becomes square rather than rectangular. Of these two limiting cases, locating the dock in the center of the warehouse is the least expensive. Locating the dock at *X* costs TC_X:

$$TC_X = 2\{[(\tfrac{1}{2})C + 2k][(\tfrac{1}{4})C + 2k]\}^{1/2}S^{1/2} \tag{11.9}$$

The cost for locating the dock at *Y* costs (TC_Y):

$$TC_Y = [(\tfrac{1}{2})C + 4k]S^{1/2} \tag{11.10}$$

The difference $TC_X - TC_Y$ is the premium that must be paid for locating the dock at X instead of at Y. It should be noted that these conclusions may not hold where a conveyorized materials-handling system is used, since conveyors tend to decouple dock location and warehouse configuration from materials-handling costs.

Jenkins expanded the above analysis by noting that when rail and truck docks are centered but at opposite ends of the building, the least expensive configuration is the square.[6] Hancock and Kraemer note, on the other hand, that movement costs may not be the primary determinant of the warehouse dimensions.[7] Rather, the length of the warehouse may be dictated by the dock requirements for rail or truck. The number of truck stalls for inbound and outbound product movement and the length of the rail siding necessary for efficient product flow would need to be compared with the theoretical findings. How to determine these dock dimensions is discussed in the next section on dock design.

DOCK DESIGN

Dock design begins with the need for a rail or a truck dock at the warehouse. Almost every warehouse requires a truck dock. The need for a rail dock is not as universal and depends on whether the product is to be received or shipped by rail. Even if there is a need, a rail siding may not be possible if the warehouse is not located on a rail spur and the railroad is not willing to provide a spur. For purposes of discussion, let us assume that both dock types are needed.

Rail Dock. A primary consideration in dock design is the length of the dock that is needed efficiently to handle the product flow. Preliminary estimates can be made by multiplying the total average demand by the average length of rail cars used and dividing this quantity by the average quantity stored in the average rail car multiplied by the number of car changes per day. That is,

$$L = \frac{(\sum_i D_i) \times S}{Q \times N} \tag{11.11}$$

where

L = length of the rail dock needed, ft.

$\sum_i D_i$ = the sum of the demand represented in i orders per day, cwt/day.

S = length of the average rail car used, ft.

Q = the average product weight placed in each car, cwt/car.

N = number of car changes per day, number/day.

For example, if $\sum_i D_i = 10,000$, $Q = 800$, $S = 50$, and $N = 2$, then

$$L = \frac{10,000 \times 50}{800 \times 2} = 313 \text{ ft}$$

In addition to dock length, there are several other dock design considerations.

[6] Creed H. Jenkins, *Modern Warehouse Management* (New York: McGraw-Hill Book Company, 1968), pp. 56–57.

[7] Hancock and Kraemer, *op. cit.*

For example, should the extra expense of enclosing the dock be incurred? An enclosed dock provides weather protection, gives some protection against theft, and contributes to labor efficiency in loading and unloading. The platform depth that is required is another question. If forklift trucks are to be used for loading and unloading, a minimum of 12 feet is necessary for safe manuvering. If the dock is also to serve as a staging area for temporary holding while order checking or palletizing, a much greater dock depth is required, perhaps 40 or 50 feet. Finally, the level of the dock in relation to the bed of the rail car is of concern. Either the dock level must be raised to meet the car bed, or the car bed must be lowered to the dock level. Because only slight inclines are possible with most materials-handling equipment and because of the expense of raising the entire warehouse floor, it is usually more economical to recess the tracks below the dock level. A "well" of 45 inches puts the car bed at the dock level. The gap between the car bed and the dock is bridged by means of a steel plate referred to as a "dock plate."

Truck Dock. Most of the factors affecting truck dock design are the same as those affecting rail dock design. A major exception is the determination of dock length. Whereas rail shipments arrive at the warehouse in "batches," truck shipments often arrive in an individual and random manner. From several studies of truck arrivals at warehouses as well as the unloading activity, the arrival-departure process at warehouses commonly takes the form of a waiting line (queuing) problem with Poisson arrivals and exponential service distribution.[8] Hence, the number of dock spaces required can be determined by balancing the costs associated with trucks waiting to be unloaded against the costs associated with unloading including the cost of truck stalls and the cost of dock workers as shown in Fig. 11-3. That is, when trucks arrive at the warehouse in a random manner, drivers may find that the existing truck docks are occupied and must wait their turn along with other drivers until they can be unloaded. The costs of this waiting include drivers' wages, amortization of the truck, and maintenance cost of idle equipment. These costs decrease when additional truck stalls and dock workers (improved service) are provided, since the average waiting time will decrease. Conversely, increases in dock stalls and workers increase both labor and capital costs. An optimum tradeoff of these costs is desired.

To make the cost computations it is necessary to determine the average waiting time that drivers must spend before unloading can begin. This computation is made for various numbers of truck stalls. When the truck arrival rate is Poisson distributed and unloading times are exponentially distributed, the long-run, or steady-state, average waiting line length for $\lambda < S\mu$ is given by[9]

---

[8] See Donald H. Schiller and Marvin M. Lavin, "The Determination of Requirements for Warehouse Dock Facilities," *Operations Research* (April 1956), pp. 233–43; and Karl M. Ruppenthal and D. Clay Whybark, "Some Problems in Optimizing Shipping Facilities," *The Logistics Review*, Vol. 4 (1968), pp. 5–32.

[9] The notation used here closely follows that of Frederick S. Hillier and Gerald J. Lieberman, *Introduction to Operations Research* (San Francisco: Holden-Day, Inc., 1967), pp. 308–9. For similar results under different input and service time distributions, see pp. 285–313 of their text.

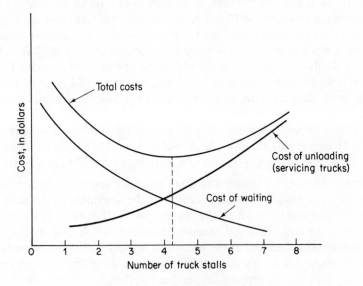

FIGURE 11-3
Generalized cost curves for truck dock sizing

$$L = \frac{\left(\frac{\lambda}{\mu}\right)^{S} \frac{\lambda}{S\mu}}{\left[S!\left(1 - \frac{\lambda}{S\mu}\right)^{2}\right]\left[\left(\sum_{n=0}^{S-1} \frac{(\lambda/\mu)^{n}}{n!}\right) + \frac{(\lambda/\mu)^{S}}{S!(1 - \lambda/S\mu)}\right]} \tag{11.12}$$

where

L = expected waiting line length, numbers of trucks.
λ = truck arrival rate, trucks/hour.
μ = unloading rate, trucks/hour/dock stall.
S = number of truck stalls.

The average waiting time W (hours) is given by

$$W = \frac{L}{\lambda} \tag{11.13}$$

These formulas look forbidding, but their solution can be facilitated by the use of Fig. 11-7, which solves Equation (11.12) for L as a function of λ, μ, and S. The solution to Equation (11.13) then directly follows. Next, the economic implications are determined for the various service times and waiting times that are considered.

EXAMPLE.[10] A grocery warehouse in San Francisco regularly receives shipments from vendors by trucks. Observed distribution for truck arrivals and unloading times are shown in Fig. 11-4. These observed distributions closely approximate

[10] Adapted from an example given in Ruppenthal and Whybark, *op. cit.*

FIGURE 11-4

Arrival and unloading time distributions for the example problem

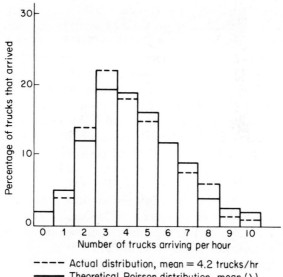

--- Actual distribution, mean = 4.2 trucks/hr
— Theoretical Poisson distribution, mean (λ)
= 4.2 trucks/hr

(a) Observed and theoretical arrival rates for
trucks at the warehouse

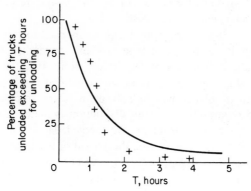

++++ Actual distribution, mean = 1.0 truck/hr
— Theoretical exponential distribution,
mean (μ) = 1.0 truck/hr

(b) Observed and and theoretical unloading times
per truck stall at the warehouse

Source: Karl M. Ruppenthal and D. Clay Whybark, "Some Problems in Optimizing
Shipping Facilities," *The Logistics Review,* Vol. 4 (1968), pp. 5–23.

the theoretical Poisson and exponential distributions, having means of $\lambda = 4.2$ trucks/hour and $\mu = 1.0$ trucks/hour/truck stall, respectively. Five truck stalls are currently used. Accounting costs for equipment amortization, maintenance cost of idle equipment, and drivers' wages amounted to $7.20 per truck per hour of waiting time. Additional dock workers cost $10,000 per year in direct wages and fringe benefits. It is possible to increase the dock space by one, two, or three stalls in the existing building at a total cost of $21,000, $35,000, and $45,000, respectively. The question is: Should additional docks be added to reduce delays?

With the five existing dock stalls, an average waiting line length L for $\lambda/\mu = 4.2/1$ $= 4.2$ is 3.4 as read from Fig. 11-7. The corresponding average waiting time for a truck is, according to Equation (11.3), $W = 3.4/4.2 = 0.8$. For 2070 warehouse operating hours annually, the annual delay cost is the operating hours $\times$ waiting time $\times$ average truck arrivals $\times$ waiting costs or $2070 \times 0.8 \times 4.2 \times 7.20 =$ $50,077, which closely approximates observed costs. Now, if a total of six dock stalls were available, the length of the waiting line would drop to 0.84 truck, and the waiting time would decrease to 0.2 hour. The total delay cost would be 2070 $\times 0.2 \times 4.2 \times 7.20 = $12,519$. The addition of one dock worker at $10,000 per year brings the total relevant cost of six docks to $22,600, a decrease from five docks to $50,077 - 22,519 = $27,558. For the addition of two docks, the waiting time decreases to 0.05 hour with a delay cost of $2070 \times 0.05 \times 4.2 \times 7.20 = 3130. Similarly, the relevant cost for eight docks would be $30,000.

The addition of one dock appears to be a good investment, since an annual savings of $27,558 can be achieved against an investment cost of $21,000 for the dock. The addition of a second dock is marginal, since an incremental savings of $-$611$ is balanced against an incremental investment of $14,000 considering that two docks are built at one time for a -4 percent simple return on investment. Adding the third dock is even more questionable.

Determining the number of shipping docks as opposed to receiving docks may or may not be a similar waiting line type problem, depending on the nature of truck arrivals and alternative uses of the drivers' time. If outside trucking companies are used for shipping, the resulting nonscheduled arrivals are likely to be random. Two design problems may be solved, in which shipping and receiving facilities are treated separately; when no distinction is made in dock design and dock labor allocation, the two problems are merged. However, if the warehouse has its own truck fleet to make deliveries, the arrival of trucks at the dock may not be on a random basis. The design problem becomes one of scheduling shipping loads with known arrivals. The number of docks required in this latter situation would depend on the need to meet peak shipping needs at certain times of the day, whether loading can be handled during off hours, and the need to respond quickly to changes in loading requirements. If the requests for loading and delivery are random, the problem is simply a waiting line problem. Whatever method is used, once the number of docks has been established, the lineal feet of dock space and the associated building length directly follow.

CONSIDERATIONS. Using queuing theory as a method of approaching the dock design problem raises some questions for consideration. First, what if the observed distributions depart from the theoretical distributions on which the method is developed? Though waiting time and associated delay costs show some insensitivity to such errors, computer simulation can be used to replicate the arrival and unloading time distributions as observed.[11] Second, the arrival rate may change depending on the time of day. This situation complicates the design problem in that many different dock designs may be suggested by the analysis. Since only one dock design is likely to emerge, deciding on the single best design is a similar problem to sizing the warehouse, as discussed earlier in the chapter. Third, there may be some concern that dock design is a balance between unloading and delay costs, and the costs for delay are not directly controllable by warehouse management. That is, delay costs accrue to the carrier, and there is no guarantee that the planned optimal design for the system will naturally result. As Ruppenthal and Whybark point out:

> ... the cost of constructing additional dock facilities would be borne by the industrial firm while the cost savings would accrue directly to the several motor carriers using that facility. In such a situation, the probable outcome is inactivity; that is, the industrial concern will do nothing about the congestion as long as it appears that the cost of such congestion will be borne by someone else.
>
> But students of economics have been taught to believe that costs of this nature are shifted. Eventually the costs of congestion will be shifted to the industrial concern through rate increases and eventually to the consumer through price increases. But this process is not immediate, and there is no guarantee that the shifting of these costs will be made in an equitable manner.[12]

Management will need to examine the impact that delays have on the price of transportation to them (some unions put penalties on delays and carrier tariffs provide for delay penalties in the form of detention and demurrage charges) and the indirect affect that delays ultimately may have on customer service. Fourth, no safety factor is allowed in dock design for contingencies and growth. That is, scheduled truck dropoffs, occassional periods of heavy loads, and future increases in shipping and receiving activity all contribute to a need for more docks than the analysis based on averages would suggest.

MATERIALS-HANDLING SYSTEM SELECTION

The primary purpose of a materials-handling system is to reduce costs through more efficient use of labor. As previously noted in Chapter 7, a tremendous variety of equipment is available to meet the materials-handling task. Selecting the particular system that will minimize costs is complicated not only by the variety of equipment but also by the changing requirements on the system. Selection begins

---

[11] For an example of computer simulation for the dock design problem, see Schiller and Lavin, *op. cit.*

[12] Ruppenthal and Whybark, *op. cit.*, p. 20.

with consideration of the warehousing system as a whole and with the demands to be placed on the materials-handling system.

The materials-handling system should be selected to be an integral part of the entire storage system activity. It is not necessarily the beginning point of storage system design nor its ending point. However, management can make some rough, first approximations to the final design without attempting to balance all factors simultaneously. In this analysis, management should take into account several things. First, do materials-handling systems external to the one being designed impose constraints on the choice? For example, if major suppliers to the warehouse make deliveries on 48 × 48-inch pallets, a materials-handling system designed for 32 × 40-inch pallets may require repalletizing the incoming goods to avoid equipment incompatibilities or storage space inefficiencies. Should the warehouse use a 48 × 48-inch pallet system, accept the inefficiencies of repalletizing, or try to persuade the suppliers to change their handling system so that some other handling system at the warehouse may be considered?

Second, does the warehouse design impose constraints on equipment choice? Low ceilings, multistory buildings, narrow aisles, and long distances within the warehouse may make some equipment impractical. That is, moving goods manually in warehouses where travel distances are long results in excessive labor costs; using forklift trucks and elevators in multistory warehouses may be inefficient.

Third, the nature and level of the system load bears heavily on equipment selection. When throughput volume in the warehouse varies considerably or the handling characteristics of the product mix are not reasonably constant, a manual materials-handling system, with its low investment cost and high degree of flexibility to be adapted to changing conditions, often is the best choice. Conversely, when a substantial, steady volume is anticipated, more mechanized equipment is justified. Capital in the form of equipment is used to replace labor, but the greater investment levels may not be recovered if the system becomes obsolete too quickly. This is a particular danger with fully mechanized systems. Undoubtedly, the reason for the wide popularity of forklift truck-pallet systems is that they offer a good balance between mechanization and flexibility.

Fourth, product characteristics can be determining. Bulk products, such as powders and liquids, may more efficiently be handled in bulk by a system of tanks and pipes rather than in packaged form by pallets and forklift trucks. A mixture of product sizes, weights, and configurations may limit equipment to the more flexible types or require that a combination of equipment types be used to meet various product characteristics.

Finally, planning for contingencies can influence system design. As materials-handling systems become more automated and integrated, they also become more subject to total shutdown when any individual segment fails. If reliability of the system greatly affects customer service, system-related costs, such as demurrage and detention charges, or system operating costs, less mechanized systems or mechanized systems with built-in redundancy may be the best direction for final system design.

Once the basic materials-handling system has been roughed out, more detailed design questions must be answered. Major among these refer to (1) the capacity of the system and (2) the equipment replacement policy.

System Capacity. Whether the materials-handling system is a forklift-pallet system, a manual system, a conveyorized system, or a combination system with different equipment types, it is necessary to determine the capacity needed to meet the volume throughput required of the system. That is, how many forklift trucks are needed, or what should the throughput of a conveyorized system be? The problem is complex because such equipment is typically user-owned and often has an economic life of 7 to 10 years. Sizing the system is conceptually the same problem as sizing a warehouse, where a certain capacity must be chosen today to meet the needs over the planning horizon. In those cases where there is no alternative to acquire additional capacity for short periods of time when needed, as would be the case for a completely automated system, the design is governed by the peak requirements on the system. Some unused capacity is likely to occur during the planning horizon, especially if capacity requirements fluctuate. This leads to the rule of thumb that such a high-investment system as a fully mechanized system is likely to be economical only if a high level and constant capacity requirement is anticipated. On the other hand, when rental units can be mixed with owned units to provide the total capacity of the system, as in the case of building a fleet of forklift trucks, the problem is one of seeking the best balance between owned and rented equipment over time. The problem solution follows the same form as that described earlier in this chapter for sizing the warehouse. Refer to Tables 11-2 and 11-3 for the general problem setup, where S_i is the number of trucks owned, L_j is the number of trucks required during each month, Q_{ij} is the number of trucks in the owned truck group that are used during the month (requirements are met first from the owned truck group and then from the rental group), $(L_j - Q_{ij})$ is the number of rental trucks to meet the remainder of the load, and C_{ij} is the combined cost of owning a fleet of size S_i and renting trucks to meet the excess load.

In the above analysis it was assumed that the size of the individual forklift trucks had already been determined. However, when the warehouse manager is faced with a choice among several forklift truck types that differ in size, operating cost, price, and salvage value, it is not clear which truck type should be used. An appropriate way to find the best type is to identify the alternative that will minimize the discounted case flows or present worth over the life of the vehicle. That is, the present worth of the investment, including capital recovery in one truck type, is given by

$$PW = I + C\left[\frac{(1+r)^n - 1}{r(1+r)^n}\right] - S\left[\frac{1}{(1+r)^n}\right] \qquad (11.14)$$

where

PW = present value of truck cost over useful life n, \$.
I = initial investment, \$.
C = annual operating costs, \$.

r = return on investment.

n = useful life of the truck, years.

S = salvage value in year n, \$.

To illustrate, suppose that two type A forklift trucks can move the same amount of goods as three type B trucks. We have the following additional data on the trucks:

	Two Type A Trucks	Three Type B Trucks
Initial investment	\$20,000	\$15,000
Useful life (planned)	7	7
Salvage value (estimated)[13]	\$5,000	\$2,000
Annual operating expenses	\$4,000	\$6,000
Return on investments before tax	0.20	0.20

Applying Equation (11.14) to both truck types, we have

$$PW_A = 20,000 + 4,000\left[\frac{(1 + 0.2)^7 - 1}{0.2(1 + 0.2)^7}\right] - 5,000\left[\frac{1}{(1 + 0.2)^7}\right]$$

$$= \$33,000$$

and

$$PW_B = 15,000 + 6,000\left[\frac{(1 + 0.2)^7 - 1}{0.2(1 + 0.2)^7}\right] - 2,000\left[\frac{1}{(1 + 0.2)^7}\right]$$

$$= \$36,040$$

Since $PW_A < PW_B$, selecting two trucks of type A seems to be the better choice.

Replacement. Depending on the particular materials-handling system selected, management is faced to varying degrees with a recurring problem of *when* to replace the existing equipment as it wears out or becomes technically obsolete. The problem is quite clear in the case of forklift truck systems, where the economic life of the trucks is not long and they must be replaced often, but the problem also occurs in various segments of bulk handling systems or conveyorized systems. It is not uncommon for management to develop rules of thumb, such as to replace forklift trucks every five years, as policy guides. Rules of thumb are based on experience and at times can be quite good. They are probably better than no guide lines at all. However, when such experience is not available from which to develop policy guide lines, or when these rules-of-thumb guide lines have not been tested by "hard" economic analysis, it is useful to have an analytical means of developing replacement policies. Analysis, which operations researchers call replacement theory, is particularly helpful, though other methods such as payback and simple return on investment may also be used.[14] To illustrate replacement theory, consider an example.

---

[13] Salvage value is what the trucks could be sold for at the end of their useful life.

[14] For a discussion of payback and return on investment for equipment replacement, see Charles S. Carew, "When Should You Replace Operating Equipment?... Sooner Than You Think!," *Handling & Shipping* (September 1969), pp. 83–90.

Suppose a warehouse uses a fleet of forklift trucks in its materials-handling system. Trucks are continually being replaced at an initial cost of $3000. The salvage value of a truck declines at a rate approximating a double declining balance,[15] and it can be sold at any time for the net undepreciated value. Operating cost for a truck, including maintenance, is $200 during the first year and tends to increase at the rate of $30 per year of age after the first year. However, because of technological improvement, it is expected that there will be a $20 per year reduction in operating expenses. A 20 percent return on investment is the guide line on all company projects. The economic consequences of replacing trucks every n years is found by[16]

$$AC_n = \left[I + \sum_{j=1}^{n} \frac{C_j}{(1+r)^j} - \frac{S_n}{(1+r)^n} \right] \left[\frac{r(1+r)^n}{(1+r)^n - 1} \right] \qquad (11.15)$$

where

AC_n = equivalent annual cost for replacement every n years, $.
I = investment (price) in a new forklift truck, $.
C_j = operating cost of a forklift truck; in our example is equal to $a + b(j-1) + c(j-1)^2$, $/year.
a = constant level of annual operating costs, $/year.
b = rate of increase (or decrease) in annual operating costs due to technological improvements, $/year.
c = rate of increase in annual operating costs, $/year/year.
S_n = salvage value of the truck at year n, $.
r = rate of return on investment projects.
n = number of years to truck replacement, years.

This formulation allows for the time value of money and the recovery of the initial investment. We seek the n with the minimum AC_n value.

Solving our replacement problem requires that we substitute our data in Equation (11.15) and determine AC_n for various values of n. For example, if we replaced trucks every year, $n = 1$. Then AC_1 would be

$$AC_1 = \left[3{,}000 + \sum_{j=1}^{1} \frac{200 - 20(0) + 30(0)^2}{(1+0.20)^1} - \frac{2{,}400}{(1+0.20)^1} \right] \left[\frac{0.2(1+0.2)^1}{(1+0.2)^1 - 1} \right]$$
$$= \$1{,}400$$

Repeating this analysis for increasing values of n produces the series of annual cost values shown in Table 11-4. The lowest average annual cost is for $n = 5$. Thus, this suggests that to minimize costs, the best policy is to replace the forklift trucks at the end of five years of service.

[15] The salvage value, according to double declining balance depreciation, is $S_n = S_{n-1}(1 - R)$, where R is $2/n$, or double the straight line rate of depreciation.

[16] This formulation assumes that there is a chain of identical truck replacements throughout an infinite planning horizon.

TABLE 11-4

Example of calculations for determining optimum equipment replacement time

	(1)	*(2)*	*(3)*	*(4)*	*(5)*
					$(1 + 2 - 3)(4)$
		Operating Costs[a]	*Salvage*	*Factor*	*Equivalent*
Year	*Initial*	$\sum_{j=1}^{n} \dfrac{C_j}{(1 + r)^j}$	*Value*[b]	$\dfrac{r(1 + r)}{(1 + r)^n - 1}$	*Annual Cost*
n	*Investment I*		$S_n/(1 + r)^n$		AC_n
1	3000	167	2000	1.20	1400
2	3000	313	1335	0.65	1280
3	3000	475	887	0.47	1220
4	3000	673	593	0.39	1200
5	3000	914	394	0.33	1160 ←
6	3000	1199	264	0.30	1180
7	3000	1525	176	0.28	1220
8	3000	1881	117	0.26	1240
9	3000	2261	78	0.25	1290
10	3000	2657	52	0.24	1345

[a] Where C_j is computed as $C_j = 200 - 20(j - 1) + 30(j - 1)^2$.
[b] Where $S_n = S_{n-1}(1 - 0.2)$.

LAYOUT DECISIONS

The final warehouse design decision concerns the internal stock layout problem. After a building configuration is known because of a design decision or because of acquisition of a building, after receiving and shipping facilities are specified, after space blocks are defined for hazardous products, for products under theft protection, and for order picking, and after consideration of the materials-handling system to be used, decisions need to be made as to where specific stock items are to be *located*, how they should be *arranged* in the warehouse, and what method should be used for *finding* stock in the warehouse. These questions have long concerned the industrial engineer in the layout of production facilities, and much of the decision method developed for production layout is transferable to the warehouse layout problem. Such methods supplement those that deal more directly with the layout problem in the warehouse and will be blended into the following discussion.

Stock Location. Stock location is the problem of deciding the physical layout of merchandise in a warehouse to minimize materials-handling expenses, to gain maximum utilization of warehouse space, and to meet certain constraints on product location such as for security, fire safety, product compatibility, and order-picking needs. It is an allocation problem that has been approached by intuitive, algorithmic, and heuristic methods.

Intuitive methods have appeal in that they provide some useful guide lines for layout without the need for higher mathematics. Layout by *popularity* is one such method.[17] This method recognizes that products have different turnover rates in the warehouse and that materials-handling cost is related to the distance traveled in the warehouse to locate and pick the stock. If stock is retrieved from location in smaller volume per trip than it is supplied, materials-handling costs can be minimized by locating the fast-moving items close to the outbound point and the slower-moving items to the rear of these. This assures that the items requiring a large number of trips for a given level of demand will have the shortest possible travel distance per order-picking trip.

Layout by product popularity neglects the size of the item being stored and the possibility that a larger number of smaller items can be located near the outbound point. This suggests that handling costs might be minimized if the *size* (volume) of the item is used as the layout guide. By locating the smaller items near the outbound point in the warehouse, materials handling may be decreased over the by-popularity arrangement, since a greater density of items can be located close to the shipping dock.

However, layout by size does not guarantee lower costs than the by-popularity method. The by-size method would be a good choice when fast turnover is concentrated in the smaller items.

The *cube-per-order index*[18] combines both turnover and product volume as two important factors in warehouse stock layout. An index for all warehouse items is formed as the ratio of the required warehouse cubic footage for the product to the number of daily orders on which the item is requested. Products with low index values are located near the shipping dock. Layout by the cube-per-order index method guarantees that the greatest stock volume moves the shortest possible distance.[19]

Intuitive layout methods are simple to use but do not guarantee that the minimum materials-handling cost layout pattern will be found. Low-cost layout will result from their application. However, an additional 10 to 20 percent cost reduction is sometimes possible if more rigorous methods are used. Various forms of linear programming are appealing for solving this type of allocation problem. The assignment method, a special case of the general linear programming problem, has been suggested,[20] as well as the more general linear programming form itself.[21]

[17] Forest L. Neal, "Controlling Warehouse Handling Costs by Means of Stock Location Audits," *Transportation and Distribution Management*, Vol. 2 (May 1962), pp. 31–33.

[18] J. L. Heskett, "Cube-Per-Order Index—A Key to Warehouse Stock Location," *Transportation and Distribution Management*, Vol. 3 (April 1963), pp. 27–31 and J. L. Heskett, "Putting the Cube-Per-Order Index to Work in Warehouse Layout," *Transportation and Distribution Management*, Vol. 4 (August 1964), pp. 23–30.

[19] *Ibid.*

[20] See James M. Moore, "Optimal Locations for Multiple Machines," *The Journal of Industrial Engineering*," Vol. 12 (September–October 1961), pp. 307–13.

[21] See Ronald H. Ballou, "Improving the Physical Layout of Merchandise in Warehouses," *Journal of Marketing*, Vol. 31 (July 1967), pp. 60–64.

The basic concepts of graph theory have more recently been proposed for use in the solution of layout problems.[22] Let us explore the use of the general linear programming model.[23]

One of the more complex warehouse layout problems is seen in the arrangement of a grocery warehouse, shown in Fig. 11-5. Product is received at rail or truck docks and is moved to semipermanent (reserve) storage. As stock is depleted in the order-picking (assembly) area, replenishment stock is moved from the storage section to the order-picking section. As orders are filled, product is moved from the order-picking section to the outbound dock. The questions become where to place each product in the warehouse and how much space should be allocated for

---

FIGURE 11-5

An example of reserve and assembly area arrangement in a grocery warehouse

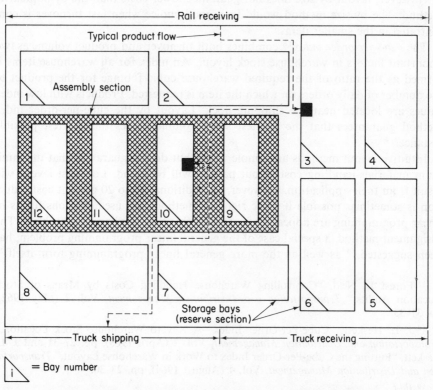

Source: Ronald H. Ballou, "Improving the Physical Layout of Merchandise in Warehouses," *Journal of Marketing,* Vol. 31 (July 1967), p. 61.

---

[22] Jouko Seppänen and James M. Moore, "Facilities Planning with Graph Theory," *Management Science,* Vol. 17 (December 1970), pp. B-242–B-253.

[23] The model and the associated example closely follows that in Ballou, *op. cit.*

each product in the semipermanent and order-picking sections. A hypothetical example of this problem using only a few products and data to show contrasts is given in Table 11-5.

TABLE 11-5

Storage bay capacities and space requirements for the reserve and assembly areas for the example grocery warehouse

Product	Mode of	Turnover	Space Requirements (units)		Bay Capacities (units)	
j	Delivery	Ratio	Warehouse	Assembly[a]	Reserve	Assembly
1	Rail	15	9,300	62	5,000	2,500
2	Truck	14	1,600	18	1,000	500
3	Truck	17	3,800	69	4,000	2,000
4	Rail	16	5,700	96	2,000	1,000
5	Rail	20	18,000	160	8,000	4,000

[a] These are the minimum requirements for the assembly section.
Source: *Ibid.*, p. 63.

Before proceeding, it is necessary to formulate the linear programming model to be realistic for this problem. Linear programming models consist of an objective function and any number of constraints that limit the objective function and the controllable variables to practical values. For the layout problem, the linear programming model can be stated as follows: The objective function is

$$Z_{\min} = \sum_{i=1}^{M} \sum_{j=1}^{N} C_{ij} X_{ij} \tag{11.16}$$

subject to:

(1) A reserve section bay capacity constraint:

$$\sum_{j=1}^{N} \frac{1}{G_j^s} X_{ij} \leq 1.0 \qquad \text{for } i = 1, 2, \ldots, L \tag{11.17}$$

(2) An assembly section bay capacity constraint:

$$\sum_{j=1}^{N} \frac{1}{G_j^a} X_{ij} \leq 1.0 \qquad \text{for } i = L+1, L+2, \ldots, M \tag{11.18}$$

(3) The minimum number of units of each product to be stored in the assembly area:

$$\sum_{i=L+1}^{M} X_{ij} \geq R_j^a \qquad \text{for } j = 1, 2, \ldots, N \tag{11.19}$$

(4) The total number of units to be stored throughout the warehouse:

$$\sum_{i=1}^{M} X_{ij} \geq R_j \qquad \text{for } j = 1, 2, \ldots, N \tag{11.20}$$

(5) A negative amount of product j cannot be stored, so

$$\text{all } X_{ij} \geq 0 \qquad\qquad (11.21)$$

where

X_{ij} = amount of product j stored in bay i.

C_{ij} = cost for handling product j when stored in bay i.

M = number of storage bays in both reserve and assembly areas.

N = number of different stock items handled by the warehouse.

L = number of storage bays in reserve section.

G_j = amount of product j that can be stored in a bay.

R_j = the required amount of product j to be stored in the warehouse.

R_j^a = the minimum amount of product j to be stored in the assembly area.

s and a = superscripts to denote the reserve and assembly sections, respectively.

This model has as its objective the minimization of total materials-handling costs in the warehouse subject to limitations on minimum amounts of product to be stored in the assembly section, the amount that can be stored in a bay, and minimum amounts of product to be stored in the warehouse. Once materials-handling costs C_{ij} are determined for the various product flow paths through the warehouse and the other parameters of the model are specified from the data in Table 11-5, the model is solved preferably by one of the "canned" linear programming computer programs now available for almost every digital computing system. Given the data for our example layout problem, the optimum product allocation to warehouse space is shown in Table 11-6.

Conceptually, linear programming is a good choice for solving the layout problem, since all possible arrangements are, in effect, searched to find an optimum, and the assembly and reserve sections can be laid out simultaneously. However, linear programming is not computationally efficient when thousands of items must be considered in the layout. To reduce the time needed to solve large-scale layout problems, Buffa, Armour, and Vollmann have developed a heuristic model called CRAFT (Computerized Relative Allocation of Facilities Technique).[24] The CRAFT model finds good layout patterns by interchanging storage units, generally two at a time, to see if an improvement in handling costs can be achieved. The interchange of storage units showing the greatest cost reduction is noted. The analysis is repeated until no further cost reductions can be found. At this point, the final layout pattern is determined. It will not necessarily be an optimum, but in comparing their results to those of a linear programming model they note:

[24] Elwood S. Buffa, Gordon C. Armour, and Thomas E. Vollmann, "Allocating Facilities with CRAFT," *Harvard Business Review*, Vol. 42 (March–April 1964), pp. 136–58 and Gordon C. Armour and Elwood S. Buffa, "A Heuristic Algorithm and Simulation Approach to Relative Locations of Facilities," *Management Science* (January 1963), pp. 294–309.

TABLE 11-6
Amount of each product assigned to respective bays to achieve minimum total handling cost for the example grocery warehouse

	Product j				
Bay i	1	2	3	4	5ᵃ
1	4,238			305	
2	5,000				
3		5		1,990	
4		510			
5		1,000			
6		67	3,731		
7				1,309	2,765
8				2,000	
9		18		96	3,472
10					4,000
11	62				4,000
12			69		3,763
Total requirements	9,300	1,600	3,800	5,700	18,000

ᵃ Much of product 5 is located in the assembly section, due to the high turnover of the product. If this creates too much of an imbalance with the other products, either the space requirements on products 1 to 4 can be increased or a constraint can be added to the model that will limit the amount of a product that should be stored in the assembly section.
Source: *Ibid.*, p. 63.

The answers generated are not as surely the best ones as the answers to linear programming problems are, but they do represent solutions that cannot easily be improved on.[25]

Stock Arrangement. Efficiency in warehousing can also be enhanced by the placement of stock within storage bays. Placement is a major consideration where palletized storage is used. Palletization is used extensively in this country. In a survey of warehouse practices, it was found that eight out of ten of the larger warehouses (150,000 to 1,600,000 sq ft of floor area) palletize 63 percent or more of all goods stored. Nearly 40 percent of the warehouses use pallets almost exclusively (83–100 percent of all goods stored).[26]

Placement specifically refers to the angle at which pallets are laid out relative to the service aisle. The most widely used placement is the on-the-square or 0 degrees placement angle [Fig. 11-6(a)]. On a sampling basis, 86 percent of the largest warehouses in this country prefer the on-the-square placement.[27] As an alternative, pallets may be placed at some angle to the center line of the service aisle [Fig. 11-6(b)]. "Angling" is not used a great deal by warehouses, probably

[25] Buffa, Armour, and Vollmann, *op. cit.*, p. 139.

[26] Ronald H. Ballou, *The Consideration of Angular Pallet Layout to Optimize Warehouse Space Utilization* (Unpublished master's thesis, The Ohio State University, Columbus, Ohio, 1963), pp. 29–34.

[27] *Ibid.*

because of the continuing controversy as to whether any efficiency results from an angular placement. Only two percent of the warehouses use "angling" exclusively.[28] The controversy can be seen in those studies that have suggested angles from 0 to 60 degrees as best.[29] More important than a generally suggested angle are the issues involved and how the correct angle, whether 0 degrees or not, can be determined.

Opponents to "angling" complain (1) that there is unused space created at the front, back, and sides of the bay [see Fig. 11-6(b)], (2) that column arrangement,

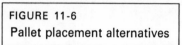

FIGURE 11-6
Pallet placement alternatives

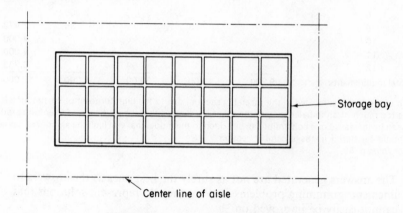

(a) On-the-square pallet placement

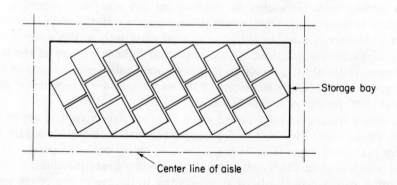

(b) Angular pallet placement

[28] *Ibid.*

[29] Joseph J. Moder and Herbert M. Thornton, "Quantitative Analysis of Factors Affecting Floor Space Utilization of Palletized Storage," *The Journal of Industrial Engineering*, Vol. XVI (January–February 1965), pp. 8–18; Donald J. Bowersox, "Resolving the Pallet Layout Controversy," *Transportation and Distribution Management* (April 1963), pp. 27–31; and Ballou, *op. cit.*

building configuration, and floor area place limitations on the implementation of an angular placement plan, (3) that angled pallets are more difficult to spot in the bay at the correct angle, and (4) that the one-way aisles that naturally result contribute to higher materials-handling costs. Proponents of "angling", on the other hand, argue (1) that the reduction in aisle width due to the less than 90 degree turn required of a forklift truck in servicing a pallet more than offsets the unused space in the storage bay and (2) that some operating efficiency is gained, since the forklift truck does not have to maneuver through a 90-degree turn to place or retrieve a pallet. Resolving this controversy is primarily a matter of balancing space utilization considerations against materials-handling efficiencies. The effect of "angling" on total space requirements has been examined, and formulas or computation forms are available for determining the exact angle for any combination of pallet size, bay configuration, and forklift truck.[30] The effect of "angling" on operating efficiency can be determined from a time study of forklift truck operations under different pallet angles. Converting space and time measures to economic terms, we say that the angle yielding the lowest cost can then be found.

Stock Locator Systems.[31]   Once stocks are located within a storage bay, it is necessary to establish a retrieval system whereby stocks can be reclaimed from storage. There are two basic systems: (1) a fixed-location system and (2) a random-location system. Each must be evaluated on the basis of its efficiency in finding stock on demand and its effect on stock layout and associated materials-handling costs.

The *fixed-location system* refers to a permanently assigned location within the warehouse that is usually identified by a code number. The product is associated with a code number, and it can always be found in that location. If relatively few products are stored in the warehouse, there may not be a formal location code. Rather, a location map or reliance on the good memories of warehouse personnel may be all that is needed for stock retrieval. In any case, the locator system is simple, but has a potential disadvantage. The capacity of each fixed product location is designed for peak inventory levels. When less than peak product levels exist, storage space in the warehouse is underutilized. Conversely, fixed-location systems are compatible with the stock layout plans that minimize materials-handling costs within the warehouse.

Random-location systems locate stock on a space-available basis. Although this system permits more complete utilization of warehouse space as excess space for one product can be matched to peak space needs of another, keeping track of stock as locations change over time is difficult. Location maps or locator code lists are constantly in a state of transition. Where many products are stored, computer-assisted locator coding systems seem most appropriate. An additional

[30] See Moder and Thornton, *op. cit.*, and Ronald H. Ballou, "Pallet Layout for Optimum Space Utilization," *Transportation and Distribution Management* (February 1964), pp. 24–33.

[31] For a more complete discussion of locator systems, see Creed H. Jenkins, *Modern Warehouse Management* (New York: McGraw-Hill Book Co., 1968), pp. 117-23.

disadvantage to be considered is that when products are not restricted to certain locations or zones within the warehouse, suboptimum layout patterns can occur.

A locator system that compromises with a layout pattern may give the lowest total cost for the warehouse. For example, the stock layout decision may roughly divide the warehouse into zones as under the cube-per-order index arrangement. A random locator system would then be applied, but with the restriction that products would be permitted to locate randomly only within their designated zones. Product location is fixed between zones but not within zones.

Concluding Comments

This is a chapter dealing with planning the design and operation of storage facilities with emphasis on the warehouse. Logisticians will have varying need for this material, depending on how storage is to be provided in their firms. If public warehousing is used, the managers of the public warehouses plan the operation and the user firms evaluate the rates and services on a comparative basis with other public warehousing firms. On the other end of the scale, if the storage space is to be company-owned, the logisticians will face the full range of warehousing design and operations decisions.

This chapter discusses the various planning approaches to the major warehousing problems once the location of the warehouse is known. The major decisions discussed are those of structure size and configuration, dock design, materials-handling system selection and replacement, and stock layout. Mathematical planning models are emphasized. Though storage and materials-handling decisions are presented here as independent of each other and of the logistics system as a whole, the logistician is cautioned to watch for economic tradeoffs of any warehousing decision and the remainder of the logistics system.

Questions and Problems

1. The Acme Manufacturing Company is concerned about its warehouse needs and how they can best be met. The company produces a line of spare parts for appliances. Due to the combination of production policies and demand patterns, warehousing space requirements vary considerably throughout the year. Space requirements are known with a great deal of certainty, since the product line satisfies a replacement market. Growth or decline in production and sales is not anticipated in the foreseeable future. Monthly storage space requirements for a typical year are as follows:

	Space Req'm'ts, sq ft
Jan.	100,000
Feb.	80,000
Mar.	60,000
Apr.	40,000
May	20,000
June	5,000
July	25,000
Aug.	45,000
Sept.	60,000
Oct.	70,000
Nov.	80,000
Dec.	90,000

Initial consideration of the problem has reduced the possible storage alternatives to three: (1) all public storage, (2) construct a 100,000-square-foot warehouse, and (3) construct a 200,000-square-foot warehouse. Only 50 percent of the total private warehouse space is usable for storage. Private warehouse space costs $2.00/sq ft, and the minimum operating cost point is 75 percent of the usable storage space, i.e., all space requirements over $(75\%)(50\%) = 37.5\%$ of total capacity will be assigned to a public warehouse. The annual variable cost for private storage is $0.50/sq ft, and for public storage it is $5/sq ft based on the storage used.

Which of the alternatives should be selected? What should the allocation be between public and private storage by month?

2. A private warehouse has a throughput of 10,000 items and an average materials-handling cost per item per foot of $0.01/ft. The total square footage of the warehouse is to be 100,000 sq ft. Annualized construction and maintenance costs are $210/ft of perimeter. The loading-unloading dock is to be located at a corner of the warehouse. What is the best length and width of the warehouse? What is the total relevant cost for this design?

3. The OK Warehouse Company maintains a fleet of trucks to make deliveries of orders placed on the warehouse. The trucks make many round trips to the warehouse each day. Deliveries to the warehouse are also made by company-owned trucks. Truck arrivals at the warehouse loading-receiving point are random and distributed according to a Poisson distribution. From observation, trucks were found to arrive at the average rate of 6 trucks/hour. Dock workers can load and unload trucks at the average rate of 1.5 trucks/hour/dock stall, and loading-unloading times are exponentially distributed. Dock workers are paid $7000/year, and construction costs for truck stalls are $15,000 each. Truck drivers receive $5.00/hour, and truck amortization and maintenance amounts to an additional $3.00/hour. The docks operate 1760 hours per year; one dock worker is required for each truck stall.

How many truck stalls should be constructed? For your selected dock design, what is (1) the average number of trucks waiting to be loaded or unloaded, (2) the average waiting time for drivers, and (3) the total relevant cost?

FIGURE 11-7

Average number of trucks waiting to be unloaded for various λ/μ ratios and number of truck stalls s when truck arrivals follow a Poisson distribution and unloading times are exponentially distributed

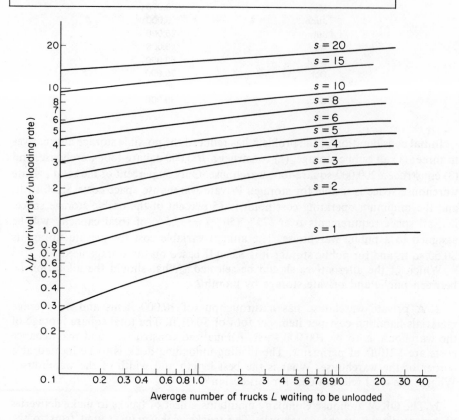

Average number of trucks L waiting to be unloaded

4. What criticisms may be directed at the use of queuing theory for dock design? Especially consider the situation in which the vehicles arriving at the dock are not owned by the warehouse.

5. A firm uses a number of narrow-aisle forklift trucks and can purchase these in three types. Type 1 costs $20,000, type 2 costs $10,000, and type 3 costs $5000. Such equipment can be sold at the end of its useful life (10 years) for 15 percent of its original cost. The annual operating costs for each type of equipment are $2000, $2500, and $3000, respectively. Three type 1 units can do the work of five type 2 units and seven type 3 units. If investments are to return 20 percent before taxes, which equipment would be the best buy?

6. A certain narrow-aisle forklift truck costs $4000. When it is replaced, it will be replaced with a truck of the same kind. Operating costs for this truck are $500 for the first year and increase at the rate of $40 times the square of the year thereafter. Technological improvements reduce operating costs by an estimated $30

per year. The salvage value S of the truck is approximated by $S_n = S_{n-1}(1 - r)$, where n is the year from present and r is the rate of return on investments. The rate of return is taken to be 20 percent per year.

When should the equipment be replaced?

7. Contrast stock layout:

    (a) By popularity.

    (b) By size.

    (c) By cube-per-order index.

    (d) By linear programming.

8. The Able Company is a local division of a large public warehousing firm. The management of this company has successfully applied the techniques of scientific management in the past and is currently looking at its layout problem to see if these techniques can indicate whether cost savings can be made in this area.

The company has selected one particular warehouse for consideration. The physical layout of this warehouse shows two receiving docks (R_1, R_2) and one shipping dock S_1. There are six storage bays in which the three major products handled by the warehouse are stored.

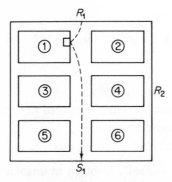

Management finds that, because of order sizes, receiving locations, quantities received, etc., different times are required to supply and distribute from a storage bay, and these service times depend on the particular product and location of the storage bay in the warehouse. There is a direct relationship between handling costs and handling times. A time study of the warehousing operation revealed the following service times for each product and storage bay.

Storage Bay	Handling Times Per 100 Units of Product Stored in Various Bays (hours)[a]		
	1	2	3
1	0.90	0.75	0.90
2	0.80	0.65	0.95
3	0.60	0.70	0.65
4	0.70	0.55	0.45
5	0.50	0.50	0.45
6	0.40	0.45	0.35

[a] For a three-month period.

Each storage bay has a certain capacity depending on the product. The following information on storage bay capacity was obtained.

Product	Storage Bay Capacity (units)
1	5000
2	3000
3	6000

Management forecasts that it must plan storage space for at least 11,000 units of product 1, 4,000 units of product 2, and 12,000 units of product 3 over the next three months. The decision problem is how to allocate the products to the various storage bays (in the proper quantities) so as to minimize the total handling time (cost) required for all products.

Hint: Solve as a linear programming problem, using the following model. Objective function

$$Z_{min} = \sum_i \sum_j C_{ij} X_{ij}$$

subject to

$$\sum_j \frac{1}{G_j} X_{ij} \leq 1.0 \qquad \text{for } i = 1, 2, \ldots, M$$

and

$$\sum_i X_{ij} \geq R_j \qquad \text{for } j = 1, 2, \ldots, N$$

where

G_j = capacity of bay for product j.

R_j = number of units of product j required to be stored.

M = number of storage locations.

N = number of products.

9. What are the space tradeoffs involved in angular pallet placement? What additional considerations would enter the decision to use angular pallet placement?

10. What alternative methods of stock location and retrieval can you think of? Discuss the advantages and disadvantages of the methods that you propose.

11. The Rubbermaid Corporation, a leading manufacturer of rubber and vinyl houseware products, uses a random stock locator-retrieval system in its plant warehouse. All orders in the country are filled through this location. The internal warehouse design shows seven-tier racks laid out in rectangular patterns. The materials-handling system involves narrow-aisle forklift trucks and palletized storage. Why would this company likely find such a storage-materials-handling system an advantage over other types?

Selected Bibliography

BOUMA, JOHN C. and ARNOLD L. LUNDQUIST, *Grocery Warehouse Layout and Equipment for Maximum Productivity*, Marketing Research Report No. 348. Washington, D. C.: U. S. Department of Agriculture, 1959.

Bowersox, Donald J., Edward W. Smykay, and Bernard J. LaLonde, *Physical Distribution Management*. New York: The Macmillan Company, 1968, especially Chapter 10.

Briggs, Andrew J., *Warehouse Operations Planning and Management*. New York: John Wiley & Sons, 1960.

Heskett, J. L., Robert M. Ivie, and Nicholas A. Glaskowsky, Jr., *Business Logistics*. New York: The Ronald Press Company, 1964, especially Chapter 14.

Jenkins, Creed H., *Modern Warehouse Management*. New York: McGraw-Hill Book Company, 1968.

Morris, William T., *Analysis for Materials Handling Management*. Homewood, Illinois: Richard D. Irwin, Inc., 1962.

Mossman, Frank H. and Newton Morton, *Logistics & Distribution Systems*. Boston: Allyn and Bacon, 1965, especially Chapter 11.

Reed, Ruddell, Jr., *Plant Location, Layout and Maintenance*. Homewood, Illinois: Richard D. Irwin, Inc., 1967, especially Chapters 6–8.

Part IV

Logistics Organization and Control

The major emphasis of this book is on planning. However, plans are of little value unless they are put into action and they achieve their intended goals. The remaining sections of this book deal with the implementation and control of plans, that is, two additional management activities necessary for the achievement of distribution and company goals. Less attention is devoted to implementation and control than to planning, since deciding what to do can be more difficult than doing it and controlling it once a course of action is selected.

A primary consideration in the implementation of plans is the organization of the logistics function. The organizational structure defines the formal lines of responsibility and authority, the personnel relationships, and the lines of communication that are useful in implementing plans. Logistics organization is the topic of Chapter 12.

Plans are made and put to work, but there is no guarantee that the desired goals will be accomplished. Plans should be monitored and corrective action taken, if necessary, to realign accomplishments with goals. This is the management activity of control and is the subject of Chapter 13.

Chapter 12

Organization for Logistics Management

Administrative organization is the structure that facilitates the creation, the implementation, and the evaluation of plans. It is the formal or informal mechanism for allocating the human resources of the firm to achieve the firm's goals. The organization may appear as a formalized chart of functional relationships, or it may be an invisible set of relationships understood by the members of the firm but not stated in any formal way, or it may be a combination of these. Whichever is the case, attempting to establish relationships in an optimal way is probably the firm's most difficult task. No algorithms exist for doing this. The best we can hope for is some guide lines that may be useful in establishing acceptable organizational structures.

The focus of this chapter is specifically on the organizational structure required for the management of the business logistics function. The discussion is separated into three parts. First is the organization of the logistics function. Concern here is with establishing coordination among those activities commonly within the scope of the logistics function. Second are the organizational considerations beyond those of the function itself. Concern is with the need for coordinating functional activities with activities of production and marketing. The third concerns the coordination of logistics decision making with other firms.

This chapter will primarily discuss the issues concerning activity relationships. Little will be said about interpersonal relationships, that is, how the people within an organizational structure can be motivated to achieve the goals of the firm. The latter is often a vital issue for management. Omission of a discussion of the issues involved should not lead to the conclusion that the attitudes, reactions, preferences, and emotions of people are unimportant to the effective management of logistics activities. Motivation of people may outweigh all the planning, organizing, and controlling that we might do. However, to open the question would digress into the complex field of organizational behavior theory. This aspect of organization is considered to be beyond the scope of the text.

Organization of the Logistics Function

The reason for and the interest in logistics as a separate and identifiable entity within the business firm centers on the notion of the total cost concept. It has often been the case that supply and distribution activities have been scattered throughout the organizational structure of many firms and in general are given little collective attention by management. As Cannon has observed,

> The fact that physical distribution, as something other than a cost factor, has received very little attention suggests that perhaps there is something peculiar or particularly difficult about this function. The fact is, however, that the technical, procedural, and operational aspects of physical distribution do not pose any more difficult problems than are found in manufacturing or selling. The real reason for the neglect of physical distribution, I believe, is that it is usually not organized very well. Too many physical-distribution functions are left to fall between the chairs, creating many "gray areas" where objectives, policies, and organizational lines are at best fragmentary, if they exist at all. Most commonly the functions of distribution are split in a haphazard manner between manufacturing and sales.[1]

For example, Fig. 12-1 shows a typical organizational design for a manufacturing firm. Logistics activities such as the selection of distribution channels, the setting of customer service levels, and control of field inventories are commonly a responsibility of marketing. Communications and inventory levels may be a respon-

---

[1] Philip F. Cannon, "Organizing for Effective Physical-Distribution Management," in *Management of the Physical-Distribution Function*, AMA Management Report No. 49 (New York: American Management Association, Inc., 1960), pp. 14–15.

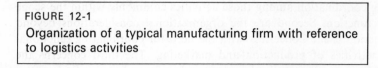

FIGURE 12-1

Organization of a typical manufacturing firm with reference to logistics activities

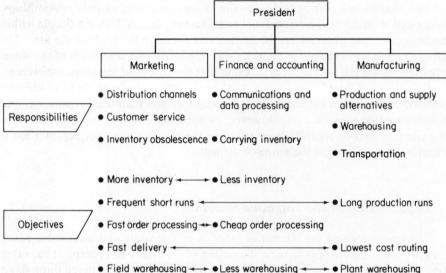

Source: John F. Stolle, "How to Manage Physical Distribution," *Harvard Business Review* (July–August 1967), p. 95.

sibility of the financial arm of the firm. Finally, manufacturing may have the responsibility for warehousing, transportation, and raw-materials supply. Individual logistics activities often show conflicting cost patterns such that a typically organized firm will also have conflicting objectives regarding logistics activities, as also illustrated in Fig. 12-1. It is clear that separate management of each of these activities can lead to suboptimum performance of the logistics function as whole. Recent recognition of these cost conflicts has led management to consider organizational structures and informal arrangements that encourage the collective management of logistics activities to exploit the inherent economic tradeoffs.

OBJECTIVES FOR ORGANIZATIONAL STRUCTURE

Any particular organizational structure by which a firm chooses to manage its logistics activities should be designed to help achieve a number of objectives. Chief among these are (1) activity and function coordination, (2) system planning and design, and (3) system administration.

Activity and Function Coordination.   All of the activities of a business firm lie on a continuum, and when these activities are divided into the various functional areas of the firm (for example, marketing, logistics, and manufacturing) there will remain some activities that are not logically the sole responsibility of a single area.

Such activities are customer service that "overlaps" between logistics and marketing, and production scheduling that "overlaps" between logistics and manufacturing. If logistics is established as a single, integrated function, such interface activities require coordination between the functional areas. The organization of the firm should be designed to handle the interface activity problem.

The second type of coordination concerns the activities within the logistics function. Logistics activities commonly include transportation, inventory management, customer service, order processing and information flows, warehousing, materials handling, protective packaging, product scheduling, and facility location. Since inventories can be traded against customer service, transportation traded against inventories, order processing costs traded against customer service, etc., coordination is necessary to achieve the best economic tradeoff among the various activities.

Setting up logistics as an organized functional area separate from marketing and manufacturing usually achieves the second type of coordination, since a single manager has the responsibility for the logistics activities. Coordination between the functions is usually not achieved with such a realignment of the firm's organization chart. Instead, it is important to build communication "bridges" between the functional areas and possibly to develop innovative ways of measuring the performance of each area that would encourage coordination and cooperation.

System Planning and Design. The second objective for organizational structure is to make provision for the planning function. The logistics system will be constantly influenced by the changes taking place in the external and internal environment. Planning and replanning for system design and operation should also be a continuing activity. In addition to the planning the line managers perform, planning assistance is provided by a staff planning group or by technical and managerial assistance purchased by the organization in the form of outside consulting services.

System Administration. The final objective is that the organizational structure should facilitate the implementation and control of plans and policies. In most companies, logistics activities are too broad and complex for one individual to handle entirely on his own. Logistics activities should be divided among different people having special expertise, and different levels of responsibility and authority should be established for implementing various phases of logistical plans. The authority should be commensurate with the responsibility. How much responsibility and authority can be delegated down the organizational hierarchy depends on the capacity of the individuals in the organization to accept it and to deal with it effectively.

The organizational structure should be skillfully designed so that its size is neither overly large in light of the importance of logistics in the firm so that excessive overhead costs are incurred nor unreasonably small so that the savings in overhead costs are a poor tradeoff against administrative performance. The best size of organization depends on the span of control (that is, the number of individuals that can effectively be supervised by a manager) that is reasonable for the firm. When the activities are involved and vary greatly, each manager can handle only a few subordinates, and large organizations result.

ORGANIZATIONAL FORMS

Many alternatives are open to top management when considering how to organize for logistics management. These range from doing nothing in a formal way to altering the existing organization to a highly formalized and integrated organization for logistics.

The Informal Organization. There are many companies that do a first-rate job of managing logistics activities, yet a separate logistics organization has not been established. Formal organizational structures are not mandatory for good management. What is important is that *coordination* be achieved. Coordination without a formal structure is encouraged in at least two ways. First, if top management believes in the principles of logistics management, coordination will be encouraged through persuasion of subordinates in the direction of top management's own thinking, and suggestions are likely to be made toward developing lines of communication that facilitate coordination. Second, interfunctional and interactivity committees are also facilitating. Even when logistics activities are fragmented among a number of functional areas (recall Fig. 12-1), committees can be used to effect communication between the logistics activities, and coordinated decisions are likely to emerge. If coordination can be achieved through informal organizational procedures, there is the obvious advantage that administrative overhead will not be increased.

Line-Staff Structure. When the decision has been made to formalize the organizational structure, the resulting organization will have varying degrees of line and staff responsibilities. The line organization usually deals with daily operational and administrative matters that are directly associated with the producing, distributing, and selling of products. The staff organization primarily engages in analysis and advisory activities to assist the line organization. Different relative proportions of line and staff create alternative organizational designs. Consider the specific activities of line and staff.

LINE. The manufacturing and marketing functions have long been recognized to contain line activities. In manufacturing, the line activities center around producing goods. In marketing, line activities center around product promotion. Certain logistics activities are also vital to satisfying customer desires in the short term and can be considered line activities. Which are the logistics line activities? They can be easily identified by simply tracing an order through the distribution system. When a sale is made, the order is transmitted to a point in the distribution system where availability of the product in stock can be determined, a freight delivery ticket can be prepared, and inventories can be updated. This is the order-processing activity. Next, the goods are obtained from the warehouse and readied for shipment. This involves warehousing, materials handling, and possibly some packaging. Finally, the order is shipped to the customer, which involves the transportation activity. As stocks are depleted, forecasts are made of future sales, and orders are placed for restocking. Inventory management comes into play. Thus, order processing, warehousing and materials handling, inventory management, and transportation would be primary line activities. It is hard to see how distribution can exist without them. Packaging and production scheduling might also be included. This activity identification might lead to the line organization shown in Fig. 12-2. A separate manager is established for each activity that is distinctly different in its demands on management.

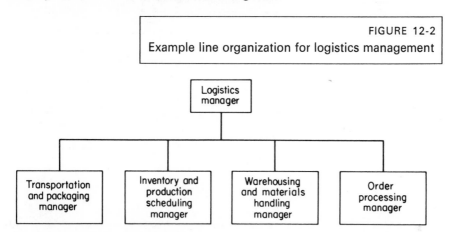

FIGURE 12-2
Example line organization for logistics management

STAFF. Line personnel often become so involved in day-to-day operations that little time remains for undertaking major analyses to improve logistics performance. Such assistance is economically provided by a staff group when there is a substantial and constant need for the group's services. Otherwise, assistance may more economically be provided by outside consultants on an as-needed basis. The staff group aids in analyzing and planning such activities as warehouse layout, warehouse location, materials-handling system design, and inventory control.

Staff groups occur in organizational structures in two ways. They may be the dominant coordinating force, or they simply may be appended directly or indirectly to the line organization.

Stolle suggests that the physical distribution organization may be staff only without a line organization.[2] The staff group in this case provides a coordinative effort in addition to planning, analyzing, and advising. An attempt is made to coordinate the various logistics line activities as they appear in marketing, finance, and manufacturing, that is, scattered throughout the organization of the firm. One way of organizing logistics around staff activities only is shown in Fig. 12-3.

Staff activities may also be integrated with the line organization. The logistics line organization may have appended to it a planning group. The group is under the direction of the logistics manager and deals primarily with logistics problems. Alternatively, the staff activities might be handled by a staff group having broad responsibilities for providing analysis, advice, and planning services to all functions of the business. The group would be located high in the organizational hierarchy and at central headquarters for the multidivisional firm.

[2] John F. Stolle, "How to Manage Physical Distribution," *Harvard Business Review* (July–August 1967), p. 97.

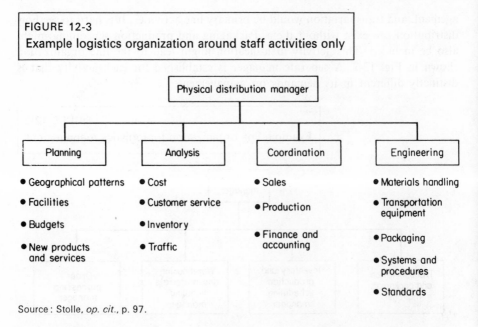

FIGURE 12-3
Example logistics organization around staff activities only

Source: Stolle, *op. cit.*, p. 97.

Line vs. Staff. The relative importance of line and staff can be debated when one is establishing a separate logistics function. However, the order in which they are developed is important. As Bowersox notes: "As a general guideline in establishing a physical distribution department, the line function should not be created unless supported by a competent staff function."[3] The line organization development should lag staff organization, but the line organization will grow in importance to equal or surpass that of the staff organization.

Placement of the line organization in the organizational heirarchy is perhaps more critical than for staff. In order to achieve effective coordination with marketing, manufacturing, and accounting, the logistics manager should be on an equal level with the managers of these functional areas. Since the functional areas of the firm are somewhat autonomous units, the ability to be persuasive in realizing functional goals and receive a fair proportion of the company's resources depends in part on the responsibility and authority delegated to the logistics manager relative to that of the other functional managers. In contrast, staff can be effective in its consulting role from most any level in the organization, though a high organizational level seems to be favored among firms.

Centralization vs. Decentralization. Placement of line and staff clearly comes to issue when the centralized and decentralized organizational structures are considered. There are many examples in which companies have created autonomous organizational units around their various product groupings. Decentralizing the organization of the company in this way makes sense when the products are

[3] Donald J. Bowersox, "Emerging Patterns of Physical Distribution Organization," *Transportation and Distribution Management* (May 1968), p. 54.

distinctly different in their marketing and manufacturing characteristics. It does not necessarily follow that the logistics organization should also be decentralized. It is possible that the products of several divisions may be enough the same in terms of either their distribution or supply characteristics that a common logistics system may be used. That is, combined use of warehouses, transportation, and order-processing linkages can yield some economies of scale that would not likely be encouraged if logistics activities were controlled decentrally. Thus, even within multidivisional companies where marketing, manufacturing, and accounting have been decentralized, logistics activities may continue to be centralized.

Establishing a separate organizational unit for logistics in each division or product grouping of a company is reasonable when the administrative advantages of decentralizing outweigh the economies that might be gained through centralized administration. However, the line organization may be decentralized while the staff activities remain centralized. The performance of staff is not affected by the volume of product flow in each division, but it is affected somewhat by the vantage point from which it must operate in the organization. In the decentralized firm, staff seems to thrive better and be less costly if it is centralized.

The issue of whether logistics activities should be centrally or decentrally organized is mainly of concern to the large, multidivisional company. Small companies naturally have a centralized logistics organizational structure. The reason for this is that there generally is too little product flow volume to support more than one logistics system.

GUIDE LINES FOR SELECTION

The form of the organizational structure that a firm chooses for administering its logistics activities depends on (1) the type of firm that it is, (2) the importance of logistics service, and (3) the enthusiasm of top management for logistics.[4]

Type of Firm. The type of firm and the nature of its activities give an indication of the importance of logistics activities to the firm and how they are likely to be organized. First, the expenditures on logistics activities in relation to sales will indicate whether separate attention can be given to logistics activities relative to the other activities of the firm. A firm in the machinery industry, where logistics costs average 10 percent of sales, is not likely to devote much organizational attention to logistics activities. In contrast, a firm in the food industry, where logistics costs average over 30 percent of sales, has a much greater incentive to establish a separate organizational unit to control the costs and performance of these activities.

Second, the type of firm gives a clue as to how logistics activities will be organized when logistics costs are significant. Four types of firms can be distinguished. First are the extractive and agricultural firms. These firms provide basic raw materials (products of mines, wells, land, etc.) to other industrial firms and the consumer. The major logistics activity is transportation on the distribution side

---

[4] These guide lines in part follow those suggested by Bowersox, *ibid.*, pp. 53–54.

of the firm. The logistics organizational structure of these firms is likely to focus on this primary need. Second are the marketing firms. Examples here are the retail stores, where products are received by the firm in large lots and distributed in small unit quantities. Unless the retail store has a substantial delivery activity, the organizational focus will be on the supply side of the firm. This usually means that purchasing and inventory control become key activities. If delivery (distribution) is important, as in mail order firms, logistics organizational structure will tend to be balanced between supply and distribution activities. Third are the manufacturing firms. Manufacturing firms typically acquire raw materials or semifinished goods, process them, and distribute them to their customers. Because both supply and distribution activities are important, all typically noted logistics activities are likely to be included in the logistics organizational structure. The structure may be balanced toward supply or distribution, depending on the specific situation of individual firms. Fourth are the service firms. Hospitals are good examples. Such firms typically consume their inventories in producing services. Thus, only supply-side activities are important to the logistician. Organizationally, we would expect to find logistics activities centered on the purchasing function.

Customer Service.   The need for distribution service may be a determinant as to whether logistics is separated organizationally from the remaining business functions. Since customer service is a function of a number of variables, including order processing, transportation, and inventory levels that may be scattered among several functions of the firm, collecting these logistics activities under a single organizational unit can lead to a higher level of customer service at lower total cost. If customers are not too service-sensitive, that is, if price and personal relationships tend to be more important to the customer than quick, reliable processing of his order, there will be no strong incentive to reorganize the firm on the basis of increased revenues that might be gained from improved service. Of course, reorganization may still be argued on the basis of economic efficiencies.

Managerial Enthusiasm.   Much has been written about the benefits to be gained from repartitioning a firm to establish a separate logistics function. A great deal of managerial enthusiasm has been generated for such a reorganization. It is clear that there must be managerial enthusiasm and support for logistics reorganization to ensure its effectiveness and continuation. However, depending on the extent of this enthusiasm, the newly formed organization can suffer from too much as well as too little enthusiasm for it. Too much enthusiasm may mean that management is expecting unrealistic performance from the new group, or that the activities and standards for the group may follow the inflated "gee whiz" stories about the potential cost reductions in physical distribution often found in the literature. Failure may come when actual performance does not match the unrealistic and distorted performance expectations of management. Too little enthusiasm may also lead to failure. A weak organization may be created that has neither adequate responsibility nor authority to deal effectively with the logistics problems as they exist in the company. Managerial enthusiasm does shape the logistics organization and contributes to its ultimate success or failure as a function.

Interfunctional Management

Much of the previous discussion has dealt with organizing logistics as a separate, integrated function so as to reduce conflicts among logistics activities. While conflict is generally reduced among these activities, an additional functional area increases the level of conflict between logistics and the other functional areas of the firm. It is probably true that all activities of the firm are economically interrelated and that to departmentalize the firm's activities along functional lines and to treat each department as an autonomous unit promotes the conflicts. Autonomy of responsibility, authority, accountability, and reward do not encourage interfunctional activity tradeoffs and can lead to suboptimum performance by the firm as a whole. Thus, the logistician as well as his superiors must be prepared to deal with the problem of interfunctional management.

EXAMPLES OF THE PROBLEM

In Chapter 1, specifically Fig. 1-2, several of the activities at the interfaces with logistics were noted. These included customer service, information flows, packaging, and retail location for the logistics-marketing interface, and plant location and production scheduling at the logistics-production interface. Recall that interface activities are those that require some form of collective management among the functional areas involved to prevent suboptimum decisions from being made with regard to them.

The benefits of interfunctional management between logistics and marketing can be seen if we consider packaging. Packaging is of concern to marketing because of its impact on sales. Protection, storage, and handling features of packaging are generally of little concern to marketing unless in some way marketing rewards are partially determined by package design. The logistics activity of the firm most often must suffer the consequences of poor package design through handling and storage inefficiencies. On the other hand, logistics performance is not typically measured by the promotional qualities of a package. Yet, the package is a single entity. Protective features cannot be divorced from promotional features. Some form of cooperation is needed to achieve a package design that will yield the best balance between marketing revenues and logistics costs. Operating unto themselves, neither function is likely to come up with a package design that is as economically beneficial as the one created by working together.

Cooperation between production and logistics on the setting of production schedules is a second example. Inventory is the common element between the two functions. Production seeks product schedules to balance inventory costs against manufacturing costs. On the other hand, logistics balances inventory costs against transportation costs in deciding production schedules. Without cooperation, there is no guarantee that an optimum balance will be achieved between transportation, inventory, and manufacturing costs.

Similar overlap between functional areas exists for the remaining interface activities.

AMELIORATING THE CONFLICTS

Interfunctional management problems are not new. They have existed ever since two functions of approximately equal status were created in organizational structures. Dealing effectively with the problem is not as obvious as the problem itself. However, several approaches might be taken to encourage interfunctional cooperation.

Top Management's Encouragement.   The most likely way in which coordination can be achieved is for the manager having authority over the functional areas of the firm to be aware of the suboptimalities in decision making caused by the arbitrary organizational division of activities. Since he is a person to whom the managers of the functional areas are immediately accountable, his awareness of such problems should lead him to encourage cooperation. However, there are some shortcomings to this approach. Obviously, if management is unaware or unconcerned about such problems, narrowly conceived decisions are likely to continue. The traditional organizational structure and rewards do not invite total cost analyses beyond the defined function. Also, top management must continually pursue coordination, or each functional area will revert to its autonomy in decision making. This requires managerial time and may be limited to selected interface problems. Top management's encouragement of interfunctional cooperation will probably be forced rather than naturally occurring.

Coordinating Committees.   Standing committees made up of members from each of the functional areas involved with the interface activities can provide the continuous analysis that top management may not be able to afford. For example, a coordinating committee of marketing and logistics personnel could be formed to monitor customer service and to suggest the best mix of relevant marketing and logistics variables for a maximum contribution to the firm's profit. However, committees alone cannot be the entire answer to the coordinating problem, since they have little or no power for implementation. The recommendations of the coordinating committee can be referred to top management for implementation, but the previously noted shortcomings concerning management would still exist.

Incentives.   Ideally, coordination of interface activities should be occurring naturally within the organizational structure and control system. The budget is a major control mechanism, but it acts as a disincentive to this type of coordinative activity. Functional area managers work to keep their costs within budget limitations and find little advantage in accepting a higher level of cost for an activity than they would individually decide for it so that the firm as a whole might benefit. This suggests that coordination might be encouraged in two ways. First is a radical approach—that is, to adopt a reward system that would encourage interfunctional cooperation. Instead of the functional area budget, possibly all profits could be pooled and then divided up for salaries according to some predetermined schedule.

Profit sharing has had some noted successes (Lincoln Electric Company), but most companies seem to be unwilling to depart too far from tradition. Second is a more moderate approach, where the reward system remains intact and payment is simply made for cooperation. A system to transfer costs, similar to those often established between divisions of large companies, could be established. Thus, the manager of a functional area absorbing higher activity level costs than those resulting from the decision made without cooperation would receive from the functional area to which the benefits occur compensation in the amount of his cost overrun plus some increment of the realized savings. The primary disadvantage of this approach is the demands that would be made on the information-decision system to determine the performance levels before and after cooperation. However, the improvements being made in mathematical models and in computer methods of providing such information give this latter approach increasing attractiveness.

Interorganizational Management

So far, we have noted the organizational problems associated with realigning the activities of the firm to achieve more meaningful economic tradeoffs and the problems associated with managing activities at the interface between functional areas. Both of these managerial problems are internal to the firm. Since the supply and distribution policies of any one firm in the channel of distribution can affect the performance of other firms in the channel, the question is raised as to whether there might be some advantage to viewing the channel as a single entity or "super-organization" and "managing" it to the benefit of all involved. This proposition is probably not new, but the processes involved are little understood. As Stern and Heskett note,

> The management of complex organizations has undergone considerable scrutiny by students of administrative processes. But only a small body of literature has been devoted to the management of interorganization systems, entities whose objectives transcend those of single organizations defined by legal boundaries.[5]

If effective organizational processes can be developed to deal with logistics matters external to the firm, the firm stands to gain in a way not otherwise possible.

NATURE OF THE SUPER-ORGANIZATION

The super-organization is a group of vertically related but legally separate firms that share a common interest in the individual decisions made by each. For example, a pricing decision of a carrier will influence the decision of a user on how

---

[5] Louis W. Stern and J. L. Heskett, "Conflict Management in Interorganization Relations: A Conceptual Framework," in Louis W. Stern, *Distribution Channels: Behavioral Dimensions* (Boston: Houghton Mifflin Company, 1969), p. 288.

much service to purchase, and the purchase decision in turn influences the pricing decision. Normally, each firm would make its decision while pursuing individual goals. If profit maximization is their goal, making the purchase and price decisions individually not only can lead to suboptimum profits for the firms taken collectively but also can result in suboptimum profits for the individual firms. Management of the super-organization seeks to take advantage of the higher-order optimum profit performance that can be achieved by encouraging cooperation and by some means whereby the profits from the cooperative effort are redistributed among the super-organization members.

Management of the super-organization will be a relatively easy task if the cooperative effort yields proportionately greater returns to each member. The situation is self-motivating for the members, and the only need is to become aware of the possibilities and benefits of cooperation. However, if the benefits of cooperation tend to "pool" with one or a few of the members, equitable redistribution of the benefits and adequate information within the super-organization to minimize individual member uncertainties become major management tasks.

Example.[6] Further to understand the issues involved in interorganizational logistics problems, consider a simple, hypothetical inventory problem. The problem involves a three-member distribution channel: a seller, a buyer, and a carrier (Fig. 12-4). The buyer periodically purchases from the seller a quantity of goods to replenish depleted inventories. The carrier is involved in moving the order from the seller to the buyer. The buyer makes the decision on the quantity to order. The seller sets the price per unit. The carrier prices his service. Quantity ordered by the buyer is a function of purchase price and transportation costs, and purchase price and transportation cost are a function of the order quantity. Thus, the interdependency of the member decision variables suggests that cooperative decision making could be fruitful.

First, consider the inventory decision problem facing the buyer. The buyer sells the units that he purchases from member 1 and would like to maximize his contribution to profit in doing so. He establishes the following general relationship between revenue received from sales and the inventory costs incurred in maintaining a supply of units for sale:

$$\text{Profit}_3 = \text{revenue} - \text{inventory costs} \qquad (12.1)$$

The subscript 3 indicates the buyer. Since the quantity ordered Q_3 from the seller (member 1) is a function of inventory costs, which include ordering costs, carrying costs, and out-of-stock costs, and carrying costs in turn are a function of the seller's price as the price paid affects the value of the inventory held by the buyer, the

[6] This example follows that shown in J. L. Heskett and Ronald H. Ballou, "Logistic Planning in Inter-Organization Systems," in Michael P. Hottenstein and R. William Millman, *Research Toward the Development of Management Thought*, Papers and Proceedings of the 26th Annual Meeting of the Academy of Management (Academy of Management, 1967), pp. 124–36.

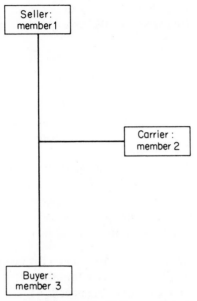

FIGURE 12-4
Members of a hypothetical super-organization

Seller:
member 1

Carrier :
member 2

Buyer :
member 3

Source: Redrawn from J. L. Heskett and Ronald H. Ballou, "Logistical Planning in Inter-Organization Systems," in Michael P. Hottenstein and R. William Millman, *Research Toward the Development of Management Thought*, Papers and Proceedings of the 26th Annual Meeting of the Academy of Management (Academy of Management, 1967), p. 126.

buyer moves to determine his optimum order quantity in light of these costs. Utilizing a fixed order quantity, variable order interval inventory model with price breaks of the form $(F + Qv)$ and warehousing costs of the form WQ, we can construct the following profit expression:

$$X_3 = r_3 D - \left\{ (F_1 + Q_3 v_1)\frac{D}{Q_3} + \frac{D}{Q_3}[S_3 + E(s)_3] \right.$$
$$\left. + W_3 Q_3 + I_3 \left(\frac{F_1}{Q_3} + v_1\right)\left[\frac{Q_3}{2} + (R - \bar{u})\right] \right\} \tag{12.2}$$

Acting unto himself, the buyer could find his optimum order quantity (Q_3^*) by applying differential calculus to Equation (12.2) with the following results:[7]

$$Q_3^* = \sqrt{\frac{2\{F_1 D + D[S_3 + E(s)_3] + F_1 I_3 (R - \bar{u})\}}{v_1 I_3 + 2W_3}} \tag{12.3}$$

[7] The first derivative of X_3 with respect to Q_3 is taken, set equal to zero, and the resulting expression solved for Q_3^*.

where

X_3 = profit to buyer (member 3), \$.

r_3 = customer price per unit, \$/unit.

D = annual demand, units.

Q_3 = quantity ordered by member 3, units.

F_1 = fixed component of the total purchase price for an order of Q units, \$/order.

v_1 = variable component of the total purchase price for each unit, \$/unit.

S = ordering cost, \$/order.

$E(s)$ = expected stockout cost, or $\pi E(u > R)$, where

π = profit penalty per unit demanded but not available.

$E(u > R) = \sum_{u=R+1}^{u\ \max} (u - R)p(u)$ = items demanded but not available during a reorder period, where

R = reorder point quantity, in units

$p(u)$ = probability of a level of usage during a reorder cycle.

I = inventory carrying cost rate, percentage per period.

$\bar{u}$ = average usage during reorder cycle, units.

W_3 = buyer's warehousing costs for demand period, \$/unit.

It is important to note that the buyer's decision on the quantity to order is dependent on the price at which he must purchase the units. This price is not under his control, but rather under the control of member 1.

The carrier (member 2) has an interest in the inventory problem, since the costs that he incurs are a function of the shipment sizes (order quantity Q) flowing in the channel. The level of revenue that he receives from each shipment depends on shipment size and the quantity price breaks that he offers. His profit function might have the following form:

$$X_2 = (F_2 + Q_2 v_2 - Q_2^2 v') \frac{D}{Q_2} - (M_2 + Q_2 m_2) \frac{D}{Q_2} \tag{12.4}$$

where

X_2 = carrier's net profit, \$.

F_2 = fixed component of carrier's revenue, \$/shipment.

v_2 = first degree term in carrier's variable revenue, \$/unit.

v_2' = second degree term in carrier's variable revenue, \$/unit².

M_2 = fixed component in carrier's cost, \$/shipment.

m_2 = variable component in carrier's cost, \$/unit.

If the carrier wishes to maximize his profits, he will apply differential calculus to Equation (12.4), as was done to Equation (12.2), to find the most desirable order quantity for him. That is, the order quantity or shipment size Q_2^* that the carrier would like to flow in the channel is

$$Q_2^* = \sqrt{\frac{M_2 - F_2}{v_2'}} \tag{12.5}$$

The Q_2^* that the carrier desires is not necessarily the same as the buyer wishes to place (Q_3^*).

The seller is the third member involved in the super-organization. His perceptions of the quantity that the buyer should order can be different from that of the other two members, since he determines this order quantity Q_1^* from his costs and not theirs. The seller determines his contribution to profit as the difference between the sales to the buyer (member 3) and the costs incurred from maintaining an inventory. The form of the seller's profit function might be

$$X_1 = \left[(F_1 + Q_1 v_1)\frac{D}{Q_1}\right] - \left\{\frac{D}{Q_1}[S_1 + E(s)_1] + W_1 Q_1\right.$$
$$\left. + (F_2 + Q_1 v_2 - Q_1^2 v_2')\frac{D}{Q_1} + I_1\left(\frac{F_1}{Q_1} + v_1\right)\left(H_1 - \frac{Q_1}{2}\right)\right\}$$

(12.6)

where the terms not previously defined are

X_1 = seller's net profit, \$.
W_1 = seller's warehousing costs for demand period, \$/unit.
H_1 = maximum stock level maintained by seller to accommodate buyer's needs, units.

This function is rather complex, and several additional comments should be made about it. First, the term $E(s)_1$ is based on the stockouts incurred by the *buyer*, not the seller. Stockouts by the *buyer* also mean lost sales for the seller. Second, the price of goods sold by the seller is the purchase price for the buyer. Third, the seller's average inventory level tends to decrease with larger order sizes from the buyer. Hence, the average inventory level is represented by $H_1 - Q_1/2$. Fourth, pricing is on a delivered basis, so the carrier's prices must be factored into the seller's profit function. Once again, applying differential calculus to Equation (12.6) to find the order quantity that the seller would most like to have placed with him yields

$$Q_1^* = \sqrt{\frac{2\{F_1 D - D[S_1 + E(s)_1] - DF_2 - I_1 F_1 H_1\}}{-2W_1 + 2v_2'D + I_1 v_1}}$$

(12.7)

Finally, we consider the super-organization as a single entity and maximize its profit. The net profit accruing to the super-organization is the sum of the individual member profits; that is, $X_S = X_1 + X_2 + X_3$. After summing Equations (12.2), (12.4), and (12.6) and seeking the optimum order quantity through the use of differential calculus, we find that the order quantity Q_S^* for the channel as a whole is

$$Q_S^* = \sqrt{\frac{2\{D[S_1 + E(s)_1] + I_1 F_1 H_1 + M_2 D + D[S_3 + E(s)_3] + F_1 I_3(R - \bar{u})\}}{2(W_1 + W_3) + v_1(I_3 - I_1)}}$$

(12.8)

The value Q_S^* gives us a single order quantity to flow through the channel. Hence, $Q_S^* = Q_1 = Q_2 = Q_3$. Although Q_S^* is the optimum order quantity for the channel, it is not necessarily true that each member will be operating at his particular maximum profit point; that is, $Q_S^* = Q_1^* = Q_2^* = Q_3^*$ is not necessarily true. Establishing this latter equality is a primary goal in super-organization management.

The conflict among the members of the super-organization can be seen if we sólve the above equations using a hypothetical set of parameter values. These parameter values are

---

FIGURE 12-5

Profit curves for buyer, carrier, seller, and channel in example super-organization problem

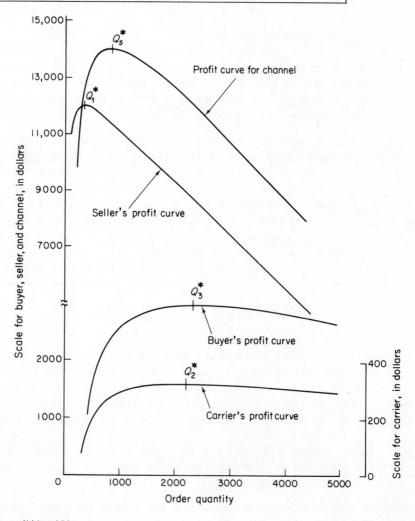

$$W_1 = 2 \qquad F_1 = 20 \qquad S_1 = 15 \qquad I_1 = 0.20 \quad m_2 = 0.04$$

$$W_3 = 0.1 \qquad F_2 = 10 \qquad E(s)_3 = 10 \qquad R = 300 \qquad v_2 = 0.06$$

$$r_3 = 1 \qquad v_1 = 0.8 \qquad E(s)_1 = 2 \qquad \bar{u} = 300 \qquad v_2' = 0.000001$$

$$D = 20,000 \quad S_3 = 30 \qquad I_3 = 0.30 \quad M_2 = 15 \qquad H_1 = 10,000$$

Fig. 12-5 shows the profit curves for the individual channel members as well as for the coalition of members. The conflict arises because the order quantities that would yield an optimum to each of the members are not equal; that is, $Q_1^* \neq Q_2^* \neq Q_3^*$. The question is: Which of the order quantities will prevail? Because the buyer places the order, we can expect that Q_3^* will be the order size, and the other members must accept the economic consequences of this decision. Whereas the buyer would appear to be satisfied by the decision, the consequences for the seller are rather severe, as a comparison of the profit level under various order policies in Table 12-1 shows. Other order size choices can be made. The most obvious would be the order sizes that would optimize any one of the other member's profits. The effect of these various order-size policies on member and channel profits is also given in Table 12-1.

Now, treating the channel members as a collective unit or coalition should increase the profits for the channel as a whole. This is to be expected, since more variables are "played" against one another simultaneously. The result is an order size that will yield the optimum profit for the coalition, but the order size will not necessarily yield any individual member its highest profit. As can be seen from column 4 of Table 12-1, each member sacrifices some potential profit in order to contribute to a higher channel total profit than could be achieved individually.

Up to this point, we have engaged in a simple total cost tradeoff analysis. The benefits that we have observed are not surprising. However, there is another

TABLE 12-1

Economic results of various order sizes under existing and revised price policies

	Order Quantity, Units				
		Under Existing Price Policy			Under Revised Price Policy
Channel Member	$Q_3^* = 2320$	$Q_2^* = 2220$	$Q_1^* = 320$	$Q_S^* = 820$	$Q_S^* = 800$
Buyer	$2,969	$2,968	$ 9	$2,367	$3,652
Carrier	310	311	67	263	368
Seller	8,688	8,873	12,032	11,409	10,152
Channel total	$11,967	$12,152	$12,108	$14,039	$14,172

Source: Adapted from J. L. Heskett and Ronald H. Ballou, "Logistical Planning in Inter-Organization Systems," in Michael P. Hottenstein and R. William Millman, *Research toward the Development of Management Thought,* Papers and Proceedings of the 26th Annual Meeting of the Academy of Management (Academy of Management, 1967), p. 133.

dimension of cooperative management. Besides the recognition that cooperation can yield higher total profits, individual members are in a position to adjust the *parameters* that they influence in order to achieve still higher channel profits. For example, the seller can adjust the unit price, which in turn influences the buyer's order quantity. The carrier can adjust his pricing schedule, which influences the seller's price and the buyer's order quantity. The buyer dominates the order quantity decision. The point is, each member exerts some influence over channel performance as well as having some interest in it. There are four price components that can be adjusted: F_1 and v_1 by the seller and F_2 and v'_2 by the carrier. Using algebra to determine the proper value for these parameters so that $Q_S^* = Q^* = Q_2^* = Q_3^* = Q_3^*$ yields the results shown in column 5 of Table 12-1. Total channel profits increase to their highest level under the revised pricing policies.

Managing the Conflict. The object of "managing" the super-organization is to establish the conditions so that each "member" of the coalition may benefit from his cooperation. Managing the super-organization is not the same as management within the firm. The reliance is more on bargaining and tacit arrangements than on formalized structural relationships. This type of management is generally little understood and is a subject for much further research. However, the direction for management seems clear. First, methods need to be established for providing relevant information among the super-organization members. Second, there needs to be some method for distributing the gains achieved from cooperation.

RELEVANT INFORMATION. An adequate information base in the super-organization is needed for at least two reasons. First, in order for each firm to "maneuver" its controllable variables so that optimum channel profits are achieved, knowledge is required of the economic factor inputs to the decision problems facing the other members, as well as accounting information on the level of profits accruing to each member. Second, an adequate information system also reduces the uncertainties among the autonomous members and contributes to their continued voluntary cooperation. An intermember information system could probably be established, but assuring adequate and accurate information among the membership is difficult because of the weak lines of accountability. The extent of accountability and control within the super-organization depends as much on how governmental antitrust agencies may view such vertical integrative arrangements as the willingness of members to relinquish a degree of their autonomy to the coalition.

DISTRIBUTION OF PROFITS. Equitable redistribution of the profits achieved by the coalition is important. Recall Table 12-1, especially column 5. Under the revised pricing policy, channel profits are at their highest level, but the change in profits from column 4 are not distributed equitably among the members. That is, both buyer and carrier stand to gain more than when acting as individuals. However, the seller stands to lose. The seller would lack incentive to cooperate, since he can profit more by acting alone, as can be noted from his profit figures of Q_1^* and Q_S^*-revised of Table 12-1. He might drop from the coalition, and the members would likely return to their autonomous stature. If a method for the redistribution of profits, possibly in proportion to the profit levels that are likely to exist under the situation where all members act alone, were established, each member could be satisfied, since he first recovers the profit level he would have gained from acting alone in addition to sharing in the additional profits achieved through cooperation. All members are likely to remain in the coalition, since all derive benefits from it. However, establishing a profit redistribution method that will keep all members acting in concert may be elusive, and, even if one can be found, uncertainties about its fair implementation tend to act against continued group cooperation.

Concluding Comments

The basic issue in logistics organization is how to achieve coordination or cooperation among activities, functions, and firms so that logistical plans can be implemented effectively. Organization should facilitate optimum logistics performance and is in general guided by the total cost concept. The organization should be considered on three levels. Grouping relevant activities together and managing them collectively as a logistics function have received the greatest attention. In certain cases, the payoffs have been great as a result of this activity realignment. Much less considered have been the problems of interfunctional and interorganizational cooperation. The potential benefits may far exceed those from direct activity management. However, achieving cooperation among functions within the firm and among firms beyond their legal boundaries, when cooperation is likely to be largely voluntary, is a highly complex organizational problem. Undoubtedly, in the future logistics organization at all levels will guide on *cooperation* as the key to organizational effectiveness rather than formalized organizational structures that create as many coordination problems as they resolve.

Questions and Problems

1. Organization is an integral part of the management activity. How does it differ from planning?

2. If a firm does not wish to establish a separate logistics function, how might the coordination necessary for effective management of logistics activities be achieved?

3. Distinguish between line and staff activities within the logistics function.

4. Should the logistics organization be centralized or decentralized for the following firms?

    (a) Westinghouse Electric Company
    (b) Proctor and Gamble
    (c) Pillsbury
    (d) Carlings Brewing Company

5. Contrast the informal logistics organization with the formal one. When would each be appropriate?

6. What activities would a logistics staff organization perform? Activities of the line organization?

7. Indicate the activities around which a logistics organization would be formed in the following:

    (a) Miller Coal Company
    (b) Titusville Community Hospital
    (c) March Department Stores
    (d) Romac Appliance Manufacturers

8. Why are (1) customer service standards, (2) packaging, and (3) production scheduling interfunctional management activities? How can they be dealt with within a functionally organized firm?

9. What is a super-organization? How does managing the super-organization compare with managing the logistics function within the firm?

10. Table 12-1 indicates that distribution channel profits can be higher if individual channel members cooperate in deciding inventory and pricing policies than if they act alone. Because the benefits of cooperation may tend to "pool" with one of the members, how might the members enjoy the increased benefits and be encouraged to continue to cooperate?

11. The Acme Products Company is planning to offer a quantity discount on widgets to its only customer. The proposed pricing policy is

Quantity, Units	Delivered Price
0–450	$300
451–∞	$290

The trucking company that serves this distribution channel offers the usual volume breaks as well. The LTL rate ($3.00/unit) applies to single shipments up to 450 units. The TL rate is $2.00/unit when quantities shipped are over 450 units.

The following additional information is known.

Acme's Inventory. The production rate for widgets is relatively constant, and the reorder cycle time is predictable. Acme carries 10 percent of the quantity ordered from its inventory as a safety stock. The combined cost for carrying in-facility and in-transit inventory is 20 percent of the average value of the inventory per year.

Customer's Inventory. The customer must account for both uncertainty in lead time and in demand, as well as provide for an adequate level of service for its customers. With this in mind, the reorder point quantity R has been set at 100 units. Other pertinent facts about the customer's inventory are

The average usage during lead time = 80 units.
The expected number of units that exceed R = 30 units.
The stock-out cost = $50/unit.
The carrying cost is 25 percent of the average value of inventory per year.
The procurement cost is $10/order.

The demand is for 5000 units per year.
- (a) Will the customer likely take advantage of the quantity discount?
- (b) Can Acme justify this discount schedule on a cost basis?
- (c) If the price schedule were changed from $290 to $299 (a reduction of only $1), would the discount offer an advantage to both parties?
- (d) What change, if any, would be caused in the service level that is being provided by Acme's customer if the quantity discount is taken advantage of?
- (e) Can Acme's customer influence Acme's pricing schedule in any way? *Note:* The concepts presented in Chapter 9 will help in the solution of this problem.

Selected Bibliography

AYLOTT, D. JOHN, and DIGBY BRINDLE-WOOD-WILLIAMS, *Physical Distribution in Industrial and Consumer Marketing*. London: Hutchinson & Co., Ltd., 1970, especially Chapter 1.

BOWERSOX, DONALD J., BERNARD J. LALONDE, and EDWARD W. SMYKAY (eds.), *Readings in Physical Distribution Management*. New York: The Macmillan Company, 1969, especially Part 3.

MAGEE, JOHN F., *Industrial Logistics*. New York: McGraw-Hill Book Company, 1968, especially Chapter 14.

Management of the Physical Distribution Function, AMA Management Report Number 49. New York: American Management Association, 1960.

SMYKAY, EDWARD W. and BERNARD J. LALONDE, *Physical Distribution*. Chicago: The Dartnell Corporation, 1967, especially Chapter 6.

STERN, LOUIS W., *Distribution Channels: Behavioral Dimensions*. Boston: Houghton Mifflin Company, 1969.

Chapter
13

Logistics Control

Logistical plans may be made and implemented, but that alone does not ensure accomplishment of the goals around which the plans were developed. It is necessary to think in terms of a third primary function of management in addition to planning and organizing. This third function is control, which may be defined as *the process where planned performance is brought into line or kept in line with desired objectives.* The control process is one of comparing actual performance to planned performance and initiating corrective action to bring the two more closely together, if required. Control is action by exception.

This chapter presents an overview of the control process and discusses the control of the logistics function and of logistics activities. The elements of control are outlined. The major elements of control information and measurement and corrective action are explored.

Overview of the Control Process

The basic need for a control activity in the management process centers on future uncertainties that alter a plan's performance. Variation from design parameters will occur, since the myriad of forces that act on the conditions of any plan cannot be predicted with certainty. In addition to what might be considered normal variations in conditions are contingencies. These are the one-time, extraordinary occurrences, usually of major proportions (strikes, fires, floods, etc.), that drastically affect a plan's performance. Besides future uncertainties, there also may be fundamental changes occurring in the logistics environment that will alter planned performance. For example, changes in the economic conditions of the country, technological changes, and shifts in customer attitudes may not have been foreseen at the time of planning but nevertheless may affect the plan. The control process is, in part, one of monitoring changing conditions with the anticipation that corrective action may be needed to realign actual performance with planned performance. Perfect planning and execution of plans would require no control. Since this is seldom possible, the logistician should provide a control mechanism to ensure the accomplishment of desired goals.

A LOGISTICS CONTROL MODEL

The management control process is analogous to the many mechanical control systems encountered nearly every day. Perhaps most familiar is the heating system in the home. The control mechanism is the thermostat, which senses the temperature of the room, compares it with the desired temperature setting, and initiates corrective action by calling for heat from the furnace. In the logistics system, the manager seeks to control planned logistics activities (transportation, warehousing, inventories, materials handling, etc.) in terms of customer service and activity costs. His control mechanism includes the audits and reports about system performance, the goals established for performance, and some means for initiating corrective action, which is often provided by the logistics manager himself. This control mechanism in relation to the associated factors in the process is shown in Fig. 13-1. These additional factors include plans, logistics activities, environmental influences, and performance.

Inputs, the Process, and Outputs. The focus of the control system is on the process to be regulated. This process may be a single activity, such as filling orders and resupplying inventories, or it may be the combination of all activities in the logistics function. There are inputs into the process in the form of *plans*. Plans indicate how the process should be designed, for example, plans on the transportation modes to use, the amount of safety stock to maintain, the design of the order processing system, etc. or plans that include a combination of all of these, depending on the goals for the control system. *Environmental influences* are a second type of input to the process. The environment broadly includes all the factors that potentially can affect the process and are not accounted for in the plans. These represent the uncertainties that alter the process output from the planned activity levels. Examples of some of the more important environmental influences would be uncertainties in the actions of customers, competitors, suppliers, and government. The output of the process is what we may in general call *performance*. Performance is the state of the process at any particular time. Say that the process is the transportation activity. Performance might be measured in terms of the direct costs

FIGURE 13-1

Generalized open-loop feedback model for logistics function control

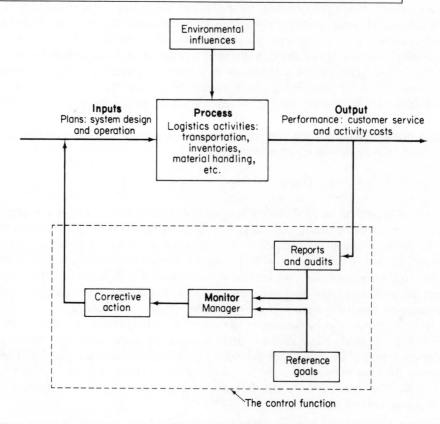

such as transportation rates, indirect costs such as loss and damage, or delivery performance.

The process with its input plans and resulting performance is the object of the control process. These factors are a result of the planning and implementation processes and are shown in relation to the control function in Fig. 13-1.

Goals. The control function requires a reference standard against which logistics activity performance can be compared. The manager strives to match process performance with this standard. Typically, this standard is a cost budget, a customer service target level, or a contribution to profit.

The Monitor. The monitor is the nerve center of the control system. It receives information about process performance, compares it with the reference goal, and initiates corrective action (see Fig. 13-1). Unlike the thermostat in the home air conditioning system, the information inputs to the logistics control system monitor often are not as electronically sophisticated. Information received by the monitor is mostly in the form of periodic reports and audits. Such information typically includes inventory status, resource utilization, activity cost, and customer service level reports.

The monitor in the system is the manager. It is the manager who interprets and compares the performance reports with the activity goals. He decides whether performance is out of control and chooses the corrective steps that must be taken to bring performance in line with objectives. For example, if customer service is too low compared with the desired service levels, the manager might call for additional safety stock to be maintained in the warehouses. The exact nature of the corrective action depends on how far out of control the process is and how permanent the manager hopes the correction to be. If the "error" between actual and desired performance is within acceptable limits, no corrective action is likely to be taken. On the other hand, if the "error" exceeds acceptable limits, the manager may choose immediate and possibly temporary tactical solutions to reduce the "error," or he may initiate strategic planning that will alter the system design. Whether he seeks a tactical and/or strategic solution is a matter of judgment and is influenced (1) by his understanding of the cause of the error, for example, random variations versus fundamental changes in performance, (2) by the benefits to be gained from major replanning against the costs involved, and (3) by the need for quick error correction.

TYPES OF CONTROL SYSTEMS

Control systems vary in design. They are generally categorized as open-loop, closed-loop, or modified feedback types.

Open-Loop Systems. The most common system for controlling logistics activities is the open-loop system. Fig. 13-1 is an example of such a system. The important feature of the open-loop system is the intervention of the manager between the action of comparing actual and desired performance and the action to reduce the process "error." The manager must intervene in a positive way before any corrective action can occur. Thus, the control process is said to be *open.*

Major advantages of the open-loop control system are its flexibility and low initial cost. The manager at his discretion can prescribe the type of information needed for control, the "error" tolerance that is acceptable at any particular time, and the form of the corrective action. This flexibility is particularly beneficial when goals, plans, and environmental influences are subject to frequent changes and when more automated control procedures are expensive and constraining. To date, most individual logistics activities plus the function as a whole are under open-loop control systems.

Closed-Loop Systems. Much work has been carried on in recent years to find ways of reducing the need for the human element in control processes. A good deal of this work has centered on physical processes, such as controlling temperatures, voltages, pressures, speed, and position. Such control devices are broadly referred to as "servomechanisms," "regulators," and "controllers." Engineers have given much attention to controlling physical processes for some time. However, relatively little attention has been given to similar control of logistics activities, but progress is being made; the automatic control of inventories is the most outstanding success to date.

In controlling logistics activities, the *decision rule* is used as a manager surrogate in closed-loop systems. The decision rule acts as the manager would if he had observed the performance error. Because the manager can be removed from the control process and control will be maintained by the decision rules, the control system is said to be *closed*.

Currently, the best example of a closed-loop control system in logistics management is the inventory control system. As early as 1952, Simon suggested that servomechanism theory could be taken from its electrical and mechanical context and applied to the problems of business concerns, especially inventory control problems.[1] It was not until the computer became useful as a business tool that inventory systems could successfully be controlled automatically. The importance of good inventory management to most firms and the quantifiable nature of inventory problems has made it one of the first activities of the firm to be controlled by closed-loop methods.

Fig. 13-2(b) shows a closed-loop control system for inventory control based on the fundamental fixed order quantity, variable order interval inventory control model with constant demand and lead time. It is contrasted with an open-loop control system for the same problem in Fig. 13-2(a). The process is one of maintaining an inventory in a warehouse from which demand is served. Demand continually depletes the stock, and positive action must be taken to replenish it. In the simple system that we are examining, process output is the inventory on hand. If we recall Equation (9.3) from Chapter 9, we can develop the performance standard and the decision rule for corrective action. That is, the decision rule would be: When the inventory on hand drops below the reorder point quantity (ROP), place a stock order for Q^* units. If conditions remain the same as those assumed when the decision rule was developed, the control system will assure optimum performance. Implementing the decision rule, reporting on inventory on hand at all times, and issuing of the stock order can all be handled by a computer.

In contrast with the open-loop control system of Fig. 13-2(a), closed-loop control systems have great capacity for controlling numerous product inventories with speed and accuracy. However, the closed-loop system tends to be rigid in terms of meeting changing conditions outside of its design parameters. It also may provide control over a portion of the total process and, therefore, may lack some of the scope of the open-loop control system. Thus, automation may offer reduced flexibility, more limited scope of control, and higher initial cost, but offers increased speed and accuracy of control.

Modified Control Systems.   In real-world application, few things are implemented in their purest form, including control systems. Managers are reluctant to transfer complete control of an activity or a group of activities to a set of decision rules.

---

[1] Herbert A. Simon, "On the Application of Servomechanism Theory in the Study of Production Control," *Econometrica*, Vol. 20 (April 1952), pp. 247–68.

Environmental influences are too unpredictable to expect that an automatic control system will remain relevant for all time. Managers even may have a degree of distrust for computers and mathematical models. As such, a combination open-

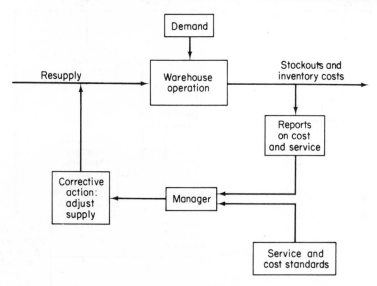

FIGURE 13-2
Examples of various control system types for inventory control

(a) An open–loop control system

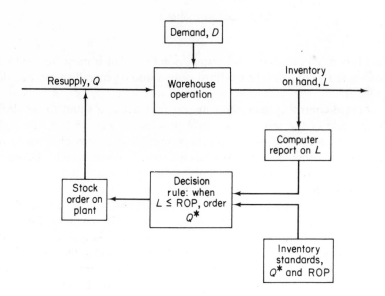

(b) A closed–loop control system

FIGURE 13-2 cont.

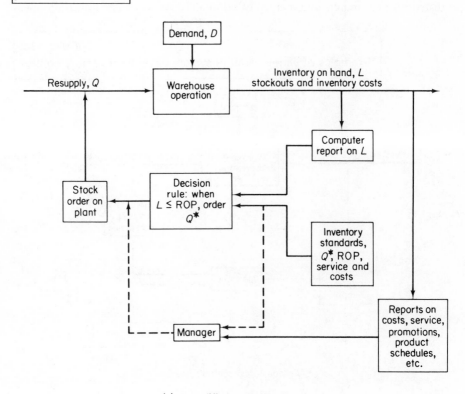

(c) A modified control system

loop, closed-loop (modified) control system is in fact what is most frequently used for logistics activity control. The modified system would generally appear as shown in Fig. 13-2(c).

In a modified control system, the manager may act as a shunt to the decision rules. In the case of the inventory control problem of Fig. 13-2(c), the logistics manager is in a position of overriding the automatic decisions of when to order and how much to order. He generally has access to a much broader information base than the automatic control system and is in a position to judge the performance of the control system. Such information might include customer service complaints, inventory cost reports, marketing promotional announcements, transportation service changes, and production schedule changes. Because the automatic control system usually does not respond to this type of information, it may no longer assure optimal inventory performance. Thus, the logistician may intervene in the control process, either to make minor adjustments in the decision rule, the reference standard, or the information base, or he may make major changes in the control system and process design. If the control system is well designed, only infrequent minor adjustments will be necessary. For example, a higher than ordinary level of inventory may be needed for temporary item promotion, and the logistician would override the automatic control system by calling for a higher order quantity for the item than the automatic system would demand.

The manager in a modified control system not only adds flexibility and scope to the system, but also acts as a "safety valve" when the automatic system breaks down. In effect, the modified control system offers leverage in controlling complex activities without requiring the manager to relinquish managerial command over the system. This undoubtedly is the reason for its use over purely open-loop or closed-loop control system types.

Control System Details

Once the type of control system for controlling single activities to the entire logistics function has been broadly defined, a number of system details need to be considered. These include the tolerance of the system to "error," the nature of system response, the setting of goals, and the nature of control information.

ERROR TOLERANCE

How great must the performance "error" be before corrective action is initiated? Just because the logistics activity costs are too high and customer service level too low may not mean that corrective action should be initiated. Corrective action does consume managerial time, especially if the control system is of the open-loop type so that to take corrective steps to reduce the error when it is unnecessary leads to unneeded expense. Corrective action is unnecessary when the error is due to ordinary random events and no fundamental changes in average process performance have occurred. In effect, a control system that tends to follow every slight performance error can have the characteristic of being "nervous." In general, a control system should not be designed to respond to random errors.

In contrast to too little tolerance for error is the control system that has too much tolerance for error. If the control monitor, say the logistics manager, is quite insensitive to performance errors, it is possible for him to miss fundamental changes in customer service and activity costs until some time after they have occurred. To bring the process back under control may require drastic alterations in activity levels even in cases where minor adjustments may have proved satisfactory if the fundamental performance changes had been detected earlier. Thus, excess control expense can result from the control system designed to be too insensitive to error.

The best control system design is obviously the one that lies between the above two extremes. That is, the best system is one that will detect fundamental errors but will not respond to random errors. Industrial engineers have long faced this problem in controlling industrial processes and frequently employ a control chart as a control guide. The concepts behind this chart are useful in controlling logistics activities as well.

An example of the control chart is shown in Fig. 13-3. Under control is customer service. Let us suppose that customer service is narrowly defined as the percentage of orders by item that could be filled from available warehouse stock per month.

FIGURE 13-3

A control chart for mean customer service level

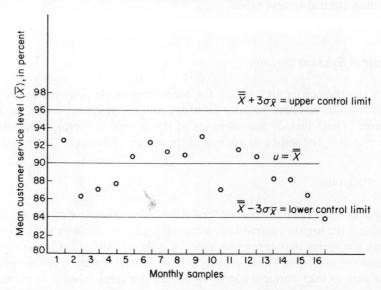

A number of random samples[2] from a large number of items carried in inventory have previously been taken. A mean of samples ($\bar{\bar{X}}$) and a standard deviation of sample means ($\sigma_{\bar{x}}$) have been calculated from these historical data. Since the distribution of sample means will be normal due to the central limit theorem,[3] we can calculate the confidence limits for mean customer service level. Suppose that we find $\bar{\bar{X}}$ to be 90 percent and the standard deviation of sample means ($\sigma_{\bar{x}}$) to be two percentage points. From the normal distribution given in Table 9-A, confidence limits of $\bar{\bar{X}} \pm 3\sigma_{\bar{x}}$ would mean that on the average mean customer service level should fall outside of these limits 0.3 percent of the time. That is, the lower control limit (LCL) would be $90 - 3(2) = 84$. Suppose also that our desired mean customer service level (μ) is equal to $\bar{\bar{X}}$.

If the desired mean customer service level μ is equal to the historically observed mean of $\bar{\bar{X}}$, the control chart provides a control guide line for the future. Customer service level would be observed from time to time, perhaps monthly, and the

---

[2] The size of each random sample should contain 20 items or more.

[3] See William S. Peters and George W. Summers, *Statistical Analysis for Business Decisions* (Englewood Cliffs, N. J.: Prentice-Hall, Inc., 1968), p. 122.

observation plotted on the graph, as shown in Fig. 13-3. When the process is under control, a random pattern of observations will be seen, and no corrective action needs to be taken. If the observations fall beyond the control limits, and especially if they display a nonrandom pattern as shown in the twelfth through sixteenth observations in Fig. 13-3, there is a strong indication that there has been a fundamental change in the process. This is a signal that corrective action is needed.

RESPONSE

When the error in a control system is no longer tolerable, corrective action must be taken. How the system responds to corrective action affects control costs. Response is a function of the characteristics of system and the form in which corrective action is taken.

Logistics control systems are much like mechanical control systems in that they have varying degrees of "mass." System mass governs how quickly actual error correction will occur and the pattern of process response. Mass in a logistics system determines the rate at which the needed change can be made. For example, if inventory levels are to be raised, the time required to realize the desired levels will be a function of the rate at which production levels can be changed. The more mass there is in the system, the longer it will be before desired levels are reached and the longer the out-of-control situation will prevail. Fig. 13-4 illustrates the effect of mass on system response.

Information time lags are a second important factor in the pattern of response. In general, when there is a time lag between when a change in the process occurs and when that change is detected in the control monitor, the system will tend to

FIGURE 13-4
Speed of response in an inventory control system depending on the "mass" of the system

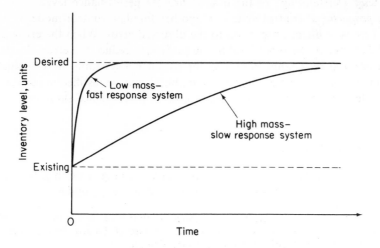

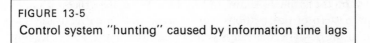

FIGURE 13-5

Control system "hunting" caused by information time lags

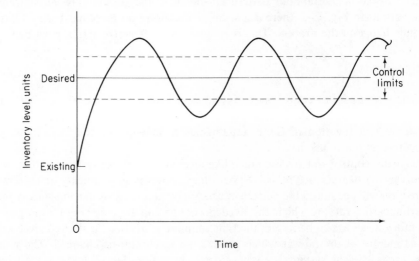

"hunt," as shown in Fig. 13-5. That is, the control system can never stabilize on the desired level. If information lags as well as system mass are not too great, the variation about the desired level will remain within acceptable limits. If not, a more responsive information system or possibly a more responsive production and delivery system will need to be designed.

Process response is also influenced by the form in which corrective action is taken. Two modes of control are common.[4] The most popular is the *on-off*, or two-position mode. When an error is detected, full and constant corrective action is taken until it is observed by the monitor that the desired level has been reached. If the mass of the system and information lags are great, the on-off control mode promotes "overshooting" of the desired process performance level.

The *proportional* control system is another familiar control mode. Corrective action here is in direct proportion to the observed error. When the error is great, so is the change in the input level to the process to reduce the error. As the error is reduced, so is the change in process inputs. Such a system is more sophisticated and more expensive than an on-off system, but it may be justified in terms of more rapid system response without a loss in process performance stability.

Control in Practice

Control systems for controlling logistics activities range from highly formalized and elegant mechanical systems to systems that are kept under control by per-

---

[4] In addition, there are *derivative* and *integral* control models. For an introductory discussion of the four control system modes, see Millard H. La Joy, *Industrial Automatic Controls* (New York: Prentice-Hall, Inc., 1954), Chapters 2-5.

sonnel who have a good "feel" of the business. So far, sophisticated control concepts have mainly been applied to product restocking. Let us recall Fig. 9-10. Most individual logistics activities as well as the function as a whole remain under manual, or open-loop, control. In practice, manual control is achieved through the aid of budgets, customer service targets, and profit centers.

BUDGETS

The most widely used device for controlling logistics activities is the budget. Budgets are cost goals set by top management in concert with the logistics manager to guide the cost performance of logistics activities. They serve as the reference standard in the control process and, hopefully, ensure the profitability of the company through cost control. They also serve as a device for measuring the performance of the logistics manager himself.

Budgets must be realistically set if the profit objectives of the firm are to be met. Nearly any budget can be met if customer service is reduced to low enough levels. However, if it is assumed that the firm desires to survive in the long run, the logistics service should be set high enough at least to ensure a competitive level of service.

SERVICE TARGETS

Opposite to the budget is the customer service target. The customer service target focuses on the revenue side of the profit equation rather than the cost side. The philosophy of control by setting the control reference standard equal to the service target is that costs will tend to follow revenues. This approach would be reasonable in cases where product sales are highly service-sensitive (for example, low-valued, highly substitutable products). However, there is an important deficiency in using service targets as a control device. Often, too little is known about the effect of physical distribution service changes on revenues.

PROFIT CENTER

An appealing approach for controlling logistics is to treat the logistics function as a separate business within the firm, that is, as a profit center. This makes sense because the logistics function employs capital, incurs costs, and adds value by distribution.[5] It even contributes to sales through the customer service level provided. All the prerequisite elements exist for establishing a profit center. Control of the logistics function is in terms of the broader concept of profit and avoids the narrow control features of either budgets or service targets.

Making the profit center concept work is more difficult than the use of budgets or service targets. The major problem centers on pricing the services provided by the logistics function. Pricing would not be a problem if there were some way of relating the customer service level provided and the contribution made to logistics

[5] Dean S. Ammer, "Materials Management as a Profit Center," *Harvard Business Review* (January–February 1969), p. 76.

function profits. If such a relationship were known, the logistics manager would balance revenue against costs incurred in providing the service. Such a relationship generally does not exist. Even if it did, another problem would still remain before the profit center concept could be effectively applied. That is, prices for incoming products to the logistics function have to be established, and the efficiency of the function in using capital needs to be determined. Ammer claims that the pricing of logistics services and the price paid for products to be handled by the logistics function is not a serious problem. He suggests that transfer prices be established in much the same way as goods are priced that move from one division to another in a multidivisional company.[6] Production would price goods to logistics and logistics, after adding value, would price goods to marketing. The price to marketing might be the price paid to production plus logistics costs incurred in supply and distribution plus a markup equivalent to the company's overall return on investment. Once prices are fixed, the logistics manager is free to improve profits in any way he wishes. Top management measures the logistics manager through his profit performance and reviews periodically the setting of transfer prices.

Control Information and Measurement

An effective logistics control system requires accurate, relevant, and timely information about activity or function performance. The major sources of this information are audits and various reports of logistics activities.

AUDITS

The logistics audit is a periodic examination of the status of logistics activities. Because of potential errors in reporting systems and the lack of reports about certain activities, it becomes necessary periodically to "take stock" of the situation. A control system may lose its effectiveness if the information available to it is inaccurate. Audit information is used to establish new reference points against which sequential reports are generated and to correct errors that can result in the performance of certain logistics activities due to misinformation.

Inventory Audits. Inventory audits are essential in inventory control systems. A typical inventory control system makes adjustments to inventory records due to demand depletions, replenishments, returns to plant, and obsolescence. But other events may occur to cause disparities between inventory records and the actual inventories maintained in the warehouses. Theft, customer returns, damaged goods, and errors in various inventory reports can lead to substantial errors in the level of inventories believed to be on hand. A physical count of the inventories from time to time determines the true level of all product items. Adjustments are

[6] *Ibid.*, pp. 72–82.

then made to inventory records so that once again the control system will provide a more accurate "track" of inventory levels.

Freight Bill Audits. Human mistakes are a common reason for incurring the extra expense of performing audits. In the control of transportation costs, many firms have found it worthwhile to audit their freight bills. Errors in rates, product description, weights, and routing are just a few ways in which errors may creep into billing. It is not uncommon for a large company to have up to three-quarter million freight bills a year, and even infrequent errors can result in sizable overcharges. Miner predicts that there is a 3 to 5 percent overcharge on an annual basis.[7]

Checking freight bills can be handled by the company's traffic department. However, many firms prefer to have this audit performed outside the firm by traffic bureaus. Traffic bureaus offer this service on a commission basis. That is, the bureau receives a percentage of the claims that are recovered. Contracting with an outside agency is particularly beneficial to the small firm that cannot efficiently provide a staff for this activity. So common are these errors that freight bill auditing is often carried out on a regular basis.

Total Function Audit. From time to time the top management of the firm will find it useful to "take stock" of how well the logistics function as a whole is being managed. Top management needs to convince itself that the function is performing effectively and efficiently. Such an audit might include an evaluation of all personnel, of the organizational structure of the function, and of the plans for improvement that have been implemented, as well as of the future plans for improved performance.

Other Audits. Any number of other audits might also be carried out on an irregular basis. Warehouse space utilization, customer service levels, transportation fleet utilization, logistics network configuration efficiency, and inventory policy performance represent specific areas that might be audited. All provide basic information necessary for effective logistics control.

REGULAR REPORTS

Whereas audits are usually irregularly scheduled status checks, a number of reports are generated on a regular basis that are important to the control process. Very often good control depends on a continuous stream of information so that performance errors cannot become extreme before they are detected. There are numerous reports produced on a regular basis, including traffic reports, sales reports, production reports, order processing reports, demand forecasts, and budget reports. All serve the purpose of keeping the manager informed of what is happening in the business so that activity performance levels can be changed when necessary to move the firm closer to its objectives. Not only do these regular reports indicate the current status of a process, an activity, or the logistics func-

[7] J. H. Miner, "The Timely Emergence of the Distribution Audit," *Handling & Shipping* (April 1971), p. 57.

tion as a whole, but when put together chronologically they show fundamental performance trends in much the same way that a series of cartoon flip-cards produces animation. Trend information is useful in anticipating the need for future corrective action so that planning may begin ahead of when it is required.

Regular reports provide the information necessary to control logistics activities on a day-to-day basis. Requirements for the information are that it be accurate, relevant, as up to date as possible, and in a format useful for control. Misinformation and information time lags contribute to instabilities in the control of activity performance with resulting inefficiency. Thus, report content, frequency of issue, and time lapse between data collection and issuance are important considerations in the design of information inputs to the control system.

Consider two illustrations of regular control reports. The first is an activity report, that is, the inventory report. The second is a logistics function-wide report covering the combined effects of managing all logistics activities. The latter is a logistics cost-service control statement.

Inventory Reports. It is common for most companies to provide regular reports about the status of inventories. Inventories usually represent a considerable expense, and careful control is justified. Inventory status is seldom fully disclosed in a single report. Take, for example, the inventory reporting system of the Usemore Soap Company. Recall that Usemore was a medium-sized company manufacturing cleaning compounds for industrial and institutional use. Usemore's computerized inventory control system was discussed under the multiple item, multiple location analysis of Chapter 9. A diagram of the inventory reports from that system is shown in Fig. 13-6. Five status reports were produced on a regular basis.

The key report was the inventory file listing report produced on a weekly basis from computer memory records; it is shown in Table 13-1. This report summarizes the product items currently stocked in the warehouse, their amounts and anticipated deliveries, forecasts, shipping information, cost rates, and decision rules currently used (shipping weight, MAX, and MIN). Since this control system is an automatic one, such information helps the logistician in evaluating the performance of the system and provides a basis for manually altering it. For example, if he is receiving a number of service complaints for a warehouse, he might after considering the economic implications simply raise the MAX value.

The four remaining reports expand on the summary information presented in the inventory file listing report. First, there is the monthly product forecast. This report provides such detailed information as actual and forecasted demand last month, next month's forecast, trend in sales, parameter values in the forecast model, the absolute deviation (MAD) of actual from forecasted sales, and exception values for MAX and MIN that override the preset values in the system. It provides the logistician with a close look at forecast model performance on a by-product-item basis and notes any manual alterations that may have been made to the automatic forecasting system.

Second, there is the value-of-inventory report. This monthly report is generated

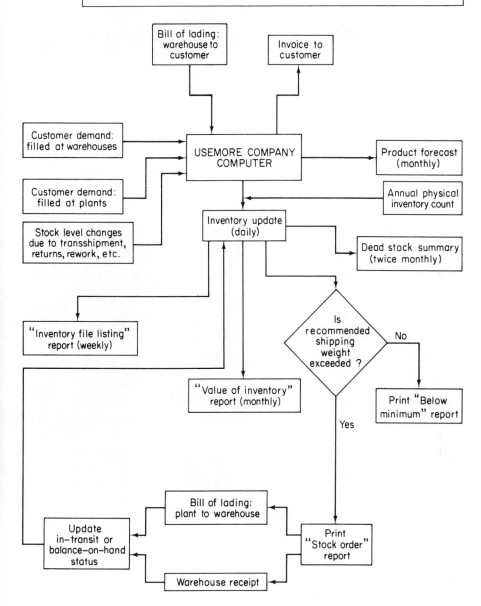

FIGURE 13-6

Diagram of Usemore Soap Company's inventory reporting system

from the inventory records maintained by the computer. It shows management the current level of investment in inventories in all warehouses.

Third, a certain amount of stock maintained in inventories will become "dead" because (1) there is no longer any demand for it, (2) it has deteriorated, been

TABLE 13-1
Example of inventory file listing report for Usemore Soap Company

Date: 01/28/72

Warehouse No.	Warehouse Name	Shipping Weight[a]	Forecast Factors		Plant No.	Storage Rate[d] $/cwt/mo	Freight Rate[e] $/cwt	Warehouse in Freezable Zone[f]
			MAX[b]	MIN[c]				
0267	Akron, Ohio	40,000	1.8	1.0	02	0.31	0.55	01

Product No.[g]	Size[h]	Product Name	Gross Weight[i]	Tare Weight[j]	Freezable Product[k]	Forecast[l]	DDS[m]	Product Line[n]	Date of Last Sale
0167820	Case	Kar Wash	22	05	00	2.60			72/01/26
0476600	MDR	TRX-93	500	50	01	4.36		365	72/01/27
0562301	1/2FDR	Ziloid	210	10	00	13.04			72/01/20
0721102	6GLPL	Oven Kleen	39	03	01	.00	.01		
0287720	Case	US Soap	56	08	01	.00		365	71/08/20

Date of Last Delivery	On Order[o]	In Transit[p]	BOH[q]
71/12/29	00	00	07
71/12/29	03	00	04
71/12/29	13	06	08
70/11/13	00	00	05
71/06/05	00	00	07[r]

[a] Recommended accumulated weight of stock deficiency in warehouse before replenishment order is sent from plant. [b] Factor times 30-day forecast to give maximum demand between stock replenishments. [c] Factor times 30-day forecast to give minimum demand between stock replenishments. [d] Rate charged by public warehouse for storage. [e] Freight rate for delivery to warehouse from plant based on shipping weight quantities. [f] 00 if no, 01 if yes. [g] Product code, where digits 1–5 represent product identification, and digits 6–7 represent the container size. [h] Package form for storage, e.g., cases, drums (DR), half drums (1/2FDR), etc. [i] Shipping weight of product item. [j] Empty container weight. [k] If product is freezable 01, if not 00. [l] Forecast of product demand for next 30 days. Products are forecasted monthly. [m] 01 indicates the item has been discontinued and no further forecasts will be made. [n] Approximate product life to indicate when stock becomes unsaleable. A blank indicates that there are no restrictions on the length of time for storage. [o] The difference between the maximum amount of product in the warehouse (MAX · forecast) and the current balance on hand (BOH). [p] Amount of product en route between plant and warehouse. [q] Current amount of product available for sale or balance on hand (BOH). [r] Since no sales have taken place in the last 120 days for this item, it would be declared dead.

462

damaged, or is otherwise unsaleable, and (3) it has been discontinued due to other product substitutions, quality control problems, etc. A dead stock report is issued semimonthly as an information report on the amount of such stock, its location, and the products involved. It provides basic information for stock disposition and for control over future dead stock levels.

Fourth, because this inventory system controls on the basis of the cumulative differential between the MAX values and the combined shipping weight, it is possible that the level of individual product items can drop dangerously low, so that stockouts are likely before the product items can be replenished in the normal manner. To control this possibility, a below minimum report is issued to provide the necessary information. By noting the items below the preset MIN levels, the logistician may take action at any time to ship these items to a warehouse and possibly avert a stockout situation.

One additional regular report that Usemore might have included is a summary report to help evaluate the overall performance of the inventory control system. This performance summary report would relate customer service and inventory cost items over time. Specifically included might be (1) percentage of orders filled on demand, (2) cost of maintaining inventories, (3) number of backorders, and (4) percentage of dead stock in inventory. Data would be presented for each warehouse and for several periods so that trends could be observed. A master summary for the system as a whole would show overall performance at a glance.

Logistics Cost-Service Control Statement. Activity reports deal with specific segments of the logistics function. To provide a balanced control over all activities, the logistician needs summary information on overall distribution and supply costs, as well as basic information on the customer service level being provided. Table 13-2 shows an example of such a report.

The report might logically be organized according to physical distribution costs, supply costs, and customer service. Distribution costs can be separated from supply costs because of the degree of independence in the systems that generate the costs. Supply warehouses may be different from finished goods warehouses, different transportation services may be used on the supply versus the distribution side of the firm, and the order-processing networks may be different as well. Because of this degree of independence, separate management of these systems is sometimes possible. Thus, it is useful to separate the costs into two categories.

Distribution costs might include transportation costs from plant to customer, finished-goods inventory costs, order-processing costs, and administrative and overhead expenses associated with the distribution system. In the example of Table 13-2, transportation costs include inbound costs to and outbound costs from a finished-goods warehouse, expenses from stock returns to plant, and charges associated with backorders. Finished-goods inventory costs include those costs for maintaining inventories in field warehouses and at the plant, as well as the cost of goods in transit from plant to warehouse and warehouse to customer. In addition, materials-handling costs at the warehouse and at the plant are listed, since materials-handling costs are often computed separately from storage costs,

TABLE 13-2
Example of an annual logistics cost-service control statement

Physical Distribution

Transportation of finished goods:

Freight charges inbound to warehouse	$2,700,000	
Delivery charges outbound from warehouses	3,150,000	
Freight charges on stock returns to plant	300,000	
Extra delivery charges on backorders	450,000	
		$6,600,000

Finished-goods inventories:

Inventories in transit	280,000	
Storage costs at warehouse[a]	1,200,000	
Materials-handling costs at warehouse	1,800,000	
Costs of obsolete stock	310,000	
Storage costs at plant[a]	470,000	
Materials-handling costs at plant	520,000	
		4,580,000

Order-processing costs:

Processing of customer orders	830,000	
Processing of stock orders	170,000	
Processing of backorders	440,000	
		1,440,000

Administration and overhead—finished goods:

Proration of unallocated managerial expenses	240,000	
Depreciation of owned storage space	180,000	
Depreciation of materials-handling equipment	100,000	
Depreciation of transportation equipment	50,000	
		570,000
Total distribution costs		$13,190,000

Physical Supply

Transportation of supply goods:

Freight charges inbound to plant	$1,200,000	
Expedited freight charges	300,000	
		1,500,000

Supply goods inventories:

Storage costs on raw materials	300,000	
Materials-handling cost on raw materials	270,000	
		570,000

Order processing:

Processing of supply orders	55,000	
Costs of expedited orders	10,000	
		65,000

Administration and overhead—supply goods:

Proration of unallocated managerial expenses	50,000
Depreciation of owned storage space	30,000
Depreciation of materials-handling equipment	40,000
Depreciation of transportation equipment	25,000

TABLE 13-2 cont.

	145,000
Total supply costs	$2,280,000
Total distribution costs	$13,190,000
Total supply costs	2,280,000
Total logistics costs	$15,470,000

Customer Service

Percentage of warehouse deliveries within one day	92%
Average in-stock percentage[b]	87%
Total order cycle time[c]	
a. normal processing	7±2 days
b. backorder processing	10±3 days
Backorders	
a. Total	503
b. Percentage of total orders	2.5%
Customer returns due to damage, dead stock, order-processing errors,	
and late deliveries[d]	1.2%
Percentage of available production time shutdown due to supply stockouts	2.3%

[a] Includes space, insurance, taxes, and capital costs.
[b] Percentage of individual product items filled directly from warehouse stocks.
[c] Based on distribution of order cycle times.
[d] Percentage of gross sales.

and the separate classifications are useful in evaluating the efficiency and effectiveness of each of these subsystems. Obsolete stock costs are listed, because in this case they are significant relative to the other costs in the category. Order-processing costs are the third major cost item in distribution costs. These costs would include both customer and stock order processing as well as the costs for processing the back orders. Finally, distribution costs would include a proration of various administrative and overhead expenses.

Physical supply costs are divided into the same general categories as physical distribution costs (Table 13-2). Because the supply system often is simpler than the distribution system for many companies, fewer costs categories are needed for effective management.

Customer service is the final category in the cost-service statement. Logistics costs mean little unless there is some measure of logistics service against which to compare them. Knowing how any particular logistics system would affect revenues would be ideal. This is rarely available, so some physical rather than economic measure is used as a substitute. For example, distribution service might be measured in terms of percentage of warehouse deliveries within one day, average in-stock percentage, total order cycle time for normal processing and for backorders, the number and percentage of backorders, and percentage of sales returned due to distribution related problems. On the supply side, customer service might be measured as a percentage of the total available production time that production was shut down due to raw-material stockouts.

In general, the cost-service statement provides the kind of aggregate data necessary for broad control of the logistics function. When further information is required for detailed control of a single cost or service category, the logistician should be able to "explode" the category to obtain the information that produced the aggregate figure. This helps to trace the reason for being out of control to fundamental causes.

Corrective Action

The final element in the control function is the corrective action that must be taken when the difference between the system goals and actual performance is no longer tolerable. Action to reduce the difference depends on the nature and extent of the out-of-control condition. In this section, three action types are delineated: (1) minor adjustments, (2) major replanning, and (3) contingency action.

MINOR ADJUSTMENTS

Whether the control problem is one of managing the overall logistics function or a subactivity of the function, some variation of actual performance from desired performance will occur and can be anticipated. Just as the direction of an automobile must constantly be adjusted as it moves along a highway, so must the performance of a logistics activity. Activity performance is under constant change due to a dynamic and uncertain business environment that acts upon it. For example, the transportation activity of service selection, routing, and scheduling will vary over time in terms of its costs due to changes in rates, available routes, equipment availability, loss and damage, etc. Such dynamics usually do not require major changes in the way that the activity is carried on. Minor adjustments to activity level and mix, decision rules, and even system goals often suffice to maintain adequate control over the system. Most corrective action is of this type.

MAJOR REPLANNING

Sweeping reevaluation of the logistics system, significant changes in logistics function goals, major changes in the logistics environment, introduction of new products and dropping of existing ones, etc. may necessitate major replanning for activity performance. Major replanning involves a recycling through the management planning process (recall Fig. 2-2) that generates new courses of action and hence a new activity performance level, control system reference standards, and error tolerance limits. Such replanning might result in a new warehouse configuration, alterations in order-processing procedures, revision of inventory control procedures, and alterations to the product flow system within warehouses and plants.

The difference between corrective action taken in the form of minor adjustments versus major replanning is that minor adjustments do not require any substantial changes to the control mechanisms. In fact, corrective action is often routine, as in the case of inventory control, where action is initiated in the form of a stock order when stock is depleted to a predetermined level. Control adjustments are automatic through the application of a decision rule. In contrast, major replanning involves substantial changes to the process inputs in the form of new plans or major revision to old ones. There is no clear delineation as to when minor adjustments to maintain activity control should give way to major system revision. In theory, the optimum changeover point is when the incremental costs associated with continuing to use minor adjustments within the control system to maintain control over the process just equal the incremental benefits to be derived from major replanning. Finding this point is more a matter of managerial judgment than of precise mathematical computation.

CONTINGENCY ACTION

The third form of corrective action is that taken when there are possibilities of dramatic changes in the activity performance level. Such dramatic changes can occur when a warehouse is shut down due to fire, when computer failure renders the computerized inventory control system inoperative, when labor strikes change the availability of transportation services, and when sources of raw-material supply suddenly dry up. The company's customer service may be severely jeopardized and/or the level of logistics costs to produce a given level of customer service may suddenly rise because of swift and dramatic changes in the conditions under which the process was operating. Minor adjustments to the process inputs often prove to be too little to restore control to a system that has suffered the shock of a contingency event. The pressures for continuing logistics operations put major replanning as a course for corrective action at a disadvantage, since good planning requires time. Many companies have found that contingency plans developed in advance of their need are a good way of meeting the problem of shock changes to the system process.[8] Contingency plans represent predetermined courses of action to be implemented when a defined contingency event occurs. For example, the privately owned warehouse of a large and well-known company was struck by fire late on a Friday afternoon, which destroyed the entire contents and warehouse. The warehouse served the entire west coast area, and sales were jeopardized in this area. Because the company had the foresight to develop a contingency plan for just such an event, inventories were immediately shipped by air freight to a public warehouse in the area to be ready for sales by Monday morning.

Concluding Comments

Logistics control helps to ensure that the goals around which logistics plans were developed are achieved after the plan is put into action. The dynamics and

[8] In a survey of the participants at the 1970 annual meeting of the National Council of Physical Distribution Management, 60 percent of the respondents claimed that their companies had contingency plans for logistics operations.

uncertainties of the logistics environment over time can cause deviations from planned process performance. To keep process performance in line with desired performance objectives, some form of managerial control is required. Control usually takes the form of an open-loop system, closed-loop system, or a system that combines both of these. All are used in practice.

The logistician is involved in the control activity on a daily basis. He often serves as the monitor of logistics activities. He measures the activity level through the various audits and reports that he receives and compares these with targets for performance such as budgets, profit standards, and customer service goals. Based on this comparison, the decision is made to take corrective steps to bring the activity back under control. In many ways, control is just short-term or tactical decision making.

Questions and Problems

1. What role does control play in the management of logistics activities?

2. A common carrier trucking firm controls its delivery performance in terms of average delivery time, delivery time variability, and loss and damage claims. Sketch a generalized open-loop feedback control model for this process.

3. What advantages does the modified control system have over either the open-loop or the closed-loop control systems?

4. Which logistics activities might successfully be controlled by a closed-loop control system? Explain.

5. What effect do you think that a mail order transmittal mode compared with a teletype order transmittal mode would have on the performance of an inventory control system?

6. Of what value is the audit in the control process? Which audits would be of particular value to the control of logistics activities?

7. Logistics managers can suffer from too many reports and reports of the wrong kind. Select a typical logistics activity and suggest the type and frequency of reports needed to control the activity.

8. Suppose you were in charge of managing a common carrier trucking operation. How would you establish the tolerance for substandard performance (average delivery time, reliability, loss and damage, etc.) before initiating minor corrective action, such as tighter standards on performance, personnel changes, etc. When should major replanning take place?

9. Westinghouse Electric Company has a large regional warehouse in Utah to store and distribute major appliances to west coast markets. If you were a logistics manager in charge of this operation, what contingency plans would you make to ensure continued good logistics performance in case disaster strikes?

Selected Bibliography

BRYSON, ARTHUR E. and YU-CHI HO, *Applied Optimal Control*. Waltham, Mass.: Blaisdell, 1969.

DAVIS, RALPH C., *The Fundamentals of Top Management*. New York: Prentice-Hall, Inc., 1954.

FORRESTER, JAY, *Industrial Dynamics*. Cambridge, Mass.: M. I. T. Press, 1961.

KURNOW, ERNEST, GERALD J. GLASER, and FREDERICK R. OTTMAN, *Statistics for Business Decisions*. Homewood, Illinois: Richard D. Irwin, Inc., 1959, especially Chapter 11.

LA JOY, MILLARD H., *Industrial Automatic Controls*. New York: Prentice-Hall, Inc., 1954.

Appendix
A

The Transportation Method

The transportation method is a solution procedure (algorithm) for a special class of linear programming problems called transportation problems and is particularly useful in solving network problems. A typical transportation problem involves finding the least-cost way of shipping goods from factories to meet the demand of warehouses. Shipping costs are linear, with the volume moving between any factory-warehouse combination. Other requirements are that supply must equal demand and that supply and demand must be expressed in integer values, i.e., whole numbers.

EXAMPLE

As an illustrative example, consider the simple problem of three factories F_1, F_2, and F_3 supplying three warehouses W_1, W_2, and W_3. The supply and demand requirements for the coming month are shown in Table A-1. The shipping costs C_{ij} are given in Table A-2. We denote the supply from factory j as b_j, the demand at warehouse i as a_i, and the shipping costs between F_j and W_i as C_{ij}. We are looking for the amount X_{ij} to be shipped between F_j and W_i for the least total shipping costs. In general terms, this transportation problem can be succinctly stated as

470

$$\text{Minimize} \quad \sum_{i=1}^{m} \sum_{j=1}^{n} C_{ij} X_{ij} \qquad \text{(A.1)}$$

subject to the following constraints:
(All demand is met)

$$\sum_{j=1}^{n} X_{ij} = a_i \qquad i = 1, 2, \ldots, m \qquad \text{(A.2)}$$

(All supply is distributed)

$$\sum_{i=1}^{m} X_{ij} = b_j \qquad j = 1, 2, \ldots, n \qquad \text{(A.3)}$$

(Supply must equal demand)

$$\sum_{j=1}^{n} b_j = \sum_{i=1}^{m} a_i \qquad \text{(A.4)}$$

and
(No negative amounts may be shipped)

$$\text{all} \quad X_{ij} \geq 0 \qquad \text{(A.5)}$$

There are m factories and n warehouses.

TABLE A-1

Supply b_j and demand a_i requirements for example problem

	Supply b_j		Demand a_i
F_1	500 units	W_1	200 units
F_2	200	W_2	200
F_3	300	W_3	200
	Total 1000 units		Total 600 units

TABLE A-2

Table of shipping costs C_{ij} in \$/unit for example problem

		Warehouses		
		W_1	W_2	W_3
Factories	F_1	3	5	1
	F_2	5	9	2
	F_3	2	2	6

Setting up the Problem. The special nature of the transportation problem permits setting up the problem in the form of a two-dimensional matrix (Table A-3), where each cell represents a unique factory-warehouse combination. The supply and

TABLE A-3
Matrix problem set up for example transportation problem

Warehouses

		W_1	W_2	W_3	W_4^a	Units Supplied
	F_1	3	5	1 200	20 300	500
Factories	F_2	5 100	9	2	20 100	200
	F_3	2 100	2 200	6	20	300
	Units Demanded	200	200	200	400b	1000

[a] Dummy warehouse added to absorb excess supply.
[b] Artificial demand equal to 1000 − 600 = 400 units.

demand requirements are displayed around the rim of the matrix and the per-unit shipping cost is shown in the small cells within the larger cells of the matrix. Because the total units demanded are not equal to the total units that can be supplied, a dummy warehouse W_4 is added to the matrix to absorb excess supply and to make supply equal demand. The dummy demand is the difference between the actual demand and supply, and the shipping costs to this warehouse are set artificially much higher than any other shipping costs in the matrix. In this problem, an artificial cost of $20 will do. This prevents all but the excess supply from being shipped to this dummy warehouse.[1] If demand had exceeded supply, a dummy factory would have been created instead of a dummy warehouse.

Getting Started. The first step in the solution procedure is to make an initial allocation of demand to supply. The closer that we can make this initial allocation to the optimum allocation, the fewer will be the computations required to find the optimum allocation. Actually, the only requirement that must be met in making this allocation is that the allocations across the rows or down the columns must sum to equal the appropriate rim value. Though the methods for accomplishing this range from a systematic method, such as the northwest corner rule,[2] which is insensitive to the particular costs in the matrix, to a sophisticated approximation

---

[1] The observing reader will note that the constraints on this problem are such that any artificial shipping costs can be used without altering the final solution. That is, the dummy warehouse must accept exactly 400 units.

[2] For an elaboration of this method, see A. Charnes and W. W. Cooper, *Management Models and Industrial Applications of Linear Programming*, Vol. 1 (New York: John Wiley & Sons, Inc., 1964), pp. 43–44.

method such as Vogel's approximation method (VAM)[3], which can yield nearly optimum solutions, the method used here lies somewhere between these. The procedure is to find the lowest-cost cell and assign as much to this cell as possible without exceeding the rim value in the cell's row or column. Proceed to the next lowest-cost cell and make another assignment. Any previous assignment must be considered when one is making subsequent assignment of the previous assignment appear in the row or column of the cell being examined. This procedure is continued until all row and column assignments equal their respective rim requirements. Table A-3 includes the initial assignment following this procedure.

The total cost of this initial allocation is determined by multiplying the cell assignment by the cell cost and summing these over the entire matrix, excluding, of course, those assignments made to the dummy warehouse, since they are artificial. Therefore, according to Equation (A.1), the shipping cost for this allocation is

$$TC = 5(100) + 2(100) + 2(200) + 1(200)$$
$$= \$1300$$

Iterating. Can the above allocation be improved? This depends on whether there is a net cost savings to shifting the assignments around in the matrix, which can be determined by evaluating those cells where there is no current assignment. Again, there are a number of methods that might be used for making these evaluations. The "stepping stone" algorithm will be used, not because it is the most efficient, but because it closely follows an intuitive explanation of the solution procedure.

The first step is to define the path through the matrix for a particular unoccupied cell over which the reassignment of units would be made if a savings could be realized by reallocating to this cell. This unique path can be determined by the following procedure.

(1) Start with the unoccupied cell being evaluated.
(2) Search for a series of occupied cells to define a closed loop, ending with the starting cell. The path resembles the movement of the rook in the game of chess and is often referred to as the "rook's tour." All turns in the path must be at right angles and can be made only on occupied cells. Jumping over an occupied square to complete the tour is permitted. The path may be generated in either a clockwise or counterclockwise direction around the loop.

Several paths are illustrated in Table A-4. The simplest type is illustrated for cell F_2W_2. The path is $F_2W_2 \rightarrow F_2W_1 \rightarrow F_3W_1 \rightarrow F_3W_2 \rightarrow F_2W_2$. A more complicated tour occurs with the evaluation of F_3W_3. Here the path would be $F_3W_3 \rightarrow F_1W_3 \rightarrow F_1W_4 \rightarrow F_2W_4 \rightarrow F_2W_1 \rightarrow F_3W_1 \rightarrow F_3W_3$. The procedure is repeated for all unoccupied cells.

[3] *Ibid.*, pp. 58–63.

TABLE A-4
Examples of rook's tours for reallocating demand

		W_1	W_2	W_3	W_4	Units Supplied
Factories	F_1	3	5	1 / 200	20 / 300	500
	F_2	5 / 100	9	2	20 / 100	200
	F_3	2 / 100	2 / 200	6	20	300
Units Demanded		200	200	200	400	1000

This path is unique, because it shows how the demand readjustment must be made to preserve the equalities in the rows and columns. Because of this, we need concern ourselves only with the costs that appear at the corners of this closed loop in searching for cost reductions. Actually, the path includes only those cells involved in a cost tradeoff. For example, to evaluate cell F_2W_2, only a marginal analysis of the costs on the path is required. To move one unit from F_3W_2 into F_2W_2 would cause a cost increase equal to the difference between the shipping costs or $9 - 2 = \$ + 7$/unit. Moving one unit onto F_2W_2 requires a compensating movement along the path from F_2W_1 to F_3W_1 so that the equality in the rows and columns is again restored. The movement of one unit from F_2W_1 to F_3W_1 reduces cost by $2 - 5 = \$ - 3$/unit. The net result of $\$ + 4$/unit could have been found by the following simple procedure:

(1) Begin with the cell to be evaluated and consider the shipping cost as positive.
(2) Alternate signs on the shipping costs, selecting only those costs at the corners of the path.
(3) Sum these costs.

Hence, for cell F_2W_2: $9 - 5 + 2 - 2 = +4$. Repeating this evaluation for all unoccupied cells, we would have

$$F_1W_1: 3 - 5 + 20 - 20 = -2 \longleftarrow \text{most negative}$$
$$F_1W_2: 5 - 2 + 2 - 5 + 20 - 20 = 0$$
$$F_2W_2: 9 - 5 + 2 - 2 = +4$$
$$F_2W_3: 2 - 20 + 20 - 1 = +1$$
$$F_3W_3: 6 - 2 + 5 - 20 + 20 - 1 = +8$$
$$F_3W_4: 20 - 2 + 5 - 20 = +3$$

Since the problem is to minimize costs, we select the cell having the most negative net cost to receive units in the reassignment (which is F_1W_1). For each unit assigned to F_1W_1 there will be a net shipping cost reduction or opportunity cost of $2/unit. We want to assign as many units to F_1W_1 as we can and still meet the equality conditions. By examining the units in the occupied cells along the path, which is $F_1W_1 \rightarrow F_2W_1 \rightarrow F_2W_4 \rightarrow F_1W_1$, we can see that a maximum of 100 units can be moved into F_1W_1. If 100 units are moved into F_1W_1 from F_2W_1, then a compensating 100 units must be moved from F_1W_4 to F_2W_4. This completes the first iteration, and the revised matrix is shown in Table A-5. The new total shipping cost will be $200 ($ − 2/unit × 100 units) less than the initial cost of $1300, for a reduced cost of $1100.

TABLE A-5

Revised matrix after the first iteration

Warehouses

Factories		W_1		W_2		W_3		W_4		Units Supplied
F_1	3	100	5		1	200	20	200	500
F_2	5		9		2		20	200	200
F_3	2	100	2	200	6		20		300
Units Demanded		200		200		200		400	1000

The iterative procedure described above is repeated until the opportunity costs for all unoccupied cells are positive or zero so that to allocate units to any cell with a positive opportunity cost will increase total costs rather than decrease them. The new set of opportunity costs are

$$F_1W_2 = 5 - 2 + 2 - 3 = +2$$
$$F_2W_1 = 5 - 20 + 20 - 3 = +2$$
$$F_2W_2 = 9 - 2 + 2 - 3 + 20 - 20 = +6$$
$$F_2W_3 = 2 - 20 + 20 - 1 = +1$$
$$F_3W_3 = 6 - 2 + 3 - 1 = +6$$
$$F_3W_4 = 20 - 2 + 3 - 20 = +1$$

Since all of the above opportunity costs are now positive, the optimum solution has been found with only one iteration. From the matrix in Table A-5, the optimum allocation would be to have F_1 serve W_1 with 100 units and W_3 with 200 units.

F_3 serves W_1 with 100 units and W_2 with 200 units. Note that F_2 serves none of the existing warehouses, which may raise questions in the minds of management as to the future of F_2 as a factory. Again, the optimum shipping cost is $1100.

Handling Degeneracy.   A common problem encountered in solving transportation problems is noted when a rook's tour cannot be completed for one or more of the unoccupied cells. This situation, called degeneracy, can be predicted when there are fewer than $m + n - 1$ occupied cells in the matrix, where m is the number of factories and n is the number of warehouses. What has happened is that one or more occupied cells has a value of zero, so that it cannot be distinguished from an unoccupied cell. Table A-6 illustrates a case of degeneracy within the context of the previous problem. For example, when one is attempting to find a rook's tour for $F_1 W_3$, the loop cannot be completed.

TABLE A-6
Illustration of degeneracy

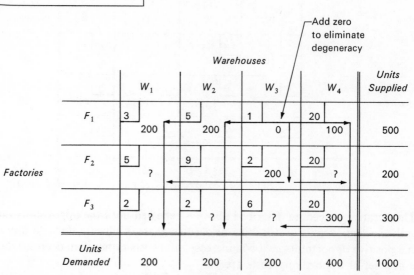

Degeneracy is easily resolved by creating enough occupied cells to equal $m + n$ -1. We merely add enough zeros to create the needed number of occupied cells and place them in the cells that will permit rook's tours for all unoccupied cells to be completed. Since, in this example, there are five occupied cells and six are needed, we need to add one zero. Experience has shown that we should consider adding the zero to low-cost cells, if possible. Inspection finds that by adding a zero to $F_1 W_3$ degeneracy can be eliminated. The solution procedure now proceeds in the normal fashion when $F_1 W_3$ is treated as an occupied cell. These zeros to eliminate degeneracy must be reallocated with each iteration.

THE MAXIMIZING PROBLEM

All discussion to this point has centered on the cost-minimizing problem. If the problem is one of maximizing the following:

$$\sum_{i=1}^{m} \sum_{j=1}^{n} C_{ij} X_{ij}$$

where C_{ij} is in terms of profit or other appropriate maximizing coefficient, the solution procedure requires only slight modification. When each unoccupied cell is evaluated, rather than choosing the most negative opportunity cost cell, we select the highest-opportunity profit cell as the one to receive reassigned units. All other operations in obtaining a solution are the same as before.

Appendix
B

Usemore Soap Company (A)[1]: A Warehouse Location Case Study

In 1968, Usemore Soap Company produced a line of cleaning compounds mainly for industrial and institutional use. Typical products included general cleaning compounds, dishwashing powders, rinse agents, hand soaps, motor vehicle washing compounds, and cleaning products for the food industry. The product line was composed of over 200 products and nearly 800 individual product items. Package sizes ranged from 18-lb cases to large metal drums weighing 550 lb.

Sales were generated throughout the continental United States, in Hawaii, and in Puerto Rico. The primary marketing effort came from a direct selling force operating under the incentive of a liberal sales commission structure. Salesmen

[1] Prepared with the assistance of Carl Kaminski.

This case is an abbreviation of a much larger problem that involved the company's warehouse configuration for the entire United States. The main features of the actual decision problem have been retained. Names, places, and costs have been disguised.

looked upon themselves as individual entrepreneurs and had a great deal of autonomy within the company. This marketing strategy had generally proved successful for the company, as it was often referred to as one of the more profitable divisions of its widely diversified parent company. Company-wide total revenues for 1968 were approximately $50 million, with 180 million pounds of product sold.

However, company management was becoming increasingly concerned about the costs for distributing the product line. Customer and salesman complaints about the frequency of out-of-stock in warehouses as well as increasing transportation and inventory costs led the company to question the efficiency of the physical distribution system. A comprehensive study of the physical distribution system was conducted. What follows is a replication of the warehouse location problem confronted, but in a more limited context so that the problem may be analyzed within a reasonable limit of analyst effort and computer time.

The Problem

The north central region of the United States, including Ohio, most of Indiana, and portions of Illinois, Michigan, Kentucky, and West Virginia, is a representative geographical segment of the larger, national problem (Fig. B-1). There are 205 counties with positive demand that is concentrated around population centers (Table B-1). Existing plants were located at Indianapolis, Indiana (grid coordinates $X = 7.7$, $Y = 4.4$) and Akron, Ohio (grid coordinates $X = 19.0$, $Y = 10.7$). The company's management had selected 23 public warehouse sites scattered throughout the region to be considered in the final warehouse configuration (Table B-2). Selections were made on the basis of salesman suggestions, favorable warehousing rates, good warehousing service, location within areas of demand concentration, space availability, and the tendency to "fill out" the distribution system. Management felt that the 23 potential sites were the maximum number that needed to be considered. It was expected that only a few of these sites would be retained, but management did not know which represented the most efficient and effective configuration. Specifically, answers to the following questions were sought:

(1) How many warehouses should be operated?
(2) Where should they be located?
(3) Which counties and their associated demands should be assigned to each warehouse and plant?
(4) Which warehouses should be supplied from each plant?
(5) Should production capacity be expanded? When, where, and how much?

SALES DATA

Usemore was one of the leading producers of industrial cleaning compounds in the United States. However, the manufacturing of soap was an easily duplicated and noncomplicated process, which contributed to severe competition in the market

FIGURE B-1

County demand (000's of lb) with the location of plants (△) and potential warehouses (●) in Usemore's north central sales region

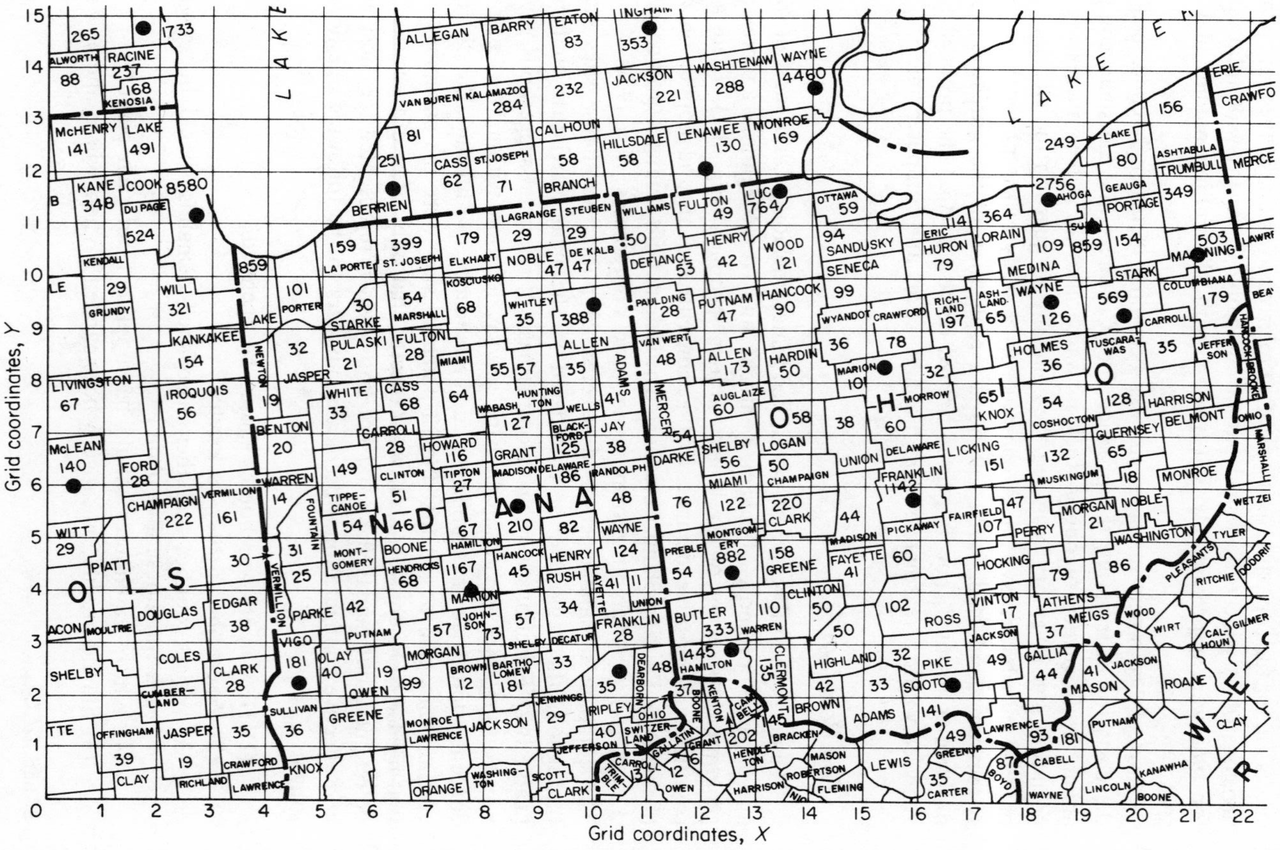

List of grid coordinates, annual demand, and county location of the 205 demand centers of Usemore's north central sales region

Grid Coordinates		County	County
X	Y	Demand	Location
2.00	5.10	221520.	CHAMPAIGN, ILL.
3.30	2.30	27676.	CLARK, ILL.
2.50	11.1	8580272.	COOK, ILL.
3.50	1.30	34709.	CRAWFORD, ILL.
0.20	5.10	28858.	DE WITT, ILL.
1.70	11.1	524309.	DUPAGE, ILL.
3.30	3.60	37718.	EDGAR, ILL.
1.40	1.30	38650.	EFFINGHAM, ILL.
1.80	6.40	27776.	FORD, ILL.
2.90	7.30	56138.	IROQUOIS, ILL.
2.50	1.20	18978.	JASPER, ILL.
1.00	11.4	348324.	KANE, ILL.
2.70	8.70	153990.	KANKAKEE, ILL.
1.10	10.2	29338.	KENDALL, ILL.
1.90	12.8	491186.	LAKE, ILL.
0.90	7.80	67477.	LIVINGSTON, ILL.
0.80	12.8	140854.	MCHENRY, ILL.
0.40	6.30	140297.	MCLEAN, ILL.
3.20	5.30	160869.	VERMILION, ILL.
2.10	9.70	320510.	WILL, ILL.
10.40	8.20	41219.	ADAMS, IND.
10.00	9.40	388384.	ALLEN, IND.
8.50	2.50	180619.	BARTHOLOMEW, IND.
4.20	6.80	19925.	BENTON, IND.
9.60	7.00	124742.	BLACKFORD, IND.
6.60	5.20	46070.	BOONE, IND.
7.70	2.30	11749.	BROWN, IND.
6.20	6.90	28325.	CARROLL, IND.
6.70	7.80	68464.	CASS, IND.
5.20	2.70	40490.	CLAY, IND.
6.60	6.10	51459.	CLINTON, IND.
11.00	2.60	47962.	DEARBORN, IND.
9.40	2.90	33485.	DECATUR, IND.
10.00	10.3	47288.	DEKALB, IND.
9.50	6.20	185561.	DELAWARE, IND.
7.70	10.8	178623.	ELKHART, IND.
10.20	4.10	40903.	FAYETTE, IND.
4.70	5.20	31289.	FOUNTAIN, IND.
10.70	3.30	28460.	FRANKLIN, IND.
6.70	8.80	28363.	FULTON, IND.
8.7	7.0	126689.	GRANT, IND.
7.8	5.5	67127.	HAMILTON, IND.
8.6	4.6	44601.	HANCOCK, IND.
6.7	4.2	68405.	HENDRICKS, IND.
6.6	5.1	81791.	HENRY, IND.

Grid Coordinates		County Demand	County Location
X	Y		
7.5	6.7	116265.	HOWARD, IND.
9.0	8.2	56559.	HUNTINGTON, IND.
4.5	8.5	31516.	JASPER, IND.
10.3	7.0	37755.	JAY, IND.
9.8	1.2	40246.	JEFFERSON, IND.
9.3	1.8	28882.	JENNINGS, IND.
7.9	3.3	73102.	JOHNSON, IND.
7.8	9.6	67530.	KOSCIUSKO, IND.
8.9	11.2	29071.	LAGRANGE, IND.
3.80	9.80	858523.	LAKE, IND.
5.50	10.4	159088.	LAPORTE, IND.
8.6	5.8	210452.	MADISON, IND.
7.7	4.4	1166790.	MARION, IND.
6.7	9.7	54266.	MARSHALL, IND.
7.4	7.8	63561.	MIAMI, IND.
6.8	2.1	99063.	MONROE, IND.
5.60	5.10	53674.	MONTGOMERY, IND.
6.90	3.20	56661.	MORGAN, IND.
3.80	8.10	19239.	NEWTON, IND.
9.10	10.3	47105.	NOBLE, IND.
11.10	1.80	6967.	OHIO, IND.
6.00	2.50	19068.	OWEN, IND.
4.80	4.00	24762.	PARKE, IND.
4.60	10.0	100826.	PORTER, IND.
5.80	8.60	21472.	PULASKI, IND.
5.80	3.70	41694.	PUTNAM, IND.
10.50	6.20	47560.	RANDOLPH, IND.
10.20	2.20	34525.	RIPLEY, IND.
9.60	4.00	34110.	RUSH, IND.
6.50	10.7	399119.	ST. JOSEPH, IND.
8.80	3.60	57026.	SHELBY, IND.
5.80	9.50	29959.	STARKE, IND.
9.80	11.3	28743.	STEUBEN, IND.
4.60	1.60	36332.	SULLIVAN, IND.
10.90	1.40	11862.	SWITZERLAND, IND.
5.40	6.30	149071.	TIPPECANOE, IND.
7.60	6.30	26522.	TIPTON, IND.
10.90	4.20	10800.	UNION, IND.
4.10	4.10	29578.	VERMILLION, IND.
4.50	2.80	181413.	VIGO, IND.
8.10	8.20	54537.	WABASH, IND.
4.10	6.10	14293.	WARREN, IND.
10.60	5.10	123842.	WAYNE, IND.
9.80	8.00	35494.	WELLS, IND.
5.20	7.50	32966.	WHITE, IND.
8.90	9.40	35049.	WHITLEY, IND.
11.70	2.00	36698.	BOONE, KENT.
17.40	0.70	87251.	BOYD, KENT.
12.80	2.00	145192.	CAMPBELL, KENT.
10.80	0.80	13334.	CARROLL, KENT.
16.70	0.30	34820.	CARTER, KENT.

| Grid Coordinates | | County | County |
X	Y	Demand	Location
11.40	1.30	6468.	GALLATIN, KENT.
16.90	1.10	48905.	GREENUP, KENT.
12.20	1.90	201890.	KENTON, KENT.
6.10	11.8	250673.	BERRIEN, MICH.
9.60	12.2	58381.	BRANCH, MICH.
9.70	13.4	232262.	CALHOUN, MICH.
7.10	11.8	61775.	CASS, MICH.
9.90	14.7	83104.	EATON, MICH.
10.70	12.2	58111.	HILLSDALE, MICH.
11.00	14.8	353426.	INGHAM, MICH.
11.10	13.5	220781.	JACKSON, MICH.
8.10	13.3	283870.	KALAMAZOO, MICH.
12.10	12.4	130114.	LENAWEE, MICH.
13.50	12.7	169139.	MONROE, MICH.
8.20	12.0	70807.	ST. JOSEPH, MICH.
6.90	13.2	80948.	VAN BUREN, MICH.
12.70	13.8	288433.	WASHTENAW, MICH.
13.90	14.1	4459801.	WAYNE, MICH.
15.10	2.10	33423.	ADAMS, OH.
12.70	8.60	173440.	ALLEN, OH.
17.30	9.50	64851.	ASHLAND, OH.
20.80	13.1	155669.	ASHTABULA, OH.
18.60	4.20	78612.	ATHENS, OH.
12.20	7.70	60462.	AUGLAIZE, OH.
14.10	2.10	42114.	BROWN, OH.
11.90	3.70	332986.	BUTLER, OH.
20.50	9.00	34887.	CARROLL, OH.
13.70	6.40	49701.	CHAMPAIGN, OH.
13.80	5.70	219854.	CLARK, OH.
13.30	2.60	134699.	CLERMONT, OH.
13.90	3.80	50186.	CLINTON, OH.
21.20	9.80	178981.	COLUMBIANA, OH.
18.30	7.60	53900.	COSHOCTON, OH.
15.60	9.20	78239.	CRAWFORD, OH.
18.50	11.6	2756363.	CUYAHOGA, OH.
11.50	6.10	76293.	DARKE, OH.
11.40	10.3	52702.	DEFIANCE, OH.
15.70	7.10	60395.	DELAWARE, OH.
16.10	11.0	113741.	ERIE, OH.
16.90	5.50	106903.	FAIRFIELD, OH.
14.80	4.60	41440.	FAYETTE, OH.
15.80	6.20	1142361.	FRANKLIN, OH.
12.10	11.3	49011.	FULTON, OH.
18.20	2.50	43690.	GALLIA, OH.
19.80	12.0	79573.	GEAUGA, OH.
13.60	4.80	158304.	GREENE, OH.
19.60	7.00	64529.	GUERNSEY, OH.
12.20	2.80	1445378.	HAMILTON, OH.
13.60	9.50	89798.	HANCOCK, OH.
13.70	8.20	49566.	HARDIN, OH.
12.50	10.5	42472.	HENRY, OH.

Grid Coordinates		County	County
X	Y	Demand	Location
14.60	3.20	49705.	HIGHLAND, OH.
18.30	8.60	36114.	HOLMES, OH.
16.20	10.3	79160.	HURON, OH.
17.20	2.90	49129.	JACKSON, OH.
17.20	7.80	64912.	KNOX, OH.
19.40	12.8	248724.	LAKE, OH.
17.70	1.60	92729.	LAWRENCE, OH.
17.20	6.60	150944.	LICKING, OH.
13.60	7.20	58213.	LOGAN, OH.
17.30	11.0	363803.	LORAIN, OH.
13.30	11.6	764289.	LUCAS, OH.
14.80	5.70	44248.	MADISON, OH.
21.10	10.6	502600.	MAHONING, OH.
15.00	8.20	100729.	MARION, OH.
18.10	10.5	109250.	MEDINA, OH.
18.80	3.50	37064.	MEIGS, OH.
11.30	7.50	54460.	MERCER, OH.
12.60	5.90	121938.	MIAMI, OH.
12.60	4.90	881624.	MONTGOMERY, OH.
18.90	5.40	21321.	MORGAN, OH.
16.10	8.00	32458.	MORROW, OH.
18.60	6.50	132406.	MUSKINGUM, OH.
19.90	6.10	18369.	NOBLE, OH.
14.70	11.5	59083.	OTTAWA, OH.
11.20	9.40	28087.	PAULDING, OH.
17.90	5.60	46607.	PERRY, OH.
15.80	4.90	59973.	PICKAWAY, OH.
16.10	2.90	32416.	PIKE, OH.
19.80	10.9	153547.	PORTAGE, OH.
11.70	4.70	54358.	PREBLE, OH.
12.40	9.40	47388.	PUTNAM, OH.
16.70	9.10	196974.	RICHLAND, OH.
16.00	3.90	102392.	ROSS, OH.
14.80	10.8	94482.	SANDUSKY, OH.
16.30	2.20	140865.	SCIOTO, OH.
14.90	10.1	99232.	SENECA, OH.
12.70	6.80	56178.	SHELBY, OH.
19.60	9.70	569281.	STARK, OH.
19.00	10.7	859025.	SUMMIT, OH.
21.00	11.7	348793.	TRUMBULL, OH.
19.50	8.30	128442.	TUSCARAWAS, OH.
14.60	7.00	38225.	UNION, OH.
11.30	8.60	48239.	VAN WERT, OH.
17.70	3.80	17185.	VINTON, OH.
13.10	3.70	109912.	WARREN, OH.
19.90	4.80	86458.	WASHINGTON, OH.
18.20	9.50	126281.	WAYNE, OH.
11.00	11.1	50126.	WILLIAMS, OH.
13.60	10.7	121428.	WOOD, OH.
14.60	9.10	36210.	WYANDOT, OH.
22.20	10.7	188952.	LAWRENCE, PENN.

| Grid Coordinates | | County | County |
X	Y	Demand	Location
18.70	1.10	180985.	CABELL, WEST VIR.
19.00	2.20	40912.	MASON, WEST VIR.
1.80	13.7	168294.	KENOSHA, WIS.
1.70	15.2	1732941.	MILWAUKEE, WIS.
1.60	14.2	237151.	RACINE, WIS.
0.40	13.9	87594.	WALWORTH, WIS.
0.90	15.2	264696.	WAUKESHA, WIS.

TABLE B-2

List of grid coordinates and county locations of the 23 potential warehouse sites to be evaluated

---

| Whse. No. | Grid Coordinates | | County Location | Dominant City |
	X	Y		
1	1.7	15.2	MILWAUKEE, WIS.	Milwaukee, Wis.
2	2.5	11.2	COOK, ILL.	Chicago, Ill.
3	0.4	6.3	MCLEAN, ILL.	Bloomington, Ill.
4	6.1	11.8	BERRIEN, MICH.	Benton Harbor, Mich.
5	11.0	14.8	INGHAM, MICH.	Lansing, Mich.
6	13.9	14.1	WAYNE, MICH.	Detroit, Mich.
7	12.1	12.4	LENAWEE, MICH.	Adrian, Mich.
8	10.0	9.4	ALLEN, IND.	Ft. Wayne, Ind.
9	8.6	5.8	MADISON, IND.	Anderson, Ind.
10	7.7	4.4	MARION, IND.	Indianapolis, Ind.
11	4.5	2.8	VIGO, IND.	Terre Haute, Ind.
12	10.2	2.2	RIPLEY, IND.	Versailles, Ind.
13	13.3	11.7	LUCAS, OH.	Toledo, Ohio
14	18.5	11.6	CUYAHOGA, OH.	Cleveland, Ohio
15	18.9	10.7	SUMMIT, OH.	Akron, Ohio
16	21.2	10.6	MAHONING, OH.	Youngstown, Ohio
17	19.6	9.7	STARK, OH.	Canton, Ohio
18	18.2	9.5	WAYNE, OH.	Wooster, Ohio
19	15.0	8.2	MARION, OH.	Marion, Ohio
20	15.8	6.1	FRANKLIN, OH.	Columbus, Ohio
21	12.6	4.9	MONTGOMERY, OH.	Dayton, Ohio
22	16.3	2.2	SCIOTO, OH.	Portsmouth, Ohio
23	12.2	2.8	HAMILTON, OH.	Cincinnati, Ohio

place. The undifferentiated nature of soap products resulted in keen competition in both price and service. Customer service was of particular concern, since it was a variable directly affected by the choice of a warehouse configuration. No specific dollar figure could be placed on the total value of good distribution service, because it depended on customers' attitudes about service and their resulting patronage. The general feeling was that service should be maintained at a high level so as not to jeopardize sales. A "high" level of service was taken to mean 24-hour delivery time or less.

In 1968, sales in the north central region were slightly over $11 million on 44,435,987 pounds of cleaning compounds sold. The average selling price per pound was $0.25, of which $0.05 per pound was gross profit. Approximately 15 percent of the sales dollar went for physical distribution costs.

DISTRIBUTION

After a sale was made, product normally was shipped from a public warehouse, a local cartage company being used for local deliveries made within approximately a 30-mile radius of the warehouse. Deliveries beyond 30 miles were made by common carrier trucking, as generally were restocking shipments to warehouses. Usemore had no significant investment in distribution facilities. Public warehouses were used, which allowed a high degree of flexibility in changing the warehouse configuration. The exception was at Indianapolis, Indiana, and Akron, Ohio, where portions of the plant facilities functioned as warehouses to serve the immediate demand area and to maintain inventories for replenishing warehouse stocks.

INVENTORY COSTS

Storage rates at public warehouses were negotiated. Rate data for the presently used public warehouses were obtained from existing company contracts. Rates for warehouse services not currently used were estimated after inquiries of potential warehouses were made, but without serious negotiation with public warehouse management taking place.

Warehousing rates were composed of two costs, one for storage and one for handling. Storage rates were generally quoted on a $/cwt/month basis, but for convenience these have been adjusted to a $/lb/month basis. Handling charges are incurred whenever in or out movement of the product occurs, and again these charges are converted to a $/lb/month basis to match the demand units. Local cartage company rates, which were also negotiated, represented an average $/lb charge for an average distance and an average shipment size. Table B-3 lists these charges for the 23 potential warehouse sites.

In addition to the above charges there were expenses incurred in the processing of stock orders to replenish warehouse inventories and in the processing of customer orders. These vary by warehouse and are also shown in Table B-3.

Charges for insurance on inventory value, tax on inventory value, and cost of capital tied up in inventories were treated as invariant with the number, location, or size of warehouses. These costs were taken to be $0.007/lb/yr, $0.0023/lb/yr, and 10%/yr, respectively. The value of a pound of product in a warehouse was $0.11/lb. The average amount of inventory in a warehouse was estimated as 100,000 lb plus 0.15 times the annual demand flowing through the warehouse.

When an order could not be filled through a warehouse due to an out-of-stock condition, the order was "split." The portion of the order that could be filled from warehouse stock was delivered to the customer in the normal way. The remainder of the order was filled from stocks maintained at the plants. Split-order delivery was direct from the plant to the customer. Split orders were expensive because (1)

TABLE B-3

List of storage, handling, order-processing, and local delivery expenses that vary by warehouse

Whse. No.	Storage (c/lb-yr)	Handling ($/lb)	Stock Order Processing ($/order)	Stock Order Size (lb)	Customer Order Processing ($/order)	Customer Order Size (lb/order)	Local Delivery Rates ($/lb)
01	.0144	.0017	30.00	57600	3.86	637	.0043
02	.0120	.0020	30.00	33200	4.16	637	.0082
03	.0132	.0019	30.00	40200	4.06	637	.0057
04	.0108	.0022	30.00	76000	3.96	767	.0057
05	.0156	.0007	30.00	27300	3.81	637	.0038
06	.0120	.0022	30.00	76000	3.96	767	.0063
07	.0108	.0031	30.00	58000	4.41	637	.0053
08	.0084	.0015	30.00	34000	3.66	637	.0057
09	.0108	.0024	30.00	76900	3.86	637	.0053
10	.0108	.0015	30.00	39200	3.81	637	.0057
11	.0084	.0011	30.00	31600	3.81	637	.0057
12	.0120	.0018	30.00	43700	4.06	637	.0057
13	.0144	.0020	30.00	76000	4.01	767	.0045
14	.0120	0019	30.00	42700	3.76	637	.0050
15	.0228	.0021	30.00	44300	3.96	637	.0081
16	.0120	.0018	30.00	41000	3.96	637	.0060
17	.0108	.0019	30.00	42400	3.81	637	.0060
18	.0060	.0015	30.00	32100	3.46	637	.0050
19	.0112	.0008	30.00	38800	3.81	637	.0057
20	.0132	.0018	30.00	43500	3.96	637	.0057
21	.0108	.0020	30.00	39000	3.96	637	.0039
22	.0120	.0020	30.00	29400	3.46	637	.0057
23	.0130	.0015	30.00	68000	3.50	637	.0055

small shipment sizes were shipped over long distances under LTL rates and rate minimums, (2) additional order-processing costs were incurred due to the extra order handling, and (3) an intangible lost sales cost was incurred due to reduced service. The total split shipment cost depends on the level of inventory maintained at a warehouse. The split shipment cost increases at a decreasing rate with the annual demand on warehouse inventory and can be estimated by

$$\text{Split shipment cost (\$/whse)} = 10(\text{demand per warehouse})^{0.5}$$

Inventory Cost Function. The inventory cost per warehouse was approximated by combining the various inventory cost components in the following way:

Inventory cost per warehouse
= [fixed inventory level + average variable inventory level × demand per whse] × [storage cost + tax + insurance + (cost of money × product value)] + handling cost × demand per whse + customer order-processing cost × (demand per whse/customer order size) + stock order-processing cost × (demand per whse/stock order size) + 10(demand per whse)$^{0.5}$ (B.1)

When the inventory costs per warehouse are summed for all warehouses and plotted as a function of the number of warehouses in the distribution system, a relationship of the type shown in Fig. B-2 results. Total inventory cost for all warehouses combined is lowest when inventories are consolidated into a few warehouses.

FIGURE B-2

Total system inventory costs as a function of the number of warehouses in the distribution system

---

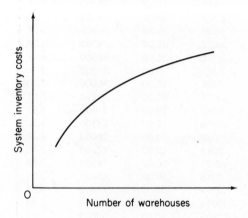

Inbound and Outbound Transportation Costs.   Warehouse inbound and outbound (beyond local delivery range) transportation costs were found to be reasonably linear with distance. After analyzing a number of point-to-point rates, the following transportation cost functions were developed. The plant-warehouse transportation cost function is

$$P - W \text{ cost (\$/lb)} = 0.0028 + 0.0000128 \cdot \text{(distance)} \tag{B.2}$$

The warehouse-to-customer transportation cost function is

$$W - C \text{ cost (\$/lb)} = 0.0157 + 0.000031 \cdot \text{(distance)} \tag{B.3}$$

Distance is in miles. Inbound costs are lower than outbound costs, reflecting the TL quantities moving to warehouses versus the LTL quantities moving from warehouses. Volume shipments moving directly to customers from plants have been removed from the warehouse location problem.

PRODUCTION DATA

All current product demand was met by the existing plants. The Indianapolis plant had an average variable production cost of $0.0842 per lb and a production capacity limit of 30,000,000 lb. Similarly, the Akron plant produced at a variable cost of $0.0807 per lb and had a capacity limit of 25,000,000 lb. Total production costs were approximately $0.10 per lb, of which 80 percent was for raw materials, 10 percent for labor, and 10 percent for overhead. Sales were increasing at the rate of 10 percent per year, which in a few years would force the plants to their capacity limits. Additional capacity could be obtained at a cost of $0.20 per lb, and the production costs would be approximately $0.09 per lb including overhead, or about $0.08 if only variable costs were considered.

Computer-assisted Analysis

To aid in analyzing various warehouse configurations, a simulation model written in FORTRAN IV and designed for use on time-sharing computing equipment[2] accompanies this problem. The analyst specifies the plant capacities in pounds, the level of customer service desired in terms of the maximum delivery distance from warehouses to customers, and the warehouses to be analyzed. The program then computes on the basis of transportation costs the best allocation of the 205 counties with demand to the specified warehouses and the best allocation of warehouses to plants, given the desired customer service level. Linear programming is used to make the allocations in an optimal way. Based on these allocations and the total demand assigned to each warehouse, inventory costs are computed. Similarly, production costs are determined. A representative report of the program's output is shown in Tables, B-4–B-6.

RUNNING THE PROGRAM

The program is stored in the computer's memory under the name of WARE-LOCA and in the FORTRAN language. After the initializing control procedure is completed, the computer will ask for the capacities of each plant. These are typed in from the terminal. Following this is another question asking the maximum warehouse-to-county distances as a measure of customer service. The distance in miles is typed in from the terminal. Next, a master list of the 23 potential warehouse sites is printed, from which the analyst makes a selection of the warehouse configuration to be analyzed by the program. The subsequent two questions ask for the number of warehouses and their identifying numbers to be typed in from the terminal. An echo check of the warehouses to be analyzed follows this input. Table B-4 shows these initial questions and output.

At the end of the summary of analysis given in Table B-5, two additional questions are typed. The first asks whether a list of the allocations of all 205 counties is desired. Typing the numeral 1 on the terminal will give the type of list shown in Table B-6. This list is lengthy and probably would be requested for only the

---

[2] The General Electric MARK II system was used initially. Other time-sharing systems may be used with minor program alterations if the system uses a high-grade FORTRAN language.

TABLE B-4

Example of initial data, master list of warehouse locations, and list of warehouse locations to be analyzed by WARELOCA

CAPACITY LIMIT ON INDIANAPOLIS AND AKRON PLANTS= ?30000000,25000000
DESIRED MAXIMUM DELIVERY DISTANCE IN MILES= ?200

MASTER LIST OF POTENTIAL WAREHOUSE SITES

NO.	X	Y	LOCATION
1	1.7	15.2	MILWAUKEE, WIS.
2	2.5	11.2	COOK, ILL.
3	0.4	6.3	MCLEAN, ILL.
4	6.1	11.8	BERRIEN, MICH.
5	11.0	14.8	INGHAM, MICH.
6	13.9	14.1	WAYNE, MICH.
7	12.1	12.4	LENAWEE, MICH.
8	10.0	9.4	ALLEN, IND.
9	8.6	5.8	MADISON, IND.
10	7.7	4.4	MARION, IND.
11	4.5	2.8	VIGO, IND.
12	10.2	2.2	RIPLEY, IND.
13	13.3	11.7	LUCAS, OH.
14	18.5	11.6	CUYAHOGA, OH.
15	18.9	10.7	SUMMIT, OH.
16	21.2	10.6	MAHONING, OH.
17	19.6	9.7	STARK, OH.
18	18.2	9.5	WAYNE, OH.
19	15.0	8.2	MARION, OH.
20	15.8	6.1	FRANKLIN, OH.
21	12.6	4.9	MONTGOMERY, OH.
22	16.3	2.2	SCIOTO, OH.
23	12.2	2.8	HAMILTON, OH.

NUMBER OF WAREHOUSES TO BE ANALYZED= ?2
THEIR NUMBERS ARE?2,23

LIST OF WHSES TO BE ANALYZED

NO.	X	Y	LOCATION
1	2.5	11.2	COOK, ILL.
2	12.2	2.8	HAMILTON, OH.

warehouse configuration that is finally decided upon. The final question asks if the analyst would like to examine another warehouse configuration. A typed 1 returns to the point in the program just following the master list of warehouses. A typed 0 (zero) will terminate the program.

SUMMARY OF ANALYSIS

Tables B-5 and B-6 show a summary of the results of the analysis by the computer program. The summary provides four types of information useful for decision

```
                                                      TABLE B-5
  Example of the summary of costs and customer service from WARELOCA
```

**SUMMARY OF ANALYSIS FOR
2 POTENTIAL WAREHOUSE LOCATIONS**

    SYSTEM COSTS

PRODUCTION COSTS	$	3654010.
INVENTORY COSTS		686498.
TRANSPORTATION COSTS		1017123.
TOTAL SYSTEM COSTS	$	5357631.

CUSTOMER SERVICE

DISTANCE WHSE TO CUSTOMER (MILES)	PCT OF COUNTIES	PCT OF DEMAND
0 TO 50	12.1	30.1
50 TO 100	21.8	12.5
100 TO 150	30.1	13.9
150 TO 200	21.4	6.9
200 TO 250	9.7	14.7
> 250	4.9	22.0

PLANT LOADINGS AND COSTS

PLANT	LOADINGS	PRODUCTION COSTS
INDIANAPOLIS, IND.	19435987.	1636510.
AKRON, OH.	25000000.	2017500.
TOTALS	44435987.	3654010.

WAREHOUSE LOADINGS AND COSTS

WAREHOUSE	LOADINGS	WAREHOUSING COSTS
COOK, ILL.	18220715.	306093.
HAMILTON, OH.	26215272.	380405.
TOTALS	44435987.	686498.

IS A LIST OF DEMAND ASSIGNMENTS TO WAREHOUSES AND
PLANTS DESIRED (YES=1,NO=0)??0
IS ANOTHER ITERATION DESIRED (YES=1,NO=0)??0

making: (1) a summary of the total costs for a given warehouse configuration, (2) a measure of customer service, (3) a breakdown of the plant and warehouse throughputs with individual cost summaries, and (4) the allocation of demand to warehouses and to plants.

Total System Costs. The decision to locate warehouses affects three important costs: (1) production costs, (2) inventory costs, and (3) transportation costs. As the number of warehouses and their locations change, the tradeoffs between these costs also change. For example, increasing the number of warehouses generally lowers total transportation costs but at the same time increases inventory costs. Production costs are also affected, as different plant loadings result from different

---

TABLE B-6

A partial list of the type of demand assignments to warehouses
and plants obtained from WARELOCA

DEMAND ASSIGNMENTS TO WAREHOUSES AND PLANTS

	DEMAND	WAREHOUSE	PLANT
1	CHAMPAIGN, ILL.	COOK, ILL.	INDIANAPOLIS, IND.
2	CLARK, ILL.	HAMILTON, OH.	AKRON, OH.
3	COOK, ILL.	COOK, ILL.	INDIANAPOLIS, IND.
4	CRAWFORD, ILL.	HAMILTON, OH.	AKRON, OH.
5	DE WITT, ILL.	COOK, ILL.	INDIANAPOLIS, IND.
6	DUPAGE, ILL.	COOK, ILL.	INDIANAPOLIS, IND.
7	EDGAR, ILL.	COOK, ILL.	INDIANAPOLIS, IND.
8	EFFINGHAM, ILL.	COOK, ILL.	INDIANAPOLIS, IND.
9	FORD, ILL.	COOK, ILL.	INDIANAPOLIS, IND.
10	IROQUOIS, ILL.	COOK, ILL.	INDIANAPOLIS, IND.
11	JASPER, ILL.	HAMILTON, OH.	AKRON, OH.
12	KANE, ILL.	COOK, ILL.	INDIANAPOLIS, IND.
13	KANKAKEE, ILL.	COOK, ILL.	INDIANAPOLIS, IND.
14	KENDALL, ILL.	COOK, ILL.	INDIANAPOLIS, IND.
15	LAKE, ILL.	COOK, ILL.	INDIANAPOLIS, IND.
16	LIVINGSTON, ILL.	COOK, ILL.	INDIANAPOLIS, IND.
17	MCHENRY, ILL.	COOK, ILL.	INDIANAPOLIS, IND.
18	MCLEAN, ILL.	COOK, ILL.	INDIANAPOLIS, IND.
19	VERMILION, ILL.	COOK, ILL.	INDIANAPOLIS, IND.
20	WILL, ILL.	COOK, ILL.	INDIANAPOLIS, IND.
21	ADAMS, IND.	HAMILTON, OH.	AKRON, OH.
22	ALLEN, IND.	HAMILTON, OH.	AKRON, OH.
23	BARTHOLOMEW, IND.	HAMILTON, OH.	AKRON, OH.
24	BENTON, IND.	COOK, ILL.	INDIANAPOLIS, IND.
25	BLACKFORD, IND.	HAMILTON, OH.	AKRON, OH.
26	BOONE, IND.	HAMILTON, OH.	AKRON, OH.
27	BROWN, IND.	HAMILTON, OH.	AKRON, OH.
28	CARROLL, IND.	COOK, ILL.	INDIANAPOLIS, IND.
29	CASS, IND.	COOK, ILL.	INDIANAPOLIS, IND.
30	CLAY, IND.	HAMILTON, OH.	AKRON, OH.
31	CLINTON, IND.	HAMILTON, OH.	AKRON, OH.
32	DEARBORN, IND.	HAMILTON, OH.	AKRON, OH.
33	DECATUR, IND	HAMILTON, OH.	AKRON, OH.
34	DEKALB, IND.	HAMILTON, OH.	AKRON, OH.
35	DELAWARE, IND.	HAMILTON, OH.	AKRON, OH.
36	ELKHART, IND.	COOK, ILL.	INDIANAPOLIS, IND.
37	FAYETTE, IND.	HAMILTON, OH.	AKRON, OH.
38	FOUNTAIN, IND.	HAMILTON, OH.	AKRON, OH.
39	FRANKLIN, IND.	HAMILTON, OH.	AKRON, OH.
40	FULTON, IND.	COOK, ILL.	INDIANAPOLIS, IND.
41	GRANT, IND.	HAMILTON, OH.	AKRON, OH.
42	HAMILTON, IND.	HAMILTON, OH.	AKRON, OH.
43	HANCOCK, IND.	HAMILTON, OH.	AKRON, OH.
44	HENDRICKS, IND.	HAMILTON, OH.	AKRON, OH.
45	HENRY, IND.	HAMILTON, OH.	AKRON, OH.

warehouse configurations. Thus, the combined or total system cost becomes the key to warehouse configuration improvement.

Customer Service. The level of customer service provided by a distribution system depends on a number of factors, including order-processing time and variability, stock availability, and delivery time and variability. Though all of these factors are affected by warehouse configuration, for a given transportation service, delivery time is the most directly influenced. After the program makes its allocation of demand to plants and warehouses on the basis of minimum transportation costs within the constraints of the maximum delivery distance and plant capacities that were typed into the program, the actual distances from warehouses to customers is summarized. When only a few warehouses are being analyzed, it is possible that a maximum delivery distance constraint cannot be met for all counties. When this occurs, the *minimum-transportation-cost warehouse* is selected to serve the county, which usually is the closest warehouse. However, at times this decision rule can result in a slight deterioration in customer service when a few warehouses are being analyzed and the desired maximum delivery distance is decreased.

Facility Loading and Costs. Plant and warehouse loadings are the demand assignments as determined on the basis of minimum transportation costs. Production costs are merely the individual plant loading multiplied by the variable production costs for the plant. The fixed portion of the production cost is not used, since it is invariant with the location decision. Warehousing or inventory costs are found by solving Equation (B.1) for each warehouse loading.

Demand Allocation. The final printed output is the demand assignments to warehouses and plants as shown in Table B-6. This listing gives the product flow through the distribution network.

Concluding Comments

WARELOCA is a vehicle for analyzing Usemore's warehouse location problem, but does not seek the "optimum" balance between all the costs involved. The program merely does some obvious computational work. Finding the warehouse configuration with the lowest system costs may not be the best decision if it is a poor tradeoff with customer service or an unwise decision in light of future plant capacity needs. A viable solution to this problem should be supported by more than the lowest total system cost.

Appendix
C

Usemore Soap Company (B)[1]: An Inventory Policy Case Study

The Usemore Soap Company purchased an electronic computer and installed a computerized inventory control system in the hope of improving stock availability and lowering distribution costs of more than 750 product items maintained at over 100 stocking points. The new system replaced a system whereby the sales-

---

[1] Prepared with the assistance of Carl Kaminski and Richard Peck. Names, places, and costs have been disguised.

This case is a continuation of the Usemore Soap Company (A) and should be referred to for further company background. The purpose is to provide some experience in dealing with the decision variables associated with the management of inventories. The actual inventory control situation that involved many product items and over 100 warehouses has been reduced to five products in one warehouse without loss in realism. The more limited problem does permit dealing with the issues of inventory management with a reasonable use of computer time and analyst effort.

men in the field controlled stock levels. Hopes for the new system were shattered when during the first year of operation inventories increased by $700,000 compared with a predicted decrease of $500,000. Management consulted with Distribution Networks, Inc., a management consulting group, in an attempt to improve the system. At the beginning of 1968, enthusiasm was once again running high; it was felt that the performance of the computerized inventory control system could be substantially improved.

SYSTEM OVERVIEW

A computerized inventory control system was designed to keep track of field inventories, make monthly forecasts of expected sales, compute desired warehouse inventory levels, call for replenishment of depleted warehouse stocks, and prepare a number of management reports. These activities were mostly performed by the computer. The entire inventory control system is shown in Fig. C-1 and includes the effect of both information and product flow delays. The operation of the system is as follows. Customer orders are prepared and transmitted to the Atlanta, Ga. warehouse by a salesman. A bill of lading is prepared, and the orders are filled from warehouse stock, if available. Warehouse out-of-stock items are shipped directly from the plant. From the warehouse, the bill of lading and the order are sent by mail to the billing department at Akron, Ohio. After invoicing, the billing department forwards the order to the computer for inventory updating. When the accumulated deficit between the product target inventory levels and the product record levels equals or exceeds the reorder quantity (called the shipping weight), a stock order is released, and the contents of the order are posted in the inventory records as "on order." The stock order is reviewed by management for possible modifications and then electronically transmitted to the plant at Akron, Ohio. If the stock order is maintained in plant inventories, it is shipped to the warehouse from stock. If not, it must be produced and then sent to the warehouse. There is a 0.7 probability that the order will be in stock. When deliveries are made from the plant, the computer is notified and the records are updated to show "intransit." Upon receipt of the stock order, warehouse personnel prepare a warehouse receipt and mail it to headquarters. The computer then transfers "intransit" to "balance-on-hand" stocks.

SYSTEM DELAYS

Time required for transmittal and processing of order data as well as production and delivery of the order caused a number of information delays throughout the system. Fig. C-1 shows where each type of delay occurs in the system. The distributions of delays are approximately normal, and each type with its observed average, minimum, and maximum in days is listed on the following page:

Type of Delay	Min.	Avg.	Max.
1. Salesman order transmission and bill of lading preparation	0	1	2
2. Transmission of order to headquarters	2	4	6
3. Invoice preparation and computer update	3	5	7
Computer update alone	0.5	1	1.5
4. Stock order review and transmission	0	1	2
5. Production time	2	7	12
Order is filled from plant stock	1	2	3
6. Stock order delivery to warehouse by truck	2	3	4
7. Stock order receipt transmission from warehouse to computer	2	4	6

DEMAND

As many as 750 product items might be stocked at a single warehouse. Each has its own demand characteristics and would individually be forecasted. Five products have been selected that represent the range of demand characteristics to be expected. The first is UBARS. UBARS is a hand soap in bars that has been in the product mix since the inception of the firm. The company does not actively promote the product, yet sales continue at a constant rate from year to year.

The second product is RINSE-EZ, which is a wetting agent used in commercial dishwashing applications. This product has enjoyed steadily increasing sales from year to year. Much of the growth was attributed to the equipment policy of the company. When a customer agreed to use RINSE-EZ, Usemore would provide and maintain dispensing equipment to introduce the product into the rinse cycle of the dishwasher. Though this was expensive promotion, it did permit a tapping of the market segment that did not have dispensing equipment on their dishwashers and that would not otherwise use the Usemore product.

DAN-DE is a concentrated liquid cleaner used for cleaning vehicles. Sales of this product roughly followed the seasons of the year. Sales would peak during the summer months and be at a low point during winter months. No appreciable growth rate had been noted in this product for some time.

In addition to soap products, Usemore produced a number of specialty items. One such item is TR-70, which is a greaseless lubricant for use in food-processing equipment. This product had a limited market, and sales tended to have a wide variation over time.

The final selected product is TRI-X. TRI-X is a specially formulated window cleaner for industrial and institutional use. Sales for this product have been growing dramatically since its introduction last year due to active promotion and general acceptance of the product in the market place. The sales pattern shows seasonal characteristics, since more window cleaner is sold during the warm months than during cold ones.

Table C-1 shows the sales by month for these five products for calendar year 1967.

FIGURE C-1

Schematic diagram of Usemore's computerized inventory control system

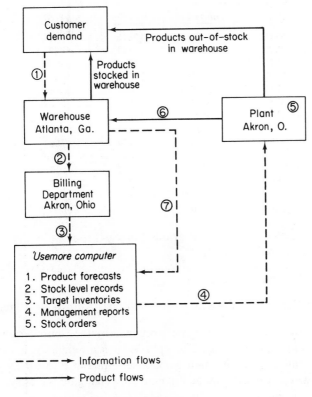

—————→ Information flows

————————→ Product flows

System delays

① Salesman order transmission and bill of lading preparation
② Transmission of order to headquarters
③ Invoice preparation and computer update
④ Stock order review and transmission
⑤ Production time
⑥ Stock order delivery to warehouse
⑦ Stock order receipt transmission from warehouse to computer

FORECASTING

In the design of the new computerized inventory control system, an exponential smoothing model was used to predict the monthly demand for all products by warehouse. The general forecasting model is

Forecast = Alpha(Actual Sales) + (1 — Alpha)(Previous Forecast)

TABLE C-1

Monthly sales for five product items in the Atlanta warehouse territory for 1967 in pounds

	Ubars	Rinse-Ez	Dan-De	Tr-70	Tri-X
Jan.	4118	8823	10878	43133	796
Feb.	3923	8857	11931	42921	2604
Mar.	4023	9054	18663	33199	11930
Apr.	3909	9200	22907	43013	20405
May	4018	9270	25842	51866	26126
Ju.	3865	9316	28637	47127	30680
Jly.	4152	9416	29981	31997	28226
Aug.	4081	9449	27234	38081	27003
Sept.	4077	9563	22184	47557	21842
Oct.	4137	9760	16470	40275	14408
Nov.	4042	10016	14117	41061	6485
Dec.	3963	9854	10785	36828	3321

Correcting for trend, we have

New Trend = Alpha(Forecast − Previous Forecast) + (1 − Alpha)
· (Previous Trend)

Final forecast with trend correction:

Corrected Forecast = Forecast + [(1 − Alpha)/Alpha] · New Trend

Previous forecasts and trend values were retained by the computer and used as a basis for developing new forecasts. The alpha value is a weighting factor that can range between 0 and 1. Usemore management set alpha at 0.15 for all products. However, there was a provision made for manually changing the alpha value for all or any of the products.

A similiar model was used to predict the variation that could occur in demand and to use this as a basis for determining safety stock levels. That is, the forecasted error in demand was determined as follows:

Absolute Error = | Actual Demand − Previous Forecast |

The forecast of the average error or mean absolute deviation (MAD) then is

New MAD = Alpha(Absolute Error) + (1 − Alpha)(Previous MAD)

Each item in a warehouse is forecasted every 30 days.

Inventory Control System Design

The inventory control system that Usemore used was a blend of fixed order quantity, variable order interval and variable order quantity, fixed order interval systems. For example, when the difference between a target maximum inventory level (MAX LEVEL) and the actual stock level for an item in the warehouse accumulated for all warehouse items to a target weight (SHIPPING WEIGHT), a replenishment order was released and transmitted to the plant. A schematic of the operating characteristics of the system for one product item is shown in Fig. C-2.

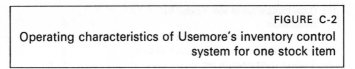

FIGURE C-2
Operating characteristics of Usemore's inventory control system for one stock item

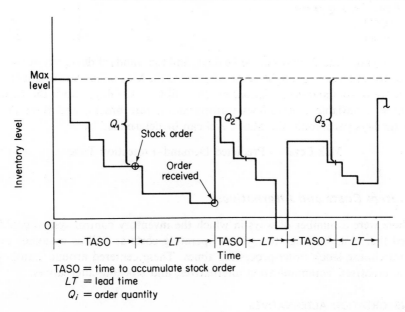

TASO = time to accumulate stock order
LT = lead time
Q_i = order quantity

Setting the MAX LEVEL for each item was done monthly at the time of the forecast and was developed from projections of item demand and lead time. The MAX LEVEL should be set high enough to provide stock for demand occurring during the time required to accumulate a stock order plus the time required to receive a stock order (lead time) plus any safety stock needed to protect against variation in demand and lead time. MAX LEVEL is developed in two parts. First, monthly demand plus its variation is projected from the monthly sales forecast and the monthly MAD projection. That is,

Predicted Demand = Corrected Forecast + Service Level · MAD

Second, the length of time over which to provide protection needed to be determined. Protection time in months was given by

Protection Time = [(Lead Time + Service Level × Lead Time Standard
Deviation)/No. of Working Days per Month] +
[Shipping Weight/Monthly Demand All Items]

The average lead time and the lead time standard deviation were determined from the effects of the various lead time components. For example, consider a set of lead time delay values.

Delay	Min.	Avg.	Max.
(1) Order transmittal to warehouse, B/L preparation	0	1	2
(2) Order transmission to headquarters	2	4	6
(3) Invoice preparation and computer update	3	5	7
(4) Processing of stock order	0	1	2
(5) Production of stock order	2	7	12
(6) Transit time	2	3	4
Totals	6	16	26

The average lead time would be 16 days, and the standard deviation of the lead time distribution can be roughly approximated as the Max minus Min delays divided by a range of six standard deviations or $(26 - 6)/6 = 3.33$ days.[2] Since the shipping weight is a variable that follows transportation rate breaks, and there are 20 working days per month, the Max Level can be determined by

$$\text{Max Level} = \text{Predicted Demand} \cdot \text{Protection Time}$$

System Costs and Alternatives

There were a number of ways in which the inventory control system could be altered that would change the system operating costs as well as customer order and warehouse stock order-processing times. These centered around transportation alternatives, communication alternatives, and stocking alternatives.

TRANSPORTATION ALTERNATIVES

Three transportation modes were considered feasible. These were truck, piggyback, and rail. Truck was the most frequently used transportation mode for delivery of stock orders to the Atlanta warehouse. However, since the throughput was increasing through the warehouse as Usemore products were gaining acceptance in the territory, the lower rates that piggyback and rail offered became more attractive. Usemore used the services of common carriers and the rates and delivery times experienced are summarized below:

Service	Volume, cwt	Rate, $/cwt	Delivery Time, Days		
			Min.	Avg.	Max.
Truck	<320	2.25	2	4	6
	≥320	1.28	2	3	4
Piggyback	≥360	1.08	3	5	7
Rail	700	0.67	8	12	16
	In excess of 700	0.55			
Rail	≥600	0.75	8	12	16

[2] The student should consider the possible error introduced into the system by estimating the standard deviation in this simple but crude manner.

While the rail rates were attractive, the traffic department had noticed an increase in damaged merchandise when rail was used. Piggyback did not show a significant increase in damage over truck deliveries.

Transportation from warehouse to customer was handled by a local cartage company at a rate of 50¢/cwt.

COMMUNICATION ALTERNATIVES

The communication delays in the current order-processing system have already been noted in Fig. C-1. However, management had entertained the idea of installing a teletypewriter at the warehouse to speed order transmittal. This would virtually drop the order transmittal time from the warehouse to headquarters to zero, but such a device would lease for approximately $80 per month. Such equipment was already in use for stock order transmission between headquarters and the plants.

Compared with the current mail transmission, additional costs would include tape preparation costs and the cost of the long-distance telephone calls.

Other transmission devices were possible such as Telex, WATS line, or the long-distance telephone. Although all were feasible, the costs of these alternatives had not been explored.

Customer order-processing costs averaged $3.00 per order, an average customer order being 600 pounds. Stock orders cost $30 per order to process, and the average order size is 35,000 pounds.

STOCKING ALTERNATIVES

Stocking alternatives refer to the various levels of product inventories that can be achieved in the warehouse. These levels are affected by the values of the variables that can be manipulated, namely, shipping weight, alpha, and service level.

Shipping weight is the cumulated weight deficit of products in the warehouse to trigger a stock order. The shipping weight for the Atlanta warehouse is currently 32,000 pounds, which follows the truck rate break schedule. Other shipping weights can be used to take advantage of alternative transportation modes.

The alpha value in the forecasting model also influences warehouse stock levels. Low alpha values can create a sluggish forecasting model such that inventory levels lag actual demand, causing excessive stockouts or excessive inventory levels. High alpha values can create a "nervous" forecasting model. Since inventory levels are responsive to forecasts, a "nervous" forecasting model can cause costly overreactions in the form of inventory levels that are too high or too low to meet actual demand conditions.

The service level variable controls the amount of safety stock maintained in the warehouse. Low service level values are related to low safety stock levels. The service level used by Usemore was 0.98.

INVENTORY COSTS

Inventory costs were of two types. First, there was the cost of holding inventories in the public warehouse. This cost includes the costs for storage, handling, insurance, taxes, obsolescence, capital tied up in inventories, and stock rework. For the average inventory level, inventory costs were $3.10/cwt per year based on a product value in the warehouse of 11¢ per pound.

Second, there was the cost of being out of stock in the warehouse. When an order could not be completely filled from warehouse stock, the order was "split." The unfilled portion of the order was supplied from plant stocks. Processing the order outside of the normal warehouse-to-customer flow created additional costs that could be associated with not having sufficient stock levels in the warehouse. A conservative estimate of the split shipment costs was $11.60 per order, which included transportation, additional order processing at Akron, telephone, plant order processing, and an extra bill of lading. Based on an average order size of 600 pounds, the out-of-stock cost per pound would be $0.02. Not included were such intangible costs as salesman's time, customer dissatisfaction, and lost sales.

Computer-assisted Analysis

To aid the analysis of this case study, a simulation model[3] (INSIM) of the inventory control system is provided. The model permits testing different inventory system designs and examining the effect of various "what if" questions.

THE INPUTS

The inputs required to operate the simulation program are summarized in Table C-2. All data shown in Table C-2 represent the current inventory control system. A glossary of the individual input items is given below:

NO. OF YEARS TO TEST The number of years the simulation is to be run.[4]

RANDOM START NO. Any six-digit number. This is a seed value to start the random number generator.

SHIPPING WEIGHT The shipping weight value in pounds.

TRANSPORT MODE SELECTION The transportation mode used to make stock order deliveries from plant to warehouse.

TRANSPORT COSTS The transportation rate associated with the above selected mode.

ORDER TRANSMITTAL MODE The means by which the order data are transferred from warehouse to headquarters.

PROB. OF FILLING STOCK ORDER FROM PLANT INVENTORY The likelihood that a stock order is maintained in plant inventory. Values can range between 0 and 1.

ALPHA VALUES The exponential smoothing constant in the forecasting model for each product. Values will range between 0 and 1.

---

[3] The model is written in FORTRAN V, and the input and output are formated for use on both batch- and time-shared computing systems.

[4] Running the simulation for a number of years will cause the simulation to replicate the demand and inventory conditions anticipated for those future years.

> **TABLE C-2**
> Example of INSIM data inputs using current system values

Input Values

NO. OF YEARS TO TEST = 5   RANDOM START NO. = 748217
SHIPPING WEIGHT = 32000 LB.   SERVICE LEVEL = .98
PROB. OF FILLING STOCK ORDER
    FROM PLANT INVENTORIES = .70
TRANSPORT RATE = 1.28/CWT
TRANSPORT MODE SELECTION: TRUCK
ORDER TRANSMITTAL MODE: MAIL

Alpha Values		*Product*			
	1	*2*	*3*	*4*	*5*
	.15	.15	.15	.15	.15

Delays (Days)	*Min.*	*Mean*	*Max.*
SALESMEN, B/L PREPARATION	.00	1.00	2.00
TRANSMITTAL	2.00	4.00	6.00
COMPUTER UPDATE	3.00	5.00	7.00
STOCK ORDER TRANSMITTAL	.00	1.00	2.00
PRODUCTION	2.00	7.00	12.00
IN STOCK	1.00	2.00	3.00
DELIVERY PLT-WHSE	2.00	3.00	4.00
ORDER RECEIPT	2.00	4.00	6.00

SERVICE LEVEL A parameter value that controls the amount of safety
    stock in the warehouse. One value is used for all products.

TIME DELAYS The distribution of the various types of time delays in the
    system in terms of the minimum, mean, and maximum number of days
    experienced.

In addition to the controllable variables, there were initializing values internal
to INSIM. Such values were the warehouse inventory levels of each product.
The late December 1967 audit of the Atlanta warehouse showed the following
stock levels:

Product	*Warehouse Stock Level, lb.*
1	4,000
2	10,000
3	10,000
4	30,000
5	5,000

INPUT DATA CARD FORMAT

Prepare the input data cards in the following manner:

Card No.	Card Content	Comments
1	No. of years to test, Random start no., service level, shipping weight, transportation rate, prob. of filling stock order from plant inventories	Data are in free format and separated by commas. No. of years, random start no., and shipping weight are integer values; i.e., no decimal points are used. All others are to have decimals.
2	Transportation mode—Columns 1–6 Order transmittal mode—Columns 7–13	A6 format
3	Salesman—B/L preparation—min, mean, max, Transmittal—min, mean, max, Computer update—min, mean, max	Free format
4	Stock order transmittal—min, mean, max	Free format
5	Production—min, mean, max In-stock delay—min, mean, max	Free format
6	Delivery plt-whse—min, mean, max	Free format
7	Order receipt delay—min, mean, max	Free format
8	Alpha values—prod. 1, prod. 2, prod. 3, prod. 4, prod. 5.	Free format

If data from Table C-2 are used, the data cards would be

Card No.	Card Content
1	1,48217,3.00,32000,1.28,0.7
2	TRUCKbMAILbb 1———6 7———13
3	0.0,1.0,2.0,2.0,4.0,6.0,3.0,5.0,7.0
4	0.0,1.0,2.0
5	2.0,7.0,12.0,1.0,2.0 3.0
6	2.0,3.0,4.0
7	2.0,4.0,6.0
8	0.15,0.15,0.15,0.15,0.15

THE OUTPUT

The output of the simulation model is of two types. The first is a monthly summary of the inventory position by product in the warehouse, a monthly summary of inventory costs and inventory related cost items, and information time delays. This report is shown in Table C-3. Second is a yearly summary of inventory position, annual variable costs, and a customer service summary. This report is shown in Table C-4.

TABLE C-3

Example of monthly INSIM report

Year 2 Monthly Reports

Month 1   *Inventories, Units*

Prod.[a]	Actual Sales[b]	Fore-cast[c]	Com-puter Records[d]	On Order[e]	In Tran-sit[f]	Total Out of Stock[g]	Avg. Level[h]	Inv. Cost ($)[i]
1	4085	3990	3239	0	1208	163	1991.	4.98
2	11448	11341	3763	3243	5857	1087	5873.	14.68
3	19108	23475	30924	4586	1611	0	33494.	83.73
4	58102	60442	60653	22173	0	4470	47818.	119.54
5	16403	22527	42605	2656	0	0	44810.	112.02

TIME BETWEEN CUSTOMER ORDER AND COMPUTER POSTING = 10.05 DAYS[j]

TRANSPORTATION COST[k]	$	1853.41
ORDER PROCESSING COST[l]		1094.21
INVENTORY CARRYING COST[m]		485.73
OUT OF STOCK COST[n]		375.02
TOTAL COST	$	3808.38

[a] 1 = UBARS, 2 = RINSE-EZ, 3 = DAN-DE, 4 = TR-70, and 5 = TRI-X.
[b] Actual unit sales occurring during the month in pounds.
[c] Forecast of unit sales for month in pounds.
[d] Current stock level in warehouse as shown by computer inventory records.
[e] Stock orders released but not yet shipped from the plant.
[f] Stock orders in transit between plant and warehouse but not yet posted as received by the warehouse.
[g] Amount of monthly demand that could not be filled from warehouse stocks.
[h] Average stock level maintained in the warehouse within the month by product.
[i] Monthly inventory carrying cost by product.
[j] Accumulated time delays resulting from salesmen delays and B/L preparation, order transmittal to Akron, and invoicing and computer update.
[k] Both warehouse in-bound and out-bound transportation costs.
[l] Both customer order-processing and stock order-processing costs.
[m] Based on an annualized carrying cost of $3.10/cwt.
[n] Based on a $0.02/pound out-of-stock cost.

TABLE C-4

Example of year-end summary report from INSIM

Year 2 Summary

Inventories

Product	Yearly Sales	Whse. Audit[a]	Computer Record	Average Level	Cost ($)
1	48405	816	2853	2277.	68.31
2	142994	0	4246	6686.	200.57
3	306844	22135	39099	24512.	735.35
4	720172	0	24405	41318.	1239.54
5	335420	28367	58348	32235.	967.04

Total Annual Variable Costs

TRANSPORTATION COST	$	32014.98
ORDER PROCESSING COST		16451.38
INVENTORY CARRYING COST		5991.49
OUT OF STOCK COST		18188.12
TOTAL COST	$	72645.97

Service

Product	Total Out of Stock (Units)	Pct. of Demand[b]
1	2490.	5.14
2	7009.	4.90
3	104799.	34.15
4	144018.	20.00
5	174181.	51.93

[a] Actual level of stock in the warehouse at the end of the year.
[b] Percentage of total out-of-stock units to the total number of units demanded.

Index

A

ABC method of inventory control, 283–86
Ackerman, Kenneth B., 198, 205
Ackoff, Russell L., 63, 340
Act to Regulate Commerce of 1887, 155–56,
    166, 173, 174
Aggregate of intermediates, 173
Air transportation:
    characteristics, 144–45
    cost, 139–40
    cost characteristics, 163
    delivery time, 140–42
    physical plant, 134–35
    products hauled, 123–26
    statistics, 121–23, 144–45
Algorithmic models, 80, 239–42
All-commodity rate (ACR), 170
American Retail Federation, 151
American Trucking Association, 123, 124
American Warehousemen's Association, 199,
    201–4, 206
American Waterways Operators, Inc., 145
Ammer, Dean S., 457–58
Angular pallet placement, 413–15
Annual volume rates, 172
Arbitrary rates, 173

Armour, Gordon C., 412–13
Arnoff, E. Leonard, 340
Association of American Railroads, 127
Atkins, Robert J., 258
Autocorrelation (*see* Multiple regression)
Automatic control systems (*see* Closed-loop
    control systems)

B

Ballou, Ronald H., 8, 32, 33, 96, 97, 227,
    257–67, 336, 341, 409–13, 415,
    436–42
Barachet, L. L., 349
Basing point pricing, 109–11
Baumol, W. J., 250–58, 341–44
Beckman, Theodore N., 11, 111
Bellman, R. E., 263
Berenson, Conrad, 56
Bergin, T. P., 270
Bill of lading, 181, 200, 205
Blanketing back, 166
Boodman, David M., 290
Bowersox, Donald J., 7, 15, 70, 229, 235,
    245, 326, 414, 430, 431
Bowman, Edward H., 395
Box, G. E. P., 232

Branch and bound, 242, 349–51
Brooks, S. H., 233
Brown, Francis, 78
Brown, Robert G., 75, 302, 314, 315
Buffa, Elwood S., 363, 392, 412, 413
Bursh, J. Parker, 78
Business logistics:
  activities, 10
  activity coordination, 428
  audits, 458–59
  committees, use of, 428
  costs as a percentage of sales, 17, 18–20,
    21
  definition, 7, 8
  GNP, 16, 17
  line organization, 428–30
  managerial level, 8
  objectives, 13
  overlap of marketing and production, 12
  profit center as, 457–59
  reports, 459–66
  staff organization, 429–30
By-popularity stock location method, 408–9
By-size stock location method, 409

C

Cahn, A. S., Jr., 306
Cannon, Philip F., 425
Carew, Charles S., 406
Carrier routing:
  appraisal, 354
  delivery scheduling, 349–54
  heuristic programming method, 350–53
  large scale problems, 353
  matrix method, 346
  routing through a network, 345–49
  savings method, 355–59
  shortest-route tree method, 345–49
  transportation method, 359–62
  uncertainty under, 348
  vehicle scheduling, 354–62
Carrying costs, 279–82
Center-of-gravity method (*see* Grid model)
Centralized logistics management, 430–31
Central limit theorem, 454
Certainty (*see* Decision theory)
Chambers, John C., 395
Charles, A., 472–73
Christofides, N., 355
Churchman, C. West, 340
Civil Aeronautics Board, 136–37, 145, 156–
    57, 180
Clarke, G., 355–59
Class rates, 170
Clelland, Richard C., 78
Closed-loop control systems, 449–50
Cochran, Harold, 349
Combination rates, 173
Commodity rates, 170
Common carriers, 144, 156–57

Comparative economic advantage, principle
    of, 5–6
Consolidated Freight Classification, 168
Containerized freight, 148–49
Contract carriers, 144, 156–57
Control system, logistics:
  audits:
    freight bill, 459
    inventory, 458–59
    total function, 459
  control methods:
    budgets, 457
    profit center, 451–58
    service targets, 457
  control model, 447–49
  corrective action, 466–67
    contingency, 467
    major replanning, 466–67
    minor adjustments, 466
  definition, 446
  error tolerance, 453–55
  reports:
    cost-service, 463–66
    inventory, 460–63
  response in, 455–56
    on-off control mode, 456
    proportional control mode, 456
  system designs:
    closed-loop, 449–50
    modified feedback, 450–53
    open-loop, 449
Control systems, 60–61
Converse, Paul D., 14, 15
Convolution, 297–98, 305
Cooper, Leon, 233, 239
Cooper, W. W., 472–73
Corps of Engineers, 145
Costs, business logistics, 16–21
Cost-service control statement, 463–66
CRAFT model, 412
Cube-per-order index, 409, 416
Cube rates, 173
Culliton, James W., 145
Customer service, 25, 95, 107, 189, 432, 454
  constraints, 102–5
  control statement, 463–66
  definition, 96–97
  functions, 102–4
  level, 14
  need, 95–96
  order cycle, 99–102
  revenue function, 235–37
Cutler, Herschel, 140–42

D

Dantzig, G. B., 360
Data coding, 67–70
Data sources, 61–63
Data transmission, 63–65
Davidson, William R., 11, 111

Dawson, Leslie M., 15
DeCani, John S., 78
Decentralized logistics management, 430–31
Decision theory, 37, 287–89
  attitudes toward, 51–52
  certainty, decisions under, 38–40
  choice criteria, 42–45
  risk, decisions under, 40–43
  sensitivity analysis, 45–48
  uncertainty, decisions under, 43–45
  utility, 48
Deferred rates, 173–74
Definitions, business logistics, 7–8
DeHayes, Daniel W., Jr., 78–79, 96, 336–41
Delivered pricing, 108
Delivery scheduling (*see* Carrier routing)
Demand variability, formula for, 285–86
Demurrage and detention, 178
Differential rates, 173
Discrimination, transportation, 155–57
Diversion and reconsignment, 174
Draper, N. R., 73
Dreyfus, Stuart E., 263, 345, 348
Dynamic programming, 238, 259–66, 306–9,
    345, 349, 394

E

Eagan, W. F., 270
Eaton, Inc., 213
Economic order quantity:
  demand-lead time certainty, 290–92
  demand-lead time uncertainty, 302–3
  demand uncertainty, 296–302
  quantity discounts, 294–96
  sensitivity, 292–94
Efoymson, M. A., 242
Eighty-two rule, 283–84
Eilon, Samuel, 81, 355
Einstein, Albert, 30
Elmaleh, Joseph, 81
Emergence of business logistics, 15
EOQ model, 80
Exception report, 61
Exempt carriers, 156–57
Exponential smoothing, 74–76, 78, 311–19
  basic model, 311–12
  constant, 311–12
  guideline values, 312
  mean absolute deviation, 315–16
  model design, 317–19
  seasonal correction, 314–15
  start-up procedures, 319
  trend correction, 312–13

F

Facility location:
  appraisal of models, 237–38
  branch and bound, 242

Facility location (*cont.*):
  calculus model, 239–42
  dynamic analysis, 259–67
  exact model, 232–34
  grid model, 229–32
  heuristic model, 247–50
  modified mathematical programming,
      250–58
  revenue-cost model, 234–37
  simulation, 242–47
  Weber's graphic method, 226–29
Feldman, E. F., 247
Fetter, Robert B., 395
F.o.b. pricing, 107–8
Forklift trucks:
  replacement, 406–8
  selection, 405–6
Forrester, J., 81
Foster, R. S., 279
Francis, Richard L., 396
Fredericks, W. A., 229
Freidman, Walter F., 113
Freight-all-kinds (FAK), 170
Freight bill, 181–85
Freight bill audits, 459
Freight equalization, 109
Freight forwarders, 149, 168
Friedman, Lawrence, 300
Fulkerson, D. R., 360

G

General Services Administration, 209
Genesis, business logistics, 14–22
Geographical coding systems, 67–70
  longitude-latitude, 245
Gerson, M. L., 245
Glaskowsky, Nicholas A., Jr., 7
Goals, 35–36
Goldstone, L. A., 233
Goldstucker, J. L., 268–69
Gonzalez, Richard F., 302
Gordon, G., 81
Great circle distance, 67–70
Grid model, 229–32
  exact, 232–34

H

Haas, Paul R., Jr., 392
Hadley, G., 284, 297
Hamburger, Michael J., 247–50
Hancock, C. E., 395, 398
Harris, Ford, 289
Hart, William L., 67
Haskell, Robert H., 116
Hausner, B., 81
Held, M., 349
Heskett, J. L., 7, 16, 102, 120, 258, 279,
    435, 436–42

Heuristic:
    definition, 82
    models, 82–83, 247–58, 350–53, 412
Hillier, Frederick S., 346–48, 399–400
Hinkle, Charles L., 82, 348
H. J. Heinz Company, 244–46
Hoover, Edgar M., 226
House, Robert E., 198, 205
Huff, D. L., 269
Hutchinson, William M., 97

I

ICC (*see* Interstate Commerce Commission)
Igelhart, Donald L., 309
IMPACT, 326
Import-export rates, 173
Industrial logistics, 7 (*see also* Business
            logistics)
In excess rate, 172
Information system:
    definition, 56
    design, 59–61
Information time lags, 455–56
Interface activities, 12, 13
    management, 434–35
Interfunctional management, 13, 433–35
Interorganization management, 435–43
    coalition of members, 441
    definition, 435
    managing the super-organization, 442–43
    super-organization, 435–36
Interstate Commerce Commission, 123, 124,
            155–56, 157, 180
Interstate highway system, 128
In-transit privileges, 174–76, 197–98
Inventories:
    cost, 279
    safety stock, 284–86
Inventory audits, 458–59
Inventory control, 200
    ABC method, 283–86
    assigned customer service, 298–99
    computer programs, 319
    control system, 450
    costs, 281–83
    dynamic demand-cost model, 306–9
    known stockout costs, 299–302
    multiple item, multiple location analysis,
            311–25
        demand-lead time variance, 323–24
        lead time distribution, 319–23
    reorder analysis, 289–94
        P-system models, 289, 303–9
        quantity discounts, 294–96
        Q-system models, 289, 290–303
    reports, 460, 463
    single order analysis, 286–89

Inventory control (*cont.*):
    variance of demand distribution, 297–98,
            302–3
Inventory reports, 460–63
Isodapanes, 226–29
Ivie, Robert M., 7, 97

J

Jamison, Paul E., 185, 188, 217
Jenkins, Creed H., 196–97, 398, 415
Joint rates, 172

K

Kaminski, Carl, 478–93, 494–506
Karel, Caroline, 349
Karg, Robert L., 349, 350, 353
Karp, R. M., 349
Karr, H., 81
Khumawala, B. M., 242
Kraemer, H. F., 395, 398
Kuehn, Alfred A., 247–50, 348

L

LaJoy, Millard H., 456
LaLonde, Bernard J., 15, 70, 245, 326
Lavin, Marvin M., 399, 403
Lawless, Robert M., 392
Lazer, William, 122
Lead time (*see* Order cycle time)
Leased warehousing, 217–18
Least squares method, 72–73
Lehrer, A., 247
Lewis, Howard T., 145
Lewis, Richard J., 67
Lieberman, Gerald J., 346–48, 399–400
Lincoln Electric Company, 435
Linear programming, 245, 250–58, 306, 345,
            410–13
Little, John D. C., 349
Local rates, 172
Locklin, D. Philip, 129
Logistics (*see* Business logistics)
Logistics Systems, Inc., 310
Long-haul, short-haul clause, 155
Loss and damage, 102
    transportation, 142

M

Maffei, Richard B., 81, 242–46, 373
Magee, John F., 16, 283, 285–86, 290
Marketing logistics, 7 (*see also* Business
            logistics)

Marketing logistics interface, 12–13
Markowitz, H., 81
Marks, Norton, E., 17, 97
Materials handling, 207–15
  automated, 215, 220
  containerization, 208
  equipment, 212–15
  functions, 194–95
    loading-unloading, 195
    movement, 195
    order filling, 195
  manual, 212, 218
  order picking, 210–12
    batching, 212
    sequencing, 210
    zoning, 210–11
  pallet-forklift truck handling, 214, 218
  palletization, 208
Materials-handling selection:
  criteria, 403–5
  model for equipment replacement, 406–8
  model for equipment selection, 405–6
Materials management, 7 (*see also* Business
    logistics)
Maximin criterion, 43–44
McConaughy, David, 15
McGarrah, Robert E., 363
McMillan, Claude, 302
Messner, W. G., 135
Meyer, John R., 158–59, 160
Military Transportation Agency, 140–41
Miller, David W., 43, 297
MILSTRIP, 140–41
Miner, J. H., 459
Min-max inventory control (*see* Q-system
    models)
Moder, Joseph J., 414–15, 416–17
Moody's Transportation Manual, 135–39
Moore, James M., 409, 410
Morgenstern, Oskar, 48
Morton, N., 235–36
Mossman, Frank H., 7, 235–36
Moving average forecasting, 74–75
Mullick, Satender K., 395
Multicollinearity (*see* Multiple regression)
Multiple regression, 76, 78–79
  autocorrelation, 77–78
  multicollinearity, 77
  number of observations, 77
  specification, 77
Multiple-vehicle load rates, 172
Murray, Donald S., 78
Murtz, Katta G., 349

N

National Council of Physical Distribution
    Management, 467

National Motor Freight Classification, 168
National Safe Transit Committee, 114
Neal, Forest L., 409
Nestlé Company, 244
Network, product flow, 31–33
Newell, A., 247
Nodal points, 224–25, 379
NOIBN, 168
Normal distribution, table of probabilities,
    328–29

O

Objectives, business logistics, 13–14
Official Express Classification, 168
Open-loop control systems, 449
Order cycle time, components of, 99–102
Order picking, 197, 210–12, 410–13
  area system, 210
  modified area system, 210
Order processing, 58, 61–62
  central processing design, 369
  design elements, 366
  order scheduling, 369–70
  order sequencing, 368–69
  order transmission design, 366–68
  priorities, 102
Organization, logistics:
  factors in selection, 431–33
  form, 428–31
    informal, 428
    line-staff structure, 428–31
    need, 425–26
    objectives, 426–27
      activity coordination, 426–27
      system administration, 427
      system planning, 427
Out-of-stock costs, 279, 282, 283
  backorder costs, 283
  lost sales costs, 283

P

Packaging, 94, 113–18, 433
Palander, T., 226
Pallets, 404
Parker, Donald D., 21
Peck, Merton J., 160, 161, 162
Peck, Richard, 494–506
Pegrum, Dudley F., 126, 155
Peters, William S., 78, 454
Peterson, Keene, 140–42
Physical distribution (*see* Business logistics)
Physical supply (*see* Business logistics)
Piercy, James, 373
Piggyback, 148
Pipeline:
  characteristics, 146–47

Pipeline (*cont.*):
    cost, 139–40
    cost characteristics, 163–64
    physical plant, 135–39
    products hauled, 123–26
    statistics, 121–23, 146–47
Place utility, 12
Plant location, 270–71
Pohlen, Michael F., 12
Pollack, Maurice, 345
Pooling, 155
Private carriers, 156–57
Private warehousing, 218–20
Proctor and Gamble, 282
Procurement costs, 279, 281–82
Production-logistics interface, 12–13
Production scheduling, 362–66
    appraisal, 366
    logistics interface with, 362–63
Product proliferation, 16
PROFIT, 326
Proportional rates, 172–73
P-system models, 289, 303–9 (*see also*
        Inventory control)
Public Utilities Commission, 200
Public warehousing, 196–205 (*see also*
        Storage system)
    costs, 216–17

Q

Q-system models, 289, 290–303 (*see also*
        Inventory control)

R

Railroads:
    characteristics, 142–43
    cost, 139–40
    cost characteristics, 160–61
    delivery time, 140–42
    physical plant, 127–28
    products hauled, 123–26
    statistics, 121–23, 142–43
Raisy, E., 229
Rate base, 170
Rate classification, 167–70
    classification codes, 168
    factors, 168–69, 170
Rate making, 178–80
Rates, transportation:
    distance-related, 164–66
        blanket, 166
        proportional, 165–66
        tapering, 166
        uniform, 165
    line-haul, 167–74
        miscellaneous, 173–74
        by product type, 167–70

Rates, transportation (*cont.*):
    special charges, 174–77
    by routing, 172–73
    by volume shipped, 170–72
        incentive, 172
    terminal charges, 177–78
        demurrage and detention, 178
        pickup and delivery, 177–78
        switching, 178
    value-of-service, 166–67
    volume related, 164
        any quantity, 164, 170–71
        less vehicle load, 164
        vehicle load, 164
Ray, T. L., 242, 247
REACT, 326
REA Express, 168
Reilly, W. J., 268
Reilly's Law of Retail Gravitation, 268–69
Released value rates, 174
Reports:
    action, 84
    information, 83–84
Retail site selection, 268–70
Rex Chainbelt, Inc., 213
Rhocrematics, 7 (*see also* Business logistics)
Richmond, Samuel B., 311
Rider, Graham W., 6
Risk (*see* Decision theory)
Robinson-Patman Act, 111
Rogers, J. D., 229, 233
Routing (*see* Carrier routing)
Rule of insufficient reason, 44–45
Rule of rate making, 156
Ruppenthal, Karl M., 399–403

S

Saaty, Thomas L., 232
Safety stock, 297–98, 299, 305, 324–25, 342
Sales forecasting, 70–78, 311–19
Sasieni, Maurice, 300
Saunders, William B., 64–65
Schiller, Donald H., 399–403
Schlaifer, Robert, 330–31
Schneider, Lewis M., 15, 207
Scope, business logistics, 6
Search methods, 232–33
    Newton's approximation, 232
    random, 232–33
    steepest descent, 232
    successive approximation, 233, 240
Sensitivity analysis, decision theory, 39, 51
Seppänen, Jouko, 410
Shaw, J. C., 247
Shriver, Richard H., 258
Shycon, Harvey N., 81, 242–46, 247
Simon, Herbert A., 247, 450
Simulation, 242–47, 302
    models, 81